THE FOREIGN POLICY OF CASTLEREAGH

1812–1815

Robert Stewart, Viscount Castlereagh
from the portrait by Sir Thomas Lawrence
in the collection of the Most Hon. the Marquess of Londonderry, K.G.

THE FOREIGN POLICY
OF CASTLEREAGH

1812-1815

BRITAIN AND THE RECONSTRUCTION
OF EUROPE

BY

SIR CHARLES WEBSTER
K.C.M.G., M.A., Litt.D., F.B.A.

Stevenson Professor of International History
London School of Economics

LONDON
G. BELL AND SONS, LTD
1950

TO MY FATHER, DANIEL WEBSTER,
FOR WHOSE AFFECTION AND FRIENDSHIP
I CAN NEVER BE SUFFICIENTLY
GRATEFUL

First published 1931
Reprinted 1950

PRINTED IN GREAT BRITAIN
BY JARROLD AND SONS LIMITED, NORWICH

PREFACE

WITH this volume I have completed a project begun over twenty years ago of describing the foreign policy of Britain during the period when Castlereagh directed it. The volume on the later period of the European Alliance, 1815–22, was published first, partly because I had already given some account of the previous period in the *Congress of Vienna* (1919) and in the first volume of the *Cambridge History of British Foreign Policy*. But in neither of these was it possible for me to aim at completeness or to display all the evidence on which the narrative rested, and I have been able to obtain from the Londonderry Papers, which have since been opened to me, much new information. A period of such supreme importance in British relations to European affairs seemed, in any case, to merit an attempt to describe it in the light of all the available evidence.

The most important evidence was in the Foreign Office Papers in the Record Office. These had been used by many historians, both British and foreign, but large portions of them had never been surveyed, and they had never been considered as a whole. I have tried to convey an impression produced by an intensive study of them all, but my task has, of course, been made much easier by the labours of those who have preceded me.

The archives of the foreign Powers are not so important for British diplomacy in this period as in that of the Alliance. For the first two years there were few foreign representatives in London, and in 1814–15 Castlereagh was for long periods in personal contact with the principal sovereigns and statesmen of Europe. Since these were concentrated in one place there was no need, as Metternich has pointed out in his memoirs, for a record to be made of their conversations. The archives in the foreign capitals do not, therefore, contain documents of the same value as the Record Office. Still, in the reports of the Ambassadors there is often evidence on the attitude of the Foreign Minister and the Cabinet which can be obtained from no other source. I was also able to supplement the imperfect information of the archives of the Great Powers by those of three smaller Courts. These papers had also been used by many historians, but not for my purpose.

A large part of this material was collected before the War, but I have been able more recently to complete my researches in the Record Office and to see once more the archives at Vienna, Paris, and Berlin, as well as to visit Dresden and Munich. Hanover and Petersburg [1] I visited in 1913.

The Londonderry Papers contained many letters which Castlereagh's brother had, either by accident or design, omitted from the collection which he edited. In some cases also letters had been altered. Those of Castlereagh to his wife were not then available. Though these last reveal the man as no others do, they do not deal much with public affairs. The most interesting of this period are those during his mission to the Continent in the first part of the year 1814, and a selection of these are given in Appendix A. The capitalisation and punctuation have been modernised in them, as in all the other documents of the period used by me.

Perhaps the most important of the new letters are those of Liverpool to Castlereagh during the mission to the Continent in 1814. Unlike those of a later date they are not to be found in the *Wellington Supplementary Despatches*, and for some reason they have been omitted from both the *Castlereagh Correspondence* and the *Life of Lord Liverpool* by Yonge. A number of them have, therefore, been printed in Appendix B.

Those of Castlereagh to Sir Charles Stuart in 1815 illustrate an aspect of his policy hitherto not sufficiently appreciated, and a selection has therefore been given in Appendix C. Much other evidence, especially in letters to and from the Earl

---

[1] I have used this name to describe the modern capital of Russia in this book since it was in common use during the period under review, omitting, however, the word Saint which so often accompanied it.

of Clancarty and Lord Stewart, too intimate to be found in the Foreign Office archives, will be found quoted in the narrative.

George IV.'s papers, in the Royal Archives at Windsor, are fragmentary. There are not many on foreign policy, but they supplied some interesting and occasionally important details on the domestic situation which affected it, especially on the formation of the Liverpool Ministry. Amongst the most illuminating documents of the period are the reports to the Prince Regent and other correspondence of Count Münster, the principal Minister of Hanover. Some of these had been printed by his son, others were to be found in the Record Office or in the Hanover Staats-Archiv. There were a few others, however, of an intimate nature at Windsor, and some of these as well as one from Hanover are given in Appendix D, while others are quoted in the text. Münster's French was peculiar to himself, but the meaning is generally clear enough. Throughout the book French is translated, except for a few obvious phrases, but in the Appendix Münster's dispatches have been left in their original French except that the capital-isation and punctuation have been modernised and some accents altered.

The papers of Sir Robert Wilson in the British Museum have been utilised, not so much for their own sake as because he was a principal source of information to Earl Grey and other leaders of the Opposition.

The total quantity of this material is hardly less than that of the longer period of the Alliance, while the amount of printed material is, of course, much larger. The task of displaying the necessary evidence was, therefore, more formid-able. It was lightened somewhat by the fact that I had printed a number of the important dispatches in the Record Office in my *British Diplomacy, 1813-15*, but I have tried to illustrate the narrative by frequent quotation so far as space allowed. References to secondary works in a period which has been studied by so many historians have had to be sparingly made where some special need arose. My obliga-tions to such writers as Sorel, Fournier, Oncken, Fyffe, and Holland Rose, to mention no others, are, of course, immense. Even as it is the notes have had to be made rather fuller than for the period of the Alliance, because the sources are more numerous and because the diplomacy is more complicated.

A bibliography of the period, if it had attempted completeness, would have been very bulky, but I have indicated in the notes those books and articles which have specially dealt with various aspects of British policy.

Of no period in history can it perhaps be said that no new material will be forthcoming sufficiently important to change radically previous conceptions. It seems likely, however, that there will be few important additions to that now made available for this part of Castlereagh's career, and that it is possible to make those provisional judgments which are necessary for the understanding of it.

The process is all the more necessary for the period of Reconstruction, because it is the only one which bears any comparison with that of our time. Indeed, while I was present at the Paris Conference of 1919 the analogues of this period were necessarily always present in my mind. But I have refused in this book to make comparisons or in any way to allow them to affect the character or form of the book. Such deductions should be left to special studies of a different character.

The sub-title of the book has been strictly construed, and I have left out of it altogether British policy towards the United States. It was kept entirely separate from European affairs, and Castlereagh had only a small share in the negotiations which led to the Treaty of Ghent, while to have given the whole story on the same scale as the rest of the book would have added greatly to its length. I may perhaps return to it in a separate study of Anglo-American relations. The Colonial settlement, on the other hand, was so much part of the European settlement that I have had to trace its course to a certain extent.

I have to acknowledge much help and advice in the preparation of the book. I must express my deep obligation to His Majesty, the King, for permission to use the papers of George IV. in the Royal Archives at Windsor. I am very grateful to the Rev. Albert Lee, then the Recorder of the Archives, and to Miss Mackenzie, who gave me most valuable guidance and help of various kinds. I owe a special debt of gratitude to the Marquess of Londonderry, who not only allowed me access to all his papers without restriction of any kind, but has taken a great interest in the book and helped it forward in various ways. The portraits of Castlereagh and his wife are taken by his permission from those at Londonderry House, and it was by his suggestion that there was added to them the view of the Temple of the Winds, which commemorates an early episode in Castlereagh's career.

To the officials of the Record Office my debt extends over a long period of years, especially to Mr. Hubert Hall and Mr. Headlam. I have had similar kindnesses from those in charge of the papers at Vienna, Berlin, Paris, Petersburg, Munich, Dresden, and Hanover. The time that can be devoted to researches in the archives is limited, and much depends on being able to utilise it to full advantage. It is only the invariable courtesy and assistance of these learned officials which makes fruitful work possible.

I also owe much to the advice and encouragement which many historians have given me in the course of the last twenty years. The late Professor Schiemann of Berlin, and my friend, the late Commandant M. H. Weil of Paris, gave me information on many points. I had also many discussions with the late Professor Fournier of Vienna, who was then engaged in the preparation of his work on the Congress, which unfortunately he did not live to write. His knowledge of the actors and events of the great drama was unrivalled, and he put it at my disposal with a generosity for which I shall always be deeply grateful. I owe thanks also to Professor A. F. Pribram of Vienna, while Professor Marczali of Buda-Pesth was kind enough to give me a copy of an unpublished letter of Metternich.

All my work owes much to my friend, Professor H. W. V. Temperley, who has always placed his unrivalled knowledge of British diplomacy unreservedly at my disposal. I owe a great debt also to my colleague, Mr Sydney Herbert, who has not only read all the proofs and saved me from many blunders, but has compiled the index. Miss Morris, Secretary of the

Department of International Politics, has assisted me in technical details. Several of my pupils in my seminars at Harvard University gave me valuable help by their researches.

To my publishers, who have always shewn the greatest interest and sympathy during the long period I have taken to complete our contract, I also owe warm thanks. I am very grateful for the consideration and kindness always shewn by my friends at Morben Issa, where most of this book was written.

Lastly, this volume, as the previous one, could not have been produced without the never-ceasing help of my wife.

ABERYSTWYTH
January 1931

TABLE OF CONTENTS

xi

LIST OF ILLUSTRATIONS

NOTE ON THE SYSTEM OF REFERENCES

I. Unpublished Official Sources

(i) The Foreign Office papers in the Record Office are referred to by the name of the country and the number of the volume (e.g. *F.O. Russia*, 83). The numbers allotted to each series in the *List of Foreign Office Records* have been omitted. The number of the dispatch is only given occasionally where it seemed necessary for identification.

(ii) The papers in the *Archives des affaires étrangères* at Paris are identified by the reference *Paris A.A.E.* They are from the series *Angleterre* and *France*. The number of the volume and folio have been given since there is a complete classification of all the papers (e.g. *Paris A.A.E. France*, 673, ff. 47–48).

(iii) In the other archives the papers are generally not bound, and the classification is hardly sufficiently detailed to make it worth while to give specific reference. The documents are therefore only identified by the writer and recipient, date, and a reference to the various archives under the following heads which explain themselves : *Vienna St. A., Pet. Arch., Berlin St. A., Hanover St. A., Munich St. A., Dresden St. A.*

II. Unpublished Unofficial Sources

(i) *Windsor Arch.* is used to denote references to the papers of George IV. in the Royal Archives at Windsor.

(ii) *Lond. MSS.* is used to denote the papers in the archives of the Marquess of Londonderry at Londonderry House.

(iii) *Wilson MSS.* is used to denote the papers of Sir Robert Wilson in the Additional Manuscripts at the British Museum. In this case the number of the volume and the folio is given (e.g. *Wilson MSS.* 30120, ff. 132, 137).

III. Published Sources

Abbreviations have been used to denote seven collections to which many references have been made.

(i) *C.C.*   =Memoirs and Correspondence of Viscount Castlereagh. Edited by his brother the third Marquess of Londonderry. 12 vols. London 1848–53.

(ii) *Gurwood.* = The dispatches of Field-Marshal the Duke of Wellington, 1799–1815, compiled by Lt.-Col. Gurwood. 12 vols. London 1837–38.

(iii) *W.S.D.* = Supplementary Despatches, Correspondence and Memoranda of the Duke of Wellington. Edited by his son. 12 vols. London 1858–72.

(iv) *Bathurst.* = Report on the Manuscripts of Earl Bathurst preserved at Cirencester Park. Edited for the Historical Manuscripts Commission by Francis Bickley. London 1923.

(v) *Münster.* = Political Sketches of the state of Europe from 1814–67, by George Herbert, Count Münster. Edinburgh 1868. This contains dispatches of Count Ernst Münster to the Prince Regent from both Paris (1814) and Vienna (1814–15), the former being omitted from the German edition (Leipzig 1867). The dispatches are translated into English.

(vi) *B.F.S.P.* = British and Foreign State Papers. Edited by the Librarian of the Foreign Office [Sir E. Hertslet]. Vols. 1, 2, 3. London 1838–41.

(vii) *B.D.* = British Diplomacy, 1813–15. Select Documents dealing with the reconstruction of Europe, by C. K. Webster London 1921.

Other works have been referred to by Author's Name and Short Title. Many of them will be found in the Bibliographies of the *Cambridge Modern History* and the *Cambridge History of British Foreign Policy*. The title of those not mentioned in these works has, it is hoped, been made sufficiently detailed to facilitate reference, if desired.

CHAPTER I

BRITAIN AT WAR: THE ELEMENTS OF RECONSTRUCTION

1. THE TRAINING OF A STATESMAN.

2. THE FORMATION OF THE LIVERPOOL MINISTRY.

3. COURT, CABINET, PARLIAMENT, AND PUBLIC OPINION.

4. THE FOREIGN MINISTER AND THE DIPLOMATIC MACHINE.

5. THE LEGACY OF PITT.

" Castlereagh relut-il alors les anciennes notes de Pitt et quelque chose de l'âme de cet implacable ennemi de la grandeur française s'infiltra-t-il dans l'âme de ses successeurs ? "—ALBERT SOREL.

CHAPTER I

1. THE TRAINING OF A STATESMAN

BETWEEN 1812 and 1815 occurred the most sudden and complete transformation of the map of Europe which had ever been produced in so short a time. In 1812 the power of the French Empire and its vassal states stretched from Madrid to Warsaw. By the end of 1815 France had been reduced to her ancient frontiers, her vassal princes had fled or changed sides, the boundaries of Europe had been entirely reshaped. To this result the example and assistance of Britain contributed greatly. Moreover, for the first time in history, she exercised a commanding influence in the reconstruction of Europe. This new influence in European affairs was due not only to the prominent part she had played in the war, but also to the personality of Viscount Castlereagh, the most European Foreign Minister in her history. It is the purpose of this book to study in some detail the principles, methods, and occasions of British policy during the period of reconstruction.

Robert Stewart, Viscount Castlereagh, was born in 1769, an *annus mirabilis* which also gave to the world Napoleon, his great enemy, and Wellington, his principal co-worker in European reconstruction. Thus in 1812 he was not yet forty-three years of age. But he had spent most of the past fifteen years in responsible office, and the times in which he lived had tested him and given him a range of experience such as few possessed. Only Liverpool, like Canning, his junior by a year, had a greater length and variety of employment behind him.

3

His family was a Scottish one which had adopted all the characteristics of the Ulster "Anglo-Irish" settlers of James I.'s reign. His father, one of the most vigorous of a vigorous stock, represented County Down in the Irish Parliament from 1771 to 1783, and became an Irish peer, Baron Londonderry, in 1789. He was advanced in the Peerage as Viscount Castlereagh in 1795, and became Earl of Londonderry in 1796, when his son had the courtesy title of Viscount Castlereagh, by which history knows him. Their family estate was on the shores of Strangford Lough, at Mount Stewart, near Newtownards, a place of grand and turbulent beauty.

His father, a man of only moderate means, connected himself by marriage with two noble families which were to be of great importance in his son's career. His first wife, the mother of Castlereagh, was Lady Sarah Conway, second daughter of the first Marquess of Hertford. Castlereagh was her only surviving child, and she died when he was only a year old. Something of his political gifts and the reserve and patience of his character he got from her, just as his energy, strong will, and persistence came from his father, from whom he also inherited his handsome features and manners. The second wife, a daughter of the Earl of Camden, had several children, including Charles, later Lord Stewart and third Marquess. Both the mother and her children Castlereagh always seems to have treated as if he had been her own son.[1] He gave them indeed far more affection than eldest sons usually bestow.

Living in Ulster until he was seventeen years of age, he followed the good example of his father and learnt to know and understand the tenants, both Protestant and Catholic, as only a young heir constantly among his dependants can do. They were not immune from the ferment of the times, but in the critical years of the nineties were kept loyal by the influence, which was more persuasion than coercion, of the father and the son. No doubt Castlereagh's physical and moral courage appealed to men who were used to both violent words and deeds. Of his possession of these qualities his youth gave many proofs. Twice when narrowly in danger of drowning

---

[1] The prefix, step-, was hardly ever applied by him to them, and I propose to follow his example.

THE TEMPLE OF THE WINDS

overlooking Strangford Lough, where on August 5, 1786, Robert Stewart and a younger companion were rescued from drowning, after so long a struggle that it seemed miraculous that they should be saved.

NORTH CRAY COTTAGE, KENT

he saved a companion's life, while, once, only his own coolness saved him from highway robbery with violence.

Fate was to make him an absentee from Ireland after 1800, but from his Irish home he brought a love of nature, dislike of display, and readiness to endure hardship which he never lost in later life. From it came also his delight in farming. His cottage at North Cray, only sixteen miles from London, had a little farm attached where he bred merino sheep. He had not much time for it in these years, but a Swiss diplomatist, who bred the same sheep in Switzerland, records how Castlereagh's coldness was replaced by an unexpected liveliness when they discovered by chance their unique and common interest.[1]

He escaped, like Pitt, the advantages and temptations of Eton, which left so great a mark on many of his contemporaries, and was educated in a private school at Armagh. A letter,[2] written when he was just over eight years old, reveals his pride and determination: "At present I am highest in my class—no boy shall get above me. I am resolved to study very close when at my book and to play very briskly when disengaged." At the end he added a line which shews that he was even then interested in politics and a Whig: "I am still a good American."

He learnt enough at school to become one of the first reading men of his year when he entered St. John's College, Cambridge, at the age of seventeen. This was unusual in one of his position, but Castlereagh, though fond of field sports and outdoor life, cared little for the usual recreations of his class. His friends were mostly of the same kind. Few of them, it may be noted, entered politics or attained much distinction in later life, unlike the brilliant coterie that Canning used to delight at Oxford. If this fact cut Castlereagh off from a kind of companionship that would have been both a stimulus and a relief in the days of power, it saved him from the burden of friends whose abilities were not equal to their demands.

---

[1] L. Cramer, *Correspondance Diplomatique de Pictet de Rochemont*, ii. 226–28. A long letter of Castlereagh to his father gives his live stock (about 1817) as 270 sheep, 130 lambs, 8 cows, 19 horses, and 5 asses. *Lond. MSS.*

[2] To his uncle, Alexander Stewart, Oct. 6, 1777: *Lond. MSS.*

He left Cambridge after little more than a year's residence
for the usual Grand Tour. His father had designed him for
a public life, and wished to get him ready for it as soon as
possible. Thus 1788 and 1789 he spent mainly in France
and Italy, without, so far as can be gathered, any very marked
effects on his character, except that it enabled him to acquire
more easily the usual polish of the times. It is probable that
his heart was in Ireland more than in Europe.

He was barely twenty-one when first elected to the Irish
Parliament; for his father was determined to wrench the
representation of County Down from the hands of the
Marquess of Downshire. He was so far successful that young
Mr Stewart obtained one of the seats at a cost of something
like the £50,000 which it had been intended to devote to a
new mansion, and the sale of some old pictures. The family
finances never quite recovered from this expenditure, but it
was no doubt considered that the influence thus acquired
brought greater honour than the house and pictures could ever
have done.

When Castlereagh declared for reform of Parliament at this
election, he meant of course reform of the Irish Parliament,
which he was himself to reform out of existence. The
Catholics had not yet the vote, which they obtained in 1793,
so that when Castlereagh sat later in the British Parliament
for his native county he represented Catholics there as well
as Protestants.[1] From 1790 to 1793 Castlereagh tended to
oppose the Government, as a young man should in his early
years. Though it is not likely that he ever belonged, as was
later alleged, to the Society of United Irishmen, he had warm
Irish sympathies and established in Dublin a "Gaelic Society"
to encourage and preserve the native language.

Being the eldest son, Castlereagh could not join the army as
his younger brothers did. But he developed strong military
instincts as Irish turmoil and unrest grew and became an
officer in the Irish militia, which Pitt had the courage to call
out. At the same time, the progress of the revolution in

---

[1] The Downshires defeated him in 1805, and Castlereagh had to take
refuge in the pocket boroughs of Boroughbridge and Plympton, but he
recovered the seat in 1812 and held it till 1820.

France tended to throw him more on the Tory side. No one was more alarmed at their Belgian conquests than he, and, unlike many of his contemporaries, he saw the danger that was latent in the call to a whole people to take up arms. "The tranquillity of Europe is at stake," he wrote to his uncle in September 1793, "and we contend with an opponent whose strength we have no means of measuring. It is the first time that all the population and all the wealth of a great kingdom has been concentrated in the field: what may be the result is beyond my perception." [1]

These fears and the increasing dangers in Ireland itself did not prevent him from winning the hand of Lady Emily Hobart, daughter of the Earl of Buckingham. The opportunity seems to have been provided by Lord Camden, who was now taking a great interest in his young relative, but the two young people fell violently in love and continued to be so for the rest of their lives. Only five of his notes to her previous to their marriage survive, but they are sufficient to shew the ardour and tenderness of his wooing. She seems to have kept every scrap that he wrote to her in later life, but the total quantity is not very large because they never separated except when some imperious duty demanded it. Some observers thought her exacting, but there can be no doubt that Castlereagh hated separation from her, counted the days until he was with her again, and wrote to her by almost every possible conveyance. She was the confidant of all his actions, if not of his thoughts, for, in spite of her love and his, the deeper processes of his mind were beyond her understanding. But his devotion equalled hers, and her pride and joy in him did not excel that which he felt for her, though her early beauty was compensated by only passable manners, and she took far more interest in the externals of his situation than he did himself. Lady Bessborough was a Whig, but her skilful and subtle pen has, perhaps, given the best picture that exists of Lady Castlereagh in Society: "No one ever was so invariably good humour'd, yet she sometimes provokes me; there is a

---

[1] To Lord Camden, Sept. 25, 1793 : Alison, *Lives of Lord Castlereagh and Sir C. Stewart*, 23. Alison is for once ponderously in the right in contrasting this judgment with those of Pitt, Burke, and Fox at the same date.

look of contented disregard of the cares of life in her round
grey Eye that makes one wonder if she ever felt any crosses
or knows the meaning of the word anxiety.   She talks with
equal indifference of Bombardments and Assemblies, the
Baby and the Furniture, the emptiness of London and the
Massacre at Buenos Ayres, Ld. Castlereagh's encreasing
debility and the doubtful success of Mr. Greville's new opera—
all these succeed each other so quick and with so exactly the
same expression of voice and countenance that they probably
hold a pretty equal value in her estimation.   How very ill
natur'd—voilà déjà tous les travers de la Veillesse qui me
viennent.   I do not believe there was a better sort of woman
or who shew'd more kindness to all around her, and above all
ten thousand times better natur'd than me . . ." [1]

But Castlereagh found in his wife complete satisfaction.
The letters could only have been written to one who was
a dear companion and a beloved mistress as well as the head
of his household and the dispenser of his hospitality.   They
reveal how much love and tenderness was hidden behind the
cold exterior with which his sensitive character guarded itself
from the quizzing world.   They had no children, and in such
cases a wife must be all or nothing.   There is no doubt that
for Castlereagh his wife meant everything in that world where
politics and war have no existence. [2]

The duties of that other world kept him from her side a good
part of the year 1796.   The dangers of French invasion called
Castlereagh's militia to the south, and he marched with them
when the French ships sailed into Bantry Bay.   They sailed
away again without doing any harm, as Castlereagh, *en route*
to his regiment, assured his wife would be the case.   There
was no fighting on this occasion, and when the real battle came
in Ireland Castlereagh was otherwise employed.   Nevertheless,
this period of active service in the militia was as useful in
another way as that of Gibbon, for it must have been of great
practical importance when, as Secretary of State for War, he

---

[1] Granville, *Corres. of Leveson-Gower*, ii. 284.
[2] Lord Londonderry has allowed me to see and quote from the typescript of these letters which was made for the use of the family.   The
quotations in this chapter are from these letters, and a selection from those
of 1814 are given in *Appendix A*.   Others will be found in the late
Marchioness of Londonderry's *Life of Viscount Castlereagh* (1904).

EMILY, VISCOUNTESS CASTLEREAGH

*from the portrait by Sir Thomas Lawrence in the collection of the Most Hon. the
Marquess of Londonderry, K.G.*

reorganised the militia, and established its connection with the regular army. Here is a letter of the soldier on the march:

" It is impossible to describe what I felt, Dearest Friend, yesterday at parting with you. I never shall forget the affection and firmness with which you went thro' a scene certainly the most trying to those who love: but the first effort made, your reason will in a great measure tranquillize your mind, and nothing on my part shall be wanting to give you frequent intelligence; but you must not look for regularity in my accounts—our situation and employment may make it impossible. I long to hear of your arrival in Dublin. Remember your promise to have a companion in your room. Fanny, I am sure, will be glad to afford you any comfort she can, and you gave me a positive assurance that you would not read at night, or sit up late—rather get up early and endeavour not to exaggerate the anxiety which I cannot expect you to be without.

" We reached Bruff last night about 6 o'clock. The weather was charming, a little cold, but marching on foot I did not feel it. Mr. Whiskey had done a little mischief in our ranks, but upon the whole for a first day's march (taking leave of Sweet-hearts, and parting with the inhabitants, who brought spirits in quantities to them when they were chilled on the street, waiting for stores which they never received) we did fairly well. I have, however, this day declared war against Whiskey and it will not retard us again. We marched this morning at 8 o'clock, and shall reach Mallow to-morrow. Nothing can be more kind and attentive than the people are to us. Our 500 men are very well taken care of, and we shall eat our Xmas dinner with the Mayor of the Town. . . .

" I rely upon your writing every post; it will be the greatest luxury, and will keep me warm in all weathers. Direct to Mallow till you hear to the contrary, and tell me everything that passes. We march to-morrow at 8. The men are in great spirits, very much afraid that the Navy will run away with their credit from them. Farewell, Dearest best friend. Ever your most devoted CASTLEREAGH."

He was called back to Newtownards to help his father keep

their own tenants loyal, a task of some difficulty, for the whole of the north was in a state of semi-rebellion. "I wish, if possible," he told his wife, "to effect something with my Father's people before I leave this country—they are at present wavering—and it is at present uncertain what may be the event." Gradually the waverers were won over. "You see then the necessity of my remaining a few days," Castlereagh explained to the impatient Emily, "for you will allow, if I should succeed in giving a turn to the unfortunate spirit which prevails in this country, that, for our future repose and present credit, it will be worth while. You can estimate my impatience to join you by your own. . . ." At last he was able to announce in triumph: "Between 3 and 4 hundred took the oath of allegiance yesterday. They did it with every mark of sincerity, after the ice had been broken and their panick a little removed. They had been much deceived and much threatened. We had a very jolly dinner. Cleland quite drunk, Sinclair considerably so, my father not a little, others lying heads and points, the whole very happy, and God Save the King and Rule Britannia declared permanent."

Castlereagh, therefore, knew a good deal of the state of Ireland when he was summoned by his uncle, who became Viceroy in 1795, to take up a position in Dublin Castle, virtually acting as Chief Secretary for Pelham from the beginning of 1797 onwards, and succeeding him officially in April 1799. Cornwallis kept him on, when it was necessary for the mild Camden to be superseded by a soldier, and he was thus in the second most responsible position in Ireland during the terrible rebellion of 1798. He was the first Irishman to hold that post. The danger was immense, for the Protestants of the north seemed no less disaffected than the Catholic south. The rebellion, which unexpectedly had its main operations in Wexford, was, however, in Castlereagh's opinion, due to both religion and politics. "It is a Jacobinical conspiracy throughout the Kingdom," he informed London, "pursuing its object chiefly with Popish instruments; the heated bigotry of this sect being better suited to the purpose of the republican leaders than the cold, reasoning disaffection of the Northern Presbyterians." [1] Fortunately for Britain, the French managed their part of the business no better than the British their expeditions against France. Vinegar Hill had been fought, and Lord Edward Fitzgerald had been captured and died of wounds before their fleet appeared and landed troops, which were easily defeated, while Wolfe Tone was taken on a French frigate. Exquisite cruelties were employed by both sides, and at least 30,000 people lost their lives.

The resolve to create a United Parliament had been taken before the rebellion took place, but it seemed to add to the urgency. Castlereagh thus became the principal instrument of Pitt and Portland in abolishing the separate Parliament of his own country, an act for which Irishmen will never forgive him. The hatred that grew around it has, indeed, obscured both the object and the method. It was meant to bring peace to Ireland as well as England. The money which Pitt and Castlereagh spent was mainly in compensation of the borough holders, opponents and supporters alike, though some money bribery was used, and much in honours and place. That Castlereagh thoroughly believed in the necessity of his actions, and used every ounce of his energy and skill, there can be no doubt. He had been disgusted with Irish politics before the rebellion, and he was genuinely convinced that the equal place which Ireland was given in the British Parliament, and her more direct association in the benefits of the British Empire, were ample compensation for the loss of her corrupt and incompetent legislature, which, after all, had but little control over the Government of Ireland. The bargain was, indeed, as time was to shew, a better one for Ireland than for England, though both suffered the greatest harm in those qualities which count most in a nation's life.

Nor did Castlereagh, in spite of his success, escape the penalty. For to it must be partly attributed his distrust of Parliamentary government, his rather cynical attitude towards politics and a certain callousness towards popular demands, his preference for secret rather than open conduct

[1] To Wickham (Portland's Under-Secretary), June 12, 1798: *C.C.* i. 218.

of public affairs, which were real defects in his character and ruined eventually some of the great objects which his diplomatic skill brought into the region of practical politics. These feelings, even more than the obloquy and hatred which have been heaped upon his name, were the heavy price he had to pay for his part in carrying out so successfully the plans of Portland and Pitt.

Pitt had promised that Catholic Emancipation should follow, though the promise was not to be used to carry the Union, and in this obvious act of justice Castlereagh had always believed. In this respect he went further than most Protestants, building his own Catholics a church and being one of the first to protest against the iniquitous tithe. When he joined the man who from now onwards was his leader and friend in the British House of Commons, he expected, therefore, to play a principal part there in conducting the necessary legislation through the House, and when the King's veto stopped the measure, he resigned with Pitt.

He was given, by his leader, such marked encouragement in his early speeches that the suggestion was immediately made that he would rival Canning in the great man's favour, as indeed was soon the case. But even less than Pitt did he make Catholic Emancipation a bar to his return to office when the question had been, at any rate for the moment, removed from the range of practical politics. Unless he was to eschew all opportunities of place and power, he was forced to recognise that other matters must take pre-eminence. Thus in a little more than a year he joined the Addington Ministry in the important office of President of the Board of Control and became one of its most successful members. But Pitt seems to have approved entirely of this act, far more so, indeed, than of the quips and gibes of the intractable Canning, who shewed his devotion to his master by vilifying those who had taken his place.

Castlereagh was admitted to the Cabinet in October 1802, and when Pitt came back he kept him in the same office, and the intimacy between master and pupil grew closer and closer in the last tragic years of Pitt's life until, at the end, transferred to the important office of Secretary of State for War in

July 1805, he had more of his confidence than perhaps any other member of his Government.

The Board of Control itself, even though the President was only an intermediary between an almost all-powerful Governor-General and an East India Company tenacious of its rights and eager for dividends, brought to him experience and connections of the most important kind. For the elder Wellesley was a great ruler, and the younger won his first victories in the Mahratta wars. Castlereagh gave them all the support that he could, wrung troops out of the East India Company, and, it may be noted, refused all patronage for himself. Arthur Wellesley had thus come to know and be known by him before he returned with his brother to take up a position in Ireland similar to that which Castlereagh himself had once held. Moreover, Castlereagh was brought into touch with Persia, where a mission was sent to hold the route to the East which now seemed to be threatened.

Even more important, however, was his connection with Pitt in the general conduct of the war,[1] and the plans for Europe which were made in connection with the third coalition. By this time he had become Pitt's principal confidant, and was far more trusted by him than Canning, who had not yet a place in the Cabinet. But Castlereagh had shewn a steadiness which Canning did not then possess, and was, moreover, a source of harmony rather than discord in the weakened team which Pitt had to drive after 1804. It was Castlereagh who planned the great expedition to the north of Germany, which Austria's defeat and Prussia's treachery made of no avail. It was Castlereagh also who discussed with Pitt the great state paper which he wrote at the beginning of 1805, in which he replied to the Tsar's extended plans for a new Europe, with others as large and more suitable to the present difficulties.[2]

Castlereagh had, perhaps, made more impression on Pitt himself than on his contemporaries and on the House of

[1] Here is his note to his wife with the news of Trafalgar : " You will weep for Lord Nelson whilst you and all around you will rejoice in his glories. After an action of only 4 hours, with only 27 sail of the line against 33, he took 19 and one blew up. We have lost no ship, but alas ! the first Admiral in the universe." *Lond. MSS.*

[2] See Section 6, p. 57.

Commons. He was a ready debater, but he had no gift of expression and never shone in a set speech like Canning. He avoided, indeed, display, and wanted, so far as possible, to fight the war in the council chamber rather than in the House, though he never shrank from defending a course of action there. But he had no coterie, either male or female, to circulate his praises, and such leisure as he had was passed in unobtrusive domesticity. His wife did not attract or please others as she did him, and, in spite of her efforts, their house did not become a social centre until Castlereagh's achievements made it so.

When Grenville and the Whigs came into power, and only redeemed one of the most feeble of administrations by their last great act of passing the Abolition of the Slave Trade, Castlereagh without Pitt did not loom large in the public eye. When Portland made his new Cabinet, therefore, though Castlereagh went back to his former office as Secretary of State for War and Colonies for three of the most fruitful years of his life, Canning, who signalised his entry into the Foreign Office by the seizure of the Danish fleet, eclipsed him somewhat in reputation. The young Etonian had a brilliant band of followers to raise his fame and mock at his rivals. Even in the Cabinet, Canning, because of his reputation as a speaker, came to be listened to more than Castlereagh or the strongly Protestant and prolific Perceval, who, as Chancellor of the Exchequer, led the House of Commons. Since the Duke of Portland was old and feeble and a fool, Canning's power and ambition grew. He was rightly conscious of great abilities, and he wished to succeed not only to the policy of Pitt, but also to his commanding position in the council.

Meanwhile Castlereagh placed great achievements to his credit, though only time could shew how great they were. He completely reorganised the system of raising men for the army in such a manner that the historian who has most right to make the judgment holds him to have been "the best War Minister that we have ever had." [1] He also played the principal, and certainly most loyal, part in the Cabinet during the tangled series of events which eventually resulted in his

[1] Sir John Fortescue, *British Statesmen of the Great War*, 228.

friend Arthur Wellesley commanding the British army in
Portugal, after having been superseded and almost ruined
by the Cintra Convention. No one can read Castlereagh's
letters to the generals at this time without being impressed
by the manner in which he was ready to bear responsibility himself, and how little he played the politician's trick
of trying to ride for safety at the expense of others. Henceforward he was one of the foremost in supporting, through
good and evil fortune, the new commander in his defence of
Portugal and attacks on the French armies in Spain.

But the Peninsula did not exhaust the military power of
Britain or Castlereagh's efforts as a War Minister. Hence
the most serious blot on his record—for the Walcheren expedition was more due to him than to any other man. As a
strategic proposition it could be defended by those who, like
Castlereagh, believed wholeheartedly in the Peninsular campaign, since the number of troops that could be usefully
employed by Wellington was limited by finance and supply.
Castlereagh wished, therefore, to use the growing strength of
Britain in a more direct attack on Napoleon's power, and, since
Prussia's weakness for the moment made an attempt further
north undesirable, the destruction of his arsenal and the new
fleet building in the Scheldt seemed the most desirable method
of striking a blow while he was occupied with the new challenge
which Austria, unaided, had the courage to make in 1809.
Castlereagh prepared the expedition with the greatest care,
and it was certainly the best equipped as well as the largest
that had ever left the shores of Britain. It was, however,
delayed until too late in the year, and ruined by the choice
of the commander, for which Castlereagh must bear the main
responsibility. The result was a humiliating defeat, instead
of, as might and should have occurred, had the Earl of Chatham
and Sir Richard Strachan possessed even a modicum of energy
and enterprise, the capture of Antwerp and the destruction
of the fleet.

This disaster would in itself have been a hard blow for
Castlereagh to bear, but the situation was made impossible
by the discovery, after the news of defeat had come, that his
colleagues had for some time been arranging behind his back

for his removal from the post which he had filled so well. This strange conduct had nothing to do with the failure of Walcheren, but was a result of Canning's ambition to obtain a commanding influence in the management of the war. Relying on the reputation which he had justly made by his conduct of foreign affairs and his ability in the House, he challenged Castlereagh's position early in 1809, and had it not been for Portland's weakness the issue would then have been tried. The Duke, however, persuaded Canning to postpone action until after the expedition, and the King and even Castlereagh's uncle acquiesced. Perceval was horrified when he heard what was arranged, but it was then too late to stop the intrigue, and, when the Government was discredited by the failure at Walcheren, Canning demanded his pound of flesh.

Castlereagh had as much grievance against his own friends as against Canning, but he could hardly challenge Portland or Camden, and he rightly saw in Canning's proposal to get rid of him the origin of the unfair treatment to which he had been subjected. His friend and helper, Cooke, has painted in vivid colours the agony and distress of his mind when the conduct of his colleagues, which at first he could hardly bring himself to believe, became clear to him. His challenge to Canning was such as would allow of no compromise and was readily accepted. The duel, in which Canning was wounded though not seriously, resulted in the resignation of both, as well as of Portland, who was already ill and soon died, and the whole Government of the country was in the melting-pot.[1]

The result did not justify Canning's expectations. In Perceval he found a tougher rival than he had expected, while no one was prepared to give him that position of primacy which he thought was his due. His offer to form an administration was contemptuously ignored by the King and his colleagues. He had not perceived that the manœuvres he used to obtain the first position destroyed the confidence that alone made it possible. Even Wellesley, whom he had planned to assist him to power, "cut him to the heart" by accepting

[1] Cooke's letter was published by me in the *Cambridge Historical Journal*, vol. iii., No. 1, 1929, where is also Professor Temperley's skilful defence of Canning, with some new letters.

the Foreign Office without caring very much that Canning was left out altogether, since he would not accept the lead of Perceval, whose honesty had won him the position which Canning had designed for himself.

Thus both Castlereagh and Canning were out of office until 1812. Both refused the offers made to them in 1810 to come back together, but, while Castlereagh's answer to the invitation was courteous to a degree, Canning was needlessly offensive to Perceval by reiterating that he would never serve under him. Meanwhile Castlereagh's own position was filled adequately by Liverpool, but Wellesley proved a gigantic failure in the Foreign Office. He, like Canning, wished to dominate the Cabinet, and his claims to special authority were no greater. Many observers attributed his failure to his private habits, which had led him to attempt to take a mistress with him on his Embassy to Spain and made him notorious for his 'harem.' However that may be, it is certain that he neglected the business of his own office and refused to attend Cabinets, while he filled the air with complaints that his brother was not adequately supported in the Peninsula.

At the end of 1810 the death of his favourite daughter caused the King to lose his reason once more. Again there was a contest over the Regency Bill, and the Tories forced the Prince to accept only limited powers for twelve months. But the King lapsed into hopeless insanity, and as the time drew near for the Regent to exercise full control of the power of the Crown, it was confidently expected that the Whigs would be summoned, or that at least drastic changes would be made in the Government. Wellesley, though a burden to his colleagues, was liked by the Prince Regent, and might easily replace Perceval as Prime Minister, thus opening the way for Canning. Few thought that Castlereagh would become the principal Minister of the Cabinet that was to be responsible for ending the war and reconstructing Europe.

2. THE FORMATION OF THE LIVERPOOL MINISTRY [1]

THE new Regency Bill which the King's madness made necessary allowed over twelve months to elapse before the Prince was free to use the power of the Crown without restriction. The Regent could hardly change his Ministers in such a position, and thus had necessarily to work with the Perceval Cabinet and discuss with them the many difficult problems, personal and political, which pressed upon him as he ascended the throne. Since Perceval had defended Caroline in 1806 and was a violent Protestant, while George had always been surrounded by Whigs and was reputed favourable to the Catholics, it was natural that friction should be expected. But during the twelve months of restricted rule the Regent changed his attitude, partly, no doubt, owing to sympathetic handling by the Cabinet, though Perceval and Eldon shewed themselves sufficiently independent in the negotiations for the new civil list.

It is unnecessary, however, to make personal motives the main reason for the Regent wishing to keep Perceval in office. Hardly any other British Sovereign has assumed power under such difficult conditions. The strain of the long war, in which Britain stood now almost alone, the new financial difficulties, the threatening attitude of the United States, the symptoms

---

[1] There is an immense amount of documentary material on these negotiations. Many of the statements were written for effect, and were published in the Press or in pamphlets, and subsequently in the *Annual Register* for 1812. All the lives and memoirs have many letters, notably the *Wellesley Papers*, and the Grenville attitude has been revealed in great detail in vol. x. of the *Dropmore MSS.*, which Mr. Francis Bickley has completed. I have also used a number of letters and documents in the Windsor Archives. Even now the exact part played by Prince Regent, courtiers, and statesmen is obscure on some points, and unfortunately especially on Castlereagh's own conduct.

of unrest in various parts of the country, shewed George that his new duties were no sinecure. In Perceval he had a man whom even Canning's friend could describe as "the most popular man in the country." But, above all, George was as determined as his Ministers to fight the war to a finish. He would not bring the Whigs into office, except under such conditions as safeguarded the policy of resistance to Napoleon and the prosecution of the war in Spain. He refused, therefore, to listen to his closest confidant, Lord Moira, who served him with rare fidelity at this time, though he recognised that he must make some approach to his old friends and supporters. Public opinion would be shocked and parliamentary controversy still more embittered if their position were not made quite clear.

The result was that in the famous letter to the Duke of York, by which the Whigs were invited to join the administration, great emphasis was laid on the successes of the last year in the Peninsula as an example to the nations of Europe. Grey and Grenville would not have accepted, in any case, a coalition with Perceval. But the terms of the letter were, in fact, an insult to them. The reference to the war was peculiarly obnoxious to the first, while Grenville was the strongest opponent of the Peninsular expedition. They took care, however, in their reply to avoid this topic and to place the Catholic question in the forefront. George considered that he was then free from the obligations of his youth and gave Perceval his full confidence, in spite of Moira's outspoken and passionate plea that he should try some other combination before confirming the Tories in office. The result was the immediate resignation of Wellesley, a step which he had only postponed since the turn of the year at the Regent's urgent request. To Wellesley's own suggestions that some one else should take Perceval's place, the Regent would not listen, though he asked him once more to discuss with Eldon whether any change could be made to satisfy his complaints.[1]

[1] Wellesley to the Prince Regent, Feb. 17, half-past 6 p.m., 1812: *Windsor Arch.* . . . " Nor would Lord Wellesley have presumed to offer any advice on the subject of forming an administration adapted to the present crisis, if he had understood that your Royal Highness had already fixed Mr. Perceval in his seat and had formed your Government on that basis " . . . This adds a new note to the correspondence of Feb. 18,

A further result, therefore, was Castlereagh's appointment as Secretary of State for Foreign Affairs, for which preparation had been made since January. How much his connection with the Hertfords helped him to office it is impossible to determine, but he certainly was Perceval's choice as well as the Regent's. There was no other obvious person to whom the Government could turn, since Canning's conduct in 1809 ruled him out so long as Perceval led the House. Castlereagh shewed no great anxiety to accept the invitation. He insisted on waiting until the Regent had full powers and had decided his course of action, saying that he "would be no stop-gap for any man." He advised also that other efforts should be made to strengthen the Government, obviously hinting that the Sidmouth party, with whom he had always worked well, should be brought in. Perceval also desired this accession, and both must have been aware that it did not increase Canning's friends in the Cabinet.

Wellington would, indeed, have preferred Castlereagh back at his old job. "I wish your brother," he wrote to Charles Stewart, "had gone to the War instead of the Foreign department. It would have been a better general arrangement. But I suspect the existing one has been made with a view to conciliate a hostile vote or two, in the notion that some parties object particularly to his management of the War department. This is weak! Their votes cannot be conciliated." [1]

This was obviously directed at Canning, but, whatever the motive, Liverpool kept the War Office, and when the Whigs had refused the Regent's offer, Castlereagh stepped into Wellesley's place, taking his seat on the Treasury Bench on February 28. His uncle, Camden, soon made way for Sidmouth to come in as President of the Council, and some of Sidmouth's followers were included in the Government. Canning, as a result, went openly into opposition. But the

published in *The Wellesley Papers*, ii. 71–78. Moira to the Prince Regent, Feb. 18, 1812 : *Windsor Arch.* Moira refused the Garter lest it should be considered as a bribe for abandoning his old friends.

[1] Castlereagh's answer to Perceval, given by the Duke of Buckingham (*Memoirs of the Regency*, i. 218–19), is confirmed in substance by Perceval himself (Spencer Walpole, *Life of Perceval*, ii. 268), and by Lord Grenville "from other *quite* authentic information" (*Dropmore Papers*, x. 204). Wellington to Stewart, March 14, 1812 : *Lond. MSS.*

Regent's judgment was confirmed, and the Government went on without much difficulty, though both Canning and Wellesley pressed the Catholic question furiously in order to embarrass it. Canning also lost reputation by his attitude towards the repeal of the Order in Council, which Brougham advocated with great skill and forced the Government to refer to a committee. But this step was already in contemplation, in face of the increasing hostility of the United States, and the Government was growing in strength, until, on May 11, the Prime Minister was assassinated by the mad Bellingham in the very precincts of the House.

Under a blow so unexpected the Cabinet were saved by their loyalty to one another. On May 13 they offered to serve under any of their number the Regent should choose, admitting, however, that their prospects of survival were doubtful. The Regent authorised Liverpool to negotiate with Wellesley and Canning, and Vansittart was brought in to take charge of the Exchequer *ad interim*, while inevitably Castlereagh became Leader of the House of Commons in succession to Perceval.

Wellesley and Canning now thought that their opportunity had come. They refused Liverpool's offers, and, in order to oust the shattered Ministry, Wortley moved a resolution in the House urging the Regent to form a stronger Government. It was carried, and there was no alternative for the Ministers but to place their resignations in the Regent's hands, offering to carry on the business of the state meanwhile.[1]

In the crisis that followed, the Regent, advised by Moira, with some help from his private secretary, MacMahon, never made a false step, while the two eager aspirants for office were soon discredited and the Opposition leaders allowed to sink back into their Olympian sulks, which it is clear they preferred to the burden of office at such a time.

[1] Minute of the Cabinet to the Prince Regent, May 13, 1812 : *Windsor Arch.*; which formally records the result of the meeting of which rough notes are given by Twiss (*Life of Eldon*, ii. 210). From the later discussions as to the entrance of Wellesley and Canning, Castlereagh absented himself so as not to embarrass his colleagues (*Annual Register*, 1812, 350).

Wilberforce says : " Canning very clever, and Wortley's motion really made for him and Wellesley, though carried by the numbers of the old Opposition " (*Life of Wilberforce*, iv. 31), but there is no proof that Canning actually planned the motion.

Wellesley was first entrusted with the task of forming a
Government, and, of course, was pledged to Canning. They
approached their old colleagues on the basis of a settlement
of the Catholic question and a vigorous prosecution of the war
in Spain, but met with a unanimous refusal; the rupture was
made complete by the immediate publication of much of the
correspondence. The Regent seems to have deeply regretted
the failure, for he insisted on each of his Ministers giving him
a separate minute of their reasons. The answers of both
"Protestants" and "Catholics" could have left him in no
doubt that Wellesley would never be accepted by them as
their leader, only Melville hinting that he could do so on any
terms.[1]

This rebuff seemed to bring the Opposition nearer to power,
but the Regent was not yet ready to yield. Wellesley was
first authorised to approach Grenville and Grey with an offer
of a coalition Cabinet, in which they should have four or five
members, while Moira and other unofficial Whigs would be
included. It was not likely that Grenville and Grey would
agree to such a compromise. Their attitude to the Spanish
war made co-operation with Wellesley impossible, as the
Regent must have known, though the Marquess seems to
have been convinced that his own talents would induce them
to join him. The exchange of correspondence lasted a week,
but no agreement could be reached. Rebuffed once more,
Wellesley offered to make a Ministry with Moira, Sheridan,
and Erskine, who were, he claimed, all ready to serve under
him, with perhaps Lord Holland as well. But the Regent
refused his assent, and Wellesley had no option but to give up
the game.

The turn of Grenville and Grey had at last necessarily come.

---

[1] Minute of Cabinet [May 27], 1813 (*Windsor Arch.*), is signed by all the
Ministers except Castlereagh and Camden, who "were absent at their own
desire." Liverpool's separate minute is given in his life (Yonge, *Liverpool*,
i. 393), the other ten are in the *Windsor Archives*. The Queen was much
shocked at the methods pursued ; for she wrote to her son : " With
infinite concern do I see by to-day's papers that the correspondence as well
as the conversation between Lord Liverpool, Marquis of Wellesley, and
Mr. Canning (not Cunning) is published. This is the first time I ever
remember such a transaction being given out in the public prints, and I
can not help reflecting how well the dear King judged the characters of
those two individuals by proving themselves such as He always described
them to me." *Windsor Arch.*

All other parties had failed to form a Government, and Moira, who was asked to approach his old friends informally, was apparently hopeful of success. That the Regent only allowed the negotiation with extreme reluctance is shewn by Sheridan's pleading that he should not proscribe Grey. But the negotiation shewed that neither Grenville nor Grey desired office on any terms. This time no conditions were laid down, but they soon found sufficient excuses, and Moira's eyes were at last opened to the real state of affairs. "It is clear," he reported to MacMahon, "that they do not mean to accept any terms whatever. The only point to be determined is whether one should take from them the last shadow of excuse which they might attempt, in saying *I* had made no overture to them; my letter having to be considered as an explanation of a matter already defunct." After another abortive attempt, therefore, to persuade Wellesley and Canning to join the Tories, Moira finally notified Grenville and Grey that he was authorised by the Prince Regent to discuss their acceptance of office. Their haughty reply, demanding a change in the Household appointments, a veiled attack on the Hertfords, was, of course, peculiarly offensive to the Regent and put an end to the negotiation.[1]

Grenville and Grey might well dislike serving such a master, but there can be no doubt that their refusal rested on deeper causes than the Household. Grey, indeed, insisted to Moira that they could only take office when the Prince Regent was ready "to give us his full confidence both as to men and measures." They were, however, conscious that they were not ready to put into practice the policies which they had urged in opposition. They were both *defaitistes* who had no wish to bear the responsibility of defeat. They shewed their

---

[1] R. B. Sheridan to the Prince Regent, June 1, 1812, congratulating him on summoning Wellesley, but not dissembling " the deep regret I have felt at an apparent alteration in your manner towards me—produced solely, I must believe, by my expressing an opinion that a proscription of Lord Grey in the formation of a new administration would be a proceeding equally injurious to the estimation of your personal dignity and the maintenance of the public interests " (*Windsor Arch.*). This may explain why Sheridan never told Grenville and Grey, as he was authorised to do, that Hertford and Yarmouth intended to resign when the Whigs came in. Moira to MacMahon, June 14, 1812 : *Windsor Arch.* See T. Moore, *Life of Sheridan,* 674–75.

patriotism best by refusing government on any terms. Perhaps Grey would have acted differently had he known that his action meant twelve more years of opposition for the Whigs.

Grenville and Grey could retire to Dropmore and Howick, making such occasional sallies into the political world as suited their convenience, and waiting for their gloomy prophecies to be fulfilled. They were quite content. But their followers set up a howl of rage. They had no contempt for office, which at one time seemed so near. They considered, with some justice, that their leaders had played into the Regent's hands. Sydney Smith, indeed, charged them with the feat of having "made the Court the object of public love and compassion, made Lord Yarmouth appear like a virtuous man, given character to the Prince, and restored the dilapidation of kingly power." Moira and Sheridan were regarded by many as traitors, and the latter could not be prevented from defending his master in the House, much as the Regent, who dreaded his garrulity, tried to stop him. As for Moira, he was heartsick and bankrupt, but the Prince rewarded him and at the same time escaped his control by conferring on him the position of both Governor-General and Commander-in-Chief in India. He barely evaded the bailiffs as he set out to enjoy his new honours. Yarmouth took his place as the foremost courtier and adviser, a fact of importance in Castlereagh's career.[1]

Meanwhile Castlereagh had thus become unexpectedly Leader of the House of Commons as well as Foreign Minister, and necessarily the second person in authority in the Cabinet. One more crisis, however, had to be passed before he was confirmed in this position. For Canning had not yet reconciled himself to the situation. He was dreadfully disappointed

---

[1] Mrs. Austin, *Letters of Sydney Smith*, ii. 93–94. Moira to MacMahon, June 14, 1812 ; R. B. Sheridan to MacMahon, June 17, 1812 : *Windsor Arch.* Moira to MacMahon, July 21, 1812 : " . . . you see I look forward to a *possibility* of a change of ministry. The state of the country tranquil but deeply dissatisfied will force that measure ; and when the necessity comes it will be very sudden. I am cutting down all establishments here [his home at Donnington] with an unsparing hand and fashioning rigidly the plan of my future life. It promises me more gratification than I have experienced in active scenes." *Windsor Arch.*

that the Whigs had not ousted his former colleagues, for he
felt sure he could outshine Castlereagh in Opposition and thus
secure the reversion of his place when the Whigs fell in their
turn.[1] But he soon shewed himself very conciliatory to
Liverpool, whom he consulted before he moved his new
resolutions on the Catholic question in the Commons. Castlereagh naturally voted with him on that subject, and it was
clear to all that nothing but personal difficulties prevented
Canning from joining the Cabinet. Liverpool was eager to
strengthen the front bench in the Lower House, and in July
Castlereagh and Canning met to discuss terms. Castlereagh
shewed his patriotism by offering to give up the Foreign
Office to Canning, taking himself the position of Chancellor
of the Exchequer, for which no one but Wilberforce thought
Vansittart very suitable.

But Canning, though he admitted that this offer was
"perhaps the handsomest that was ever made to an individual," could not bring himself to allow to Castlereagh that
lead which he had formerly refused to Perceval. It was
in vain that Castlereagh assured him, at Liverpool's request,
that he should control absolutely the Foreign Office business.
He demanded complete equality either under some other
person, though none was available, or by some division of
business, which Castlereagh rightly declined as impossible.
No one suggested that Castlereagh should give way entirely,
for he was already Leader of the House, and to surrender
the position to another was obviously to confess incompetence. Moreover, he had offered to resign his office for
one less well paid and less preferable to himself. The Regent,
though full of praise of Castlereagh's handsome conduct,
was most anxious to bring Canning in, and explored every
avenue to put pressure on him to reconsider his decision. "He
takes as much courting as a woman, and a great deal more
than most," he told Lady Bessborough, whom he urged to

---

[1] See his statement to Huskisson a little later, given in Aspinall, *Lord
Brougham and the Whig Party*, 271 : "Between Castlereagh in office, and
me where I am, the Pittites, with Charles Long for their guide, probably
will not hesitate to choose Castlereagh as their leader. Let us be *both out* ;
and *then* let them make their choice and let Lord Castlereagh *then* state his
pretensions."

induce Lord Granville Leveson-Gower to support the bargain. But that friend of Canning was altogether on the other side. Though even Lord Sidmouth seized an opportunity to make it up with Canning, who confessed that he believed his overture to be sincere, the distrust and jealousy of Castlereagh remained. Canning wrote bitterly to Granville: "Had Castlereagh half the Dr.'s [Sidmouth's] art (if art it be) or his nature (as I take it to be) *his* point would have been carried in our tête-à-tête; but (luckily perhaps for me) *he* can neither feel nor feign." He accepted, therefore, the value which his too partial friends placed upon him and refused all concession. Though the new elections brought him a triumph at Liverpool, he had thrown away as great a chance as ever came to any man. Only his rival's death renewed the opportunity, of which at last his genius availed itself.[1]

Castlereagh was thus left to bear nearly the whole burden of the Government in the House, while he conducted the Foreign Policy of Britain at the most critical moment of her fortunes. But he had behind him a Cabinet united as no Cabinet had been since the early days of the war. They had passed through a crisis which had drawn them together in a common defence of a vigorous prosecution of the war, and in this they knew they had the Regent's full backing. Liverpool himself regretted his failure, but rejoiced in the unity of his Cabinet and the confidence of the Prince Regent, whom he told Wellington he should protect against "the complete and uncontrolled dominion of the Opposition." As for Wellington, who had just been again promoted in the peerage, he inquired, "What the devil is the use of making me a

---

[1] For these negotiations, see Yonge, *Life of Liverpool*, i. 401–25. *Life of Wilberforce*, iv. 37–41. Stapleton, *George Canning and his Times*, 208–10. Countess Granville, *Corres. of Lord Granville Leveson-Gower*, ii. 439, 441, 443, 445–46, 469. F. Leveson-Gower, *Letters of Harriet Countess Granville*, i. 35–37. In a letter to MacMahon, no doubt intended for the Regent's eye, Canning boasted of his success at Liverpool and gave vent to his spleen and rancour against the Government in a manner which shewed how much he exaggerated his own importance : "If therefore the Government intended the dissolution (as I hear they do not scruple to avow they did) against *me*, they are as great bunglers in their miserable home politics as they have shewn themselves abroad in their *vigorous* war measures, against America, for instance. . . . But though I have not suffered from their good intentions, you may believe I do not less *gratefully* acknowledge them." *Windsor Arch.*

Marquess? " but he accepted the new Ministry with considerable satisfaction and urged his brother Henry not to resign.
He was ready to serve any Ministry which would prosecute
the war; but Liverpool, Bathurst, and Castlereagh he already
knew and was grateful for past support, however much he
might grumble at times. All the Cabinet except Liverpool
were glad that they had escaped from Canning's brilliance.
Whatever Castlereagh's other qualities, he could be trusted
to be loyal to those working with him. In a short time both
Wellington and the Cabinet were to discover that he had other
unsuspected merits.

3. COURT, CABINET, PARLIAMENT, AND PUBLIC OPINION

THERE is little recognition by historians of the Regent's merits as a politician which he had so clearly displayed in the appointment of the Liverpool Government. Still less have they given him any credit for the successful ending of the Napoleonic war. Many at the time, however, were not slow to admit it, and he certainly claimed it for himself, even for events of which the main responsibility was scarcely his. In December 1812 he wrote to the Queen of "the great and glorious news from Russia of which I have, under Providence, the heartfelt consolation, without unbecoming vanity, to ascribe in a great degree to my own original and indefatigable endeavours in drawing that Power to those measures which have since been pursued." To celebrate the battle of Leipzig he sent her a snuff-box bearing his portrait, "*one* who I hope you will *now* think is *no disgrace* to *you*, to his family or to his country, and who, as far as his mind could go, has contributed *that to his utmost* in aid of and towards the accomplishment of all the great and splendid events and successes which it has pleased Providence to bless and to crown our joint combined and allied exertions and arms." Of the news of the capture of Paris he could only write with a trembling hand: "I think, my dearest mother, that you will think that I have fulfilled and done my duty at least, and perhaps I may be vain enough to hope that you may feel a little proud of *your son*." [1]

This attitude towards these great events was of a certain

[1] The Prince Regent to the Queen, Dec. 6, 1812 : *The Taylor Papers*, 82 ; Nov. 3, 1813 ; April 9, 1814 : *Windsor Arch*. It is only fair to add that no one praised Wellington more ; and the draft in the Windsor Archives of the letter of July 3, 1813, making him a Field Marshal, shews how carefully George composed his eulogies.

importance. It was, as has been seen, one of the reasons which kept the Whigs from power in 1812. It had also an influence in 1814 and 1815, when the Prince Regent was one of the foremost of those who wished for no peace with Napoleon. Naturally it would not have had much effect without the assistance of determined Ministers and of public opinion. But the support of which the Cabinet were assured from their royal master was one factor in their decisions, and public opinion was much influenced, at any rate in aristocratic circles, by the example of the Court.

George, indeed, took a constant interest in all military matters, and in one at least, uniforms, he was something of an expert. Nor was he without influence in the diplomacy of the period. His dislike of the Tsar after the unfortunate visit of 1814, his admiration of the Emperor of Austria, his kindness to the Bourbons, all played a part in British policy, even though in the last resort he allowed his Ministers to decide it. He always followed closely all the complicated negotiations of the war and the peace, and in the interviews, which foreign representatives reported in great detail, he shewed himself completely conversant with the subject in hand. He was, indeed, apt to talk too much, and sometimes gave away information which his Ministers would have preferred to remain secret. But nearly always he acted in this period as they desired, and no one could exercise a greater charm on even the most suspicious of diplomats.

Moreover, he was ruler of Hanover as well as Britain, though in 1812 the Electorate was swallowed up in Jerome Bonaparte's kingdom. In spite of this, however, he retained as Regent of Hanover diplomatic relations with both Austria and Prussia, which were of vital importance in linking Britain to the Continent, were indeed the main channel through which she still obtained information from and conveyed ideas to those Courts. His principal Hanoverian Minister, Count Münster, who had sacrificed his patrimony in Hanover to serve in London, had the Regent's full confidence. Fortunately he was a man not only of energy but of moderation and common sense. Though he was anxious to advance the interests of his own country, he saw that to do so he must subordinate them to the interests of Britain. Indeed, the argument might perhaps now have been turned the other way; for, while Hanover supplied troops of splendid quality for the British service and a diplomatic network on the Continent, Britain gave no guarantee of Hanoverian territory, and though Hanover became a kingdom in 1814 it was not enlarged on a scale corresponding with the subservient south German states. Münster accompanied the Duke of Cambridge to Hanover at the end of 1813, and then represented his master at headquarters and during the peace negotiations at Paris and Vienna, where his advice and assistance were freely used by Castlereagh. George, however, was not even allowed to visit the new kingdom until 1821, though he made a determined effort to do so during the Hundred Days.[1]

George was connected through his wife with the Brunswick family, and the return of their duchy was therefore always part of the British programme. This was not a great matter and hardly compensated for the treatment to which Caroline herself was subjected. The private life of the Regent is beyond the defence of the most casuistical of pens, even if Lord John Russell's considered opinion that "a worse man has not lived in our day" is obviously too harsh. Now that the Regent was in power the position of Caroline became again a burning political question. It was the irony of fate that the Chancellor and Prime Minister of the Regent's first Government should be Eldon and Perceval, who had defended Caroline in 1806 against the insinuations of the Delicate Investigation. But no one could deny the Regent's right to control the upbringing of his daughter Charlotte, now reaching marriageable age, and there was much to be said for the view that her mother was not a suitable person to look after her. This controversy, which began in 1813, unfortunately became mixed up with politics, and the Tory Government were thrown more and more on the side of the Regent by the violence of the Opposition. Brougham for his own purposes, and Whitbread out of decent feeling, led the attack. The

---

[1] Liverpool to the Prince Regent, June 1, 1815 (*Windsor Arch.*), which reports the Cabinet's refusal to apply to Parliament for a Bill to enable the Prince Regent to leave the country.

family quarrel was to be a source of great anxiety and real detriment to British interests in 1814.

If George's relations with his wife bear no defence, he was a dutiful and affectionate son to his stiff and obstinate old mother, exceedingly kind to his sisters, and for the most part on amazingly good terms with his extraordinary brothers. Partly, no doubt, his attentions to Windsor were due to the necessity of keeping them loyal in his marital quarrel. But the letters of his sisters shew a genuine and artless affection for him, which he retained by little acts of kindness. He made a great effort to rescue them from the living tomb of Windsor, where their mother exercised a relentless tyranny over them, partly that they might chaperon Charlotte, and, though he was not very successful, they were full of gratitude. The Windsor Court, however, exercised no influence on politics.

By 1812 the Regent had become tired of the beautiful Lady Jersey, who was reduced to begging for a pension in these years. Caroline's place was now supplied by Castlereagh's aunt, the Marchioness of Hertford, a mistress who was fifty years of age and the mother of a son, Lord Yarmouth, who was later to be the most notorious of the family. Her husband was made Lord Chamberlain of the new Court, while Yarmouth became Warden of the Stannaries. They were good Tories, and his cousin Yarmouth was, as has been seen, Castlereagh's friend, while Lady Castlereagh was an intimate of Lady Hertford.

But little of their influence can be traced in public affairs. Yarmouth's services for the Prince mainly concerned those delicate family matters which needed so much care, though occasionally he was used as an intermediary with some politician. He had a quarrel with the Government late in 1814, which seems only to have been healed by the Regent himself; but though this caused tongues to wag and gave the Whigs a fleeting hope of royal sunshine, it had no effect. In fact, after a short period, no one had a greater influence on George than Castlereagh himself. Charles Arbuthnot was consulted in minor affairs. The King's Private Secretary, little Colonel MacMahon, whose appointment caused a great row in Parliament, a discreet and tactful man, Sir William

Knighton, whom Wellesley recommended, and Adam, the Attorney-General, were no more than useful instruments.

There was still great difficulty about the Regent's debts and expenditure, but a partial reform took place at this time. When peace came, though George never ceased to be extravagant, he was made to feel the economy campaign, Castlereagh writing stern letters and many useless functionaries being dismissed. This George took easily enough. His building craze was waning, though Carlton House was made very magnificent, and his artistic nature sought other outlets. He was devoted to music and was an intelligent patron of the fine arts. Had not Bavaria changed sides he would have added the Ægina to the Elgin Marbles, and he even sought to bring some of Napoleon's ill-gotten treasures to London.

By this time, in theory at least, all George's brothers had reached years of discretion. With only one, the Duke of Sussex, was he now on really bad terms, and one of the consequences was that the Duke was a violent Whig and always suspected, rather unfairly, of a hand in the worst intrigues against the Regent. The doors of Carlton House were closed to him. The Duke of Gloucester, his cousin, was also altogether on the Opposition side and one of the channels through which Sir Robert Wilson circulated his misleading reports from the war area. Of the others the Dukes of York and Cambridge were both of great service. George had soon replaced the former in the position of Commander-in-Chief which he had lost through the scandal of Mrs. Clark. As has been seen, he played some part in the political crisis of 1812, but his influence did not generally extend so far outside his office. In spite of his curious menage at Broadlands he was a decided asset to his family and country.

For the Duke of Cumberland, however, no one had a good word save George himself. This violent, ugly, and vicious man, Court, Cabinet, and public alike detested; and when the Princess threatened exposure of past letters abusing the Regent, with whom he was now on the best of terms, he thought it well to depart for the Continent early in 1813, with the hope that he might obtain a military command, the Governorship of Hanover, and a wife. In only the last object

was he successful, and the twice-divorced Princess Solms
added to the difficulties of his position when he returned in
1815. The Cabinet, while relieved at his departure from
England, refused him all help to the smallest of commands.
His relatives at Mecklenburg received him with courtesy and
Bernadotte with extravagant flattery. But the Tsar refused
to invite him to headquarters, whither, however, he proceeded and there did his best to inflame the jealousies of the
Austrians and Prussians of Alexander's primacy in the
military councils of the coalition. He entered Hanover as
soon as it was free from French troops, and his mortification
when superseded by the Duke of Cambridge was intense. His
sister, the Queen of Wurtemberg, appealed to the Regent in
the highest alarm to save her from a visit. One result of this
melancholy expedition was to sow suspicions of the Tsar in
the Regent's mind, for while he had no illusions as to his
brother's popularity, his own person was to some extent
involved in the treatment meted out to him.

The Duke of Cambridge, on the other hand, was a quiet,
sensible, competent, and even religious man, who seems to
have handled the government of Hanover, to which he was
appointed in 1813, if not with the most liberal outlook, at
least with skill and tact. The Duke of Clarence, the Lord
High Admiral, of whom hardly anyone thought as a future
King, was of assistance when the royal visitors came to
England after the peace. The Duke of Kent's opportunity
had not yet come, though he asked in 1811 to be made either
Commander-in-Chief in the Mediterranean or Master-General
of the Ordnance. It must be admitted that the financial
affairs and domestic relations of all the brothers were terribly
complicated, and, as none of them was popular, due provision
for them at this time harassed the Government by affording the
more extreme Opposition an excellent opportunity to annoy.

George's eldest sister he had not seen since 1797, for she
was the wife of one of Napoleon's most faithful vassals, the
King of Wurtemberg, which did not, however, prevent her
from receiving an allowance from Britain during the war, or
from claiming for loss of exchange on the money when her
husband changed sides. Her new position was signalised by

a flood of letters, most of which ended in a request for subsidies or other favours for Wurtemberg. This importunity
was, however, undoubtedly mainly due to her jealous and
selfish husband, who watched closely her relations with her
family, which he wished to exploit for his own benefit. George
nevertheless treated her personally with great kindness, and
sent her an invitation to London by one of his favourite
courtiers, little Sir Thomas Tyrwhitt (known in the family
circle as the "shortest night"). But her husband would not
let her come, and it cannot be said that her begging letters had
much effect on the Regent or his Ministers.

Such was the world of the Court which Castlereagh soon
learnt to understand and use for his own purposes. If it gave
him some trouble, it also provided opportunities not otherwise
available. Above all, in the Prince Regent he had at least
one man in London who was vitally interested in the shape of
the new Europe and took pains to inform himself about it.
Undoubtedly this mutual and exceptional interest did much
to give Castlereagh that commanding position in the Regent's
councils to which he gradually attained. But he kept it as a
member of the Cabinet and Foreign Minister. He had hardly
any private correspondence with George except on family
matters.[1]

Thus, though there are hints that the Prime Minister was
occasionally a little jealous of Castlereagh's high favour with
the Prince, which he certainly never quite obtained for himself, on the whole the two were on the most excellent terms.
Liverpool was not a man who wished to impose his ideas
on others, and so long as Castlereagh avoided commitments
which threatened Parliamentary difficulties, he was quite content to give him a free hand. But though his confidence in
Castlereagh grew in these years he never quite appreciated
the difficulties of his task. During the war he was always as
persistent and courageous as he was cool and circumspect.
But when peace came his eyes were too much fixed on Parliament and not enough on reconstruction. He only yielded

---

[1] So I conclude from an examination of the Londonderry Papers and
Windsor Archives, though the contrary was often stated. The Prince
Regent in 1814 ordered Castlereagh to write direct " if anything occurred
that was not of an official nature." C.C. ix. 210.

reluctantly to the risk and effort involved in Castlereagh's determination to make a new Europe which would stand the test of time. His mind was too much occupied with domestic and party politics to realise all that was involved in the issues of the Congress of Vienna, and he regarded Castlereagh too much as Leader of the House of Commons and not sufficiently as Secretary of State for Foreign Affairs. But his long experience of the Foreign and the War Offices, his unfailing calm and common sense, and his profound knowledge of Parliamentary tactics were of great importance in enabling Castlereagh to carry out policies for which few of his country-men cared. No one could make a better debating speech than Liverpool on a thorny question. He was, as a Whig critic confessed, "one of the most prudent ministers and debaters in Parliament he ever knew, and that he is besides a man in the House of Lords who is ready to turn out in all weathers—a form of speech formerly much in use in Ireland to describe ready and daring speakers." [1] However much Liverpool had hung back before the decisions were made, he was a tower of strength when they had to be defended at home.

With the other member of the Government who was most concerned with foreign affairs, the Earl of Bathurst, Secretary of State for War and Colonies, Castlereagh worked most harmoniously. Bathurst, who also had held the Foreign Office for a short time and acted as locum-tenens in Castle-reagh's absence abroad, was one of the most assiduous, modest, and equable of Ministers. His correspondence shews a breadth of view to which none of his colleagues except Castlereagh attained. He supported Castlereagh as loyally as he did Wellington. Their minds often ran on similar lines, and Bathurst was more in sympathy with Castlereagh during the crisis at Vienna [2] than any other member of the Cabinet. Bathurst was in any case an ideal colleague; for while he did his own job well enough, he was always ready to help and give credit to others. No other member of the Cabinet did so much to preserve its unity.

---

[1] W. Sichel, *The Glenbervie Journals*, 203–204. The remark was Tierney's, one of the mildest of Whigs at this time.

[2] Castlereagh took his son, the young Lord Apsley, to the Congress as a member of the British delegation.

Of the old brigade neither Eldon, the Chancellor, nor Sidmouth, the Home Secretary, took much interest in foreign affairs. They were absorbed in domestic politics. Harrowby, who was really experienced, seems to have been foremost in his confidence in Castlereagh and was generally content with a hint or two from the side lines. Another ex-Foreign Secretary, Mulgrave, nearly always shewed the same confidence. Camden, who was made a Marquess in September for giving up his office to Sidmouth, was, of course, delighted with his relative's return to power. Melville at the Admiralty was too mediocre a man to have much influence, while the Earl of Buckingham at the Board of Control was something less than that. Of the two Cabinet Ministers in the Lower House, Vansittart, a *pis aller*, who had the terribly difficult job of Chancellor of the Exchequer, occasionally protested at Castlereagh's distinctly aristocratic attitude towards finance, but he was always induced to give way in the end. Bragge Bathurst, who had been given the Duchy of Lancaster because of his loyalty to Sidmouth, was even duller than his patron.

That the Cabinet was obviously not one of All the Talents was one of the main reasons why Castlereagh was able to carry out his bold and adventurous policy in foreign affairs. But he could not have done so unless he had won the confidence of his colleagues by his superior knowledge, powers of work, and loyal and consistent conduct. The Duke of Buckingham had at the time characterised Castlereagh's appointment as an "intrigue," but he later testified to the rapidity with which the new Foreign Minister established his ascendancy over men who had until then never appreciated fully his merits: " . . . so opposed was his nature to display, that his previous colleagues had never given him credit for the resources he possessed. In a very little time he proved that a more accomplished statesman had rarely entered a Cabinet, and the stability Lord Liverpool's administration enjoyed was due as much to the interest and affection with which Lord Castlereagh inspired his coadjutors as to the conscientious discharge of duty, of which he continued to set them an admirable example." [1]

[1] Buckingham, *Memoirs of the Regency*, ii. 11.

Of the younger members of the Ministry, Robinson, Treasurer of the Navy, was a good subordinate to Castlereagh in 1814, while his devoted friend Clancarty, President of the Board of Trade, was brought into the Diplomatic service. Huskisson succeeded him in 1814. The young Croker was already Secretary of the Admiralty and, through the *Quarterly* and his connection with the *Times*, exercising an influence on Tory tactics, which he shared with Charles Arbuthnot, the Treasury Secretary, who was a confidant of the Prince Regent and, through his wife, of Wellington. The modest Secretary at War, Viscount Palmerston, who had already refused Cabinet office, does not seem to have taken exceptional interest in foreign affairs.

None of these young men, however, had yet much influence with the House of Commons, and it was there that the Government was weakest, neither Vansittart nor Bathurst commanding much respect. This sufficiently explains Liverpool's anxiety to bring in Canning. The Catholic question was raised repeatedly in 1812 and 1813, and as the Government was more than ever divided, it was no light burden on Castlereagh's tact to continue his support of liberal measures without offending his colleagues. Moreover, though the Government could always rely on a majority for the war, there were cross-currents of opinion which needed careful watching. The revolt against the Orders in Council was rightly regarded as a sign of the growing influence of the commercial classes. Their spokesman, Alexander Baring, was anxious to settle all differences with the United States as soon as possible, and though no one advocated the abandonment of 'maritime rights,' the new war, in which but little glory was won, continued to embarrass the Government. The unrest in the provinces gradually died down in 1812, but throughout the period the London mob were always a source of anxiety. Most important of all was the necessity of raising huge sums not only for Britain's own efforts but also for her Allies. The strain on the power of Britain to send money to a Continent from which her trade was shut out by the Continental System was tremendous. Cash payments had been suspended and the paper pound depreciated by 30 per cent. in 1811. In spite of Ricardo's pamphlet and Horner's Committee neither the Government nor the community properly appreciated the causes of this fact—perhaps fortunately so. At any rate, in spite of all obstacles, the cash was found, largely through the financial genius of two men—J. C. Herries, the Commissary General, and Nathan Rothschild, whose services in 1813 in collecting gold, even from Paris itself, made a deep impression on British statesmen. These were, however, quite unable to learn the rudiments of international finance. Herries bitterly complained that, in spite of his instruction, the mistakes of 1813 and 1814 were repeated in 1815. But somehow or other obligations were always met.[1]

The House accepted these burdens comparatively easily, for the heaviest did not come until victories also could be reported. Only on one question did it shew itself to have a mind of its own. The Abolition of the Slave Trade had now been made a permanent feature of British politics, and the Government had constantly to take it into consideration in the arrangements which it made with its Allies over colonial matters. This preoccupation added immensely to Castlereagh's burden in the period of reconstruction. But he coped with all these difficulties far more successfully than had been expected, and easily held his own until the turn of the tide in 1813. In spite of his reputation as a bad speaker, he learnt how to manage the House remarkably quickly. In 1814 the great successes kept the House quiet until he returned in the summer, but while he was at Vienna his colleagues proved quite incapable of maintaining the Government's advantage, and only the short length of the autumn session and Castlereagh's return saved the situation. The lead was a terrific strain on the Foreign Minister at such a time, yet was perhaps necessary to give him the position of vantage and authority in carrying his own policies through the House.

---

[1] An account of the methods of financing the Allies is much needed. Some glimpses into the fascinating story can be obtained from E. Herries' *Memoirs of John C. Herries* and various accounts of the Rothschilds, including Count Corti's *The Rise of the House of Rothschild*. But I hope that Prof. J. H. Clapham is wrong in claiming that his interesting article on " Loans and Subsidies in Time of War, 1793–1914," in the *Economic Journal*, Dec. 1917, is " probably all that economists will care to know about British subsidies in time of war " during that period.

For now less than ever had the war brought a party truce. On the contrary, it seemed to increase and embitter the rivalries of parties and persons. Fortunately for Castlereagh, the Opposition were split into factions, which even their dislike of the Government could not weld into a formidable body. Though Grenville and Grey seemed firmly united in 1812, they were divided by fundamental differences of principle and outlook. Lord Holland did not agree with them about Spain, which he had seen with his own eyes, though he had an unreasoning admiration for its attacker. In the Lower House the Whigs were perpetually harassed by the irresponsible conduct of the little band of men who were now called the "Mountain" and were soon to be known as "Radicals." These, so far as they admitted of being controlled at all, looked for guidance to Whitbread rather than to George Ponsonby, the official Whig leader, Tierney his principal colleague, or their chiefs in the Lords. Whitbread, though warm-hearted and honest, had no sense of reality, and his conduct, which Grey, his brother-in-law, scarcely ventured to defend, gradually drove Grenville almost frantic. Creevey's attacks on the sinecures were also repulsive to the Grenvillites, who enjoyed a huge revenue from them. Neither the economist Horner nor Romilly, the Reformer and best of all the Whigs, knew much about foreign affairs. Brougham was ready to choose any route to advancement, and after his great triumph over the Orders in Council offered to serve under Castlereagh to negotiate a peace with the United States. He was out of Parliament after the elections of 1812 until 1816, but as legal adviser to the Princess he was able to harass the Government as much as anybody. Sir James Mackintosh, just returned from India, was ardent in his researches in the Archives, but his historical knowledge, as is sometimes the case, made his excursions into practical politics terribly doctrinaire.

Above all, the Whigs lacked both deep conviction and reliable information. They dreaded the might of Napoleon as much as those they opposed, and their cowardly opportunism did not do justice to themselves or to their country. Had they come into power they might have abandoned Spain,

but they could not have made peace with France. No wonder
Grey preferred domestic to Parliamentary duties at such a
time. It is, however, almost incredible that he should have
relied so much on the inaccurate and unfair reports of Sir
Robert Wilson, who served in the Russian campaign as a
volunteer and then in a military capacity as part of the
British mission. Brave and energetic as Wilson undoubtedly
was, his stupid vanity and itch for fame led him into the most
ridiculous criticisms of the Government he was serving. Yet
Grey seems to have accepted him as a reliable authority even
after his information and his confident prophecies had repeatedly been proved false.

Until Vittoria the Opposition were in a strong position.
After that overwhelming triumph their morale was shattered.
Even Grey recanted in private, and, if a Grenville could never
be wrong, henceforward there was a new spirit at Dropmore,
where Napoleon had always been hated. As for Canning,
Vittoria and Leipzig completed his discomfiture. The refusal
of the Foreign Office at such a period of his country's history
had, as he himself confessed, begun to look not merely un-
patriotic but ridiculous. But if he suffered intensely, his
character was strengthened and ennobled by the time of trial.
He celebrated the victories in speeches which put into words
what Castlereagh felt but could not express. Such criticisms
as he made were generally well founded and moderately
phrased. He set his too-devoted followers free to follow their
own fortunes, and after peace was made, accepted the Lisbon
Embassy to his own detriment, partly at any rate for their
sake.[1] He was thus removed from all influence during the
period of reconstruction.

But even after the tide of war had turned, the Whigs were
led into untenable positions by their foolish appreciations
of the situation. During the peace settlement they had
greater opportunities for obtaining information, and their
conduct is all the more reprehensible. Wilson established

---

[1] Professor Temperley makes this point clear in his article " Joan
Canning on her Husband's Policy and Ideas " (*English Historical Review*,
July 1930, p. 425). Huskisson and Sturges Bourne were given office ; and
the peerage granted to Leveson-Gower, whose bad advice in 1812 Canning
bitterly recalled in 1813, was also probably part of the bargain.

connections with all those who opposed British policy, and he was, of course, supplied by them with the most biased and inaccurate account of events. Thus, while it was sometimes possible to embarrass the Government by the production of confidential papers, the manner in which the information was used destroyed the effect it might have produced.

This incompetence made the task of Castlereagh much lighter than it might have been, but it exercised a bad effect on the process of reconstruction. For on many points the Opposition might have exerted a beneficent influence on events had they applied their principles with more knowledge and understanding. As it was, they were led by faction and ignorance into the grossest of blunders. Only the great contribution which Grey later made to history can palliate the weakness and selfishness of his conduct during this period.[1]

If the Opposition was factious and unreasonable, the Press was sometimes even worse behaved. Wellington, who never ceased to denounce it, was of course unusually petulant and unfair when he told Croker that, "owing to the ignorance and presumption and licentiousness of the Press, the most ignorant people in the world of military and political affairs are the people of England." The British Press was, in fact, the best in the world; and Gentz, a prince of publicists, confessed that in 1812 it was his greatest enjoyment. It was, indeed, the only uncensored and free expression of opinion in Europe.

It must be admitted, however, that Wellington was so far right that its pages were continually disfigured by bias and sensation. It had no sense of fairness either to domestic or foreign enemies, yet one of Wellington's most serious complaints was that it gave away information to the enemy, even when it was misleading the British public. It was with one or two exceptions highly patriotic, and in these years the crescendo of abuse of Napoleon and France swelled into a loud and vindictive clamour. Only the *Morning Chronicle*, under the brave and skilful Perry, continued to advocate the unpopular view of a negotiated peace. The *Times*, owing to the energy and foresight of Mr. Walter, was by far the best

[1] Professor G. M. Trevelyan, in *Lord Grey of the Reform Bill*, naturally passes somewhat lightly over this period of Grey's life, of which the late H. W. C. Davis has indicated the weakness in his *Age of Grey and Peel*.

informed, but its editorial columns were packed with abuse. Wellesley had a great influence on its policy until 1814.

For the most part, the Government left the Press alone as impossible to control. It seems to have been the Prince Regent who first thought of influencing it, or at any rate possessing advocates amongst it to circulate or contradict opinions as policy might suggest—a course to which he was driven by the delicacy of his family affairs. Charles Arbuthnot, the Secretary of the Treasury, was his agent, assisted by MacMahon. Even the "diabolical *Morning Chronicle*" was tackled, and Perry was induced at one moment to profess his belief in the Prince's case against his wife, and to promise silence on his family affairs, though he reserved his right to deal with anything affecting public policy. The Regent wanted, however, active support, and Arbuthnot considered many schemes for getting it. From his efforts came the unpaid but influenced semi-official support of the *Courier*, and later the hired subservience of the *New Times* and the *Anti-Gallican*, which developed into something like a Government Press. But the effect was small, and the Press continued its irresponsible and, it must be admitted, often inaccurate dissemination of news without control.[1]

That the bulk of the Press was violently chauvinistic was an index of public opinion. Of the steadfastness of the mass of the nation under the ordeal of battle there is, indeed, abundant proof. Only in 1811 and 1812, when an economic crisis added greatly to the burden, were there riots and burnings, but these had little to do with the war. It is true that the fleet could only be recruited by a press gang, but that was partly due to adventure and freedom of private trading. The merchant classes, too, were growing richer in spite of the

[1] The general attitude of the Press towards Napoleon has been analysed in F. J. MacCunn's *The Contemporary English View of Napoleon*. Wellington's stricture is given in *Croker Papers*, 41. For typical comments to and by him, see *W.S.D.* vii. 62, 303, 353, 427, 457; and *Gurwood*, xi. 431. Wellesley's influence on the *Times* is in a letter of Goldsmith's (*F.O. Great Britain*, 23). He employed ' Vetus,' Edward Sterling, to write in it. The Regent's attitude is revealed by letters from Arbuthnot in the Windsor Archives. A scheme for an organised propaganda bureau to influence both domestic and foreign opinion, submitted to Carlton House by the notorious Lewis Goldsmith through the Duke of Cumberland, seems to have been wisely refused. Large sums were spent later by the Regent in buying up malevolent caricatures and pamphlets.

blockade, and though they overthrew the Orders in Council their support of the war never failed.

The country gentlemen and the governing aristocracy supplied the leaders on the field of battle. Their patriotism was, however, peculiar to the class and the time, and often seems strangely diluted. The highest generals were always apt to refuse to serve for some personal motive, and suffered little thereby. It was impossible for this reason to arrange for a second-in-command to Wellington. Sinecures were seized by all who could obtain them, and the Marquess of Buckingham thought he was generous in offering to give back one-third of his swollen receipts from that source. But little stigma rested on those who made no effort to serve their country at such a time, and English literature shews how much national energy remained unabsorbed and even unaffected by the war. Britain had, indeed, so long been cut off from the Continent that only a few could follow the shifting kaleidoscope with any intelligence.[1]

The habits of the upper classes had, of course, been much changed, for only the most adventurous civilians were able to obtain foreign travel, and the Grand Tour ceased to be a normal part of the education of the young aristocrat. No wonder that as soon as peace came the British flocked to Paris and Italy in shoals. This exodus caused some resentment in those classes at home which had received the money now spent abroad, while it hardly added to the popularity of Britain on the Continent. There was much vulgar curiosity displayed as well as a genuine interest in the new Europe. The panic of the travellers caught in 1815 by the return of Napoleon and the adventure of Murat also hardly added to British prestige. There was something to be said for the dictum of a British consul: "I think the English are never so respectable as when they are shut up in their own island and at war with the whole world."[2]

[1] "How can you ask who is Prince Metternich? I thought everybody knew the fame of so great a person," Lady Burghersh had to write to a friend as late as January 1814. Rose Weigall, *Letters of Lady Burghersh*, 160.
[2] Rachel Weigall, *Corres. of Lord Burghersh*, 181.

4. THE FOREIGN MINISTER AND THE DIPLOMATIC MACHINE

IT was fortunate that Castlereagh brought to his new position great powers of work, for Wellesley's slackness had caused considerable arrears to accumulate. A new energy, however, soon penetrated every part of the official machine. In a sense, the war had reduced the work of the Foreign Office considerably by 1812, for Britain was cut off from formal diplomatic relations with almost all Europe. But the problems were there and all the more difficult because the information about them was often sparse and unreliable. As Napoleon's power waned, state after state came back into the circle of British friendship, and it thus fell to Castlereagh to appoint almost the whole of the diplomatic service by the end of 1815.

In 1814 and 1815, however, Castlereagh was in himself almost the whole diplomatic machine, since for sixteen months of the two years he was on the Continent in close proximity to the sovereigns and statesmen of the Great Powers and many of those of second rank. The usual methods of diplomacy were in abeyance, and affairs were discussed round the council table rather than by dispatch from Court to Court. The Foreign Minister learnt to know the personalities as well as the problems of Europe to a degree none of his predecessors had ever attained. But the number of problems was so great during the period that he needed all the assistance which could be given by capable subordinates, of whom, however, he had but few.

To the Foreign Office he took with him, in accordance with custom, a new Under-Secretary of State. This could be none other than Edward Cooke, of Eton and Kings, his friend and follower ever since he had first taken office in Ireland. He was placed in control of the Northern Department, but he kept an eye on all important subjects. There was complete harmony of outlook and method between the two men, and Cooke knew the affairs of the family as well as Castlereagh himself, though he was always a subordinate, and his attitude to Castlereagh was one of respect and admiration. He was, like his chief, an indefatigable worker, but unfortunately his health had already become impaired. His illness in 1813 threw much extra work on Castlereagh, and he collapsed completely under the strain of the Congress of Vienna, one reason, no doubt, why Philip Morier, one of a famous family of diplomats, acted temporarily as an Under-Secretary of State in 1815.

The other Under-Secretary, William Hamilton, who had the Southern Department, had been brought into that position by Harrowby. He has to his credit a share in bringing both the Rosetta Stone and the Elgin Marbles to Britain. Without ever possessing the same intimacy with Castlereagh as Cooke, he was on sufficiently friendly terms with his chief to write a jesting letter at times. The more technical part of the office was in his hands. Castlereagh also inherited Joseph Planta, his private secretary, who accompanied him on all his expeditions to the Continent, an efficient civil servant of good manners, very popular with both foreigners and his own countrymen, but with no desire to initiate or influence policy. He had other Etonians in the office, of which the discipline and hours of work were rather lax, according to some observers.

The diplomatic service had almost ceased to exist in 1812. Only six missions were in existence, five of them to Courts whose monarch was either in exile, imprisonment, or had lost the greater part of his dominions. With the rest of Europe British connections were maintained by other channels which had gradually come into operation during the course of the war. Most important of these was that through the Hanoverian residents at the Courts of Vienna and Berlin, whose correspondence with Münster was used to keep Austria and Prussia in touch with Britain, even at the height of Napoleon's power. Count Hardenberg, who had won

Metternich's confidence, was by far the more important of the two and, as will be seen, had considerable influence on events in the critical period after Napoleon's return from Russia. Ompteda, whose brother was fighting in the Peninsula, was less trusted by the Prussian Chancellor and Münster, but supplied a large amount of useful information. That they should have been allowed to continue their functions in so open a fashion is one of the curiosities of the extraordinary situation in which Europe found itself. Hanover had no Minister at Petersburg, but there the Duke of Serra Capriola, who continued to represent unofficially the King of the Two Sicilies, provided the necessary link. He helped Stratford Canning in his delicate negotiations in 1812, and was later rewarded by Castlereagh for his services to Britain with a diamond snuff-box. The Spaniard Zea Bermudez played a similar rôle.

There were also a number of British agents employed in obtaining information. These men generally travelled with false passports as merchants, and were, of course, always liable to be disowned by the Government. Most of them had foreign wives and often they were of foreign origin. That they ran serious danger was shewn by the mysterious murder of Bathurst, an accredited envoy, in 1809. Of the four who were employed in South Germany and Austria in 1812–13, King at Vienna was the most promi-nent. Johnson, the most efficient, was also in Austria for a time and established communications through the Adriatic with Bentinck. George Mills, less reputable and fortunate, was expelled from Vienna in 1812. The most extraordinary amongst them was Horn, who returned to the Continent in 1813 and much annoyed the poor Queen of Wurtemberg by pretending that he had been sent by the British Government to establish relations. The information supplied by such men was, of course, unreliable in the extreme. They were all anxious to magnify the importance of their position and full of schemes which would enable them to handle money. There were also secret agents at Paris, of whom Darby was the best known, who sent over quantities of not very illuminating information.

Not only was this information suspect, but it was

exceedingly difficult to obtain it in anything like reasonable time. From 1810 to 1812 the supervision of the north coast grew ever stricter, and when Napoleon at last invaded Swedish Pomerania the last easy place of entrance had gone. Ompteda sometimes had to wait long periods before an opportunity presented itself of forwarding his own and Hardenberg's dispatches. Attempts were made to organise a route to Vienna from Scutari, and Count Hardenberg had to receive his remittances *via* Constantinople. Not until Hamburg was finally secured in the end of 1813 was there a quick route to central Germany and Austria.

By that time a regular diplomatic service was in process of formation. The principal posts went by favour in accordance with the custom of the times. Moreover, since Europe was at war, the two principal Ambassadors, the Earl of Cathcart and Sir Charles Stewart, were both soldiers. While it is not fair to call them, as Gentz did, "real caricatures of Ambassadors" whose "whole behaviour is an epigram on England," [1] yet they hardly added to our diplomatic reputation. The Earl of Aberdeen was too young for his job, and the only one of these important appointments which gave real satisfaction was that of the Earl of Clancarty to the Hague. For the Paris Embassy Wellington himself was selected, and one of the results of his short stay was the purchase of Pauline Borghese's hotel as the British Embassy. Wellington, though not without some grave defects as a diplomatist, was of great assistance to Castlereagh by reason of his great prestige, energy, and knowledge. No one else gave so much help in the reconstruction of Europe. Fortunately, the two men were already close friends, and there does not seem ever to have been a shadow between them during the complicated and delicate negotiations of 1814 and 1815. In Wellington's brother Henry, who continued to represent Britain in Spain, Castlereagh had also an efficient and reliable subordinate. Sir Charles Stuart was not quite so happy in Portugal but he was promoted in 1814, first temporarily to Paris and then to Brussels, where he had the unexpected and difficult task, which he performed very creditably, of being

[1] Mendelssohn-Bartholdy, *Briefe von Gentz an Pilat,* i. 21.

attached to the twice-exiled Louis XVIII. Viscount Strangford shewed courage and resource in Brazil. In Sicily Lord
William Bentinck's extraordinary conduct was eventually
to cause great inconvenience. Thornton in Sweden did not
entirely satisfy Castlereagh, who refused him the K.C.B.
which was granted to Wellesley and Stuart.

Castlereagh was not responsible for the appointment of
old Robert Liston, who eventually relieved young Stratford
Canning from his temporary position of such great importance
at Constantinople, but he had the discernment to send the
young man at the age of twenty-seven to the difficult position
of Minister to the Swiss Confederation, not only for his cousin's
sake, but also because he saw in him "precision of understanding and a stock of principle in his mind."

There was no lack of applicants for junior office, since many
peers and others rich enough to bear the expense were anxious
to give their sons the insight into the European world thus
acquired. Until the end of 1815 such appointments were in
the hands of the Office, and Clancarty warned Castlereagh not
to let the patronage slip, as it later did, into the hands of the
Ambassadors and Ministers themselves. These young men
had no special training, and if we are to believe George Rose,
a steady worker, who was first at Bavaria and then raised to
Berlin, most of the Secretaries of Legation knew neither
German nor French, "the one the key to the North, the other
to the South of Europe." Thornton, when in need of a
secretary, was also contemptuous of the training of the
Foreign Office. "I do not think your discipline strict
enough," he told Cooke, "or your employment regular and
methodical enough to suit my purpose." It was only natural
that the service should need overhauling after the suspension
of employment during the war, and this it received, though
in a mild way, when peace finally came. The consular service
was in even greater need of drastic treatment, and in 1812
every consul in the Mediterranean was on his way home on
account of either misbehaviour or ill-health. It was never
satisfactorily staffed in Castlereagh's time.[1]

[1] To Liverpool, April 27, 1814: *C.C.* ix. 509. From Rose, Nov. 23,
1815: *Lond. MSS.* Thornton to Cooke, April 24, 1813: *F.O. Sweden*, 82.
From Clancarty, Dec. 13, 1815: *C.C.* xi. 99.

Indeed, it must be confessed that Castlereagh made no great contribution to the machinery of the Diplomatic Service. While he treated his subordinates with the greatest consideration, he never set himself to overhaul the whole machine of which he was head. Like many industrious men, he relied too much on himself and did not seek the relief which better organisation and less care for the interests of family and friends would have given him.[1]

Castlereagh preferred to keep the threads of a negotiation in his own hands, and he wrote most of his dispatches, on policy, with his own pen. Parliament kept him in town a great deal, and his position forced those entertainments after the play in which Lady Castlereagh delighted and her husband acquiesced. He was always happiest, however, in the country. He escaped whenever he could to his cottage at North Cray, celebrated for its flowers, and there he was able to work serenely at the most important dispatches amidst the clamour of a family party, which he preferred to the isolation of his study. "He liked the society of young people," his favourite niece, Emma, tells us, "and far from checking their mirth and their nonsense, he enjoyed and encouraged it, with his own fun and cheerfulness. His tastes were simple: he loved the country and a country life, and it was delightful to see his look of quiet happiness while taking a saunter after an early dinner, in his pretty grounds at Cray, and finishing with an evening ride or drive, often prolonged until after dark. On his return home he would sit down and write at the same table, round which we all sat. If an air were played that pleased him, he would go to the pianoforte and sing it; if a waltz, he would say, 'Emma, let us take a turn,' and after waltzing for a few minutes, he would resume his writing. His power of abstraction was indeed remarkable; our talking and laughter did not disturb him; once only do I recollect that he rose from his chair laughing, and saying, 'You are too much

---

[1] He did, however, improve the financial position of the service and thus made it easier for those without private means to make it a profession. Salaries were raised in 1815 and special allowances regulated. These included " loss by exchange," which in some cases Castlereagh had paid out of his own pocket, and another item which the previous three years had shewn very necessary : " Fêtes and illuminations on occasions of public rejoicing." *F.O. Great Britain*, 10.

for me to-night,' carried off his papers, to what was called his own room, but in which he rarely, if ever, sat, always preferring the general drawing-room. The next morning at breakfast, he good-humouredly observed, 'You fairly beat me last night. I was writing what I may call the metaphysics of politics.'" [1]

Later the representatives of foreign Powers were often invited to Cray, and some of Castlereagh's most important conversations took place there. But in this period they played but a small part, since Castlereagh, during most of 1814 and 1815, was in personal contact with their masters. His French, which was not good when he entered office, improved considerably through the practice of these years. Only four were resident in London in February 1812, and as they gradually appeared in 1813 and 1814 it took them some time to settle down. Austria, it is true, was never without some kind of representation, for an old deaf and blind secretary, Reigersfeld, had been left behind when war was declared. General Nugent had been used by Metternich as his special agent in 1811, and he returned in 1812 after a very long journey. Wessenberg, sent on a special mission in 1813, remained, of course, unofficial until Austria joined the Allies. Though a man of great ability, he was quite unsuitable for this difficult and thankless task, and was relieved by General Merveldt in 1814, who, too, shewed little tact until his sudden death in July 1815 made the office vacant once more.

Count and Countess Lieven began at the end of 1812 their long residence as representatives of Russia. The Countess is, however, of but small importance in this period. She was at the outset unhappy and unpopular, and the visit of the Grand Duchess Catharine made her more so. Her peculiar position in London Society and the hearts of British statesmen took some time to establish. Baron Jacobi, who represented Prussia, returned to an old post with plenty of experience— too much in fact, for age and infirmity had made him of little account. Louis XVIII.'s representative, Count de la Châtre, was an *émigré* of no great sense or weight. The Spanish Duc

[1] Countess Brownlow, *Slight Reminiscences of a Septuagenarian* (1867), 191–92.

de Fernan Nuñez created much embarrassment by his struggle
for precedence, which absorbed much of his energy at this
crisis in his country's fortunes. The Sicilian Castelcicala tried
without much success to defend the strange conduct of his
master, while the Portuguese Court transacted little business
through Count Funchal. The truth was that the state of
Europe, and the fact that Castlereagh in 1814 and 1815 spent
most of his time in conference with the sovereigns and First
Ministers of Europe, deprived of much importance their
representatives, most of whom did not reach London until
the end of 1813. Those who tried to influence affairs behind
Castlereagh's back, like Lieven or Merveldt, soon found out
their mistake. Their position, indeed, was not an enviable
one. Most of their countries found it difficult to send them
funds, while the cost of living they thought ruinous.[1]

If foreign Ambassadors were few in the earlier years of the
period, there was no lack of other foreigners of every kind who
had been driven from the Continent by Napoleon's hostility.
They supplied some information and advice, but for the most
part were too much out of touch with affairs to be very helpful.
On the whole, Britain's conduct towards these unfortunates
does credit to her sensibility. Most important of all was
Louis XVIII., whose little Court at Hartwell was almost
forgotten in 1812. The Regent, however, always treated him
and his family with the greatest kindness, even when there
seemed not the slightest ch nce of his restoration. His
conduct had been perfect, the Duchess of Angoulême told
Fanny Burney.[2]

Many French émigrés received pensions from British funds.
Perhaps the most notable amongst them was Doumouriez,
the conqueror of Belgium, whose memoirs on every con-
ceivable strategical and diplomatic project cumber the public

---

[1] The debts which the Austrian Stahremberg left behind him in 1810
were attributed to parsimony rather than penury, but his successors were
put to hard shifts. Wessenberg estimated his expenses at 8000 guineas
per annum, but Merveldt put it at the lowest at £12,834 without any
luxuries such as theatres. Indeed, he thought £17,000 the least sum on
which an Ambassador could live decently. He reported that Lieven's
allowance had been increased to more than double that amount. During
1811 Reigersfeld had sold the Embassy plate to keep himself alive, and
Merveldt replaced it out of subsidy payments much to Metternich's anger.

[2] C. Barrett, *Diary and Letters of Madame D'Arblay*, 139–40.

and private archives of the period.   Wellington received large
quantities, but only corresponded with him, he said, to keep
him from caballing with the Princes.   The young Corsican,
Pozzo di Borgo, Napoleon's fiercest enemy, was gradually
establishing confidence, while other refugees, such as the
Swiss Sir François d'Ivernois, brought useful talents to the
service of the state.   Amongst those who had quarrelled with
Napoleon and sought refuge in Britain was his brother
Lucien, whose literary labours at Dinham and Thorngrove
have been the subject of Masson's bitterest irony.   His
sojourn, which seems hardly to have aroused as much interest
as might have been expected, was allowed without great
suspicion on the part of the authorities.   When, however,
Mlle. George, the notorious French actress, applied through
Bernadotte for permission to come to Britain to perform,
Thornton thought a line ought to be drawn.   The most
famous of all the visitors was, of course, Madame de Staël.
The persecution of Napoleon assured her a warm welcome
even amongst those who did not appreciate her literary
labours, but the memoirs abound with anecdotes of the
sensation caused by the manners and table talk of this ardent
blue stocking.[1]

[1] Stanhope, *Conversations*, 70.   F. Masson, *Napoleon et sa famille*, vii.
169–82, 409–422 ; viii. 321–27.   There are five volumes on Lucien in the
Foreign Office Archives (*F.O. France*, 84, 85, 89, 93, 110).   On Dec. 21, 1811,
Wellesley commented to the Regent on a proposal to entertain Lucien at
Cheltenham : " It is unnecessary to state to your Royal Highness the
impropriety of this request and the impossibility of granting it without
great public inconvenience " (*Windsor Arch.*).   From Thornton, April 4,
1813, on Mlle. George : " . . . though the lady herself may not come under
the character of an *intrigante*, yet I think the mistress of Bonaparte is not
exactly the most proper person to be admitted into England " (*F.O.
Sweden*, 82).

5. THE LEGACY OF PITT[1]

"In his public life he has never had and never will have an equal, as a private individual he honoured and adorned human nature." If history has not quite endorsed this eulogy of Pitt by Count Vorontzov, the Russian Ambassador, at the time of his death, his figure will always remain as a monument of genius and virtue. Though he died with his task unfulfilled, he left behind him a legacy of courage and perseverance to his pupils, of whom Castlereagh was the most trusted and the most imbued with the ideas of his master. But Pitt left more than that behind him; for before he died he had worked out a complete scheme of European reconstruction, which was to be Castlereagh's guide when in happier circumstances he enjoyed something of Pitt's power in the councils of Britain and Europe.

The plan was due not only to the necessities of the time, but also to the dreams of the young monarch with whom Castlereagh was to share so much of the responsibility for the reconstruction of Europe. For Pitt, as a true Englishman, avoided generalisations and aspirations, and would probably never have constructed so comprehensive a scheme or touched on such debateable topics if he had not been challenged by the impulsive fantasies of the Tsar Alexander. He tried to turn a vague and emotional proposition into a practical and comprehensive plan for uniting Europe against Napoleon, and reconstructing it in such a manner that, if peace were won, it could be maintained. Castlereagh himself had later more than once to apply the same process to Alexander's lucubrations.

[1] For the background of this section I have, of course, relied on Professor Holland Rose's *Pitt and Napoleon*, and also the essay " Pitt's Plans for the Settlement of Europe " in his *Napoleonic Studies* (3rd edn., 1914) and his *Dispatches relating to the Third Coalition* (1904).

In 1804 Alexander was still in the first flush of his liberalism.
He wished to apply the ideas he had learnt from his Swiss
tutor, La Harpe, to a new crusade on behalf of Europe, to
whose assistance his father, the mad Paul, had already sent
Russian troops as far as Italy and Switzerland, a new phe-
nomenon in the balance of European power. The young Pole,
Czartoryski, full of ambition and love of his country, and
anxious to use his new position to serve both, was now in
charge of foreign affairs, and he and a group of young Russians
encouraged the Tsar in these schemes. An understanding for
common defence had already been made with Austria. But
British gold was needed to bring a coalition into being, and
at the end of October 1804 the young Novosiltzov was sent by
the Tsar and Czartoryski to London on a special mission, since
Count Vorontzov was considered too old-fashioned for the
purpose. The Russian was vain and presumptuous, but he
had the complete confidence of Czartoryski and of himself,
and certainly brought new ideas and methods to London.

His instructions, written by Czartoryski, breathed a spirit
of lofty idealism in which, however, the objects of the Tsar
and his Minister found an appropriate place. The old Europe
was gone for ever. The new Europe must take into account
the spirit of the times. The old feudalism must be replaced
by liberal governments, founded on "the sacred rights of
humanity." All monarchs must endow their subjects with
modern constitutions. Even the Ottoman Empire must be
encouraged to reform itself, if by joining France it did not lay
itself open to more drastic treatment. France herself must
not be made an exception, for it was not the French people
but Napoleon who was responsible for the difficulties of
Europe.

Once the new Europe had been constituted, it was to be
endowed with a new system of international law. Why
should not states accept an obligation not to go to war without first invoking the mediation of a third party for an inquiry into the causes of the dispute? Any state that defied
the new Europe might be expected to bring upon itself
immediately a coalition of all the others, but the privileges
of "neutrality" should also be assured, and this point led

naturally to the hope that British 'maritime rights' might be reconsidered—another of Paul's favourite objects.

Finally, Britain and Russia must take the new Europe under their special protection as the only Powers "who by their position are invariably interested in the reign there of order and justice, the only ones who by their position can maintain it, and being free from conflicting desires and interests will never trouble this happy tranquillity."

Some concrete suggestions were included. The King of Sardinia should be restored to Piedmont, if he would grant a constitution to his subjects. The Italian republics should be rescued from French control. Switzerland's independence should be re-established, and she should be enlarged and endowed with a democratic constitution. Holland should also be rescued from French influence and placed under a Stadtholder, who, of course, must be a constitutional ruler. As for the German states, they should be united in a Federation from which Prussia and Austria were excluded, thus making a balancing power between the two. One of the features of the dispatch was, indeed, the neglect of the interests of these two Powers.[1]

It is impossible to tell how completely or in what form these far-reaching and grandiloquent ideas were brought to Pitt's notice. He seems to have judged Novosiltzov's character pretty accurately, and tried, so far as he could, to transfer the negotiation to Count Vorontzov, with whom he was on good terms. But the Ambassador was by the Tsar's orders not at first informed of Novosiltzov's instructions, and it was necessary to discuss them with the young envoy and to humour his vanity and presumption. Gradually the various propositions appeared and much discussion took place, but it was not until two months had passed that Pitt was prepared with his reply.

There was much in the Russian proposition that must have been either incomprehensible or obnoxious to Pitt's mind.

---

[1] The mission of Novosiltzov can be followed in Czartoryski, *Mémoires* (2 vols., 1887), vol. i. chap. xi., vol. ii., pp. 27–66. The 'secret' instructions probably never reached Pitt or Novosiltzov. The account of the negotiations by the envoy (F. Martens, *Recueil des Instructions*, xi. 95–105) shews that most of the ideas were brought at one time or another to Pitt's notice. Sir William Scott was consulted as to 'maritime rights'!

The last thing which he desired was a crusade either for constitutional liberty or republican freedom. Nor could the references to British maritime rights, nor the hint as to the partition of the Ottoman Empire, have been very palatable to him. But Russia was the key to the new coalition, which he hoped would overthrow Napoleon. The great thing was to get her to move, and draw Austria and Prussia in the same direction. For this reason the objects of the war must be defined and the outline of the new Europe sketched in such a manner that each of the Great Powers would see its main interest in joining it. The Tsar had hardly alluded to the objects which the other two Great Powers might be expected to desire. He must be encouraged to envisage plans which would attract them to his side. Moreover, while the immediate object was to overthrow Napoleon, Pitt also wished Austria and Prussia to be guardians of European peace quite as much as Russia—indeed, in a sense, more so, for he wished them to be so against Russia as well as against France, though this object naturally could not be avowed.

Fortunately most of the Tsar's territorial proposals were aims which Pitt could support and had already formulated on more than one occasion. The independence of Holland, Switzerland, and Sardinia was essential to the liberties of Europe. Indeed, in spite of the Peace of Amiens, no English statesman could be content with that line which left the mouth of the Rhine and Scheldt, including Antwerp, in French possession. Pitt had already therefore, in 1795 and 1799, put forward plans, first for restoring Austria to her old possessions in Belgium, and later, after Austria had signed them away, for adding Belgium to Holland in order to establish the northern 'barrier' against France. In the same way he had always wished to strengthen Sardinia, to enable her to check French expansion in the Mediterranean, and had already suggested that she should incorporate Genoa, so as to keep that important harbour out of French control.

The Tsar's challenge and the hope of combining the three Great Powers in a common effort against Napoleon now led him to a more extended review of the reconstruction of Europe than he had ever before attempted. Since it was written at a moment when one Foreign Minister, Harrowby, owing to illness, was yielding place to another, Mulgrave, who was admittedly of no great capacity, it seems improbable that either had much to do with it. Canning saw it and admired it, but his confidential relations with Pitt had been destroyed by his opposition to the inclusion of Addington in the Cabinet, and he confessed that he had nothing to do with it and regarded it as Pitt's work. " I have read . . . ," he told his friend Leveson-Gower, at this time Ambassador at Petersburg, "the Instructions sent to you (the long Instructions, I mean, in the shape of a draft to Vorontzov) *as his*. He is very proud of them, I think—and I think, very justly." [1] It was in the "draft to Vorontzov" that Pitt made his extended survey of European reconstruction, perhaps so that it might reach Petersburg uncontaminated by Novosiltzov.

One Minister had, however, enjoyed his confidence and discussed his plans during the period of incubation—Castlereagh.[2] It was thus in a sense the joint production of master and pupil, though doubtless Pitt's commanding genius was responsible for the greater part of it. The pupil, however, never forgot it; it was the text of all his efforts when, in a happier position than his master, the coalition which Pitt had dreamed at last came into being and made its application possible. By then time had made, as Castlereagh confessed, some of its suggestions perhaps inapplicable, and one fundamental principle Castlereagh was eventually to discard. But the main points of the document were sufficiently reproduced by Castlereagh in the reconstruction of Europe to enable him in May 1815 to lay large portions of it before Parliament to justify the actions of the last three years. It is necessary therefore to consider it in some detail.[3]

[1] Countess Granville, *Corres. of Granville Leveson-Gower*, ii. 30.
[2] To Cathcart, April 8, 1813 : *C.C.* viii. 356. See below, Chapter III., section 1, p. 125.
[3] Historians have used Garden's translation of the truncated form of this document which was laid before Parliament in May 15, 1815. Alison retranslated this (*History of Europe*, chap. xxxix.). The original, bound in a separate volume (*F.O. Russia*, 60), was first printed in part by Professor Colenbrander in his *Gedenkstukken der Algemeene Geschiedenis van Nederland*, vol. iv., and will be found as Appendix I. in *B.D.* 389–94, with the exception of the military discussions. Professor Alison Phillips first shewed the relation between these ideas and those of the later European Alliance in his *Confederation of Europe*, 38–42.

Pitt began by reducing the Russian suggestions to three principal objects with which he said he entirely concurred: "(1) To rescue from the dominion of France those countries which it has subjugated since the beginning of the Revolution, and to reduce France within its former limits as they stood before that time. (2) To make such an arrangement with respect to the territories recovered from France as may provide for their security and happiness and may at the same time constitute a more effectual barrier in future against encroachments on the part of France. (3) To form at the restoration of peace, a general agreement and guarantee for the mutual protection and security of different Powers, and for the re-establishing a general system of public law in Europe."

Such a programme, he pointed out, however, implied the complete overthrow of Napoleon, which could only be expected if Prussia, as was unfortunately doubtful, as well as Austria joined the coalition. If she did not, he considered it unlikely that the whole of the Netherlands and the left bank of the Rhine could be recovered from France. Even in that case, however, he thought it essential that Antwerp and a ' barrier '. should be added to Holland.

As for the rest of Europe, he pointed out that some of the countries which had lost their independence had been so completely changed and subjugated that it was impossible to restore it to them. Amongst these he placed Genoa, the three Legations of the Papal States, Parma and Placentia in Italy, and on the other side of Europe the Austrian Netherlands and the German territory on the left bank of the Rhine. They were too weak to protect themselves, Spain by her conduct had forfeited her rights in Italy, and neither Genoa nor the other states had been renowned for just or liberal rule. Austria had abandoned the Netherlands, and the Ecclesiastical states had obviously disappeared for ever.

These territories, then, could be used to induce the other Great Powers to join the Coalition and at the same time strengthen them for their future task of protecting Europe against France. It was, above all, necessary to remove the cause of rivalry between the two great German Powers, which had been one of the many reasons of French predominance. Austria, therefore, should be encouraged to seek expansion in the south and Prussia in the north of Europe. In each quarter there was, however, a small Power which must act as the first barrier against France. In Italy this was Piedmont, which Pitt wished to see enlarged not only by the acquisition of Genoa, but by part of the Milanese and perhaps by Parma and Placentia as well. The rest of the Milanese and the three Legations would then go to Austria, while the restoration of the Grand Duke would make Tuscany virtually Austrian also. Austria would thus dominate the north of Italy, supporting the greatly enlarged state of Piedmont and a firm *bloc* be constructed against France.

It was in the north, however, that Pitt made the most revolutionary suggestions. Here Holland was to have a similar and even more important responsibility than Piedmont in the south, and she should be given Antwerp and a 'barrier' of a portion of the southern Netherlands. The rest might go to Prussia, as well as a considerable portion of the left bank of the Rhine. This suggestion was made, as Pitt confessed, partly to persuade her not to accept Hanover, which Napoleon was sure to offer and thus embroil her with Britain. This threat hung over him, then, like a nightmare. He had to take it always into account, for George III. would of course not sanction any arrangement which deprived him of his electoral possessions. But Pitt wished the extension of territory also to make Prussia strong enough to undertake the defence of northern Europe against France, and pleaded earnestly that this might be done even if it were thought wiser to give more of the southern Netherlands to Holland. If Prussia refused to come in, he reluctantly confessed that only Antwerp and a small 'barrier' could be regained from France. At this point his military instincts, stronger at this time than ever before, overcame him, and he used a great deal of paper discussing the means and method of the plan of campaign, insisting on the urgent need of Prussia's assistance and pressing the Tsar to use his influence to persuade her to give up ideas of Hanover and join the Allies.

Only after this excursion into strategy, which, it must be

admitted, he had better have left to another hand and occasion, did he discuss the third point, the preservation of the new Europe when it had been reconstituted. Here again he transformed the rather vague phraseology of Czartoryski into something more concrete and definite—a general territorial guarantee by all the Powers of Europe of their possessions as established by the final treaty. Russia and Britain, who he had already agreed were in a spécial position and had no separate territorial designs to prosecute, he suggested, should take the new treaty under their protection by a special guarantee in a separate treaty of their own. He also suggested that it might be possible to unite the Italian states together in a special alliance for their own mutual protection, while he considered a similar union very desirable for the German states, whose jealousy, however, he thought, would make it impossible. He added, therefore, a last safeguard—a line of barrier fortresses between Germany and France similar to the barrier in the Netherlands, which both Britain and Hanover would aid with money and men. These two Powers also, as well as Russia, might enter into special engagements for the defence of Holland and its barrier.

Such a Europe would be able to resist even a France with Napoleon on the throne. However desirable, therefore, his fall might be, Pitt did not think it ought to be one of the avowed objects of the coalition. Only if France herself demanded it would it be possible, and such a sentiment could only arise if every appearance of foreign dictation were scrupulously avoided.

This remarkable paper might well inspire Pitt with pride and Canning with admiration. It turned the vague suggestions of the Tsar into a practical scheme for the reconstruction of Europe. It was so phrased that it appeared to accept the basic principles of Alexander, but it utilised them in a manner more consonant with the interests of the other Great Powers and Britain than the Tsar and his advisers had attempted or perhaps desired. It was founded on the idea of the balance of power in Europe, to which, indeed, every statesman outside France paid tribute, now that the balance had been so completely overthrown. The ideas of a strong Germany and a united Italy were there, though they were adapted to the more pressing need of a strong Prussia and Austria, from which alone the salvation of Europe could come. It even accepted, if necessary, the 'natural frontiers' of France, with the exception of Antwerp and perhaps Savoy, though it insisted that the Germans on the left bank of the Rhine should not be sacrificed to that idea unless it was impossible to prevent it. Its practical value was proved by the fact that so much of it was put into operation ten years after it was written. It was more than a plan; it was a prophecy.

Two points in Czartoryski's dispatch, it will be noted, Pitt omitted altogether—the Ottoman Empire and 'maritime rights.' A discussion of such thorny subjects would obviously cause dissension between Britain and Russia. He was, however, not allowed to leave them in obscurity. For the Tsar and his Ministers were by no means satisfied with the paper, and endeavoured to modify Pitt's position on several questions and to raise others on which he had been silent. Chief of all these were the 'maritime rights' of Britain—which the Tsar's father had challenged and which Alexander equally refused to admit—and Malta, on which Paul had also set his heart. But it was, of course, out of the question that Britain should abandon the right of visit and search, and the discussion terminated in an uncompromising refusal of that demand, though Pitt, after much resistance, went so far as to offer to exchange Malta for Minorca.[1]

Another subject brought up by the Tsar was the question of the colonial conquests, and on this the collector of 'sugar islands' shewed himself strangely moderate. Early in 1805, as the special contribution of Britain towards peace, he offered to return all the "conquests made in this war from France or from any of her European allies in any quarter of the globe" if France would accept the British basis. Doubtless Pitt knew that there was not much chance of his offer being accepted, and merely wished to impress the Tsar with his moderation. But he had laid down the important principle that Britain was prepared to use her monopoly of the colonial

[1] The main points of these discussions are admirably summarised in Rose's *Pitt and Napoleon*, 525–28, and the details given in the other two works mentioned in the note on p. 53.

world to obtain as good a European peace as possible. Of its application, however, she must be the judge. It will be seen that Castlereagh followed this principle of his master, and that it was a powerful weapon in his hands when the time of reconstruction came.

That time, however, was still far off. Russia and Britain came to a complete deadlock, and the European coalition suggested in January seemed quite impossible. Only the arrogant policy in Italy of Napoleon, who annexed Genoa while Britain and Russia were talking about it, at last made the Tsar accept the lesser evil of British arrogance on the sea, and a treaty was signed which embodied some, but by no means all, of Pitt's ideas, and for which he promised heavy subsidies to Russia and Austria, who also was driven into action by the threat to Italy. Prussia, on the other hand, could not resist the bribe of Hanover and her own fears, while she was by no means ready to accept the forward position on the Rhine which Pitt had designed for her. The result was the Ulm disaster. Still Pitt persevered, and after Austria's defeat delivered his more famous and shorter prophecy in the magnificent phrase which inspired his followers even in the darkest days which followed. Prussia seemed almost won by the conduct of Napoleon, though Pitt could not give her Hanover except at the cost of his King's reason, while Castlereagh, at Pitt's commands, prepared for the north a greater expedition than had ever sailed before from British ports. But Napoleon was too swift and subtle both in diplomacy and strategy. Prussia had already decided to accept his bribe before Austerlitz put an end to Austria's efforts, and the double blow brought Pitt to his grave. All the scheme of reconstruction seemed now but idle strokes of the pen. The map of Europe might be rolled up so far as Britain was concerned.

Pitt died at a dark hour, but darker ones were to follow. Castlereagh had been on duty in London while Pitt was dying, encouraging his master to the last. Even when Prussia's desertion had rendered it necessary to withdraw the great expedition which he had prepared with so much care, he urged Pitt to find consolation in the thought that it would bring back with it the Hanoverian forces, which had been raised to assist it for future service against the conqueror —no vain hope. But after Jena, Friedland and the Peace of Tilsit had put all the north of Europe at Napoleon's feet and made the Tsar his ally, Pitt's plans seemed relegated to oblivion. When Castlereagh entered office he could hardly have dreamed that in a little over twelve months he would be asking Cathcart to remind a new Alexander, whose armies were on the Oder and the Elbe, of Pitt's scheme for the reconstruction of Europe.

CHAPTER II

*THE TURN OF THE TIDE : RECONSTRUCTION
FORESHADOWED, 1812*

1. THE MEDITERRANEAN AREA.

    (i) THE PENINSULA.
    (ii) SICILY.
    (iii) THE NEAR EAST.

2. THE RISING OF THE NORTH.

3. RELATIONS WITH PRUSSIA AND AUSTRIA.

" Les Anglais enrichissent tous les peuples chez lesquels ils vont et payent leurs vassaux au lieu d'exiger d'eux des tributs, comme nous l'avons toujours vu dans l'histoire, et comme le font les Français."—THE KING OF THE TWO SICILIES (March 17, 1813).

CHAPTER II

1. THE MEDITERRANEAN AREA

(i) THE PENINSULA [1]

THE strange shape of Europe had by 1812 brought France and Britain into contact in many diverse places. The two inland seas of the north and south vastly extend its coasts and give access to its interior regions far away from France. Hence Napoleon's amazing annexations; hence the extension of British influence along the coasts in inland seas, where in the previous century she had shrunk from hazarding her forces. Wherever resistance occurred and it was geographically possible, British ships carried British arms, money, and goods.

Throughout the years 1812–13, however, the struggle in the Peninsula continued to absorb the greater part of the military and financial resources of the British Government, and in spite of the disappointment of the retreat from Madrid in 1812, after the victory of Salamanca, they were rewarded in 1813 by the great campaign which ended in Vittoria and the expulsion of the French armies from the soil of Spain. Wellington, as his military prestige grew, gradually obtained more and more influence over the civil administration of Spain and Portugal as well as over the policy of the Home Government. Through his brother, Henry Wellesley, Ambassador at Cadiz, and Charles Stuart, Minister and a member of the Regency at Lisbon, he was constantly advising the Peninsular

---

[1] Sir Charles Oman has described with great skill the war problems, which are only touched on here, in vol. v. 136–56 and vol. vi. 194–238 of his great work. He has not used the *F.O. Records*, which, as well as the dispatches of Fernan-Nuñez, are the basis of the Marqués de Villa Urrutia's *Relaciones entre España é Inglaterra*, iii. 1812–14, an interesting commentary on much intimate British as well as Spanish history.

Governments on a great variety of subjects, nearly always with wisdom and patience, though occasionally failing to see any point of view but his own. He kept also the attention of his own Government fixed on Spain, and discouraged them from adventures elsewhere when Europe again was in movement. His own success was the justification of his policy.

The rôle of the Foreign Minister was, therefore, a circumscribed one in the Peninsula. Castlereagh had always been Wellington's friend and defender, and he was his most earnest supporter in the Cabinet. One of his first actions as Foreign Minister was to reject with indignation Napoleon's offer of peace on the basis of leaving in Spain the '*dynastie actuelle*,' a term which inquiry shewed was meant to describe Joseph. His own share in the game was most concerned with harmonising the interests of his Peninsular Allies with the rest of Europe, and supporting all steps in Spain and Portugal which the Commander-in-Chief recommended.[1]

The Spanish Regency, so far as the Cortes left it any power, under the new constitution of 1812, which was based on the least practical of the French revolutionary models, was a poor enough ally; but it was at least loyal to the fight against the common enemy. On the main question, in spite of some subterranean temptations, the Spaniards never wavered throughout these years. There was, however, some anxiety at the proposal which Palmella, the Portuguese Minister at Cadiz, was pressing, that the Princess of Brazil should be nominated Regent for her captive brother Ferdinand. The Princess may perhaps be considered as the most noxious of all the Bourbon brood with whose fortunes British interests were now intertwined. Moreover, she was constantly sending letters to Cadiz accusing the British of every crime. Her chief adviser, one Presas, was "a man of a most vile and unprincipled disposition, the known enemy of England and the person who first had inspired the Princess with the

---

[1] There are two projects of Maret's final letter in the Paris archives (*Paris A.A.E. Angleterre*, 606, f. 217), one more conciliatory than the other, but each insist that the re-establishment of the Bourbons in Spain is incompatible with French security : " It would be as easy to propose as a basis of negotiation the establishment of the Comte de Lille [Louis XVIII.] on the throne of France." The two branches of the House of Bourbon were indeed restored within three months of each other.

strange notions concerning the designs of the British Government with which Her Royal Highness is now entirely possessed." Thus, while Castlereagh did not approve of Wellesley interfering directly in the appointment of Regents, he was entirely in sympathy with his efforts to keep the Princess of Brazil away from Spain. In January a decree was passed that no royal personage should be made head of the Government, but when the Princess was placed next in the succession to Don Carlos, excluding the Queen of Etruria and Ferdinand's youngest brother (who was Godoy's son), her partisans revived, and the question still kept cropping up. Fortunately, Strangford's influence on her husband at Rio, and Wellesley's on the Cortes at Cadiz, prevented it from becoming really dangerous.[1]

After Salamanca the Cortes at last agreed to appoint Wellington Commander-in-Chief of the Spanish armies, an act which Henry Wellesley had always desired, though both Wellington and his Government had been more doubtful about it. After securing the consent of the British Government, Wellington visited Cadiz, and though he did not get as much power as he wanted or as much as Wellesley's enthusiasm had promised, the step did make a great difference to the Spanish armies in the ensuing campaign. Indeed, in fundamentals the objects of the two Governments were so much identical that, in spite of the irritating and ridiculous conduct of the Cortes over the details of policy, which sometimes almost drove Henry Wellesley frantic, the appearance and even reality of cordial relations was on the whole maintained.

This was all the more creditable because on one vital question the two Governments were in entire disagreement throughout these years. The important, tedious, and indeed insoluble problem of the Spanish Colonies Henry Wellesley

---

[1] From Strangford, March 11, 1812 : *F.O. Portugal*, 123. To Wellesley, Jan. 17, Oct. 19, 1812 ; July 3, 1813 : *F.O. Spain*, 127, 128, 142. From Wellesley, Jan. 13, March 10 (with enclosure from Strangford, Nov. 22, 1811), Sept. 10, 1812 : *F.O. Spain*, 129, 132. Later Wellesley even suggested agreeing to the Regency of the Princess in return for a settlement of the Colonies, but it seems to have been only a passing thought (*W.S.D.* viii. 87). The King of Sicily at an early period protested against his own claims being passed over (From Wellesley, April 24, 1812 : *F.O. Spain*, 130). See also, on the whole subject, Villa-Urrutia, *Relaciones*, iii. 127 ff.

rightly described as the "principal cause of all the trouble and vexation" with the Spanish Government. Castlereagh had inherited from his predecessor a proposal for mediation on terms for which he was to press in vain throughout these two years and indeed to the end of his life. In 1812, however, there did seem some hope that Spain in her desperate condition would listen to the good advice which Castlereagh poured out unstintingly throughout the year. He approached the problem from the broad point of view, using British experience to reinforce his arguments. The Spanish Government were still demanding that Britain should promise to use force if the mediation failed, refused altogether to include Mexico, where they considered their chances were good, and, above all, would not give up their monopoly of trade. In sending his instructions to the recently appointed Commissioners of Mediation on April 1, 1812, Castlereagh endeavoured to overcome this opposition. "The conviction of the British Government is," he wrote in a remarkable dispatch, "whatever may be the commercial prejudices of the Spanish Government and whatever may be their jealousy of us, that, if they cannot bring themselves to place the inhabitants of America upon a commercial footing of corresponding advantage with the inhabitants of European Spain, and that without loss of time, their separation from the parent state is inevitable and at hand. . . . In pressing this view of the situation upon the Spanish Government it may be desirable to suggest for their consideration the commercial system which we find it not only necessary but advantageous to apply to our East India possessions . . . where we have an Empire to govern, as in India we govern it as far as relates to commerce upon a national and not a colonial principle. Whether the trade to Great Britain be carried on as heretofore by an exclusive company, or as it is now proposed, it be thrown open . . . the commerce of India is open to all neutral nations, and as sovereigns we claim nothing but a commercial preference. If this system be, as it has been found to be, no less advantageous than just, even as applied to a country where our political power is exercised without control, how much more necessary is its application to provinces whose rights have

been acknowledged to be equal to European Spain and which have been admitted to a share in the natural representation."
. . . He even used a bolder example: "You may point out to the Spanish Government . . .," he concluded, "that Great Britain has derived more real commercial advantage from North America since the separation than she did when that country was subjected to her dominion and part of her colonial system."

These general principles he reinforced throughout the year with every possible argument in a long series of dispatches. Mexico, he insisted, was the most important and most promising place for the mediation to begin, and if she were rescued from anarchy, Spain's resources would be immensely increased. He agreed, at Wellesley's request, to guarantee a settlement, if one were arrived at under British mediation, however much such guarantees were normally distasteful to British policy. He took the Spanish side in the dispute with Portugal over Buenos Ayres, and was able to shew that Strangford, as a result of his instructions, had induced the Brazil Government to moderate its action there. He pointed out that the resources of South America were necessary to carry on the struggle against Napoleon, and that Spain might draw a vast revenue out of duties levied on British trade.[1]

It was all necessarily in vain. The city of Cadiz controlled the policy of Spain, and both parties in the Cortes were united in refusing all concession. Only the South American deputies and a handful of enlightened Spaniards gave Wellesley any encouragement. He was, indeed, able to prevent troops being withdrawn from Galicia for South America (though some were sent in 1813), and Pizarro agreed after great pressure that Britain should not be expected to use force. But the Cortes were obdurate both on that point and on throwing the trade open. They refused also to include Mexico. On the contrary, the national policy was that "no concessions should be made to the insurgent provinces." They believed "that all offers of this kind would rather tend to increase the spirit of insurrection and that the insurgents must be reduced to

---

[1] Wellesley to Wellington, July 18, 1811 : *W.S.D.* vii. 183. To Wellesley, April 1, May 19, June 15, 1812 : *F.O. Spain*, 127. To Strangford, May 29, April 10, July 13, 1812 : *F.O. Portugal*, 122.

unconditional submission by force of arms." In the final vote on July 18, 1812, only nine European deputies were in the minority. Castlereagh, however, refused to accept this defeat as final. The American War had made him more anxious than ever that some attempt should be made. He agreed to exclude Mexico on condition that, if a settlement were arrived at elsewhere, Spain would apply it to all South America. He hinted that Britain might be compelled to take action herself if Spain remained obdurate. Miranda was still writing from Venezuela, and Castlereagh told Wellesley that, though the Venezuelan agents in London were not recognised, he had had to see them and explain the situation.[1]

But all this made very little impression at Cadiz, where the Cortes had been encouraged by recent victories in Mexico and Venezuela. There was no hope of mediation, Wellesley reported. Indeed, in February 1813 he considered that it would be dangerous to reopen the question, so irritated were the Cortes at the British intercourse with the insurgents and the assistance they were receiving from British volunteers. It could hardly be denied that the British Government were "encouraging trade from which the insurgents were indebted for the resources which have enabled them to persevere in their resistance." In 1813, therefore, Castlereagh had to suspend his pressure, except to defend Britain against the unjust suspicions of the merchants of Cadiz to which the offer of mediation was in itself, he said, sufficient answer. The use of force by Britain to aid Spain would merely have united the colonies in their resistance and eventually thrown them into the arms of the enemy. But these arguments were of no avail at Cadiz. Castlereagh could only hope that, when the Cortes were transferred to Madrid and became more representative of the nation, British conduct would be better appreciated.[2]

With Portuguese problems Castlereagh had less difficulty. The Prince Regent at Rio, though callous as to the fate of his

[1] From Wellesley, March 10, April 24, May 24, June 20, July 5, 18, 1812: *F.O. Spain*, 129, 130, 131. To Wellesley, Aug. 29, Oct. 27, Dec. 31, 1812: *F.O. Spain*, 128.

[2] From Wellesley, Oct. 1, Nov. 19, 1812; Feb. 16, 1813: *F.O. Spain*, 132, 143; Wellesley to Wellington, Feb. 4, 1813: *W.S.D.* vii. 546. To Wellesley, July 3, 1813: *F.O. Spain*, 142.

people and actually drawing money from Portugal during this difficult time, was fairly amenable to Strangford's influence. He only pressed the claims of his wife, perhaps, in order to get rid of her. The difficulty over Buenos Ayres continued, but the Regent always gave way when British pressure was put on him. At Lisbon, Stuart and Beresford were both members of the Regency, and though the financial and economic difficulties were great and the records are full of disputes as to trade under the treaty of 1810, yet on the whole the Government was moderately competent. Though two of the Regents were dreadful, Wellington later confessed that the principal Minister, Forjas, was "the ablest man I had to do with on the Peninsula." Stuart lost patience on occasion, and Hamilton had to write to him at Castlereagh's request to moderate his protests to the Portuguese Government: "He thinks you have expressed your feelings too warmly, not perhaps more so than the subject merited or than the conduct of that body called for, but more than prudence and sound policy would recommend." Portuguese merchants might reasonably be expected to be jealous of the new privileges conferred on British trade. "As to national gratitude," it was pointed out, "we must not expect much on that score, and what little we may expect must come voluntarily and not as a right."

The spirit of jealousy, indeed, grew as the danger of invasion diminished, and Castlereagh became anxious as to the connection between Portugal and the Royal Family in Brazil, which seemed so indifferent to its fate. "Considerable advantages . . . might be expected to result," Strangford was told, "from the return of the Royal Family to Europe at the present auspicious moment. It is not, however, a point which they feel themselves entitled to press. If the Prince Regent should from any motive desire to protract his stay in Brazil it is very desirable that H.R.H. should send his son to Europe without delay. His evincing some military ardour at the present juncture could not fail to elevate the family in the eyes of their own subjects and of Europe. It is not less material should the Prince Regent determine to return himself to Europe that some branch of the Royal Family should continue to be resident with efficient power at Brazil. Any attempt to lower the South American Dominions again to the colonial standard would, I am satisfied, prove at once fatal to the interests of the monarchy in that quarter of the globe." [1]

With the Peninsula was intimately connected British policy towards the Barbary Powers, whence supplies of food were obtained for the Spanish and British troops. The Vice-Consuls, a poor lot, were under Wellesley, but he had little control over them, and the special officers sent over were thwarted by his own subordinates. The Barbary pirates preyed on Britain's allies as much as they dared, and were a continual source of friction between Britain and the Mediterranean Powers. Sicily was especially concerned, and a number of her nationals were released at a low cost in 1812. But the evil grew to such an extent that A'Court was sent on a special mission at the beginning of 1813. This was, however, only a palliative, and not until the struggle on the Continent was over could Britain take the action which duty and interest demanded. [2]

(ii) SICILY

While the main land attack of Britain upon Napoleon's power was proceeding in the Peninsula, it was never the intention of the British Government that Sicily should be more than a point of defence fulfilling its essential purpose of guarding the central Mediterranean. Nor did it become in any real sense a base of attack during these years. But owing to the extraordinary character of the man sent out by Wellesley in 1811, and the curious situation which he found and tried to use for his own schemes, Sicily during these years became the centre of an amazing drama which has attracted the attention of many historians. [3]

[1] Stanhope, *Conversations*, 91. [Hamilton] to Stewart, Nov. 2, 1813 : *F.O. Portugal*, 150. To Strangford, Nov. 22, 1813 : *F.O. Portugal*, 144.
[2] From Wellesley, May 1, 24, June 20, Sept. 10, Nov. 10, 1812 : *F.O. Spain*, 130, 131, 132. To Wellesley, Jan. 6, 1813 : *F.O. Spain*, 142. To Stuart, May 19, 1812 : *F.O. Portugal*, 126. From Pro-Consul MacDonald, May 15, Sept. 16, 1812 : *F.O. Algiers*, 14. R. M. Johnston, *Mémoire de Marie Caroline*, 120.
[3] The story was first told from the documents in the Record Office by Oscar Browning (" Queen Caroline of Naples," *English Historical Review*, ii.

Lord William Bentinck was only thirty-six years old when he was sent by Wellesley to Sicily with greater powers than any of his predecessors, being made Commander-in-Chief of the Mediterranean (except Malta), as well as Minister to the Sicilian Court. His Presidency of Madras had ended in an embarrassing failure, partly owing to his own rash actions, and the military posts that he had subsequently filled had hardly disclosed qualities specially suitable to the very delicate position he was now to occupy. But the son of the Duke of Portland could not be denied a high military or diplomatic post. He had shewn, at least, that he possessed great energy and a masterful mind, and both were needed in Sicily. The intensity of his Whig faith, still less his immense vanity and rashness, were not appreciated by Bathurst and Wellesley. They did not suspect that they were sending to cope with Marie Caroline and her weak and treacherous husband, a brilliant and unbalanced egoist, all the more dangerous because he was also imbued with a species of idealism. As it was, Bentinck attempted to make Sicily serve his ambition to rival Wellington as the saviour of Europe, and gradually evolved grandiose plans for the future of Italy, which were in direct contradiction to the wishes of his Government and produced a situation of such complexity that Castlereagh was led by it into the most equivocal conduct of the whole of his career.

Bentinck, on his arrival in 1811, found Sicily still governed by the sensual, pleasure-loving, and false King, who was still at moments of crisis liable to be influenced by his wife, Marie Caroline, the fierce, drug-ridden, almost mad daughter of Maria Theresa. In 1811 an attempt to override the constitutional

482, reprinted in *The Flight to Varennes* (1892)) with skill and judgment, but with few references. The most important Italian account is that of Bianco (*La Sicilia durante l'occupazione inglese, 1806–1815* (1902)), who used the archives at Palermo. Helfert's defence of the Queen in his *Maria Carolina von Neapel* (1878) was based mainly on Austrian archives. R. M. Johnston's *Mémoire de Marie Caroline Reine de Naples* (1912), whatever may be thought of the origin of the manuscript, contains a large number of *pièces justificatifs* and valuable extracts from the Bentinck MSS. and the correspondence in the Record Office. Two articles by Miss Lackland in the *English Historical Review* ("The Failure of the Constitutional Experiment in Sicily, 1813–1814," April 1926, and "Lord William Bentinck in Sicily, 1811–1812," July 1927), which are based on the Bentinck MSS., and researches at Palermo, bring out some new points. It may be hoped that her full study will soon appear.

rights of the Sicilian Estates (nobles, clergy, towns) by the imposition of special taxes had resulted in a protest of the Sicilian nobility who saw their privileges threatened and the imprisonment of five of their leaders, including the liberal Prince Belmonte and his father-in-law, Villa Ermosa. Bentinck's instructions, which ordered him not to meddle with internal affairs, were not sufficient to cope with this situation, and he returned to England to obtain wider powers. Wellesley, who probably paid no greater attention to Sicily than elsewhere, gave Bentinck new instructions which emphasised the necessity of Sicilians sharing in the government of Naples, and empowered him to suspend the subsidy at will, and, if necessary, break off the alliance and remove the British troops from Sicily. He returned to Palermo on December 7, 1811, and began his struggle for the overthrow of Caroline, the regeneration of Sicily, and the creation of an Italian state under British influence. In only the first of these objects was he successful; the second produced the new Sicilian constitution modelled on that of Britain, not altogether by Bentinck's wishes; and the third led to Bentinck's struggle with Murat, which eventually resulted in the Austrian control of the Italian Peninsula.

Though Bentinck already suspected the Queen of treasonable correspondence with the enemy, he did not at first insist on her complete removal from the centre of affairs. Only gradually did he see that it was necessary and possible to exclude her from Palermo and eventually from Sicily altogether. Now with the threat of suspending the subsidy he only demanded the return of the exiles, the removal of the illegal taxes, and the creation of a Ministry of Sicilians instead of Neapolitans. The King, whose main object in life was pleasure, evaded this onslaught by pleading ill-health and appointing his son Vicar-General. The task, according to the Duke of Orleans, Ferdinand's son-in-law, who was now always on the British side, was not an uncongenial one, but the Prince was too much in dread of his parents ever to act a very decisive or manly part. His father appeared only to intervene occasionally and at moments of crisis, but was perhaps more potent behind the scenes than has been generally recognised. His son was, after all, only a temporary Regent, and the King could assume power at any moment. His mother fought continually and hopelessly the relentless attack by which Bentinck gradually ousted her from influence and at last residence in Sicily. While, therefore, the Hereditary Prince responded to Bentinck's stern admonitions and appeared to accept the conditions which he laid down, he was continually breaking away from a policy in which he did not believe and was always liable to yield to the entreaties of his mother or the commands of his father.

Bentinck began with an open threat of force if he did not have his way. In this he appears to have exceeded his instructions, but he reported his conduct to his Government with the same openness and detail as he narrated all the subsequent series of events. "I told him frankly," he wrote, "that not only the British army but the country generally believed in the existence of an understanding between the Court and the enemy. . . . I concluded a very long conversation by saying that I should use force if my representations were not attended to. This force was not against but for the benefit of the King and his family." [1]

In this uncompromising fashion Bentinck began a campaign for the reform of the Sicilian state, which lasted till July and resulted in the unexpected adoption of the British constitution. The affair originated in a contest about persons and policies. Bentinck insisted on the employment of the liberal Sicilian nobles, and he wished the whole system of government to be overhauled. The state was indeed practically bankrupt: the Hereditary Prince was as extravagant as his open-handed mother, and the people were subjected to arbitrary rule, to which. however, they were accustomed by long practice. The victory was delayed by the opposition of the Queen and a visit to Malta. Perhaps it would never have come, certainly not in the form which it assumed, had not the question of the Sicilian constitution become associated with what was naturally the main anxiety

[1] From Bentinck, Jan. 1, 11, 1812 : *F.O. Sicily*, 51. I agree with Miss Lackland that the King was a more active agent than had been supposed by those writers who concentrated on the dramatic struggle between Bentinck and the Queen.

of the Court, the recovery of their ancient possessions on the mainland.

At last, after a fierce fight with the Queen, of whose treachery Bentinck offered to shew the King and him alone convincing proofs, the Sicilian Estates were summoned to a special session so that the reform might be carried out in the approved constitutional manner. When the Prince doubted whether such a course was "safe," Bentinck declared it was "indispensable" and offered to guarantee him against the "revolution," which both he and his father dreaded would be the outcome. In May, therefore, the Estates were "elected" under the influence of the new liberal Ministry, which naturally secured as many supporters as possible in all three houses. When they met in June the question arose as to where the programme of reform was to begin. It was then the King and not Bentinck who suggested that the model of the British constitution should be adopted. This might be deemed a piece of delightful irony from such a monarch, but it had behind it solid motives. It completely counterchecked Bentinck and the liberals, and turned their energies into establishing a British constitution instead of the more dangerous course of concentrating on judicial and financial reform. Moreover, it would designate Sicily as a model state, the only continental one which possessed that mysterious constitution which had enabled the British people to defy the conqueror of all the rest of Europe. The King would therefore be able to appear to his old subjects as a reformed character and carry the torch of liberty to Italy, perhaps even increase his old realm. Doubtless the King had little belief in the desire of Italians for liberty, but Bentinck had already indicated to the Prince that it was the determining factor and combated the schemes of Moliturno, a Neapolitan adventurer, who was assuring the Court that they could conquer an Italian Empire without granting a constitution. British aid was necessary to effect anything on the Continent, British principles must therefore be adopted, in theory if not in practice.[1]

[1] From Bentinck, March 19, 30, May 5, 6, June 27, 1812 : *F.O. Sicily*, 51, cf. R. M. Johnston, *Mémoire*, 126–27. The Queen was playing for time,

When, therefore, the Parliament at last assembled, the idea of a British constitution immediately appeared. The Prince was, indeed, at first little inclined to accept his father's suggestion, and, as Bentinck confessed, was only won over by the fact that without a constitution in Sicily, Naples could not be recovered. This was, indeed, Bentinck's own condition for an expedition, though he had not for one moment expected that the Sicilians would adopt the British model—a thing so sacred and intangible that it was difficult to imagine any other people copying it successfully. "I must confess," he reported in one of the most remarkable of his dispatches, "that at first I was very much against the adoption of the English constitution. I doubted very much whether the people have sufficient steadiness or wisdom to execute it. I was, however, very much better disposed to it when I saw that no other plan presented so few difficulties, and my fears were very much lessened when I read the outline of a constitution formed upon that of England, but with great moderation and wisdom adapted to the depraved state of this society by certain salutary restraints upon the Liberty of the Press and by suspending for the present the Trial by Jury." Its authors, Belmonte and Villa Ermosa, as Bentinck reported, inspired by a Sicilian, Professor Balsamo, as modern researches have indicated, were indeed no more democrats than the aristocratic Whig whose actions had made the constitution possible.

But even this magnificent adaptation of the British model did not, in Bentinck's opinion, make Sicily the natural inheritor of Napoleonic Italy. The Neapolitan Royal Family, he solemnly told the Hereditary Prince, was so disliked in Naples, owing to its past conduct, that it could hardly be the standard-bearer of liberty. Indeed Italy—all Italy and not merely Naples—must be allowed to choose for itself: "I told him that the only chance of success was to declare at once to the people that the deliverance of Italy from the French yoke was our sole object. The choice of a constitution and

thinking that Bentinck would be disowned. In this she was encouraged by Sir Robert Wilson, who, with his usual disloyalty and vanity, meddled in affairs during his visit to the island in May. Randolph, *Private Diary of Sir R. Wilson*, i. 52–63. He, of course, wrote to Grey about the situation. *Wilson MSS*. 30119, f. 47.

a chief must be left to the free will of the people." The poor
Prince was much dismayed: "He asked, if in the first proclamation I would make no mention of the Royal Family.
My answer was that such a measure would inevitably
produce resistance. He suggested that in the event of such
an expedition it would appear extraordinary to the Neapolitans that while there were two Princes of the family in
Sicily, neither of them should come forward to aid in the
deliverance of their country. I told H.R.H. the sentiment
did him much honour, but that private feeling in a case of
such high moment must give way to the public advantage.
He added also that it was far from his wishes to appear as a
conqueror. He meant merely to offer himself as the choice
of the people. I told H.R.H. that in an invasion there would
be no time to convince the people of his real character, that
it would have been fortunate had H.R.H. many months ago
done that in Sicily, which would have been the best explanation and security to the Neapolitans of his intentions towards
them. Now, upon seeing a Prince of the old family arrive,
the general alarm would be that they were about to have
imposed upon them the ancient system." The only concession, indeed, that the poor Prince could wring from Bentinck,
with regard to the crusade which the Captain-General of his
own army was planning, was that he would not take any other
Prince with him.

This conversation seems, not unnaturally, to have left the
Prince somewhat bewildered as to the advantages to the Royal
Family of the new British constitution. The King also cooled
off, a fact which Bentinck attributed to the Queen's influence
and caused him to lament the moderation with which he had
treated her, but to which the above conversation may have
contributed. But the die was now cast; an anonymous
paper threatening the Spanish constitution made the Prince
see some advantages in the British; Bentinck was, indeed,
induced to give a kind of guarantee that it would be maintained, and so the Speech from the Throne announced to the
new Parliament that the Crown and the Government were
prepared to take the momentous step.[1]

---

[1] From Bentinck, June 30, 1812 : *F.O. Sicily,* 51.

The final stage in this curious negotiation is contained in the paper which Bentinck sent to the Prince of his conditions for an expedition to the mainland, which, amongst other technical clauses, contained the following: "3rdly, That the independence of the whole of Italy and not the partial conquest of any particular province or state shall be the acknowledged object. 4thly, That such portions of the territory of the Continent as are relieved from the yoke of France shall be left to the free choice of their own constitution and their own chiefs. 5thly, That the British Commander shall guarantee to them this liberty."

The Hereditary Prince was to promise not to interfere with this programme, and all who opposed it were to be treated as enemies whatever their rank or condition. It was a poor consolation that the last three clauses ran: "Lord William Bentinck engages to do all in his power to persuade the Neapolitans to accept the Hereditary Prince for their Sovereign. He engages to resist with all the means at his command any pretender who, either by force or intrigue, shall endeavour to establish himself on the throne of Naples in opposition to the will of the people. He engages not to take any Prince or person of royal extraction on the expedition." [1]

No wonder that the Prince's response was considered by Bentinck "highly unsatisfactory," "passing over in silence almost every part of my paper," and "shewing in the clearest manner the continuance of the same weak policy with regard to Naples and of the same confidence in Prince Moliturno, who had been the constant adviser of the Queen and whose character is, in general, discredited." Even the adoption of the British Constitution had placed the Sicilian Royal Family merely in the position of a favoured candidate rather than that of a sovereign who could claim restoration to his old dominions as a right.

The final touch to the comedy was given when Bentinck announced that there would be no expedition to Italy at all, but only the dispatch of a Sicilian force to the east coast of Spain. The discussion therefore, he reported, was of no

[1] Secret Memorandum given to the Hereditary Prince, June 20, 1812, enclosed in the dispatch of June 30, 1812 : *F.O. Sicily*, 51.

immediate consequence. This was, of course, quite in accordance with the wishes of his own Government, but it left the King and the Crown Prince with but little confidence in the power or wish of Bentinck to bring them back to their lost kingdom.[1]

It was only natural, therefore, that the Hereditary Prince now shewed little zeal for the new constitution, while Bentinck regretted the weakness with which he had treated him, and explained that the excellent Speech from the Throne accepting the British constitution had only been made in view of the expedition to Italy, which the Prince then thought at hand. The opposition to the new ideas was secretly encouraged, while their supporters were depressed. For the moment even Bentinck was discouraged; but Belmonte and his party were still strong, and Bentinck's control over the cash was a powerful factor on their side. In spite of the manœuvres of the Court, therefore, Parliament accepted fourteen articles, which for the first time laid down in writing the glorious principles of the unwritten constitution of Britain.[2]

This was, of course, only a barren victory until the formal sanction of the Crown could be obtained, and a long and bitter struggle ensued. Bentinck made the Queen the centre of it all, though it is probable that the King in his intervals of energy exercised a more malign influence, while the Prince himself was more hostile to the constitution than his father, who saw its futility but usefulness as a means of absorbing Bentinck's reforming zeal. It was the Queen whom Bentinck singled out as his real enemy, and his dispatches are full of her appeals to the King and the Prince, and his own denunciations and threats to the same pair, who were really as wishful to get rid of her as he was, if the boon could be obtained without too much scandal. The struggle was won step by step. The Queen was first forced to leave Palermo in spite of an unwelcome return to the bedside of her son, whose sudden illness was thought, most unjustly, to be caused by his mother's poison. Then came a final struggle for her

---

[1] From Bentinck, June 30, 1812 : *F.O. Sicily*, 51. Nugent subsequently claimed to have helped Bentinck to this decision. Nugent to Metternich, Oct. 15, 1812 : *Vienna St. A.*

[2] From Bentinck, July 9, 25, 1812 : *F.O Sicily*, 52.

removal from Sicily altogether, when her husband did shew a flash of real spirit and announced his intention to resume the royal power. But Bentinck threatened to break off the alliance and the King collapsed. The Prince returned to his station with even wider powers than before. The Queen's debts, which her extravagance and generosity had made overwhelming, were paid for her through an arrangement made by Bentinck. Even then her final decision was only obtained by a threat of force and the disposition of the British troops to keep her away from her husband. However, she sailed at last on a British warship for Vienna *via* Constantinople—the only route available in April 1813.[1]

From the point of view of British policy the most important part of all this tortuous struggle was that it kept the Commander-in-Chief from discharging any other part of his functions. He was unable to accompany the force of 6000 men, which was all that he could send to Spain in 1812, though Murat and the flower of his army had accompanied the Emperor to Moscow. Meanwhile he had concluded a new treaty to which the Prince at last forced his father to agree, which gave the British much greater control over the Sicilian forces than before. In return, Bentinck gave a guarantee of the possession of Sicily to the King in any treaty of peace which Britain should sign, though he refused the Prince's request to add a promise to endeavour to recover the kingdom of Naples. The guarantee he defended on the ground that the new constitution in Sicily had made the compact one "not only between the two sovereigns but between the two nations, sealed by the unanimous gratitude of the Sicilians and indissolubly fixed in the feelings of political interest of liberty and of independence common to both." [2]

During these exciting events the attitude of the British Government towards its Commander-in-Chief was one of resigned acquiescence in his actions. Whatever charges may be made against Bentinck, that of concealment from his Government is not one that can be substantiated, at any rate

[1] For the details of the struggle, see the works noted on p. 75. Bentinck's long dispatches and enclosures give every stage of the negotiation.
[2] From Bentinck, Sept. 13, 1812 : *F.O. Sicily*, 52. The new treaty is given in *B.F.S.P.* i. 683–90.

until the end of 1813. His dispatches naturally gave his own view of events, but they narrated all his actions in great detail and enclosed the voluminous series of notes and letters with which he bombarded the King and the Prince. The Government therefore shared fully his responsibility. Castlereagh, it is true, always placed the objects of British policy in a rather different perspective, but he accepted in general Bentinck's methods. In March 1812 he approved all his conduct "in the delicate and arduous circumstances" in which he was placed, only asking for further details of the Queen's treachery on which he might be questioned in Parliament. In May Bentinck was told that he could not be given instructions in detail, he was to follow those which Wellesley had drawn up. He was to try to secure a loyal army and "to recommend such necessary reforms of the Sicilian constitution as may ensure the affections of the people and make the Neapolitans anxious to receive equal advantages together with the return of their lawful sovereigns." [1]

Castlereagh was, however, rather perturbed at Bentinck's dispatch about the terms of the expedition to Italy, which he criticised in a private letter. There was no question of Ferdinand submitting to "election" by the people of Naples. In the eyes of the British Government he was their lawful sovereign, who should be "restored" not "elected." But he approved the reform of the Sicilian constitution as likely to secure this object, as well as all Bentick's actions towards the Queen. He seems to have been as convinced as Bentinck of her treachery, and this, doubtless, made him view the Ambassador's conduct favourably. Castelcicala's protests therefore made no impression. On February 9, 1813, a special instruction was sent to Bentinck authorising him to pay the Queen's debts to get rid of her, and to go to the limit of his powers to produce that desirable result. Force was, indeed, only to be used in case of treason and as a last resource: "It is of infinite importance in point of *impression* that the object should be accomplished by arrangement and not by force, . . . as it would be difficult to make the world at large understand, whilst the whole military power of

---

[1] To Bentinck, March 6, 12, May 19, 1812 : *F.O. Sicily*, 50.

the island is in your Lordship's hands, that there existed an adequate necessity for forcibly removing the wife of the sovereign, more especially if no tumult existed, from her family and dominions." But Castlereagh refused Castelcicala's suggestion that Catania or Sardinia would be a distant enough exile for the Queen; only at Vienna would she be at a safe enough distance, and the dispatch ended by assuring Bentinck, who learnt at the same time that he had been given the K.C.B., of the Government's "fullest confidence" in his discretion and "very cordial support." [1]

When the news came therefore of the final struggle even Bentinck's use of force was approved, especially as he had explained that Castlereagh's dispatches of February 9 had come too late to convince the Court that he had his Government behind him.   There was, however, a note of regret in Castlereagh's approval, and he urged that in the future the use of force should be unnecessary, and control by means of the subsidy should be sufficient to effect all British purposes. It is clear that Castlereagh did not yet understand all that Bentinck's dispatches implied with regard to Italian policy. His attention was concentrated on the new situation which was arising in the north, and so far as the Mediterranean was concerned, on Spain.   Several of his colleagues, however, were very critical of Bentinck, whose wild schemes of combinations with Russia and expeditions in the Adriatic had alarmed both Mulgrave and Bathurst.   Liverpool was disappointed at the paucity of his support in Spain.   But, after all, great latitude had to be allowed to a man so far away and admittedly in such a difficult position.   His schemes for Italy were not taken very seriously, especially as all depended on the attitude of Austria, which was yet in doubt. [2]

Bentinck was therefore left undisturbed, and it must be admitted without much guidance.   His victory over the Queen had at last, he believed, set him free from military duties, and in June he sailed for Spain, leaving Lord Montgomerie to watch over the new constitution.   On

[1] To Bentinck, Dec. 5, 1812 : *F.O. Sicily*, 50 ; Feb. 9, 1813 : *C.C.* viii. 298 (where wrongly dated) ; Feb. 9 (No. 4), 1813 : *F.O. Sicily*, 56.
[2] To Bentinck, May 19, 23, 1813 : *F.O. Sicily*, 56 ; *Bathurst*, 223 ; *W.S.D.* vii. 374, 401.

the way he had his first important negotiation with Murat.

(iii) THE NEAR EAST [1]

While Bentinck had been imagining great deeds in Sicily, an important crisis had been faced at Constantinople with wonderful skill and courage by a man not less resolute and much more practical than he. Stratford Canning had received the onerous charge which Adair handed over to him in 1810, without for one moment imagining that he would have to bear it for two years. But Wellesley during all this time not only did not send him a single dispatch but, on the pretext that he was awaiting Russia's action, allowed the old and dilatory Liston, who was eventually appointed to succeed Adair, to delay month after month in England. It was only Castlereagh's accession to office which at last sent Liston off with a large bundle of instructions, to arrive too late to affect the main issue. [2]

No man better served the state by incompetence than Wellesley in this case, since Stratford Canning played a part in which Liston would almost certainly have failed. Circumstances indeed made peace between Russia and the Porte practicable; for Alexander was about to fight Napoleon, while the Turkish army had been severely defeated and was rapidly deteriorating. But the Sultan might very well consider that the French attack on Russia would be his opportunity, as the energetic and skilful French Chargé laboured to prove with the constant assistance of the Austrian and Prussian Ambassadors, while the Russian generals were convinced that they could easily overcome the remnants of the Grand Vizir's armies. Moreover, the Porte's usual weapon in diplomacy was always delay, which seemed especially suitable at this juncture. Without Stratford Canning's mediation, therefore, it is doubtful if peace could have been made until the news of Napoleon's invasion had reached Constantinople, and then it

---

[1] The story is well told by Lane Poole in his *Life of Stratford Canning,* but the dispatches, of some of which a very short précis is given in the *Cambridge History of British Foreign Policy,* i. 599–602, add many details.
[2] For Liston's dilatoriness, see *Bath Archives,* i. 216, 278, 287 ; and Buckingham, *Memoirs of the Regency,* i. 128.

might never have been made, with incalculable consequences on the whole campaign.

The diplomatic situation at the beginning of 1812 indeed appeared hopeless. The Tsar had rejected the Porte's offer of the Pruth, and demanded the Sereth as a boundary and the Phasis in Asia, insisting also that Turkey should make an alliance. The French were triumphant at this news, but in spite of a terrible row over Turkish un-neutral action, which was proceeding at the time, Canning's offer to write once more to Italinski, the Russian diplomatic agent, was accepted by the Reis Effendi, and the Turks restrained from breaking off negotiations. In the interval the French, as a result of frequent couriers from Paris, made a determined effort to prevent peace, while Canning had to confess he had no instructions. "I must not omit to inform your Lordship," ran his dignified protest, "that having had occasion to see the Reis Effendi this morning he questioned me respecting the long silence of His Majesty's Government towards the Porte, in a manner which betrayed much anxiety and disappointment on that account, feelings which I have but too much reason to believe he only partakes in common with his colleagues. I think it my duty to mention this circumstance and to entreat your Lordship's attention to what I have repeatedly urged upon the same subject in my former dispatches." [1]

In spite of this handicap he held his own, and when Baron Stürmer, the Austrian Ambassador, announced to the Porte, with a great flourish of trumpets, the new Franco-Austrian treaty directed against Russia and guaranteeing the integrity of the Ottoman Empire, Canning countered by revealing to the Porte the plan of invasion of Turkey, drawn up in 1810, which Adair had procured from his friends in Vienna. When the Ambassador returned to the attack with the offer of active co-operation against Russia and the dispatch of officers to the front, indignation with Austria added to Canning's resolution. " I assure your Lordship," he wrote, "that if other motives were wanting, the sole desire of helping

[1] Stratford Canning to Wellesley, Jan. 11, Feb. 6, 21, March 11, 1812 : F.O. Turkey, 77.

in some degree to make the degraded Government of Austria feel that the only points to be gathered from the sacrifice of her honour are mistrust and contempt would urge me to redouble my exertions." He even contemplated the offer of £300,000 to the Porte under the terms of a secret article of the treaty of 1809. Fortunately, the Reis Effendi shewed sufficient resolution to spare the young Minister this grave responsibility.[1]

The issue, however, was still in doubt, and the announcement of the dispatch of General Andreossi, as French Ambassador, increased Canning's anxiety. It was difficult to make the Russians realise the situation by letters, which the Turks conveyed and saw, and in this emergency Canning made use of a Scotch traveller, Gordon, to convey to Bucharest his urgent warnings. By this time his letters to Petersburg had begun to take effect, and the result was that on May 28 a treaty was signed at Bucharest. Even now, however, though Russia had conceded the Pruth frontier—thus giving up the Principalities and keeping only Bessarabia—and agreed to return her conquests in Asia, there were difficulties in the fact that she still demanded a treaty of alliance, and the Asiatic article was doubtfully worded. Ratification was still uncertain, and Canning had again to intervene with letters to Italinski, urging the Turkish point of view on these points. Gordon, who seems to have been an excellent diplomatist, had frightened the Russians by lurid accounts of Austria's hostile intentions, and by the time Liston appeared on the scene the ratifications had been sent off, though the Porte still meant to alter the Asiatic article of the treaty if it could. Though the real author of the treaty was Napoleon, whose threatened attack forced the necessary concessions from the Tsar, yet the courage, energy, persistence, and resource of Canning under the most difficult circumstances will always remain on record as a fitting prelude to the career of the greatest British Ambassador of the nineteenth century.[2]

[1] Stratford Canning to Wellesley, March 17, 26, April 12, 25, 26, 1812 : F.O. Turkey, 77.
[2] From Stratford Canning, May 11, June 10, 12, 29, 1812 : F.O. Turkey, 77. Bernadotte's influence on the Tsar also contributed to the result, though his envoy, Tavast, arrived too late on the scene at Constantinople

In the midst of his anxieties Canning did not neglect to ensure that Liston should have a magnificent reception by the Turkish authorities. The old gentleman had still an important part to play in keeping the Turks quiet through the vicissitudes of the next eighteen months, but his qualities were sufficient to soothe and placate the nervous Sultan and his Ministers. Castlereagh endeavoured to help him by information from Paris that "there is every reason to believe that the ultimate object of Bonaparte is the taking of Constantinople and placing himself on the throne of Constantine. He has packed up with his equipage his coronation robes and imperial crown." This news possibly did not much disturb the Sultan, but it was important that Liston put his foot down on Admiral Tchitagov's absurd scheme of marching across the Balkan Peninsula to the Adriatic, much to that gentleman's annoyance, but to the great relief of the Turks, who had threatened war to prevent it. He deprecated any attempt to force into active alliance against the French, the Turks, who were now discontented that they had not taken greater advantage of Russia's difficulties. The Sultan, whose personal interference had alone made the Peace of Bucharest possible, at one time seemed to contemplate a renewal of hostilities, and he relieved his anger by cruel and capricious conduct towards the Ministers who had signed it.

It was long, indeed, before the Porte realised the defeat of Napoleon. Throughout 1813 the Sultan wavered from side to side, growing steadily more uneasy at Russia's triumphs. The armistice of June was hailed as a decided check to her arms, and the Reis Effendi insisted on Liston supporting the Turkish demand to be represented at the proposed Conference at Prague. But the rapidity of events made Turkish actions of small importance, and the Sultan could only await the final stage of the drama with great anxiety, relying almost entirely on British support to save him from his enemies in the north when they were freed from French pressure.[1]

to help Stratford Canning. The French view, which exaggerated the effect of English ' bribes,' is given from Latour Maubourg's dispatches by Vandal, *Napoleon et Alexandre I*, iii. 443-48.
[1] Cooke to Liston, May 15, 1812; from Liston, July 11, 18, Aug. 12, Sept. 14, Sept. 18; (to Cooke) Nov. 12, Dec. 12, 1812: *F.O. Turkey*, 79. Jan. 15,

Meanwhile on the extreme wing of the battle front—Persia —an attempt was also being made to promote peace. It must be admitted that this effort was as much due to obtain relief from a subsidy of 200,000 tomans per annum as to assist the Russian cause. British officers were aiding the Persian army in Georgia to win considerable successes and a flotilla on the Caspian sea was planned. Still Sir Gore Ouseley, the British Ambassador, continued to press for peace though he was of the opinion that a weak Persia was far less dangerous to India than a strong one. The first successes of Bonaparte, however, had an even greater effect at Teheran than the treaty of Bucharest, which the Shah considered a base betrayal by the Turks. News came very slowly, and in the middle of 1813 the Persians still hoped Petersburg would share the fate of Moscow. At last, by promising to use his personal aid to get further concessions from Russia, Sir Gore negotiated a peace at the end of September 1813. He did it, he said, at the risk of his health, because his Government seemed to consider "that strengthening Persia is better policy than leaving her in her former state of weakness," obviously still believing the contrary himself. He made the journey to Petersburg in order to carry out his promise without much effect, though he was convinced that, if only Russia would leave the Georgians alone, they would act as a splendid buffer state. Young James Morier meanwhile had to negotiate a new treaty with Persia, which was not concluded until November 25, 1814. It made due provision for British assistance to Persia in time of war, beginning, after praising God, the All-perfect and All-sufficient: "These happy leaves are a nosegay plucked from the thornless garden of concord and tied by the hands of the Pleni-potentiaries of the 2 great states in the form of a definite

March 27, Aug. 10, 13, 1813 : *F.O. Turkey*, 81. It is quite likely that Napoleon did take the emblems of Charlemagne with him to Russia, but, if so, the coronation was meant to take place at Moscow, not at Constantinople (Vandal, *Napoleon et Alexandre I*, iii. 587). Liston to Wilson, Sept. 20, 1812: *Wilson MSS.* 30106, f. 324; Dec. 25, 1812; Jan. 5, 7, 1813. Randolph, *Wilson's Journal*, 395, 400, 402. Wilson was employed by Liston to stop the Russians' march on Dalmatia. Ali Pasha of Janina, a valuable ally of the British because of the strategic position and ship timber of his territory, had also protested, and Castlereagh constantly urged attention to his interests both to Liston and Bentinck (*e.g.* To Liston, March 27, 1812 : *F.O. Turkey*, 77. To Bentinck, June 10, 1812 : *F.O. Sicily*, 50).

treaty, in which the articles of Friendship and Amity are
blended." [1]

[1] To Cathcart, July 24, 1812 : *F.O. Russia*, 78. From Sir Gore Ouseley,
March 15, July 6, 1812 : *F.O. Persia*, 6 ; Aug. 10, Oct. 12, Dec. 24, 1812 :
F.O. Persia, 7 ; Jan. 16, July 10, Sept. 28, 1813 : *F.O. Persia*, 8. Sir
Gore Ouseley to the Earl of Buckingham, Feb. 11, 1814 ; To Morier,
April 28, 1814 ; from Morier, June 25, Nov. 30, 1814 : *F.O. Persia*, 9.
See also *C.C.* ix. 162, x. 107. Sir Gore Ouseley to the Prince Regent,
March 20, 1812 ; Oct. 31, 1813 : *Windsor Arch.* The last letter betrays
some bitterness and an obvious hint : " Although the affairs relating to
Persia (unfortunately for me) create little interest in England yet, the
reverse being the case in Russia, I have already received the most grateful
acknowledgments from General Rtischev, Governor General of Russia and
the Lion of the Caucasus." Yet Sir Gore Ouseley suffered the humiliation
of being offered passage home from Petersburg in a horse transport, which
he refused as " disparaging my representative character so much at the
close of my mission." *F.O. Persia*, 10.

2. THE RISING OF THE NORTH

THE Spanish rising, important as its ultimate influence was on British policy and Napoleon's power, was immediately only local in its effects. The first breaking up of the European Empire of Napoleon came in the north. In 1812 the invasion of Russia dominated the political scene, and all eyes in Europe were fastened on one of the most dramatic and unexpected tragedies of history. Castlereagh could do but little to influence such a titanic struggle so far away, though Napoleon's success might be disastrous to British imperial and economic interests. On either flank, however, Britain had a footing, and, as has been seen, at Constantinople Stratford Canning had contributed a good deal to ease the pressure on the Russian armies. Castlereagh himself had played little or no part in this development; but the Baltic was much nearer, and it was to the Baltic that Castlereagh's main attention was directed in the year 1812. No attempt was made to influence Russia during the long period of suspense while the Russian and French armies were gathering against one another. Both the Tsar and his Francophil Chancellor, Rumantzov, who still nominally directed foreign affairs, knew through Spanish and Sicilian agents that Russia's actions were being watched sympathetically in London, and that aid would come to her if she threw down the gauntlet. But Russia must take all the responsibility of her actions upon herself. "It has never been the policy of this country," wrote Castlereagh in his first dispatch on the subject, "to incite Russia to war. It has been, on the contrary, the uniform wish of the British Government to leave the decision of that question entirely to Russia upon a view of her own situation and resources." [1]

[1] To Thornton, March 13, 1812 : *F.O. Sweden*, 71. Extracts and *Précis* from a number of Thornton's dispatches for 1812 are given in the *Cambridge*

For the moment, therefore, it was Sweden from whom something might be expected immediately, small in itself, perhaps, but of great importance because of its ultimate effect on Russian policy. There the Gascon, Bernadotte, who against Napoleon's wishes had become Prince Royal and heir to the old King, who had succeeded in 1809 to the mad Gustavus, was planning with rash words but subtle brain a new orientation of Swedish policy. Wellesley's negotiations in 1811 had completely failed, partly because he had wanted to obtain results too quickly. The French invasion of Pomerania and the clouds threatening over Russia had, however, produced a new situation, and Bernadotte, in February, had approached the Tsar and secured his assent to the conquest of Norway. He still looked to Britain to aid him in the same object. Castlereagh disliked the idea of associating Britain in the attack on Norway on which Bernadotte had set his heart, but he appreciated his wish to isolate Sweden from Germany and consolidate her power in the peninsula. Thornton was authorised, therefore, at once to promise naval protection, some military equipment, the cession of a West Indian island—one of Bernadotte's strange desires—and even on the question of Norway to hint that British countenance would be given, though peace must be made before further discussion could take place. "In the present situation of Europe," ran the dispatch, "when all the minor states on the southern shores of the Baltic have sunk into the vassalage of France, should Sweden, instead of engaging in distant operations, consider it necessary for her own safety to consolidate her internal system, and with this view deem it wise to look for her security to the protection of Russia on one flank, and the naval power of England on the other, excluding from the

History of British Foreign Policy, i. 590–99, but they are often inadequate and sometimes misleading. A Swedish translation of British Records, 1809–13, is given in Scaevola (Pseud.), Utlandska diplomaters minnen fràu Svenska Hofvet (three parts, 1885), while some of them are printed in English in S. Wollebaek's Om Kielertraktaten (1928). Vandal's dramatic and scientific account of the negotiations of 1812 (in his Napoleon et Alexandre, vol. iii. 1911) is too prejudiced against Bernadotte, as is the slighter and less reliable book of Pingaud (Bernadotte Napoléon et les Bourbons, 1901). There are many Swedish narratives which do not, however, take British policy into full account, especially that part revealed in Cathcart's dispatches.

northern coast of that sea the influence of a Government so subservient to France as Denmark must be—to such a view of her policy it would be difficult for Great Britain to oppose any objection."

Sweden was, therefore, to be encouraged to hope. It was something at any rate to keep her from helping France, but, of course, an attack on Norway would have but little effect in the main theatre of war when the great clash of arms came— if come it did. For long, therefore, Castlereagh coquetted with the idea that Denmark might be induced by compensations in Germany (which must not affect Hanover) to come to some arrangement with Bernadotte, "as the only chance . . . of the Allies being able to command a disposable force for continental operations within the period which may probably decide the fate of the campaign." [1]

Meanwhile Thornton, who arrived at Stockholm on April 6, had found that the Swedish Ministers had just made a treaty with Russia by which Norway had been guaranteed to her and assistance offered for an attack on the heart of Denmark—the island of Zealand, on which Copenhagen itself is situated. It was only natural that the Swedish Minister should press hard for similar terms from Britain, hinting that this was the way to get in touch with Russia, whose Chargé, Nicolai, was apologetic to Thornton as to the silence of his Government towards Britain. Bernadotte himself, however, took excessive pains to check his Gascon exuberance, and in an informal interview admitted that Britain's caution was only natural, though unjust. He was anxious to prove "that he had made himself what he was by his own sword and by no favour from Napoleon," but he quite charmed Thornton by his "natural, open, and unaffected manner with nothing of the fanfaronade usual with Frenchmen of which the Prince seems to have as little as almost any Frenchman I have ever seen." Later Bernadotte urged the attack on Zealand as his best contribution to the campaign. Swedes of all classes, indeed, insisted that Norway must come first for fear of Russia as well as of France. They could not risk another Tilsit in their

---

[1] To Thornton, March 13, April 14, 1812 : *F.O. Sweden*, 71 ; March 13, 25, 27, April 14 : *Cambridge History of British Foreign Policy*, i. 591–92.

present position: "But the union of the whole northern peninsula under one monarchy gave to it at once a sort of insular security against any invasion with military force alone . . . it would impose upon them the eternal and (they added) the agreeable obligation of cultivating a constant union with Great Britain, whose maritime superiority was the sole guarantee of their safety by sea." [1]

There was much truth in these arguments, so skilfully adjusted to British pride, but Castlereagh refused to admit their force in the immediate situation. Sweden must first make peace with Britain, he wrote on May 7, before the question of Britain joining the Swedish-Russian alliance could be considered, nor could Sweden's demands for large subsidies be granted. The situation was made very difficult by the fact that Russia, in spite of her critical position, had as yet made no direct approach to Britain. True, Thornton had sounded Suchtelen, the new Russian Minister at Stockholm, and Nicolai, after a visit to Petersburg, had brought a message from Rumantzov that he wanted peace, a subsidy, and Lord Wellesley as Ambassador. But, as Castlereagh pointed out, it was admitted that Russia was still in discussion with the enemy and the moment for action had not yet come.

The month of May was thus one of great suspense. The French consul and the Austrian Minister, Neipperg, used every form of blandishment and threat to win Bernadotte to the French side, while news came of new Russian offers at Paris of which Rumantzov had told Sweden nothing—still less, of course, Thornton, when he sent his message by Nicolai. Nevertheless Castlereagh, convinced that war was inevitable, sent Thornton full powers to make a treaty of peace with Russia, and promised an Ambassador of high rank. But nothing could be done with either Sweden or Russia while the issue still remained doubtful on the Continent. Bernadotte, pleading illness, sent word that he could not make peace with Britain and refuse France's tempting offers, though he knew they were illusory, until the Russian situation was clear. Rumantzov's conduct still appeared treacherous. Suchtelen had to confess to Thornton that the Chancellor had acted

---

[1] From Thornton, April 9, 16, 27, 1812 : *F.O. Sweden*, 72.

dishonourably; and when, on June 24, Rumantzov offered to make peace only on condition that Britain assumed her large debt in Holland and subsidised Sweden, it seemed as if he were purposely playing for time. But Bernadotte had at last realised that it was no time to bargain with Britain, and he pressed this view on the Tsar; and when on July 4 news came that the French had crossed the Niemen, British help, naval and financial, became urgent. On July 18, therefore, at Orebro, Thornton was able to sign treaties of peace with Sweden and Russia. They did no more than put an end to the technical state of war. The real negotiation had yet to begin.[1]

Thornton had fully carried out his instructions, but the result was terribly disappointing; for Bernadotte soon announced that he could take no part in the campaign without large sums of British money, and this aid Thornton had no authority to give. The Prince Royal had no intention of making an irretrievable step until it was seen on which side victory lay. He was still at peace with France. Thornton, therefore, after using every argument in vain to move Bernadotte, accepted his suggestion to return home for instructions, and was about to do so when, to his great surprise, Cathcart arrived on his way to Petersburg.

The Ambassador had been sent off as soon as the news of the outbreak of war had been received. The choice was in a sense a curious one, for Cathcart was the commander at the attack on Copenhagen in 1807. Nor had the old gentleman much diplomatic experience or those qualities which seemed to be needed in the delicate state of Baltic politics. But he was an Earl and of high military rank—an indispensable condition if he was to accompany the Tsar in the field, and not be a mere cipher at Petersburg. He had complete confidence in himself and was never ruffled by adverse circumstances, qualities which enabled him to pass unscathed

[1] From Thornton, April 29 (with extracts from Rumantzov to Nicolai, April 6), May 6, 21, 30, June 6, 17, 23, Aug. 2, 8, 1812: *F.O. Sweden*, 72, 73, 74. May 3, 6, 15, 20, 30, June 24, July 4, 18 : *Cambridge History of British Foreign Policy*, i. 597–99. To Thornton, May 7, 8, 1812: *F.O. Sweden*, 71. May 7, 22, 1812 : *Cambridge History of British Foreign Policy*, i. 592–93. F. Martens, *Recueil des Traités*, xi. 156–62. It was apparently the Tsar himself who asked for Wellesley.

through situations which might have daunted a more imaginative and subtle envoy. In all the vicissitudes of the next two years only once is it recorded that he shewed signs of uneasiness, and that was produced by the presence of both John Quincy Adams and Madame de Staël—it must be admitted a formidable combination.

The Ambassador had been waiting for two months to set out. Castlereagh had been anxiously watching the tortuous diplomacy of May and June, afraid to commit himself while the issue was in doubt. It was obvious that Sweden's action depended on the larger Power, whose conduct, Thornton was ordered to tell Suchtelen, seemed quite inexplicable: "You will acquaint him that H.R.H. the Prince Regent has been long expecting some satisfactory communication from the Russian Government which will enable Lord Cathcart to proceed to his destination which nothing but the hesitating counsels of the Court of St. Petersburg has prevented. It is to be remarked as extraordinary that Russia should avail herself of the mediation of Great Britain to procure peace with the Porte and hesitate as to concluding peace with the Power she has chosen to negotiate for her." Nevertheless, the situation was obviously so urgent that Cathcart was dispatched on the news of war even before the Russian peace treaty reached London.

His instructions in the extraordinary state of affairs on the Continent were very general and threw on him immense responsibility. He was not authorised to offer subsidies to either Russia or Sweden, but a sum of £500,000 was placed at his disposal "to be applied to the service of Russia or Sweden as circumstances may point out." His gaze was directed, however, far afield. Naturally he was to promote peace with Turkey and Persia, but he was also to watch the policies of Prussia and Austria, especially the latter, and even to take under his care national uprisings in Dalmatia, the Tyrol, or Switzerland, should such occur—a sufficiently difficult job from Petersburg. But of course the instructions were framed to meet any emergency. No one could tell which way the tide of battle would flow. How undecided Castlereagh's own mind had been is shewn by the fact that nine days afterwards he sent a supplementary instruction authorising Cathcart to use the whole of the £500,000 to get Sweden into the war at once, even offering to agree as to Norway if Sweden would postpone her operations against Denmark and attack France immediately.[1]

This last dispatch reached Cathcart in time for him to make the offer at the important conferences held between the Tsar and Bernadotte at Abo in September. He had found Bernadotte full of schemes as usual, including a temporary occupation of Finland to save it from the French. But the Crown Prince refused to postpone the acquisition of Norway, and the Tsar agreed to help him in his attack on Zealand with 20,000 men. This was not a great contribution towards defeating Napoleon; but the Tsar told Cathcart that, "from the situation and feelings of the Government and people of Sweden, he did not think it possible to obtain it, and that, as he was fully satisfied of the zeal and of the generous and loyal principles of the Prince Royal, he did not think it fair to press him on that subject." Perhaps a clause in the Abo Convention by which Sweden agreed to Russia's advance to the Vistula helped him to this decision. Cathcart seemed to think that these objections were a little premature, while Napoleon's armies were marching into the heart of Russia, but took care to point out Britain was never likely to agree to Zealand remaining in Swedish hands, while "the proposition of extension of territory to the Vistula had, I believed, never occurred to the imagination of the Court of London."

The main result of the Conference therefore was merely to renew the friendship between the Tsar and the Prince Royal. It brought no Swedish help across the Baltic, and Cathcart's money remained idle in his pocket. It was soon seen, indeed, that Bernadotte had no intention of leaving Sweden at all so late in the season, and the auxiliary Russian corps was needed in Russia itself. Cathcart could, however, report a warm welcome to himself from the Tsar, while the Chancellor attempted to justify his past conduct and agreed cordially with all Cathcart's criticisms. He had, however, obviously

---

[1] To Thornton, July 3, 1812 : *F.O. Sweden*, 71. To Cathcart, July 24, Aug. 5, 1812 : *F.O. Russia*, 78.

lost his master's confidence—one of the most cheering factors in the situation.[1]

For the next three months the great conflict in Russia with its dramatic reversal of fortune almost hushed the mouths and stopped the pens of the diplomatists. Cathcart remained at Petersburg, while Sir Robert Wilson, fresh from Turkey, sent him vivid reports of the fighting, which were unfortunately mixed up with too much politics, and Lord Tyrconnell, one of the attachés, lost his life following the French retreat. The Tsar in an agony of mind, though sustained by the national steadfastness and the letters of his favourite sister, could make no plans for the future until the will of Providence was known. But Cathcart was always able to report his resolution to persevere to the end. When news came of the fall of Moscow, Alexander declared that, "the more reliance was placed by the enemy on that event, the more his determination to persevere would prove to all Europe the sincerity of his declarations and the zeal with which he was supported by his people." A little later, though Petersburg was not yet directly menaced, he said he should continue the conflict if necessary in Siberia, and sent his fleet to join the captured ships of Copenhagen under the protection of the Power whose tyranny he had once so vigorously denounced. During this critical time Cathcart could do little except maintain an imperturbable mien in the Petersburg salons. He even had a pleasant conversation with John Quincy Adams. He plied Rumantzov with entreaties to admit British commerce, which had little or no effect, and seized every opportunity to encourage the Tsar to get rid of his Chancellor at the earliest opportunity. He also directed his attention to the importance of conciliating Austria in every way possible.[2]

As for Sweden, she remained armed but quiescent during all this period. Bernadotte had not the slightest intention of risking himself in the general *mêlée*. His main anxiety was

[1] From Cathcart, Aug. 14, 17, 30, 1812 : *F.O. Russia*, 79. Thornton also thought that the article about Zealand shewed " a pretty unequivocal proof of a desire to add the possession of that island to that of Norway." From Thornton, Sept. 12, 1812 : *F.O. Sweden*, 74.

[2] From Cathcart, Sept. 13, 15, 17, 22, 30, Oct. 18, 1812 : *F.O. Russia*, 79. Cathcart hired a house for three years at the most critical period of 1812 in order to reassure the inhabitants of Petersburg.

to get Britain's accession to the Abo Convention so that he
should possess another guarantee of Norway and, as Thornton
believed, of Zealand also. Cathcart was also pressed to take
the same step at Petersburg, but replied that Britain wished
to get the voluntary consent of Denmark, which he seems to
have thought could be obtained by colonial restitutions.
Meanwhile Bernadotte tried to use the British desire that he
should make peace with Spain to bargain on this subject,
evincing also "a great repugnance to do anything which
might shock the feelings of his brother-in-law Joseph." Not
until the tide had turned in Russia did he take this step, on
which Thornton had refused to be cajoled. Bad harvests
and the late season now made action against Norway impossible, and it was not until the end of December that the
French Chargé was dismissed from Stockholm.[1]

Nor could Castlereagh give much help during these critical
months, though he sent a constant stream of dispatches to the
Baltic. The problem of Norway exercised his pen, and
gradually and reluctantly Bernadotte's obstinacy produced
its intended effect. The island of Guadeloupe was offered
to encourage Sweden to resist France. The declared intention
of treating the Norwegians in a conciliatory fashion was
warmly welcomed, though Castlereagh insisted that Sweden
must shew herself completely identified with Britain and
Russia before he could make any engagement, and he was
careful to claim a voice in the future of Zealand. The inactivity of Sweden induced him at the end of November to go
further than he had ever done before. He was ready, he told
Thornton on November 29, to sign a treaty concerning
Norway, but not on the lines laid down at Abo which included
a guarantee of possession to Sweden. This problem in one
form or another was to occupy his mind a good deal during
the rest of his life, and his attitude at this moment is an interesting one. "The point that I am most desirous of having
fully represented, especially to the Prince Royal," he wrote
in a long and carefully prepared dispatch, "is the insuperable
difficulty, I may say impracticability, of being a formal party

---

[1] From Thornton, Sept. 18, 28, Oct. 13, 24, Nov. 3, 10, 26, Dec. 18, 29,
1812 : *F.O. Sweden*, 74.   From Cathcart, Oct. 26, 1812 : *F.O. Russia*, 79.

to the guarantees these treaties contain, more especially when
Sweden is not prepared to carry her arms to the Continent.
It is almost impossible to make foreigners understand the
delicacies and difficulties of our Parliamentary system. We
can do much in support of foreign states (I believe no Power
so much), but we must do it our own way. The continental
Governments that have no account to render to a Parliament
can commit themselves to guarantee possessions and never
to lay down arms till others are acquired, well knowing that
they are amenable to no authority for the prudence of such
engagements, and that when they become impracticable the
engagements are dissolved either by circumstances or by
mutual consent. They can also keep such engagements
secret as long as it suits their convenience. In our system
concealment is not practicable for any length of time, and
when the stipulations are canvassed they are impeached
upon every extreme case that ingenuity can suggest as falling
within their possible operation. . . .

" It is not, then, to be inferred that the British Government
do not mean to maintain a point for a friendly Power because
they refuse to guarantee it. Guarantees have been given, it
is true, of Portugal and Sicily, but these were established
features in the policy of the country to the maintenance of
which our military exertions have long been expressly
directed, but, close as the connection is, such an engagement
has never been taken with respect to Hanover, nor with regard
to Spain, nor with relation to various other objects of which,
either from the point of honour or a sense of common interest,
we have been most tenacious." [1]

Meanwhile, the far greater question of what help should be
given to Russia had not yet been solved. Munitions had been
already dispatched, and the Government were preparing to
send out 150,000 muskets for the victorious levies. Parliament, in spite of Whitbread's opposition, cheerfully voted
£200,000 for the relief of the inhabitants of Moscow, and
public subscriptions were made for the same end. In
November Nicolai resumed his old position as Secretary of

[1] To Thornton, Oct. 10, 20, 1812 : *Cambridge History of British Foreign
Policy*, i. 593 (where last wrongly dated) : Oct. 10, Nov. 29, 1812 : *F.O.
Sweden*, 71.

Embassy at London, and he was soon followed by Count Lieven. Both made demands for large subsidies, which they considered were no more than Russia's due after her successful resistance. The Tsar himself, however, never asked for money, telling Cathcart that he preferred arms to guineas, and the question hung fire until it was seen what policy Alexander would pursue now that the French were expelled from his own territories.[1]

Obviously much depended on how he would be received if he carried the war into Germany. For long this question had been occupying Castlereagh's thoughts, and in particular he had constantly directed Cathcart's attention towards Austria. Bernadotte might help to raise the north of Germany. Could Austria also be brought over, and a greater coalition than ever Pitt had seen be brought into being?

[1] From Cathcart, Dec. 6, 1812 : *F.O. Russia*, 80. F. Martens, *Recueil*, xi. 166–68. Hansard, *Commons*, Dec. 18, 1812. Canning, who claimed that the war in the north was " child of that great effort on the Peninsula which has enabled Europe to reflect on its condition and has raised it to a struggle for emancipation," thought that the way to help Russia was by action in Spain. Hansard, *Commons*, Nov. 30, 1812.

3. RELATIONS WITH PRUSSIA AND AUSTRIA

THROUGHOUT the year 1812 Napoleon dominated the two monarchies of central Europe. They were, in fact, his vassals, constrained to support his attack on Russia and supply auxiliary corps to protect the flanks of his huge army. The situation of the two countries was, however, vastly different—they were only united by a common subterranean hatred of their master. Prussia was far more completely under control. In 1811 she had by an appeal to the Tsar, which met with but little response, vainly attempted to escape from her humiliating and dangerous position. In her despair, fearing a last partition at Napoleon's hands, she had no alternative but to accept all his conditions, and agreed to facilitate the passage of his troops through her territory and provide the protection of his left wing. Austria, on the contrary, affected independence, and her relations were ostensibly guided by the close harmony between the two Imperial Courts, now so intimately united by marriage. The treaty with Austria was, in theory, between two equal sovereign states, and the tide of the French armies was kept away from her territory, while her auxiliary corps was no larger than that of her weaker neighbour. Moreover, the treaty guaranteed the Ottoman Empire, so dangerously threatened by Russian troops, and thus Austria's interests were taken into consideration and received protection.

Both countries were, however, in secret full of men resolved to break the chains, whether iron or silken, which bound them to Napoleon's chariot. In Prussia, the Chancellor, Hardenberg, was in his innermost soul fully sympathetic to them, but the dangerous position of his country made him for the moment seek safety in a policy of complete acquiescence, while the King was in constant dread lest he should lose the rest of his kingdom. In Austria, the Empress, Stadion, and numbers of other soldiers and statesmen resented the French connection. Metternich, himself the author of the French alliance, always tried to keep a door open for retreat, informing the Tsar secretly that the Austrian corps was only meant for display and would do no harm if left alone. But both he and the Emperor never dreamed at this moment of breaking from the French connection. At the magnificent entertainment which Napoleon gave at Dresden to his vassal kings and princes the Emperor affected a personal intimacy. The King of Prussia came late and hardly ventured more than a timid subserviency. Metternich and Hardenberg exchanged the most secret confidences, a marriage alliance between Prussia and Austria was planned, and Metternich obtained a sort of ascendancy over Prussian policy and encouraged her distrust of Russia. The weakness of Prussia was so obvious that few observers in Europe looked to her to raise the standard of opposition in Germany. Certainly during this year British hopes were not placed high. The Prussian Chancellor appeared terribly disappointed that the French offer of peace in April had been rejected. England, he said, was preparing her own ruin. This may have been merely calculated language, but it was significant that for a long period he hardly saw Ompteda, and British intercourse with the Prussian Government almost ceased.[1]

In these circumstances Britain naturally looked elsewhere for leadership of that popular resistance which events in Spain had convinced her leaders was latent in Germany. As Münster pointed out in a Memorandum written about this time: "A more *general resistance* and a *popular war* must destroy a system which carries the principle of self-destruction within itself, in having made the whole population of continental Europe poor, whilst at the same time it has trained it to the use of arms and has left no choice but that of fighting for or against the Tyrant. All this authorises me to expect a great popular insurrection on the Continent the moment the people

---

[1] Ompteda to Münster, May 30, June 26, July 4, 1812; Ompteda, *Nachlass*, ii. 270, 280, 285.

shall find an army to which they may, in the first moment, look for protection and which will render their first union possible."

For this reason Münster from the first strongly supported Bernadotte's plans. He preferred, perhaps, that Prussia should not take too prominent a part, owing to her past treatment of Hanover. Indeed, throughout most of this year many German patriots, as they looked at Prussia apparently reduced to as low a level as any member of the Confederation of the Rhine, planned a new Germany in which she should be reduced to a second- or third-rate position. This is the explanation of the design imputed to Münster and the Prince Regent of creating a new and powerful north German state, with Hanover as its centre, ruled by a member of the Guelph House, to take the place of Prussia. But Münster's allusion to this idea in a letter to Stein was called forth by a specially tactless letter of the latter's, and it was never a very serious part of his policy. He was merely putting Hanover's right to an increase of territory in the north of Germany on an equality with that of Prussia. The utterance was purely defensive, and, as the sequel was to prove, Münster was moderate enough when the time for action came, while neither Castlereagh nor the Cabinet ever gave the slightest encouragement to the creation of a great Hanover at the expense of Prussia.[1]

But as Bernadotte's promised attack failed to materialise a substitute was hard to find. Gneisenau, in disgust at the policy of Prussia, had come to England to obtain support for his plan of a German legion which he should throw into Colberg, so magnificently defended in 1807, and, with British help, make the centre of a popular movement. Münster was greatly desirous that some such plan should be carried out, and addressed the Prince Regent a memoir on the subject, accompanied by a grandiloquent letter reminding him that he belonged to the cadet branch of the "oldest house in the

[1] Memorandum by Münster " on the intended alliance between the Courts of Russia and Sweden," [May] 1812 : *F.O. Hanover*, 4. Seeley in his compilation and German historians, especially those who wrote under the influence of the events of 1866, have always exaggerated the " Austrasian " project. *Cf*. Seeley, *Stein*, iii. 18 ; Treitschke, *History of Germany* (Eng. trans.), i. 522 ; Pertz, *Stein*, iii. 238–40.

Universe," which once ruled over the greater part of Germany. Providence, it is true, had compensated the Guelph House by an even fairer domain "the first throne in the world." But even that position was subject to mortal chances, and meanwhile there was no reason why its German dominions should not be increased. The Duke of York, he suggested, might be placed at the head of the expedition.

The Prussian Chancellor had been much alarmed at Gneisenau's plan when he heard of it, and had urged Ompteda that an expedition to Holland was greatly to be preferred. In any case the claims of the Peninsula made British co-operation impracticable unless her efforts were to be entirely diverted from that area, and the plans were still being canvassed when the Prussian people forced their King into the position of leader of the north. British hopes were then immediately transferred to Prussia, and the enthusiasm was all the greater because expectation had been so small.[1]

It was natural, however, that throughout 1812 much greater attention should be paid to Austria than to Prussia. She was still a great Power, and if the French policy of Metternich was regrettable, both Minister and policy might be changed when the opportunity came. Indeed, Metternich himself took care never to lose touch, and, while no great confidence could be placed in him, care was taken to keep the connection as close as possible. Metternich never gave his confidence to the vain, rash, and conceited young man, King, whose reports, except in so far as they were an echo of Count Hardenberg's, were untrustworthy. He was used as one who could be disavowed, if necessary, to foment insurrection in the Tyrol—a service which he performed without great discretion. Still, he was a link. He saw Metternich occasionally and reported his conversations, while one of his duties was to pay Gentz, that prolific journalist and publicist, who was not unmindful of his old connection as a British propagandist. Gentz had been very cautious all the year 1811. Nevertheless he yearned, he

---

[1] Memorandum of Münster, Dec. 6, 1812 ; Münster to the Prince Regent, Dec. 7, 1812 : *F.O. Hanover*, 4. Ompteda to Münster, Nov. 23, 1812 : Ompteda, *Nachlass*, ii. 313. Lehmann, *Gneisenau's Sendung nach Schweden und England im Jahre* 1812, in his *Historische Aufsatze und Reden*, 292–93.

said, for news from England and undoubtedly for English gold.   In April 1812 he sent a pathetic mixture of flattery and entreaty, which eventually met with some response, for Cooke wrote to King on November 3: "Say everything flattering to Gentz and give him £600 and draw for it, and you may promise more if he will be useful." But Gentz' contribution was only a pamphlet defending the Orders in Council at the moment when they were withdrawn.   He had not yet much influence with Metternich.[1]

The principal and responsible channel was Count Hardenberg, who maintained his connection with Metternich with considerable skill throughout the year.   It was through him that Metternich conveyed the view which he wished British statesmen to take of his policy even after more direct contact was established at the end of the year through General Nugent and Lord Walpole. For Metternich never left Britain outside the complicated game in which he was secretly engaged.   Before the campaign he sought to add to his secret assurances to Russia by her aid, and later on he tried to make her the instrument of peace. This process began even before the war with Russia.   "Metternich's overtures on the subject," wrote Münster in a private little note to Cooke on July 5, "seem to aim at a double game: he wishes England to understand and persuade Russia that the alliance is not meant seriously, and that Austria intends no harm to Russia, if not provoked. The fact is that the Austrian Ministry is silly enough to imagine they may now safely overthrow the constitution of Hungary."   No notice seems to have been taken of this communication; but in August Metternich opened himself more fully to Hardenberg, feeling no doubt that Austrian policy at Constantinople needed some explanation.   He defended it by Austria's natural fear of a Russo-Turkish alliance and the advance of Russia in the Principalities.   Above all, the scheme for the march of Russian troops to the Adriatic had caused great anxiety,

---

[1] King's correspondence is in *F.O. Austria*, 99.   Gentz to the Prince Regent, April 19, 1812 : *F.O. Austria*, 98.   . . . " Je ne desire au monde que les moyens de m'acquitter des dettes que j'ai contractées, pendant un nombre d'années où le Gouvernement Britannique a paru m'avoir complètement oublié. Ma tranquillité, mon honneur, mon existence future tiennent à une somme d'environ 1500 £."

because Napoleon would immediately have taken action against it and thus Austrian territory might have become a theatre of war. He complained bitterly of Russia's silence towards him which had forced him into his active French policy. It was obvious that his hatred and distrust of Rumantzov were as strong as ever, and that he constantly dreaded that Russia and France would make a peace at the expense of Prussia, leaving Austria isolated. He hinted also that Napoleon would reply to the last British answer, and that Austria would be prepared to facilitate the negotiation.

There was no hurry to reply to this insidious epistle. As Münster told Cooke soon after its arrival: "I believe, of course, that the best answer would be to say that Great Britain had no reason to press Bonaparte's reply, especially after the recent events in Spain and Russia, and that she was much averse to negotiations whose result would most likely merely tend to discourage her allies." Castlereagh, however, at once informed Cathcart of its contents, not for communication to the Tsar, but in order that he might urge that "an assurance of firmness on the part of Russia and a real demonstration of goodwill towards Austria may induce that Power not only to adhere to its present line of qualified hostility, but under wise and liberal management to adopt a policy which the general interests demand and the present position of affairs invites." [1]

The answer to Austria was not dispatched till the beginning of November in the form of a letter from Münster to Hardenberg and a personal letter from the Prince Regent to the Emperor. It emphasised the firmness of Russia, of which there were now unequivocal proofs, and urged Austria to continue her policy of inactivity. If Austria helped Bonaparte to subdue Russia she would only destroy herself; if she remained neutral the issue was certain: "Remote from all his resources, and now for the first time engaged in two wars, in neither of which plunder can, as in former campaigns, be made to replenish his Treasury, Buonaparte cannot long find the means of continuing the exertion. He has failed in Spain. He must fail in Russia, whose powers of resistance are

[1] Münster to Cooke, July 5, Sept. 11, 1812 ; Hardenberg to Münster, Aug. 6, 1812 : *F.O. Hanover*, 4. To Cathcart, Sept. 4, 1812 : *F.O. Russia*, 78.

infinitely superior, if Austria is true to herself and to the nations in Europe that desire to be free." In an autograph letter the Prince Regent told the Emperor that the deliverance of Europe from oppression depended on his actions. Before this appeal was dispatched Nugent had arrived in London. He had been long in travelling by the Mediterranean route, and knew nothing of Metternich's recent thoughts. He was, of course, warmly received, and had several interviews with the Prince Regent, who reiterated his desire that Austria should not reinforce her auxiliary corps, but take advantage of Napoleon's defeat when it came, as come it must soon.[1]

No hint of the possibility of peace with Napoleon was allowed to appear in these communications. But it was of peace that Metternich was constantly thinking, and in the early days of October he told the Prussian Chancellor that he intended soon to make a secret move in that direction. He became more and more anxious as the French offensive developed. King, who had two interviews with him at the beginning of November, was inaccurate in thinking that "Count Metternich has thrown himself entirely into the arms of France." But it was true that the capture of Moscow had thrown him into something like a panic, which the announcement that a French retreat was contemplated did nothing to remove. He dreaded more than ever that peace would be made between France and Russia in such a manner as to leave Austria exposed to the enmity of both Powers. He did not conceal, according to King, his hatred and distrust of Russia and his most anxious wish for a general peace. This need for peace was the burden of a more formal communication which Hardenberg sent to Münster on November 9. It expatiated on the resources of France and the security of her position in Germany even if not successful in the north, and pleaded earnestly for peace negotiations. Austria had already sounded Napoleon, had made recommendations to Prussia and intended to do so to Russia. Would Britain assist her in the good work?

[1] Memorandum of Instructions for Count Münster ; Münster to Hardenberg, Oct. 31, 1812 ; Prince Regent to the Emperor of Austria, Oct. 31, 1812 ; Münster to Metternich, Oct. 31, 1812 : *F.O. Hanover*, 4 ; Nugent to Metternich, Oct. 15, 29, Nov. 3, 1812 : *Vienna St. A.*

This appeal, which did not reach England until after the first news of Napoleon's disaster, had a profound effect on the British attitude towards Austria not only in the immediate future but throughout the years of reconstruction. Some of the Cabinet, including the Prime Minister, never quite forgave Metternich for his attitude at this critical period. Castlereagh was, perhaps, the least affected and more ready to make allowances for Austria's position than any of his colleagues, but his comments to Cathcart on the offer were severe enough: "It is impossible, however, not to trace throughout the whole a language and spirit of submission which, it is feared, the late animating events may not have sufficient influence to overcome. If we are to implicitly believe Count Metternich's declarations, there is no extent of disaster which can befall the French armies beyond the Vistula which would in his conception justify in prudence a change of system on the part of Austria. He represents France as capable of creating and bringing forward another army, were that in the north destroyed, which, united to the troops of the Confederation of the Rhine, would enable her still to hold Germany in subjection against Russia, Austria, and Prussia united. If such is really his opinion, there is no extent of submission to the will of France, whether in peace or war, to which that Minister must not be prepared to counsel his master."

This pessimism, which he thought purposely exaggerated, Castlereagh then proceeded to combat with an elaborate calculation of the forces that might be expected to be raised by either side, which gave the Allies a superiority of over 200,000 men, if Austria and Prussia joined the coalition against France. He recommended Russia to do all that was possible to win Austria to her side, hinting that she might even consider giving up Bessarabia. Meanwhile Britain would remain staunch to Russia and Sweden, and notify Austria that no action would be taken without consultation with them. Indeed, it was doubtful if Austria was entitled even to a reply, "bringing forward as she has done a proposition altogether vague to Great Britain, which she has not even ventured to do more than insinuate to the French Minister, Maret, as a *rêve politique of Count Metternich's own*, on which Maret's opinion is desired as to the expediency of opening it to Bonaparte. Connected as Austria is with France, it would be difficult for her under any circumstances to assume the character of a mediator, but to present herself in that character holding, as her Minister does, the language of submission under every imaginable circumstance to France, renders an overture from her, in the present temper of her councils, little indistinguishable from one from the enemy, with the additional inconvenience that the enemy may, at his option, disavow it." [1]

The weakness of Austria was all the more distressing since it was likely to prevent Prussia from taking advantage of Napoleon's disaster. Indeed, the Prussian Chancellor had, at Metternich's request, sent a letter to Gneisenau supporting the Austrian proposition. He confessed to Ompteda that if he could himself make the decision, it would be a very different one. "Such a course," he said, "could only be taken by a sovereign who has enough character, spirit, and energy to take the risks of a fairly hazardous step." Meanwhile Prussia had to shew extreme caution, and, as has been noted, he hoped Gneisenau's expedition would leave her alone.

The effect of Austria's weakness, therefore, appeared to paralyse the movement of resistance just at the moment when deliverance seemed at hand. It dashed the hopes of the Cabinet for the recovery of Germany. "I wish we could see any prospect of a wiser policy being adopted by Austria and Prussia, and particularly by the former," Liverpool wrote to Wellington, "for I have no doubt the latter would act if she could rely upon the support of Austria. If these two Powers would really take advantage of the Russian successes, we might have hopes of effecting the deliverance of the Continent; but nothing can be more abject than the councils of Vienna at this time, and I fear that neutrality is all that can be

[1] From King, Nov. 5, 7, 1812 : *F.O. Austria*, 99. Count Hardenberg to Münster, Nov. 9, 1812 : *F.O. Hanover*, 4. To Cathcart, Dec. 15, 1812 : *F.O. Russia*, 78. Memorandum of Cooke [Dec. 15], 1812 : *C.C.* viii. 276. (Placed by the editor in November, but obviously a little later.) See also Metternich's remarkable letter to Baron Hardenberg of Oct. 5, 1812, in which he sketches his peace plans : Oncken, *Oesterreich und Preussen im Befreiungskriege*, i. 378.

expected from them." Still the situation was such that there was hope of a change. "We are doing our best, however, to rouse them"; he added, "and the wise and magnanimous conduct which the Emperor of Russia has adopted towards them ought not to be wholly without effect." [1]

The Tsar had, indeed, shewed resolution and wisdom. It is true that Rumantzov still remained, but he was daily losing influence. Alexander meanwhile had encouraged Cathcart on the question of Austria, though he distrusted Metternich a great deal more than his master. In order to take advantage of this situation, Cathcart, who had failed to get in touch with Hardenberg and King, accepted the "gallant offer" of Lord Walpole to go to Vienna. He sent him off with instructions to win Austria over if possible, if not to ensure her benevolent neutrality towards Russia, and also stir up the Tyrolese and Swiss. For this purpose Walpole was authorised to spend the £500,000 which Cathcart still had untouched. He was also to offer Cathcart as a channel to the Tsar, if Metternich wished to avoid dealings with his enemy, Rumantzov. [2]

Lord Walpole was perhaps more 'gallant' than diplomatic, but he carried out his difficult mission with great energy. Metternich was dismayed at his appearance, which threatened to force confidences at a moment when he was most anxious to avoid them. He had recovered some spirit, now that he realised the extent of Napoleon's defeat, and was secretly engaged in *pourparlers* not only with Prussia but also with Count Stackelberg, the Russian Ambassador, who had remained behind in Austria. But he was still determined to keep out of trouble and, above all, to save Austria from invasion by either side. He consented to talk to Walpole, but his talk was all of peace and he said his master was indignant at the idea that he would break his treaty with France and join the enemies of his son-in-law. Of Russia he was obviously jealous and afraid. Walpole explained this attitude by the Russian diplomacy of 1811–12 which had caused so deep a division between the two Courts. Napoleon's

---

[1] Liverpool to Wellington, Dec. 22, 1812 : *W.S.D.* vii. 503.

[2] From Cathcart, Sept. 30, Nov. 10 (enclosing Instructions to Lord Walpole, Oct. 31), 1812 : *F.O. Russia*, 79. Lehmann claims that Stein was responsible for Walpole's mission (*Stein*, iii. 194).

message from Dresden that he was raising a new army had also helped to draw Austria back to the French side. Hence Metternich's great desire for a general negotiation: "Count Metternich hopes to escape by that means from his present dilemma. So great is his fear that a continuation of the war will eventually overthrow his system and engage Austria in hostilities, that to avoid it he would willingly abandon all view of aggrandizement, but he will also be induced by the same motives to press forward a peace not of restitution from France or independence for Germany, but on the *status quo ante* this Russian war, if such can be made."

This was not altogether true, for Metternich did not of course give Walpole his full confidence. He was trying to prepare for different eventualities which he could not accurately gauge. He had sent Bubna to Napoleon to talk peace and professed to be satisfied with the result. He was preparing now to talk to Russia and Britain, where, he had assured Maret, only Austria's great influence on public opinion could produce any effect. But at any rate he was not going to entrust his policy to a subordinate English diplomat who represented neither London nor Petersburg with any real authority. Indeed, Walpole had to leave Vienna for a country town outside it; for the English newspapers had mentioned his arrival and Metternich feared Napoleon's wrath. He, however, still promised to see him, and Walpole by the middle of January thought he detected a change for the better, and held out hopes that Austria would become neutral, though this attitude would only be made possible if a negotiation for peace were opened. Metternich's dislike and jealousy of Russia were still in evidence, but he told Walpole that he would gladly confide in a British envoy accredited from London. A few days later, however, Metternich gave him his *congé*. Walpole's presence was known to all the diplomatic corps and therefore he must go. When he went to say good-bye to Metternich he found him in no mood for talk. "His temper seemed extremely ruffled by some news he had received; he in general appears incapable of any emotion, but he really seemed to be greatly agitated with something which has happened. . . . The capitulation of the Prussian

contingent has caused him the greatest uneasiness; he spoke
of it as a kind of revolution." [1]

The famous convention of Tauroggen, by which Yorck on
January 1 made terms with the Russians and declared against
Napoleon, was at any rate a revolution in the diplomatic
situation. Metternich was rendered all the more uncertain
as to his course of action. He dreaded a German uprising
against their rulers as well as against Napoleon. He tried to
draw closer to Prussia and Russia, sending Lebzeltern, one
of his most skilled subordinates, to meet the Tsar at Vilna.
"His conduct," Walpole warned Cathcart, should be
narrowly watched. If it is not his object to conclude a
separate peace, there is no doubt but that he is sent with a
view to bring about an instantaneous pacification."

This was true enough, as Metternich's correspondence with
Lebzeltern shews. The Austrian Chancellor had, indeed,
now determined on formal offers of his services to all the
belligerents with a view to forcing them to make peace. The
situation in Germany, the advance of Russia in Poland,
Napoleon's efforts to collect another army, all seemed to him
to bring danger to Austria. Britain, the relentless enemy,
ready to supply arms and money to all combatants on her
side seemed especially to stand in his way. He determined
therefore to send Wessenberg, one of the most competent and
trusted administrators in Austria, to London to enforce his
views there. [2]

Thus at the end of the first two months of the year 1813
the situation from Castlereagh's point of view was full of
hazard and uncertainty. The war with the United States
remained as an irksome and indefinite charge on British
energies at this moment of supreme crisis in Europe. Wellington had been forced to retire to Portugal with serious loss
of men and prestige, and the Opposition in the autumn
debates had taken full advantage of the unexpected disap-

---

[1] Walpole to Cathcart, Dec. 19, 22, 28, 1812; Jan. 3, 12, 13, 18, 1813:
F.O. Russia, 84. Metternich to Floret, Dec. 9, 1812: Oncken, *Oesterreich
und Preussen im Befreiungskriege*, i. 384. Metternich to Stackelberg, Jan. 10,
15, 1813: *Lettres et papiers du Nesselrode*, iv. 3, 8. From King, Dec. 31,
1812; Jan. 9, 15, 23, 25, 1813: *F.O. Austria*, 99.
[2] Walpole to Cathcart, Jan. 19, 1813: *F.O. Russia*, 84.

pointment.   Bernadotte could only be won by a large subsidy and an engagement about Norway, which was very distasteful and must meet with much criticism in Parliament.   The attitude of Prussia was vacillating and uncertain, while Austria seemed about to play the part in 1813 which Prussia had played in 1805.   The elements of a great coalition were there as a result of Napoleon's disaster, the magnitude of which every report tended to increase.   But would the jealousies of the three Great Powers prevent it from being formed?

Fortunately every report shewed that the Tsar was standing firm.   He had left Rumantzov behind in Petersburg and taken the young and ambitious Nesselrode with him to headquarters.   At home public opinion was, on the whole, steadfast and expectant.   Above all, Castlereagh had done well as Leader of the House of Commons and won the confidence of the Prime Minister, who told Wellington: "We have gone through our short session in the most satisfactory manner.   Lord Castlereagh has done admirably and has raised himself very considerably in the eyes of the House of Commons." [1]

[1] Liverpool to Wellington, Dec. 22, 1812 : *W.S.D.* vii. 502.

CHAPTER III

THE LAST COALITION: RECONSTRUCTION MADE POSSIBLE, 1813

1. THE SUBSIDY TREATIES WITH SWEDEN, PRUSSIA, AND RUSSIA.

2. THE ARMISTICE AND AUSTRIA.

3. FIRST ATTEMPT AT AN ALLIANCE.

4. THE FRANKFORT PROPOSALS.

" War had hitherto been the conflict of Government against Government : it had changed its character : it was now for the first time the war of the people."—LORD LIVERPOOL (October 4, 1813).

CHAPTER III

1. THE SUBSIDY TREATIES WITH SWEDEN, RUSSIA, AND PRUSSIA

DURING 1812 Britain had made peace with Sweden and Russia and sent out some arms and money to the Baltic, but no contracts had been entered into for the future. Experience had made her cautious of such commitments. But the time had now come when she must adopt an attitude towards the northern Powers, if the movement of resistance were not to be checked.

The first to receive a definite contract was Sweden, and so anxious was Castlereagh to raise the north of Germany, where Prussia still lay apparently supine, that he was ready to grant very generous terms. Münster also was enthusiastic over the prospect of Bernadotte's appearance on the Continent and insisted that the King of Denmark hated England. When, therefore, the Danish Minister at Petersburg sounded Cathcart for an accommodation, Castlereagh's answer was quite definite that he would stand by Russia and Sweden, however much he regretted Bernadotte's insistence on Norway. He wished, however, to get as much value as possible out of Bernadotte for the common cause, and General Hope was sent out to assist in the negotiations and report on the military situation, a task for which Thornton, who had been putting forward some very wild ideas, was not very competent. Bernadotte's Swedes were to be reinforced by the Germans whom Gneisenau, it was hoped, would rally to his standard. The result would be a northern force of considerable dimensions which would strike at Napoleon's flank while Russia attacked his front, and summon all Germany to arms. For this purpose money was freely given and, though with reluctance, the promise of Norway, without, of course, a guarantee of its permanent possession. In return it was stipulated that Bernadotte should abandon immediate attack on Denmark, sail for Pomerania and the Hanse Towns, and advance into Holstein, which would bring him to the frontiers of Hanover.

Thornton was alarmed when he heard of this plan, but Bernadotte was encouraged to accept it by Yorck's rising. It was obvious that Prussia, with whom he had secret negotiations, was undergoing a change of heart, and if she went over she would be a competitor for British gold as well as an ally. The result was that a treaty of subsidy and alliance was signed at Stockholm on March 3, 1813, by which Britain agreed to co-operate with her naval forces in the reduction of Norway, if Denmark refused to give way, and ceded Guadeloupe with due provision for the Abolition of the Slave Trade. A secret clause by which Bernadotte attempted to safeguard his position, if Russia was unable for any reason to carry out her obligations, was refused by Castlereagh as shewing " distrust of the permanency of the Triple Alliance " and likely to "give umbrage to Russia." At the same time Bernadotte, encouraged by a subsidy of one million pounds and the promise of a German legion under his command, agreed to transport 30,000 troops to the Continent. He was given a free hand, and it was notable that no mention of Hanover's interests was made in the treaty. Since the German levies were expected to cost a million pounds more, the treaty set a scale which could not be maintained throughout the year. But at the time the instructions were sent, the defection of Prussia and all north Germany had not taken place, and was not immediately anticipated unless action was taken. It seemed vital, therefore, to encourage Russia to advance and to attack the tottering structure of the French Empire before Napoleon could recover and support it with new armies. It was hoped also that the opening of the north to British trade would enable the subsidy to be more easily paid, Sweden agreeing to regularise the use of

Gothenburg and Stralsund as bases for British commerce in the Baltic.[1]

The treaty with Sweden had hardly been signed when news came of a complete change in the German situation. The advance of the Russian troops had produced the agreement with Yorck which had so startled Metternich. His defection shook the counsellors of the King of Prussia and made an immense impression on the German people. As the Russian armies advanced, and Alexander shewed no signs of weakness or hesitancy, Hardenberg and others began to consider seriously going over to his side. The King was induced to go to Breslau to obtain some freedom of action. Even Metternich's advice was not against such a step, for he preferred the Prussian monarchy to lead the revolt rather than that a popular rising should take place uncontrolled. Moreover, as soon as he heard of Yorck's action, the Prussian Chancellor resumed confidential relations with Ompteda and encouraged him to hope the King could be won over, until at last, on February 19, he made a definite overture and begged that Britain would excuse the recent conduct of his master, which had been dictated by imperious necessity. Negotiations with Russia had so far advanced, he said, that the change of sides would soon take place and British help would be asked in munitions and money, especially the latter, for which Prussia's need was desperate.

The negotiations between Russia and Prussia had gone slowly. Each side wished to commit the other as far as possible. Prussia demanded not only a guarantee of her reconstruction to a position equivalent to that she held before her last war with France, but also assurances as to her lost Polish provinces. Russia was ready to agree to the first point

---

[1] To Cathcart, Dec. 20, 1812: *F.O. Russia*, 78. Memorandum of Münster, Dec. 6, 1812: *F.O. Hanover*, 4. To Thornton, Jan. 16, March 26, 1813: *F.O. Sweden*, 80. From Thornton, Jan. 8, 19, Feb. 14, 1813: *F.O. Sweden*, 81 ; Feb. 3, 18 (to Cooke), 1813: *C.C.* viii. 316, 325. From General Hope, Feb. 14, 1813: *F.O. Sweden*, 79. For the supposed strategic situation see the interesting memorandum of Colonel Bunbury of Dec. 31, 1812: *W.S.D.* viii. 457 (where wrongly dated). Thornton agreed to cede Guadeloupe to the Swedish House as a personal possession and also advocated a wild plan of Bernadotte for the abolition of privateering in the Baltic, for both of which actions he was snubbed by Castlereagh. (To Thornton, March 3, 1813: *F.O. Sweden*, 80.)

but adamant on the second.   Czartoryski and other Poles had
come to headquarters, and the Tsar was already considering
their plans of uniting Poland under his own rule.   Lebzeltern
had arrived meanwhile from Metternich and was urging a
general peace negotiation under the intervention of Austria,
who, however, withdrew her forces on the Russian flank and
shewed herself determined not to engage in hostilities.

The times were too critical to settle the question of Poland,
and on February 27, at Kalisch, a treaty of alliance against
France was signed between Russia and Prussia, by which the
former engaged to keep 150,000 men in the field and the latter
80,000, while in secret articles Russia promised that Prussia
should be made as strong as before the war of 1806.   No
mention was made of Russian claims on Poland, except by
implication, for while Prussia was promised that East Prussia
should be united to Silesia by a strip of territory, it was also
laid down that she was to seek compensation for lost territory
in the north of Germany.   Presumably, therefore, the duchy
of Warsaw was meant for Russia.   Meanwhile the British
Ambassador had stayed at Petersburg, talking vainly of
commerce to Rumantzov, who had been left without instructions or influence, though he now professed a change of heart.
Cathcart only reached headquarters at the beginning of March,
where he was able, at Castlereagh's orders, to encourage the
Tsar to resist Austria's suggestions for peace negotiations by
an assurance that Britain, to whom it was known Wessenberg
had been sent, would do nothing without the fullest communication with her Allies, whom she was prepared to assist
in every way.[1]

Meanwhile Metternich's peace messengers, who were all
ordered to use the word 'intervention' rather than 'mediation' as the part their master wished to play, were all receiving rather rough handling.   The Tsar shewed dislike of
Lebzeltern, and Napoleon shewed no signs of wanting peace.
Indeed, his first reception of the idea was so discouraging
that Metternich drew back, but after Napoleon disavowed
Maret's public speech, Wessenberg was sent to London on

[1] Ompteda to Münster, Jan. 7, 10, 31, 1813 : F.O. Hanover, 6 ; Feb. 19,
1813 : Ompteda, Nachlass, iii. 16.   From Cathcart, Jan. 29, Feb. 6, March
6, 26, 1813 : F.O. Russia, 84.

February 8. Metternich was further agitated by the discovery that the Archduke John and others had been receiving
money from King to start a revolution in the Tyrol for reunion with Austria.   The British agent, who had quarrelled
with both Cathcart and Hardenberg, had no one to defend him
when he was ordered to leave Austria.[1]

This *contretemps* was not likely to have much effect on
relations with Britain, but Wessenberg found a new situation
when he at last reached London.   Misfortune had pursued
the unhappy envoy from the first.   He was stopped at Hamburg as an Englishman and detained in Sweden as a Danish
spy.   He was further delayed by bad weather in the North
Sea for over a fortnight and did not reach his destination
until March 29.   There he met with the coldest of wel-
comes.   Napoleon, to whom Metternich had also sent an
Austrian envoy, had anticipated the 'intervention' by a
rousing speech in which he declared that the integrity of the
French Empire must be maintained.   In any case, the
accession of Prussia to the Allied side had made Britain less
anxious for peace than ever.   All her energies were devoted
to supporting the new coalition, which it was hoped would
drive Napoleon out of Germany.   The English newspapers
had got wind of Wessenberg's mission, in spite of his elaborate
incognito, and greeted him with a chorus of abuse.   Castlereagh, who explained that an Austrian envoy could only be
received informally, gave him no encouragement, though, like
Münster, he treated him with great politeness.   But the
Kalisch treaty, he said, had changed the whole situation on
the Continent, and Wessenberg's instructions were already
out of date.   The Prince Regent, who received him privately,
was also as polite as could be, but the interview developed into
an excellent royal lecture "made with great heat and remarkable eloquence," much of which Wessenberg reported

[1] To Cathcart, April 9, 1813 : *C.C.* viii. 358. From King, Feb. 19, 27,
March 1, 6, 8, 16, 1813 : *F.O. Austria*, 99. King, who had been pluming
himself that he was to receive letters of credence from Castlereagh, had
annoyed Cathcart by his strictures on Walpole's mission, and Count
Hardenberg by his jealousy and concealment of the Tyrol plot. Metternich
did not scruple to stop his messenger and prevent his dispatches from
reaching Kalisch. Even Gentz, who had received so much money from
him, found it difficult to defend him. (*Lettres et Papiers de Nesselrode*,
i. 52.)

verbatim, on the iniquities of Napoleon and the necessity of Austria assuming once more her old position as a Great Power, one of the most cherished wishes of the Regent's heart. Both the Prince and Castlereagh insisted that Napoleon's words had shewn that no peace was possible, and this was the keynote of the answer, which was sent to Metternich on April 9, formally refusing Austria's good offices. The Emperor, it was hinted, had no right to make them "under his existing relations to the enemy," and an appeal was made to him to answer the present call and come forward as "the ancient and natural Protector of the Germanic Body." [1]

Poor Wessenberg, who had not anticipated such treatment, was much dismayed, and the new instructions which reached him on April 14 to ask Britain for subsidies to assist Austria to advance from 'intervention' to 'armed mediation' did not help him much. Count Hardenberg had encouraged the British Government to believe that something more than this would be offered. There was no chance, Castlereagh told Wessenberg politely enough, of money being given for such an object. All they had was needed for arming Germany. Münster nastily added that Parliament still remembered that Austria owed large sums to England for previous campaigns. The envoy found himself, indeed, in a most unenviable position. The Prince Regent and Münster circulated Hardenberg's private gossip. The Press became more and more violent against Austria, especially after Metternich had sent Schwarzenberg to Paris for further discussions. Wessenberg was excluded from Court and Society, and of the Government only Castlereagh treated him with any attention or courtesy. In this painful situation, without sufficient money to live decently in a terribly expensive capital, he pleaded for recall, information, and instruction—in vain, until the issue of peace and war had been settled on the Continent. [2]

This mission was, however, only a minor interlude. Castlereagh had now to rivet the Russian-Prussian alliance by

---

[1] Wessenberg to Metternich, April 1, 2, 5, 6, 9, 13, 16, 1813; Castlereagh to Metternich, April 9, 1813: *Vienna St. A.* Arneth, *Wessenberg*, i. 158–61.

[2] Wessenberg to Metternich, April 13, 16, 20, 1813: *Vienna St. A.* Metternich to Wessenberg, March 10, 1813: Arneth, *Wessenberg*, i. 162.

assistance in arms and money.   He was also well aware that the weapons forging for the overthrow of Napoleon would also reshape the Continent in the process.   However he tried to keep his hands free, each Power of the coalition would seek its own special purposes in the treaties which must be made. Castlereagh had already pledged himself to Norway.   What other obligations would he have to take before the struggle was over and the victors met to discuss peace terms?

That he did not shrink from the responsibility is shewn in the remarkable letter which he sent to Cathcart with the instructions for the new treaties.   Now that Europe was to be reshaped, he turned back to his master, Pitt, for guidance and inspiration.

"The political arrangement of Europe in a larger sense," he wrote on April 8, "is more difficult at this early moment to decide on.   So much depends on events, that it is perhaps better not to be too prompt in encountering litigated ques- tions.   The main features we are agreed upon—that, to keep France in order, we require great masses—that Prussia, Austria, and Russia ought to be as great and powerful as they have ever been—and that the inferior States must be summoned to assist, or pay the forfeit of resistance.   I see many inconveniences in premature conclusions, but we ought not to be unprepared.

"As an outline to reason from, I send you, as a private communication, a despatch on which the confederacy in 1805 was founded; the Emperor of Russia probably has not this interesting document at headquarters: (interesting it is to my recollection, as I well remember having more than one conversation with Mr. Pitt on its details, *before he wrote it*) some of the suggestions may now be inapplicable, but it is so masterly an outline for the restoration of Europe, that I should be glad your lordship would reduce it into distinct propositions, and learn the bearings of his Imperial Majesty's mind upon its contents.   An unofficial communication of this nature between two Powers that have no partialities to indulge may prepare them the better to fulfil their duties at a future moment." [1]

[1] To Cathcart, April 8, 1813 : *C.C.* viii. 356.

This confidence shews how far his mind was already travelling; for, as has been seen, the dispatch of 1805 was no less than an outline of a new Europe with a special guarantee of its maintenance. But the immediate object was much less in extent, and the new instructions only traverse a very small portion of this ground. They were addressed not only to Cathcart, but also to the new Ambassador to Prussia—Sir Charles Stewart, whose experience and character, it must be confessed, were hardly such as to qualify him for such a position had they not been weighed by a brother's affection. Sir Charles had, it is true, a gallant and distinguished military career behind him, and was anxious to continue it in the Peninsula. But Wellington, despite his liking for him personally, his regard for Castlereagh, and the wishes of the Duke of York, refused to give the cavalry command, which had been Sir Charles' ambition, to a man who was too shortsighted (owing to a wound), too deaf, and, above all, not possessed of those qualities of discretion and foresight which were necessary. Sir Charles had, therefore, reluctantly to choose another avenue for fame, and the post which he was now given was at least partly military, for, like Cathcart in Russia, he was to act as chief intelligence officer to the Prussian and Swedish armies as well as Ambassador to the Prussian Court. Castlereagh, knowing his brother's impetuous character, had intended at one time that he should be subordinate to Cathcart, but Sir Charles claimed and obtained an independent position, though, of course, Cathcart was his senior in appointment, rank, and very considerably in age.

The new envoy at any rate possessed abounding energy and a soldierly *bonhomie* which were to carry him through some pretty difficult times. He loved display as much as fighting, was as vain as he was brave, as rash and impetuous as he was ready to take responsibility at a critical time. He was to be of real use as a soldier. As a diplomatist it was scarcely fair to expect much. Indeed, even Stewart's confidence in himself was temporarily dashed at the thought of the unaccustomed responsibilities he had now to assume. "I hope, my dear friend," he wrote to Cooke, "you will give me your advice freely on everything relating to my concerns, for I feel devilish nervous about it all." [1]

If Stewart rarely shewed such modesty, George Jackson, his Secretary of Embassy, never had any doubts of his own ability, but though this young man had been carefully coached by his more famous elder brother Francis, whom he had accompanied on his mission to Prussia in 1806–1807, he was too young to exercise much influence on events. Sir Robert Wilson was, of course, still there high in favour with the Russians, especially Platov, the famous Cossack, but on even worse terms than ever with Cathcart, who was rightly suspicious that he was too ready to push political questions in direct opposition to his chief's wishes. The fact that he immediately tried to transfer to Stewart's staff did not predispose the latter in his favour. [2]

Stewart took with him instructions for both envoys to negotiate subsidy treaties with their respective Courts, though Cathcart was given a kind of supervision over the whole. The demands of Sweden and the new German legion had reduced the amount of money available to two million pounds, of which it was suggested that Russia should have two-thirds, since by the Kalisch treaty she was to supply twice as many troops as Prussia. As Lieven had thought himself moderate in asking for four millions, and Jacobi, the new Prussian Minister, who hoped to negotiate the treaty in London, had been ordered to press for very large sums, this was not likely to satisfy the expectations of their Allies. But, as Castlereagh pointed out, heavy obligations had already been accepted before the situation changed: " It was not possible to calculate upon the career of Russian successes enabling them to march in the depth of winter without a halt from the banks of the Moskva to the shores of the German Ocean; that the barrier of the Oder would be passed; that Prussia

[1] Wellington to the Duke of York, June 25, 1811: *W.S.D.* vii. 165. *Bath Archives*, ii. 20–28. Stewart to Cooke, April 20, 1813 : *Lond. MSS.*
[2] The two had, however, some things in common and became good friends. They were both brave to a fault and enjoyed the zest of life. Ompteda records with amazement that, after a diplomatic meeting of the two with himself and a colleague, which, it is true, ended in a good dinner, the two Germans were put inside a rather small coach while Sir Charles and Sir Robert, each in the full regimentals of a British general, rode the one on the box and the other on the roof of their vehicle.

would so soon be incorporated in exertion and alliance against France; and that so wide a field for British commerce and enterprise should be thus suddenly opened throughout the north of Europe."

As a means of making up the deficiency he agreed to negotiate what some people called a "deferred subsidy," a treaty of financial assistance through the issue of paper money by Prussia and Russia, of a large part of which Britain should guarantee the repayment when the war was over. This elaborate design, invented by Stein, had been brought to London by Lieven and accepted with some misgivings by the Government. It was discussed throughout the year, but as it was never practicable to put it into operation, it served rather as a psychological than a financial inducement to the Allies.[1]

Of territorial objects Castlereagh was ready to give the same guarantee as Russia had done, viz. to restore her to a position equivalent to 1806. No Hanoverian claims were allowed to stand in the way. Münster, it is true, was already alarmed at Stein's influence with the Tsar, which reached its high-water mark in March and resulted in the Convention of Breslau. By this instrument the German states, as they were recovered from the enemy, were to be placed under a council which Stein was to control, and their revenues were to be used for the prosecution of the war. Hanoverian interests were only partially safeguarded, and the measure obviously hinted at a new organisation of Germany such as Stein had adumbrated in 1812. He made, indeed, no secret of his designs, which soon earned him the soubriquet of the "Emperor of Germany." Münster naturally wished that Hanoverian interests should be protected, and in two memoranda at the close of March urged his claims on the British Government. These were, however, modest enough. The only territorial increases which he demanded were the

---

[1] To Cathcart, April 9, 1813 ; Instructions to Jacobi, March 26, 1813 : Oncken, *Oesterreich und Preussen*, ii. 688, 615. Report of Lieven, April 6, 1813 : F. Martens, *Recueil*, xi. 167. Jacobi was much hurt to find the negotiation transferred to the Continent, a course which Wessenberg attributed to Castlereagh's desire that his brother should obtain a diamond snuff-box. But Jacobi did not arrive till May 10.

small Prussian territories of Minden, Ravelsberg, and Hildesheim, *enclavé* in Hanover and already incorporated by
Napoleon.

This moderation shews that the so-called Austrasian
project of an enlarged Hanover was never seriously intended,
and was only made because of the apparent hopelessness of
Prussian revival. But Münster was naturally alarmed at
Stein's proposals, which seemed to threaten Hanoverian
independence altogether. The smaller Princes, he asserted,
might perhaps give up the right of separate armies and
foreign relations, but the greater German Powers must retain
full sovereignty. He hinted that this might keep the
Hanseatic towns in Hanover's system rather than Prussia's
—thus preserving for Britain easy entrance into Germany.
To Stein's new plans, so far as he understood them, the
Princes, he claimed, would never submit.

This memoir raised the terribly difficult question of the
internal reorganisation of Germany which Castlereagh was
anxious to avoid, though he was always desirous of as strong
and compact a Germany as possible. He refused to be the
agent of Münster's alarms. All that he would do at the
moment was to demand representation for both Hanover and
Britain on Stein's German council. It was Metternich and
neither Münster nor Castlereagh who was to defeat, in the
course of the year, Stein's plan of a centralised Germany.[1]

While these discussions were completing in London, aid
was already overdue. The military situation had changed
with startling rapidity. The defection of Prussia had enabled
Russian troops to cross not only the Oder but the Elbe, with
the result that Hamburg escaped from French clutches —
an immense satisfaction to Britain, which thus had at last a
convenient port of entry into Germany. Saxony had been
overrun, and its King, the most loyal of Napoleon's allies,
had sought refuge in Austria, whose neutral position he had
supported in a special treaty. Russian and Prussian troops,
however, occupied Dresden, and Stein began there his career

---

[1] Memorandum of Münster, March 30, 1813 ; From Münster, March 31,
1813 : *F.O. Hanover*, 6. Münster's observations on the Treaty of Breslau :
Ompteda, *Nachlass*, iii. 75. To Cathcart, April 9, 1813 : *B.D.* 2. To
Stewart, April 20, 1813 : *C.C.*, ix. 6.

as administrator of liberated provinces with a zeal which rather defeated its object.

Napoleon was disconcerted at this rapid advance, for the new army, which he had been organising with magnificent energy, was not yet ready. But the chance which the Moscow campaign had offered had to some extent been lost by Prussia's delay. There was as yet no general rising in Germany. On the contrary, nearly all the Confederation of the Rhine remained loyal, and half Germany fought under Napoleon's banners in the war of liberation which was about to begin. The Emperor, himself startled at the rapid advance, set out for headquarters in April.

When, therefore, Stewart with his horses and aides-de-camp landed in Hamburg on April 17, the two armies were converging towards one another in the Saxon plains. He hastened towards the scene of the combat, travelling day and night after he had arranged for a Hanoverian corps to join the Swedes, visited Berlin, and refused to help the Prussian Minister, Golz, who seemed to think that the best way of reducing the French fortresses was through bribery with British gold. He reached Dresden on April 25. It was hardly a convenient moment to negotiate a treaty, especially for Cathcart and Stewart, both burning with military ardour and anxious to take part in the fast approaching battle. Hardenberg and the King gave him a warm welcome and were very anxious to get their money and munitions. Cathcart received his instructions and thought there would be no difficulty about Hanoverian claims. He took advantage of his seniority to go off to the armies, and order Stewart to remain at Dresden and open negotiations. Sir Charles hated handling the pen instead of the sword, but he obeyed like a good soldier and soon discovered that there was great objection to the Hanoverian demands. Hardenberg absolutely refused Minden and Ravelsberg, which "contained, he said, the oldest and most faithful of His Majesty's subjects." Though Nesselrode had promised Cathcart support, Stein was behind Hardenberg and no progress could be made. At last the impatient Stewart could wait no longer, and left for the front only to arrive just too late to join in the battle of

Lützen (May 3), a disappointment for which he never quite forgave Cathcart.[1]

This was bad enough; but Napoleon's victory, even though he had lost more men than the Allies, meant a hasty evacuation of Dresden. For a fortnight the retreat continued, headquarters were split up, and diplomacy was almost out of the question, even if the generals could have spared the time from their military duties. Instructions were being awaited from Castlereagh on the Hanoverian question, and the details of Federative Paper Money Sir Charles found so depressing that he threatened to send for a financial expert. Meanwhile Saxony had returned to Napoleon's obedience, and Austria, far less ready to desert him since Lutzen, was skilfully pressing her 'armed mediation' on the defeated allies. On May 18 they were beaten again at Bautzen and driven to retreat to Silesia, this time Sir Charles, as well as Cathcart and Sir Robert, having his full share of battle. He was, indeed, a master of the art of campaigning and fared better than Cathcart, whose freedom from worry, however, even at the suspicious conduct of Austria, he could not imitate. The threatened visit of the Duke of Cumberland was another anxiety. "The plot thickens," he wrote to Cooke from Wurschen two days after the battle, ". . . I do not think C. is in the secret. Military men are *envisaged* with a jealous eye, and if a good continental peace can be obtained our Allies would leave us to make our own . . . I suppose we shall have him [the Duke] here . . . but as Cathcart sleeps on straw and dines without a tablecloth and is to all intents and purposes the officer on picket and not the Ambassador at Court, I am apprehensive the fare afforded will be bad. I have not thought it necessary to be *so warlike* as my chief; consequently I am rather more sought. . . . There is a great deal of difficulty in getting on smoothly with C. He is at times so strangely important and so little communicative on perfect trifles." [2]

---

[1] From Stewart, April 19, 23, *C.C.* viii. 360, 377 ; April 26, 27, 1813 : *F.O. Prussia*, 87 ; May 5, 1813 : Oncken, *Oesterreich und Preussen*, ii. 694. From Cathcart, April 27, 1813 : *F.O. Russia*, 85. *Bath Archives*, ii. 77–87.

[2] From Stewart and Cathcart, May 24, 1813 : *F.O. Prussia*, 87. From Stewart, May 18, 20, 31, 1813 : *C.C.* ix. 11, 14, 21. Stewart to Cooke, May 20, 1813 : *Lond. MSS.*

Under these circumstances it is amazing that so much progress could be made with the negotiations before the allied headquarters had reached Reichenbach, especially as Stewart later complained: "Lord C[athcart] takes two days to consider a dispatch, and two to write one, and he never begins to think till other people have done." Fortunately, Sir François d'Ivernois had arrived on his way to Switzerland *via* Petersburg and was able to take over the Federative Paper discussions. The demand of the Allies that the subsidy should be paid in gold values was peremptorily rejected. Hardenberg fought strenuously about Hanover and at one time withdrew his offer of Hildesheim. Stein, who had studied English history, was even more offensive, threatening to expose the delegates to Parliament and overthrow the Government if they persisted in their demands. Sir Charles answered that he had been sent neither by the nation nor by Parliament, but by the Prince Regent. But the British Government were by no means ready to risk their relations with Prussia for a few miles of territory. "You are not to press the object," Castlereagh ordered, "as a *sine qua non*. The claim is felt to be a reasonable one, but it must not be the obstacle to larger views." Münster was forced to consent, and asked for East Frisia as a substitute. But this had nothing to do with Prussia, and the British Government evaded an obligation which might, in the future, conflict with the aims of either Holland or Denmark.

Sir Charles, therefore, did not press matters. He perhaps did well enough to secure Hildesheim for his royal master. The possessions of the ducal house of Brunswick were also specially mentioned. "I hope I have pleased Carlton House on the Hanover points," wrote Stewart to Cooke, when it was all over, "without militating general interests." [1]

These discussions prolonged the debate until the middle of June, when the treaties with Russia and Prussia were signed at Reichenbach. Britain agreed to the restoration of Prussia

---

[1] From Cathcart, June 16, 1813 : *F.O. Russia*, 85. From Stewart, June 16, 1813 : Oncken, *Oesterreich und Preussen*, ii. 698 ; June 19, 1813. *C.C.* ix. 28. Münster to Castlereagh, May 25, 1813; To Stewart, May 26, 1813 ; Stewart to Cooke, June 19, 1813 : *Lond. MSS.* Ompteda, *Nachlass*, iv. 121.

to the condition of 1806, being saved by Ompteda from being tricked by Hardenberg into accepting the year 1805, when Prussian territory was rather larger. In return, Prussia only promised Hildesheim to Hanover. Russia, for her part, was too proud or too wary to ask for territorial clauses. The question of Poland was not mentioned. For the rest, the treaties merely consisted of promises by Prussia to place 80,000 and by Russia 150,000 in the field, and by Britain to divide between them the two million pounds as Castlereagh had suggested. The Prussians were quite ready to raise 100,000 men, but as the Tsar could not guarantee more than 150,000 and insisted on two-thirds of the cash, the original numbers were left. The result was, of course, unfair to Prussia, who was bearing at least an equal share of the fighting, while the highly paid Bernadotte had as yet done nothing but complain.[1]

The Crown Prince had, indeed, some reason to be dissatisfied. During the great advance of the Allies the Danes had been encouraged to negotiate by Russia, whose envoy Dolgourouki had, so it was afterwards asserted, far exceeded his instructions and suggested that they might retain Norway after all, if they joined the Allies. Bernadotte himself had a little earlier almost agreed to be content with Drontheim, the northern part of Norway, and compensations in Germany. But he had been inspired to action by Prussia's example, and by the end of April 11,000 Swedes had landed at Stralsund. He was loud in protest when the news of Dolgourouki's mission reached him, and demanded the Russian corps to which, by treaty, he had every right, though it was obviously more usefully employed against Napoleon's main army.

The Danes had also approached Britain and sent Count Bernstorff to London. But Castlereagh insisted that treaties made in adversity "must not be forgotten in the day of prosperity," and Bernstorff was sent home without an audience. Cathcart was warned that Russia must manage

[1] For the treaties, see *B.F.S.P.* i. 58, 63. The vexed question of the Federative Paper Money was only settled in a separate convention signed at London on Sept. 30 (F. Martens, *Recueil*, xi. 189). On the whole subject, see D. Karmin, "Autour des negociations financières Anglo-Prusso-Russes de 1813" in *Revue Historique de la Revolution et de l'Empire*, xi. 177–97; xii. 24–49, 220–52.

the Crown Prince in order to get the best out of him, and General Hope was sent back to help Thornton get the Swedish forces into action.

The Tsar, meanwhile, sent to Stralsund Pozzo di Borgo, who had left his British exile to resume service at a spot where his hatred of Bonaparte could have more scope for action.   But even his adroit diplomacy could not manage to conciliate the Crown Prince, who remained inactive organising his army while the great events were in progress in the south, causing, as Cooke explained, an "anxiety and impatience of the public mind" which boded ill for the ratification by Parliament of the onerous Swedish treaty.   But it was in vain that he was urged to take part in the general campaign.   He made plans for attacking Zealand and meanwhile was deaf to all diplomatic pressure, while the Danes finally went over to Napoleon, and Davoust reoccupied Hamburg, on which terrible punishment was inflicted.   For this loss, his kindly attentions to the Duke of Cumberland, to whom the Tsar had refused hospitality, and the issue of a number of warlike bulletins were poor compensation.   Nor was the offer, which he later made to Thornton, of handing over Zealand to Britain, taken as an adequate excuse for his conduct.[1]

The coalition was, indeed, undergoing a severe strain and at moments seemed as if it would suffer the same fate as its predecessors.   By their treaties, it is true, Russia and Prussia had promised not to make peace without Britain. But already, after two defeats, they had accepted an armistice without consulting her.   The opportunity of Austria had, at last, arrived.

[1] To Cathcart, April 20, 28, 1813 : *C.C.* viii. 376, 382.   To General Hope, April 30, June 6, 17, 1813 ; Cooke to Hope, May 26, 1813 : *F.O. Sweden*, 79.   From Thornton, June 21, 1813 : *C.C.* viii. 399.

2. THE ARMISTICE AND AUSTRIA

THE treaties had been long in making, and they were perhaps only just made in time. For before the signatures had been affixed an event had taken place which threw all the ideas of the British plenipotentiaries into confusion. On June 4 Russia and Prussia concluded an armistice of six weeks with Napoleon, and negotiations for a Congress to lay the basis of a peace had begun—a step due to the initiative of Metternich, who throughout the month of May had conducted, with the greatest skill, an energetic diplomatic offensive.

He had been much chagrined, as Count Hardenberg, who shared his own grief and surprise, reported, at the contemptuous refusal by Britain of the offer of mediation. He was even more afraid of Russia's advance since he had heard something of Alexander's Polish plans, and the dread that Russia and France would come to terms at his expense increased. He redoubled his efforts, urged military preparations to strengthen Austria's power of resistance in any event, and now came forward as a more imposing mediator to obtain at least a continental peace, even though Britain refused to accept the good offices of Napoleon's ally.

Two carefully chosen envoys were sent to either side. Bubna, a Francophil, who went to Napoleon, was instructed to confess that there was, in view of the British attitude, no hope of a general and maritime peace, which could only be obtained by her 'compensations' as well as by France's cessions. But England must be led into negotiations by the attitude of other Powers. She could only be forced to yield by the conclusion of a "continental peace," which would "leave her entirely isolated and abandoned to the efforts of France." He proposed, therefore, negotiation under Austrian auspices at Prague. An armistice could be arranged if necessary.

To Stadion, the leader of the war party, who was sent to the Allies, the same point was made, but in rather a different fashion. If France had conquered on land, so had England on the seas: "The domination of England on this element is not less monstrous than that of France on the continent. . . . The last direct news from England proves only too well how much the system of war without end seems to be still the policy of that Government. We have reached the conclusion, if we had not already possessed it, that a peace between France and England, and even a negotiation which might lead to a maritime peace, can only be brought about by a continental arrangement." If the Allies insisted on their obligations to Britain, Stadion was to reply that Austria wished to reduce the French power to its proper limits as well as bring about a peace, but was determined not to be hampered by maritime questions. He was, therefore, to press the Allies to state their views as to the future of the Continent —in a word, to say what they meant by peace.[1]

Though Metternich always professed that Austria's policy was founded on principle and did not depend on the military situation, he instructed both envoys to adapt their arguments to the results of the impending battles. Lützen had already been fought, and the Saxons had joined the French army at Dresden while the Allies retired behind the Spree. But both the Prussians and Alexander were still possessed of high hopes, and, moreover, were anxious to conclude the subsidy treaties with Britain. They could not afford to ignore the Austrian pressure, but the terms which they first adumbrated at Wurschen (May 16) included Britain's special obligations in Spain, Sicily, and Hanover, and her interests in Holland, as well as their own intention of freeing Germany from French control. When Bautzen had been lost on May 20 the

---

[1] Metternich to Stadion, May 11, 1813; Metternich to Bubna, May 11, 1813; Oncken, *Oesterreich und Preussen*, ii. 641–46. Fournier's comment is: "What idle words these must have seemed to Napoleon, who for years back had been striving with all his might to isolate her [Britain] and yet had failed!" (*Napoleon*, ii. 274). But Britain had been isolated before, and she was now at war with the United States. How could she resist peace if the Continent were determined to have it?

necessity of Austrian co-operation became much more urgent, and they were far more inclined to accept Metternich's plans for an armistice and a negotiation without making any previous stipulation as to its basis.

Meanwhile Napoleon had also made a response. He had, before Bautzen, agreed to a Congress, to which he even suggested the Spanish "insurgents" might be summoned, the first sign that he was prepared to consider yielding in Spain, and insinuated that the representatives of the United States, and consequently "maritime rights," should be included in the discussions, though this invitation was not to delay the negotiations. Meanwhile he made an effort to come to an agreement with Russia at the expense of the German Powers. But Alexander refused to receive his envoys and ostentatiously associated Stadion in the offer of a truce made in order that the Austrian mediation should be carried out. After Bautzen, therefore, Napoleon had to choose between delay and negotiation or the prosecution of his victories, since he had failed to divide his opponents. He made the decision almost entirely on military grounds. He thought delay would enable him to add more to his own resources than the Allies could to theirs, and so, after fierce controversy as to details, an armistice for six weeks was agreed upon, Napoleon allowing Silesia to remain neutral ground, but stipulating that if Hamburg had been recaptured he should hold it.

Metternich had thus obtained the opportunity for negotiation which he had sought for so long. If neither side had yielded much, an interval had been obtained during which discussion might proceed in a different atmosphere. It in no wise detracted from his satisfaction that Britain was not included in the truce and that Napoleon was left entirely free to act in Spain, if he thought fit.

From a British point of view the significant fact about these negotiations was that Cathcart and Stewart were told but little about them, and never consulted, until all had been settled. The subsidy treaties had already been initialled when the news came of the conclusion of the armistice, but the Tsar told Cathcart that he could refuse to sign if he wished. Cathcart, however, wisely preferred to conclude the treaty,

which at least gave Britain by its terms some right to watch
over the negotiations. He was but little disturbed at the
manner in which the armistice had been arranged. But
Stewart, though he sent a discreet official dispatch for
publication, was highly indignant and suspicious. "I fear
political treachery," he wrote in a private letter, "and the
machinations that are in the wind more than any evils from
Bonaparte's myrmidons. We must keep a sharp look out,
especially since our refusal of Austrian mediation. We are
not considered (from all I see going on) in the Cabinet." He
was alarmed at the idea of negotiation for which he felt rightly
he had himself little talent, and was indignant at Russia's
domination over the Prussians, in whose good faith he had far
more confidence than in that of the Tsar. Every day deepened
his distrust, which, indeed, Hardenberg himself appeared to
share: "Hardenberg dined here," he wrote excitedly on
June 10 to Cathcart, "and I have had some information since,
and I think it of the utmost importance that your Lordship
should have distinctly from the Emperor what is passing.
I do not believe Count Nesselrode is to be firmly relied on,
but you certainly know best; however, I would give a great
deal for your Lordship to see the Emperor under present circumstances before you see Nesselrode, or before he can state
your conversation to H.I.M. From Hardenberg's conversation, Count Stadion only awaits a courier to enter into general
negotiations, and they (the Allies) are to solicit your Lordship
and myself to take a part in the consultations for a general
peace; I told Hardenberg Great Britain had refused the
Austrian mediation, that I could not answer for your Lordship's sentiments, but I did not see how we could be a party
without instructions. He added, because England had
refused some time since, there was no reason for her not taking
a part under a new state of affairs. Hardenberg admitted
Prussia had not a Sous—nothing in the shape of supplies can
be obtained from Bohemia without money. Prussia is in
the greatest state of uncertainty as to what may arrive and
is evidently unsettled. You will not, I am sure, find Nesselrode
yet ready to sign our treaty. The crisis requires the most
explicit avowals of everything that passes. I will give you

authority when we meet; it is from an individual whom you respect and who is not apt to see things *en noir*."

Cathcart, who accepted the Tsar's claim that the negotiation was necessary to draw Austria to the allied side, tried to soothe his colleague, and insinuated that Hardenberg's alarms were partly due to a desire to get his subsidies as quickly as possible.

"Your intelligence, my dear Sir Charles," he answered, "coincides in every thing with what I told you. Prussia has no separate view unless to obtain a present supply of money, which I also explained. I explained also the game that Austria will play to render perfect the consistency of her proceeding. She is treating and negotiating to obtain the general peace she has sighed for, but if her terms are considered inadmissible in the French Cabinet, then, alas! she finds herself under the necessity of making war with all her forces. She will exact on the part of the Allies that they will give their assistance to this *Marche Politique*. But you may rely upon it I shall use my best endeavours to know correctly every step in progress. You will assist me if you avoid giving any answers to my friend Hardenberg, otherwise than in a diplomatic way, that is, such as may not commit your opinion, because, depend upon it, Prussia will not act independently, and will be guided by Russia. But to get at opinions, I may think it right to keep back; the Russian Government may desire thro' Hardenberg to get at your opinions which they will guess must be the same with mine." [1]

It had been arranged that there was to be no direct communication between Napoleon and the Allies. Everything was to go through Metternich, who thus kept the negotiations in his own hands. This was his stipulation and not the allied choice, but it was represented to the Ambassadors as an evidence that war was still the most probable result and the only method to obtain war with Austria on their side. They reported as such to their Courts, but Stewart was still in a state of great anxiety. He refused to allow Hardenberg any addition to the £100,000 already advanced. He had the greatest distrust of Austria, and her recent proceedings added

[1] From Stewart, June 6, 1813 : *C.C.* ix. 22. From Cathcart, June 6, 1813 : *F.O. Russia*, 85. Stewart to Cathcart, June 10, 1813 ; Cathcart to Stewart, June 10, 1813 : *Lond. MSS.*

to his suspicions. Nor had he, and perhaps with reason, much confidence in Cathcart's ability to cope with this delicate situation. He expatiated to Cooke in a very private letter on his colleague's dilatoriness, jealousy, and inability to controvert the returns which the Russians made of their numbers. "C[athcart] will be more of a Russian than an Englishman soon, he is so bigoted to his Emperor . . . you will not much mind what I write. However, this will not arrest my opinions; you cannot pay M[etternich] so high as he is paid elsewhere. His master is worse than him and nothing will come of it." [1]

Stewart had some right to his suspicions, which were, however, not sufficient to keep him from going north to inspect Bernadotte's forces. Metternich with his Emperor had moved to Gitschin in order to get into close contact with Imperial headquarters at Reichenbach. Thence he ordered Stadion to extract from the Allies their terms of peace, excluding them, as has been seen, from all direct communication with Napoleon. He made also an explicit and emphatic condition that neither Sweden nor Britain were to be informed of the negotiations. They could join in the military discussions which Austria was also initiating in case of war on the allied side. But from all discussions as to terms both, and especially Britain, were to be rigorously excluded. The excuse was that it was vital that Napoleon should not learn what was going on, and that no account of these transactions should appear in the dispatches of Stewart and Cathcart, which might be laid before the British Parliament. But it cannot be doubted that Metternich wished also to exclude from the terms, which he was to offer Napoleon and upon which the issue of war and peace depended, all special British interests such as Spain. She had refused to allow him to act in maritime and colonial questions. She was to get her reward by being excluded from all influence on the

<hr>

[1] From Stewart, June 16, 1813 : B.D. 66–71 ; June 26, 1813 : Alison, Lives, i. 674. From Cathcart, June 16, 1813 : F.O. Russia, 85. Stewart to Cooke, June 16, 1813 : C.C. ix. 28, where it is wrongly addressed to Castlereagh, and the above sentences, presumably because of their bitterness, omitted : Lond. MSS. Sir Robert Wilson, who painted the military situation in the gloomiest colours, wrote to Grey on the 6th, " I have myself no doubt of a continental peace . . . a continental peace seems to be the first wish of Austria " : Wilson MSS. 30109, f. 171.

continental basis which was to be offered to Napoleon. She would thus be forced to use her colonial conquests to obtain those points in which she was specially interested.[1]

These negotiations went on apace and Metternich himself went to Reichenbach to complete them. There by June 24 he had concluded his bargain. Austria would support the Allies absolutely on four points: the dissolution of the duchy of Warsaw, the enlargement of Prussia, the restitution of Illyria to Austria, and the re-establishment of the Hanseatic towns or at least Hamburg and Lübeck. If Napoleon refused to concede these terms, she promised to make war on him. The dissolution of the Confederation of the Rhine, and the restoration of Prussia to a position equivalent to 1806, Austria also regarded as important, but Metternich would not make them conditions *sine qua non*. He had thus to offer Napoleon a peace based on four points, two of which had already been practically conceded. Undoubtedly, therefore, when Metternich set out for Dresden at Napoleon's invitation on June 24, leaving Stadion to sign the Treaty of Reichenbach on June 27, so that he might declare that he had no engagements, he had still considerable hopes of laying the basis for a peace between the continental Powers. He had terms of extreme moderation to offer, and he could face Napoleon with the alternative of having all Europe against him if he refused.

But in the celebrated interview at Dresden Metternich made less impression on Napoleon than he had anticipated. Though Napoleon's marshals hoped for peace, the Emperor was determined not to abandon his conquests. He still hoped to divide the Allies and make an arrangement with Russia at the expense of the German Powers. All that

[1] There is in the Berlin archives a dispatch, dated June 12, 1813, to Jacobi "concertée avec M. Stadion et Nesselrode," which gives a full account of the reasons for the armistice, quotes Stadion, as asserting that a "continental" peace would necessarily lead also to a "maritime" peace, and suggests that the British Government should send a special plenipotentiary to take part in the negotiations. But this dispatch seems to have been withheld, doubtless at Metternich's wish. Humboldt's careful *Projet d'instruction* for the Prussian representatives at the Congress (June 15–18) endeavoured to prove that Britain had no right to complain whether the issue was peace or war, as she would gain something in either case, a continental peace at least giving her access to the Continent! B. Gebhardt, *Wilhelm von Humboldt's Politische Denkschriften*, ii. 49.

Metternich could get was an agreement to send a negotiator to Prague to discuss, and as the armistice was drawing to a close it was agreed to extend it to August 10, a date which Schwarzenberg had fixed as one which suited Austria. But though a negotiation was decided, there was no sign of agreement even on the four points to which Metternich had reduced the ultimatum. Henceforward he must have had less hope of a continental peace. In July, therefore, the Austrian Court gradually drew nearer to the Allies, who accepted, after protest, Metternich's unauthorised extension of the armistice. The Emperors met and the staffs began to confer. Though the issue was still in doubt when, on July 11, Metternich formally invited Napoleon to send his representatives to Prague, war seemed more probable, and war in which Austria would be on the allied side.

From all these negotiations the British representatives were entirely excluded as Metternich had wished. Stewart was in the north engaged mainly on the military work that he liked. Cathcart remained at Reichenbach throughout June, but he acquiesced easily in the situation, made no endeavours to find out what was in progress, and recorded no protests. In July he went to Trachenberg, where Bernadotte met the Tsar and the King of Prussia with an Austrian representative to draw up a plan of campaign for the coming struggle. Bernadotte was far from satisfied with his position, for Sweden, like Britain, was excluded from the negotiation. He yielded, however, to the influence of the Tsar, placed his military science at the disposal of the Allies, and promised, though with mental reservations, to join in the general attack. Cathcart was well satisfied at the unity obtained and the plan prepared, the principle of which, he wrote, had already been anticipated by Castlereagh.[1]

While he was there news came of the battle of Vittoria (June 21), which had a profound effect on the minds of all the parties to these delicate transactions. The report reached Dresden immediately after Metternich's visit, and it was

---

[1] From Cathcart, July 12, 1813 : *F.O. Russia*, 86. From Thornton, July 12, 1813 : *F.O. Sweden*, 82. He described the Trachenberg scheme : " in short, to use the expression of the Prince Royal, that the rendezvous of the three great armies should be at the centre of the enemy's camp."

soon spread throughout the whole Continent. The British representatives were much excited by such news arriving at a time when their own interests seemed to be so neglected by their Allies, and they attached perhaps too much importance to its effects. Even Cathcart was uplifted when Alexander ordered a *Te Deum*, the first ever sung for a victory in which no Russian troops were engaged. "Wellington will save Europe yet," wrote Stewart exultingly to Hamilton. Jackson, when the final decisions were made, considered that Vittoria had been the main influence in producing them. This is, of course, an exaggeration. It was Napoleon and not Wellington who was the deciding factor. Yet the effect was considerable and played its part from now onwards in increasing British prestige and influence on the Continent. The Emperors even went so far as to invite Wellington to the command of their armies, which was at this time a matter of dispute amongst them, though only perhaps because they knew that distance made the offer no more than a compliment.[1]

At the moment, however, the effect could not be relied upon. Jackson, who had been left by Stewart at Reichenbach, found no relief in the pony races which the British staff organised to fill up the tedium of waiting. The first news that came from Prague, where the young Addington had been sent, was very ominous. Binder, Metternich's First Secretary, had indicated that a continental peace was most likely, and complained that "all the world knew that England was determined on an eternal war." Jackson watched even more zealously, and after Hardenberg and Nesselrode had been to Ratisborsitz to see Metternich, plied the Prussian Chancellor with notes and questions which the latter found it difficult to evade without direct lying. Jackson could do no more, however, than report the gradually growing optimism that Austria would come in, which, however, he distrusted himself.

---

[1] From Cathcart, July 20, 1813 : *F.O. Russia*, 86. From Stewart, Stralsund, July 16, 1813 : " The sensation it has exerted is indescribable. Everything may be hoped from it and from it *alone*. . . . It is only to be regretted that this news could not have reached the Allies before the prolongation of the Armistice. In the papers that have passed it is somewhat singular Great Britain's consent seems not to be noticed or hinted at." Stewart to Hamilton, July 19, 1813 : *F.O. Prussia*, 88. Nugent to Wellington, July 27, 1813 ; *W.S.D.* ix. 132. *Bath Archives*, ii. 204.

Ompteda, who had come to Reichenbach, was left in similar darkness and doubt, and though Count Hardenberg, who had accompanied Metternich to Ratisborsitz, knew more, he was under Metternich's ban to send nothing to Reichenbach but compliments.[1]

Meanwhile these anxieties were just as acutely felt in London, where the news of the armistice from French sources came as a great shock. They had no information from their own representatives, since Hamburg's fall, besides shutting out their commerce, kept them from quick communication. No wonder that Fain said its capture was worth two victories against Britain. Wessenberg was completely neglected by Metternich, who, in pursuance of his principle of isolating Britain, did not send him a single dispatch from March onwards, in spite of his reiterated entreaties. Münster's letters from Count Hardenberg, all the direct news available, were not encouraging, and so disturbed the recipient that he drew up a memorandum couched in most desponding terms. Metternich was said to be using the same foolish language as immediately after the French marriage, and pretending that Britain had refused her every kind of assistance. "Fear is evidently the chief motive of the Austrian policy," he wrote, suggesting that, in order to stiffen it, a British expedition should be immediately dispatched to the north of Germany. He offered to let Metternich know in a fortnight if the British Government consented. "At this awful moment," he urged, "when the hopes of the Continent are on the point of being perhaps for ever blasted, when England is likely to have again to contend alone against the power of the French Empire, it would certainly be important to make a great effort in order to bring Austria over to our side."

The British Cabinet necessarily shared this despondency, and Bathurst consulted Wellington whether in the case of a continental peace, which he anticipated, Britain had better not offer France the Ebro as a boundary. Castlereagh's anxiety was also acute. He subjected Wessenberg to sharp and detailed questioning, but could, of course, obtain no

[1] From Jackson, July 8, 9 13, 1813 : *F.O. Prussia*, 92. Addington to Jackson, July 10, 15, 1813 : *F.O. Prussia*, 88. Ompteda, *Nachlass*, iii. 163–68.

information from him. Jacobi was also without any news, and could only report the despondency of the Cabinet and their fears lest French hegemony should be re-established in Europe. Castlereagh confessed these fears to Cathcart, but, in the absence of all information, could give no instructions except to urge him to get in direct touch with Metternich and offer him British subsidies.[1]

He easily piloted his Swedish treaty through the Commons in spite of the attacks of the Opposition and the general depression. It was to be their last chance before victory came and they "made a sad job" of it, as Ward confessed. In spite of the clause concerning Norway, which Ponsonby in a violent speech compared to the Partition of Poland, and the fact that Bernadotte had done so little, Castlereagh routed the Opposition in one of the best speeches which he ever made. Madame de Staël thought it "the most eloquent, most rhetorical, and persuasive speech that was ever made in Parliament." He confessed afterwards that he had been doubtful of the result. "Half our own friends came down to the House determined either to vote against us or go away," he told General Hope, "I never recollect impressions so adverse. The transfer of Norway—the supposed loss of Danish concert—the Armistice—the fall of Hamburg—the Swedish army inactive—It was a most formidable combination of untoward circumstances. All, however, is right by decided conduct, and so it will be on the Prince Royal's part if his demands are not pushed too far. It is true the treaties are precise, but we know that parties who are *bona fide* can never expect to realise *extreme rights*." [2]

This unexpected success gave great encouragement and,

[1] Count Hardenberg to Münster, May 24, 31, 1813 ; Memorandum by Münster, June 25, 1813 : *F.O. Hanover*, 6. Jacobi to Hardenberg, June 15, 18, 22, 1813 : *Berlin St. A*. To Cathcart, June 30, 1813 : *B.D.* 5.

[2] Hansard, *Commons*, June 18, 1813. Canning also joined in the attack, but could not adapt his criticisms to those of the Whigs. " Castlereagh perceived his advantage and availed himself of it in the best and most dexterous speech I ever heard him make, and Canning, angry, dispirited, and embarrassed, was as much below as his adversary had been above himself. So the Government gained its greatest victory upon its worst case, and for anything I see may last as long as Liverpool and Castlereagh live." Not a bad prophecy ! S. H. Romilly, *Letters to Ivy*, 206–208. A. F. Steuart, *Diary of a Lady in Waiting*, 64. To General Hope, June 22, 1813 : *F.O. Sweden*, 79.

even before the news of Vittoria, Castlereagh had regained
some confidence in his Allies and was ready to discuss subsidy
payments, as Jacobi noted with delight. The news from
Spain not only dissipated all clouds and made the Government impregnable, so great was the joy and pride of the whole
nation, but it enabled new instructions to be sent abroad.
Spain might now be considered as won by force of arms.
When, therefore, Castlereagh received from Cathcart the
Russian terms of peace (he did not know, of course, to what
they had been reduced by Metternich) he sent off new instructions, which might be of vital importance in the negotiations which seemed about to commence. He insisted, first,
that Britain had given pledges to Spain, Portugal, Sweden,
and Sicily and could accept no peace which did not fulfil
them.   Secondly, Britain would support Austria and Prussia
to any extent in their demands for the restoration of their
territories. He hoped they would include Holland and he
expected the restoration of Hanover. But on these points,
even the last mentioned, he admitted that the final word lay
with the Allies and, still more so, on the rescue of the rest
of Germany and Italy from French domination. If Austria
would join the Allies all this might be won, but the decision
must be hers.   In fact, if the Allies insisted on negotiation,
he told Cathcart, Britain could not stand out, however much
she regretted it.   He could not trust the imperfect ties of the
subsidy treaties if they were determined to make peace.

"The risk of treating with France is great," he wrote, "but
the risk of losing our continental Allies and the confidence of
our own nation is greater.   We must preserve our own faith
inviolate to Spain, Portugal, Sicily, and Sweden.   We must
maintain our most important conquests, employing others to
improve the general arrangements on points which are not
likely to be carried by other means; and with respect to the
Continent we must sustain and animate those Powers through
whose exertions we can alone hope to improve it, taking care,
in aiming at too much, not to destroy our future means of
connexion and resistance." [1]

[1] Wessenberg to Metternich, June 21, 1813 : *Vienna St. A.*   Jacobi to
Hardenberg, June 25, 1813 : *Berlin St. A.*   Bathurst to Wellington,

A week later he made a further advance. The Russian and Prussian Ambassadors at the orders of their Courts, inspired by Metternich, had been urging him to accept the Austrian mediation. To this step he now consented, since the Spanish difficulty had been removed. Moreover, he sent a note promising to use the colonial conquests for the common advantage of Europe, though refusing to make specific proposals, since none had been made on the other side. He refused, however, to pay any subsidies while the armistice existed. At the same time he insisted that maritime rights must be altogether excluded from the negotiation. He had already refused to consider the idea which Napoleon had circulated for his own purposes that the Americans should be invited to the Congress. He reiterated Britain's refusal to allow any discussion on this point: "Great Britain may be driven out of a Congress but not out of her maritime rights, and if the continental Powers know their own interests they will not hazard this." He also peremptorily refused the insistent requests which were put to him by Jacobi to increase Prussia's subsidy. These important instructions were not revealed to the unfortunate Wessenberg, who was merely told that, as he appeared to have lost the confidence of his Court, communication would be established with Metternich through the agency of Cathcart.[1]

A further reinforcement to the British representatives abroad at this time was hardly an asset. The Duke of Cumberland set off at the end of April to represent the Guelph House on the Continent, taking with him much good wine. He was anxious to raise a north German force to serve under him, but Castlereagh regretted to have to damp his ardour because there was no money to raise a corps adequate to His Royal Highness's rank and station. All that could be done was to beg that he might be allowed to see something of the fighting.[2]

June 23, 1813: W.S.D. viii. 17. Castlereagh to Cathcart, June 30, July 5, July 6, 1813: B.D. 5–11.

[1] To Cathcart, July 13, 14: B.D. 12–13; C.C. ix. 34–36. Wessenberg to Metternich, July 10, 1813: Vienna St. A. Jacobi to Hardenberg, July 10, 14, 1813 · Berlin St. A. Jacobi was expressly forbidden by Castlereagh to inform Wessenberg of the acceptance of Austrian mediation by the British Government.

[2] Bathurst to Wellington, April 7, 1813: W.S.D. vii. 601. Wessenberg to Metternich, April 27, 1813: Vienna St. A. From Cathcart, April 28,

There was now good prospect that this would be continued, for Napoleon proved to be even more adamant than Metternich had imagined, and the Congress which had been staged with so much care at Prague was no more than a dreary farce. Metternich had intended to keep all the threads of the negotiations in his own hands, but he found that there was little opportunity for his diplomatic skill. Napoleon shewed his intentions by refusing his envoys all instructions. The mediation ended in miserable quibbles as to the form of procedure until the Emperor, who up to the last seems to have hoped for peace and was even prepared to sacrifice Illyria to obtain it, was at last convinced that nothing could be obtained from his son-in-law. Metternich had come to that conclusion somewhat earlier, and Gentz's assurances to his British friends now began to sound the ring of truth. At last, on August 8, Metternich sent an ultimatum, and so certain was he of rejection in any case that, in order to please those to whose side he must now turn, he included in it all the six points of the Reichenbach agreement. When no answer came in time, the armistice was denounced, and a line of bonfires signalled the Allied armies to their march to Austria's assistance in Bohemia. Even now, however, a slender thread of negotiation was still kept across the chasm of war, for Metternich's answer to the rather insulting note which Maret sent him was studiously moderate. But it took Britain into consideration, and said that her reply must be awaited. Now that Austria was at war, British subsidies were necessary, and British interests must be considered to some extent.

During this period the hopes of the British representatives had naturally been rising higher. The attitude of the French at Prague could not be concealed, and Metternich grew more friendly as his hopes of peace dwindled. Jackson, who attributed the change too completely to the Vittoria victory, never lost his suspicions altogether, but even he had to admit that Napoleon's conduct made peace all but impossible. As late as August 2 he was still painting awful pictures of the possibility of a continental peace, but more to ensure his

1813 : *F.O. Supplement (Russia)*, 343. The Duke of Cumberland to the Prince Regent, June 7, 18, 1813 : *Windsor Arch.* Castlereagh to the Duke of Cumberland, July 13, 1813 : *F.O. Hanover*, 5.

position if it took place than because he thought it likely.
Cathcart became completely complacent. The Tsar professed himself ready to accept all the points of Castlereagh's
instructions of July 5. He was confident concerning Austria,
for Stadion, at Metternich's orders, began to negotiate concerning subsidies, while Nugent was allowed to receive money
to complete the long-planned Tyrolean insurrection which
Metternich had once so frowned on. Metternich, indeed,
refused to see Cathcart personally to receive the letter which
Castlereagh had sent, but that was due to the negotiations
going on at Prague.[1]

It was fortunate that when Stewart returned from the north
the die had been cast. For his first action was to wrest from
Hardenberg by a violent denunciation the secret of the
Reichenbach treaty of July 27 between the three Powers, and
Hardenberg had a very bad quarter of an hour. Jackson
could hardly help insisting that Cathcart had scoffed at his
suspicions and that Hardenberg had lied to him about it.
Stewart endeavoured to excuse Hardenberg on the ground of
age and infirmity; but he was convinced that, if Napoleon
had yielded even one point, a continental peace would have
been signed without any regard being paid to Britain's
interests. That such a treaty by Prussia and Russia should
have been signed only a few days after the subsidy treaties
with Britain, which bound them not to negotiate separately
and to communicate everything regarding policy to each other,
was, to say the least, as Stewart pointed out, "a very strange
proceeding." Only the obstinacy and recklessness of
Napoleon had saved the Allies from another of those breaches
of good faith with which the history of coalitions abounds.[2]

All could, however, be forgiven now that Austria had been
driven to war by Napoleon's intransigeance. Imperial headquarters were transferred to Prague, and although difficulties
immediately arose as to the supreme command of the Allied
forces over which Schwarzenberg's authority was disputed

[1] Jackson to Stewart, July 27, Aug. 2, 7, 1813: *B.D.* 72–75. From
Cathcart, July 20, 24, 26, 29, 1813; Metternich to Cathcart, July 30,
1813: *F.O. Russia*, 86. From Cathcart, Aug. 5, 1813: *B.D.* 15. Nugent
to Cathcart, July 27, 1813: Oncken, *Oesterreich und Preussen*, ii. 706.
[2] From Stewart, Aug. 12, 20, 1813; Jackson to Stewart, Aug. 12, 1813:
B.D. 76–79. *Bath Archives*, ii. 211.

by the Tsar, who had now brought Moreau from America to advise him, preparations were made to carry out the plan of campaign drawn up at Trachenberg. Gentz was delighted to see his English friends once more, and no one was more capable of placing all the recent transactions in the best possible light. Metternich had no treaties to explain away, but he was aware that his recent conduct was hardly such as to win back British confidence. He now began to put forward the view, which he subsequently elaborated in his memoirs, that he had all the time intended to join the allied side, and that his tortuous methods were rendered necessary by the painful position of his country. Cathcart and Stewart accepted these explanations, which by now were merely academic, and began to plan how Austria's sore need of money and material could be supplied from British sources. Cathcart immediately promised a subsidy of half a million and gladly accepted all Metternich's assurances. Stewart still kept some suspicions, but was impressed with the Austrian army, whose unexpected size and excellence compensated, in his mind, for much diplomatic chicanery.[1]

Metternich could also at last take notice of poor Wessenberg, and on August 28 he sent him an account of these transactions meant for British consumption. "My silence must have astonished you," he added in an intimate note, "but it was completely calculated. We were in so difficult a position, and our relations with England were so vulnerable, that to talk to her without knowing what to say would have only done harm. . . . I wished to make it possible for you to say with all frankness that you knew nothing about anything. Your mission was limited to the offer of the mediation, and there was no reason why you should discuss other objects as yet so little defined. Stadion was able to treat concerning them confidentially with the English agents at headquarters." Hardenberg pointed to the triumphant issue as the best excuse for his concealment, made at the orders of Austria "for fear of publicity."[2]

---

[1] From Stewart, Aug. 20, 1813 : B.D. 79. From Cathcart, Aug. 12, Sept. 1, 1813 : F.O. Russia, 86. Londonderry, Narrative, pp. 104–106.
[2] Metternich to Wessenberg, Aug. 28, 1813 : Vienna St. A., 1813. Hardenberg to Jacobi, Aug. 24, 1813 : Berlin St. A.

It was evident, however, that Austria would need more attention, and Castlereagh had already sent out a special Ambassador whose arrival was hourly expected. Nothing could better illustrate the outlook of the age than the choice of the young Earl of Aberdeen for this important post. He was not yet thirty years of age, had practically no diplomatic experience, and could not speak French. He was chosen partly at the Prince Regent's desire, but also because such a position could hardly be filled by a *diplomate de carrière*, but demanded a man of high rank. Aberdeen, the ward of Pitt and Dundas and son-in-law of a very great magnate, the Duke of Abercorn, had always been regarded as destined for a high career in the Tory ranks, though he had shewn himself diffident and reluctant to accept it. He had already refused in 1812 a difficult job—the negotiation with the United States. Now domestic sorrow caused him to accept as important and responsible a mission as had been sent out from Britain during the war. Though he had not sought it and was sincere in lamenting the trouble which it gave him, he was by no means dismayed at the task, and was quite prepared to negotiate peace for Europe all by himself. He insisted that he should at least be placed on a full equality with Cathcart, and was quite prepared to lecture Castlereagh. As will be seen, so stiff and yet so diffident and so inexperienced a character fell an easy prey to the wiles of Metternich.[1]

Nevertheless, this was the envoy Castlereagh chose to send out on August 6, even before he knew that Austria would be an ally. He was given wide instructions. Britain was ready to fight on to confine France to her 'natural' frontiers, if the Allies would fight with her. For the rest, Castlereagh repeated the principles he had already laid down for Cathcart in July, to which were added further encouragement to go on with the Tyrolean insurrection. In one important point, however, Aberdeen was given great latitude. Austria was known to be already in negotiation with Murat. Britain was pledged as regards Sicily, and wished that the Bourbons should get back Naples. Aberdeen was ordered to suggest that Murat should

---

[1] Balfour, *Life of the Earl of Aberdeen*, i. 72. Jacobi to Hardenberg, Aug. 3, 1813 : *Berlin St. A.*

be offered compensation elsewhere in Italy, if he would change sides. But in a separate and secret dispatch he was allowed to agree to Murat's retention of Naples in the last resort, provided Ferdinand was given an equivalent elsewhere, an idea which had already been suggested by Lord William Bentinck. The negotiation was obviously a delicate one, and in the hands of men like Aberdeen and Bentinck it could hardly fail to bring confusion and uncertainty.[1]

The fact that Aberdeen had been given such discretion at all shewed that Castlereagh was seeking every possible means to encourage the Allies to attack Napoleon in every quarter. He was cheered by the accounts of the Trachenberg decisions, which he warmly approved, but he redoubled his exhortations. He could not believe, he wrote, that peace was possible, adding further news of Wellington's progress in Spain. But he revealed his anxieties in the closing words of his letter, which were meant to warn the Allies of their danger:

"Fatal would it be for them, and for the world, if they could for the moment think of seeking their safety in what is called a continental peace. We have done wonders in the Peninsula, but don't let the experiment be tried of single combat again in that quarter. We *may* sink before the undivided power of France, and, if we do, Germany, and even Russia, will soon resume their fetters. We are protected against this evil by the obligations of good faith; but we are also protected against it by the plainest dictates of common sense. We have now the bull close pinioned between us, and if either of us lets go our hold till we render him harmless, we shall deserve to suffer for it." [2]

Shortly afterwards he learnt of the secret Treaty of Reichenbach; for Metternich had at last allowed Count Hardenberg to communicate it to Münster under a strict injunction of secrecy. He must have known, however, that Münster could not conceal it from the British Ministers, and by the time it reached them the crisis would be over. An apology was sent for the concealment from Cathcart and Stewart, on the ground

---

[1] To Aberdeen, Aug. 6, 1813: *B.D.* 94–97. For the Italian negotiation, see below, Chapter IV, Section 4, p. 253.
[2] To Thornton, Aug. 7, 1813: *F.O. Sweden*, 80. To Cathcart, Aug. 7, 813: *C.C.* ix. 39.

that their dispatches might have to go before Parliament. When the news of the rupture finally came to Britain it was received with immense relief. "We were deeply anxious," Castlereagh now confessed to Cathcart, and he commented with some acerbity on the way the British representatives had been treated. The negotiations with Murat, of which Münster had been informed, had also been concealed from them as well as the Reichenbach treaty. Castlereagh's indignation, though restrained, is apparent: "Engagements of secrecy against us are of bad precedent, and must not be." [1]

How could he be confident of the completion of the immense task of overthrowing Napoleon's dominion with Allies of this kind? Was it not possible to make more definite provision by treaty to bind Europe together than had ever been done before? His thoughts naturally went back to the dispatch of 1805, and a few days later he had completed the first project of an Alliance which should bind Europe together against the power of France and give some guarantee against further manœuvres of this kind.

[1] Münster to Castlereagh, Aug. 24, 1813 : *F.O. Hanover*, 6.   To Cathcart, Sept. 1, 1813 : *C.C.* ix. 45.

3. FIRST ATTEMPT AT AN ALLIANCE

For the first time since 1795 all the Great Powers of Europe were now combined together against France, with Sweden, Spain, and Portugal in their train. It was, indeed, a very different coalition to that of the Kings against the French Revolution. Nearly twenty years of French domination had made this new coalition one of peoples as well as monarchs. But it was the monarchs who directed the whole, without much reference to the wishes and desires of their subjects, and the same jealousies, ambitions, and tergiversations were present in this coalition as in those that preceded it. Austria's entry had brought 150,000 men into the field against Napoleon, but it had added greatly to the difficulties of combination. The Austrians had secured the entry of Russian and Prussian troops into Bohemia as a result of their negotiations and intended Schwarzenberg to have the supreme command. But the Tsar, who had now got Moreau as well as the Swiss Jomini to advise him, was by no means ready to subordinate his armies to foreign control, while the Prussian soldiers, animated by a much more eager and national spirit than the Austrians, were impatient of the restraints placed upon them. The result was that, though the principle laid down at Trachenberg was accepted by all, the methods by which it was to be carried out were a continual subject of dispute. Since Napoleon's exertions during the armistice had raised his forces to a number only slightly inferior to the allied total, the central position and unified command of the French forces might well be expected to make the combat a doubtful one.

Fortunately for the Allies, the field was so vast that Napoleon found it almost impossible to control the operations with his usual certainty and skill. His marshals had not the same confidence in him or in themselves as before the Russian campaign, while his troops were young and unable to sustain the hardships to which they were condemned by his wretched commissariat. Though Bernadotte was more than sluggish in the north, his raw Prussian troops stood fast, and Blücher and Gneisenau gave the Army of Silesia both fire and prudence. Napoleon's first marches and counter-marches were rendered futile, his marshals were defeated, and though he won his last victory on German soil at Dresden, he failed to take advantage of it, and the disaster of Kulm more than counter-balanced the success. Meanwhile his army was melting away faster than that of the Allies, who had learnt something from the risk they had run of overwhelming defeat, while Moreau's death in action had checked the Tsar's desire to overrule Schwarzenberg.

Cathcart and Stewart were in their element once the fighting had begun. Both were in the thick of it, especially Stewart, who was wounded at Kulm and for a couple of weeks had to stay quiet. Their reports revealed the difficulties of the situation and their own. "No Commander-in-Chief ever had before two Emperors and a King superintending and controlling not only movements in agitation, but also operations decided on," wrote Stewart. "In a residence where there are three Sovereigns, three Courts, three Ministers, and three Headquarters," explained Cathcart, "there are, of course, many parties, many rumours, and great variety in stating the same matters of fact." "It is difficult to ascertain the truth," he confessed, but with his usual optimism vouched for the general zeal in the cause and was confident of ultimate success. Neither he nor Stewart had much time for diplomacy, yet important discussions were going on between the three Powers at this time with regard to new treaties amongst themselves in which the war aims were to be restated. From these discussions, as at Reichenbach, the British plenipotentiaries were excluded, though, of course, they knew what was in progress.[1]

Nor did Aberdeen, who arrived at Toeplitz on September 5,

---

[1] From Stewart, Sept. 4, 1813: *B.D.* 81. From Cathcart, Sept. 7, 1813: *F.O. Supplement (Russia)*, 343.

supply this deficiency. He made at first a bad impression by his cold demeanour and his lack of French. But within a few days the ice melted under Metternich's genial handling, and in a short time Aberdeen was ready to adopt the Austrian views as his own. With subtle flattery Metternich and his Imperial master treated Aberdeen with even greater distinction than the Tsar gave to Cathcart. Though the young man affected to disdain such worldly trifles, he was in fact much influenced by them, and in a short time was ready to place unbounded trust in Metternich and to share his views about the future of Europe and the best methods of bringing the war to a close.[1]

If Aberdeen was communicative to Metternich, he was the reverse with his own colleagues. Cathcart and Stewart were too much men of war for his liking, though he yielded somewhat to Stewart's good nature and *bonhomie*. The only British colleague who appealed to him was Sir Robert Wilson, who at last saw an opportunity of making a recognised position for himself. At the Russian headquarters, though made much of personally, he was overshadowed by Cathcart, who was military representative. But Aberdeen was a civilian, and Sir Robert soon won his confidence and arranged a transfer to the Austrian headquarters, where his bravery and energy as well as his flattery of Schwarzenberg and Radetzky soon made him a favourite. He too began to expatiate on the advantages of peace and added to the influence on Aberdeen in this direction, which Metternich was already exercising in a hundred different ways.[2]

Aberdeen had, indeed, but little opportunity to contribute to the treaties between Austria and her Allies, signed at Toeplitz a few days after he reached headquarters, which, besides providing for the conduct of the war in common, restated its aims in separate and secret articles. These

[1] Wittichen, *Briefe von und an F. von Gentz*, iii. 134, 149. On Aug. 31 Gentz wrote to Metternich: " Ich finde ihn sehr verlegen, embarrassé et embarrassant, finster, steinern, tot-kalt, und wie es mir vorkam, des Franzoschen nicht recht mächtig," but on Sept. 13 he could say, " Er ist ein andrer Mench geworden. . . . Ihr Glanz strahlte von seinem Gesicht zurück."
[2] Balfour, *Life*, i. 143–44; Randolph, *Wilson Diary*, ii. 113–14. From Cathcart, Sept. 25, 1813 : *F.O. Supplement (Russia)*, 343.

included the dissolution of the Confederation of the Rhine, the freedom of Germany to the Rhine, and the reconstruction of the Austrian and Prussian monarchies on a scale equal to 1805. The restoration of Hanover was specifically mentioned, but none of the other British aims such as Spain or Norway or Holland. Jackson was much exercised at these omissions when he discovered them, and Humboldt's explanations that Britain was left to make her own proposals and that there would be no peace made without her consent did not completely satisfy him. But none of the Ambassadors supported him.

Meanwhile Aberdeen's negotiation of the Austrian-British treaty went on only slowly. He had told Metternich of the acceptance of Austrian mediation by Britain, the news of which had reached Cathcart on the eve of the rupture and had been kept concealed from Austria at the Tsar's request. This confession only caused surprise, but Aberdeen at times had doubts about Metternich's perfect sincerity, though he did not waver for long. "Metternich continues to be as cordial and as confidential as possible," he wrote on September 23, "I think this man must be honest; yet it may be after all that he is only a most consummate actor. I will be sufficiently cautious, but I will also retain the favourable opinion I have of him until I see some good ground to change it." Cathcart, who had received Castlereagh's severe comments on the armistice negotiations, also promised to be circumspect with regard to Russia: "I do not think this Cabinet is more successful than others in keeping its secrets, but it is the principle to be secret and to make no sort of communication which is not absolutely called for." He had protested against being told of measures only after they were settled, and hoped for better results in the future.[1]

The treaty which Aberdeen signed on October 3 was on the model of the British treaties with Russia and Prussia. It contained the clause promising unreserved communication and that peace would only be signed by common accord. Of the subsidy of a million pounds, payable at £100,000 per

---

[1] From Aberdeen, Sept. 23, 1813 : Balfour, *Life*, i. 105. From Cathcart, Sept. 25, 1813 : *F.O. Supplement (Russia)*, 343.

month, half had already been given by Cathcart on August 18, so that the rest would last till April 1. The treaty had been, however, preceded by long discussions on the terms of peace. Metternich assured Aberdeen that he was ready to accept all the British points on which Castlereagh had insisted in the instructions. Though the Rhine had been mentioned as a geographical frontier in the treaties with Russia and Prussia, he did not mean to adhere to it too strictly and thus Holland would be provided for. He was very reluctant to support Bernadotte's claim to Norway, but at last agreed to try to obtain Denmark's consent by negotiation. At the same time he made Aberdeen his confidant as regards Germany. He claimed but little merit for Austria's refusal to resume the Imperial Crown, but gradually revealed his alarm at Stein's plans, which Aberdeen came to share: " Instead of imitating Bonaparte we ought to pursue a conduct directly opposite and avoid everything of a revolutionary tendency. . . . There is a spirit in the north of Germany which is dangerous. The *friends of virtue* ought to be attended to. It is impossible to say what may arise from this discontented and restless disposition; but it is clear we ought to put down as much as possible the mischievous effects produced by these speculating philosophers and politicians. . . . The real sum of the matter is, that while we are fighting to destroy the Confederation of the Rhine, we shall raise up another as odious and unjust." [1]

Aberdeen was also loud in praise of the subtle diplomacy by which Metternich was detaching Napoleon's vassals. The negotiations with Bavaria were, indeed, a masterpiece; for they struck equally at Napoleon and at Stein, whose plans were fatally ruined by the complete independence of outside control which Bavaria obtained with Hardenberg's assent. With Denmark slower progress was made, and there was much risk of offending Bernadotte, who objected to Bernstorff even being received by Metternich. As to Italy, Aberdeen found it hard to get exact ideas from Metternich. Negotiations were still going on with Murat, who, to the general surprise,

---

[1] From Aberdeen, Oct. 1, 1813 : Balfour, *Life*, i. 110. A. F. Pribram's *Oesterreichische Staatsverträge, England*, 543, 546–50, gives the secret articles of the Treaty of Toeplitz.

appeared at Dresden at Napoleon's imperious summons and was put in command of the cavalry. He kept, however, his link with Austria, and it did not take much longer than a week for Metternich to obtain from Aberdeen a written statement that Britain would agree to Murat retaining Naples, though his instructions were that this was only to be yielded as a last resource.[1]

Meanwhile in Britain they were endeavouring to take stock of the new situation caused by the accession of Austria to the coalition. They could hardly believe the news. According to Wessenberg, the Prince Regent was still full of distrust of Metternich and maliciously repeated all the gossip assiduously collected by Count Hardenberg. Münster, he added, lamented Austria's views on Germany. It was evident that it would be long before the unpopularity of Austria wore off. Münster sent a different, though perhaps less veracious, view of his master's attitude to Hardenberg, but he added his solicitations to those of Russia and Sweden that Austria would resume the Imperial crown—a measure which would solve the problem of Germany by ensuring just sufficient independence to the Princes who would now be restored.[2]

Castlereagh, who alone, according to Wessenberg, had behaved with dignity towards Austria during the trying interval of the armistice, was not slow to send his official congratulations to Metternich "on the dignity and firmness with which he has conducted these delicate and important transactions to a close." He was anxious to give all possible help, and readily agreed that the arms and munitions sent to Austria should not come out of the subsidy. But, as has been seen, he was far from approving of the manner in which the recent negotiations had been carried on, and while Austria's assistance was invaluable, her disposition to treat was suspect, and the risk of a premature peace which would leave the Continent still at Napoleon's mercy at some future date seemed to be much increased.[3]

[1] From Aberdeen, Sept. 14, 24, 1813 : Balfour, *Life*, i. 91, 93, 101.
[2] Wessenberg to Metternich, Sept. 1, 3, 7, 1813 : *Vienna St. A.* Jacobi to Hardenberg, Sept. 7, 1813 : *Berlin St. A.* Ompteda, *Nachlass*, iii. 231–36.
[3] To Aberdeen, Sept. 1, 1813 : Balfour, *Life*, i. 82. Wessenberg to Metternich, Sept. 21, 1813 : *Vienna St. A.* Wessenberg asked for half the

It was now, therefore, that he first produced the scheme for an Alliance against France which should continue in peace as well as in war and give some unity to Europe in future danger. He began to draft the project early in September, and the documents were signed on the 18th, but could not be dispatched till nearly the end of the month, the Packets being detained by contrary winds. They were in a sense a reply to all the discussions of Reichenbach and Prague as well as a plan for the establishment of what he considered to be the basis of a permanent peace. They were also an effort to assert Britain's place in the negotiations to prevent such discussions being carried on again without her knowledge. And, finally, they were an attempt to weld the system of treaties between the individual Powers into one comprehensive instrument, which should place the coalition beyond the reach of dissolution by Napoleon's diplomacy. In fact, he wished to turn the coalition into an Alliance to win the war and safeguard the peace.

Cathcart was to be the principal negotiator and the Tsar's consent was first to be secured, though Prussia, Austria, and Sweden were to be approached at the same time, so that the treaty might include all the Great Powers. Spain, Portugal, and Sicily, he thought, might accede at a later date. "The present Confederacy," he wrote, "may be considered as the union of nearly the whole of Europe against the unbounded and faithless ambition of an individual. It comprehends not only all the great monarchies, but a great proportion of the secondary Powers. It is not more distinguished from former Confederacies against France by the number and magnitude of the Powers engaged than by the national character which the war has assumed throughout the respective states. On former occasions it was a contest of sovereigns, in some instances, perhaps, against the prevailing sentiment of their subjects; it is now a struggle dictated by the feelings of the people of all ranks as well as by the necessity of the case. The

muskets in the British arsenals, more than he expected, so that the demand could be cut down " car dans ce pays-ci on marchande en toute chose." Jacobi for his part appealed to the Prince Regent himself on the question of arms, on the ground that at his first audience the Prince had told him that Prussia would find in England all that she needed ! (Jacobi to the Prince Regent : Aug. 31, 1813, *Berlin St. A.*).

sovereigns of Europe have at last confederated together for their common safety, having in vain sought that safety in detached and insulated compromises with the enemy. They have successively found that no extent of submission could procure for them either safety or repose, and that they no sooner ceased to be objects of hostility themselves than they were compelled to become instruments in the hands of France for effectuating the conquest of other unoffending states. The present Confederacy may, therefore, be pronounced to originate in higher motives and to rest upon more solid principles than any of those that have preceded it, and the several Powers to be bound together for the first time by one paramount consideration of an imminent and common danger."

The objects were fully avowed. Cathcart was authorised to "urge the importance of such a direct pledge and avowal between all the Powers engaged in the war, from the distrust which the late negotiations for what was termed 'Preliminaries of a continental peace to serve as a basis of a general peace' were calculated to inspire." Castlereagh was convinced, he said, "that the Allies never thought for a moment of signing an engagement in separation from the Prince Regent." But he pointed out the risks run by the British army in Spain if the armistice had been protracted, and ordered Cathcart to "press the necessity not only of mutual engagements but that any preliminaries to be hereafter listened to must be general and not partial. They must explicitly provide for the main interests of all the Powers, and not leave it open to the enemy, first to satisfy certain claims in the hope of sowing jealousy and disunion. . . ."

He hardly alluded to the clauses which committed the Powers to "a perpetual defensive Alliance for the maintenance of such peace and for the mutual protection of their respective states," and "that in case of attack hereafter by France on any one of the said High Contracting Parties, the several Powers will support the party so attacked with all their forces if necessary, and see justice done." The idea as yet had only a secondary place in his mind, since the war had yet to be won, but this proposal in which it was first given expression was the foundation of all the subsequent attempts to construct a European Alliance.

Such a treaty, which implied common negotiation, obviously necessitated a restatement of war aims. These Castlereagh also supplied, in nine articles which, as he explained, were founded on those laid down by Russia and Prussia at Wurschen. He had, however, made considerable extensions. The independence of the whole of Germany and Italy was more rigidly laid down, the separation of Holland from France was added, and for the first time the phrase "with an adequate barrier" appeared, while provision was made for Norway and Naples.[1]

Nothing, it should be noted, was said about maritime rights. Lieven, when Castlereagh communicated the draft to him, asked what was to happen if France insisted on discussing them. Castlereagh replied that maritime rights never had been discussed at a Congress, and he was not going to allow them to be so now. Still less was he prepared to bring into discussion the dispute with the United States. He devoted a special dispatch to this subject, because he had reason to suspect that both Lieven and the Tsar held very different views regarding it.

Nor was anything specific said as to the colonial conquests. These were thus held in reserve as a control over the conclusion of peace. It must be admitted that in so doing Castlereagh was asking much from his Allies. Britain was to be consulted on all points of the European settlement, but they had not been informed, except in the most general manner, as to the conquests which were to be returned from France. Yet if there were serious negotiations for a general peace, this subject must infallibly be raised by Napoleon.

Castlereagh seems to have thought that this great project could be obtained by his Ambassadors with comparatively small trouble and energy. Parliament was to meet on November 4, and it was essential that the Cabinet should be assured of the intentions of the continental Powers before they asked for financial support for them in the coming year. The financial weapon was, indeed, what Castlereagh relied

[1] To Cathcart (Nos. 65, 66, Private), Sept. 18, 1813 : *B.D.* 19–29.

upon to secure his ends. Lieven immediately asked about
subsidies when the treaty was submitted to him. Castlereagh made it abundantly clear that future subsidies were to
depend on the Allies agreeing to his terms.

He did not, he explained for the benefit of Metternich,
object to all negotiation, but he deprecated negotiation while
the Allies were still without a common instrument on which
negotiations could be based : "When the Confederacy is
placed beyond the reach of Bonaparte's cunning, as I flatter
myself it is of his arms, they may receive a proposition for
peace or they may make one at a suitable moment, but don't
let them countenance proceedings which are calculated to
create a doubt whether they are fighting or negotiating. . . .
The only invigorating remedy is a common Alliance." [1]

This point he made more emphatic to Aberdeen, though he
had been inclined to accept his Ambassador's view of Metternich: "I am inclined to think it best to make a hero of him,
and, by giving him a reputation, to incite him to sustain it."
He sent Aberdeen Münster's views on Germany, but warned
him to keep out of German politics as much as possible. But
when, a day or two later, he received from Wessenberg the
correspondence between Metternich and Maret after the
Congress of Prague, he reiterated with great emphasis the
point which he had made to Cathcart. In a long dispatch he
insisted on the dangers of a Congress before the basis of peace
was fixed. Such a proceeding could only enfeeble the Allied
efforts without obtaining any corresponding advantages.

"The question is still at issue," he urged, "whether an
individual shall hold the rest of Europe in subjection, or
whether, after long suffering and hopeless submission, the
Great Powers shall now deliver themselves from bondage,
and resume their former station in the Commonwealth of
Europe. This is, in its nature, an issue of arms and not of
diplomacy, and it seems as yet undecided in the temper of
either parties.

" When Bonaparte proposes a Congress let him state the
principles on which he is ready to negotiate, and it will be
then in the power of the Allies, comparing them with the

---

[1] To Cathcart, Sept. 21, 27, 1813 : *B.D.* 29, 31.

acknowledged principles which bind them together, to judge
whether discussion can be advisable on such a basis. It may
also be open to the Allies to propose, at a suitable moment,
terms of their own, but in dealing with such an enemy, and
meaning to require an arrangement which is to give peace to
Europe, they ought not to hazard a premature proposition,
which, if unsupported by corresponding successes, would
afford advantages in point of impression to their antagonist."

To Wessenberg, too, he spoke in the same manner, though
he protested that England did not want war without end.
"Do not think," he added of Napoleon, "that we are aiming
at his dynasty"—words which Wessenberg thought might be
passed on to Napoleon himself. The Ambassador pretended
to be convinced that the Government would have refused all
negotiation but for fear of the Opposition, "who much approve
of the moderation of the Court of Vienna and desire peace,"
though at the same time he admitted that the mere word of
peace had become "almost a signal of alarm" in Britain.
The truth was that Castlereagh did not want negotiations
until Napoleon was either overthrown or pushed back beyond
the Rhine, but his consent to discuss the question arose, not
from fear of the Opposition, but from doubts as to the steadfastness of his Allies.[1]

It was, perhaps, this deep anxiety that caused his health to
break down at this time. For long news was denied to him,
since heavy gales kept his own instructions from reaching his
envoys, and at the same time delayed their accounts of the all-
important negotiations entrusted to them. The report from
France of a vast conscription was disquieting, and he could
hear of nothing of the same kind from his Allies. He awaited
anxiously word that the Tyrol was up once more. In the
middle of the month he heard from Lieven of the Toeplitz
treaties. He approved the general outline "*so far as it goes*,"
he told Cathcart, but by no means accepted the Ambassadors'
complacent acquiescence in the omission of all reference to
Spain. They were ordered to protest vigorously forthwith,
and it was again hinted that British subsidies depended on

[1] To Aberdeen, Sept. 21, 28, 1813: *B.D.* 97, 98. Wessenberg to
Metternich, Sept. 21, 24, 27, 28, 1813: *Vienna St. A.*

some notice being taken of her special war aims.   Aberdeen's precipitate action with regard to Murat was also approved, but he was warned that only active assistance on the part of the King of Naples could justify it.   Some reference was also made to the colonial conquests.   The restoration of the Dutch colonies, it was now first insisted, depended upon "the absolute separation of Holland from France," and "the adequacy of the securities to be provided for the future independence of that country."

These instructions were written from Dover Castle, where he and Liverpool had gone to repair their health, which the labour and anxiety of the summer had visibly affected.   He added to them urgent appeals not to rely on negotiation for victory, but to organise the national spirit of Europe.   "It is become a contest of nations to all intents and purposes," he told Cathcart.   "The people are now the only barrier," he warned Aberdeen, and betrayed extreme anxiety less Metternich's cleverness might play into Napoleon's hands.   To his brother he even sent advice on the strategy of the campaign, but he ended in the same note: "They must tell their people the truth, namely that they have nothing to trust to *but their own exertions.*" [1]

Ill-health, no doubt, is partly responsible for the tone of these appeals.   But relief was soon to come.   While they were being penned, the armies of the Continent were converging into a veritable battle of the nations, the result of which was to change entirely the whole European situation.

[1] To Cathcart, Oct. 14, 1813 : *B.D.* 34 ; Oct. 15, 1813 : *F.O. Russia,* 83.   To Aberdeen, Oct. 15, 1813 (Private) : *B.D.* 102 ; Oct. 15, 1813 (Nos. 20, 21) : *F.O. Austria,* 101.   To Stewart, Oct. 14, 1813 : *Lond. MSS.*   Jacobi to Hardenberg, Oct. 12, 1813 : *Berlin St. A.*

4. THE FRANKFORT PROPOSALS

In October, all the three armies of the coalition gradually converged on Leipzig, though it was only with difficulty that Bernadotte's forces were got on to the scene in time to make the victory complete. For this Sir Charles Stewart is entitled to a good deal of credit; since he certainly added volume and power to the reproaches which Bernadotte's Swedish, as well as Prussian subordinates were addressing to the Crown Prince. Written were at last added to verbal entreaties on the critical day, and the result was an explosion of Gascon wrath. But the victory of Leipzig wiped out all the past, at least for the moment, and there was general reconciliation and mutual congratulation when the Sovereigns and their generals met on October 19, after the most sanguinary and decisive battle of the war. Stewart's energy was redoubled by the victory, and his description of the battle, sent off on the morning of October 19, outstripped by many days those of Cathcart and Aberdeen, and appeared in the *Gazette*. He forwarded at the same time an account of Napoleon's important conversation with Merveldt, which Wilson had obtained and sent to Aberdeen. Both of these were furious at what they considered a shabby trick to obtain all the credit. Napoleon, whose strategy and tactics were alike unworthy of him, drew off enough troops, nearly all Frenchmen, to defeat his latest foe at Hanau, where Wrede only made his Bavarians fight for political reasons. But only a handful of the Grand Army found refuge behind the Rhine, and Napoleon's German vassals hastened to make peace with the victorious coalition. All got favourable terms modelled on, though not equalling, those given to Bavaria. To the King of Saxony alone was mercy denied, though some of his troops had changed sides in the course of the battle. Austria could do nothing for him, and he was sent as prisoner to Berlin, whose monarch intended to make Saxony the compensation of his own efforts.[1]

Only where Davoust and the Danes still held fast in the north was there now any resistance in Germany to the conquerors, and Stein's opportunity seemed to have come. Except on the great point of Saxony, however, Metternich had already out-manœuvred him, and elsewhere his Council had little real power. But this was hardly yet apparent, and Stewart was much concerned for Hanoverian interests, which he considered threatened by "the influence that Baron Stein has had in all this concern."

Bernadotte was also at last free to attack the Danes, which meant that he would occupy the Electorate. Stewart was urgent to protect it from him and also from the Duke of Cumberland, who seemed likely to take advantage of Bernadotte's favour to exercise royal authority. He went off himself to supervise British interests, writing the Duke a stiff letter warning him not to come.[2]

Cathcart and Aberdeen meanwhile accompanied the Emperors across Germany to Frankfort, which was for the next two months to be the scene of negotiation. Castlereagh's important instructions had not been received by his Ambassadors until October 18. The whole situation had now changed, and it was difficult to deal with such a project amidst the tumultuous scenes which accompanied the great victory. Stewart wished to attack the problem at once, but Cathcart refused and he had the final word. He had but little idea as to the magnitude and difficulty of his task. "I think there is nothing proposed," he wrote from Leipzig, "which will occasion much difficulty or delay, and if it had arrived a day sooner it might perhaps have been signed here." When, however, he tackled the Tsar at Ansbatt, he found that

[1] From Stewart, Oct. 17, 1813: Alison, *Lives*, ii. 107; Oct. 23, 1813: *F.O. Prussia*, 90. From Thornton, Oct. 17, 22, 1813: *F.O. Sweden*, 83. Thornton claimed credit for suggesting the joint letter to Bernadotte, which is dated Halle, Oct. 18, and was signed by Thornton, Vincent, Pozzo di Borgo, Krusemarck, and Sir Charles Stewart. Suchtelen's influence was against action. Blücher's resolution decided the crossing of the Elbe.

[2] From Stewart, Oct. 23, 1813; Stewart to Cathcart, Oct. 30, 1813 (at night): *F.O. Prussia*, 90. Stewart to the Duke of Cumberland, Oct. 31, 1813: *Lond. MSS.*

Lieven's report had arrived and he was immediately confronted with the questions of maritime rights, colonies, and subsidies. He gave such answers as he could, but all that he obtained was permission for Aberdeen and Stewart also to open the question with their Courts. Bernadotte, at the express desire of the Tsar, was to be left out—a step of great significance in the history of the Alliance, but the motive of which was at present no more than a distrust of his immediate conduct.[1]

If the Tsar was lukewarm, Metternich was occupied with matters which he hoped would make all such negotiations unnecessary. The objects of the coalition had, in his opinion, now been attained and he was eager for peace. In his new plan he was to have the earnest co-operation of Aberdeen, who had been deeply moved by the terrible scenes which he had witnessed. The ride across the Leipzig battlefield, while the screams of the wounded lying amidst the masses of dead fell unheeded on the ears of the cavalcade, made an indelible impression on the sensitive nature of the young envoy and affected all his future life. He realised the horror of war as no other British Minister has ever done, and was more than ready to listen to Metternich's proposals.[2]

Metternich was already almost as much afraid of his allies as of Napoleon. He had not forgotten Poland, but for the moment it was the question of Prussia's attitude towards Saxony, so clearly revealed at Leipzig, on which he expatiated to Aberdeen. "The question of Prussian aggrandisement," reported the Ambassador, "is viewed by the Austrian Government with the utmost solicitude. . . . Nothing would induce

---

[1] From Cathcart, Oct. 21, 1813 : *F.O. Supplement (Russia)*, 343; Oct. 30, 1813 : *B.D.* 35. From Stewart, Oct. 21, 1813; Cathcart to Stewart, Nov. 1, 1813 : *F.O. Prussia*, 90. *Bath Archives*, ii. 315–16.

[2] " Oct. 22. For three or four miles the ground is covered with bodies of men and horses, many not dead. Wretches wounded unable to crawl, crying for water amidst heaps of putrefying bodies. Their screams are heard at an immense distance, and still ring in my ears." Nov. 3. " The most affecting sight I think I ever beheld, I have seen to-day. Houses were burning : the owners of these cottages in the deepest misery and their children were playing around, and were quite delighted with the fire which consumed the whole property of their parents and condemned them to cold and hunger. . . . I do not know when I have felt more severely the wretchedness of mankind. . . . I pray God we may be near to a termination of these horrors." Balfour, *Life*, i. 125, 129.

Austria to agree to the incorporation of Saxony in Prussia."
It was only natural, therefore, that Metternich should convince Aberdeen that Castlereagh's letters of September were
sufficient warrant to open negotiations. He enjoined on him
the strictest secrecy and persuaded him easily enough to
conceal the plan from Cathcart and Stewart, who, he knew,
were not likely to be sympathetic. "In consequence of the
British answer being received," reported Aberdeen with
obvious satisfaction, "it has been determined to open a communication with Bonaparte, but in such a manner as to give
rise to as little speculation as possible, and indeed the whole
affair is to be kept a profound secret." [1]

Accident had furnished the opportunity. Baron St.
Aignan, Caulaincourt's brother-in-law, French Minister at
Weimar, who had been taken prisoner and threatened with
captivity in Russia, appealed to Metternich, who procured his
release and invited him to Frankfort, where the sovereigns
and their suites assembled in the early days of November.
Bernadotte was absent in the north and Stewart was with
him, looking after Hanover. The British representatives
were reinforced by Lord Burghersh, Lord Westmorland's
son, who had been sent out as military representative to
the Austrian Army. He received but a cold welcome; for
Wilson was furious, and the Austrian soldiers and Metternich,
to whom Wessenberg had already described Burghersh as a
"disagreeable spy," supported Wilson's complaints at being
superseded. Aberdeen took the same point of view, and
Burghersh found himself in a very unpleasant position until
the result of his energetic protests to Castlereagh and Lord
Westmorland could be known at headquarters.   He was
consoled by the appearance of his charming wife, a niece of
the Duke of Wellington, who insisted on joining him at
headquarters and was made much of in the brilliant society
which gathered round the banker's wife, Madame Bethman,
whose charms, though a little faded, brought some relief to
the harassed soldiers and statesmen. [2]

---

[1] From Aberdeen, Oct. 29, 30, 1813 : *F.O. Austria*, 101.
[2] Burghersh's private letters on this subject are in *Lond. MSS.*
Wessenberg to Metternich, Sept. 17, 1813 : *Vienna St. A.* Balfour, *Life*,
i. 145. Randolph, *Wilson Diary*, ii. 219–21.

It was in this interval of comparative peace that Metternich again approached St. Aignan on November 8. He
wished, he said, to send an answer to the offer which Napoleon
had made to Merveldt during the battle of Leipzig. In this
conversation Napoleon had shewn himself disposed to give
up all control over Germany, perhaps over Italy as well; but
he had inveighed against the *intransigeance* of Britain, who
was determined, he said, to limit France's fleet to thirty sail
of the line, an indignity to which she would never submit.
This, said Metternich, was a false view, the Allies were ready
to make peace, and England, above all, was far more reasonable
than Napoleon allowed. He now offered France her 'natural
frontiers' as a basis of negotiations, which would leave
Belgium, though not Holland, in French territory. But by
far the best method of approach to his allies was the informal
and confidential, and Metternich proposed that St. Aignan
should see Nesselrode and Aberdeen, as if by accident, at his
rooms on the morrow. With these he then had a long conference, and Aberdeen entered with enthusiasm into his views.
He had already written to Gentz: "England is satisfied:
for the power of France is now reduced within legitimate
bounds, and this is all that England ever desired." But he
knew that Stewart and Cathcart would not support this view,
and he was even more urgent for secrecy than Metternich,
insisting that St. Aignan should not see either of the Emperors
before his departure, as had been intended. He also wished
the terms of peace to be fixed as low as possible, instead of
stating them high for bargaining purposes, in order that they
might be made "with the hope of being accepted. . . . If the
proposition were made without any such hope, I deprecated
the whole proceeding as being most erroneous in principle,
and calculated to produce the greatest injury to the common
cause."

Next day these plans were carried out to the letter. Metter-
nich again saw St. Aignan and discussed the terms with him.
Nesselrode entered claiming to represent Hardenberg also.
St. Aignan now proposed that he should reduce the terms to
writing. Metternich had suggested the natural frontiers,
France giving up all influence in Germany and Italy, while

independent states were to be established between the
Austrian and French frontiers. The absolute independence
of Holland was stipulated, but its precise frontier as well as
form of government was to be a matter of discussion. St.
Aignan refused to be impressed by this moderation, but added
by various subtleties to the content of the offer. Thus when
it was stated that France was not to exercise any influence
in Germany outside her natural limits of the Alps, Rhine,
and Pyrenees, he excepted "the natural and indispensable
influence which every powerful state must exercise over its
weaker neighbours." He made also a special point of
Metternich's statement about maritime rights which he
developed into the phrase "que l'Angleterre était prête à
faire les plus grands sacrifices pour la paix fondée sur ces
bases, et à reconnaître la liberté du commerce et de la navigation, à laquelle la France a droit de prétendre." [1]

Then Aberdeen entered, as had been planned, and the note
was read over to him. He naturally demurred at the phrase
about maritime rights, which had to be read a second time,
complaining that it was too vague. Metternich would have
erased the last part of the sentence, but when St. Aignan
replied that it was then made even more vague, Aberdeen
agreed that the original phrase should be restored. He seems
to have had no suspicion that its inclusion might very well
make the maritime rights one of the subjects of the future
discussions.

"I particularly cautioned him," he explained to Castlereagh,
"against supposing that any possible consideration could
induce Great Britain to abandon a particle of what she felt
to belong to her maritime code, from which in no case could
she ever recede, but that, with this understanding, she had
no wish to interfere with the reasonable pretensions of France.
I took this opportunity to contradict the assertion which
Bonaparte had made to General Merveldt of the intention of
the British Government to limit him to thirty ships of the
line, and declared that, so far as I knew, it was a prejudice
without any foundation. Of course the whole transaction and

[1] Aberdeen in his account translates the phrase " could with justice
pretend," but the French word 'droit' carries, of course, a much wider
implication.

interview were understood to be perfectly unofficial, and merely following up the conversation which Bonaparte had recently held with General Merveldt. . . .

" I trust your Lordship will not disapprove of the part which I have taken in this affair. My great object, if any propositions were made, was to frame them so as to afford the greatest probability of success consistent with the fixed policy of the Allies. I hope the communication which has been made will be found to embrace the most essential points, and to demand as much as our actual situation entitles us to expect. My next object was that the whole transaction should be conducted with the utmost secrecy and expedition." [1]

It might have been expected that in dealing with a matter of such great importance Aberdeen would at least have consulted Cathcart. On the contrary, he was even more anxious than Metternich to get St. Aignan on his way to France and his own account forwarded to London before his colleague heard a word about the transaction. Cathcart only knew on the 9th that Aberdeen had sent off a courier without informing him, and protested mildly to Castlereagh at such a step. It says much for his equable temperament that, when he was informed by the Tsar of the interview with St. Aignan, he should have taken the whole affair very easily and even approved of it—so far as he was allowed to know what had happened.

The vigilant Jackson was not so easily satisfied. He also had only a vague account from Hardenberg, who suggested that the whole affair was not of great importance, but casually mentioned that of course they must await the issue before going any further with the treaty of Alliance. Hardenberg had no wish to leave the left bank of the Rhine in French hands, but he was powerless against Metternich, and had been misled by a stupid report of Jacobi's that the British Government were anxious for peace. Jackson hastened to inform Stewart, who shared Bernadotte's indignation at their exclusion from these negotiations. He was far from approving of all the conduct of the Prince Royal, whom he thought

---

[1] From Aberdeen, Nov. 8, 9, 1813 : *B.D.* 107, 109. Report of St. Aignan and his note, Nov. 9, 1813 : D'Angeberg, *Congrès de Vienne*, i. 73–76. *Cf.* Mendelssohn-Bartholdy, *Briefe von Gentz an Pilat*, i. 92.

quite mad, but he agreed with him in his criticism of the new plan of campaign, from the making of which the author of the Trachenberg scheme had been entirely excluded. He came to Frankfort, therefore, in no sweet temper and roundly condemned both the manner and the substance of the transaction with St. Aignan, of which, however, he was as yet only imperfectly informed, not having seen the famous minute.[1]

Had Napoleon immediately accepted the basis of the Frankfort proposals there can be no doubt but that peace negotiations would have begun immediately. But the answer which Maret sent back on the 18th was entirely noncommittal and simply asked for a Congress. Metternich's reply, which merely insisted on the basis being first accepted, was harmless enough, though it made the transaction an official one, but Aberdeen had again agreed to the answer without consulting or informing his colleagues, and Stewart was denied all information by Hardenberg. It was only a threat to ask for his passports which at length extracted from the harassed Chancellor St. Aignan's minute and the last correspondence. Jackson and Stewart then sent home a long dispatch which protested strongly against the omission of Norway and Sicily, and of course at the introduction of the maritime rights into the discussion. It was only Jackson's persuasion that induced the indignant Stewart not to demand his instant recall.[2]

Meanwhile Aberdeen had gone imperturbably on his way. He had begun to discuss the treaty of Alliance, and Metternich encouraged him to believe that he would be able to complete this negotiation also on his own account, offering to be the intermediary with the Tsar. So great was Aberdeen's trust

[1] From Cathcart, Nov. 8, 1813: *F.O. Supplement (Russia)*, 343; Nov. 10, 1813: *B.D.* 36. Jackson to Stewart, Nov. 11, 1813: *B.D.* 87; Nov. 8, 1813; From Stewart, Nov. 15, 1813: *F.O. Prussia*, 91. *Bath Archives*, ii. 352–53. The report of Jacobi's caused much trouble and correspondence, as Castlereagh insisted on an explanation. Wessenberg attributed the unfortunate mistake, which had some influence on affairs at this crisis, to old age, lack of memory, an imperfect understanding of English, and an excessive itch for writing (Wessenberg to Metternich, Dec. 3, 1813: *Vienna St. A.*). Jacobi's dispatch had, as a matter of fact, been exaggerated in Berlin and the old gentleman never ceased to protest bitterly against the charge of misrepresentation made against him (Jacobi to Hardenberg, Nov. 30, Dec. 1, 3, 1813: *Berlin St. A.*).

[2] From Stewart, Nov. 28, 1813: *B.D.* 89. *Bath Archives*, ii. 368, 371, 375.

in Metternich that he presumed to lecture Castlereagh on his insular suspicions. "Do not think Metternich such a formidable personage," he wrote on the 12th; "depend upon it, I have the most substantial reasons for knowing that he is heart and soul with us: but, my dear Castlereagh, with all your wisdom, judgment, and experience, which are as great as possible and which I respect sincerely, I think you have so much of the Englishman as not quite to be aware of the real value of foreign modes of acting. . . . Now do not be afraid of me. There is a sort of half confidence and intimacy which Ambassadors may enjoy which perhaps is likely to mislead. My intercourse with Metternich is of another description. Living with him at all times, and in all situations, is it possible I should not know him? If indeed he were the most subtle of mankind, he might certainly impose on one little used to deceive, but this is not his character. He is, I repeat it to you, not a very clever man. He is vain; but he is a good Austrian. He may, perhaps, like the appearance of negotiation a little too much, but he is to be trusted. . . . He is at this moment the main support of warlike measures."

With this view it was only natural that he should accept Metternich's assurances about the treaty of Alliance: "Prince Metternich considers the affair, so far as Austria is concerned, a work of supererogation: but he is not less anxious to fulfil the wishes of the British Government." It was with the Tsar, explained Metternich, that the difficulty lay. Cathcart had, indeed, been long trying, in vain, to overcome Alexander's objections to signing the treaty immediately; for the Tsar, apparently, viewed the whole proposal with profound suspicion. The demand to exclude Sweden, the Ambassador easily accepted, though both Stewart and Aberdeen protested; but to two other conditions he had not the authority, even if he had the desire, to agree. The Tsar wished the treaty to include the subsidies for the coming year and the details of the colonies which Britain would return for the sake of peace. He carried his suspicions so far that he even wished to insert a clause concerning the continuance of the British army in Spain. Moreover, he refused to accept the outline of the new Europe which Castlereagh had attached to the treaty. Various objections were made, but the motive was clear; and it was Metternich's as much, probably more, than the Tsar's. If Britain would not bind herself to details on the colonial side, why should the Allies do so on the continental? These were fundamental difficulties with which, we shall see, Castlereagh himself found it hard to deal and of which Cathcart had only just begun to perceive the importance. The discussions, therefore, dragged on without result throughout the month of November. The Tsar and Metternich, indeed, were much more interested in the consequences of St. Aignan's overture than in the treaty of Alliance.

Aberdeen had been quite ready to take on Cathcart's job as well as his own, and his senior shewed no jealousy. He relied on his intimacy and influence with Metternich, who left all the opposition to Nesselrode and professed himself ready to agree. When Nesselrode was stubborn, Metternich still assured his friend that he would "*answer for making* Nesselrode agree to it at last," adding, "And now, my dear A[berdeen], make my compliments to Lord Castlereagh and ask him what is the next proof of our zeal and confidence which he requires." [1]

Aberdeen fully believed all these promises, though there is reason to suspect that the three Powers had already agreed that the treaty should not be signed forthwith. He boasted of them to Stewart and Jackson, who had already fulfilled their part by getting Hardenberg's consent to the Alliance in writing. But somehow the treaty hung fire. It was pushed on one side by numerous other matters, the preparations of war and the Declaration to the French people which Metternich was preparing. At last, on November 28, the Ambassador was able to announce triumphantly his complete success: "The treaty of General Alliance *will positively be made forthwith.* The difficulties have not been few or slight, but M[etternich] has made a point of bringing your unjust suspicions of Austria to shame. Now, pray observe, these are not fine words only but *facts*, and pretty important too. I await your *amende honorable.* There is only this difference,

[1] From Cathcart, Nov. 11, 1813: *B.D.* 37; *F.O. Supplement (Russia)*, 343. From Aberdeen, Nov. 12, 1813: Balfour, *Life*, i. 154; Nov. 14, 1813: *F.O. Austria*, 103.

that the Emperor wishes the treaty should be executed in London. To this there can be no objection."

The Ambassador had, however, been completely gulled. He soon found that Metternich had promised more than he could perform, or, as we may suspect, than he ever intended. Russia continued to make the same objections, and in the final stages Metternich shewed himself also stubborn, insisting on the necessity of obtaining a list of the colonial conquests, without which he still lacked the necessary control over the negotiations for peace which he still hoped would soon begin. Russia also remained firm, and refused to compromise at the last minute when Cathcart, now that Hardenberg had promised to sign, still had hopes of success. Metternich professed the greatest concern at this unfortunate situation and offered Aberdeen a written undertaking of his readiness to accept the Alliance—a safe enough concession since Russia had prevented its signature. Aberdeen nobly refused this gift lest it might prejudice Metternich in the eyes of the Tsar, who had already other serious grievances against him.[1]

The final *dénouement* caused an explosion at headquarters. It was decided by the three Powers to refer the whole matter to London. This step had been previously discussed, but its sudden adoption at this moment was due to the receipt of another note from Napoleon on December 5, signed by Caulaincourt (whose appointment to Maret's post was an earnest of peace), which accepted the Frankfort terms and asked that negotiations should be begun. Had it come earlier it might have been at once accepted; but the Tsar had become much less disposed to peace in the course of the last week, owing to Stein's arrival in Frankfort and to growing suspicions of Metternich. Nevertheless, some preparation must be made to discuss terms with Napoleon, and one of the difficulties was the position of the three representatives of Britain, who were not in agreement with one another and had not powers to act with authority. It was determined, therefore, to appeal to London, and special instructions of the greatest importance were sent by Pozzo di Borgo, who set

[1] From Cathcart, Nov. 17, 24, Dec. 4, 1813: *B.D.* 39, 41, 45. From Aberdeen, Nov. 25, 28, Dec. 4, 1813; Balfour, *Life*, i. 162–67; Dec. 5, 1813: *F.O. Austria*, 103.

out on December 6, not only to get the project of the Alliance altered to include the subsidies and the colonial conquests, but also to ask that one person should be designated to represent Britain at headquarters with authority to make grave decisions. Metternich's letter to Wessenberg was especially insistent on this point. He had by this time apparently had enough of Aberdeen and hoped that either Wellesley or Canning would be sent out. Hardenberg, for his part, tried to impress Jacobi with the necessity of soothing British feelings on the question of maritime rights.[1]

Even Aberdeen was not informed of these decisions until Pozzo di Borgo had left, and then only to a degree. Neither he nor Cathcart made much objection, since it was obvious that nothing more could be done at headquarters. But Stewart, who had been kept much more in the dark, was furious at this unexpected decision. When he was not immediately informed of Caulaincourt's note, he obtained it by bribing one of Metternich's clerks and sent Jackson home with instructions to get there before Pozzo di Borgo. Cathcart, whom neither Stewart's outbursts nor Aberdeen's secretiveness could ruffle, mildly deprecated this conduct, which naturally produced something like a sensation at headquarters. He had himself a much better idea of the whole position than either of his brother Ambassadors. It had been Metternich quite as much as the Tsar, in spite of all his protestations to Aberdeen, who had been responsible for the rejection of the treaty. "I have neither on this nor on any former occasion," Cathcart summed up, "found the Emperor so much averse to a general treaty of Alliance offensive and defensive, as proposed by your Lordship, as the Ministers are. The language of Prince Metternich on the subject of specifying in a treaty of this sort the conquests, which Great Britain would keep or bring into negotiation, has been stated. I do not see the object of calling for this declaration unless it be to take out of the hands of Great

---

[1] Metternich to Wessenberg, Dec. 6, 1813: *Vienna St. A.* Nesselrode to Lieven, Dec. 6, 1813: *Vienna St. A.* Hardenberg to Jacobi, Dec. 6, 1813: *Berlin St. A.* From Cathcart, Dec. 9, 12, 1813: *B.D.* 51, 55. From Aberdeen, Dec. 9, 1813: *B.D.* 118; do. *F.O. Austria*, 103. Metternich to Hudelist, Dec. 16, 1813: Fournier, *Congress von Châtillon*, 246.

Britain the preponderance in the negotiations which must arise from the important circumstance of being the only Power which has conquests to restore. But His Imperial Majesty will not decide without the Allies to agree to this treaty, and although Prince Metternich attributes the opposition to Russia, he is the only person who is eloquent in supporting that opposition, and it neither occurred to the Emperor nor to Count Nesselrode till after consultation with him."

That Metternich should take this attitude was to be expected. He had as much right to wish to extend his influence over the negotiations as Castlereagh. That he cared but little for Belgium and much for Saxony and Poland was in the nature of things. But the deceit which he practised on Aberdeen was hardly fair towards one so honest and sincere; yet Aberdeen's self-confidence—indeed a harsher term is needed—above all, his desire to obtain the credit for the negotiations and to be put in a different position to Cathcart and Stewart, an ambition for which Lord Abercorn was largely responsible, deserved the punishment which they obtained. It is impossible not to agree with George Canning's view that he was "entirely unequal to his situation—probably from thinking himself imó suprà." Fortunately he never realised how much he had been Metternich's dupe; but the receipt of Full Powers, in which Cathcart's name by a natural routine decision was placed first, put the finishing touches to his discomfiture by reminding him that he was not in sole charge of Britain's interests. He would have carried out his desire to return home, for which he had also urgent private reasons, had not Metternich and Nesselrode previously informed him that they had asked that he should represent Britain at the impending negotiations.[1]

Leipzig brought headquarters much nearer Castlereagh, but as Hamburg was still in French hands it was not until December that a short route was open to the Continent, and even then bad weather held up the Packets. He was thus too far off these extraordinary events to exercise control over them, and it was not until the close of the year that their

[1] From Cathcart, Dec. 12, 1813 : *B.D.* 55. Balfour, *Life*, i. 167, 173. *Bath Archives*, ii. 361. Lane Poole, *Life of Stratford Canning*, i. 202.

real significance became clear. The Leipzig victory naturally increased the desire and will for complete victory over
Napoleon. New plans were made for Germany and, above all,
for Holland. Indeed Holland was considered as of little use
without its 'barrier,' which it was now hoped would comprise
the whole of Belgium. While the Allies were still offering
the 'natural frontiers,' public opinion in Britain had gone
much further and was already looking forward to driving
back France inside the 'ancient frontiers' from which she
had emerged twenty years before. The ancient frontiers
naturally turned men's minds to the ancient family, and the
Bourbons were at length remembered as something more than
unfortunate refugees. Whispers began which soon grew into
murmurs, and before the year was out swelled into a loud
uproar that Napoleon must be dethroned. They were loudest
at Carlton House, but soon spread in all directions.

Castlereagh and his Cabinet shared these feelings, but they
were more aware of the difficulties of translating them into
fact through the armies of other Powers. Wellington was
already crossing the Pyrenees. They wished to add to this
pressure a British effort in the Netherlands. The Prince of
Orange had been in England since the end of April, having
travelled *via* Stockholm, where Bernadotte's good wishes had
been added to those which he claimed to have received from
the Tsar and the King of Prussia. His equivocal conduct in
past years made him rather an unwelcome guest, and Bathurst
at any rate would have preferred that his son, who continued
to receive Wellington's warm praise, should be made the
leader of any expedition. But the young Prince, though he
visited England, refused to act in any way as the rival of his
father, who, advised by the old Lord Malmesbury and Henry
Fagel, behaved with discretion, and Castlereagh intimated that
he was prepared to support him when the time was ripe.

Early in November a memorandum had been sent to the
Allied Powers which stated that Holland was ripe for revolt
and that steps were being taken to collect arms and even
Dutch levies to assist it when it broke out. At the same time
it was pointed out that, though the allied treaties specified
the Rhine as the frontier of France, additions must be made

to the Dutch state, at least the whole of the territories of
1792, as well as Antwerp and "an adequate military frontier,"
unless one of the great military Powers of Germany was interposed as a protection between France and Holland.   Amongst
other arguments used to induce the Allies to agree to this
scheme were the importance of Holland "as the natural centre
of the money transactions of Europe," and the fact that unless
Britain felt secure from the threat of Antwerp she would have
to develop her navy and thus be unable to assist the Continent
with men and money in a future war.[1]

If Austria wished to resume her old possessions in the Low
Countries the British Government would, of course, have
been ready to support her.   But that was not very probable,
and Austria was still considered the least likely of all the
Allies to press the victory home.   Indeed, when Parliament
had assembled on November 4, she was put in the same paragraph with Bavaria in the King's speech, a slight which
caused grave offence to both Francis and his Minister.   But
Castlereagh, however much he might criticise Metternich
to Aberdeen, never intended the public to share his suspicions.
He sent glowing congratulations to Metternich on the success
of his negotiations with Bavaria, and when the Austrian
subsidy treaty came before Parliament gave such a fervent
defence of Austrian policy that even Wessenberg was moved
to admiration.   That Minister was, however, the last person
to wish the war aims of the Allies to be extended, and reported
with dismay that the British Ministry viewed the possibility
of peace with anguish.

At any rate events could not wait on Austria.   On November
15 a revolt broke out in Holland at the approach of Prussian
and Russian troops from Bernadotte's army, and was immediately successful, perhaps as much from the disorganisation of

---

[1] Bathurst to Wellington, April 28, 1813 : *W.S.D.* vii. 612.   Minute
of interview between the Prince of Orange and Castlereagh, April 27,
1813; Memorandum respecting Holland (Nov. 7, 1813) : Colenbrander,
Gedenkstukken, vi. 1876, 1950.   Professor H. T. Colenbrander's great
collection, *Gedenkstukken der Algemeene Geschiedenis van Nederland van
1795 tot 1840* (22 vols., 1905–22), contains documents from many public
and private archives, including the Foreign Office Papers in the Record
Office.   There is also an admirable study by G. J. Renier, *Great Britain
and the Establishment of the Netherlands, 1813–15* (1930), which is based on
the larger work.

the French as from any great enthusiasm on the part of the inhabitants. But the cry of 'Oranje Boven' had been raised and William had obviously to act immediately. In great haste a British fleet and an improvised force was put at his disposal, together with £100,000 in hard cash, and he was soon established at the Hague, not as Stadtholder but in a new position as "Sovereign Prince," which implied that the old republic would be transformed into a monarchy. With him Castlereagh sent the most faithful and assiduous of all his assistants during these years—the Earl of Clancarty, who was so far from intending to embrace diplomacy as a profession that he still retained, for some time, the positions which he held in the Ministry. His intimacy and affection for Castlereagh were such that the most delicate matters could be discussed between them with perfect confidence— a fortunate circumstance with regard to Holland, which was to raise some very delicate matters indeed. Thus, though Clancarty had no diplomatic experience, and was in some ways a rather reactionary Tory, he was specially fitted for this post, in which, indeed, he won the affection and praise of the Dutch statesmen by his zealous care for their interests.

Though this great success acted like wine on the spirits of the nation it also brought a new charge on both British strategy and diplomacy, which was to cause much anxiety in the following months. The past history of British expeditions to Holland was not reassuring, and the present one was to win but little military glory. Moreover, it was essential that the Peninsular forces should not be weakened by it, unless, as at one moment Bathurst even hinted, the main British effort should be transferred to the north, and Wellington was not unnaturally alarmed at its possible effects.[1]

More was hoped from Bernadotte's assistance. But he, after handing over Hanover to the Duke of Cumberland, preferred to prosecute his Danish plans and began to carry on a campaign in the north which had but little to do with the main operations against Napoleon. He deprecated moving across the Rhine and was at first strongly against the idea of

[1] Wessenberg to Metternich, Nov. 4, 12, 20, 22, 1813: *Vienna St. A.* Bathurst to Wellington, Dec. 10, 1813: *W.S.D.* viii. 413. Wellington to Bathurst, Dec. 21, 1813: *Gurwood*, xi. 386.

detaching from France the Belgian provinces, which he had himself helped to conquer. However, when he found himself left entirely out of the discussions by the allied monarchs, he yielded to Thornton's urgent entreaties, changed his tune, and said "that he was prepared to go to the utmost lengths with England in the support" of the Low Countries as an independent state, and admitted that he had previously been influenced "by a sort of repugnance at seeing the destruction of what might be considered as in part his own work." [1]

Affairs in Hanover also went through a critical stage. For though it was perhaps better that the Duke of Cumberland, in spite of the official warning from Stewart not to go, had beaten Bernadotte by a short head and received the welcome of the inhabitants, he was not likely, if left in charge, to increase their loyalty to the absent King whom they had never seen. That it still existed in full measure, Stewart proved by reporting a touching anecdote of the preservation of George III.'s bust in the University of Hanover. The Duke only enjoyed his position for a month, when he was superseded by the Duke of Cambridge, who had been hastily dispatched with Münster for that purpose. Though the Prince Regent sent Bloomfield in advance to explain the royal command as tactfully as possible, the poor Duke was reduced to tears at the loss of his new honours. But he obeyed with many protestations of loyalty, and the Duke of Cambridge and Münster soon brought order to the Electorate. Wessenberg, though he did not completely agree with Münster's views, suggested to Metternich that the Hanoverian Minister was the man to complete the defeat of Stein. Castlereagh was by no means anxious that these thorny German questions should be raised before France was defeated, and secured Münster's promise that he would not press his views on the reconstruction of the Empire at this critical moment. Castlereagh saw clearly that some Federal bond was necessary to keep out French influence, but that the time was not ripe to solve so difficult a question. [2]

[1] From Thornton, Nov. 9, 13, 28, Dec. 10, 1813 : *F.O. Sweden*, 84 ; Nov. 16, 1813 : *C.C.* ix. 76.

[2] The Duke of Cumberland to the Prince Regent, Nov. 9, 13, 26, Dec. 9, 1813 ; Bloomfield to the Prince Regent, Dec. 9, 1813 ; Duke of Cam-

When, therefore, the first news of the Frankfort proposals and the delay in the conclusion of the Alliance reached Castlereagh, the situation was already a strained and anxious one. He was naturally somewhat indignant at the Tsar's insistence on points which, he thought, he had already anticipated in his conversations with Lieven: "I cannot suppose that His Imperial Majesty can seriously expect us to propose to Parliament now to vote a scale of subsidy for an indefinite period of war, still less that we should disqualify ourselves from treating at all by stipulating by anticipation the surrender of our conquests—these suggestions would be inadmissible on the part of any Power, and are, to say the least, not very appropriate to a nation that has acted the part we have done. If these species of negotiation is persisted in, better at once decline the measure altogether. And I am yet to learn why Great Britain is more interested in cementing the Confederacy than Russia."

Of the Frankfort proposals Aberdeen's first dispatches only gave him an imperfect account, since St. Aignan's note was not included in them. He agreed to the basis of the 'natural frontiers' which Aberdeen had described, provided that the colonial conquests were employed to obtain what was necessary to the indefinite frontiers of Savoy and Holland, whose cause he particularly recommended. In a private letter he made no disguise of the unpopularity of any peace which did not confine France to her ancient limits or left Bonaparte on the throne. "We are still ready," he concluded, "to encounter with our Allies the hazards of peace, if peace can be made on the basis proposed; and we are not inclined to go out of our way to interfere in the internal government of France. . . ." He deplored the internal difficulties of the Confederacy, but pointed out the necessity of keeping it together. Above all, he pressed the necessity of wresting Antwerp from France in the well-known words: "The destruction of that arsenal is essential to our safety. To leave it in the hands of France is little short of impos-

bridge to the Prince Regent, Dec. 22, 1813: *Windsor Arch.* Instructions to Münster from the Prince Regent, Dec. 9, 1813: *F.O. Hanover*, 6. From Stewart, Nov. 2, 1813: *F.O. Prussia*, 90. To Stewart, Dec. 4, 10, 1813: *Lond. MSS.*

ing upon Great Britain the charge of a perpetual war establishment."

The same point was made in a private letter to Cathcart: "We shall feel very anxious here whilst discussions are afloat. I trust you will all enter as warmly at headquarters about supporting Holland as we do here. I must beg you never to lose sight of Antwerp and its noxious contents—recommend also the Orange cause to the Emperor's warmest protection. The popular spirit which has shewn itself there I look upon as amongst the most fortunate events of the war. It has operated here as magical—there is nothing beyond the tone of the country at this moment."

He was naturally, therefore, indignant at the conduct in the north of the Prince Royal, who was refusing to co-operate in the attack on France and was trying to buy off Denmark with territory in north Germany which could not be disposed of except as part of the general settlement. "His language of 'Every one for himself' is an unworthy instrument," Castlereagh told Thornton, "till the enemy is effectually subdued . . . the only natural course, then, is to stir no unnecessary controversy, to finish the war with vigour, and to trust to the future for an equitable settlement amongst ourselves: in which settlement it is of the first importance that Sweden should receive her advantages beyond and not on this side of the Baltic. This is of the greatest consequence, both to the future independence and the peace of the north of Europe, which can never be permanently consolidated whilst the territories of Sweden and Denmark are *morcelées* and intermixed on the opposite coasts." [1]

Bernadotte did not, however, send his troops south, and, though the position in Holland was well maintained, the Belgians shewed little disposition to emulate their northern neighbours. Nor were the Dutch people, apparently, as anxious as the Prince of Orange to extend their territory in that direction, and Clancarty much preferred that Austria should resume her ancient sway there, since the mutual

[1] To Aberdeen, Nov. 30, 1813 : *B.D.* 114 ; Nov. 30 (Private) : *C.C.* ix. 73 (where given as Nov. 13 in error). To Cathcart, Nov. 30, 1813 : *F.O. Supplement* (*Russia*), 343. To Thornton, Nov. 30, 1813 : *F.O. Sweden*, 80.

jealousy of Amsterdam and Antwerp, he thought, could never be overcome. Castlereagh shared this view to some extent at this time; but the great thing was action and military success somehow in the Netherlands, so that they might be taken from France.[1]

The anxiety about Holland was naturally much increased when the details of the Frankfort proposals became known by the subsequent dispatches. Castlereagh did not, indeed, accept his brother's criticisms of the basis, because it left out such matters as Norway. Though Clancarty supported Stewart with much fervour, Castlereagh administered a diplomatic caution against excessive zeal. But he was deeply concerned at the omission of all reference to the 'barrier' which he wanted for Holland; indeed, he now objected entirely to the phrase 'natural frontiers,' and much more to its extension to a 'natural influence' over the smaller German states, which he rightly saw might be used by Napoleon to interfere in the reorganisation of Germany. Above all, he was alarmed at the reference to maritime rights, and Aberdeen was ordered to make at once an official protest against it in a note which was, to avoid error, drafted in London. A few days later he added to this an instruction that no negotiations were to take place until the exclusion of maritime rights was accepted.[2]

His indignation had thus already grown considerably before he received the news of the failure of the negotiations for the Alliance by the arrival of Pozzo di Borgo with his instructions to the allied Ministers at London, and Jackson with his brother's warnings and entreaties. Apart from these protests, there could be no doubt of the attitude which Castlereagh would adopt. He would not even discuss officially the conditions which the Tsar and Metternich had laid down. They were peremptorily refused, and in unofficial interviews Castlereagh let the Ambassadors, and especially Lieven and Pozzo di Borgo, realise clearly what his feelings were on the subject. The whole purpose of his proposal, he said, had been mis-

---

[1] From Clancarty, Dec. 1, 14, 17, 1813: Colenbrander, *Gedenkstukken*, vii. 2, 9, 11.
[2] To Stewart, Dec. 10, 1813: *Lond. MSS.*; Dec. 17, 1813: *B.D.* 92. To Aberdeen, Dec. 7, 1813: *B.D.* 116, 117.

understood and misrepresented. It was in the interests of the Continent that the proposal had been made, not in those of Great Britain, who had shewn that she could look after herself. If he could be sure that Napoleon would no longer rule over France, he would never have advanced it: "But whilst Bonaparte shall continue to rule France, perhaps even while the system itself, which he has matured, shall continue to give impulse to the military resources of that great Empire, the only safety for other Powers of Europe is to impose upon the ambitious propensities of France that constraint in time of peace, to which alone they will owe the concessions, which may by war be extracted from the enemy." [1]

The only point which he yielded to the views of his allies was to limit the Alliance, in the first instance, to the Great Powers, a step which he now perceived was logical and necessary. Thornton had already protested against Sweden's exclusion from any knowledge of the negotiation. The Prince Royal, however, knew a good deal of what was going on, and in his indignation insinuated that the three Powers wished "to bring Great Britain alone, without an ally, into the Congress for a general peace, and by that circumstance to find themselves in a condition to dictate the terms of peace to Great Britain, meaning to threaten her, in case of refusal, with the same exclusion from the Continent which she suffered under Bonaparte, and, in fact, to renew against her that man's continental system." Even Thornton could not take this gasconade very seriously, though he supported Berna-dotte in his main contention. But Castlereagh had already dismissed Sweden's claims to be included in the negotiations, since the treaty would probably assume the form of contracting to furnish "stipulated succours" which would "far exceed her means." "The repugnance," he added, "to including the Allies generally has naturally increased since their number has been so largely augmented. It is not so much a reluctance to provide for the interests of the Allies generally as the inconvenience of multiplying the councils of the Confederacy which is felt as an objection to the original Projet." He had

[1] To Cathcart, Dec. 18, 1813 : *B.D.* 56. Wessenberg to Metternich, Dec. 12, 13, 1813 : *Vienna St. A.*

already expressed to Rehausen, the Swedish Minister in London, his doubts as to the possibility of Sweden being included in the treaty in her own interests, and Thornton was ordered to take the same line and calm "the susceptibility which prevails in the temper of the Swedish Councils and weakens their just influence and counteracts the objects they have in view." [1]

But though this difficulty was adjusted, there was no hope of concluding the Alliance at London, for the Ambassadors had no powers to deal with Castlereagh's main criticisms. The only step which they could take was one which Castle-reagh insisted should be done at once, viz. to send him formal notes agreeing to the exclusion of maritime rights from the discussions. For the rest, they supplied him with a *Projet de Traité de l'Alliance*, which they considered embodied the views of their Courts, so that he might draw up his own instructions in the light of it. This precious document restricted the Alliance to the present war and made a large number of demands, besides those connected with the colonies and subsidies, which shewed a marked distrust of Britain, even including the stipulation that Wellington should continue his offensive in France.

It was clear that British policy needed better exposition on the Continent than it had obtained in the last year. The Cabinet, therefore, found no difficulty in agreeing to the demand that the negotiations there should be placed in a single and authoritative hand. The confusion and uncertainty that had arisen was obviously partly due to the quarrels between the British representatives. None of them were adequate to a crisis in which the whole future of the Continent was involved. The delay in receiving views and transmitting instructions made it impossible to control them from London. Someone must be present on the spot who could speak with commanding authority. This could be none other than Castle-reagh, whose two years of work had already won the confidence of all his colleagues. He did, indeed, suggest Harrowby, but that shrewd statesman remembered his experiences in 1806,

---

[1] From Thornton, Nov. 29, Dec. 16, 1813 ; to Thornton, Dec. 17, 1813 : *F.O. Sweden,* 84, 80.

and with modesty and good sense insisted that Castlereagh himself should go. This decision was made on December 20 after a long Cabinet meeting, and Liverpool informed the allied representatives at a dinner-party the next day that Castlereagh had been chosen because he not only knew all the ideas of the Government but had their full confidence. They hastened to emphasise the importance of the choice to their Governments, dwelling on Castlereagh's delightful manners, but not concealing that he would bring his own views to the Council in a manner that they could scarcely forecast.[1]

So it was decided, and every day shewed the need to be more urgent. Metternich's attempts at settling the Danish question by diplomacy had naturally alarmed Bernadotte, who refused all help in Holland and wished to allow Davoust's force to return to France so as to get them away from the Danes. "His conduct," reported Colonel Lake, "makes me really sick." Thornton endeavoured to excuse him at Austrian expense, but it was clear that he had no desire to do more than secure his own objects. News had also begun to arrive of the dispute between the Tsar and Metternich over Switzerland. Metternich got his way by engineering a mild revolution, and the allied armies were thus able to infringe Swiss neutrality without opposition. But the Tsar, who had promised La Harpe to protect his birthplace, was much mortified. Though the negotiations with Murat were going well, German questions were giving anxiety, and Aberdeen wrote that "one of our new friends clearly deserves hanging," meaning the King of Wurtemberg, who had entered into a clandestine correspondence with Napoleon.[2]

Ere this letter reached him, Castlereagh had set out for the Continent. He announced his intending arrival to his three Ambassadors in letters which shewed the greatest attention

---

[1] Lieven to Nesselrode, Dec. 22, 1813: *Pet. Arch.* Wessenberg to Metternich, Dec. 22, 25, 1813 : *Vienna St. A.* Jacobi to Hardenberg, Dec. 19, 24, 26, 1813, enclosing *Projet de Traité de l'Alliance. Memorandum des plénipotentiaires de la Russie, de l'Autriche et de la Prusse. Berlin St. A.*

[2] From Stewart, Dec. 9, 1813 : *F.O. Prussia,* 91. From Aberdeen, Dec. 24, 1813 : *Lond. MSS.* The caution of the editor had altered this expression in *C.C.* ix. 110.

to their feelings. He praised what they had done, glossed over their faults, and attributed their rivalries to the inevitable friction of diplomacy, taking blame to himself that he had not arranged for them to work more closely together. Stewart and Aberdeen were encouraged to go on as if nothing had happened. He wrote as a colleague rather than a superior. "I feel confident," ran the letter to his brother, "that when we all get together at headquarters *we shall give to the whole the ensemble it requires.*" [1]

[1] To Cathcart, Dec. 22, 1813 ; to Aberdeen, Dec. 22, 1813 : *B.D.* 62, 120. To Stewart, Dec. 21, 1813 : *Lond. MSS.*

CHAPTER IV

FROM COALITION TO ALLIANCE: RECONSTRUCTION PLANNED, *JANUARY–APRIL*, 1814

" Aucun homme n'était plus propre que Lord Castlereagh à remplir une pareille mission. . . . Avec son caractère, avec ses instructions, on pouvait dire de lui que c'était Angleterre elle-même qui se déplaçait pour se rendre au camp des coalisés."—THIERS.

CHAPTER IV

1. CASTLEREAGH'S MISSION TO THE CONTINENT

PEACE now seemed to be fast approaching. Indeed, in some quarters it was expected that it would be practically concluded before Castlereagh arrived on the scene. The Cabinet only gave him leave of absence to the beginning of March. The situation was by no means clear; but the Frankfort proposals were so moderate an offer that it was expected that Napoleon would soon accept them. At any rate, events seemed likely to move very quickly, and the Government agreed to the view, which their Allies had so definitely expressed, that their representative must have power to make the most vital decisions as to peace or war without reference home. The instructions on which he was to act were therefore of great importance, and deserved and obtained the earnest consideration of the Cabinet. Castlereagh prepared for them by obtaining from Lieven, Jacobi, and Wessenberg a statement of the views of their Courts so far as they knew them, but these were, of course, already out of date, and the reports of his own Ambassadors were conflicting and inadequate. In these circumstances he was, no doubt, anxious to obtain as wide a latitude as possible. Thus while he went over the points with his colleagues in several long Cabinets, the document in which the decisions were finally embodied—a Cabinet memorandum passed at a meeting in which the whole Cabinet except Camden were present, and signed by the Prince Regent—was neither so comprehensive nor so explicit as might have been expected. The sentences appear to have been drafted on different occasions as a result of Cabinet debates, for there is but little order and arrangement, and the same topic is repeated. They were, indeed, an obviously hastily compiled *résumé* of points which had been discussed in the Cabinet meetings, and there was no attempt to make them into a complete and formal document.[1]

Since the exclusion of all discussion of maritime rights had already been admitted by the allied Ambassadors, his attention was mainly directed to two points—the 'barrier' to Holland, especially Antwerp, and the colonial conquests on which the Allies had so long desired to be informed. The first was now the cardinal point of British policy. The Frankfort proposals seemed to leave Antwerp and Belgium in French hands, and but little progress had been made by the British force in Holland to remedy the situation. It was Castlereagh's main task to see that Antwerp, the Netherlands, and as much of the left bank of the Rhine as possible should be taken from France. Italy and the Peninsula must also be free, but these objects had now been specifically agreed to by the Allies if not by Napoleon. But the fate of Belgium was, to say the least, still doubtful. Nor could it be assumed that it would be added to Holland, even if France was compelled to surrender it, since Austria had not yet definitely abandoned all her old rights and might wish to place an Austrian Archduke there. Such a proposal would have been welcomed, but it was not expected. The great point was to wrest as much of Belgium as possible from French control.

It was for this purpose that Castlereagh was instructed to use the colonial conquests. If the Allies agreed about Belgium, then Britain was prepared to use these to procure French assent. Both her French and Dutch colonial conquests were to be used for this purpose. Holland could not be given back her possessions unless her independence was made secure, while France must be induced to consent to the sacrifice of Belgium by getting back what she could not otherwise obtain. It was left to Castlereagh to decide how far the 'barrier' was satisfactory, and the restorations were to be proportionate to the territory secured. The marriage of the Hereditary Prince of Orange to Princess Charlotte, already

---

[1] Memorandum of Cabinet, Dec. 26, 1813: *B.D.* 123; Colenbrander, *Gedenkstukken*, vii. 16.

confidentially proposed, was now to be officially suggested to his father and to the Allies, but this was not to influence the negotiations in any other respect.

It was also stated, though less explicitly, that the conclusion of the Alliance guaranteeing the new Europe from attack by France was a condition of the restoration of the conquests. As a result of the criticisms of the Allies it was agreed that the *casus fœderis* should be confined to Europe, and in deference to the Tsar's wish, that Sweden should not be included in the first instance, though it was still suggested that both Spain and Holland might join as original members of the Alliance.

The treaty of Alliance was "not to terminate with the war, but to contain defensive engagements with mutual obligations to support the Powers attacked by France with a certain extent of stipulated succours." It was meant, of course, to protect Europe from Napoleon, who throughout was assumed to be the ruler of France after peace had been made.

For these two great objects, Belgium and the Alliance, the colonial conquests were to be bargained. Not all were to be given back, for some were held to be essential to the strategic security of the Empire. None were claimed on other grounds, though some had now been for a long time in the hands of the British, and British traders and planters had begun to invest capital there. On this matter there was some difference of opinion in the Cabinet, and Castlereagh was subsequently ordered to retain one French colony, Tobago, and the Dutch settlements of Demerara, Essequibo, and Berbice in Guiana, but the principle on which the Cabinet proceeded is well stated in the instructions and in a document on the maritime peace which was drawn up a little later: "Great Britain has declared her disposition with certain exceptions to sacrifice these conquests for the welfare of the Continent, being desirous of providing for her own security by a common arrangement rather than by an exclusive accumulation of strength and resources. Her object is to see a maritime as well as a military balance of power. . . . [The Government] do not desire to retain any of these colonies for their mere commercial value—too happy if by their restoration they can give other states an additional motive to cultivate the arts of peace." [1] This was, perhaps, putting the matter on rather a high plane, but it was substantially true and reveals how little the Cabinet was moved by commercial sentiments.

The conquests which were to be retained included, of course, Malta, to which Napoleon had already agreed, the Cape, Mauritius, Bourbon, Les Saintes, and Guadeloupe, which was required for Sweden. These exceptions were made as a result of the experience of the war, being claimed by the Admiralty as essential bases for the squadrons. In the case of the Cape it was admitted that the cession was substantial, and an offer of two million pounds was to be made to Holland for it, which she was to use in fortifying her new possessions against France. The Danish colonies in the West Indies were to be restored subject to Denmark's agreeing to Sweden's terms.

It was Holland rather than France which gained by these surrenders, though the West Indian colonies were rich possessions. The return of the Dutch East Indies, where Stamford Raffles had already begun to make his mark, testified to the truth of the principle by which the Cabinet claimed to be actuated. It should be noted that no conditions were laid down as to opening the trade of the restored colonies to Britain, though it might be presumed that it would remain a monopoly of the mother countries. Such a stipulation was doubtless felt to be too dangerous a precedent. Nor was anything said as to the Abolition of the Slave Trade to these colonies, which of course had been brought about by their capture by Britain. This was an omission against which Wilberforce and his friends were soon to make protest.[2]

While Britain's special interests were carefully considered, it was perhaps only natural that the instructions dealt with the continental objects very sketchily. In Italy it was hoped to gain as much of Savoy as possible to protect the military

[1] Memorandum on the Maritime Peace, *B.D.* 126. An undated document which in my *British Diplomacy* I placed rather too early. It was written after the news of the Danish peace (Jan. 14), but it sums up the discussions of the Cabinet memorandum of Dec. 26, 1813.

[2] An estimate was made at the time of the value of the West Indian conquests, including the slaves, as follows : French, £31,048,000 ; Dutch, £39,157,540 ; Danish, £5,014,440 : *F.O. Great Britain*, 25.

line of the Alps, and it was considered "highly expedient" that Piedmont should be restored to its King and perhaps also incorporate Genoa so that it could act as a buffer against France. The Pope also was to be restored, while Tuscany and Elba were suggested as compensation for the Sicilian family if Austria "connected herself" with Murat. Nothing was said as to Germany, except that Britain was to offer her "mediation." Hanoverian claims were not even mentioned. Five million pounds were placed at Castlereagh's disposal as subsidies for the coming year, provided that British interests in Holland and the Peninsula were safeguarded in a treaty with the Allies. For the rest, so long as French power was reduced, the Cabinet did not feel much interest, and Castlereagh was left a free hand, of which, as will be seen, he took full advantage. He was authorised to state that Britain was prepared to make peace with the United States on the principle of the *status quo ante bellum*, if the continental Powers pressed for information on this point.

The omission of one question of great importance is not easily explained. Nothing was said as to the possibility of dethroning Napoleon. It was, indeed, assumed throughout that the peace was to be made with him. This subject must have been brought up in the Cabinet discussions, for it was already a topic of discussion in the Press and in political circles. But Liverpool and Castlereagh were, as will be seen, convinced that the time was not yet ripe to open it, and it was probably felt by all that so delicate a matter should be left out of a formal document which it was possible might be laid before Parliament. Nor was it yet realised how much the ancient frontiers and the ancient family were connected together.

While these instructions were being drafted anxious news continued to arrive. Bernadotte's conduct in the north was especially viewed with the greatest distrust. The Austrian mediation had apparently delayed the signature of peace with Denmark, and meanwhile Bernadotte refused all help to Sir Thomas Graham's force in Holland, which met with a decided check. Castlereagh sent to Thornton an unusually angry dispatch, inveighing against Bernadotte's actions which "can not longer be tolerated," and even threatening to suspend the subsidy if he did not join in the attack in the Low Countries, or at least detach some of his forces for that purpose. "We are all in arms here against the Prince Royal," he wrote to his brother in a hasty note. "The reinforcement of Antwerp and Bergen-op-Zoom, whilst His Royal Highness breaks faith three times, as I enumerate to Thornton, has exhausted all our temper. . . . There never was such a cruel disappointment. The withdrawal of Blücher from Cologne and the P.R.'s promenades on the Elbe seem to have been most ingeniously combined to ruin *our greatest objects.*" [1]

This was his mood when he set out on the 28th. His wife accompanied him to the Hague, where she was to remain until April, despite her repeated entreaties to join him at headquarters. To assist him, Castlereagh had Robinson, later Viscount Goderich and Earl of Ripon, then Treasurer of the Navy and a Privy Councillor, who was thus competent to possess secrets though not likely to dispute the authority of his chief. Planta also went with him and two other Foreign Office clerks, a small enough staff for duties so onerous and under conditions so difficult, as Hamilton soon confessed. Fog and calms held up his ship so that he was able at the last minute to receive important communications from Liverpool and Bathurst of Wellington's views on the Bourbons. This did not affect the decision which Liverpool and Castlereagh had already reached, that nothing could be attempted for the present. [2]

At the Hague he discussed with the Prince of Orange the marriage and the problems of succession which it involved. He secured his assent to all the propositions of his instructions, and persuaded him without difficulty to leave his case in British hands at headquarters. The rest of his journey was

---

[1] To Thornton, Dec. 17, 1813 : *F.O. Sweden*, 80. To Stewart, Dec. 24, 1813 : *Lond. MSS*.

[2] Castlereagh's personal expenditure of £10,546 seems little enough when the length and circumstances of the mission are taken into account. The fog which enveloped London in darkness for several days became famous for its intensity and long duration. It was a prelude to one of the most severe winters Britain and Western Europe ever experienced. The Thames was frozen so hard that cards were printed and oxen roasted on it. The Rhine was also frozen. For the question of the Bourbons, see below, Section 3, p. 235.

made at express speed over the wretched roads, and only one night was spent at an inn.[1]

Special orders had been given by the impatient Allies to expedite his journey, and he took all the post-horses for the four carriages of his little party. He had, however, time for reflection, and we know something of the designs which were in his mind. They went far beyond his instructions. He regarded himself as something more than a British Minister concerned only in British interests. These were part of the general interests of Europe, and Castlereagh, no less than Pitt, could not separate one from the other. Above all, he regarded himself as a mediator in the continental disputes, of which he had already only too much information, and one of his great desires was to bring harmony between the rival parties.

"In the course of our journey from Frankfort to Bâle," wrote Lord Ripon, "he stated to me that one of the great difficulties which he expected to encounter in the approaching negotiations would arise from the want of an habitual confidential and free intercourse between the Ministers of the Great Powers *as a body*; and that many pretensions might be modified, asperities removed, and the causes of irritation anticipated and met, by bringing the respective parties into unrestricted communications common to them all, and embracing in confidential and united discussions all the great points in which they were severally interested."

Thus early did he emphasise the importance of the new method of diplomacy that had grown out of the war, the frank and formal, though confidential, discussion of the most delicate problems directly between the principal statesmen. Only by that means, he thought, could he solve the difficult questions of reconstruction, which had already begun to cause doubt and suspicion, and he hoped that the representative of Britain, which had no direct interest in the Continent, might play an important part in reconciling the interests of others. He was as yet unaware how formidable the task was to be, but he was to shew himself peculiarly fitted for the work which he was now called upon to perform. The Earl of

---

[1] To Liverpool, Jan. 8, 1814 : *C.C.* ix. 152. Klinkowström, *Oesterreichs Theilnahme*, 222. To his wife, *Appendix*, pp. 503–504.

Ripon gave him no more than his due when he added: "No man was ever better calculated so to transact business himself and to bring others to act with him in such a manner than Lord Londonderry. The suavity and dignity of his manners, his habitual patience and self-command, his considerate tolerance of difference of opinion in others, all fitted him for such a task; whilst his firmness, when he knew he was right, in no degree detracted from the influence of his conciliatory demeanour." [1]

The next three months were to test these qualities fully. The task of obtaining peace on terms Britain could accept, while at the same time harmonising the councils of the coalition, could, indeed, be only partly fulfilled. It was carried on in the most difficult circumstances. Headquarters was in the midst of enemy territory, and sovereigns, generals, and statesmen alike were constantly harassed by the rigour of the climate and the uncertainty of the military situation. They were deprived of almost all personal comfort and their councils were often cut short by the hazard of war.

The mission reached Bâle on January 18 and caused some amusement by its warlike exterior. "Planta does nothing but flourish about with a long sword and a military cloak," wrote a pert observer, "while the noble Viscount himself presses the war in a pair of red breeches and jockey boots amerced of their tops." He was soon in the thick of intimate discussions, for he was impatiently awaited by all concerned. Aberdeen, no less than Stewart and Cathcart, described his arrival as "providential," so thorny had the problems become. Metternich, who awaited him at Bâle, wrote to Hudelist that such a mission was without precedent, and claimed that headquarters had become the world centre. Hardenberg was also there; but the Tsar had moved forward to the armies which were now far advanced into France. He left word with Cathcart entreating Castlereagh to join him and, if possible, to refuse all previous consultation with others. This was ominous of the relations between the Tsar and Metternich, but at least neutralised the insinuation which the latter

---

[1] The Earl of Ripon to the Marquess of Londonderry (Charles Stewart), July 6, 1839: *C.C.* i. 128.

inspired Aberdeen to make to Castlereagh that the Tsar had purposely avoided him. Stein also wrote to Stewart to warn Castlereagh against Metternich, to whom the warning was betrayed, thus increasing their mutual dislike. Castlereagh could have no doubt of the atmosphere of suspicion and distrust which pervaded headquarters.[1]

However, though these suspicions were soon apparent in the intimate conversations which he had with Metternich, Stadion, and Hardenberg, yet there was much on which he could congratulate himself. Metternich did not wish for territory on the Rhine and had already refused the offer of Alsace made by the Tsar to obtain Galicia. He accepted, however, Castlereagh's views on the Netherlands, and was also prepared to consider the question of depriving France of the left bank of the Rhine to Düsseldorf, though he had been previously opposed to all such claims. Hardenberg was, of course, anxious to go as far as possible, and supplied Castlereagh with many statistics of his plans for the recon-struction of Prussia. In these circumstances Castlereagh was inclined to bring Prussia beyond the Rhine, a course which Stewart advocated in long dispatches which shew the influence of the Prussian General Staff. He also reminded the Cabinet that this idea was a favourite one of Pitt's. All this was satisfactory, and even on the problems of Poland and Saxony he was optimistic, though in this case it was because he had received from Cathcart a dispatch giving him an entirely erroneous impression of the Tsar's intentions.[2]

At the same time he could not disguise that in other matters the situation was exceedingly dangerous. Not only were Bernadotte's strange actions causing grave suspicion, but the Tsar was accused of wishing to make him the ruler of France. Metternich's indignation was extreme and he at once raised the subject. Not one Austrian, he insisted, would

---

[1] Lane Poole, *Life of Stratford Canning*, i. 203. From Aberdeen, Jan. 6, 1814 : *C.C.* ix. 142 ; Balfour, *Life*, i. 177. Metternich to Hudelist, Jan. 3, 1814 : Fournier, *Congress von Châtillon*, 248. Seeley, *Life of Stein*, iii. 222. From Cathcart, Jan. 8, 1814 : *C.C.* ix. 149.

[2] Hardenberg to Castlereagh, Jan. 22, 1814 : *F.O. Cont. Arch.*, 5. From Stewart, Jan. 10, 1814 : *W.S.D.* viii. 498 ; Jan. 14, 1814 : *F.O. Prussia*, 96. From Aberdeen, Jan. 9, 1813 : *W.S.D.* viii. 528. From Cathcart, Jan. 16, 1814 : *C.C.* ix. 171.

move forward for such an object. Castlereagh took the opportunity of this confidence to discuss the whole question of the future government of France. He was able by condemning the Tsar's project to secure also the repudiation of the idea of a Regency, which it was suspected Austria desired, and to reduce the alternatives to Napoleon or the Bourbons, the latter being preferable if France desired it, but not otherwise. It was decided, however, that it was neither politic nor honourable to take part in an attempt to overthrow Napoleon while they were in negotiation with him.

That an attempt must be made to negotiate a peace with Napoleon both were agreed. Indeed, Metternich had already answered Caulaincourt's impatient inquiries from Lunéville that he was only awaiting Castlereagh's arrival to instruct his plenipotentiaries. Caulaincourt's answers insisted that as Aberdeen had already agreed to the Frankfort proposals, which Napoleon had accepted, he could see no reason for delay. But the Frankfort proposals were now not only opposed by Prussia but by the Tsar. Alexander had, indeed, wished to exclude France from all knowledge of the arrangements beyond her own limits. Castlereagh considered this proposal as too strong a measure, "calculated to give Bonaparte popular grounds on which to refuse the terms to be proposed, and bearing too much the character of a blind and dishonourable capitulation, as the security or insecurity of any given extent of limits must depend on the relative state of possession in which the other Powers, at least those of the first order, are to be left." He wished, therefore, that the outline of the new Europe should be agreed upon and communicated to Caulaincourt, who was not, however, to be allowed to discuss and criticise the whole. The terms were to be given as an ultimatum, which, as at Prague, he was to be called upon to accept or reject within a given time.[1]

Metternich had, no doubt, his own views on the expediency of this scheme, but for the moment he allowed Castlereagh

[1] Aberdeen to Bathurst, Jan. 20, 1814: *Bathurst*, 263. To Liverpool, Jan. 22: *W.S.D.* viii. 535; Jan. 22: *C.C.* ix. 185; Jan. 22, 1814: *B.D.* 137. Thornton's last account had, however, asserted, though with some hesitation, that Bernadotte was now prepared to accept the Bourbons: "I think I can venture to say that he does *not* now at least look to the highest place." (From Thornton, Dec. 27, 1813: *F.O. Sweden*, 84.)

to think it possible, and the Ministers moved forward to headquarters at Langres to obtain the agreement of the Tsar. Each had made a good impression on the other, as their intimate correspondence shews. Castlereagh had obtained Metternich's consent to most of his own programme, while Metternich found great relief in the authority and energy of Castlereagh, and already regarded him as his ally to restrain the impetuous actions of the Tsar.[1]

Of these, Castlereagh was soon made aware at Langres, which he reached on January 25. Here took place his first real diplomatic battle, which lasted five days and ended in establishing some sort of political and strategic unity amongst the Allies. It began with two frank conversations with the Tsar—the first of many such in the course of the next two years. Castlereagh at once broached the question of Bernadotte, and though the Tsar denied that he had given occasion for the rumours, he made no secret of the fact that he desired neither peace with Bonaparte nor the return of the Bourbons. Let the allied armies press on to Paris, he said, and France could choose her own ruler. Castlereagh, while anxious that military operations should go on, insisted that negotiations must be begun with Caulaincourt, while at the same time he defended the Bourbons. The Austrians would not consent to march unless negotiations were opened, and, though Castlereagh was not yet sure of Metternich's views, he agreed with him entirely on this point. The political distrust was embittered by military disputes, for the Tsar had no confidence in Schwarzenberg's judgment, and in this attitude he was supported by the Prussian generals. For the solution of this deadlock Castlereagh advocated the method which he had already explained to Robinson on his way to Bâle. "I cannot but feel," he wrote after two days, "extremely anxious for a discussion face to face, perceiving how progressively points of difference are exaggerated in unofficial interviews."

---

[1] Metternich to Hudelist, Jan. 23, 1814: "Ich bien ausserst zufrieden mit ihm, und ich darf mir schmeicheln, auch er mit mir" (Fournier, *Congress*, 251). Metternich to Schwarzenberg, Jan. 21, 1813: "Lord Castlereagh est ici et j'en suis fort content. Il a tout; aménité, sagesse, modération. Il me convient de toute manière et j'ai la conviction de lui convenir également" (Klinkowström, *Oesterreichs Theilnahme*, 800).

What was needed was a formal council of all the four Powers, so that the whole matter could be thrashed out with all parties represented.

It was some time before the Tsar gave way. But he found almost everyone at headquarters opposed to him. Metternich, indeed, went so far as to threaten a separate peace unless consent was given to negotiation, and his Emperor supported him. Eventually the Tsar agreed that discussions should be begun, and a conference of the Ministers was summoned as Castlereagh had desired. In the interval he had had much conversation with Metternich on the Tsar's Polish plans, and realised how extensive were the Russian claims and how deep their differences with Metternich went. Austrian and British fears on this point were mutual and naturally brought them to look at other matters from a similar point of view. "Castlereagh behaves like an angel," wrote Metternich to Schwarzenberg.

Alexander also shewed himself anxious to get in the closest touch with Britain. He accepted an invitation, which he—erroneously—considered the Prince Regent had sent him, to visit England, and meanwhile asked that his dearly loved sister, Catherine, should precede him. She was to cause much trouble there, but for the moment her visit was accepted as a sign of friendship, and Castlereagh took steps to secure that the necessary attentions should be paid to the distinguished guest.[1]

It was good news too that Denmark, on January 14, at last signed a peace with Sweden and Britain. She gave up Norway, and in return received monetary compensation and Swedish Pomerania. Britain gave her back her West Indian colonies but kept Heligoland, which had been so useful a base during the war. Danish troops were taken into British pay to the tune of £400,000 per annum, a bribe which was not relished in London. Still, it was hoped that Bernadotte's army would soon appear in force on the right wing of the

[1] To Liverpool, Jan. 29, 1814 : *B.D.* 138 ; Jan. 30, 1814 : *C.C.* ix. 212. To the Prince Regent, Jan. 30, 1814 : *C.C.* iv. 210. Metternich to Schwarzenberg, Jan. 30, 1814 : Klinkowström, *Oesterreichs Theilnahme*, 805. From Stewart, Jan. 27, 1814 : *C.C.* ix. 536. Fournier, *Congress*, 56 ff. Oncken, " Lord Castlereagh und die Minister-conferenz zu Langres," *Hist. Tasch.*, Sechste Folge, Jahrgang 4, 34–40.

Allies and make easier the final overthrow of Napoleon which now seemed imminent.

The first formal council of the coalition met on the morning of the 28th. The military situation was first considered, and the Austrians proposed a cessation of hostilities while negotiations were going on. Castlereagh's opposition was naturally supported by the Russians and Prussians, and Metternich was easily overborne. In return, Castlereagh enabled Metternich to carry his point that negotiations should be begun with Caulaincourt, and thus the whole question of the terms to be offered came up for discussion.

It took some time before they could be settled. Castlereagh claimed that the progress of the war since November entitled the Allies to lay down an entirely different basis from that offered at Frankfort, and that France must be reduced substantially to her ancient limits. Metternich demurred at first, but eventually agreed, only stipulating that some concessions in Savoy and the left bank of the Rhine should be offered, if necessary, so as to fulfil the promise made in the allied Declaration of December 1. Castlereagh was satisfied with this great advance. "We may now be considered," he reported, "as practically delivered from the embarrassments of the Frankfort proposals."

The method had then to be found of carrying out the negotiation on this basis. It was decided to send joint instructions to the negotiators at Châtillon embodying a draft treaty. Castlereagh was alone in insisting that this should give information to the French on the outline of the new Europe He defended his action on the grounds that any other course would dishonour France; but, as soon appeared, he had another object in view. He wished to force his Allies to an agreement as well as Napoleon, having already learnt how dangerous their controversies about Saxony, Poland, and other points had become. He hoped to get these settled in outline immediately, not yet realising that over a year would have to elapse before so great a task could be accomplished. The others, however, agreed to his demand, though, as we know, with little hope of satisfying it. In return, Castlereagh could do no less than offer to specify, in accordance with his instructions, the colonial conquests which Britain would restore to obtain a continental settlement of this nature.[1]

This discussion cleared the air, and Castlereagh was able to report that temper all round had improved "from the natural vent which this species of Cabinet has afforded to the diverging sentiments of the respective Governments." But in the two further conferences which followed (January 30 and 31) it was found impossible to work out the principles which had been adopted, and the instructions drafted by Metternich were exceedingly vague. Castlereagh could, indeed, claim that on several points he had secured what he wanted. Caulaincourt was to be informed that the maritime rights were to be excluded from the discussions, and when Metternich's drafting of this paragraph seemed unsatisfactory, since it implied the existence of a British maritime law as distinct from common maritime law, Castlereagh was allowed to choose his own phrasing. Moreover, the document distinctly laid down the ancient limits as the basis of the discussion with France, though these might be modified by mutual agreement in return for "compensations"—a word which Castlereagh preferred to "restitutions"—made by Britain out of her colonial conquests. He was, at any rate, now practically assured of the Netherlands to the Meuse by all the Allies, and could write to Clancarty to authorise the Prince of Orange to encourage the inhabitants to look to him as their future sovereign.[2]

But the information on the disposition of the territories conquered by France was meagre in the extreme. The Allies were far from any agreement on the subject. The importance of this part of the document lay in its indication of the great changes which were almost unconsciously being made in the principles of the European polity. The Allies claimed to represent not only themselves but all Europe, and they intended to settle all the main points by themselves. As

[1] From Thornton, Jan. 14, 15, 1814: *F.O. Sweden*, 90. To Liverpool, Jan. 29, 1814: *B.D.* 141.

[2] To Liverpool, Feb. 1, 1814: *F.O. Continent*, 2. First instructions for the Plenipotentiaries at Châtillon, Feb. 2, 1814: Fournier, *Congress*, 306. To Metternich, Jan. 29, 1814: *C.C.* ix. 203. To Clancarty, Feb. 1, 1814: *C.C.* ix. 224.

yet, however, they had made hardly any progress. They could therefore give only the vaguest outline of what that Europe was to be, which they yet claimed to represent and control. "The great European Powers actually existing," as they called themselves in a significant phrase, would decide their own limits amongst themselves. Nothing more could be said except that Switzerland and Holland should be free, the latter receiving an increase of territory, while Italy and Germany should be composed of independent states, the former "between the possessions of France and Austria," the latter "united by a federal bond." All the disputed points in the settlement were left out—the disposition of Saxony, Poland, and the left bank of the Rhine was unknown. These questions were to be finally settled at a Congress to be held at Vienna, at which both the Tsar and the King of Prussia promised to be present. Castlereagh was far from satisfied, and he therefore refused to specify in detail the colonial restorations, though he indicated verbally the line he should take.

In the course of this statement he laid down some very important principles. The colonial restorations, he said, were made not only to obtain peace with France but also a peaceful Europe. He made, indeed, three conditions for their surrender: (1) "that France should submit to retire, if not literally, substantially within her ancient limits"; (2) "that Great Britain should have an assurance by an amicable arrangement of limits between the three Great Powers, that, having reduced France by their union, they were not likely to re-establish her authority by differences amongst themselves"; (3) "that we should be satisfied that the arrangements in favour of the Powers of whose interests we were more especially the guardians were likely to be attended to, and especially those of Holland and Sicily—the point of Spain being abandoned by France herself." These last two points, he reminded them, depended on the Allies not on France, and he suggested that they should be discussed at once. These observations were received politely, though Metternich suggested Spain and Holland might be called on to sacrifice some of their colonial possessions to France, a course immediately vetoed by Castlereagh. That Castlereagh should have brought these points forward at this period shews that he already intended to play the rôle which was to be his in the course of the next twelve months. The reconstruction of Europe in such a manner as to produce a peaceful Continent he considered as a primary British interest, and he wished to use the advantage of the colonial possessions to compel his Allies to come to an agreement. If his haste shews his inexperience it reveals also his broad outlook and magnificent courage.

That he hoped to advance this work in the course of the negotiation with France was undoubtedly one of the reasons for his decision to go himself to Châtillon to supervise the proceedings, though not as an official negotiator None of the other principal Ministers were to accompany him, and that he should leave headquarters at such a time indicated that he was not satisfied that the instructions were such as to lead to peace with Napoleon or to agreement amongst the Allies, unless they were treated in the spirit which he desired to prevail.[1]

Another reason was, no doubt, the difficulty he had in deciding how Britain was to be represented. Each of the other Powers appointed one plenipotentiary—Austria, Stadion; Prussia, Humboldt; and Russia, Razumovski. Aberdeen would have been the obvious person to have represented Britain, and he had expected to occupy that position with the powers which Castlereagh himself now exercised. Stewart and Cathcart were with their respective armies and not at all eager to resume the diplomatic profession. But Castlereagh felt that Aberdeen was too much under Austrian influence, and that his appointment would shake the confidence of Russia and Prussia. Accordingly he had appointed all three Ambassadors as plenipotentiaries, and when Cathcart and Stewart protested at being recalled from their military duties he sent a sharp order that they must obey without question.

[1] To Liverpool, Feb. 4, 1814: Instructions to the British Plenipotentiaries at Châtillon, No. 1 and No. 2 (Confidential), Feb. 2, 1814: *F.O. Continent*, 2. To Liverpool, Feb. 6, 1814: *B.D.* 146. Münster to the Prince Regent, Feb. 2, 1814: *Hanover St. A.* Münster, who had been ill, arrived at Langres on the 29th. His general impressions are given in the dispatches in Fournier, *Congress*, 295, 296.

Aberdeen's feelings were soothed by being given a kind of special position, and he was told that the jealousy of Stewart and Cathcart must be humoured.[1]

Castlereagh could hardly regard such a trio as a satisfactory body to carry out his plans.   But he had to make the best of them, and he tried to make them appreciate the view which he held of Britain's own position in the coalition by a special instruction, which was "intended to apply . . . to the conduct of the King's affairs in all matters of general policy so long as the allied sovereigns shall continue together."   "It is impossible," he wrote, "to have resided at allied headquarters even for the short period I have myself passed at them without perceiving how much the interests of the Confederacy are exposed to prejudice and disunion from the want of some central council of deliberation, where the authorised Ministers of the respective Powers may discuss face to face the measures in progress, and prepare a result for the consideration of their respective sovereigns. You must all be aware how deep was the distrust and alarm which existed some days ago as to supposed divergencies of opinion, which it was feared were irreconcilable in themselves, and how soon these differences disappeared when the allied Ministers were ordered officially to enter upon their discussion.   To such a degree did this happen, that every individual question which they have been called upon to deliberate has been decided, not only unanimously, but with cordial concurrence."

British Ministers, he said, were equally liable to differences of opinion, which tended to divide rather than unite the Courts to which they were accredited, and they must seek a remedy in the same manner: "The power of Great Britain to do good depends not merely on its resources but upon a sense of its impartiality and the reconciling character of its influence. . . . To be authoritative it must be impartial. To be impartial it must not be in exclusive relations with any particular Court."   For this purpose, he said, a council of Ministers was, in many respects, more suitable than a single

[1] To Cathcart, Jan. 31, 1814 ; to Stewart, Jan. 31, 1814 : *C.C.* ix. 215, 216.   Aberdeen was quite unaware of the real feelings of Stewart and Cathcart on this question (Balfour, *Aberdeen*, i. 185).

person, if they acted cordially together. "It will be your duty to consider yourselves as a British Cabinet on the Continent, bound to pursue the general interest of the Alliance and not the particular interest of any state. . . . The interests of Great Britain neither require to be asserted with chicane nor with dexterity—a steady and temperate application of honest principles is her best source of authority."

This was both an encouragement and a warning—a stern comment on their past behaviour and at the same time an incentive to work together with Castlereagh for the common end. Otherwise, he hinted, he would have to place the task in other hands: "I persuade myself that with union amongst themselves and concert with me they are most competent to conduct the great work now in hand to a happy and glorious issue. Having brought it to the present auspicious point, I wish them collectively and individually to have the reputation of bringing it to a close. It depends on themselves to do so."

Before he left, news had been received of the victory over Napoleon at La Rothière (February 1), an event which he hoped would increase the courage as well as the unity of the Allies. His last word from Langres, therefore, to Liverpool was one of assurance, which had been also increased by an intimate conversation with the Emperor of Austria, who had entirely dissipated any fears that he was aiming at establishing a Regency under his daughter. Metternich also accepted with equanimity the news of Monsieur's intended visit to Switzerland, which Liverpool had just announced. Castlereagh set out for Châtillon, therefore, full of confidence. He was to need it all in the course of the negotiations there.[1]

[1] To the British Plenipotentiaries (Confidential), Feb. 2, 1814: *F.O. Continent*, 2. To Liverpool, Feb. 3, 1814 : *W.S.D.* viii. 566.

2. THE TREATY OF CHAUMONT

ALL the plenipotentiaries were by now kicking their heels at Châtillon awaiting the word to begin. The little town, though in the allied lines, was neutral territory, a fact of which the inhabitants took advantage to organise raids on the allied communications. They were, indeed, far more hostile than most of those in the occupied territory, and the Maire was in terror lest something should happen to one of the plenipotentiaries. These had expected to be there only a few days, and when the sojourn was lengthened to seven weeks they complained bitterly of their fate, which they endeavoured in vain to relieve by the exercise of the arts of hospitality—a matter of some difficulty under the conditions, but sufficiently accomplished to cause two or three to fall ill "from the effects of their intemperance." Most of them soon lost hope of obtaining peace, except perhaps Aberdeen, whose *innocence diplomatique* caused Stadion much amusement. Stadion himself preferred war, but he was loyal to his chief, to whom he sent many cynical and amusing letters. Humboldt had been chosen by Hardenberg because of his ardour, and Razumovski was merely a cipher awaiting orders from headquarters. Stewart and Cathcart could do little, though the former used his energy in making copious notes. Aberdeen sat in dumb despair at the cynicism of his companions. Caulaincourt alone increased his reputation for sincerity and ability. He had no illusions, and if his master had given him a chance would have obtained the best possible frontier within a few days. Napoleon had, however, still no intention of yielding Antwerp or the left bank of the Rhine, and this determination reduced the discussions to a *mauvaise comédie*, as Stadion termed it.[1]

[1] Fournier's account in his *Congress von Châtillon* (1900) is a model of historical skill and insight.

The absurdity of the situation was fully revealed at the first conference on February 7. Caulaincourt was offered the ancient limits with some modifications, and told that Britain would, in return, restore some of her conquests as compensation. He naturally asked for more information, not only as to the conquests but as to the shape of the new Europe which the plenipotentiaries claimed to represent in its entirety.[1] Since Castlereagh had refused to specify the first until the second could also be known, the Allies were bound to be silent on both points, though Caulaincourt pressed them again and again. When the plenipotentiaries retired after this exposure, Castlereagh again insisted to Stadion and Humboldt that they must be able to furnish information as to the intentions of their Governments before he would specify the colonial conquests. All that could be done, therefore, was to invite Caulaincourt to submit his ideas of the treaty of peace in the form of a *contre-projet*. Meanwhile news came of further victories over Napoleon at Brienne, and it seemed likely that the Allies would soon be at Paris. Caulaincourt, in despair, sent privately to Metternich to offer the ancient frontiers if an armistice could be granted immediately.

While the plenipotentiaries were discussing the effect of the allied victories, peremptory orders came from the Tsar that the negotiations must be suspended. He had taken this step on his own initiative, and Metternich in great distress urged Castlereagh to come to Troyes, which headquarters had now reached. Castlereagh had anticipated this wish. It was clearly at headquarters rather than at Châtillon that the vital decision must now be made. After long conversations, therefore, with Stadion on the whole European settlement, he had already decided to return there in order to bring the Allies to agreement, so that the peace with France could be made. The method was to be the same as that which he had begun at Langres; formal discussions between the four Ministers, so that all the cards would be on the table.

"Lord Castlereagh appeared decided," reported Stadion to his chief, "and I have done my best to support his idea, to

[1] " I see by your Protocol," wrote Edward Cooke, " you treat in the name of Europe. What corollaries follow ! What questions start ! And how difficult to answer ! " From Cooke, Feb. 12, 1814 : *Lond. MSS.*

treat of the objects which cause his return only in conferences of the four Ministers. It is only by such conferences that ideas will become clarified, and it is only by this method that the exaggerated claims and scandalous demands of Prussia can be got rid of at the outset, since she will have difficulty in formulating them, and still more in defending them, when they are subjected to a formal and official discussion. I have also tried to confirm the English Minister in his opinion that in this ministerial reunion it is, above all, necessary to force Russia to declare herself on her plans concerning ci-devant Poland, because all our calculations depend on them. He has seemed to be quite convinced that we must not admit a distinct kingdom or a duchy of Poland, either in fact or in name, either openly avowed or concealed under some subterfuge." What Stadion thought wise for Prussia and Russia, Castlereagh doubtless thought applied to Austria also, but when he arrived at Troyes he found conditions hardly suitable to carry out such a plan.[1]

The coalition was within an ace of dissolution. The Tsar was convinced he could now reach Paris, where, he announced, he would summon an assembly to decide Napoleon's fate. Metternich had exhausted his protests, and Castlereagh was urged to take his place. In two long and stormy interviews on February 13 and 14 Castlereagh tried in vain to impose his will upon the Tsar, who was determined not only to march on Paris but to refuse all negotiation with Napoleon, even though Caulaincourt had offered to accept the ancient limits. Alexander still considered the Bourbons incapable of rule, especially Louis XVIII., but, in view of the sentiments of his Allies, thought that one of the younger members, possibly the Duke of Orleans, might be chosen. Castlereagh tried to shew the hazards of such a course—the absence of any movement against Napoleon and the chaos which might ensue—if they refused to treat with him while he was still the ruler of France and when Caulaincourt was apparently ready to accept their terms. How was a representative assembly to

[1] Minute of Second Conference at Châtillon : *C.C.* ix. 544–45. To Liverpool, Feb. 6, 1814 : *B.D.* 146. Stadion to Metternich, Feb. 9, 1814 : Fournier, *Congress*, 317. Caulaincourt's letter of the 9th is given in Fain, *Manuscrit de 1814*, 265.

be obtained, he asked, and if a new ruler was chosen, how was he to be supported against Napoleon? Was he likely to have an army of his own, and, if not, how long would the Tsar undertake to keep his army in France to fight a Bourbon's battles against Bonaparte?

The Tsar had but few arguments, but he suddenly tried to refute Castlereagh by claiming that the British Government did not support his views, producing a letter from Lieven which asserted that the Prince Regent was decidedly against all peace with Bonaparte and anxious that the Bourbons should be recalled. This, as will be seen, was true enough so far as the Prince Regent was concerned, but Lieven's letter was entirely unauthorised. Castlereagh was naturally indignant at the insinuation that he had not the confidence of his Government, and his letter to Liverpool portrays, as Lord Salisbury noted, "almost the only angry shade that passes over the calm imperturbable style of his correspondence during this exciting period." His protests were as strong as he could make them to a reigning monarch, though we may imagine that his coolness and impassiveness, which had now become celebrated at headquarters, did not desert him even at this moment. But the Tsar refused to give way, and the interview ended without result. It was the first real passage of arms that Castlereagh had experienced, and must in no small degree have affected all his future attitude towards Alexander.

Meanwhile the Ministers held formal conference as Castlereagh desired. Metternich drew up a questionnaire on the situation (his favourite mode of proceeding), and Hardenberg, as well as Castlereagh, supported him in insisting that the negotiations should continue. But this was hardly the time to redraw the map of Europe. Though it was agreed that the answer to Caulaincourt should take the form of a draft treaty of peace, its terms remained as vague as at Langres. Nevertheless, Castlereagh now consented to specify the colonial conquests, which he did on the lines laid down in his instructions, only insisting on adding the Abolition of the Slave Trade to them and a reserve on the question of Tobago. In return, however, he obtained from the Allies a convention agreeing to the essential British interests on the

Continent—the Netherlands, the left bank of the Rhine, an indemnity for the King of Sicily, and the confiscation of the fleet in Antwerp harbour, to which the Cabinet attached great importance. With this he had to be content, for it was clearly impossible to do more, and yet he could not go on with the negotiations without making a real offer to France. At the same time he came back to the treaty of Alliance, which the prospect of a peace with Napoleon made more than ever necessary. A draft treaty was submitted to the Ministers on February 12, which contained the same outline of Europe as was submitted to Caulaincourt. They received it with assurances of favourable consideration, to which their need of money doubtless added fervour. Castlereagh now confined the scope of the treaty to an attack on the European dominions of the signatories, which Nesselrode said had removed the Tsar's objections. This was satisfactory; even though Nesselrode, as always, wished to make Russia's consent to Holland's increase depend upon Britain and Holland taking over the Russian debt in Amsterdam.[1]

Even now the Tsar's consent had not been obtained to negotiate, though Metternich went so far as to threaten that peace would be made without him. But by the time Castlereagh got back to Châtillon with the new instructions, the enterprise of Napoleon had accomplished what argument had failed to win. Hitherto he had given few signs of his military genius, but now, taking advantage of the fact that Blücher's troops had moved forward unsupported, he dashed amongst them and won a series of combats. His prestige and the ardour of his troops revived, and Schwarzenberg became even more nervous than usual for the safety of his communications. The Tsar's hopes were dashed, he sent the necessary word to Razumovski, and the negotiations were resumed.

But at Châtillon the situation was now reversed. Caulaincourt had hitherto been pressing for decision, going beyond the limit of Napoleon's instructions. But success had now

---

[1] To Liverpool, Feb. 16, 18, 1814: *B.D.* 147, 157. Lieven to Nesselrode, Jan. 26, 1814: *C.C.* ix. 267. To Metternich, Feb. 12, 1814: *Vienna St. A.* Münster to the Prince Regent, Feb. 17, 1814: *Hanover St. A.* Draft treaty in D'Angeberg, *Congrès de Vienne*, i. 110. Convention of Feb. 17, 1814: Martens (F.), *Traités conclus par la Russie*, xi. 200. To Clancarty, Feb. 20, 1814: *C.C.* ix. 284. Salisbury, *Biographical Essays*, 58.

revived his master's hopes, and he received peremptory warning not to make peace except on the Frankfort basis. When, therefore, the draft treaty was presented to him on February 17, he naturally played for time by again raising the unanswerable enquiries as to the fate of Italy and Saxony, and meanwhile awaiting Napoleon's counter-proposals which had been promised, but which were hardly to be expected while the tide of his success flowed on.

Castlereagh did everything in his power, as Stadion admitted, to make peace possible. He was perhaps pushed further in that direction by the Tsar's attack on his authority. He had sent Robinson home with an indignant letter to make sure of the Cabinet's support. It was an anxious moment, but Castlereagh shewed little signs of the strain. Lady Burghersh, it must be admitted, was partial to him because he had supported her "dear B" against Wilson, and her charm seems to have made an impression on him, and made him sparkle if not thaw. "I quite delight in Cas," she wrote. "I had no idea he had so much fun in him, though he is impenetrably cold." [1]

Another crisis summoned him back to headquarters. Blücher's defeats had put the main army in such a state of nerves, that, when it received a blow itself, Schwarzenberg prevailed on the two sovereigns to agree that he should accept the armistice which Caulaincourt had offered on the 9th, and a *parlementaire* was sent to the French army. This weakness seemed to threaten the whole fabric of the peace, and the urgent appeal which Castlereagh sent to Metternich on the 18th betrayed his deep emotion at the news. "I feel it more than ever necessary," he wrote, "to conjure you and your colleagues at headquarters not to suffer yourselves to descend from the substance of your peace. You owe it, such as you have announced it, to the enemy, to yourselves, and to *Europe*, and you will now more than ever make a fatal sacrifice both of moral and political impression, if under the pressure of those slight reverses which are incident to war, and some embarrassments in your Council which I should hope are at an end,

---

[1] Stadion to Metternich, Feb. 17, 1814 : Fournier, *Congress*, 323. Rose Weigall, *Letters of Lady Burghersh*, 185.

the great edifice of peace was suffered to be disfigured in its proportions. Recollect what your military position is. . . . If we act with *military* and *political* prudence, how can France resist a just peace demanded by 600,000 warriors. Let her, if she dare, and the day you can declare that fact to the French nation, rest assured Bonaparte is subdued. . . . There can be in good sense but one interest among the Powers; namely, to end nobly the great work they have conducted so near to its close." [1]

How far the Allies would have descended had Napoleon been anxious to accept their offer it is hard to say; but he was by now uplifted by his wonderful successes against such superior force. He sent a letter to his father-in-law which characterised the new offer as dishonourable, and though the discussions as to an armistice continued for some time he never seemed ready to accept the allied conditions, which included the abandonment of Antwerp, on which, as yet, Carnot's hold had not been shaken. Nevertheless, the allied leaders were very downcast. When Castlereagh joined headquarters at Troyes he found it packing up for retreat, and next day he learnt from Metternich that Schwarzenberg was still pressing for an armistice. The Austrian was nervous about his left wing, having received news that Augereau was advancing from the south, and the whole allied army had orders to retire until they got in touch with their reserves. No doubt, as some critics have averred, there was much military prudence in this retreat, but it gave an impression of weakness which might have disastrous effects on the sovereigns and generals.

Meanwhile Blücher was left in the air with his forces already roughly handled, and though no one questioned his courage or ardour, his ability to cope with Napoleon was a matter of grave doubt. At this critical moment Castlereagh played an important part in rallying the coalition by strengthening not only their confidence but their military position. "I could not but perceive," ran his official report, "the altered tone of my colleagues—their impressions being strongly tinctured with the demoralising influence of a rapid

[1] To Metternich, Feb. 18, 1814 : *B.D.* 158.

transition from an advance made under very lofty pretensions, to a retreat of some embarrassment and of much disappointment and recrimination. There was no disposition, however, to shrink from the substance of the line laid down at Châtillon. . . . I strongly urged to Prince Metternich the importance of a contemporaneous answer from the Emperor to Bonaparte to dissipate all hope of the Allies conceding in their terms of peace, and also to put an end to this mode of approaching the Emperor so derogatory to his dignity." A more intimate letter written at the same time shews that he had grave fears of both Austria and Russia, who were loud in their accusations against one another: "The criminations and recriminations between the Austrians and Russians are at their height, and my patience is worn out combating both. Austria both in army and government is a timid Power. Her Minister is constitutionally temporising—he is charged with more faults than belong to him, but he has his full share, mixed, however, with considerable means for carrying forward the machine—more than any other person I have met with at headquarters." This was a just estimate of Metternich, who was rarely at his best when direct and rapid action was necessary.

Nor could the Tsar be now used to correct this fault, for he seemed to be as urgent for peace as he had been warlike a few days before. In his haste to get to Paris he had prevented the Allies from listening to Caulaincourt's offer of the ancient frontiers, and now he was, to Castlereagh's disgust, pressing for the armistice. That there were some military reasons for this step is shewn by Burghersh's reports from the Austrian army, which had grown in gloom throughout the month of February. He emphasised the panic which the name of Bonaparte had reawakened in the minds of the officers since he had begun his offensive, and the increasing hostility of the civil population roused to desperation by the brutal methods of the allied armies. The paralysis which had attacked the Austrians and appeared to be spreading to the Russians was also, no doubt, partly due to the political distrust between Austria and Russia, which the defeat had intensified. The Tsar told Castlereagh that Schwarzenberg had secret orders not to fight a battle. This was not true;

but the idea bred suspicions that each was now reserving his own forces to win Poland rather than Paris. "I have no doubt," wrote Münster to the Prince Regent, "that the Austrians are inclined to keep their army intact in order to preserve their influence on the affairs of Poland, while the Russians are accused of sparing their beautiful cavalry."

In these circumstances Castlereagh was beset on all sides, but he stood fast: "Nothing keeps either Power firm but the consciousness that without Great Britain the peace cannot be made; but I have explicitly told them that if the Continent can and will make a peace with Bonaparte upon a principle of authority, Great Britain will make the greatest sacrifices; but that if they neither will nor can, we must, for their sake as well as our own, rest in position against France."

Stewart's account was even more gloomy, and he bitterly regretted that the Allies had not signed peace with Napoleon while they had the chance. He was loud also in his praise of Castlereagh, whose firmness alone had saved the situation: "What Castlereagh has achieved is really wonderful. But for him I do believe we should have been off, the Devil take the hindmost. I have told you we were wrong from the commencement, and your d——d Bourbon blood was doing all you could to urge us on. . . . Anything, my dear friend, more madly inconsistent and childish than our proceeding has been I cannot figure to myself, first accepting or rather giving the Frankfort basis, then changing it to immense sacrifices for France, then finding we could have this we are not pleased, we must have a *Bow* at Paris. Some Bourbons, some Charles Jeans, some for a republic, some for dividing France, the poor French people looking on quietly, awaiting their fate and having no more inclination about Louis XVIII. than about Edward Cooke. Whatever of bad happens to us we rightly deserve it; whatever of good we must thank Providence and Castlereagh." [1]

---

[1] To Liverpool, Feb. 26 (No. 19), 1814: *F.O. Continent*, 3; (No. 20): *B.D.* 160. Münster to the Prince Regent, Feb. 25, 1814: Fournier, *Congress*, 303. Nesselrode to Lieven, March 10, 1814: *Pet. Arch.* From Burghersh, Feb. 24, 1814: "The allied army is certainly stronger than that of Bonaparte, yet if its retreat is continued I dread its total disorganisation. The licentious proceedings of the soldiers of late, the pillage of the country wherever they have passed, has driven the inhabitants from their

There was also a military problem to be solved—how to succour Blücher while the main army retired. In this also Castlereagh played a decisive part. A conference was held on the 20th at which the sovereigns, Schwarzenberg and other generals, and the Ministers were present. The Commander-in-Chief stated his precarious position. He had 50,000 sick and no magazines, and could not risk a pitched battle. He had tried to obtain an armistice and had failed. He had to detach troops to the south. He was now separated from Blücher, who had adhered to his own line of operations. After such a review no one could oppose his suggestion of a retreat behind the Marne. He was also allowed to accept an armistice, leaving part of the Netherlands in French hands. It was Castlereagh who insisted that the Russian and Prussian corps under the command of Bernadotte, which had as yet hardly been used, should be detached from his force and placed under Blücher's command. "I ventured to make this proposition," he reported, "and the order to preserve the command in Blücher, who is too daring to be trusted with a small force, but a host at the head of one hundred thousand men." This piece of strategical insight was to have important results, but Castlereagh was aware that it would not please Bernadotte, who was already bitterly complaining of the exclusion of Sweden from all the important negotiations, and especially of the refusal to allow a Swedish representative at Châtillon. He tried to soothe him by placing the whole of the Netherlands forces under his command, and urged that the best way to obtain Norway was by a successful attack on Antwerp.[1]

houses and has converted them into most bitter enemies. Bonaparte was received yesterday at Troyes with every mark of attachment; the inhabitants fired upon the Austrian troops that were last retiring from it and dragged the sick and emaciated soldiers that had been left in hospital to grace the triumphal entry of their ruler ": *F.O. Austria*, 110. Stewart to Cooke, Feb. 28, 1814 : *Lond. MSS.* This vivid and unguarded letter, which produced considerable effect at home, was much edited by the writer when he published it in *C.C.* ix. 553.

[1] To Liverpool, Feb. 26 (No. 19), 1814 ; Protocol of a Conference at Bar-sur-Aube on Military Procedure : *F.O. Continent*, 3. To Clancarty, Feb. 27, 1814 : *C.C.* ix. 291. From Thornton, Feb. 17, 1814 : *F.O. Sweden*, 90. To Thornton, Feb. 27, 1814 : *C.C.* ix. 292. The idea was not, of course, Castlereagh's, but had been for some time advocated at Blücher's headquarters, which had long wished to be strong enough to cut loose from Schwarzenberg (see Fournier, *Congress*, 161 ff., and the authori-

By these means the morale of the armies was steadied. The answers sent to Napoleon by Francis shewed no sign of intimidation; in fact Castlereagh considered that Metternich had carried out his advice "handsomely." Instructions were also sent to Châtillon that the answer from Caulaincourt must be required within a definite period of time, and must conform to the spirit of the basis laid down by the Allies. Metternich's private letter to Stadion for the edification of Caulaincourt was, indeed, more yielding, but of this Castlereagh was not aware. By the end of the month the soldiers were cheered by a check given to Victor, and though armistice discussions still persisted, the tone all round was better.[1]

Throughout this dramatic and exciting month Castlereagh had kept his Cabinet as well posted as possible and, when a passage had been opened through Paris, fairly quickly informed. But, of course, they only obtained a partial view of events after a considerable interval of time, and it was impossible for them to control the negotiations. For this they had been prepared, and entrusted Castlereagh with the widest powers for peace and war ever held by a British Minister abroad, but they naturally were more affected than he was by public opinion in Britain, and these influences dictated one or two official instructions which, as will be seen, had no practical influence on the result. Liverpool and Bathurst, however, kept their colleague in touch by a constant stream of private letters, commenting in the frankest possible way on the negotiations, and making their influence felt by suggestion and information as to the situation at home rather than by any obvious attempt to enforce a point of view.

The most delicate of all the questions was, of course, that of the Bourbons, which is dealt with in the next section. On this subject the views of the Cabinet gradually grew somewhat

ties there quoted), but that Castlereagh sponsored it in the council, secured its adoption, and found the means to pacify Bernadotte is shewn not only by his own account but also by Robinson's recollection (*C.C.* i. 129). The letter to Thornton was a masterpiece of tact, and secured Bernadotte's acquiescence after some protest. (From Thornton, March 9, 17, 1814: *F.O. Sweden*, 90.) Bernadotte was subsequently allowed to send a plenipotentiary to Châtillon at the Tsar's request.

[1] To Liverpool, Feb. 28, 1814: *C.C.* ix. 299. Metternich to Stadion, Feb. 26, 1814: Fournier, *Congress*, 328.

different to those of Castlereagh, but, as will be seen, did not affect his actions to any important extent, though the outcry at Carlton House and in the Press, which were reported at length by the foreign Ambassadors, perhaps did something to make his task more difficult.

The Ministers, though they made no secret of their dislike of peace with Bonaparte, did not attempt until much later to restrain Castlereagh from concluding it. They continually insisted, however, on the necessity of the peace terms, such as would satisfy the expectations of public opinion, and were continually pressing Castlereagh not to allow the negotiations to drag on. They had little idea of all the difficulties in the way of submitting a clear-cut issue to Napoleon. "Surely," wrote Bathurst immediately after Castlereagh's departure, "you can make the Allies feel all the advantages of having a clear and distinct basis first agreed upon by Bonaparte before we enter into a Congress, where the very existence of a Congress will so essentially strengthen him." Bathurst was, indeed, always more bellicose and more distrustful of the Allies than the more phlegmatic Liverpool. Moreover, as responsible for the colonies, he was anxious that the principles on which the conquests were to be returned should be made clear at the outset. They were sacrifices made with the purpose of obtaining what could not otherwise be taken from Napoleon. As peace would be unpopular in any event, it must be shewn to be necessary. "However gallantly our Allies fight the enemy in the field," he went on, "I am at times apprehensive that in the Cabinet they mistake us for the enemy and France for the ally. At the very moment that they at Frankfort declared France should have at the peace a more extended territory than she had ever enjoyed before the Revolution, they required us to be reduced to what we were. What could an enemy do more in negotiations than require us to give up as a price of peace what, by war, they could not take from us. Or could a friend do more for an ally in distress than secure to him the remainder of his conquests and stipulate the restoration of the possessions he had lost?" This was, perhaps, putting it a little unfairly, and Liverpool never went so far. But he also stressed the necessity of a peace that would soothe if not satisfy public opinion.[1]

These were general principles—in the details they had little to say, and indeed could hardly appreciate what Castlereagh was doing. They made no comment on his attempts to act as a mediator between the Allies. They were interested exclusively in the peace as it affected British interests. Bathurst had naturally to watch very carefully the commercial interests affected by the surrender of the conquests. Representations were being made, as Liverpool recorded, against any colonies being given back by merchants who were interested in their trade. In most cases property had been acquired which seemed to be in jeopardy. The Cabinet, however, only pressed for one colony which had not been expressly mentioned in the instructions—Tobago, which had only belonged to France since the American war, and where British property interests were especially strong. Liverpool took a rather wider view of these questions, insisting, for example, that Spain and Holland should not be made to compensate France for her cessions to Britain—a bargain which, as has been seen, Metternich actually suggested at one time.[2]

Though Bathurst acted nominally as Foreign Minister in Castlereagh's absence and signed the dispatches, it was Liverpool who did such work of importance as was not concentrated at headquarters. He saw the foreign representatives and soothed or reproved them as might be necessary. He also kept a special eye on the Prince Regent in Castlereagh's absence, and instructed him what language to use— not always, however, winning his obedience. Thus Loevenheilm, who was specially sent over by Bernadotte to explain his master's very equivocal conduct, was allowed to have no doubts of the opinion of the British Government about it, and when he complained of the exclusion of Sweden from the peace negotiations he was told that Castlereagh would decide all such points. The Cabinet accepted with reluctance the

---

[1] From Bathurst, Jan. 7, 1814; from Liverpool, Jan. 20, 1814: *Lond. MSS., Appendix,* p. 516.

[2] See the letters in the *Appendix,* pp. 517, 522–23. The archives contain many memorials from the planters and merchants on this subject.

treaty with Denmark, not considering the Danes worth the
£400,000 which Thornton had promised. Spain had to be
handled with more gentleness than Sweden. The Spanish
Government were deeply moved by the news that peace
negotiations had opened without their concurrence. They
reproved Pizarro, who was at headquarters, for not asserting
himself, and ordered Fernan-Nuñez to join him from London to
vindicate the rights of Spain. They had many demands to
make—a rectification of their French frontier or even larger
surrenders, and a revival of their claim to Louisiana. They
still considered themselves a Great Power, and this claim,
which had a great past but was already out of date, was to
cause a good deal of trouble throughout all this period.
Liverpool treated it with some respect, though he did not
encourage their demands. He was moved by the Treaty of
Valençay, by which Napoleon tried to use the captive Ferdinand to make peace—a step which was considered in London
to shew how impossible it was to trust Napoleon's professions
of peaceful intentions.

Castlereagh was thus left for the most part to himself to
work out the details of the Alliance and the peace. How
unpalatable any peace with Bonaparte was to the Cabinet
will be seen when the question of the Bourbons is considered.
But they remained loyal to the policy which Castlereagh was
trying to carry out. "Our policy should be to keep the
Alliance together," wrote Liverpool, "and not to separate
ourselves from it either in peace or war. But we ought not
to conceal from ourselves that any peace with Bonaparte
will be only a state of preparation for renewed hostilities." [1]

Nevertheless, they submitted to the delays produced by
Bonaparte's military genius and the strategic faults of the
Alliance. Castlereagh's stay was early extended beyond
March 1, the period which originally the optimism of the
Cabinet had fixed to complete his mission, and when it was
clear that the campaign would be prolonged, Liverpool wrote
that Parliamentary business was not urgent till the middle

---

[1] From Liverpool, Jan. 20, 26, Feb. 4, 8, 12, 1814 : *Lond. MSS., Appen-
dix*, pp. 515–22. From Bathurst, Feb. 12, 1814 : *F.O. Cont. Arch.*, 1.
From Hamilton, Feb. 8, 1814 : *C.C.* ix. 254. Wessenberg to Metternich,
Feb. 1, 1814 : *Vienna St. A.*

of April, and that " we all think that it is of the utmost importance you should not leave the headquarters of the Allies before you have brought all your arrangements to a satisfactory conclusion." Castlereagh had no intention of doing otherwise. He had moved with headquarters to Chaumont —"a dirty and dull town which has nothing to reconcile one to it but a sense of public duty." "I have only one small room," he told his wife, "in which I sleep and work and the whole Chancellerie dines, when we can get anything to eat." It was here that he completed what was in some sense the greatest diplomatic act of his career.[1]

For Castlereagh did not return to Châtillon. In view of all that had happened it was now clear that his presence was more needed at headquarters, and that the most obvious necessity was the treaty of Alliance. Though this had been pushed on one side by the rapid course of events, it had never been out of Castlereagh's mind, and still less out of the recollection of the Allies who saw in it a necessary step to the subsidies of the next year. It is true that in December Castlereagh had indignantly rejected the proposal that these should be specified in the treaty. But his experience had shewn him that there was no other way to secure what he regarded as an indispensable instrument both for the present war and for the future security of Europe. He had already given up the colonial conquests, but in return he had obtained substantially allied agreement to a peace based on the ancient limits. He had failed, however, to obtain agreement on the reconstruction of Europe. The subsidies were his last great weapon. Could he use them to make the Allies guarantee the new settlement not only against France but against one another?

The difficulties proved to be greater than he could surmount. By this time he had come to realise something of what the disputes over Poland and Saxony portended. The Polish leaders, who had the Tsar's confidence, Czartoryski and Radziwill, had arrived at headquarters on February 26, and made Castlereagh's labours to produce an understanding still

---

[1] From Liverpool, Feb. 12, 17 : *Lond. MSS., Appendix*, pp. 520, 522. To his wife, March 12, 1814 : *Lond. MSS., Appendix*, p. 507.

more difficult. The Tsar had receded somewhat from his claim to all Galicia, but his intention to reconstitute almost the whole of Poland into a state under his own sovereignty was as firm as ever. Castlereagh, as has been seen, was determined to prevent this. He succeeded in persuading Czartoryski to leave headquarters, but made little progress on the main point. Nor were German questions in a much healthier condition. It is true that Hardenberg held Metternich's verbal promise of Saxony, but the rest of the territorial distribution and the new constitution of Germany were entirely undecided. Practically nothing, therefore, could be added to the outline which the Allies had already used as the basis of their last offer to Napoleon on February 17. Castlereagh, to Münster's relief, was defeated in an attempt to obtain a specified frontier in the Netherlands for Holland. The German Powers insisted that the territory on the left bank of the Rhine beyond the Meuse should be left open. Hardenberg had, indeed, said he would refuse all territory there for Prussia unless it was large enough to give strength, while Münster urged that if Holland became too strong she might again be a maritime rival to Britain.[1]

This was not a very happy situation in which to formulate a treaty to safeguard the world's peace. It was, however, something that the military and political position as regards France had become more solid. It could survive anything but calamity, Castlereagh thought. On March 4 the armistice negotiations were broken off, and Castlereagh pressed the Allies to prepare for a long campaign. No one at Chaumont now imagined that the war would soon be over. The lack of provisions, reported Castlereagh, were a hindrance to immediate operations, but he hoped that at the close of the harvest a great effort would be made "upon a scale which must envelope and overwhelm the enemy." He had practically no hope that the negotiations still in progress at Châtillon would result in peace: "My own impression is, as it has always been, that whilst anything of an army remains

[1] From Castlereagh, Feb. 26, March 3, 1814 : *B.D.* 160, 163. Münster to the Prince Regent, Feb. 17, 1814 : *Hanover St. A.*; Feb. 23, 25, 1814 : Fournier, *Congress*, 302, 303. From Hardenberg, Feb. 15, 1814 : *F.O. Cont. Arch.* 5.

to him, he [Napoleon] will not easily submit to sign such a peace as the Allies require; and I am induced to believe he will put his main resistance upon Antwerp, 1st, as the point of most pride as well as power, and, 2ndly, as that interest in support of which he expects the continental Powers will be least disposed to continue the war." Nor was it likely, he added, that peace would come from the people, though he painted a terrible picture of their sufferings: "So far as concerns the part of France through which I have passed, viz. from Bâle to Troyes, I never saw any country in a state of more abject misery and decline." But the pride of the middle class, he said, was yet unbroken and would support Napoleon in fighting for the frontiers of the Rhine and the Alps.[1]

In these circumstances it was only natural that his treaty should be mainly concerned with the present war with France and the protection of Europe from France after the war. The allied Powers each promised to keep 150,000 men in active service during the present war, and they pledged themselves not to make peace except with common consent. Britain in return promised subsidies amounting to five million pounds, in equal proportions to each, Prussia being thus raised, as her efforts entitled her, to a level with Russia and Austria. Monthly instalments were to be paid so long as the war lasted, if necessary beyond the year 1814, and for a month after the treaty of peace had been signed.

Ample provision was thus made for the continuation of the war until Napoleon was beaten, but, after all, this was only a consolidation of subsidy treaties such as were already in being. The novel part of the treaty extended its action into the peace. More extended guarantees might have to be postponed, but the four Powers at any rate bound themselves for twenty years to protect Europe against every attempt which France might make "to infringe the order of things resulting from such pacification." For this purpose they promised 60,000 men, Britain reserving her right to employ foreign troops paid by her as her contribution.

The stakes, as Castlereagh confessed, were high, and Britain's

[1] To Liverpool, March 3, 1814: *B.D.* 163; March 4, 1814: *F.O. Continent*, 3.

immediate contribution was, according to his calculation, double that of any of the Allies. Five million pounds was in itself equivalent to 150,000 men, and Britain contributed another 150,000 men besides. The Allies had each, of course, more than 150,000 men under arms, since the subsidy was paid for active forces only, but Britain also at that moment had on the Continent, Castlereagh claimed, 225,000 men in her direct pay: "What an extraordinary display of power. This I trust will put an end to any doubts as to the claim we have to an opinion on continental matters." It must be remembered that of the 225,000 not more than 70,000 were British. The rest were hired from foreign Powers according to her old methods. Yet it must be admitted that the exploits of Wellington now entitled her to rank as a military Power, though none of her soldiers were to be found in the main army fighting against Napoleon. Castlereagh had gone rather beyond the limits of his instructions in promising so much, as he admitted to Liverpool. But he pleaded that he had thus added powerfully to the impression which the treaty would produce, and he could not refuse, he said, "to assume that station in Europe as one of the great military Powers to which the exploits of her armies and the scale of her resources have so justly entitled her to claim." "I think your Lordship will agree with me," he added, "that if the war must go on, upon no principles could it be consistent with our policy to economise in point of exertion to the degree that would still remain open to us." [1]

The Cabinet, indeed, made no objection. They were prepared for any effort against France, and they warmly praised their colleague for securing at last the permanent Alliance which had been so long sought. Castlereagh's subordinates, who knew all the obstacles which he had had to surmount, joined in the chorus of congratulation. It was,

---

[1] To Liverpool, March 10, 1814 : *B.D.* 165; do. (No. 33): *F.O. Continent*, 3. To Hamilton, March 10, 1814 : *C.C.* ix. 335. He also promised to recommend his Cabinet to relieve Russia of her Dutch debt : E. Wawrzkowicza, *Anglia a Sprawa Polska, 1813–1815*, 330–32. Colenbrander, *Gedenkstukken*, vii. 87. To Liverpool, March 8, 1814 : *C.C.* ix. 327. This obligation, to which the Cabinet were very averse, henceforward acts as a sort of barometer of Russian relations with Britain. The Polish work noted above collects much evidence on this subject as well as on other points.

perhaps, the greatest moment of Castlereagh's career, and the treaty will always be a monument to his patience and diplomatic skill. But, as has been seen, it only accomplished half the objects which Castlereagh had set out to obtain. It had been designed, as its phraseology shews, to guarantee the settlement not only against France but against any disturber of the peace. The four Powers spoke in the name of all Europe, and they reserved "to themselves to concert together on the conclusion of a peace with France, as to the means best adapted to guarantee to Europe, and to themselves reciprocally, the continuance of the peace" (Art. V.). But this task lay in the future, and Castlereagh could now realise how difficult it was to be. As yet he was the only signatory who desired to find practical means to carry out the intention so stated, and it will be seen that he was never fully to accomplish the task.

As has been often pointed out, the treaty marks a stage in the evolution of the distinction between the Great Powers and the other states of Europe. It had been drafted and signed by them alone, and the main obligations of the treaty were such as only Great Powers with large resources could undertake. But the significance of this aspect was hardly realised by the signatories at the time. They wished to associate the most considerable of the smaller Allies in their Alliance after it was signed. By a secret and separate article Sweden, Spain, Portugal, and Holland were invited to accede to the treaty. Nevertheless, accession meant something very different from original signature. The four Powers were "Europe," as they had been in the negotiations with Napoleon, and they remained Europe in the future so long as they were united. Even the term Great Powers had begun to be current in diplomatic phraseology.[1]

[1] Hanover and Bavaria would have been specifically invited had not the Tsar insisted that Wurtemberg should accompany them, an act which it was considered would have undermined the rights of the German Federation in process of construction. Castlereagh at last terminated this dispute by drafting the clause so that any state might be invited in the future, and he explained to his Cabinet that Germany would accede as a whole when the Federation had been brought into being. Münster to the Prince Regent, March 10, 1814 : Fournier, *Congress*, 304. Pizzaro to the Secretary of State, March 12, 1814 : *W.S.D.* viii. 643. From Castlereagh, March 10 : *F.O. Continent*, 3. To Clancarty, March 14, 1814. "You will

Meanwhile at Châtillon the representatives had been "spitting over the bridge," as Castlereagh phrased it. No answer had come from Napoleon. On February 28, at the orders of headquarters, Caulaincourt had been allowed ten days in which to obtain his master's orders. He was still without them on March 10, but faced the Allies with a long disquisition, drawn up by the skilled public servants who were helping him, Rayneval and La Besnardière, which re-called the promises of Frankfort and the phrase in the King's Speech of October 1813, that France would not be humiliated. When an immediate rupture was about to follow, he made verbally another offer and kept the negotiation alive. As Stadion told Metternich, he could break off or not as he liked. Aberdeen said the same thing, adding that Caulaincourt had pleaded specially for Castlereagh's return: "If he were but here and would listen to my propositions, so that we might understand one another, we should speedily conclude the affair." Castlereagh had, however, concluded his treaty and was anxious to break off negotiations, but the rupture was delayed by the wish of Metternich, which his colleagues could not overcome, for some statement from Caulaincourt on which to found an ultimatum. Stadion was thus able to get the plenipotentiaries to allow more time, though Stewart protested vigorously at the delay, which had the additional disadvantage of keeping him from Blücher's army, which was fighting the critical battles of Craonne and Laon (March 7–10). Aberdeen quarrelled once more with his colleagues, to Stadion's great amusement.[1]

Metternich, however, was gradually placed under great pressure at headquarters, where Schwarzenberg's inactivity was strongly criticised by the Tsar and the Prussians, and Castlereagh became anxious to get rid of the negotiation, which he thought, with some truth, hindered operations. He urged on the others, and above all on Metternich, that the whole military situation should be surveyed and comprehensive

perceive the great Powers have been quite explicit in their offer of protection": *C.C.* ix. 355. *B.F.S.P.* i. 128 does not give the separate and secret articles of the treaty which are in F. Martens, *Recueil*, iii. 163.

[1] Stadion to Metternich, March 13, 1814 : Fournier, *Congress*, 349. From Stewart, March 13, 1814 ; from Aberdeen, March 10, 15, 1814 : *C.C.* ix. 334, 358, 567.

plans made for reinforcing the armies for a big campaign. "I cannot but express," he wrote on the 12th, "my individual anxiety to see the negotiations at Châtillon brought to an early issue. They enervate the temper of the army, and until we can make it clear whether it is to be war or peace to which we are to look for future security, the operations will languish and the enemy enjoy a double advantage." The Tsar agreed with him and they got on better terms.

This agreement had been helped by the Russians having at last agreed to the Dutch extension in Belgium. Castlereagh had only secured the assent by the promise to recommend to the British Government favourable consideration of the Russian demand that their loan to the Dutch bankers should be taken over by Britain or Holland. This was something like blackmail, as Castlereagh admitted, but he considered that Russian support was worth the price. It was, indeed, an important moment for his plans, since a deputation had arrived from Belgium to entreat the Emperor of Austria to allow them to be governed by a prince of his house. A refusal of this request had been promised, but Castlereagh was anxious that the "Brabanters," as he called them, should be reassured when their severance from France was announced to them. This was done in a note, drawn up by Castlereagh himself, which promised protection to their religion and commerce, and announced that an Austrian would take charge of their provisional government. This Castlereagh considered highly important, since it proclaimed publicly the Allies' intention of severing Belgium from France.

"I hope you will not disapprove our committal to the Brabanters," he wrote. "My colleagues here desired me to draw the declaration, and I certainly did it meaning *to tie you all hard and fast to the people*, if they did their duty by them- selves. The value of this measure is not *local*; it is *universal*. It will give confidence in the vigour of our councils, and it is doubly important to place Austria at the head of them. The effect of this on the enemy must be highly important." [1]

[1] To Liverpool, March 8, 1814: *C.C.* ix. 327; March 12, 15, 1814: *F.O. Continent*, 3. To Clancarty, March 13, 14, 1814: *C.C.* ix. 354, 365. Van Staen to Hogendorp, March 14, 1814: Colenbrander, *Gedenkstukken*, vii. 522. Liverpool was writing at the time that all information shewed

It was a relief to Castlereagh, therefore, that on the 17th instructions were sent from Troyes, where headquarters had moved, to Châtillon to break off if Caulaincourt had not accepted the basis. This put an end to the proceedings, though Caulaincourt, impressed by Napoleon's failure against Blücher, made last efforts to prolong them. But he had no word from his master, and on the 19th the end came. Castlereagh considered that the negotiation had shewn beyond "reasonable doubt in the view even of the French nation that Napoleon is the true and only obstacle to an early, honourable, and solid peace." [1]

The hands of the Allies were now free to prosecute schemes for his overthrow. The Bourbon princes were already in their rear, and an overture had at last been received from Paris. Though the Tsar was still hostile, Castlereagh was now able to take up their cause with the conviction that Louis would be accepted both by the French nation and the allied Governments as the future monarch of France.

the Belgians to be averse from a connection with Holland, and that they should form a state with Trêves or Mainz under an Austrian Archduke. From Liverpool, March 11, 1814 : *Lond. MSS., Appendix*, p. 525.

[1] From Castlereagh, March 22, 1814 : *B.D.* 168. Confidential Circular to the Allies, March 10, 1814 : *Vienna St. A.* From Cathcart, March 18, 1814 : *C.C.* ix. 366.

3. THE RESTORATION OF THE BOURBONS

TALLEYRAND in the early eighteen - twenties, very conscious of the lack of Bourbon gratitude towards himself, questioned the necessity of that expressed by Louis XVIII. in his famous tribute to George IV. "The British Government was convinced," he wrote, "until the last moment that peace could be signed with Napoleon at Châtillon, which reduces somewhat the merit which Louis XVIII. is said to have attributed to the Prince Regent when he asserted that, after God, it was to him that he owed his throne." [1] There is, however, in this, as in many other of Talleyrand's statements, a *non sequitur*. Were the Bourbons necessarily the successors of Napoleon if Europe could make no peace with him? Why were the other alternatives rejected? What caused the surprising ease with which they returned after twenty-three years to a nation which had almost forgotten their existence? Was it Talleyrand's skilful manœuvring in the last crisis of his Emperor's fortunes, or had the course of events been already determined by other means?

If the return of the Bourbons was inevitable, it took a very long time for those who were directing the allied councils to find it out. The discovery was certainly first made by Britain, and its application at the critical moment was more due to her than to any other Power. It was, indeed, an indispensable item of British policy during these fateful months, and, as such, merits a special examination of the intricate and subterranean process by which the final result was achieved.

The origin of the policy, like most else in this period, goes back to Pitt. He had always regarded a Bourbon restoration

---

[1] Broglie, *Mémoires du Prince Talleyrand*, ii. 146.

as the best guarantee of the peace of Europe, both before and after the Peace of Amiens. "The restoration of the French monarchy," he said in 1800, in response to a challenge by Tierney, "I consider as a most desirable object, because I think it would afford the strongest and best security to this country and to Europe." In the dispatch of 1805 the same principle was, as has been seen, again asserted. This object though highly desirable was, however, always subordinate. "*But* this object may not be attainable; and *if* it is not attainable, we must be satisfied with the best security we can find independent of it," he said in 1800; and in the dispatch it is laid down: "It is one with a view to which no active or decided measures can be taken, unless a series of great and signal successes shall previously be obtained by the Allies, and a strong and prevailing disposition for the return of the Monarch shall then manifest itself in the interior of France." [1]

This was the policy of Castlereagh, and it was the one accepted, though with great reluctance, by his Cabinet until the end. It did not, however, preclude sympathy with and support of the Bourbon cause within the limit Pitt had laid down. The Bourbons found in Britain their last refuge from a Continent no quarter of which was safe from Napoleon's power and influence, and this circumstance made the connection closer than it would otherwise have been. The Prince Regent and public opinion also went beyond the policy of the Cabinet in the final stages. But these circumstances, though they made the policy more difficult, did not determine it. The policy of Pitt was the guide, and if the final condition of a "strong and prevailing disposition" on the part of France was never secured, yet there was, in fact, no resistance, indeed complete acquiescence with the Restoration when it came.

The first suggestion of Britain, which was made in September 1813 to Austria, was received with a coldness that amounted to rejection. This may have been one reason why Castlereagh's instructions contained no word on the subject. Before his vessel left the country, however, a letter had been

---

[1] R. Coupland, *War Speeches of William Pitt*, 286. *B.D.* 394.

received from Wellington which gave more hope than had hitherto existed of a movement in the Bourbons favour. A request had come for a Bourbon prince to join Wellington's army and raise the south. Wellington allowed the Comte de Grammont to carry this request to England, but he sent also a memorandum for the Bourbon princes, pointing out that no movement was yet noticeable, and emphasising the difficulties and dangers of the proposition. This direct communication with the Bourbons forced the Cabinet's hand, and Liverpool at once saw Monsieur, who naturally insisted that if a Bourbon prince were allowed to join Wellington's army all France would rise to his support. Bathurst was disposed to do something—at least to announce that an immediate armistice by sea and land would follow a Bourbon restoration. Liverpool was more cautious, but he suggested that it would be impossible to stop the princes going to the south if they wished to, and that Wellington desired their presence. Castlereagh's answer strongly deprecated anything being done: "My impressions are against any step which should even in appearance mix our system with that of the Bourbons, whilst we are embarked in discussion for peace, and ignorant how our Allies would relish such a step at the present moment." [1]

The subject had, however, necessarily to receive the extended consideration of the Cabinet. Liverpool had a second interview with Monsieur, who refused all suggestions of delay and intimated firmly that his sons would try to embark for the south, and if refused a passport would appeal to the nation. The majority of the Cabinet were, however, of Castlereagh's opinion, and it was decided that though the princes must be allowed to go on their own responsibility, yet they could not be received at Wellington's headquarters. Liverpool's letter to Castlereagh, and still more Bathurst's, shew how distasteful the policy was to them. Wellington was, however, instructed accordingly, though doubtless Colonel Bunbury, who was sent over by Bathurst at this time,

---

[1] Wellington to Bathurst, Dec. 22, 1813; Memorandum, Dec. 20, 1813: *Gurwood*, xi. 390, 381. From Liverpool, Dec. 29, 1813; from Bathurst, Dec. 29, 1813: *Lond. MSS., Appendix*, p. 510. To Liverpool, Dec. 30, 31, 1813; to Bathurst, Dec. 30, 1813: *C.C.* ix. 123, 125, 130.

conveyed his chief's private desire that as much should be done as possible.

The Bourbons therefore made preparations to depart—Angoulême to the south, Berri to the north of France, if he could land, and Monsieur himself to Switzerland. Wellington was now given rather more latitude to take advantage of any movement on their behalf, but the whole enterprise was still kept strictly unofficial and at the princes' own risk. Monsieur had, however, an interview with the Prince Regent, whose warm hopes for his success he published in the Press the next day. The Prince Regent, indeed, made no secret of his opinions, which the Foreign Ambassadors hastened to tell their Courts—one eventual result being, as we have seen, the unfortunate incident between Alexander and Castlereagh at Troyes.[1]

Liverpool expressed his disgust at Monsieur's disregard of the proprieties, and had it been possible would no doubt have used similar language about the Prince Regent. Monsieur, however, informed him before his departure that the Bourbons, if restored, would accept the ancient limits. This was bidding high for support, as they had never thus committed themselves before. But the Cabinet were steadfast in their adherence to Castlereagh's policy.[2]

Castlereagh meanwhile, as has been seen, had found little support for the Bourbons at headquarters. He had, however, got Metternich's apparent agreement to the alternatives of Bonaparte or the Bourbons in order to check the Tsar's supposed plans for Bernadotte. But the Tsar was obviously hostile, and Castlereagh had merely laid down at Langres that peace should be offered to Bonaparte, leaving entirely undecided what should happen if he refused it, or if he was to lose the support of the French people.

This situation continued throughout February and the

---

[1] Liverpool's memorandum and correspondence with Monsieur : *W.S.D.* viii. 485–90. Bathurst to Wellington, Jan. 7 : *Lond. MSS.* From Liverpool, Jan. 6, 1814 ; from Bathurst, Jan. 7, 1814 : *Lond. MSS., Appendix*, p. 512. The Cabinet was scattered as usual when Parliament was up. Mulgrave was strongly against action, Harrowby inclined to it : *Bathurst*, 255, 260.

[2] From Liverpool, Jan. 20, 21, 1814 : *Lond. MSS., Appendix*, pp. 516, 518. Bathurst to Wellington, Jan. 18, 1814 : *W.S.D.* viii. 519.

first half of March. Angoulême went to Passages, but kept away from Wellington, who found but little demand for him amongst the occupied provinces, though the British troops were received with but little hostility. Monsieur went to Vesoul, whence he wrote to the Tsar, who sent a cold reply. The Cabinet continued to support Castlereagh in his policy of negotiation with Bonaparte, though public opinion in Britain became more and more vehement for his dethronement.

The St. Aignan documents were now published by Napoleon and caused an outburst of indignation in London. "You can scarcely have an idea how *insane* people are in this country on the subject of any peace with Bonaparte," wrote Liverpool on February 12, "and I should really not be surprised at any public manifestation of indignation upon the first intelligence of a peace with him being received"; and he drew again the moral that though peace might have to be made it must be such as would stand the scrutiny of a hostile public. The reports of the Ambassadors confirm this point of view, and there were about this time hints that the Prince Regent would send for Wellesley. His organ, the *Times*, was especially violent in its denunciation of Bonaparte. Liverpool never wavered, but he admitted that the Cabinet did not want a peace with Bonaparte, who must be worse for Europe than any other Government whatever in France.[1]

This letter cannot have been very pleasing reading to Castlereagh, who received it at Bar-sur-Aube when the Allies were in retreat and threatened with dissolution, but the same mail brought some cheering words from the faithful Cooke: "We have great confidence in what you will settle, and I think it will not be a hard matter to put the public mind right. It is difficult to enter any measures for that purpose, whilst it is of consequence to keep the designs of the Government in obscurity." Liverpool also loyally gave encouragement when Castlereagh's later reports began to arrive and he realised more of the situation. The *Courier* got hold of the terms which had been offered at Châtillon, as Cooke thought, through some leakage in London. Cooke, however, was stout in defence of

[1] From Liverpool, Feb. 8, 12, 1814 : *Lond. MSS., Appendix*, pp. 520, 521. From Hamilton, Feb. 8, 1814 : *C.C.* ix. 254.   Wessenberg to Metternich, Feb. 17, 1814 : *Vienna St. A.*

Castlereagh's policy, and Liverpool did not waver. The only criticism on the draft treaty was that Sardinia had been omitted. "Peace is as unpopular as ever," Liverpool reported on the 17th; but he reassured him that the Cabinet was united and would not fall and that Castlereagh would have their full support. When, therefore, he received the news of the Lieven intrigue and Robinson's account of all that had happened, his private letter was all that Castlereagh could desire. The official instruction expressly allowed him to conclude peace with the *de facto* ruler of France, while Lieven was made to feel the weight of Liverpool's displeasure and anxiety at what had taken place. This was doubtless all the more genuine since the incident caused friction between the Prince Regent and the Cabinet, and it took all Eldon's influence to make George give way to the opinion of his Ministers.[1]

Then came the check to the allied armies which, as has been seen, nearly dissolved the coalition. This made all but the most violent of the supporters of the Bourbons hesitate. Even Bathurst had admitted that if Bonaparte were dethroned there was no agreement as to his successor, while there was the undoubted fact that no overt Bourbon movement had been detected in France in spite of allied occupation in north and south, as Liverpool pointed out to the Marquis of Hertford for the edification of the Prince Regent. Meanwhile Wellington was informing the Duc d'Angoulême that he saw no chance of a movement for the Bourbons unless the Allies took their adherents under their protection.[2]

---

[1] From Liverpool, Feb. 17, 27, 1814 : *Lond. MSS., Appendix*, pp. 522, 523. From Bathurst, Feb. 17, 1814 : *B.D.* 161. From Cooke, Feb. 12, 1814 : *Lond. MSS.* ; Feb. 19, 1814 : *C.C.* ix. 280. Wessenberg to Metternich, Feb. 15, 17, 22, 1814 : *Vienna St. A.* Jacobi to Hardenberg, Feb. 15, 18, 1814 : *Berlin St. A.* Lieven to Nesselrode, March 1, 1814 : *Pet. Arch.* Sir Charles Flint to Peel, March 2, 1814 : " The Prince, I hear, is in a very bad humour and has been so ever since Robinson's arrival. He cannot bear the idea of peace with Bonaparte. I suspect the Chancellor [Eldon] has had a very difficult task in making H.R.H. yield to the opinion of the Cabinet. He used to pass three hours at a time with the Prince and almost every day while Robinson was here." Parker, *Life of Peel*, i. 127. Horner, though himself against the restoration, wrote on the 22nd that " public opinion is an amusing subject of observation at this moment ; I never knew it more violent or more nearly unanimous." Horner, *Memoirs*, ii. 159.

[2] See *supra*, p. 219. Bathurst to Wellington, Feb. 26, 1814, in sending the Châtillon terms of peace : " The Allies cannot agree who to favour.

It was not till the middle of March that the patience of the Cabinet gave way. Then they began to chafe at the long delay at Châtillon. Bathurst, always the most ardent, controverted Castlereagh's assertions that the Bourbons had no adherents and urged on him Wellington's view that a declaration of the Allies was necessary before a rising could be expected. By March 19 the dissatisfaction had gone so far that an official instruction was sent to Castlereagh to bring the Châtillon negotiations to a close or withdraw the British offers of colonial concessions. The majority of the Cabinet were now in favour of no peace with Bonaparte, the Prince Regent openly supported them, and the Press were frantic. Grenville was on the same side, though Grey and a portion of the Whigs did not follow him. Only Liverpool's steadfast adherence to the principle on which Castlereagh was acting, that no steps should be taken to overthrow Napoleon while the negotiation was going on, prevented definite orders being sent that no peace was to be made.

The effect of the news of Bordeaux's declaration for the Bourbons was, however, irresistible and affected all classes. "The Methodists and the women are particularly warlike," noted Stratford Canning, while Merveldt in great alarm pleaded for the return of Castlereagh, who alone could bring his countrymen to reason. "The only man is absent," he lamented, "who, according to general opinion, is the soul of the present ministry . . . Lord Castlereagh. Lord Sidmouth and Mr. Vansittart, who are the strongest after him, are not strong enough to support the fears of their other colleagues, and especially of Lord Harrowby and Lord Liverpool. The last named especially is even more timorous and quite incapable of maintaining his opinion against his colleagues and the unanimous voice of the City of London without some external aid." Jacobi was less certain of the weakness of the

It is therefore difficult to protest against the existing Government if we cannot agree on a successor." Liverpool to Hertford, March 9, 1814 : " I think it is highly probable that there is scarcely a large town in France in which there are not some friends to the Bourbon cause—but that this sentiment is at all general in the eastern and central provinces of that country thro' which the allied armies have been marching is at direct variance with every report, official or unofficial, political or military, received by the Government." *Lond. MSS.* Wellington to d'Angoulême, March 3, 1814 : *Gurwood*, xi. 543.

Cabinet, but he had no doubts of their decision, and Lieven, who alone seems to have been told of it, was delighted at the result.

For Liverpool and the Cabinet had immediately decided that no peace must now be signed with Napoleon by Britain, whether the Allies wished it or not, and official instructions to that effect had been sent to Castlereagh on March 22. Even if he had signed, ratification must be considered doubtful until the situation was known. Liverpool's private letter displayed his anxiety and embarrassment: "We never should be forgiven if we made peace with Bonaparte under these circumstances, unless forced to by the Allies." Cooke, who had promised all support for a peace until this moment, sent a similar word of warning.[1]

Fortunately for Castlereagh no such problem was presented to him. By the time the dispatches reached him not only had the Châtillon negotiations been broken off, but other events had happened which made action for the Bourbons not only justifiable but also practical.

The exact processes by which France was induced to accept the Bourbons is still a matter of dispute. The evidence is obscured by the self-interest and vanity of the actors who took part in it, many of whom subsequently compiled memoirs in which truth is generally subordinated to the display of the writer's own importance. Nevertheless, even in such a delicate negotiation a good deal of contemporary evidence was accumulated in letters and notes, and from this a fair idea of Castlereagh's share in it can be obtained, however much he was himself inclined to minimise it. He had moved with Metternich, Hardenberg, and the Emperor of Austria to Bar-sur-Aube. The Tsar, on the other hand, had remained with Schwarzenberg when the latter had at last been induced to join in a forward movement, which largely by

---

[1] Lane-Poole, *Life of Stratford Canning*, i. 204. From Bathurst, March 11, 1814 : *Lond. MSS.* ; March 19, 22, 1814 : *B.D.* 166, 171. From Liverpool, March 19, 21, 22, 1814 : *Lond. MSS., Appendix*, pp. 527–30. From Cooke, March 22, 1814 : " If . . . after knowing the proceedings at Bordeaux, you shall authorise the signature, I fear the case must be of extreme urgency to make it any degree supportable here." *C.C.* ix. 382 (where wrongly copied). Merveldt to Metternich, March 25, 1814 : *Vienna St. A.* Jacobi to Hardenberg, March 25, 1814 : *Berlin St. A.* Lieven to Nesselrode, March 25, 1814 : *Pet. Arch.*

Alexander's influence was continued by the Austrians as well as the Prussians and Russians when Bonaparte threw himself on the rear of the allied armies in a vain effort to stop the advance.

The allied sovereigns were thus about to be separated when at last a communication came from Paris with the object of concerting with the Allies for the overthrow of Bonaparte. This emissary, Vitrolles, a returned *émigré*, whose station was below his ambition, had set out before the rupture of negotiations to Châtillon. He came with a note to Metternich from d'Alberg, while Talleyrand was cognisant of the mission though not of all the Bourbon plans of the emissary and was anxious to avoid responsibility. Stadion sent him from Châtillon to Troyes to Metternich, who gave him no encouragement, being still in negotiation with Caulaincourt and having not yet abandoned hope of peace with Napoleon or a Regency. After this check, Vitrolles obtained through Nesselrode an interview on the 17th with the Tsar, who was about to join Schwarzenberg. The Tsar was in complete accord with Vitrolles that no peace should be made with Napoleon, but he shewed no wish to ensure a Bourbon restoration. The choice, he said, even if it were a republic, must be left to France. He agreed, however, that a march on Paris would mean the end of Napoleon, and it is probable that he was by this time far more reconciled to a Bourbon restoration than he had ever previously been, otherwise Castlereagh would hardly have written two days before: "I have seen a great deal of the Emperor, and his tone of thinking is perfectly satisfactory to me." But the Tsar was absorbed with military plans; time enough to settle the question of the dynasty when he had entered Paris and displayed his power and magnanimity to the French people. Vitrolles went on to Bar-sur-Aube, where on the 19th he again saw Metternich and this time Castlereagh. He demanded that the Allies should no longer treat with Napoleon but with France, or, better still, with Monsieur, who should be encouraged to administer the occupied provinces and supplied with funds. According to his own account, they received him with suspicion and reserve—especially Castlereagh. It is easy to believe him when he reports the "impassibility" and "imperturbable silence" with which Castlereagh received these communications, but hardly when he claims that Castlereagh eventually replied that the Bourbon cause was unpopular in England.[1]

Nevertheless, Castlereagh and Metternich were impressed with Vitrolles' possibilities, however much they took pains not to commit themselves. Castlereagh told his Cabinet two days later that the communication had been conveyed "through a channel peculiarly competent in point of ability to develop the views of those concerned," "persons of no mean weight in France." They wished to send Vitrolles straight back to Paris, where they rightly concluded that the issue would be decided. But when Vitrolles insisted on going first to Monsieur at Nancy, they sent with him a cautious document drawn up by Metternich, which, however, offered him the revenues of any province he could get to support him, while the plotters in Paris were encouraged to go on and assured that an amnesty would be obtained for them if they were unsuccessful. Castlereagh also offered cash, but he wished it to pass to its destination through allied hands in order to avoid the political difficulty "which must always attend, in a Government like ours, the voting of a sum of money for effectuating a change in the Government of France." He was, indeed, very anxious to avoid direct responsibility, his object being, as he explained, "to bring Great Britain forward in whatever may regard the interior of France rather as the ally and auxiliary of the continental Powers, than as charging herself in chief, and making herself responsible for what cannot be conducted under the superintendence of her own Government." His parting words to Vitrolles were: "Let those act who are stronger than we are and more free to make decisions."[2]

At this interesting stage developments were checked by the fact that headquarters were chivied from one town to another by Napoleon's rapid movements, with the result that while the Tsar and the King of Prussia remained with the

---

[1] To Liverpool, March 15, 1814 : *F.O. Continent*, 3. Vitrolles, *Mémoires*, i. 119, 139 ff.

[2] To Liverpool, March 22, 1814 : *B.D.* 168. Vitrolles, *Mémoires*, i. 140.

armies which were pressing on to Paris, the Emperor of
Austria with Metternich, Hardenberg, and Castlereagh found
refuge in Dijon, where they arrived on March 24.   Castlereagh seems to have thrived on these hardships, for Lady
Burghersh, who had herself an exciting escape from the
French, was in raptures over his appearance and his reputation: "You never saw such a beauty as Lord Castlereagh
has become.   He is as brown as a berry with a fine bronzed
colour and wears a fur cap with gold and is really quite
charming.   There never was anybody so looked up to as he
is here."

It was in Dijon that in the course of the next few days the
fate of the Bourbons was decided.   The declaration drawn
up on the rupture of the Châtillon negotiations still lacked
the Tsar's signature and was not issued until the 28th, but
by that time it was out of date.   Münster was able to report
on the 23rd that it had been decided to support the Bourbons,
though the Tsar's absence had delayed matters.   The
Emperor of Austria was still in some doubt, but Metternich
and his master finally yielded to the logic of events and the
unceasing pressure of Castlereagh.   All hesitation was finally
removed by the news which reached Dijon on the 26th that
Bordeaux had declared for the Bourbons.   On the 27th
Metternich sent a cold answer, concerted with Castlereagh,
to an urgent appeal from Caulaincourt, and on the 28th, in
what seems to have been a very gay party at Castlereagh's
house, Metternich, Hardenberg, Razumovski, Münster, the
envoys of Holland, Bavaria, and Spain, and their host drank
openly to the success of the Bourbon cause.[1]

The Emperor of Austria now consented to send an envoy,
Bombelles, to Monsieur with the conditions of allied recognition of the Bourbon cause.   These were drawn up in a broad

---

[1] Rose Weigall, *Letters of Lady Burghersh*, 205. To Liverpool, March
29, 1814 (enclosing Metternich to Caulaincourt, March 27, 1814) : *F.O.
Continent*, 3 ; March 30, 1814 : *B.D.* 173. Münster to the Prince Regent,
March 23, 30, 1814 : *Hanover St. A.* Verger to King of Bavaria, March
28, 29, 1814 : " Le Comte de Stadion porte le premier toast au brave Maire
de Bordeaux qui avait arboré la cocarde blanche, Milord à Louis XVIII.,
puis au peuple français, en suite aux princes alliés. Tout le monde fit
chorus. Ce dîner memorable qui assure le pavillon blanc prouve que dans
ce sens nous avons passé le Rubicon." *Munich St. A. Cf.* also *Bath
Archives*, ii. 417.

spirit, for they required that Monsieur should undertake to rule constitutionally, to recognise the confiscation of the lands of the nobility, to guarantee the public debt of France, and to maintain the existing civil and military officials in their situations.   Castlereagh had no doubt of success, and hastened to tell Wellington for the edification of the Duc d'Angoulême: "The Congress is over. The Allies support the King. . . . The old family must take the Government as they find it, confirm the proprietors without reserve, and use the public men, civil and military, of latter times." These decisions had arisen out of the nature of things and had hardly been affected by the instructions which Castlereagh had received on the 28th, though Metternich used them as a justification for his actions.   But as Castlereagh wrote officially to his Cabinet: "I need hardly assure your Lordship that upon a manifestation of national sentiment so striking against the authority of the existing Government, I should have felt it my duty, unsanctioned by an order from home, to have acted upon the reservation of the 29th of January, and should have suspended further negotiation till the Prince Regent's pleasure was declared.   As it is I have only to rejoice that the allied councils are now wholly unembarrassed on this subject by the previous rupture of the conferences at Châtillon." This, of course, since it was written possibly for publication, did not tell all, but Castlereagh had all along made clear that rupture with Napoleon was to be followed by active assistance to the Bourbons.[1]

When Napoleon himself, therefore, was induced to make one final attempt to save his throne for his son by an appeal to his father-in-law, there was no chance of a hearing. This approach was made through no other than the unfortunate Wessenberg, who, at last released from his painful mission in London, was taken by French soldiers on his way to rejoin his master. Napoleon, in a long interview, offered to resign in favour of a Regency under Marie Louise, but even now it

[1] Instructions to Bombelles: *F.O. Continent*, 3. To Wellington, March 31, 1814: *F.O. Cont. Arch.*, 5, and *W.S.D.* viii. 708 (where it is wrongly presumed to be for Bathurst). To Liverpool, March 30, 1814: *F.O. Continent*, 4. Metternich to Hudelist, March 30, 1814: Fournier, *Congress*, 266.

is interesting to note he could not bring himself to sacrifice the place which had been Castlereagh's main object since he came on the Continent. "I must keep Antwerp," he said, "since without this place France will not soon again possess a fleet. I am ready to give up all the colonies if by this sacrifice I can keep the mouth of the Scheldt for France." "England," he added later, "is now the most reasonable of the Allies, and Castlereagh seems to me a most estimable man." But words like these, which we may be sure Wessenberg would not have reported had they not been uttered, were now of no avail. Steps had already been taken on Castlereagh's initiative to ensure that wife and son shared Napoleon's downfall.[1]

For, meanwhile, important communications had been taking place with Paris. Since Vitrolles did not return, Castlereagh opened another route through the agency of a friend there, "whom I knew to be with the party likely to conduct the expected movement." This was fortunate, for the Bourbon party were hoping to obtain assistance from Bernadotte, who was intriguing in a mysterious way with both them and Joseph. His emissary, Vielcastel, had already given out in the south that his master was to be made Lieutenant-General and to govern in the name of the Bourbons. Bernadotte himself left his army and made a hurried journey in the direction of Paris, refusing Thornton's advice to visit Monsieur "on the ground of his entire ignorance of the wishes and sentiments of the Allies, and on the bad effect which in this state of ignorance such conduct might produce upon the minds of the Swedish people." But the Count de Montagnac, sent out from Paris to get in touch with him, failed to find him, and learnt from Bülow that the Prince Royal was in no way authorised to act for the Allies as those in Paris had imagined. Montagnac was therefore, when Castlereagh's message arrived, sent back to Dijon, and he was able to return with the promise of allied support under the signatures of Castlereagh, Hardenberg, and Metternich. Favourable answers were received from Paris quite decisive in favour of the Bourbons.

It was even more important that the Tsar was now also

---

[1] Arneth, *Life of Wessenberg*, i. 188 ff.

prepared to acquiesce. "The Emperor is weaned of his false notions on this point," stated Castlereagh, "and we have a secret intimation from Nesselrode through Schwarzenberg that the Prince Royal's intrigue with Joseph is understood, and that Talleyrand and others in authority will counteract it." At the same time Bombelles returned on April 4 from his mission to Monsieur, bringing back "most satisfactory assurances of His Royal Highness's readiness on the part of the King to adopt every measure that can tranquillise and conciliate the nation."

Bernadotte was thus completely frustrated in the design which Castlereagh believed, in the light of subsequent disclosures, he had harboured to the last. The intercepted letter of an emissary of Napoleon to Berthier appeared to shew that he was ready to abandon the allied cause, and his conduct certainly needed explanation. "It is clear," wrote Castlereagh on May 3, after a review of these events, "he never meant more than to make the Bourbons the instruments of his own elevation, notwithstanding his assurances to me thro' Thornton (who has been his dupe throughout) that there was no middle line between Louis XVIII. and Bonaparte." [1]

Castlereagh and Metternich were therefore able to remain in tranquil confidence at Dijon while the momentous events were in progress at Paris. Neither, it may be imagined, was very anxious to be present at the capital. The Emperor of Austria could not fail to be embarrassed at appearing on the scene while matters were still undecided and refusing all support to the claims of his daughter and grandchild, while Castlereagh had continually insisted on his anxiety to keep his share in the restoration as much out of sight as possible. They alleged, therefore, that the roads were unsafe for travel, and Castlereagh's annoyance with Lady Burghersh, who hastened to join her husband in Paris, for proving these

---

[1] To Liverpool, March 30, April 4, 1814: *B.D.* 173, 174; April 4, May 3, 1814: *F.O. Continent*, 4. The friend in Paris may have been the English agent Darby, or another of his kind, or perhaps the Princess de Vaudemont, of whom Vitrolles informs us there was mention at their first meeting. Castlereagh had met her at Hamburg during his first visit to the Continent (Vitrolles, *Mémoires*, i. 135). From Thornton, April 8, 1814: *F.O. Sweden*, 91.

fears false may well have been real, though not for the motives she had imagined.[1]

The allied armies, meanwhile, inspired with energy by the Tsar, were on the 29th outside the capital, which no foreign army had entered since the days of Jeanne d'Arc, and Marmont was beaten in a last battle on the heights of Montmartre. But by this time the adherents of the Bourbons had already made their plans, and Talleyrand had at last decided to place himself at their head. It was he who visited the Tsar and arranged for the capitulation of the capital. On March 30 the Tsar and the King of Prussia, with the allied generals and suites, made a magnificent entry. Stewart and Cathcart and seven other British officers were amongst them—"Lord Cathcart in scarlet regimentals, his low, flat cocked hat forming a striking contrast to all the others. Sir Charles Stewart was covered with orders and conspicuous by his fantastic dress, evidently composed of what he deemed every army's best." The Tsar was Talleyrand's guest, since there were rumours that the Palace Élysée was mined, and between him and Talleyrand was arranged the capitulation of Marmont, the declaration which refused to treat with Napoleon or any of his army, and, finally, the restoration of the Bourbons as constitutional monarchs on terms such as Talleyrand thought best for France and for himself.[2]

It was the Tsar who made all these decisions on the part of the Allies, for the King of Prussia without his Minister was powerless, while Schwarzenberg was put on one side completely. Lord Stewart, who depicted in vivid and excited language the dramatic scenes of the allied entry, gradually became much perturbed and wrote daily that Castlereagh's presence was urgently needed. But the progress of events was already decided between Talleyrand and the allied Ministers, and Castlereagh made no haste to join his brother.

---

[1] Rose Weigall, *Letters of Lady Burghersh*, 221–23.
[2] [Underwood] *A Narrative of Memorable Events in Paris in the Year 1814*, 105. The best account of these events is in M. Dupuis' *Ministère de Talleyrand en 1814*, vol. i. chap. 5 (1919). M. Lacour-Gayet's *Talleyrand*, vol. ii., 1799–1815 (1930), adds but little to our knowledge, though the author has had access to the Talleyrand Archives. Like many French writers, he has neglected works in any other language but French.

Though the marshals made an attempt to secure a Regency
and the Tsar hesitated for a moment, the issue was never
really in doubt.   On the 5th Stewart was able to announce
that the marshals' attempts had been defeated.   On the 6th
Napoleon himself had agreed to the Tsar's terms, and all
obstacles in the way of a Bourbon restoration were at an end.
The principle on which Castlereagh had insisted on his first
entry into the allied councils had prevailed, and the Tsar was
himself the instrument of the restoration of the family which
he had so much despised and detracted.[1]

In two respects, however, the absence of allied Ministers
influenced events at Paris.   The way was made easier for the
constitution which the Senate adopted at Talleyrand's in-
stigation.   This certainly went further than either Metternich or Castlereagh preferred, and they were not satisfied with
the manner in which the Tsar had given it encouragement.
"The declaration, which had been signed by the Emperor of
Russia," wrote Castlereagh, "is not a very orthodox instrument—in so far as it is a pledge to guarantee a constitution
without knowing what it is."   This declaration, made by the
Tsar in the name of the coalition on March 31, was indeed the
work of Talleyrand, who was determined to make constitutional government a *fait accompli* before the legitimate
King's representative appeared on the scene.   It made no
mention of the Bourbons, but declared that the Allies would
not treat with Napoleon nor any member of his family, that
France should have at least her ancient limits, and that the
Allies would respect and guarantee the constitution which the
French nation should choose.   We may imagine that if
Metternich and Castlereagh had been present they would
not have been so complacent.   Nor would they have given
Talleyrand the support which the Tsar proffered, so that he

[1] To Liverpool, April 4, 1814 : *B.D.* 174.   From Stewart, April 1, 4,
5, 6 : *C.C.* ix. 415, 418, 436, 440, 441, 442 ; April 5, 1814 : " [The Regency]
has been most peremptorily refused, and if there were no other reasons
there is indisputable proof, I am told, that this child is not the son of the
Empress Maria Louisa, but that she was delivered of a dead child and this
infant was substituted from a girl of one or two that Bonaparte had at the
moment at hand in case of accidents.   I have heard this from such
authority that I can hardly doubt it," *F.O. Prussia,* 97.   This passage,
which repeated a current slander, was wisely omitted from the same letter
printed in *C.C.* ix. 441.

was able to get a constitution adopted by the Senate before
the abdication of Napoleon was consummated or there was
any possibility of interference by Monsieur. But Castlereagh and Metternich had, after all, already committed
themselves to some form of constitution in their correspondence with Monsieur, and the final result of Talleyrand's
efforts was not harshly judged by Castlereagh. Though
Cooke's susceptibilities were shocked ("Such a House of
Lords! without family, property, character!") Castlereagh
was not altogether displeased at Talleyrand's work. "The
concession of the hereditary principle to the existing Senators
is a great fault," he said, after he had had time for consideration, and this view has been supported by most modern
critics. For the rest, he was mainly concerned that the new
bodies should have the right to modify the *Charte* without
reference to the people, and thus build up something which
was more likely to correspond to the needs of France than
Talleyrand's hasty improvisation. He had no great confidence that any form of words could replace experience and
experiment in constitutional matters.[1]

Far more serious in his view was the arrangement that had
been made for Napoleon. It was the Tsar's magnanimity
that secured for the fallen Emperor his title and the island of
Elba in full sovereignty. Talleyrand and the provisional
Government had no share in the offer. Stewart was instantly in alarm and made a notable prophecy when he
suggested that "it might be well to consider, before the act
is irretrievable, whether a far less dangerous retreat might not
be found, and whether Napoleon may not bring the powder
to the iron mines which the island of Elba is so famed for."
Many others, and not least the British Government, shared
these fears, while Liverpool pointed out that Elba was considered by many persons as the best naval station in the

---

[1] To Liverpool, April 4, 1814 : *B.D.* 174. From Cooke, April 14, 1814.
To Liverpool, April 20, 1814 : *C.C.* ix. 462, 481. Münster to the Prince
Regent, April 20, 1814 : " I venture the belief that, if the Ministers of
England, of Austria, and of Prussia had been present at the taking of the
capital of France, they would not have agreed to the declaration made in
the name of the Allies by the Emperor Alexander on the 31st March. This
declaration (made by M. de Talleyrand) is a veritable Pandora's box."
Münster, 151.

Mediterranean. But when Castlereagh arrived in Paris on the 10th he found the decision irrevocable. It was considered imperative to get Napoleon off the scene as soon as possible so that the allegiance of the army to the new *régime* could be secured. Nor was it easy to find any other refuge for him less objectionable to which he was at all likely to consent. His Corsican home was just as dangerous, and in any case his rival Pozzo di Borgo, now in great favour with the Tsar, would never have allowed it. "I did not feel," reported Castlereagh, "that I could encourage the alternative which Caulaincourt assured me Bonaparte repeatedly mentioned, namely, an asylum in England." Thus he had reluctantly to agree, refusing, however, to recognise the title of Emperor on behalf of Britain, to whom Napoleon remained legally General Bonaparte until the day of his death. Nevertheless, Napoleon continued during his journey to Elba to express the wish to reside in Britain, and Castlereagh was inclined to consider it. He had less hesitation in recognising the grant of Parma duchies to the Empress and her son. It was, in a sense, a concession to the Emperor of Austria rather than to Napoleon. It was by Castlereagh's suggestion, however, that the imperial titles of the Napoleonic family were limited to the lives of the holders, so that a dynasty which Britain had never recognised would ultimately cease to exist even in name so far as treaties could accomplish the fact.[1]

These reservations shew the passion which inspired British statesmen who had lived under the shadow of Napoleon's ambition almost the whole of their political life. But to France and her restored King, Castlereagh and his colleagues were in a kindlier mood. To this they were helped not only by their especial interest in the Bourbon restoration, but also

---

[1] Stewart to Bathurst, April 7, 1814 : *C.C.* ix. 450. From Liverpool, April 9, 1814 : *Lond. MSS., Appendix*, p. 532. To Liverpool, April 13, 1814 : *B.D.* 175. It is impossible to believe Napoleon's assertion (O'Meara, *A Voice from St. Helena,* 497-98) that Castlereagh actually offered him an asylum in England. But he would have preferred him there to Elba. To Liverpool, May 5, 1814 : " If his taste for an asylum in England should continue, would you allow him to reside in some distant province ? It would obviate much alarm on the Continent " : *C.C.* x. 10. Fouché urged Napoleon to go to the United States. Yonge, *Liverpool,* i. 507. *Münster,* 166.

by some natural jealousy of the position which the Tsar had obtained by his magnanimous and liberal attitude. His protection of the constitution had aroused much enthusiasm amongst the Opposition in Britain, and at Paris he stood out far above his fellow - sovereigns. Though a separate and magnificent reception was arranged for the Emperor of Austria, Francis was ill at ease and had none of the Tsar's popular gifts. When, therefore, Monsieur arrived in Paris and negotiations were begun, Castlereagh was anxious to be as accommodating as possible. It had, at first, been decided to make a preliminary treaty of peace with France, but as it was urgently necessary to arrange for the withdrawal of the allied armies and the restoration of the allied fortresses still in French hands, some simpler instrument was necessary to effect this quickly. Accordingly, negotiations were at once begun for this purpose with Talleyrand, who was accepted by Monsieur as Foreign Minister, though in domestic matters his opinions were by no means approved. Castlereagh was anxious to allow France to retain the fleet captured in Antwerp, but the Cabinet's consent could not be obtained and this point was left open in the Convention signed on the 23rd. The discussion of the terms of peace had already begun, and Castlereagh hoped that they would not take longer than a month. As the line to which the armies retired was that of the 1792 frontier, it was clear what the territorial basis of the peace would be.[1]

Meanwhile, the return of Louis XVIII. to his kingdom had been delayed by a severe and inopportune attack of gout. The British Government treated him with the greatest consideration and loaned him £100,000 to pay off his debts and prepare for his new magnificence. They also agreed to continue their allowances to the distressed émigrés until the restored monarch was in command of a revenue. When at last he was able to move, he was received by the Prince Regent and the enthusiastic applause of the populace. He replied to the Prince Regent's congratulations: "It is to the counsels of your Royal Highness, to this glorious country, and to the

---

[1] To Liverpool, April 19, 20, 1814: *C.C.* ix. 472, 480, 482. From Liverpool, April 14, 1814: *Lond. MSS., Appendix*, p. 534.

steadfastness of its inhabitants that I attribute, next after the will of Providence, the re-establishment of my house on the throne of its ancestors." The tribute was genuine and truer than most royal speeches, but it was hardly likely to commend him to his faithful subjects. It had, however, a reassuring effect on the British Cabinet, of whom the Prime Minister and several of his colleagues accompanied Louis and the Prince Regent to Dover, whence the King sailed on Sunday, though Wilberforce was much distressed that these duties interfered with the higher ones due to the Sabbath day. Liverpool was not afraid that the Tsar would have too much influence on the restored monarch. On the contrary, he welcomed the efforts which Pozzo di Borgo, whom the Tsar had sent over to accompany and advise the King, made to overcome the prejudices of the *émigrés* by whom Louis was surrounded. "Strange as it may appear," Liverpool wrote to Castlereagh as the royal yacht was escorted from Dover by the Lord High Admiral, "[the French] are in better humour with the Austrian Government, and more inclined to confide in them, than in any of the Allies, except ourselves." [1]

The exception was, however, important. Louis was genuinely grateful, and if gratitude was not an emotion in which Talleyrand indulged, other motives led him in the same direction. They were shared by few other Frenchmen, who saw in Britain the most successful and obvious of her foes, but they were to affect profoundly the reconstruction of Europe. First of all, however, France had to make her own peace with her victorious enemies.

[1] From Liverpool, April 26, 1814 : *Lond. MSS., Appendix*, p. 538. Liverpool to De Chastre, April 22, 1814 : *Paris A.A.E. Angleterre Supplement*, 22, f. 6.

4. BENTINCK AND MURAT

By June 1813 Bentinck had driven Marie Caroline from Sicily, and, convinced that the future of the constitutional system was thus ensured, he had sailed to join in the grand attack in Spain. It was on the way there that he had his first negotiation with the man who possessed some of the same qualities of mind as himself and the same ambitious view of the future of Italy. Murat, urged perhaps by his wife, was already considering treachery to the Emperor and in secret negotiation with Metternich. Since April he had been seeking a means to get in touch with Bentinck through the British Commander on the isle of Ponza. Bentinck did not refuse the approach, being anxious to sound Murat's mind, and he informed the Prince of the suggestion and asked him whether he, while maintaining fully his own rights, would agree to Murat keeping Naples until the Allies found an equivalent elsewhere. The Prince evaded the question, but Bentinck went himself to Ponza and made the offer in a written communication to Murat's representatives, one of whom, Jones, was a British subject. Though nothing came of this attempt, it had an influence on the instructions which Castlereagh sent out in August.[1]

These were drafted for Aberdeen, while Bentinck was conducting his unsuccessful diversion in the east of Spain

[1] The Ponza negotiations are fully described by M. H. Weil in his *Prince Eugène et Murat 1813-14*, i. 60-75. This work (5 vols., 1902), the result of prolonged researches in French, Austrian, and Italian archives and in the Record Office, will always be the principal authority for the subject, but its translations of British documents are untrustworthy and some of the most important are not included. R. M. Johnston ("Bentinck and Murat," *English Historical Review*, April 1904, xix. 278) exaggerated these defects. Masson's analysis of Murat in *Napoleon et sa famille* is based on much documentary evidence which, however, he always refused to make clear by annotation.

and Murat in sudden repentance was joining the Emperor at Dresden. As has been seen, they contemplated as a last resort that Murat should keep Naples and Ferdinand be compensated, though Castlereagh much preferred the alternative which Bentinck had suggested at Ponza. Aberdeen had hastened, however, to inform Metternich of the extreme limit to which he could go, and after Leipzig, where Murat fought at the Emperor's side, the negotiations were resumed on this basis. Austria preferred to re-establish herself in north Italy by negotiation rather than conquest, thus saving her army, while the pressure on Napoleon would, of course, be greatly increased if Murat came over to the allied cause immediately. By December, therefore, as a result of an agreement between Aberdeen and Metternich at Frankfort, in which the former stressed the necessity of finding an equivalent for Ferdinand, Count Neipperg was sent to Naples to conclude a treaty with Murat on that condition, while Aberdeen wrote to Bentinck to urge him to do likewise, so that the Neapolitan and Anglo-Sicilian forces might combine with the Austrian army under Bellegarde to overthrow the skilful and determined resistance of Eugène Beauharnais in the north and begin a new invasion of France south of the Alps.[1]

Meanwhile the new constitution had not been fulfilling expectations, and Lord Montgomerie, whom Bentinck had left in charge, was soon writing despairing letters to his chief. For the moment even Bentinck's courage seems to have failed; for he asked to be relieved of his political duties and even for leave to come home to look after his seat in Parliament, but Castlereagh refused on the plea that no satisfactory substitute could be found. Bentinck accordingly returned to Sicily in October, where his energies were soon absorbed in the constitutional struggle. The newly elected House had, alas! abandoned British principles and turned to Jacobinism. Bentinck administered immediately stern reproof. "The British power," he insisted, "had been interposed to ameliorate the condition of the people and to bring forward the

---

[1] See above, Chapter III., Section 3, p. 159. Aberdeen to Bentinck, Dec. 12, 1813: Weil, *Eugène et Murat*, iii. 229.

resources of the state; but it was never intended to permit the introduction of a wild democracy or to allow the Crown to be endangered and the island to be reduced to still greater weakness by a misguided Parliament." He expressed his firm determination to stop these errors, got a new Ministry appointed and Parliament dissolved, issued a proclamation and went himself on an election campaign all over the island. The results were apparently of the best so far as Parliament was concerned, but one less happy was that for over two months Bentinck had no time for continental affairs and did nothing to prepare for the new situation in Italy. In particular, he made no mention to the Sicilian Royal Family of the instructions which Castlereagh had sent to him in July and August.[1]

At any rate, when Murat approached him with a view to concluding a treaty, he refused to listen. The whole situation had changed, he informed Castlereagh, since he had received his instructions. So far from Murat getting better terms than had been offered at Ponza in June, Bentinck was now doubtful whether he ought to be given any terms at all. It was in vain that Murat's agents told him that British approval had been given to the Austrian offer. Bentinck replied that he knew nothing of it, and refused even to discuss the terms of an armistice much less a treaty.

For these excuses there was much to be said. Until, at any rate, Bentinck heard from Aberdeen he might be pardoned for refusing to take any step which would jeopardise the rights of the Sicilian crown. But it is clear that he was thinking of far other things than the interests of King Ferdinand. For while he made no mention of Castlereagh's instructions to the Prince, it was in early December that he made, on his own responsibility as a private individual, the amazing suggestion that the British crown should become the sovereign of Sicily. The Prince's reception of the proposal made him admit that the idea was only a 'philosopher's dream.' When two months later, as a result of the inquiries in London of Prince Castelcicala, who saw in the incident a chance of getting rid of

[1] To Bentinck, Sept. 16, 1813: *F.O. Sicily*, 56. From Bentinck, Aug. 31, 1812: *C.C.* ix. 44 ; Sept. 3, Oct. 19, Nov. 1, Dec. 20, 1812: *F.O. Sicily*, 59.

Bentinck altogether, he was forced to confess this action to Castlereagh, he seems to have had but little idea of the absurdity and danger of such a request. "I perhaps ought to apologise," he wrote, "for having taken upon myself to originate propositions of such high interest without any knowledge of the wishes of the British Government. But the moment offered and there was no time for reference, and I considered myself as much bound by duty as prompted by inclination to put it in the power of the British Government to have made an arrangement which, in my judgment, would have been beneficial to all parties, but especially to Sicily and Great Britain—to the first by the restoration of its ancient greatness and of its long lost happiness, to the latter by adding to its possessions a source of infinite honour and strength without the ordinary disadvantages of foreign dominions."

Castlereagh's comments on this performance were, as Bentinck gratefully admitted, full of "kindness and consideration." Both he and Liverpool tried to throw as much blame as possible on Castelcicala for founding an official inquiry on a private communication, but the incident shewed, as they were just realising, how dangerous the unbalanced schemes of Bentinck might become unless he was checked by peremptory orders from above.[1]

For the moment the only effect of this extraordinary action was to bring the King back to Palermo and unite the Sicilian family, including Orleans, more closely together than they had been for a long time. They were naturally less in love with the philosopher's constitution than ever, and it was only Bentinck's stern reminder of the events of 1799 and the necessity of the constitution to regain the Neapolitan throne that kept them from open attack upon it. For Bentinck continued to oppose with every means at his disposal the treaty with Murat. He sent Graham over to Naples with instructions to sign nothing, but find means of getting to

---

[1] The incident is well known from the letter of Bentinck of Feb. 6, 1814 (*C.C.* ix. 238), and Castlereagh's reply, April 3, 1814 (*C.C.* ix. 429). The letter quoted above is in *F.O. Sicily*, 63, and encloses the letters exchanged between Bentinck and the Hereditary Prince, the last of Dec. 20, 1813, saying : " I see with real satisfaction that what you write to me was only a philosophic dream." See also Liverpool to Castlereagh, March 11, 17 1814 : *Lond. MSS., Appendix*, pp. 526–27.

headquarters with Bentinck's protests. After losing a good deal of time arguing with this powerless but imperturbable envoy, Count Neipperg at last signed the treaty with Murat alone, guaranteeing him his Neapolitan throne, with an extension of frontier to Ancona at the expense of the Pope, on condition of joining with the Allies to expel the French from Italy and, as Aberdeen had insisted, winning compensation for Ferdinand. Bentinck considered the Allies had been overreached, and roundly condemned the treaty. "Upon Murat," he told Castlereagh, "no reliance can ever be placed, and therefore the less power given to him the better. But Austria by the terms of the treaty will have created not only a rival but perhaps a master in Italy. When the Viceroy is driven to the Alps, as seems probable, with whom will his great Italian army take part?   The Italians have evidently no disposition towards the Austrians. The fact of Beauharnais having been enabled with an Italian army to maintain himself, is a clear proof of the national feeling towards the Austrian Government. Of the two they will undoubtedly prefer Murat, now become an Italian prince and declaring himself the champion of Italian independence. If the British protection and assistance had happened to be within their reach, that great floating force would certainly have ranged under their standard. The national energy could then have been roused, like Spain and Germany, in honour of national independence, and this great people instead of being the instrument of the ambition of one military tyrant or another, or as formerly the despicable slaves of a set of miserable petty princes, would become a powerful barrier both against Austria and France, and the peace and happiness of the world would receive a great additional security—but I fear the hour is gone by."

It had, indeed, passed, and Bentinck was all unprepared, one of his wild schemes being in direct opposition to the other, so he vented his spleen on Murat, a man "whose whole life had been crime, who has been the intimate and active partner of all Bonaparte's wickedness and whose last act of treachery to his benefactor has been the result of necessity." When, therefore, Aberdeen's letter at last reached him on January 18, he still refused to do more than go to Naples himself, and before he went he took care to obtain the refusal of the suggested compensation by the Hereditary Prince and the King.[1]

On his arrival at Naples, therefore, Bentinck refused entirely to make a treaty with Murat on the same terms as Neipperg. All he could be persuaded to do was to sign an armistice (February 3) to which Graham had at last consented after pressure from Neipperg and Sir Robert Wilson, who had now arrived in this part of the arena, excluding from it a clause which promised the conclusion of a treaty at a later date. To joint operations against the enemy he did agree, and returning to Palermo to make his final preparations, he embarked his army for Leghorn, reaching that city himself by land on March 8. Even now, with the Austrians unable to cope with Beauharnais and the Allies at their most critical stage in France, Bentinck's force might have been of great importance if he had co-operated wholeheartedly with Murat, and if Murat had really been willing to attack his countrymen. But if Murat's conduct was equivocal, Bentinck gave him every excuse. He was, perhaps, not responsible for the insulting and hostile proclamation which the Hereditary Prince issued as his troops embarked for Tuscany. But Bentinck treated Murat with the greatest distrust and held up the whole campaign by.a stupid claim for the control of Tuscany, through which Murat's line of communication ran. Murat, ill at ease in his new position, undoubtedly wavered and wrote compromising letters to the Viceroy and Fouché. But of this Bentinck was unaware, and his conduct was the despair of the Austrians and so violent and ill - humoured as to make all joint operations impossible, and enable the loyal and capable

---

[1] From Bentinck, Jan. 14, 30, 1814 : *F.O. Sicily*, 63. Bentinck to Wellington, Jan. 14, 1814 : *W.S.D.* viii. 511. The Prince hesitated, and but for Bentinck's obvious wishes might have consented to bargain. Bentinck told him that the proposition would be " objectionable as far as regarded Great Britain and embarrassing to myself individually, because I should pledge my government to a recognition to which it had hitherto never consented." Words difficult to reconcile with his instructions ! The King was violently opposed, and said he was the son of Charles III. and " would never disgrace the family." His discourse was, however, " of the nature of a rhapsody," and his only definite request to Bentinck was to take a " Pheasant Pye to a gentleman at Naples who from extreme cowardice had refused to follow the King to Sicily."

Viceroy to maintain his position until peace was won in France.

Bentinck's proclamation had summoned the Italians to follow the example of Spain, Portugal, Holland, and Sicily, and hinted that they could make a free and united Italy. At any rate, Murat had protested against it and threatened that he might follow the example in his own interest. Yet Bentinck, when he met the Pope at Modena hastening back to Rome, encouraged him in every way to assume his old position, promised him support, if Murat tried to stop him, and even supplied him with four thousand crowns from the secret service funds when he "learnt that His Holiness was in great pecuniary distress, that he never would consent to receive anything from Bonaparte, and that his wardrobe literally consisted of four shirts only." [1]

Meanwhile, Castlereagh had only gradually realised what was going on in Italy, and his instructions to Bentinck had been powerless to check his extravagances. It must be admitted also, that while he strongly condemned his conduct, when Metternich brought it to his notice as a result of Bellegarde's indignant reports, he was from the first not sorry that no treaty had been made with Murat. Bentinck was ordered to make an armistice, but his action in refusing to make a treaty was emphatically approved. Only when a suitable indemnity for the Sicilian House was provided could peace be concluded, and it was thought that if Murat realised this fact it would stimulate him to greater exertions against the enemy. But Castlereagh of course never contemplated such conduct as Bentinck pursued. After he had seen Graham and received a special report from him he wrote to Bentinck on February 21: "The British Government never liked the measure; but, being taken, they are perfectly ready to act up to the spirit of the Austrian treaty and to acknowledge Murat upon a peace on two conditions: 1st, that he exerts himself honourably in the war; and 2ndly, that a reasonable indemnity (it cannot be an equivalent) is found for the King of Sicily. I should hope with this basis to work upon you may not only quiet any

<hr />

[1] For Bentinck's actions in Tuscany, see Weil, *Eugène et Murat*, iv. 388 ff., and Randolph, *Diary of Sir Robert Wilson*, ii. 338–52. From Bentinck, April 3, 1814: *F.O. Sicily*, 63.

alarms Murat may have felt as to the nature of our armistice, but furnish him with two very powerful incentives to come forward effectually." [1]

How Bentinck carried out this instruction has been seen. Castlereagh was far from attributing all the blame to him, but the rising tide of complaint produced an instruction at the end of March, urging further co-operation and warning him against any action committing his Government to any political view in Italy, whose settlement must await the peace discussions. On April 3, from Dijon, these warnings were reiterated in a tactful but much more peremptory fashion. Castlereagh had now had time to realise the extent of Bentinck's views on Italy, and he was anxious to confine him to the business in hand—the defeat of the French forces. He was critical of Bentinck's proclamations, of which Murat had complained, and he insisted that he must not advocate ideas which ran counter to the "arrangements understood between the Great Powers of Europe." By this, of course, he meant appeals to Italian nationality in order to raise a levy *en masse*, such as Bentinck had often hinted he could organise: "It is not insurrection we now want in Italy, or elsewhere—we want disciplined force under Sovereigns we can trust." [2]

This judgment was pronounced even before the news of the fall of Paris and the final overthrow of Napoleon had come to Dijon. It was obvious that once that end had been achieved, the ideas of Italian nationality, which Bentinck and Murat alike were prepared to use for their own purposes, would receive short shrift from the victors. The outline of the new Italy was, indeed, already foreshadowed in the treaties and agreements which had been necessary to win the victory.

[1] To Bentinck, Jan. 22, Feb. 4, 15, 21, 1814 : *C.C.* ix. 184, 235, 262, 286.
[2] To Bentinck, March 30, April 3, 1814 : *C.C.* ix. 409, 427, 429, 434, 435.

CHAPTER V

THE FIRST PEACE OF PARIS: RECONSTRUCTION BEGUN, APRIL–AUGUST, 1814

" France, reduced to its ancient limits, was still the equal, and far more than the equal, of any of the Continental Powers."—FYFFE.

CHAPTER V

1. THE TREATIES WITH FRANCE

"It may be presumptuous in me to say so," wrote Castlereagh, "but my remaining till this new scene takes a shape
is beyond all comparison more important than my original
mission." The claim was confessedly a bold one, but there
was much to justify it. The results of the victories had
yet to be obtained. Peace with France had to be made, and
with it, perhaps, the whole of the reconstruction of Europe.
Though a Convention was made with Monsieur on April 23
regulating the suspension of hostilities, it was important that
a more definite basis should be quickly obtained. The four
Powers wished to arrange their affairs with France as soon as
possible, and though one or two Frenchmen would have
preferred to leave their settlement to the Congress which was
finally to determine the affairs of Europe, that was not the
opinion of Talleyrand or his wisest colleagues. It was early
decided, therefore, to negotiate a definite peace between
France and her principal enemies. How far the rest of
European reconstruction could be dealt with in these treaties
depended on how far the four Powers could agree in time;
but now that the fighting was over there was some chance that
the outstanding problems could be settled with comparative
celerity.

It is clear that Castlereagh's mind was quite as much
occupied with the wider problems as with the peace with
France. He had failed to solve them while the war was in
progress, but he had always regarded the reconstruction of
Europe as a vital British interest. If he could not settle it
at Paris, he meant to continue the discussions in London until

the whole was complete. Even now no one realised how intricate and stubborn the problems were.

For six weeks, therefore, Castlereagh remained at Paris, dealing with the joint problem of peace with France and the reconstruction of the rest of Europe. The main responsibility of both, so far as Britain was concerned, rested almost entirely on his own shoulders. He had, it is true, a certain amount of assistance. He kept the three Ambassadors with him to sign the treaty of Peace, but they were very little use in the negotiations. Aberdeen, indeed, wondered why he was still there: "It can be of no use to him and is not very agreeable to us." It was only natural that Castlereagh could not make much use of him nor of Stewart, who, however, enjoyed himself thoroughly in the best house in Paris, in spite of losing, by a valet's robbery, all those stars and decorations which he loved so much. Cathcart was no better, and Castlereagh relied on Münster as his principal agent though Münster had his own Hanoverian problems. Robinson also was of such assistance that Castlereagh resisted Liverpool's urgent appeals to get him home to help in the Commons, and Herries was sent out by the Treasury to afford support in the financial discussions, which were complicated. Wellington arrived on May 4 for a short visit and made a fine impression, but the new Ambassador was still in command of an army, and was urgently needed to settle Spanish troubles which the King's return had occasioned.

Thus Castlereagh had to do the bulk of the work himself, and indeed most of it was of such a delicate character that it was impossible to entrust it to anyone else. He did not complain of its extent, but lamented the time wasted in social duties. Pleasure was the order of the day, and Castlereagh had necessarily to take part in an unending series of balls, dinners, reviews, and gala performances. Paris, too, was filled with English travellers of high rank who expected attention.

After the arrival of his wife on April 18 Castlereagh therefore entertained extensively, giving frequent dinners where "the conquerors and the conquered were seated at the same table," while Lady Castlereagh "received and had *des*

petits soupers every night, to which all she knew, both English
and foreign, could come without invitation, and those with
whom she was not previously acquainted were introduced."
No doubt the result was a little mixed; but Aberdeen's
wounded pride was probably responsible for the tone of his
description: "Lady Castlereagh's suppers after the play
might just as well be in St. James Square, except that they
are attended here by Englishmen of a worse description and
scarcely by any women at all." There were, however, women
enough in Paris, amongst them Madame de Staël, a constant
guest at Castlereagh's, whose attentions were almost Talleyrand's heaviest anxiety. The cost of this hospitality in
money was repaid by the state, but the expenditure of time
and energy could not be made up. "I really work as hard
as a man can well do in such a town as Paris," he wrote in
apology, when Liverpool complained of delay.[1]

The negotiations with France itself were divided into two
parts, continental and colonial. The last was, of course,
entirely entrusted to Castlereagh, but he had also to keep an
eye on the former, for the Netherlands were involved, an
interest which he, like Napoleon, thought quite as important
as the other. The Dutch had, of course, their own representatives, but it would never have done to have left matters in
their hands, and they had merely the fears and anxieties of
observers. Their Prince was anxious to make an early
appearance on the scene, but Clancarty thought that his zeal
for acquisitions in Belgium, which had recently had to be
damped somewhat, would do more harm than good, and got
Fagel to dissuade him on the ground that he could not be
spared from Holland. He only put in an appearance at the
end of May when the main question was already settled.[2]

The basis for both settlements could be found in the terms
which had been offered to Napoleon at Châtillon in the allied

---

[1] Balfour, *Life of Aberdeen*, i. 187, 188. Londonderry, *Narrative*, 327.
Weigall, *Letters of Lady Burghersh*, 231. Countess Brownlow, *Slight
Reminiscences*, 92–93. [Underwood] *Narrative*, 179. To Liverpool, May 5,
1814 : *W.S.D.* ix. 64. The accounts of the special missions to the Continent,
including the cook's book, are in *F.O.* 95 (Misc.), 506. The quantity of
crayfish consumed at Paris is startling. The total cook's bill, April 21 to
May 31, was £1596, 2s.
[2] From Clancarty, April 19, 1814 : *Lond. MSS.*

project of February 17. But though the "ancient limits" had been expressly mentioned, the Tsar was supposed to have encouraged expectations, and it was claimed that a Bourbon France had claims to better treatment. Liverpool, indeed, had hastened to point out as soon as these ideas reached him that Monsieur did not expect to obtain anything beyond the limits of ancient France when he left England, and Castlereagh made that assumption the basis of a request to the Cabinet to be liberal on other questions: "Points may occur in the discussions upon which I can refer, but I wish to know your wishes as to the spirit in which we should conduct ourselves. I am myself inclined to a liberal line upon subordinate questions, having secured the Continent, the ancient family, and the leading features of our own peace." [1]

But, though Castlereagh hoped as late as April 27 to sign the treaty by May 15, delay arose from two causes. Talleyrand had not sufficient authority to overcome the opposition in France until the King arrived on the scene, while the German Powers wished to include "the main principles of the continental arrangements" in the treaty with France before Britain gave back the colonial conquests. This important development is considered later, but it delayed the main negotiation, so that on May 5 Castlereagh had to confess that he had made little progress. By this time Louis had returned and further complicated matters by refusing to accept the constitution without a re-examination of its principles by his own partisans. In domestic matters Talleyrand was no more trusted by Louis than by Monsieur, but the King accepted his guidance in foreign affairs where his position was now regularised. Nor was Louis likely to be stubborn on British interests even if the offer of another loan of £100,000, which Liverpool suggested, did not influence him. [2]

The negotiations were now carried on with greater speed. On May 9 a conference of the principal Ministers of the four Powers and France was set up—Spain being excluded by the usual device of terming them "informal conversations." By

---

[1] From Clancarty, April 19, 1814 : *Lond. MSS.* From Liverpool, April 9, 1814 : *Lond. MSS., Appendix,* p. 531. To Liverpool, April 19, 1814 : *C.C.* ix. 472.

[2] From Liverpool, April 29, 1814 : *Lond. MSS., Appendix,* p. 540.

this body two commissions were appointed—a territorial and a financial, on both of which Münster represented Britain, an indication of Castlereagh's view of the diplomatic abilities of the negotiators of Châtillon. The final decisions were, however, still left in the hands of the principal Ministers, to whom their representatives had constantly to refer.

To the territorial commission an allied project was presented which gave France about half a million of population more than in 1792, including such territories as Avignon, which had previously been under foreign sovereignty though inside the French frontier. The main addition outside this was in Savoy, the frontier to the Netherlands being kept almost the same as in 1789. In reply, the French representative, the Marquis d'Osmond, claimed "that the King of France, according to the promises of the allied Sovereigns, thought himself entitled to expect an augmentation of a million of subjects, therefore his astonishment was great on seeing that he was offered only acquisitions which he valued at 212,611 inhabitants, leaving out the part of Savoy which was offered to him and which he could not accept as it formed part of the states of a Prince who is nearly related to him." He demanded, therefore, considerable increase of territory, especially in the Netherlands, "a proposal which would have surrendered a great part of Belgium to France and left the rest defenceless."

The higher powers had to intervene. Louis had taken his tone from his marshals and talked to the Emperor of Austria of war. But it was to Talleyrand that Castlereagh, who was already in anger at the French proposals on the maritime peace, spoke without hesitation. None of the other Powers cared much about the Belgian frontier, but to him it was vital. "I have been compelled peremptorily to oppose this," he wrote, "as incompatible with the only defence of Brabant, and as disclosing a desire to encroach in that direction which has been the source of so many wars. I spoke yesterday strongly to Talleyrand on the subject, and shall feel it my duty before I leave Paris, to represent to the King the necessity, if he wishes the peace to last, of extinguishing in the minds of the army this false notion of Flanders being necessary to

France." At the same time, to put an end to French delays, he got his Allies to agree that if the peace was not signed by the end of the month the negotiations should be transferred to London.[1]

Talleyrand, indeed, had expected no other result. "I am not surprised," he told d'Osmond, "at the difficulties which you have met with concerning Belgium, the English having always appeared to me very positive on this point." An interview with Metternich shewed him that there was no support in that quarter, and the King's council were told that they had to accept what they could get. The King consented, therefore, to receive a part of Savoy in spite of the fact that it belonged to a near relation. The only other point on which France insisted was the Pays de Gex, on the northern shore of the Geneva lake, which united the canton to the rest of Switzerland. The Genevois had hoped much from the literary reputation of their town in London, and their representative, Pictet de Rochemont, had loosed the intrepid Madame de Staël on the "glacial" Castlereagh. Her ardour failed to thaw him, though he was, as a matter of fact, not unfriendly to the Genevan claim. But he refused to force France to give way, and when de Rochemont in a last interview urged every possible strategic and political reason why the Pays de Gex should be given to Geneva, Castlereagh answered: "These arguments about natural defences and strategic boundaries are pushed too far. Real defence and security comes from the guarantee which is given by the fact that they cannot touch you without declaring war on all those interested in maintaining things as they are."

With this victory and one or two other minor concessions France had to be content. Her new frontier was substantially that of 1792, and thus the whole of Belgium and the left bank of the Rhine up to that boundary was surrendered, though to whom had not yet been determined. Castlereagh had, however, expressly inserted in the treaty that Belgium to the Meuse should belong to Holland. "You will see," he wrote, "that I have secured the assent of France to the in-

[1] Münster to the Prince Regent, May 15, 1814 : *Münster*, 173. To Liverpool, May 19, 1814 : *B.D.* 185.

corporation of the Low Countries with Holland." "I felt it of the last importance," he added, "not to go to a Congress without having this most essential point acquiesced in by that Power." Britain was thus the only one of the four Powers which had secured her vital interest in the continental settlement before peace with France was signed—an important fact, for it made much easier her future rôle as mediator. She had nothing now of cardinal importance to ask for. "The noxious contents of Antwerp," the fleet which Napoleon had had built and whose menace had been so feared, turned out not to be so noxious after all, since many of the ships were built of unseasoned wood, and Castlereagh secured the reluctant consent of the Cabinet to allow two-thirds of those completed to be retained by France. Antwerp itself was to be kept a commercial port without fortifications. The navigation of the Scheldt was to be free to all nations, and the same principle was to be applied to the whole of the Rhine. Liverpool was critical of this clause, which abandoned an old British principle of an indefensible kind, but his protest was ignored by Castlereagh, and indeed the Austrians had already issued instructions for the river to be opened. On the whole, Castlereagh could claim that the foundations of the new state of the Netherlands had been solidly laid at Paris, though its final shape was still to be seen, and the marriage on which he placed much importance was already in jeopardy. That the "Brabanters" had shewn so much reluctance to accept the new king had no effect on his mind. A Belgian nationality was, indeed, far to seek, and the strategic necessity of a "barrier" in any case outweighed all other considerations.[1]

Meanwhile, Castlereagh had been conducting the negotiations as to the colonies directly with Talleyrand. He had tried to reduce his demands to a minimum. Sweden had been

[1] Talleyrand to d'Osmond, May 16, 1814 : Dupuis, *Ministère de Talleyrand*, i. 354. From Castlereagh, April 19, May 23, 1814 : *C.C.* ix. 473 ; x. 10. From Liverpool, April 26, 1814 : *Lond. MSS., Appendix*, p. 536 ; May 27, 1814 : *W.S.D.* ix. 114. From Clancarty, May 13, 1814 : Colenbrander, *Gedenkstukken*, vii. 123. *Münster*, 174. L. Cramer, *Correspondance diplomatique de Pictet de Rochemont et de François d'Ivernois*, i. 27, 43–44, 76, 79–81. E. Pictet, *Biographie de C. Pictet de Rochemont*, 127, 132.

persuaded to give up Guadeloupe, and Castlereagh pressed his Cabinet to give up Les Saintes also: "With respect to our own peace, I consider Malta, the Cape, Mauritius, and Tobago as *sine qua non*; also the regulations limiting the French to a commercial occupation of their factories in the East Indies. I should wish, as at present circumstanced, not to press the Saintes. It is not worth swelling the catalogue with a demand of this nature. It is easily reduced at the outset of a war and will not be strengthened by the Bourbons." The Cabinet were not convinced by this argument: "We have no harbour in that part of the West Indies. The French have two excellent ones at Martinique and Ste. Lucie. The Saintes are of no value whatever except for their harbour, and are the least invidious possession we could propose to retain." However, it consented to substitute St. Lucia for Les Saintes and also abandoned Bourbon. This reduced the direct cessions from France to three small islands, and Liverpool had some right to claim that "after the six or seven hundred millions we have spent in the course of a war which has led to the restoration of the Bourbon Family, the demand can scarcely be considered as unreasonable." [1]

Castlereagh was therefore indignant when Talleyrand proposed to send him an answer which failed entirely to meet British demands. It was silent on St. Lucia and Tobago, asked for extensive fishing rights in Newfoundland, and did not discuss the Slave Trade. The same influence which had affected the continental peace was at work. "I thought it therefore wise," he reported, "to be quite explicit and recall the French Government to a sense of our claims, to the for-bearance shewn, and to the true relations of the parties."

Liverpool sent a strong reply reinforcing this attitude. He was prepared to sweeten the pill by giving up financial claims, but the colonial cessions he considered as a minimum which France ought to grant with ease. "We demand," he claimed, "nothing which is of any value to them except the Mauritius; for there is not a Frenchman on the island of Tobago, and the only value of Ste. Lucie is its port, which they do not

---

[1] To Liverpool, April 19, 1814 : *C.C.* ix. 474. From Liverpool, April 26, 1814 : *Lond. MSS., Appendix*, p. 537.

want, having a much better in Martinique.   Our moderation, indeed, is great compared with that of any of our Allies." Whether Talleyrand agreed or not he made no further op-position.   St. Lucia and Tobago were given up, the French settlements in India confined to commerce, and the Newfound-land rights limited to those existing before 1792.[1]

It was on the Slave Trade that Talleyrand found the greatest difficulty in meeting British demands, which he, however, recognised as just.   In this matter he had the King on his side, for Louis had been witness of the extraordinary interest in this subject of his late hosts and perhaps shared their con-victions; but the King stood almost alone.   The commercial classes thought the demand was made merely to prevent the restoration of the trade of their colonies.   Hardly a person of substance in France supported Abolition therefore, and Talleyrand, who entreated Castlereagh to impress this view on his colleagues, could only agree to offer Abolition after a number of years so that French colonies might be stocked with slaves as required, and thus put on an equality with the British. Castlereagh himself was inclined to accept this offer as the best expedient, for he was aware that to make Abolition effective he must secure something more than treaties, how-ever stringent.   He hoped that the French would not add much to the traffic in five years, and rightly disbelieved that they would ever be able to recover their position in St. Domingo.   "My feeling is," he concluded, "that on grounds of general policy we ought not to attempt to tie France too tight on this question.   If we do, it will make Abolition odious in France, and we shall be considered as influenced by a secret wish to prevent the revival of her colonial interests. The friends of Abolition ought also to weigh the immense value of having France pledged to this question, and the subject brought before the Congress with the aid of France and Russia, both of which I can in that case answer for." The Cabinet were by no means ready to accept this point of view, which Liverpool urged as inconsistent.   They were

[1] To Liverpool, May 19, 1814 : *B.D.* 183.   British Projet and French Counter-Projet : *F.O. Continent*, 4.   From Liverpool, May 19, 1814: *W.S.D.* ix. 89.   *Cf.* Yonge, *Liverpool*, i. 510.   Dupuis, *Ministère de Talley-rand*, i. 378 ff.

more acutely aware of British feeling than Castlereagh. The House of Commons had passed a resolution on May 3 against surrender of the colonies without Abolition, and Wilberforce and his friends became frantic when they heard that this policy could not be carried out. They had received assurances from the Ministry that general Abolition would be obtained, and it was a cruel blow to find that France, to whom they were about to return colonies, in which the Slave Trade had been abolished for a considerable period, was to be allowed to continue it. Wilberforce had just prepared an address to the Tsar when the news reached him. He thought at first of going himself to Paris, but rightly concluded that his strength lay in the House of Commons. Zachary Macaulay was therefore dispatched in his stead, but could make no impression on French public opinion. Malouet, the French Colonial Minister, asked him if the English meant to bind all the world. No support could be obtained even for the abolition of the Trade on that part of the African coast north of the Line, from which it had been fairly effectively stamped out, but Talleyrand promised in a secret note that he would see to this point. In these circumstances the Cabinet had no alternative but to accept Talleyrand's proposals unless they were prepared to refuse to return the colonies altogether. Talleyrand's final notes were meant for public consumption in Britain and were profuse in humanitarian sentiment, but the feelings of Wilberforce and his friends were outraged.[1]

This was a grievous blot on the treaty, but otherwise the Cabinet and the nation were satisfied. They were too happy at the general result to haggle after a colony or so. Even the Admiralty did not grumble much. In Malta, the Cape, Mauritius, Tobago, and St. Lucia they considered that they had obtained the necessary strategic control over the Mediterranean, the long route to India, and the West Indian seas. The demands of the planters and merchants to retain conquests in which their capital was already invested went

[1] To Liverpool, May 19, 1814: *B.D.* 183. From Liverpool, May 19, 1814: *W.S.D.* ix. 88. From Talleyrand, May 26, 27, 1814; to Talleyrand, May 24, 26, 27, 1814: *W.S.D.* ix. 110-11. *Cf.* C. Schefer, *La France moderne et le problème coloniale* (1815-30), 71-72.

almost entirely unheeded. The same spirit was applied to the Dutch colonies, a far richer prize than the French West Indian islands. "I still feel doubts," Castlereagh had early written, "about the acquisition in sovereignty of so many Dutch colonies. I am sure our reputation on the Continent as a feature of strength, power, and confidence is of more real moment to us than an acquisition thus made." This principle prevailed, and if the final settlement left Britain supreme on every sea and in final possession of India, France and Holland were left with the bulk of their overseas possessions. It may be doubted, perhaps, if as much credit was won at the time by this restraint and wide outlook as Castlereagh had prophesied, while history was slow to recognise that such enlightened self-interest is rarely forthcoming at the critical moments of international relations.[1]

This moderation Britain shared with Russia and Austria in the financial settlement. These two Powers were compelled indeed to make in some ways greater sacrifices, for, if they had received subsidies and Britain had paid them, Napoleon had inflicted far greater loss on them than on Britain. The fact that their own armies had lived in France for nearly six months and wreaked a savage vengeance on her inhabitants, their belief that France's finances were exhausted, and the desire to win the Bourbons to their side explains in part, no doubt, this moderation. Prussia did not share it, but she could not prevail in the face of the opposition of her allies. Some voices were raised in Britain also for another view. "I hope the Allies will not forget," urged Edward Cooke in the first flush of victory, "that we deserve something for the £700,000,000 we have spent in the contest, and that we cannot pay a soldier, a clerk, or a magistrate before we have spent £40,000,000 for interest and redemption of our debt. It will be hard if France is to pay nothing for the destruction of Europe, and we are to pay all for saving it."[2]

This attitude was, however, not adopted by the Government. They asked for no indemnity and were content to

---

[1] To Liverpool, April 19, 1814 : *C.C.* ix. 474.
[2] From Cooke, April 9, 1814 : *C.C.* ix. 454.

renounce the payment for prisoners of war, which it was customary at that time to claim. Since few British were in Napoleon's hands and 70,000 were held in Britain the sum was a considerable one. All that they required was compensation for the injuries inflicted on the private property of British citizens, including, it may be noted, their losses in French state funds owing to the depreciation of the currency. Napoleon had granted these claims in the Treaty of Amiens, but his promises had remained unfulfilled when the war was resumed.

Thus Castlereagh's instructions to Münster, who was his not very suitable representative on the financial commission, were to give up the claims for the prisoners of war, provided the principle was recognised and full justice done to the private claims. "Count Münster may represent," he wrote, "that the claims of individuals against the Government of France, although of vital importance to them, cannot, if liquidated by an inscription amongst the mass of the national debt, be a very inconvenient, certainly not an impracticable, measure of justice to adopt. The dilapidations committed by the late Government on Foreign Powers it is impossible for the King to repair; but the individual property of British subjects seized in France to the profit of the state must lie within moderate limits, and the public credit of the new Government would derive a benefit from an early act of moral justice performed in favour of private persons. . . . The present Government of France must consider itself as the more bound in good faith to see justice done to British subjects in this case, as the claim is principally founded upon the treaty of 1786, the provisions of which have been strictly fulfilled in favour of French subjects by the British Government." [1]

Münster had no difficulty in getting France to accept this principle, but Prussia was not so easily convinced. In the opening Conferences of May 11 and 13 she tried to obtain compensation for the sums which Napoleon had sucked out of her for the campaign of 1812. All shrank, however, from the prospect which this precedent opened up, for similar exactions had at one time or another been inflicted on almost

[1] To Talleyrand (undated, but May), *Paris A.A.E., France*, 673 ff., 47, 48.

every country of Europe.   The French representative, Count
de la Forêt, therefore, was secure in support when he said—
according to Münster—"that the King of France would
rather deprive himself of necessaries than not satisfy a just
demand, that his Majesty regarded what was here in question
as unjust, and that sooner than satisfy it *he would submit to
be arrested and kept shut up in his palace*, and that he would
resign himself to his fate, as the Holy Father had done."
M. de la Forêt added "that the King, his master, had consulted the *Emperor of Russia* on this subject, and that it was
after this conversation that he gave him the order which he
now executed."   Louis XVIII. had, however, no need to
follow his long exile by imprisonment.   Prussia obtained no
support.   There were long wrangles about the complicated
domain rights with which Napoleon had saddled many
countries in favour of his marshals, while the claims of the
Bank of Hamburg, which Davoust had so outrageously
plundered, received a good deal of sympathy.   But France
managed to do remarkably well, and eventually the whole
financial matter was settled on the basis which Castlereagh
had first suggested.   "You will see," he said as he sent home
the draft of the treaty, "by the extent of the matter comprised that the pecuniary reclamations have been a most
troublesome and difficult concern.   After endless controversy
they have all, with a good grace, come into the principle I
recommended from the first, viz. clear scores in respect to
state claims, France engaging to do justice to individuals
whose claims rest upon contract, in contradistinction to
military spoliation and warfare."   Though Liverpool confessed that he did not understand the article and was afraid
the British Government might be held responsible if the
French Government did not keep its promises—as he seemed
to anticipate—the only alteration made was to emphasise
the surrender which had been made of the maintenance of
prisoners of war.[1]

Napoleon had, however, not only drawn the wealth of
Europe to Paris, but had filled the Louvre with its fairest art

---

[1] *Münster*, 177 ff.   To Liverpool, May 23, 1814 : *C.C.* x. 10.   From
Liverpool, May 27, 1814 : *W.S.D.* ix. 113.   From Hamilton, May 27,
1814 : *Lond. MSS.*

treasures. It occurred to many that these ought to be restored to their original owners—not least to the French, who hid the best as deep as possible in the cellars of the Louvre and substituted bad copies in their place. But Louis's weakness supported his refusal to give them up, and "the effect which it was feared the removal of the greater part of the Museum of Napoleon—amassed by spoliation committed over all Europe—would produce on the Parisians, served as a specious argument for withholding what was incontestably due." So for a time France kept her ill-gotten gains.[1]

Thus France obtained treatment such as she had never granted to others during her twenty years of domination. The peace might, indeed, be described as a generous one, though it is true that other Powers were to receive territorial gains while France was reduced to nearly the position which she had held at the beginning of the war. But when the experience of Europe in the last twenty years is taken into account, and the huge debt which Britain had accumulated, of which France, having lived on Europe, was comparatively free, the conquerors must be allowed to have shewn both moderation and wisdom far above the average.

[1] *Münster*, 178, 182. Aberdeen had also another reason : " I have been strenuous in recommending the preservation here of the pictures and statues, principally as a lover of art, for they would infallibly be destroyed by a journey into Italy. They have, many of them, suffered much in being transported here, although done with the greatest care which a great Empire could bestow. . . . I am sure the surrender would do more to discredit the French Government than anything in the world. The cession of the Netherlands and Antwerp is not felt as such a national disgrace as the surrender of these trophies would be." Balfour, *Life of Aberdeen*, i. 189.

2. ATTEMPTS AT RECONSTRUCTION

(i) AT PARIS

ONE cause of the moderation of the Allies was undoubtedly their own disagreement over the reconstruction of Europe. It was much simpler to draw France's boundary than to determine the fate of the French Empire, which in one form or another had stretched from beyond Warsaw to the southern shore of Italy. The frontiers of every European state outside the Balkans had to be determined, and the interests of the three Great Powers were at stake. These impending decisions had, as has been seen, hung like a cloud over the Coalition ever since the Rhine had been reached, and it was only the appearance of Castlereagh at headquarters which had prevented them from paralysing the armies and causing the failure of the campaign in France. But the task which he had set himself of mediating between these conflicting interests had as yet made little progress, and now that the victory was won the problems had become acute.

In these circumstances it was no wonder that many hoped that the decisions on these questions might be taken at Paris before the peace with France was made. Castlereagh does not, however, seem at the outset to have been one of them. At the beginning he certainly wished to delay the settlement until the allied sovereigns came to London, where he hoped to resume his rôle of mediator with all the prestige of a brilliant host. He had designed this visit as soon as Napoleon's fate was settled as the culminating point of all his efforts. The failures at Langres, Châtillon, Troyes, and Chaumont to determine the basis of the new Europe were to be made good under his guidance in England itself. Thus would she put the final touches to the twenty years' struggle and establish such a peace as Pitt had dreamt of before he rolled up the map of Europe.

For this purpose it was necessary to turn the visit which Alexander had so long planned into a reunion of all the four Powers of the Alliance. As soon as he reached Paris, therefore, Castlereagh urged Liverpool that the Tsar's brother sovereigns should be invited to accompany him. It was essential, he insisted, not to single out Russia for special compliments. The Tsar had attracted quite enough notice already by his acts at Paris, and Castlereagh particularly wished attentions to be paid to Austria, knowing how unpopular she was in comparison with Russia. Her influence in France and the Netherlands was of great importance to Britain. Lest he should be misunderstood he added in a postscript: "When I recommend you to dilute the libation to Russia, I am the last to wish it should be less palatable. The Emperor has the greatest merit, and must be held high, but he ought to be grouped and not made the sole feature for admiration. The interview in England will have a sensible influence on the politics of the Continent." [1]

Three days later he returned to the subject, anticipating possible objections on the score of practicability, and adding that "Hardenberg spoke to me to-night with much earnestness about his King and the Emperor of Austria going to England. The anxious wish of himself and others is to keep the intermediate Powers together to guard against an inordinate influence in the Great Powers at the extremities." The design was clearly to use the visit to keep Austria and Prussia united against Russia, to whom France seemed likely to gravitate. Münster sent similar advice to the Prince Regent, whom there was apparently no great difficulty in persuading to write letters of invitation which Liverpool considered "very proper." The King of Prussia promptly accepted, but the Emperor of Austria refused. The reason alleged was that his presence in Austria was urgently needed, but it seems more likely that he was afraid of the reception that awaited him. In spite of Castlereagh's renewed efforts and the evident pressure of Metternich and

[1] To Liverpool, April 20, 1814 : *C.C.* ix. 478.

Stadion, he persisted in his refusal, which was only mitigated by sending Metternich in his place.[1]

Though this refusal spoilt somewhat the scheme of "grouping" the Tsar, yet the rest of the plan was maintained. But to many at Paris such a long delay in settling the outstanding questions seemed intolerable, and it was not long before an attempt was made to solve them before peace was made by France. Of these momentous discussions we know hardly anything definite. The Prussian statesmen alone put their thoughts on paper. The other three Powers did no more than discuss, and no accurate records of these discussions exist, while since the three sovereigns and Ministers were assembled together, there was no need to write any full account. Castlereagh did not supply the deficiency as he did later at Vienna, doubtless because he did not think the time ripe to take his Cabinet into his confidence in these questions, which were still so indefinite. He only sent home, therefore, one dispatch on the subject, and Liverpool had but little to say to him except on the one point of Murat. Talleyrand was left completely outside the discussions.

Such information as we possess comes, therefore, mainly from minor actors on the edge of the conflict, deeply interested in some part of it but outside the inner circle on which the decisions depended. The Ministers told their subordinates something, for they had need of advice and assistance, and these were not always as discreet as their masters. There were also in Paris representatives of the smaller Powers, who were naturally desirous of finding out as much as possible. But the four Great Powers were at least agreed on one point. They would settle these matters themselves. Neither France nor the secondary Powers were to be placed in a position of equality with those whose armies had decided the conflict. Only when these latter had agreed were the other to be allowed to intervene. But of course they could not be kept altogether without information, and their representatives

---

[1] To Liverpool, April 20, 23, 23 (at night) : *C.C.* ix. 478, 492, 493. *Münster*, 161, 168. From Liverpool, April 26, 1814 : *Lond. MSS., Appendix*, p. 537. Aberdeen to Harrowby, May 15, 1814 : " Knowing as he does the feelings which prevail in England, I am not surprised that he should decline the risk of mortification incompatible with the dignity of his situation." Balfour, *Aberdeen*, i. 187.

were able to send home to their Courts reports which contain some facts, though they are largely guesses and half-truths. The most complete account of these transactions comes, indeed, from Münster, who combined two capacities. He was Castlereagh's principal assistant and at the same time he was the representative of Hanover, deeply interested in the discussions and bound to send home to his master some report of them. Stewart also must have learnt a good deal from his brother, but he was discretion itself at the time, and the narrative which he wrote sixteen years after the event is so vague and apparently so confused with what happened later at Vienna that it adds but little to our information.

At first it seems to have been Prussia which insisted on an attempt at settlement, but Metternich, who, as has been seen, had already made a promise to sacrifice Saxony to save Poland, also desired it. The conferences took place at his house in profound secrecy. The two Ministers were afraid of the popularity which the Tsar had obtained in Paris by his magnanimity and assurance during the change of dynasty. He had won the first position in Europe. "When the settlement of France, and the treaty of Paris came under discussion," wrote Stewart, looking back on these days of glory, "it may be affirmed, without exaggeration, that the Emperor of Russia stood upon the most elevated pinnacle of human grandeur that was ever attained by monarch." Stewart's idea of exaggeration was perhaps personal to himself, but all felt Alexander's ascendancy, and to it was added the fear that France would repay his services with support as soon as she was free. Therefore, as Castlereagh explained, there was "a strong desire felt by Prussia and Austria to bring both Russia and France to some understanding upon the main principles of the continental arrangements, in a secret article or otherwise, previous to our stipulating away our conquests." [1]

Hardenberg was fully primed for the fray, and after some preliminary discussions with Stadion he laid before his colleagues a long memorandum, dated April 29, which with true Prussian thoroughness attempted to settle the whole

---

[1] Dupuis, *Ministère de Talleyrand en 1814*, ii. 54: Londonderry, *Narrative* (1830), 324. To Liverpool, May 5, 1814: *B.D.* 180.

complicated question in all its details, though he was modest
enough to describe it as only a draft for discussion. These
details need not detain us, though to Münster they gave much
food for thought over the future of Hanover. The key
questions were three—Poland, Saxony, and Mainz. The
Tsar, far from giving way in the claims which he had been
making, was pressing them with renewed vigour. Prince
Czartoryski stood higher in his confidence than ever, and the
Poles in France, who had served Napoleon so well, were
rallying to the Tsar, who was now asking for Cracow and Thorn
to round off his new kingdom, which he meant to endow with
a constitution. "My predictions about Poland are fully confirmed," reported Münster, apparently with exact knowledge,
on May 9. "The Emperor Alexander will yield nothing to
Austria of the claims. He wishes to keep Cracow, Zamosk,
and the 400,000 souls ceded to him at the Peace of Vienna
[1809]. What is more astonishing, he does not keep his
promise to Prussia, and instead of increasing the communications between East Prussia and Silesia he wishes to encroach
further on the line of the Thorn on the Warta, promised at
Bâle. Now Russia demands not only Thorn, but also a
radius of 300,000 souls further on. The position is very
dangerous for the neighbours of Russia, and Austria is
seriously vexed by this new claim."

Since both Prussia and Austria were threatened, interest
drove them to unite. But Saxony and Mainz kept them
apart. Metternich had, it is true, made a promise about
Saxony to Hardenberg in January, but he was under pressure
from all sides and wavered. Moreover, it was vital to his
plans that Bavaria should receive the key-fortress of Mainz,
which the Prussian soldiers had occupied and insisted on
retaining. Not only would it bring Prussian influence
dangerously near southern Germany, but without it Bavaria
refused to make to Austria indispensable cessions in the
Tyrol. These difficulties, as well as those concerning the
German constitution, proved so difficult that about the middle
of May it was decided to adjourn them to London.[1]

[1] Münster to the Prince Regent, May 5, 9, 1814 : *Münster*, 162–69.
Hardenberg's " Plan pour l'arrangement futur de l'Europe," April 29,

Of Castlereagh's part in these discussions there are only one or two indications. Stewart states his brother's policy as follows: "He must have felt the danger which threatened the adjustment of any equilibrium in Europe, if the Russian designs, aided by Prussia, were to be carried into effect, contrary to the consent of Austria. It was evident, or at least feared, that the two Powers who could dictate such arrangements must command in all others. He felt also equal danger, I should suppose, in case Austria, by similar management, should be induced to join in the plan, and lest it should lead to the complete subjection of Europe to a triple alliance. He felt equally the inexpediency of a new war, upon grounds which could be stated to be of very limited import, and which might not be generally felt or understood; and he was sensible of the danger of bringing France forward in the scene. The last objection also made him naturally averse to any public appeal, because such a measure would give open grounds to France for interference and action. His object, therefore, was naturally to effect the abandonment of her designs by Russia through a similar kind of management; to dissuade the Emperor of Russia from perseverance in his projects by statement and argument; and by shewing the dangers which threatened the two Courts, to endeavour to separate Prussia from Russia and to induce the former to join Austria in a close alliance; under which, aided by Great Britain and the German Powers, they would be enabled to form a complete barrier against Russia on one side and France on the other." [1]

That this was an accurate description of the trend of Castlereagh's mind later events at Vienna were to reveal. But how definite this plan was at this time it is difficult to decide. The obduracy of the Tsar had yet to be proved. But Castlereagh, at any rate, kept a vigilant watch upon events, tried so far as he could to bring Austria and Prussia together, and used every means to defeat the Tsar's Polish plans. "I know that His Majesty is piqued at the interposition of England in this matter," wrote Münster on

1814, enclosed in Castlereagh's dispatch of May 5, 1814 : *F.O. Continent*, 4, is printed by Colenbrander, *Gedenkstukken*, vii. 113. *Cf.* Treitschke, *History of Germany* (Eng. ed.), i. 661.

[1] Londonderry, *Narrative*, 315–16.

May 5, "and certainly it is a matter of too much general interest to Europe for a Power like Britain to leave it alone." The question was certainly already grave enough. "I am anxious in the meantime," Münster added, "to represent as strongly as possible the necessity of avoiding at present, almost at any price, a new war, which would embarrass everything, and which will be kindled less easily when all the military have returned to their homes, and all the states feel the effects of the extreme exhaustion produced by their late struggle." No wonder that Castlereagh was anxious to bring Prussia and Austria to agreement. "England is behaving perfectly in all this," wrote Wrede, who was negotiating the Bavarian exchanges with Metternich, "Lord Castlereagh is always the mediator and he has much helped to get Prussia to desist from her claims to Dresden and its neighbourhood."

It may be doubted, however, if Wrede knew Castlereagh's whole mind on the Saxon question. He kept an impenetrable reserve upon it. Baron de Just, the representative of the captive King, had hopes that Britain would see in the maintenance of his country the preservation of the balance of power. He urged his King to write to the Prince Regent, and himself plied Castlereagh with letters and attempted to obtain an interview. But both he and General von Watzdorf were denied all access, and had to content themselves with some kind words from Stewart when he gave the general his passports to follow the sovereigns and Ministers to London.[1]

All efforts at Paris, however, proved vain. Perhaps Castlereagh did not even anticipate success there. The unending succession of social duties made it almost impossible to get business done. "This capital is as bad as any other big city for business," complained Wrede. "We eat, drink, dance, see the sights and the women, but business does not move forward as one would desire." Metternich, as later at Vienna, succumbed to these temptations and would not work sufficiently diligently or carefully to please Wrede. Castlereagh, as has been seen, made the same complaint, though

[1] Münster to the Prince Regent, May 5, 1814: *Münster*, 163. Wrede to the King of Bavaria, May 6, 1814; Dupuis, *Ministère de Talleyrand*, ii. 72. Baron Just to the King of Saxony, May 20, 1814; General von Watzdorf to Einsiedel, June 9, 1814: *Dresden St. A.*

he was really diligent enough. But he seems fairly soon to have come to the conclusion that but little of the main problems could be settled at Paris. At any rate, by the middle of the month he had definitely agreed with Metternich to postpone their solution to London. "His Imperial Majesty will send Metternich on a special mission," he wrote on May 15, "to make his excuses to the Prince Regent. I have very much encouraged this plan, as his presence in London would enable us (Hardenberg and Nesselrode being also there) to decide finally on several important points previous to the Congress at Vienna." That Metternich shared Castlereagh's hopes is clear from a letter to Hudelist: " I follow the Emperor of Russia to England. There we will chiefly go into and settle the Polish question under the mediation of England. This present place is not suitable to this affair, since it is too much under the influence of wretched Polish Frenchmen and French Poles. We are at one with England, and I guarantee that most intimate relations will continue; the Russian farce (*schwindel*) has sunk very low.[1]

But the Tsar was also doubtless aware that Paris was more favourable to his plans than London was likely to be. Stein and Pozzo di Borgo as well as his Polish friends pressed him to settle Poland and Germany before he left, and Münster and others were inclined to support them because of the dangers of leaving Germany in such an unsettled state. Metternich consented that one last attempt should be made to settle the German questions, and the Tsar tried to establish his claims on Poland. But their efforts all ended in failure. There was nothing left for it but to hope that in London a new situation would arise. To many it seemed that Britain would then be able to perform her rôle of mediator with success. "The discussions on the grand duchy of Warsaw ought to be ended there through the mediation of the British Cabinet," wrote Wrede to his King; and a little later: "The affair of Poland ought to be definitely settled in London. Castlereagh continues to behave very well in this question as in all which pertains to your Majesty's interests." Though

---

[1] Wrede to the King of Bavaria, May 12, 1814 : *Munich St. A.* To Liverpool, May 15, 1814 : *W.S.D.* ix. 72. Metternich to Hudelist, May 24, 1814 : Arneth, *Wessenberg*, i. 212.

General Watzdorf and Baron de Just could obtain no answer from Castlereagh to their demands, the latter still insisted that "England holds in her hands the balance to decide the fate of our country"; and he pursued him with letters and entreaties.[1]

If the fate of Poland and Saxony was left undecided, only small progress was made as regards Italy, but that was of an important character and practically decided its future. The ideas of liberty and nationality, which Murat had reluctantly laid on one side and Bentinck had encouraged as far as he dared, were given no chance at Paris. Bentinck himself during April still caused a good deal of trouble. When at last he attacked Genoa he secured the surrender of the town by promising the Genoese their ancient freedom, a piece of vanity which was to lead the Opposition into one of their most foolish crusades. Murat sent him a sword for this achievement, which Bentinck only managed to acknowledge with courtesy by "doing severe violence to his feelings." Meanwhile he gave as much sympathy as possible to all anti-Austrian elements, and General MacFarlane, who foretold it, and other English officers were supposed to have encouraged the resistance which eventually broke at Milan. At the same time Bentinck was not without zeal for the interest of his own country, and an expedition to Corsica, whose port, he said, was probably the best in the Mediterranean, was only stopped by orders from Paris.[2]

All these actions Castlereagh viewed with growing distrust, and it must have been with relief that he granted Bentinck a leave of absence, which, however, he shewed no anxiety to use. The Italy which Castlereagh envisaged was one under the guidance of Austria, with the old families restored so far as possible and French influence excluded. He had no sympathy whatever with the liberal and national movement in which Bentinck and Sir Robert Wilson saw such hopes. It is true it was confined to a handful of men, and the ex-

---

[1] Münster to the Prince Regent, May 30, 1814: *Münster*, 183–84. Wrede to the King of Bavaria, May 22, 29, 1814: Dupuis, *Ministère de Talleyrand*, ii. 81. Just to Einsiedel, June 6, 1814: *Dresden St. A.*

[2] From Bentinck, April 17, 1814 (about Corsica): *F.O. Sicily*, 63; April 27, 1814: *B.F.S.P.* ii. 317. From Lt.-Genl. MacFarlane, May 4, 1814: *F.O. Italian States*, 6. Weil, *Eugène et Murat*, iv. 568–70.

travagant reports of these two vain egoists was not likely to increase his faith on it. Bentinck "seems bent on throwing all Italy loose," he wrote to Liverpool in a phrase often quoted against him, "this might be well as against France, but against Austria and the King of Sardinia, with all the new constitutions which now menace the world with fresh convulsions, it is most absurd." National movements were excellent things to encourage as a weapon against Napoleon, but now that the battle had been won they were to be damped down as far as possible. Time enough to stimulate such movements when some experience had been gained as to the best method of dealing with them. " I am desirous that your Lordship should not take steps," he instructed Bentinck, "to encourage the fermentation which at present seems to prevail in Italy on questions of Government." " It is impossible not to believe," he warned him in a private letter, "a great moral change coming on in Europe, and that the principles of freedom are in full operation. The danger is that the transition may be too sudden to ripen into anything likely to make the world better or happier. We have new constitutions launched in France, Spain, Holland, and Sicily. Let us see the result before we encourage further attempts. The attempts may be made and we must abide the consequences; but I am sure it is better to retard than accelerate the operation of this most hazardous principle which is abroad." He used similar arguments to the Milanese deputation which came to Paris to plead their case against Austria.[1]

Castlereagh had, in fact, already agreed that Austria should obtain Venice and Milan, and, as no other member of the Alliance had any objection, her Italian frontiers were settled

[1] To Liverpool, May 5, 1814; to Bentinck, May 6, 7, 1814: *C.C.* x. 10, 15, 18. The protocol of the conversation with the Milanese is given by G. Gallavresi, *Carteggio del Conte Federico Confalionieri*, Part I., 131–38 (1910). It is doubtless this attitude of Castlereagh which produced the forged letter of May 26, 1814, from Metternich, asserting that a secret treaty had been made at Prague between Britain and Austria giving the latter control over Italy. This was printed by Bianci (*Storia Documentata*, i. 333–34), and many historians believed it. But, as Rinieri (*Il Congresso di Vienna e la Santa Sede*, 35–43) and Fournier (*Napoleon*, ii. 307–308) have demonstrated, there is no truth in it. The document itself shews by internal evidence its falsity, and the British and Austrian archives and all the rest of the correspondence of these years prove conclusively that no such treaty was made.

by a secret clause of the treaty. It was laid down in the public treaty that Italy should consist of sovereign states, though who the sovereigns were to be was not specified. At the same time, in the secret clauses it was agreed that Genoa should be transferred to Sardinia to compensate her for the loss of Savoy to France, Genoa being created a free port. This of course nullified Bentinck's promises, which he had no right to make.

The fate of the rest of Italy, however, remained open, except that the Treaty of Fontainebleau had assigned Parma to the Empress. Austria was not ready to recognise the Pope's claims until the question of her own occupation of the Legations and Murat's of the Marches had been settled. As for Murat's future, it was quite uncertain. Bentinck had at least saved Britain from recognising him as legitimate sovereign of Naples. He had no friend amongst the Powers now that his army was no longer needed, and Castlereagh had no difficulty in acceding to Liverpool's urgent request that he should receive no recognition in the treaty of peace.[1]

Meanwhile, in the treaty with France the four Powers had shewn that, however much they might disagree amongst themselves, they had no intention of allowing the rest of Europe to interfere in their concerns. By a clause in the public treaty, it is true, all Powers who had taken part in the war were invited to a Congress at Vienna to complete the settlement. It had also been ostentatiously given out that France was to take part in it, now that Bourbons had replaced Napoleon. But the four Powers still intended that the main points should be decided before the Congress met. By a secret clause they bound France to submit to the decisions which they should make amongst themselves, though they seem to have given Talleyrand some assurance that he would be consulted before the final decisions were made. As for the secondary Powers, Spain, Sweden, and Portugal had not even been consulted about the treaty with France, which they were now invited to sign without alteration, the secret clauses, however, being reserved for the four Powers alone. Spain was especially indignant at this treatment, which she

[1] From Liverpool, May 16, 1814 : *Lond. MSS., Appendix*, p. 543.

considered as a humiliation, and it was some time before her plenipotentiary could be induced to sign a treaty constructed without his participation. The four Powers had still less intention of allowing the three Powers to interfere in the major problems of the reconstruction, and still less the smaller Powers. The Congress, which was not expected to last longer than six weeks, was only intended to be a convenient reunion of the states of Europe to ratify decisions already made, to adjust minor details, and to give some semblance of legality to the claim which the four Powers made to represent "Europe." Castlereagh was in agreement with this point of view. It was not Vienna but London which he designed as the place where the reconstruction of Europe should be determined.

(ii) At London

While these discussions were going on at Paris the Grand Duchess Catharine had been awaiting the Tsar at London. She had been invited at her own request, but was paid every honour and attention that her brother could have desired. The Duke of Clarence, who was on a visit to Holland, immediately fell a victim to her charms, and himself arranged her journey to England.[1] It was by her own wish that she stayed in the comparative privacy of Pulteney Hotel, "hired at the enormous cost of 210 guineas a week," rather than in a royal palace, and she was received by the people as well as the Court with enthusiasm. Catharine, the young widow of the Duke of Oldenburg, now only twenty-four years of age, was the Tsar's favourite sister. His correspondence with her, indeed, breathes more than a brother's tenderness. She had always had great influence upon his emotional nature, which had been increased by her constancy during the trial of 1812. Unfortunately, though possessing many feminine attractions,

---

[1] He was much perturbed to find that the Admiralty had only sent a Cutter and made haste to secure a Frigate. " I hope yet to see this elegant and fascinating lady landed on our shore in a manner suitable to the sister of the Emperor Alexander. . . . George the First sent an Admiral and a whole British fleet to fetch Peter the Great, and now a *Cutter* is sent for the Grand Duchess ! " Duke of Clarence to the Prince Regent, March 23, 1814 : *Windsor Arch.*

she was wayward and impulsive, and apt to put her personal predilections before the political interests of her country. The account which Countess Lieven gives of her extraordinary conduct, though perhaps too bitter to be quite accurate, is confirmed in the main by her letters to her brother and from other sources. The Prince Regent produced in her from the first a feeling of repulsion which she hardly attempted to conceal. Her out-of-hand rejection of his two royal brothers, the Duke of Clarence and the Duke of Sussex,[1] who hastened to seek her hand, was only to be expected, and offended no one. But shocked, as she said, by the grossness of the Prince Regent, she was soon in almost open hostility to him. Her distaste for music, the usual relief of a royal entertainment, irritated her host. This was perhaps an inevitable cause of friction, but in her desire to shew her contempt of his character Catharine associated markedly with the Opposition leaders, encouraged the Princess Charlotte to assert herself, and even talked of calling on the Princess of Wales.

The visit of the sovereigns naturally brought to a head the quarrel between the Prince Regent and his wife. The Queen had to receive once more, and the Prince Regent insisted that the Princess should be excluded from her court. His wife's dignified protest was communicated to Parliament, and gave to the Opposition what was now almost their only chance of harassing the Government. The controversy had reached its height when the royal visitors arrived.

Moreover, the Princess Charlotte was involved. Since a marriage was already arranged for her, it was held to be all the more necessary that she should be sheltered from the influence of her mother. It may be doubted whether that of her father was any more salutary for a young girl, but the Prince Regent appears to have been genuinely anxious to place his self-willed and excitable daughter under suitable guardianship. It can be imagined, therefore, how keenly he resented Catharine's sarcastic comments on his marital and

---

[1] According to Merveldt, the Prince Regent formally asked Lieven for the hand of the Grand Duchess for the Duke of Clarence. To the Austrian Ambassador, with whom she had many conversations, she seemed not averse from the Duke of Cambridge as a husband (Merveldt to Metternich, May 5, 1814 : *Vienna St. A.*).

paternal duties, and her open sympathy with the Princess of Wales and her daughter. Such conduct must have recalled to the Regent's mind the bitter criticisms of the Tsar, which the Duke of Cumberland had sent from the Continent in 1813.

Thus there was much to make George suspicious of his guest before the monarchs crossed the channel, escorted by the Duke of Clarence as Lord High Admiral. They received an uproarious welcome; for to the British people the visit appeared not only an occasion for celebrating the end of twenty years of war and isolation, but also a tribute by Europe to Britain's constancy in the conflict and generosity to her Allies. The Tsar had a glorious opportunity. He had become a hero to the whole people, and had he also attached to himself the Prince Regent and the Court it would have been more difficult for Castlereagh to have stood out against his plans. Indeed, the Government by no means took Castlereagh's view of the respective importance of Russia and Austria. The Tsar came first in the estimation of all, then Prussia for her heroism in 1813, with Austria a very long way behind. The most distinguished attentions, therefore, which Britain had ever paid to a royal guest awaited Alexander. He had indeed to share them with the King of Prussia and a large number of soldiers and statesmen who accompanied them, but he stood forth *primus inter pares*. The Prince Regent invested him with the Garter with his own hand, an honour not shared by the King of Prussia, to whom the order was now at last given, and the same pre-eminence was everywhere designed for him.

But the Tsar made blunder after blunder. That he might enjoy his sister's society he insisted on staying at her hotel instead of St. James's Palace, which the Regent placed at his disposal. It was an added injury that this was in the heart of London where the Tsar could and did receive the never-ceasing plaudits of the mob, who had nothing but abuse, and even worse, for his royal host. He and the Prince Regent vied in inflicting petty but noticeable slights upon one another. The Tsar followed his sister's example in especially favouring those members of the Opposition whom the Regent most disliked, notably Grey and Holland. He paid great attention to the discarded mistress, the beautiful Lady Jersey, while he had not a gracious word for the reigning one, Lady Hertford, whose charms did not attract him. He even threatened to call on the Princess of Wales, and was only prevented by the determined opposition of Lieven. Even his impression on the public diminished as time went on. It is true that he could always get applause from the mob, but he shocked the more solid portion of the London public by deliberately avoiding their recognition on his first entry into London and by humouring the whims of his sister, who not only insisted at being seated at the Guildhall banquet given by the City of London, but actually on occasions tried to prevent music being played to the royal toasts. The Tsar, therefore, never was really popular. It was Blücher, always ready to drink a bumper and make uncouth speeches, which were translated with tact and *bonhomie* by Sir Charles Stewart, soon made a Baron, a Lord of the Bedchamber, and Ambassador to Austria, who stood first in popular estimation, with Platov, the Cossack, a good second.

The Prince Regent, the Court, and the Government were astounded at the attitude of their royal guest. That Alexander made liberal friends and got into touch with Bentham and other reformers as well as the Whig Lords was no doubt a testimony to his breadth of view. Even on the Opposition, however, he made no great impression of sincerity and ability, while it was a fatal diplomatic blunder for a monarch, to whom the goodwill of the British Government was a priceless asset, to shew so marked a preference for their opponents. How far there was calculation in his conduct—a plan to enlist the Opposition on behalf of the liberties of Poland or even the expectation that they would be called to office—and how much was mere personal pique, it is hard to decide. But the men whom Alexander courted never had much influence in Britain during his lifetime, the Prince Regent remained his determined foe until his death, while Castlereagh's difficulties with his Government were made much less in the momentous year which followed the visit.[1]

[1] . . . " The Emperor of Russia sent for Lord Grey, Lord Grenville, Lord Holland, Lord Lansdowne, and Lord Erskine, and had long con-

Meanwhile Metternich represented his royal master with far more tact and skill than Francis himself could have mustered. The Prince Regent was given the magnificent Order of the Golden Fleece, which no other Protestant had ever obtained, as well as the rich uniform of an Austrian regiment. He was treated with the most flattering deference, and encouraged to magnify the part which he had played in the war and to regard himself as the arbiter of Europe. Metternich scrupulously avoided all intercourse with the Opposition. No wonder that henceforth George regarded Metternich as the wisest of Ministers and affected a special deference towards the Emperor of Austria.

This diplomatic rivalry would in any case have made it difficult for Castlereagh to carry through the schemes which he had made at Paris, but the excessive hospitality which was offered by the British made anything like systematic consideration of the important problems impossible. Within a week the visitors were tired out by the balls, receptions, and dinners—above all, by the dinners with which they were surfeited. The feast at the Guildhall surpassed everything that had hitherto been seen in Britain, and cost twenty thousand pounds. For three nights the Metropolis was illuminated, Lord Eldon's house in Bedford Square displaying in large letters formed of lamps the words: "Thanks to God." Transparencies, fireworks, and bonfires surrounded by ill-regulated and often drunken mobs met the visitors at every turn. Only when they escaped from London and remarked with surprise that all England was a garden did they have time or inclination to admire.[1]

Castlereagh himself, who with Liverpool was given the Garter by his sovereign, had to devote much of his attention to

versations with all of them. Lord Grey represents him as having very good opinions upon all subjects, but quite royal in having all the talk to himself, and of vulgar manners. . . . In truth he thinks him a vain silly fellow." Creevey to his wife, June 14, 1814 : *The Creevey Papers*, i. 195.

On the whole visit, see "Extrait des mémoires de Princess Lieven" in Grand Duke Mikhailovitch, *Correspondance de l'Empereur Alexandre I. avec sa sœur Catharine*, 225–46, a highly coloured account.

[1] Gentz might well record his opinion that Metternich's conduct at London was a " chef d'œuvre de perfection." *Dépêches inédites*, i. 90. The Guildhall banquet is described in all its magnificence by the committee which arranged it, in *Annual Register*, 1814.

formal hospitality [1] and thus to undergo a terrible strain, while at the same time he had to resume his place in the Commons and take up the innumerable administrative duties of his office, which had been postponed while he was on the Continent. It soon became evident that but little could be done on the main problems. The Tsar, as at Paris, refused to allow the question of Poland to be officially discussed by his Ministers, though it was canvassed on all sides. No doubt he felt that he had too much against him and wished for time to prepare public opinion in Britain. Metternich and Castlereagh seem to have acquiesced easily enough in this decision.

What informal discussions took place amongst the Ministers of the Four we do not know. Some there were; but of Metternich's five reports to his master only one remains of no great interest. The British archives are naturally silent, nor was there any need for the Russian and Prussian Ministers to make written reports. All that is known are a few Protocols of the decisions, mainly on procedure, that were made, and a few rumours reported by the diplomatists of the minor Courts in which but little credence can be placed.[2]

The only subject on which substantial progress was made was that of the Netherlands, which is narrated in the following section. There were also discussions on the German questions, in which Castlereagh acted as mediator. After consulting with him, Münster and Hardenberg were able to sign a Convention that both Luxemburg and Mainz should be fortresses of the future Confederation. This was, of course, not to the liking of Metternich, who still intended Bavaria to have Mainz, not only to keep Prussia in check but in order to get back the Tyrol. But Castlereagh tried to help Austria also by

---

[1] Pfeffel to the King of Bavaria, June 10, 1814: "It is hardly possible to give any idea of all the duties which fall to him [Castlereagh]; besides his functions in the Cabinet and Parliament he has almost sole control over all questions of ceremony, no department for it having been organised in this country in such a manner as corresponds to the multitude and importance of the duties that belong to it at this moment." *Munich St. A.*

[2] Klinkowström, *Oesterreichs Theilnahme*, 393. Nesselrode to Pozzo di Borgo, June 22, 1814: *Transactions Imperial Russian Historical Society*, cxii. 25. To Liverpool, Nov. 25, 1814: "Having in successive interviews during the campaign, at Paris, in London, . . . employed in vain every conciliatory representation to place the question upon a footing to which a mediation could be applicable". . . *W.S.D.* ix. 451.

urging Bavaria to come to an agreement with her. Mainz would need at least thirty thousand men as a garrison, he pointed out, and would thus prove an onerous charge. It was in any case Bavaria's interest to support Austria as a mainstay of the balance of power. "As enemies," he said to Pfeffel, "you can do one another much evil; as friends you will make each other stronger. The provinces which you cede to Austria were acquired with hostile intent, while those you will get in exchange will suit you much better in every way." This is a good example of the manner in which he was exerting his influence in these questions, though for the moment but little effect was produced. Both Metternich and Pfeffel were disappointed that Mainz had not been obtained and that a long delay must ensue before the settlement could be arranged. Metternich pointed out that Bavaria must keep up her army, but dissuaded Pfeffel from asking Britain for a subsidy for that purpose.[1]

No other decision as to territory could be made. No doubt the Saxon question was discussed as well as that of Mainz, but nothing was allowed to leak out about it. It was in vain that General von Watzdorf, with Metternich's secret approval, tried to enlist Castlereagh's aid on behalf of his sovereign. He could not even secure an interview with him and was refused all access to the Prince Regent. The question of Saxony, he was curtly informed, was reserved for the future Congress. Castlereagh was indeed little likely to commit himself on a question on which he had already decided that the union of Austria and Prussia in common opposition to the Tsar chiefly depended. The only person to whom the Saxon Minister was able to appeal was Lord Aberdeen, who, though he shewed sympathy, obviously knew little more about it than Watzdorf himself. All that the envoy could do, therefore, was to find consolation in the fact that decision was at least delayed and to enumerate those on the side of his King an imposing catalogue that included Providence, Austria, France, all the states of Germany, and "the English nation which is

---

[1] Memorandum of Münster and Hardenberg, June 15, 1814: *F.O. Continent*, 5. Pfeffel to King of Bavaria, June 26, 1814: *Munich St. A.*

too moral in its principles to applaud the overthrow of an ancient and virtuous dynasty." [1]

Important changes of plan were, however, made as to the Congress. Though it was clear that agreement was not likely to be reached in London on the outstanding points, the intention to keep the decision in the hands of the "Four" remained as strong as ever. They were also anxious to complete the work as quickly as possible. But Castlereagh could not leave until Parliament rose. By June 16, therefore, the Ministers agreed that the Congress should be summoned for August 15, that the seven Powers who had signed the Treaties of Paris should be a preliminary committee, but that the "Four" should first determine the plan of reconstruction. The Tsar, however, refused to accept the date fixed. The negotiations had already lasted longer than had been foreseen at Paris, and he was now asked to remain idle several weeks before the Congress met. He insisted, therefore, on returning to Russia before the meeting took place, with the consequent postponement of the opening to the end of September. The three Powers were somewhat taken aback by this decision, which raised fears and doubts as to the intentions of the Tsar. They suspected some design for action in Poland. But it could not very well be refused. In a joint note, therefore, while stressing the necessity of the Tsar's presence, they lamented the anxiety which further delay would cause to the sovereigns of the second and third order whose fate was undecided, and especially to the inhabitants of those countries in provisional occupation by foreign armies. They asked for an assurance of his return by September 1 and also a formal engagement that nothing should be done in the meantime to prejudice the decisions which had to be made especially in those countries under provisional occupation. But the Tsar would not accept the date suggested. He proposed that the Congress should be deferred until October 1, the four Powers meeting together previously to decide their affairs. He offered, however, no objection to making a declaration that nothing should be decided in the interval.

[1] Watzdorf to Einsiedel, June 26, 1814: *Dresden St. A.* The correspondence with Castlereagh is given in Dupuis, *Ministère de Talleyrand en 1814*, ii. 133–38.

Two months would thus pass before the Congress met, and there was general anxiety at such an interval while the fate of Europe remained uncertain. The only remedy that the four Ministers could devise was to renew amongst themselves the promises made at Chaumont. A Convention was signed between them, agreeing to keep 75,000 men on foot until the future repose of Europe and the maintenance of the balance of power was assured. It was not so much France as one another that they distrusted. That they also promised that the armies should only be employed by common agreement was an attempt to reassure one another of their intentions. The Convention, indeed, seems to have been designed by Castlereagh to secure from the Tsar another pledge that he would not attempt to settle his difficulties by the sword. Alexander had left behind him in Cabinet and Court distrust and resentment. The future encounter at Vienna was obviously to be a stern one, and in the interval that remained Castlereagh, like all others in Europe, got ready as best he could for the conflict.

3. PRELIMINARY SETTLEMENTS AND DISCUSSIONS

(i) THE NETHERLANDS [1]

IF in the breathless interval between the peace with France and the Congress but little could be decided on the great problems which divided the Allies, there was still much for Castlereagh to do on other matters. The affairs of the centre of Europe must wait, but attention had to be given to the circumference where British power had gained special influence by its exertions during the war. During the three months he was in Britain Castlereagh was therefore constantly pre-occupied with the settlement of a number of problems which were part of reconstruction. The Netherlands, Norway, Spain, and Italy all demanded some kind of action. As Parliament was sitting, the Opposition and especially the "Mountain" were on the look out for means by which to harass the Ministry, in spite of the fact that it now seemed so secure after the final triumph. Holland House and the official Whigs were indeed in a very despondent mood at the apparently impregnable position of their rivals both in the Prince Regent's and the country's favour. But Brougham —all the more a free lance since he had no seat and seemed unlikely to be given one by the Whig magnates—saw that peace would eventually bring almost as many problems as it solved, and would provide many opportunities for attacking the Government.

Most important of all was the question of the Netherlands, which involved not only the key position in Europe and colonial possessions of great importance, but also the future of the dynasty. For the new state, as has been seen, was to be connected to Britain by the closest possible ties of marriage,

[1] See note on p. 180.

the heiress of Britain being united to the heir to the new kingdom. This important step, foreseen since 1812 by the Prince of Orange, had matured at the end of December 1813, in spite of his son's reluctance, comprised part of Castlereagh's instructions, and been announced to Europe and regularised by formal letters between the Prince of Orange, the Hereditary Prince, and the Prince Regent in February and March 1814. If neither of the young people had shewn great eagerness at the outset for the match, that was after all not expected in a royal marriage, and their relations had grown at any rate cordial and even tender before the Hereditary Prince left for his new dominions, it being hoped that his charm and reputation would encourage the Belgians to accept the new sovereignty to which they were destined.[1]

Had Princess Charlotte been left to normal influences, no more than the usual difficulties of a marriage of this nature would have had to be overcome. She had lately shewn herself more submissive to her father, and her Confirmation in January 1814 had appeared to indicate her readiness to undertake new responsibilities. But the situation was highly abnormal. The impending visit of the sovereigns brought to an acute stage the friction between her father and mother. The Princess of Wales' consent had not been asked to the marriage, nor was it required. But she obviously could not view it with complete indifference, and was instinctively against it as her husband favoured it. Her own abnormal position was one of the few things which unscrupulous members of the Opposition could now use to make the Prince Regent and his Ministers uncomfortable, and the marriage therefore soon came to be viewed by them with a jealous eye. Opportunity was thus given to foreign intrigue, for despite official assurances some Russians at any rate saw in opposing the match a chance to extend the influence of their own country

---

[1] The Regent had been much alarmed at Charlotte's attachment to his cousin, the Duke of Gloucester, of which the Duke of Cumberland wrote: " I own to you when I left England [in April 1813], and from all I knew, I was very much afraid she would prefer the *cheese* to the *orange* " (*Windsor Arch.*), while Münster, as late as October 22, 1813, told Ompteda that the Prince Regent believed the young Prince of Orange did not want to marry Charlotte, and asked for a list of eligible Protestant princes in Germany. Ompteda, *Nachlass*, iii. 249.

in a most important quarter of Europe. It was natural that the Grand Duchess Catharine, who had, as has been seen, made special efforts to obtain the friendship of the young Princess, and who disliked her father intensely, should be suspected of influencing her protégée against the marriage. There is no direct evidence against her, but other Russians had been residing in London whose later history shewed them to be masters of intrigue, Tatischev, Minister designate to Spain, and his wife, whose intimacy with the Princess had been so openly boasted of that Lord Walpole had written from Petersburg to warn the Government against it.[1]

At any rate, before Castlereagh got back from Paris Charlotte had already begun to rebel. Moreover, the Mountain leaders were assisting if not inspiring her. There were obviously difficult questions as to the future residence of one who was likely to be Queen of England. These were stated at length in the *Morning Chronicle*, and at the same time the Princess informed Lord Liverpool that she could not go on with the marriage unless she had power to choose which country she would live in. Neither the Prince Regent nor the Government felt that they could accede to a request which seemed to shew great distrust for her future husband. Liverpool's belief that the Tatischevs were responsible for this sudden and unexpected demand in order to make a marriage with either Nicholas or Constantine possible was so strong that he asked Castlereagh, at the Prince Regent's orders, to prevent the expected arrival of the Grand Dukes in England. The indignant Tsar immediately sent Tatischev to his post at Madrid, and as a result neither Nicholas nor Constantine accompanied him to London.[2]

The only remedy seemed to be to send for the young lover, and in the greatest haste and secrecy Lord Clancarty managed

---

[1] From Lord Walpole, March 23, 1814 : *Windsor Arch.*

[2] For the correspondence of Charlotte, see Rose Weigall, *Princess Charlotte*, and Colenbrander, *Gedenkstukken*, vii. 541, 549, 551–53. From Liverpool, April 30, 1814 : *Lond. MSS., Appendix*, p. 541. Lieven (to Nesselrode, May 21, 1814 : *Pet. Arch.*) reported that the Prince Regent had told him that he knew that the Tatischevs had first suggested to the Princess the idea of detaching herself from the Prince of Orange in order that she might marry a Grand Duke. He also alluded to the influence of the Grand Duchess on the Princess. *Cf.* F. Martens, *Recueil des Traités*, xi. 206.

to smuggle him out of Holland incognito. The Prince's
position was painful enough, for though Charlotte said she
loved him, she did not love him enough to entrust her future
to his hands. His own great desire for the marriage was
sufficiently proved by the fact that he entreated his father
to suggest such alterations in the marriage contract as would
satisfy the Princess. The Sovereign Prince agreed, with
some reluctance, and for a few days it seemed as if the matter
was settled. Only in the first week of June, just as the royal
visitors were at hand, did Charlotte again announce that she
refused the terms. Since she had obtained all that she
demanded, this second refusal is even harder to explain than
the first. According to Creevey, it was due to the machinations
of Brougham, who suggested that the marriage would result
in the departure of the Princess of Wales to the Continent, a
subsequent divorce of the Prince Regent, and a new marriage
which might deprive Charlotte of the throne. Neither
Creevey nor Brougham can be believed on any matter without confirmation, and it may be that Charlotte's act was due
to a strong revulsion of feeling against her lover owing to an
incident which might have influenced any one of her age and
character.[1]

At any rate, by the middle of June it was recognised that
the marriage could not take place, though a formal pronouncement was delayed as long as possible. In July occurred
the dramatic flight of Charlotte to her mother, an act of
desperation which was, however, followed immediately by

[1] From Clancarty, April 30, 1814: " Tho' it is no easy matter to smuggle
an heir apparent out of the dominions I think we have accomplished
this. . . . Had Lady Castlereagh been here I should have consulted her
on the best means of smuggling him into England." *Lond. MSS.*
Cf. *Bathurst*, 273, 275, and *Creevey Papers*, i. 197–98. The desire of the
Prince and his influence on his father can be followed in Colenbrander,
Gedenkstukken, vii. 561–86. The incident referred to in the text was the
bad behaviour of the young Prince in the Princess's presence owing to
drunkenness. He was led astray by Prince Paul of Wurtemberg (Queen
of Wurtemberg to the Prince Regent, June 30, 1814: *Windsor Arch.*).
Mrs. Warrenne Blake, *An Irish Beauty*, 226. There is other evidence
of his drunken habits at this time, and it may well be that the Princess's
disgust is the real explanation of her conduct. Whig observers, of course,
placed the whole responsibility on the Prince Regent, who was accused of
desiring to get his more popular successor out of his sight. *Cf.* Horner,
Memoirs, ii. 169. Dr. F. G. Renier puts well the evidence for the Russian
influence in his *Great Britain and the Establishment of the Kingdom of the
Netherlands*, 181–90.

complete submission to her father, who placed her under closer supervision than before.

This signal failure of the Government's favourite plan caused great rejoicing to the Mountain, but their joy was short lived. For it was on the Princess of Wales herself that they mainly relied to harass the Prince Regent and his Government, and her sudden decision to accept a Parliamentary grant and go abroad deprived them of their most dangerous weapon for a period of five years.

Castlereagh had, however, to carry out his negotiations concerning the Netherlands with every obvious disadvantage. But he made it immediately quite clear that the failure of the marriage plan made no difference to the main problem. He attributed the failure to the influence of the Duke of Sussex, a conjecture which the Sovereign Prince thought impossible, and which shews what difficulty the Government found to account for Charlotte's action.

Castlereagh was anxious that the Prince of Orange should not enter into a Russian alliance, for the Tsar's visit to the Hague was considered by the Dutch Royal Family to be intended to lead to a suggestion that the Grand Duchess Catharine should marry the Prince. Van Nagell declared that this would make him the most miserable of men and disrupt the whole Orange family, and it was partly to guard against this danger that no steps were taken formally to withdraw Charlotte's hand, and that an offer which Prince Leopold of Saxe-Coburg immediately made was peremptorily refused by the Prince Regent. Castlereagh could not, however, help being impressed by the lavish attentions which the Tsar and his sister heaped on the Hereditary Prince during their visit to the Hague and the cordial invitation to visit Petersburg, which the rejected lover appeared to catch at somewhat eagerly. That he still had hopes of Charlotte is shewn by the fact that he did not encourage the suggestion of an Austrian match for the Prince, which had been already communicated to him privately, for Austria was as alarmed as Britain at the idea of the Russian marriage. The Regent also did not quite give up hope, for the Queen reported to him a satisfactory change in the conduct of Charlotte, who had declared to the Duchess of York that "being convinced that you have the power over her person she was determined to submit entirely to your will." But the young Prince, though both he and his father considered resuming negotiations, did not eventually take the chance of another rebuff, and next year confirmed the worst fears by marrying Catherine's younger sister, Anne.[1]

The important thing now, however, was to shew that the caprice of a young girl had made no difference to the British attitude towards the Netherlands and the House of Orange. The Hereditary Prince therefore was not only invested with the Order of the Bath, but put in command of the army of Hanoverian and Dutch troops, which, by agreement with the Allies, Britain had to maintain in Flanders. This was a signal mark of confidence and a sign, moreover, of British desire to ensure the authority of the House of Orange over Belgium. The final disposition of the Low Countries had, indeed, to be postponed to the Congress of Vienna. But by an agreement of June 14 the four Powers had decided that the provisional administration should be handed over to the Prince of Orange.

The principles on which the two countries should be united had already been warmly canvassed in London, and Liverpool had even suggested the Irish Union as a model [2]—at any rate on the financial side. In order, however, that the interests of his new subjects should be fully protected, it was laid down that their rights should be established along the lines already

---

[1] From Clancarty, June 28, 1814: *C.C.* x. 65; June 29, 1814: *Lond. MSS.* To Clancarty, June 26, 1814: *C.C.* x. 60; July 14, 1814: *Lond. MSS.* Merveldt to Metternich, July 9, 1814: *Vienna St. A.* Colenbrander, *Gedenkstukken*, vii. 630. The Queen to the Prince Regent, Sept. 11, 1814: *Windsor Arch.* Of the Grand Duchess, Charlotte said "that she felt no partiality towards her and that the last visits of which passed between them were most disagreeable and that she was a very intriguing woman. The Prince of Orange was, of course, not named. . . ." This lends itself to various interpretations.

[2] Protocol, June 14, 1814: D'Angeberg, *Congrès de Vienne*, i. 182. Colenbrander, *Gedenkstukken*, vii. 588, 596. Liverpool's principles were, however, soundly based: " Depend upon it, it will require the utmost management and indulgence to reconcile the people of Brabant to this connection. A new connection cannot be governed with as tight a rein as an old one. Recollect how Ireland is governed now, and what lost America to the crown of Great Britain." Liverpool to Clancarty, May 30, 1814: Yonge, *Liverpool*, i. 514.

discussed between Clancarty and the Prince at Paris, by special guarantees of religious toleration and commercial equality. The Dutch sovereign, whose reported grant of a constitution "as liberal as the English" had already won the applause of the British Press and allowed Mackintosh to withdraw the ill-informed criticisms that he had made in the House of Commons on the destruction of an ancient republic, was ready without pressure to agree to all that was required. But he was not sorry to be subjected to outside authority in order to avoid the criticism of his Dutch subjects, and its exertion, repeated in the Vienna Treaty, is the first instance of the protection of the rights of minorities by the Great Powers. On August 1 he formally took over the administration of the Provinces to the Meuse.

Meanwhile, Castlereagh was anxious to arrange as speedily and with as little friction as possible the important question of the Dutch colonies. To a large extent the main lines of the settlement had already been determined. The British Government had committed itself to the restoration of the majority of the Dutch colonies, provided that an independent and enlarged Netherlands was secured. This had now been agreed to in the Peace of Paris, though its eastern frontier had still to be settled, and it was obvious that the promise must be met. There was thus no dispute about the surrender of the rich prize of the Dutch East Indies, which, though "a point of strength and Empire," as Liverpool had termed it, in contrast to the West Indian Isles, the Dutch might now be considered strong enough to guard from attack. Nor was there any claim or even desire on the part of the Dutch to receive back the Cape, which had been in British hands since 1806, and was considered essential to the protection of the long route to India. The West Indian islands and Guiana, on the other hand, which had been a long time in British possession, had begun to be exploited by British capital, especially the settlements on the Demerara, Essequibo, and Berbice rivers, where Liverpool merchants had made serious commitments. At one time these had been suggested as compensation to Sweden for the renunciation of Guadeloupe, which France insisted on retaining, but fortunately

Sweden was induced to accept £1,000,000 in compensation, a charge which it was at first intended to throw on Holland as a contribution to the general cause in return for restoration and the acquisition of Belgium. The Dutch had also agreed to take over the Russian debt in Holland in agreement with Britain, in order to obtain Russia's consent to the union of the Belgian provinces to Holland. Moreover, the Dutch Government was quite ready to abolish the Slave Trade, and this was actually done by a decree of June 15.[1]

This was the situation which Castlereagh had to deal with on his return. As has been seen, he had always wished to treat Holland as generously as possible, and perhaps all the more as the discussions at Paris had shewn that her land territory would not be extended as far as he had at one time imagined. In Hendrik Fagel he found a negotiator who fully appreciated the English point of view and realised that a good financial settlement was the best bargain that the Dutch could make. An agreement would therefore soon have been reached had not Van Nagell, the vain and self-opinionated Dutch Foreign Minister, sent instructions which attempted to assert in a most unfriendly manner the extreme Dutch view on every point, both on the colonies and the Russian debt, without paying any regard to British interests. Fagel himself realised that this was a false step and wrote to his sovereign direct to protest against it. He was bound, however, to submit the proposition to Castlereagh, who said it was "a bit hard" to be treated thus by a state which owed so much to Great Britain. If such conduct continued, he threatened to refer the whole question of the colonies to the Congress of Vienna, when their disposition would have to depend on the rest of the settlement there. This threat was hardly meant seriously and was probably concerted with Fagel to bring the Foreign Minister to his senses. The Sovereign Prince had, at any rate, no illusions on the subject, and immediately repudiated Nagell without even informing him and accepted all Castlereagh's demands.[2]

---

[1] From Liverpool, March 15, May 3, 1814: *Lond. MSS., Appendix*, p. 540. In March Liverpool had suggested ceding Trinidad to Sweden instead of Guadeloupe. Colenbrander, *Gedenkstukken*, vii. 142.

[2] Colenbrander, *Gedenkstukken*, vii. 142, 167, 614, 622, 640–41, 648.

The result was a settlement with which both sides could profess themselves contented. Britain kept the Guiana settlements but allowed the Dutch to trade with them. In return she took on herself the charge to Sweden for Guadeloupe (£1,000,000), half the Russian debt (£3,000,000), and paid £2,000,000 besides for the Cape, which, however, was to be spent on fortifications against France. By this means the whole charge of £6,000,000 could be represented to Parliament as expended for British colonial interests, but the fact was that the Dutch only got £2,000,000, and that they had to expend on an object which was an European interest as well as their own—the barrier against France. Then and later they protested against the view that they sold part of their colonies to Britain, as the transaction has often been represented by British historians. They had really no alternative but to accept such portions of their Empire as Britain was willing to return, and the money they received was meant for a special purpose for which the British Government would have found it difficult otherwise to get Parliamentary sanction.

Nevertheless, Castlereagh's claim that Britain was acting generously was justified by the facts, if the principles of the age be taken into account. The colonies she took were not considered at the time of much commercial value, and their cession was justified by the fact that the Dutch were incapable of defending them from the enemies of Britain in a world war. The Empire she surrendered was a rich and noble possession, though it is true that its great value was not fully realised at that time, and Stamford Raffles was considered a nuisance. There can be no doubt, however, but that Britain could have kept it with the acquiescence of the Great Powers if she had desired. The European settlement provided her with plenty of opportunities to make such a bargain. Napoleon indeed thought her foolish not to have done so. But Castlereagh and his Government in attaching more importance to the welfare of the new kingdom they had created and to the public opinion of Europe, than to the demands of their own merchants or an attempt to create a monopoly of colonial trade, were building for the future better perhaps than they realised.

(ii) NORWAY

Another embarrassing problem, though one bearing less directly on British interests, was that of Norway, over which, by the Treaty of Kiel, Denmark had surrendered her sovereignty and in return received considerable concessions from the allied Powers. Britain, as has been seen, had agreed to return to her the whole of her colonial possessions except Heligoland, and to endeavour to procure her compensation in Europe. The Norwegians, however, refused to be transferred to Sweden by treaty, proclaimed their independence, and elected Prince Christian of Denmark, the heir to the Danish throne, as their King. One of their first steps was to send Carsten Anker to London to announce their unshakable determination never to be united to Sweden and to ask for the approval and help of Britain. He was received by Liverpool (March 26), who made it absolutely clear that the Norwegian movement for independence would be condemned by the British Government. He pointed out that Norway had been for years in hostility to Britain, and only declared her independence after Denmark was conquered, and that Britain was bound by treaty to Sweden. He assured him, however, that Norway would not be incorporated in Sweden, and offered, if the Norwegians submitted, to mediate on this point with the Crown Prince. Anker refused all such proposals and left Liverpool's presence reiterating that the people of Norway would never submit. He refused also to leave England, where an illness and an unfortunate prosecution for a supposed commercial offence helped him to remain, thus encouraging his countrymen to imagine that the British Government was inclined to negotiate about their independence.[1]

The reluctance of the British Government to use force against the Norwegians was increased by the equivocal con-

[1] Memorandum of Liverpool, March 26, 1814; Liverpool to Thornton, March 28, 1814: *F.O. Sweden,* 89. The memorandum was to be read to Bernadotte, but Liverpool trusted to his honour "that, if the Norwegians should within a reasonable time submit to the annexation of Norway to Sweden, he will not be disposed on this account to take any vindictive measures either against Mr. Anker or any persons who may have been connected with him."

duct of the Crown Prince in the closing days of the struggle
with Napoleon, and, above all, by his suspicious attitude
towards the Bourbon restoration, in which, as has been seen,
Castlereagh at last regarded his actions as definitely treacherous. Bathurst, who had even suspected him of selfish
designs on Antwerp, lamented the necessity of a blockade,
for which the Swedes were pressing, but, though Castlereagh
admitted that "Charles Jean has certainly forfeited all claim
to personal favour," he thought that, as Russia was prepared
to carry out the treaty, Britain could not use what were after
all only suspicions to justify refusal. The blockade was therefore continued against Norway after the peace with Denmark
had been ratified.[1]

By now, however, the Opposition began to be alive to the
situation, and questions in both Houses led to a long debate
on May 12. Liverpool confessed his apprehension at taking
part in it, and his surprise at finding that Vattel and Grotius
defended self-determination. Grey quoted these and other
masters in one of his most eloquent speeches, but Harrowby
and Liverpool were, of course, able to shew that the good faith
of the country was involved, and the Opposition was easily
defeated in both Houses. Nevertheless, the Government was
anxious to escape as soon as possible from an odious necessity,
and gladly joined in a plan which Liverpool had first suggested
in March of sending allied representatives to try to bring the
Norwegians to accept the sovereignty of Sweden.

Indeed, before a joint attempt could be made, the Government sent J. P. Morier on a special mission to Norway, to
explain the British position and urge Prince Christian to give
way. He did his best, but was so much impressed by the
Norwegian dislike of Sweden that he gave passports for deputies
from the newly elected Diet to go to England, a step which
at any rate tended to delay acceptance of the situation, and
for which he was mildly censured by Castlereagh when he
got home. Meanwhile, Augustus Foster had been sent to
Copenhagen, where he found Austrian, Prussian, and Russian
colleagues, of whom the last, General Orloff, was taking a

[1] From Bathurst, April 14, 1814 : *Lond. MSS.* To Bathurst, April 27,
1814 : *Bathurst,* 274.

very high line, which alarmed the Danes, all the more since there was a strong Russian force in Holstein. Foster acted with skill and tact, and by the time the mission set out for Gothenburg and Christiania he had got on good terms with his colleagues. After an interview with Bernadotte, who indulged in some characteristic gasconades, the mission tackled Prince Christian and used every possible argument to overcome his natural reluctance to abandon the Norwegians to their fate. But even after a second visit to Bernadotte and a return to Norway it seemed as if no terms could be arranged. A sort of war indeed ensued. But fortunately Prince Christian's honour could be saved by the *douce violence* of an invasion, while Bernadotte, whose actions were always wiser than his words, was, in spite of his threats, prepared to grant what under the circumstances must be considered as very favourable terms. Thus in August the fighting, which had never been very serious, ceased, and by November the Prince Royal, in the name of the King of Sweden, had accepted all the essentials of the Norwegian constitution, which made the union between the two countries little more than a personal one. Liverpool heaved a sigh of relief when his responsibility ceased. "Though our policy respecting the union of Norway to Sweden has always appeared to me right," he told Castlereagh, "I confess I felt for some time that the question was the most awkward and embarrassing of any in our European politics." [1]

Bernadotte, however, continued to hold the Danish Government responsible for the trouble which had been caused, and insisted that Prince Christian should be disinherited. Foster on his return to Copenhagen refused to accept this point of view, though he admitted, as did other observers, that public opinion was violent in favour of Prince Christian, with the result that he used his conditional powers of presenting his letters of credence immediately on his return to Copenhagen, so that Great Britain "would thereby have the gracious appearance of being the first Power to pardon the past errors

---

[1] The dispatches of Morier and Foster are given in full in vol. i. of Yngvar Nielsen's *Aktstykker vedkommende Stormagternes Mission* (2 vols., Christiania, 1896-97). From Liverpool, May 3, 1814: *Lond. MSS.*; Sept. 2, 1814: *W.S.D.* ix. 213.

of the Danish Cabinet and to afford protection to the most distressed country at present in Europe."

This action was quite approved by his Government, who were thoroughly suspicious of the Russian troops in Holstein and the threats of Bernadotte. Thornton was ordered to make vigorous protest. But though Norway was settled, the Swedish-Danish situation, which Bernadotte exploited for his own ends, continued, as will be seen, to give Britain much trouble throughout the Congress of Vienna.[1]

(iii) Spain

On the shores of the Baltic Britain had only a secondary rôle to play. In the Spanish Peninsula she was by far the most important outside influence in settling the affairs of a country which her armies had assisted to regain its independence, and throughout these months the responsibility was as irksome to her as to the proud and entirely unreasonable Spaniards. As has been seen, the relation between the British and the Regency was a continual struggle against incompetence and arrogance, which made Sir Henry Wellesley's life a prolonged torment and even impaired at times the apparently inexhaustible patience of Wellington. The victory of Vittoria, which almost freed Spain completely from the invader, did little or nothing to improve matters. The Cortes at Cadiz still maintained their jealousy of Britain's South American plans. Castlereagh urged the Government to remove to Madrid, but fear of the Cadiz mob delayed an obvious measure indefinitely. In a long review of the situation towards the close of the year 1813, Wellesley described the absurdities of the constitution of 1812, and the resentment against the British at Cadiz, which, however, he believed existed nowhere else in Spain. Wellington's supreme command was constantly disputed by the Regency and the Council of State.[2]

In the all-important matter, however, of refusal of all compromise with France, both Governments were at one. Some

---

[1] From Sir C. Gordon, Aug. 1, 1814 : F.O. 38 (Holland Frontiers), 16. To Wellington, Aug. 7, 1814 : C.C. x. 77. Foster's dispatches, as in previous note.

[2] To Wellesley, July 7, 1813 ; from Wellesley, July 25, Aug. 19, Sept. 7, Nov. 30, 1813 : F.O. Spain, 142, 145, 146.

of the Regents were, indeed, of the French party, but the feeling of the country was too strong for them to allow their secret wishes to influence their actions. Even before Vittoria they refused all participation in the negotiations during the armistice, to which, as has been seen, Napoleon tried to entice them. Nor when in desperation he forced on the captive Ferdinand the Treaty of Valençay and sent him back to Spain was there the slightest danger of the offer being accepted. A new Regency was at last allowed by the Cortes to transfer the seat of Government to Madrid (January 11, 1814), for yellow fever had broken out at Cadiz, and in the breathless months of the final struggle the Government shewed every disposition to seek British aid to secure its objects in the approaching world settlement, for which it had an ambitious programme, including the return of Louisiana by the United States. The Foreign Minister, Luvando, indeed went so far as to suggest a treaty of alliance, which would bind Spain not to renew the Family Compact, and Wellesley, "knowing from experience the disposition of Spaniards in moments of anger or of enthusiasm to pledge themselves to acts of the greatest importance without any reflection as to the consequences which are to follow," was of opinion that it would be good policy to accept the offer.

There was, however, no time to deal with such high questions before Ferdinand returned to Spain. The King was from the first determined to overthrow the constitution, and at once asked Wellesley for the aid of Wellington's army for that purpose. This was naturally refused, with some good advice for the future, and for a time Wellesley hoped that Ferdinand's promises to grant a constitution were sincere, but the extravagant demonstrations of his subjects both in the provinces and at Madrid gave the King and his Camarilla of reactionary clericals the necessary courage, so that by the middle of May it was swept away, and the King began a reign of undiluted autocracy, which re-established the Inquisition and proscribed many of those who had done most to drive the French out of Spain.

Both Wellesley and Wellington, who made a hasty return from his Paris honours to lend his authority to his brother's protests, endeavoured in vain to curb the extravagances of the new *régime* and persuade Ferdinand to grant a new constitution. In this they, of course, had the support of their Government, though Castlereagh, sickened by the experience of the last two years, wrote that "it is impossible to conceive that any change tranquilly effected can well be for the worse. We are entitled to pronounce now upon a certain extent of experience that in practice, as in theory, it is amongst the worst of the modern productions of that nature." "I hope," he continued, in language that reveals a good deal of his mind on this subject, "if we are to encounter the hazards of a new constitutional experiment in Spain, in addition to the many others now in progress in Europe, that the persons charged with the work will not again fall into the inconceivable absurdity of banishing from the legislature the Ministers of the Crown: to which error, more perhaps than to any other, may be attributed the incapacity which has distinguished the march of every one of these systems, which has placed the main authorities of the constitution in hostility, instead of alliance, with each other." [1]

It was with Ferdinand's new Government, therefore, that the peace negotiations had to be transacted. Its predecessor, protesting against exclusion from the Châtillon and Chaumont negotiations, had sent full powers to Fernan-Nuñez to take part in the Peace Conference. It was, however, only Castlereagh's urgent summons and promise to accept responsibility which brought him, in doubt and trepidation, to Paris at the end of April. Ferdinand, indeed, shewed himself sufficiently hostile to France. He accepted the Treaty of Chaumont with alacrity. But the Duke of San Carlos, his Foreign Minister, was immediately up in arms at the manner in which Spain was treated at Paris. He refused to recognise Fernan-Nuñez, and sent to Paris Labrador, whom Wellington described as "*la plus mauvaise tête* that I have ever met with." Wellington left behind him a masterly memorandum urging Spain to give up her claims on Italy and rely on her almost insular position.

[1] From Wellesley, Jan. 6, 11, Feb. 26, March 22, April 19, 23, 24, May 15, 1814: *F.O. Spain*, 158; *W.S.D.* ix. 17. Wellington to Stuart, May 25, 1814: *Gurwood*, xii. 27. To Wellesley, May 10, 1814: *C.C.* x. 25.

Meanwhile, Castlereagh had been trying to induce Fernan-Nuñez to accept the treaty with France, but the Spaniard, much piqued at being left out with all the other secondary Powers from the inner councils of the peace negotiations, was trying to negotiate separate articles with Talleyrand, which would have reopened every territorial change since 1792. Castlereagh got for him the retrocession from France of the Spanish part of St. Domingo—a barren enough gift—but he had to refuse to take up the question of Louisiana, explaining that France had no money to buy it back from the United States. Fernan-Nuñez, profoundly disheartened, would have left Paris but for Castlereagh's urgent request, and welcomed the news that Labrador would replace him. Labrador had but little more success than his predecessor, and the treaty with France, when finally signed on July 20, added nothing of importance to the main treaty drawn up by the Four, except that Talleyrand promised the good offices of France at the coming Congress in support of Spanish claims in Italy.[1]

There was thus hardly a favourable atmosphere in which to arrange special British interests with Spain. Two questions especially, besides that of the colonies, on which there was not much hope for a settlement, were uppermost in the mind of the British Government—the Slave Trade and the restoration of Olivenza to Portugal. Wellesley soon saw that but little could be done as regards the first, though he continued his unavailing efforts until the autumn. The second also, Wellington thought, could only be settled by strong support of Spain in the colonial question, while San Carlos, who received the demand with great surprise, suggested that Louisiana would be fair exchange. He also asked for a loan of ten millions and the continuation of the British subsidies to the end of the year. Wellesley had to subdue these demands but the treaty of Alliance was nevertheless concluded on July 5. It contained no clause of importance except one which ensured most favoured nation treatment to Britain, if Spain opened her South American trade, and a separate article, which San Carlos insisted on keeping secret,

[1] From Wellesley, June 5, 1814: *F.O. Spain*, 160. Wellesley to Wellington, June 17, 1814 : *W.S.D.* ix. 139.

by which His Catholic Majesty agreed not to enter into any treaty with France of the nature of the Family Compact or affecting its independence or alliance with Britain. No commercial treaty could yet be obtained, much as it was needed.

Castlereagh was nevertheless glad to obtain the treaty, which at least removed a fear necessarily present at the simultaneous restoration of the Bourbons in France and Spain. He regretted the necessity of keeping the clause secret from France, and when in August his relations with Talleyrand grew closer, he succeeded in getting San Carlos to allow it to be divulged. For the rest, except for the interminable Slave Trade negotiations, British influence was confined to protests against the conduct of Ferdinand, who was now completely in the hands of his secret advisers. His arbitrary actions had already begun to make him most unpopular in England, and Wellington on his return was warned by the Lord Mayor that he must not propose the King of Spain's health at a Guildhall banquet.[1]

(iv) ITALY

If in Spain some progress had at least been made with British interests, however unsatisfactory Ferdinand's conduct towards his own subjects, in Italy during this period nothing could be accomplished. The new constitution in Sicily was, indeed, put in the greatest danger by the King assuming the royal power once more, now that the war was over. Bentinck, who had insisted on returning to Palermo, was still in charge when this event happened, and though he was quite aware of what Ferdinand's return to power meant, he tried to make the best of it. He assured the Sicilian constitutionalists that Britain would continue to protect them, while he affected to believe that the King, who had received much good advice from both the Tsar and the Emperor of Austria, was now

[1] To Wellesley, May 11, 1814: *C.C.* x. 27; July 30, Aug. 3, Sept. 9, 1814: *F.O. Spain*, 158. From Wellesley, June 17, July 5, 6, 22, 23, Aug. 31, 1814: *F.O. Spain*, 160, 161. Wellesley to Wellington, June 17, 1814: *W.S.D.* ix. 139. Wellington to Wellesley, July 20, 1814; from Wellington, May 25, Sept. 12, 1814: *Gurwood*, xii. 77, 28, 109: *F.O. France*, 100 (from which the blanks in *Gurwood* can be filled up).

ready to adopt liberal principles in order to obtain the return of Naples. He released him from the promise he had made in October 1813 not to resume the throne, and the reconciliation was celebrated by the King visiting Bentinck's house for the feast of Santa Rosalia—an unprecedented honour. Bentinck could therefore, in the last dispatch he wrote as British envoy, congratulate Castlereagh "upon this happy termination of the long and embarrassing relation which has existed for so many years between the two Governments. The King returns to an independent throne, saved by the valour and forbearance of Great Britain. He returns with expressions of gratitude to his ally, with a desire apparently most sincere to support the improved institutions of his country, with feelings of universal conciliation and goodwill." [1]

How far Bentinck had been able to persuade himself that the King had changed his spots it is difficult to say. He could believe almost anything. But A'Court, his cool, capable, and cynical successor, had no illusions and was thankful that he had no responsibility for the King's recall. His most secret instructions, drawn up by Liverpool in Castlereagh's absence, ordered him to secure a modification of the constitution to strengthen the power of the Crown. A'Court's opinion of the Sicilian people was that they were "totally and radically unfit to be trusted with political power." He deplored "their natural depravity at bottom, which will always rise, when the hand of power be removed, to ruin and destroy the fairest projects of philanthrophy." Yet he had to try to defend the constitutional party from the persecution which the King and his new advisers immediately began. "I am forced to become its advocate and its chief," he lamented, "because neither the honour of the British name nor humanity itself will permit me to think of deserting it." The partisans of the constitution, he reported, fearing the King's vengeance, were already fleeing the country.

His battle was from the first a losing one. The King was determined to destroy the constitution as soon as it was safe to do so. A'Court, much as he hated democracy, dreaded the despotism of a King like Ferdinand even more. His own

[1] From Bentinck, July 4, 5, 1814 : *F.O. Sicily*, 64.

position, he said, was an impossible one. Bentinck had done sufficient to fill the King with rancour against the British, while he had failed to secure his abdication. The result was that he had called back to power a set of Ministers who hated both the constitution and the British. A'Court thus found himself powerless to protect the constitutional party. He asked for authority to suspend the subsidy in order to obtain some control, while the only chance for the Sicilians, he thought, was for the Vienna Congress to restore Ferdinand to Naples on condition that the Hereditary Prince was left in independent control of Sicily. This proposal somewhat embarrassed both Castlereagh, now on his way to Vienna, and the Cabinet. The former was ready to protect the constitutional party, "even to the extent of breaking off relations" with the Court, but he pointed out that Britain could not use force for that end and could not assume "a control which cannot belong to us and which could not, if attempted, be persevered in." The Cabinet went as far as possible in a draft instruction which they sent to Vienna for Castlereagh's approval. Both Liverpool and Bathurst disliked the Sicilian constitution, but they thought Britain in honour bound to protect their "friends." A'Court was therefore to concentrate on that point and leave the constitution to take care of itself as much as possible. He was given full control of the subsidy and ordered "to insist on the most positive terms with the Sicilian Government that no person whatever shall suffer in his person or property for the part he may have taken in the establishment and support of the constitution." But, on the second point, it was impossible to say what could be done. Nevertheless, the bait of Naples was to be used to restrain the King: "You will give the Court of Naples most distinctly to understand that if they make so ill a return for all we have done for His Sicilian Majesty as to persecute those with whom we have acted, it will be impossible for us to take any effective part in the measures which may be proposed for the restoration of His Sicilian Majesty to the crown of Naples."

These instructions were sent to Castlereagh, who before forwarding them to A'Court had an interview with Ferdinand's

representative at Vienna, Ruffo. After explaining that the
British troops could not stay for ever in Sicily, which was
now in no danger, he urged the King to make his peace with
those of his subjects who had been on the constitutional side,
thus avoiding the necessity of an "interference which must
more or less lower his authority and embarrass our relations."
"With respect to the constitution," Castlereagh continued,
"we considered it too servile an imitation of a system inapplicable to the state of society in Sicily, and especially
defective in not giving adequate power and influence to
the Crown. That the King might rely upon our support
in any temperate and prudent modification of the Government, but that nothing ought to be done abruptly; any party
measure, which gave the impression of reaction before a plan
was well considered and opinions prepared, would injure the
King's interests generally and especially counteract any hopes
of returning to Naples." [1]

These instructions implied that the British Government
were perhaps prepared to join in an attack on Murat, and
throughout this period their policy had obviously tended in
that direction. As has been seen, Liverpool as early as April
had hoped to get rid of him, and such continued to be the
desire of the Government, though of course it could not be
avowed. In June the Duke of Orleans visited France to
plead his father-in-law's cause, and Louis, while full of sympathy, sent him to London where, he said, the matter would be
decided. The Prince Regent received him warmly, and openly
avowed his desire to get rid of Murat. His Ministers were,
however, more circumspect. Liverpool, though he made no
secret of his opinion, refused to admit that Britain could do
anything, and tried to throw the responsibility for the removal
of Murat on the Bourbon courts. Castlereagh was much less
positive, and dwelt on the difficulties of the situation without
in any way committing himself, while Metternich was embarrassed and hesitating.

[1] Memorandum for Mr. A'Court, March 9, 1814; Bathurst to A'Court
(" sent to Vienna by Mr. A'Court's request to be considered by Lord
Castlereagh "), Sept. 17, 1814: *F.O. Sicily*, 65. From Bathurst, Sept. 16,
1814: *Lond. MSS.* To Liverpool, Sept. 9, 1814: *C.C.* x. 112. To
A'Court, Sept. 29, 1814: *F.O. Continent*, 7. A'Court to Hamilton, July 3,
1814; from A'Court, July 23, 24, Aug. 6, 17, 1814: *F.O. Sicily*, 65.

Nevertheless, the British Government shewed pretty clearly its dislike of Murat. It refused to receive his representative as an accredited envoy, and Castlereagh's reply to a question of Canning on June 29 indicated that the Government felt free to follow any line of action, being only bound by the armistice. Though Murat continued to receive many British visitors, and through them endeavoured to work on public opinion at home, his envoys were not very well chosen.[1]

Meanwhile another distinguished visitor had arrived who also shewed no favour to Murat—Cardinal Consalvi. For the first time since the days of Mary Tudor a Cardinal was received in London. The Pope's defiance of Napoleon had enabled Castlereagh to tell Consalvi at Paris that "all England was Catholic in wishing to restore the Pope to his patrimony," and to allude pleasantly to the British scheme to rescue His Holiness by a daring raid in 1812. Consalvi began his campaign with a note to the Ministers of each of the Four Powers, asking for the return of the whole of the patrimony of St. Peter, including the Legations and the Marches. But having once formally established his claims, he was careful not to press the British Ministers too hard. He knew that the affair depended mainly on Metternich, who gave him evasive replies. During his visit, therefore, he behaved with the greatest tact, avoiding public occasions so as not to raise the dangerous question of precedence, being satisfied with the fact that the Prince Regent had received him wearing a Cardinal's costume. The Prince showered compliments on him, and the Ministers treated him with great courtesy. They were eager to get the assist-ance of the Pope in dealing with the Catholic Powers, who now alone supported the Slave Trade. They promised him their support at the coming Congress, but when he tried to obtain something more definite on the question of the Legations and the Marches they evaded any definite promise.

In this situation Consalvi shewed the greatest discretion. There were big issues at stake. The question of permanent

---

[1] Weil, *Murat*, i. 127 ff., gives the long letter of the Duke of Orleans which is in *F.O. Sicily*, 65, having been communicated to A'Court. La Châtre to Talleyrand, June 23, 1814: *Paris A.A.E. Angleterre Supplement*, 21, f. 268.

diplomatic relations between the Papacy and Britain was bruited, and of course that of Catholic Emancipation, in which the consent of the Pope to such safeguards as its supporters thought necessary to secure the assent of Parliament and the Regent was of the utmost importance. In February the Vice-Prefect of Propaganda had sent a letter which seemed to shew that the Pope would agree to the restrictions necessary to carry the measure, especially the Lay veto on the appointment of bishops, and the Irish Catholics were already in open protest against it. But the Cardinal did not grant or press for decisions on any question. He was content to have established amicable relations with Castlereagh and cultivated the goodwill of the principal Protestant Power.[1]

(v) General

In the midst of all these transactions affecting the British position in the Mediterranean and the North Sea the main preoccupation of the Foreign Minister, as of the sovereigns and statesmen of the other great Powers, continued to be the struggle at the coming Congress for the future of Germany and Poland. Neither Metternich nor the Tsar had left England satisfied with the results of the visit. The former, indeed, professed himself delighted with his reception, which Montgelas said had made him an "Anglomaniac." But though he might be satisfied with the impression which he had produced on the Government and the Prince Regent, who, he claimed, had offered him an alliance against Russia, he had secured nothing definite for the large concessions which he had made on Saxony, however much he might minimise them to the Saxon representatives or their friends. The question of Mainz had not gone well, and he was doubtful, to say the least, how far Castlereagh's plan of declaring, in the first instance, for an independent Poland would work out. At Vienna these misgivings must have been increased by find-

---

[1] There is a full account of the visit in Consalvi's letters to Pacca in P. I. Rinieri's *Il Congresso di Vienna e la Santa Sede*, 143–82. *Cf.* also *Mémoires du Cardinal Consalvi*, ed. J. Cretinau-Joly (1866), 82–84, and Bernard Ward, *The Eve of Catholic Emancipation*, II. chaps. xx. and xxi. and pp. 91–94.

ing a strong party organised against him, even though he was secure in the Emperor's favour.

As for the Tsar, he made no secret of his irritation at all that had occurred in London. He wrapped himself in inscrutable mystery as to his Polish plans, but he was aware of the combination forming against him. It was perhaps some consolation that emissaries came to Petersburg from the sovereigns of the smaller Courts, and even from the Italians, asking for his protection at the Congress. Nesselrode was at this time appointed Foreign Secretary, but it was recognised that he was only a secretary and that the Tsar kept affairs in his own hands.

Only Prussia had obtained anything of substance. The agreement with Münster over Mainz and the countenance of his Saxon plans by Castlereagh seemed of great importance to Hardenberg and Humboldt. The conduct of their soldiers in the Netherlands, which General Sack refused to evacuate and where he levied large contributions, shewed the spirit in which the army approached the coming settlement.[1]

Castlereagh was kept hard at work in the House of Commons throughout July, for besides the irritating question concerning the Princess of Wales, he had to obtain a vote of credit for his reconstruction arrangements in Holland and his army of 75,000 men on the Continent. The overwhelming superiority of the Government was, however, much in evidence. The Opposition had lost caste by the manner in which the Princess of Wales had thrown over Whitbread, and Castlereagh covered them with ridicule. The Whigs were losing all their possible allies. Canning's acceptance of the Embassy to Portugal was considered a great triumph. The Wellesley party also seemed destroyed, and Wellesley Pole soon joined the Cabinet as Master of the Mint. Castlereagh might prepare then to go to the Congress with the Government apparently in a secure position at home, though it was to be proved that without his aid it could scarcely survive a short session of Parliament.

---

[1] From Rose, July 20, 1814: *F.O. Bavaria*, 40. Metternich passed through Munich on his way home and was very nice to him but told him nothing: Fournier, *Die Geheimpolizei*, 96. Wilson saw Alexander at Bruchsal on his way back: *Wilson MSS*. 30120, f. 29. From Lord Walpole, Aug. 9, 1814: *C.C.* x. 83. To Clancarty, Aug. 14, 1814: *C.C.* x. 85.

In August he began to prepare seriously for the task. It was Prussia whom he was most anxious to keep in the right faith, for the subservience of her King to the Tsar had been most noticeable in London. On August 8 he wrote Hardenberg a long letter, calling his attention to the organisation of a Polish army in Poland and the concentration of Russian troops in the north of Germany. Hardenberg's reply shewed almost as much jealousy of Austria as of Russia, though he and Metternich were in constant communication over the German constitution. At the same time Castlereagh put in a good word for Talleyrand, who was impressed with the same danger and whose general conduct was most satisfactory. Hardenberg sent a long answer which revealed a very different outlook. He admitted Russia needed watching, but shewed far more jealousy of Bavaria for her claim to Mainz, and even of Austria, who, he said, was aiming at frontier rectifications at the expense of Saxony. The remedy he urged was to give all Saxony to Prussia, to confine the left bank of the Rhine to Prussia and Austria, and to induce the Netherlands to enter a strong German Confederation as the "Burgundian Circle"—this last idea being one to which Castlereagh was strongly opposed.

With Metternich himself Castlereagh seems to have had no direct contact during this time, and Merveldt was totally inadequate to act as a link. After a long conversation with Czartoryski on Poland, he went to Castlereagh to recount it, and talked of war with Russia in the most nonchalant fashion. Castlereagh snubbed him unmercifully, and hinted that Austria was the least ready for war of all the Great Powers. He continued to insist that the right way to treat the Polish question was to propose the re-establishment of Poland as an independent state, which would rally the Poles and, above all, public opinion in England to their side, and thus prepare the way for driving back Russia to the Vistula. Merveldt was, however, quite incapable of appreciating this point, and merited the censure which Metternich sent him later. He could, however, plume himself that the Prince Regent distinguished him above all the other Ambassadors.[1]

[1] To Hardenberg, Aug. 8, 1814; from Hardenberg, Aug. 27, 1814: F.O. Continent Archives, 20. Merveldt to Metternich, Aug. 2, 12, 15;

There was still Talleyrand, who had remained completely isolated during the discussions at London.   He was much disturbed at the news of the postponement of the Congress and the preliminary meeting of the Four Powers at Vienna. According to Sir Charles Stuart, who was temporarily at Paris until Wellington arrived, the visit of Metternich on his way back to Vienna only increased these fears, for Metternich had shewn an open jealousy of the supposed desire of France to support Alexander.   Castlereagh immediately sent his excuses for not having informed Talleyrand officially of the London decisions, and explained the motives which had led to them.

It was natural, therefore, that Talleyrand, who was already preparing his famous instructions for the Congress, which he hoped would bring back France to a position of equality and influence in Europe, should see in Britain his best chance to break his way into the circle of the Four and obtain some insight into their plans.   At the end of July he approached Sir Charles Stuart with proposals of co-operation in the coming Congress, urging France's views on Italy but especially stressing Louis' desire to support any wishes the Prince Regent might have for Hanover.   At the same time the Duc de Berri was sent to London by the King to ascertain how the land lay. These overtures, which Stuart encouraged, continued at frequent intervals, based on the theme that Britain and France had a common interest and duty in the approaching discussions, in which both might be considered impartial arbitrators.

Castlereagh, for his part, was anxious to know Talleyrand's views on Poland and Naples, and to make sure that he was not being drawn into a Russian combination.   He had, of course, to take the greatest care that neither the other Ministers of the Four nor Talleyrand himself should get the impression that he was breaking away from his old connections.   The secret clause of the Treaty of Paris still governed the situation. Nevertheless, Wellington, who was consulted, warmly advocated a meeting, though he shewed his usual prescience and breadth of view when he pointed out: "The situation of

Metternich to Merveldt, Nov. 4, 1814. Merveldt had continued to talk in a similar strain to Liverpool after Castlereagh's departure : *Vienna St. A.*

affairs will naturally constitute England and France as arbitrators at the Congress, if those Powers *understand* each other, and such an understanding may preserve the general peace. But I think your object would be defeated and England would lose her high character and station if the line of [Prince Talleyrand] is adopted, which appears to me tantamount to the declaration by the two Powers that they will be arbitrators of all the differences which may arise. We must not forget that only a few months ago it was wished to exclude the interference and influence of France from the Congress entirely."

With this caution Castlereagh thoroughly agreed, but an interview was an obvious necessity if he was not to run the risk of driving Talleyrand to take his confidences elsewhere. Accordingly, he was quite ready to accept the invitation which Talleyrand sent him to visit Paris on his way to Vienna.[1]

He left for the Continent on August 16 with the expectation of a two months' stay (so he told the Bavarian Minister), visited Brussels, was much impressed by Antwerp, and made more determined than ever that France must never possess it, and went to Ghent to confer with the British Commissioners on the negotiation for peace with America. Then, leaving his wife and the rest of his party to proceed direct to Dijon, he made a hasty visit to Paris. There in interviews with the King and Talleyrand he discussed all the points of European policy. It was merely an exchange of views, but one so satisfactory that Talleyrand now professed no jealousy of the preliminary meeting of the Ministers of the Four at Vienna, and even gave Castlereagh authority to support his own arguments by quoting Talleyrand's views if he thought it desirable. Indeed, so great was the desire on the part of the King and his Minister to establish a close connection with Britain that Castlereagh found it necessary "rather to repress the exuberance of this sentiment and to prevent its assuming a shape which by exciting jealousy in other states might impair our respective means of being really useful." Münster, who also passed

[1] To Stuart, July 16, 1814 : *F.O. France*, 96 ; Aug. 13, 1814 : *W.S.D.* ix. 185–86. From Stuart, July 4, 28, Aug. 18, 22, 1814 : *F.O. France*, 97, 98 ; Aug. 1, 8, 9, 1814 : *W.S.D.* ix. 180 ff. From Wellington, Aug. 18, 1814 : *Gurwood*, xii. 81.

through Paris shortly afterwards, was able to testify to the deep impression which the visit had made. It is a tribute to the tact and foresight of both Talleyrand and Castlereagh that each at once saw how far they could go together without hindering their common interests.[1]

[1] Pfeffel to the King of Bavaria, Aug. 16, 1814: *Munich St. A.* Münster to the Prince Regent, Sept. 2, 1814: Dupuis, *Ministère de Talleyrand en 1814*, ii. 285. To Liverpool, Sept. 3, 1814: *B.D.* 191. Castlereagh told Pfeffel that he would have preferred the Congress " in a spot where business would be less liable to be interrupted by pleasure," but he counted on being home by Christmas. To Metternich, Aug. 22, 1814: (from Brussels) ". . . I propose separating from Lady C. here and making an excursion for 48 hours to Paris to see how the land lays there . . . everything here goes well. The Prince gains ground daily and is highly sensible of the loyalty with which General Vincent prepared the way for his reception. I conclude Aberdeen has apprised you of his change of plans. I don't know whether there is any truth in the newspaper report of *his being in love. . . ." Vienna St. A.*

CHAPTER VI

THE CONGRESS OF VIENNA I: THE CRISIS OF RECONSTRUCTION, SEPTEMBER 1814–JANUARY 1815

1. THE PERSONNEL AND PROCEDURE.

2. CASTLEREAGH AS MEDIATOR.

3. THE SECRET TREATY.

"Le véritable but du Congrès était le partage entre les vainqueurs des dépouilles enlevées au vaincu."—GENTZ.

CHAPTER VI

1. THE PERSONNEL AND PROCEDURE

SINCE the only invitation to the Congress of Vienna was a public announcement that it would open on October 1, almost every sovereign and statesman in Europe might cherish some hope of being present at what was naturally regarded as a unique occasion. Some were necessarily disappointed, including the Prince Regent, but a large number of states were represented, not only by their principal Ministers, but also by their crowned heads. By September they had already begun to assemble at Vienna, whose resources were hardly able to cope with their numbers, for almost all the guests brought their wives and other female relations, and a mass of visitors poured into the city merely to enjoy the spectacle. The impoverished Austrian Court and the principal nobles strained their resources to the utmost to provide hospitality for all, but where crowned heads were so numerous lesser men had to be content with very narrow quarters.

Castlereagh was well within his promised date when he arrived on September 13, ready to discuss with the other Ministers of the Alliance the programme and procedure of the Congress, as well as to make a last effort to settle the main problems of reconstruction before the other plenipotentiaries arrived. Nesselrode and Hardenberg arrived two days later, and though Metternich had to give up his plan of a little preliminary party in the quiet of Baden, a pleasant resort near Vienna, private discussions at once began.

The quantity of business was, indeed, formidable. Outside France hardly anything had been settled as to the territorial reconstruction of Europe. From the Rhine to the Vistula, from the North Sea to the Mediterranean, the frontier of every state had to be reconsidered.   Germany and Switzerland had also to be given constitutions, while the Pope and the Sultan raised special problems.   Nor were the questions merely territorial.   The old dynasties were hastening to Vienna to claim their "rights," so that questions of succession were involved.   Lastly, there were such general problems as the Abolition of the Slave Trade, the Navigation of International Rivers, the Emancipation of the Jews, the Regulation of Diplomatic Etiquette.   In the background was the all-important question whether some new method was to be instituted for the new Europe, once it was made, to prevent the recurrence of the evils of war.

Though Britain's own claims had been largely satisfied at the Peace of Paris, Castlereagh was still convinced that these European questions were of vital concern to the peace and prosperity of his country.   For twelve months he had been preparing for the settlement, which could no longer be postponed.   Now at last the principles and expedients which he had so often discussed with Pitt were to be applied.   The "balance of power" or "just equilibrium," as he more often called it, had now to be transferred from the preamble of state papers to the map of Europe.   The experience of the last eight months had shewn how difficult it was to obtain agreement amongst the continental Powers.   Failure to do so now threatened disaster of great magnitude—at the worst, war; and even if an immediate outbreak was avoided, a Europe so badly reconstructed that war would follow in a short interval. To avoid such a catastrophe was to Castlereagh's mind the chief duty of a British statesman.   Alone of all the plenipotentiaries he had no territorial claims to urge.   It is true that the frontiers of the Netherlands had still to be settled and the claims of Hanover to expansion adjusted.   But these were, after all, secondary matters; while Russia, Prussia, and Austria were vitally affected by the settlement.   Britain could act, therefore, as the mediator in their disputes, with an eye to Europe as a whole rather than any special interest.

As has been seen, Castlereagh had to some extent compromised this situation by the attitude which he had adopted at an early period on the questions of Poland and Saxony. He had already shewn himself violently opposed to the Tsar's schemes, and was preparing to combine all Europe against him. He had already taken sides. But his position was still that of a mediator and not of a principal in the dispute. He was convinced that without him the other Great Powers would be unable to come to satisfactory conclusions, and that he must take the lead in the discussions. He could not remain merely as a judge; action was necessary. The dead-lock had already come, and no one else appeared to possess the energy, resolution, and courage to solve it.

The British delegation seems small enough to cope with its formidable task. Castlereagh had no one to help him of first-rate calibre. He was perhaps glad to have no other Cabinet Minister with him, yet it seems strange that in view of the magnitude of the problems and the distance of Vienna from London no suggestion should have been made to send one of his colleagues to share his responsibility. The other British plenipotentiaries were diplomatic assistants. "You would find the others useful in matters referred to subordinate commissions to report upon, but they take no part in trans-actions between Cabinet and Cabinet," Castlereagh explained to Wellington when he offered him his own place.[1] Wellington carried out his duties with his usual efficiency and coolness, and as a good soldier with careful attention to the orders which Castlereagh left behind him. The main questions of reconstruction were settled before he took charge, but it was of great importance that he was at Vienna when the news of Napoleon's return arrived, where his prestige and authority did much to make the military plans of the Allies less dilatory than in previous years and to compose the inevitable rivalries of strategy and command which immediately arose.

Lord Stewart, as Ambassador to Vienna, had necessarily to be a member of the delegation, but his brother's affection would have given him the opportunity wherever the Congress had been held. No one enjoyed its magnificence more than he did, but the energy and heartiness, which was often useful while the campaign was in progress, now made Stewart a

[1] To Wellington, Dec. 17, 1814 : *C.C.* x. 220.

terrible handicap.   His love of display and social prominence
led him into some dreadful situations, nor could he resist as
his colleagues did the social dangers of the Congress.   The
result was that he became the *enfant terrible* of Vienna and
earned the nickname of "Lord Pumpernickel."   No snub
could damp his effervescence, and his exploits, which included
a free fight with a coachman, apparently thoroughly enjoyed
by both combatants, shocked and disgusted the aristocratic
Society in which he moved.

Lord Cathcart was included because of his intimacy with
the Tsar, but he played no part until after the return of
Napoleon.   It was the third Plenipotentiary, the Earl of Clancarty, who was Castlereagh's principal assistant.   He was a
man of limited outlook but of amazing industry and real
diplomatic courage.   His reverence and affection for Castlereagh were such that the orders of his chief were almost
sacrosanct.   He supplied therefore but little check or criticism
of Castlereagh's plans, but gave him constant assistance in
carrying them out, while his work in the final stages of the
Congress was of great importance.

Criticism as well as assistance was supplied by Edward
Cooke, whom Castlereagh took with him as chief of staff.
His long years of devotion to the Secretary of State enabled
him to adopt when necessary a more detached attitude than
any other of Castlereagh's helpers.   He was undoubtedly his
chief confidant while he remained at Vienna.   He established
valuable contacts with Metternich's officials in the Foreign
Office and was a mine of information and advice.   He assisted
Castlereagh with his memoranda, and the phraseology of some
of them is undoubtedly his.   His cynical letters to the Prime
Minister added just the right touches to Castlereagh's
dispatches.   Unfortunately, his health, which was already
much impaired, could not stand the strain of the hot rooms
and harsh climate of Vienna, and he had to leave at the
critical moment to recuperate in Italy.[1]

[1] I must again correct the statement made in the *Cambridge History
of British Foreign Policy* (iii. 554), that Cooke resigned as a result of a
difference with Castlereagh over Poland, which is founded on a remark
of Stapleton, Canning's Private Secretary, who claimed that he had it
from Planta.   This malicious lie of Stapleton's, which was only published
after both Planta and Cooke were dead, is not only proved false by the

The other most important member of Castlereagh's staff was Planta, who was by now well versed in continental journeyings, and who was to succeed Cooke. The ten other members of the staff were mainly young men, some of them regular members of the Foreign Office, others relations of Castlereagh or his friends. Their command of French appears to have been limited, since Gentz had frequently to be employed by Castlereagh to translate his notes and memoranda.[1] Clancarty also brought two assistants of his own. The Duke of Wellington brought three assistants when he replaced Castlereagh in February. Stratford Canning was summoned, apparently as an afterthought, to assist in Swiss affairs, which he had already mastered in a few months' stay, and to which he was to contribute a good deal during the Congress. Münster of course represented Hanover, and was at Castlereagh's disposal as at Paris. But a severe accident kept him in the background throughout October and most of November, and he had necessarily to devote much attention to purely German affairs in which he was a prominent figure. His ideas on the Saxon question were by no means the same as those of Castlereagh. He was, however, used by the latter on occasion, was always a source of information, and responded loyally when called upon to make sacrifices for the general good.

On October 12 he announced to the allied Courts that George III had taken the title of King of Hanover, a step which, according to the Duke of Cambridge, caused great joy to his faithful subjects, though the Duke himself postponed his rejoicing until he saw whether Münster succeeded "in procuring sufficient additional territory to the Electorate to make it worthy of its new title." [2]

The staff though small was well organised, and on the whole seems to have been adequate to its purpose. There is no

whole of Cooke's relations with Castlereagh, but is shewn to be without foundation by the fact that Cooke's letters take an even stronger position towards the Polish question than Castlereagh himself. Cooke indeed wrote part of the memoranda in which Castlereagh laid down his position.

[1] *Tagebücher von F. von Gentz*, i. 320, 324, 327, 356. Gentz received £1600 from the British in addition to such presents as all the principal Powers gave to him at the end of the Congress.

[2] Duke of Cambridge to the Prince Regent, Oct. 24, 1814 : *Windsor Arch.*

complaint of delay, though a large number of long documents and memoranda had to be dealt with, and the amount of copying work must have been at times overwhelming. Moreover, it remained, almost alone amongst the embassies of the Great Powers, impervious to the ubiquitous secret agents of Austrian police. Castlereagh hired his own servants, gave special orders as to the disposal of his papers, and seems to have warned his staff against feminine seductions.[1]

He inhabited a suite of twenty-two rooms in Minoriten Platz, rejecting the Auge Gottes prepared for him by his hosts as too small. There Lady Castlereagh and her sister, Lady Matilda, dispensed a hospitality which it must be admitted was, as at Paris, more appreciated by English travellers, of whom eighty were present, than by foreign guests, of whom, however, said Cooke, a curious medley appeared at her suppers nearly every night. Dancing was held every Tuesday, and Castlereagh seems always to have been glad of it as a form of exercise. Her obvious attachment to her husband amused Viennese Society, where such a spectacle was rare. Lord Apsley complained of the excessive Sabbatarianism, which was perhaps increased as a protest against the licence of the place. The performance of Beethoven's new sonata had to be postponed from a Sunday owing to this reason. Lord Stewart also kept open house at great expense. Divine service was celebrated at the Embassy every Sunday.[2]

In the never-ending series of public entertainments Castle-

---

[1] The papers were well kept while Castlereagh was there, but after his return there was some difficulty. A light wagon was sufficient to take them home at the end of the Congress. Two ciphers were lost in March, but it was found that they were only mislaid. The courier service was better than that of any other Power, not only because more money was available. The secret police, who had agents in all other hotels, apparently failed entirely in Castlereagh's. Nothing was left in the waste-paper baskets. Fournier, *Die Geheimpolizei auf dem Wiener Congress*, 25. Weil, *Les dessous du Congrès de Vienne*, i. 211.

[2] The cost to the State was £15,000 for the period of Castlereagh's stay (*F.O. Great Britain*, 10), while Stewart was given an extra £5000, besides special allowances of £5274, both moderate amounts considering the general scale of expenditure at Vienna. These sums were, of course, for personal expenses only (Bathurst to Stewart, June 9, 1815, which intimates that in future he must strictly limit himself to his salary. *Lond. MSS.*). Yonge, *Life of Liverpool*, ii. 95. According to Consalvi, Castlereagh laid in 10,000 bottles of wine for his dinners and receptions (Weil, *Murat*, i. 391–92).

reagh was always an impressive figure, his beauty and imperturbability being generally renowned as well as the simplicity of his dress. His wife, on the other hand, was a mark for the wits on such occasions, especially when she wore her husband's Garter ornament in her hair. Castlereagh, however, unlike Metternich, cut down his social duties to the minimum, and the unavoidable interruptions to his work were generally used to further some negotiation.

He kept his team working in laudable harmony while he was at Vienna. There were, however, considerable heart-burnings amongst the British plenipotentiaries at Wellington's appointment, which they felt as a reflection on their own competence, though all acquiesced in Castlereagh's wishes without complaint. The Duke fully carried out the hint of Castlereagh to keep matters in his own hand, and the others were treated by him as subordinates and not told too much. Clancarty was, however, made contented with the K.C.B., which he had long coveted, and Lord Stewart had to stifle his discontent. This was increased when Clancarty succeeded to Wellington, but Clancarty's tact and friendship made the position bearable. It became, however, worse when Cathcart took the Duke's position on the military committee, and broke bounds when it was thought that Clancarty would assume a position at headquarters such as Castlereagh had held in 1814. Clancarty forwarded Stewart's pathetic letter of protest to Castlereagh and generously offered to serve in any capacity so that harmony might prevail. Fortunately, events rendered this sacrifice unnecessary, though Castlereagh in a kind note to his brother pointed out that he had no cause for complaint.[1]

The statesmen of the Great Powers Castlereagh, of course, now knew intimately after six months' constant intercourse with them. There was but little change in personnel. The Tsar appointed as his principal plenipotentiaries, Nesselrode, Razumovski, his Ambassador at Vienna, a rich nonentity who only attracted attention when his magnificent palace was destroyed by fire, and Stackelberg. But none of the

---

[1] From Clancarty, May 19, 1815 ; from Stewart, May 15, 1815 : *Lond. MSS*. To Stewart, June 9, 1815 : *C.C.* x. 378. Of Cathcart's feelings we have no record, but it is improbable that they were disturbed.

Tsar's real confidants were Russians. Czartoryski wrote most of his memoranda on Poland. That he was the lover of the Tsarina appears to have made no difference to the Tsar's trust in him. Stein was used in German questions, and Capo d'Istria was also increasingly in evidence. He was given a free hand as regards his native Ionian Isles and was responsible for Swiss affairs, in which he tried to carry out La Harpe's wishes. Pozzo di Borgo, summoned from Paris, fell from favour because he disapproved the Tsar's plans.

The King of Prussia still relied on Hardenberg, but Humboldt played in some ways the more important part. He was suspected of trying to supplant his chief, and his manœuvres were undoubtedly one cause of Hardenberg's inconsistencies. Baron Jacobi was brought from London to check him, perhaps, but he was too bewildered to do much. Prussia had as usual a very capable staff, which continued the unending series of memoranda on every possible occasion. Their generals were too much in evidence for comfort and helped to give an appearance of rapacity to their demands.

Metternich might have been more easy and efficient if he had not been at home. Wessenberg, who was appointed to be his second, was, on the other hand, far happier than in London and did much to supply the deficiencies of his chief. The officials of the Ball Platz, including the indispensable Hudelist, also kept the machine moving, and Gentz reached the pinnacle of his fame when he became Secretary of the principal conferences. He acted also as Metternich's publicity agent. But Metternich's critics and enemies were also necessarily on the spot, watching for an opportunity to displace him in the Emperor's favour. Neither Stadion, who had been given the Finances, nor Schwarzenberg were entirely satisfied with Metternich, while other officials and generals were violently hostile. Metternich himself, though his subtlety and patience never deserted him, was not at his best. He lacked energy and was "most intolerably loose and giddy with women," an opinion of Cooke's which is confirmed from many other quarters. Nevertheless, his Emperor remained faithful to his Minister to the end.

Talleyrand brought with him three plenipotentiaries of but

moderate parts, of whom the Duc d'Alberg was the most efficient. His own brilliance would have been obscured by more assertive colleagues. He relied for help principally on La Besnardière, one of the most reliable of Napoleon's civil servants, whose pen was much in use for the composition of his chief's memoranda and even of some of the brilliant but untrustworthy reports sent to Paris for the edification of the King.

Both Labrador, who asserted Spain's rights in a spirit of pride and protest, and Count Palmella, who represented Portugal, gave Castlereagh a good deal of trouble. Sweden had now fallen almost completely out of the picture, except for her stubborn refusal to carry out her obligations to Denmark. Admiral Sydney Smith, the advocate of the deposed mad King Gustavus IV., was considered "as eccentric as his client." Gagern and Von Spaen, the Dutch plenipotentiaries, confessed that Castlereagh held "the tiller of their policy," but were sometimes restive under the control. Other plenipotentiaries with whom Castlereagh had a good deal of intercourse were Wrede, who was a fighting representative of Bavaria, Cardinal Consalvi, who was on excellent terms but too apt to bargain for small favours, and Mavrogeni, the unofficial representative of the Sultan, sent as a result of Liston's efforts at Constantinople. With the Kings of Bavaria, Wurtemberg, and Denmark, as well as a number of smaller princelings, Castlereagh seems to have had as little intercourse as was possible. Nor could the representatives of the smaller Powers see him without great difficulty. He remained in the inner circle which was dominated by the three sovereigns and their principal advisers, to which Talleyrand was afterwards admitted, the real Congress of Vienna, which carried out the reconstruction of Europe.

Castlereagh sent home a constant stream of reports to his Cabinet, together with copies of all the official memoranda. They were nearly all sent through Paris under flying seal so that Wellington could keep himself informed of the progress of events. Castlereagh also received a series of private letters from Liverpool as well as a few from Bathurst, which conveyed to him the sense of the Cabinet. He does not appear to have carried with him any special instructions.[1]   At any rate, none have been discovered and there is no explicit reference to them.   His powers were as wide as in his earlier mission, and he certainly extended them to their utmost.   Such official instructions as he received were signed by Bathurst, but only one was of importance, and that he flatly disobeyed.   Though the Cabinet were to grow very anxious at the course of events, Castlereagh was not checked in his vigorous policy even when a number of his colleagues disapproved of it.   Only when Parliament was in session did the Cabinet meet to consider foreign policy, and at the moment of the greatest crisis were scattered all over England at their private seats.   It was Liverpool and Bathurst alone who followed events closely, though, of course, the papers were accessible to other members, and these two were ready to give Castlereagh the greatest possible latitude.   The Prince Regent received long accounts from Münster and had his own opinions about Saxony, but he made no effort to influence events as he had done earlier in the year.

The British Press was ill-informed as to the Congress, and public opinion in Britain was never greatly interested in it. The fate of Poland appealed to that section of liberal opinion which Czartoryski had inspired during his visit, and at a later stage Saxony was to arouse some emotions.   But the Cabinet succeeded in cutting down the autumn session of Parliament to three weeks, and the mass of the people knew but little of the Congress.   It was only the Abolition of the Slave Trade which could excite their emotions.   The attempts which were to be made by those at Vienna to influence Castlereagh through the Regent, the Cabinet, or Parliament, were thus doomed to failure from the outset.

The first task was to make a plan for the Congress, and until this moment no one seems to have quite realised the difficulty which now appeared.   The idea of a "Congress" had been adopted without consideration of what such an assembly signified.   Who were to compose it?   How were its decisions to be made?   The statesmen of the Four Great Powers had now to face these questions in earnest, for the representatives

---

[1] So I now conclude, though for long I thought some instructions had been given.

of all Europe were pouring into Vienna to take part in its deliberations. The Four were just as much determined as ever that they alone should decide the territorial questions, but agreement had yet to be reached. Nothing was ready to be laid before Europe for approval. How were they to obtain the legal position which would enable them to keep the problems in their own hands until their differences were settled? [1]

The discussions on these questions began on September 15, and were continued for a week. There was unanimity, "that the conduct of business must practically rest with the leading Powers," and, except for a doubt on the Tsar's part as to Sweden's claims, the 'leading Powers' were held to be "the six Powers of the first order"—the Four, with France and Spain. It was an arbitrary distinction resting on no legal basis, re-asserting the claim of the "Great Powers" to have a special position in the European polity, which they had already made at Châtillon, Spain's historic past placing her for the moment alongside the five Powers whose resources really gave them a title to claim the epithet. But the Four had no intention of admitting France and Spain to a real equality. They reserved the "initiative" on all the territorial questions to themselves, and by the "initiative" they meant, as their Protocol confessed, practically the decision. Only then were France and Spain to be allowed to make criticisms and objections, and it was clear that these could then have no effect. This position was justified by the secret article of the Treaties of Paris, which, however, though it could be quoted against Talleyrand, had no validity for Spain or any of the other states, who were not even aware of its existence.

Castlereagh, fresh from his interview with Louis and Talley-rand, was not quite happy at the manner in which this claim to the "initiative" was stated. He would have liked to have shewn more delicacy towards France. But he found, as he told his Cabinet, that "the three continental Courts seem to feel equal jealousy of admitting France either to arbitrate between them or to assume any leading influence in the arrangements consequent upon the peace." He could do no more,

[1] " Not even the English, whom I thought more methodical than the others," wrote Talleyrand on his arrival, " have done any preparatory work on the subject." Pallain, *Correspondance inédite de Talleyrand*, 4.

therefore, than record his opinion that "the arrangements when so brought forward, to be open to free and liberal discussions with the other two Powers as friendly and not hostile parties." Moreover, he thought it necessary to reserve his right to protest against the decisions of the Four, if they were not to his liking.[1]

The Four had now to consider how these decisions were to be enforced on the rest. It was clear that the Congress could not be constituted at once without bringing up not only the delicate point of its authority, but the vexed problem as to who had the right to take part in it. It was Prussia who was, as usual, ready with memoranda to settle even these complicated questions, and Humboldt produced two papers which proposed to deal with them in a very masterful manner. The other Powers should simply be told that the Six Powers had assumed direction, and committees should be set up to deal with the various problems, the territorial questions being reserved to the Four. Only when the Four had decided, and the Six had promulgated, the decisions was the Congress to be summoned to ratify them.

This open assertion of the rights of the Great Powers was not much liked by Castlereagh, because "it too broadly and ostensibly assumed the right to do what may be generally acquiesced in if not offensively announced, but which the secondary Powers may protest against if recorded to their humiliation in the face of Europe." In two papers of his own composition he suggested that the smaller Powers should be persuaded rather than compelled to agree to the proposals of the Four. But this involved a meeting of plenipotentiaries, and immediately, therefore, the consideration of such questions as who was to represent Saxony or Naples. Humboldt therefore pressed his point of view, and Castlereagh had to give way. The Four prepared to meet Talleyrand with a Projet which deferred the opening of the Congress on the lines which Humboldt had proposed. None of them seem to have realised the opportunity which it gave to him.[2]

---

[1] To Liverpool, Sept. 24, 1814 : *B.D.* 193. Protocole de la Conference des 4 Cours, Sept. 22, 1814 : *B.F.S.P.* ii. 554, with Castlereagh's reservation.

[2] Castlereagh's proposals are given as Appendices II. and III. of my *Congress of Vienna*, where will also be found as Appendices IV., V., VI.,

For Talleyrand, when he was summoned to a quiet gathering in order to be informed of these proposals, refused entirely to agree with them. He had unanswerable objections. Who were these Six who were to be the directing committee? By what treaties were they constituted? The only body that he would recognise at all were the eight Powers who had signed the treaties of Paris by which the Congress had been summoned; and even these, he claimed, had no rights until their position was established by a meeting of the whole Congress. Let that body be summoned forthwith, he demanded, adding that France and Britain were constitutional Powers with special responsibilities. This view he immediately embodied in a formal note which he addressed pointedly to Castlereagh and not to Metternich. The Four were much perturbed at this method of handling the question, but they had no intention of giving way. They abandoned the idea of the Six and accepted Talleyrand's substitute of the Eight. But they refused to summon the Congress, and clearly indicated that the Four would continue their discussions of the territorial problems without any authorisation. Castlereagh, in vain, endeavoured to obtain Talleyrand's consent to these decisions, drafting himself another form of declaration. But Talleyrand would not give way. He was appealing to what he knew was a universal sentiment amongst the smaller Powers, to whom he speedily made known the facts of the controversy. He continued to insist that the Congress should be summoned, sending another note to Castlereagh which dwelt on British respect for the law because it was founded on consent and not on dictation.

But these appeals had no effect on Castlereagh. As he had told Talleyrand at Paris, he had no intention of separating Britain from her Allies. He gave him no support when, at the next meeting, Talleyrand, in answer to a challenge, proposed a formula for summoning the Congress, which would have included the King of Saxony's representatives and excluded those of Murat. He tried to persuade him to acquiesce in the decision that the Congress could not be

Humboldt's papers. Other details of organisation will be found in Part II. of the same book.

summoned. Talleyrand was thus in effect isolated: in fact his attitude had driven the Four closer together. He had therefore, after some flattering from Metternich, to agree to the postponement of the Congress for a month, to November 1, a decision which was formally announced in a declaration drawn up by Gentz. He had only succeeded in preventing the formal acceptance of the Prussian plan. Everything still depended on the discussions of the Four, from which Talleyrand was entirely excluded. These were continued without abatement, and a German Committee, such as had been originally suggested, also came into existence to discuss the Federal Constitution. As Castlereagh explained to his Cabinet, these decisions arose out of the nature of things, since a negotiation was in progress and not questions to be decided by voting.[1]

Talleyrand's chagrin was extreme, and he attributed his exclusion to Castlereagh more than to anyone else. He continued, however, to work for the opening of the Congress, and throughout the month of October there was an intention to hold some kind of a meeting on November 1. Castlereagh's plans indeed, as will be seen, included a threat to the Tsar that the Polish question would be brought before the assembled delegates if Russia did not give way, and Metternich, at his suggestion, actually told the Tsar that some such step would be taken. Talleyrand was invited by Castlereagh to make plans for the holding of a meeting of the plenipotentiaries, and readily consented. But the situation did not work out as had been expected, and it was found that a further postponement was necessary. This time Talleyrand shewed himself more yielding. He brought, indeed, before the Committee of Eight, which met on October 30, an elaborate plan of organisation, but he shewed little resentment when this was rejected, and all that was done was to appoint a committee to receive the full powers of the plenipotentiaries. These soon arrived in shoals, but the organisation of the full Congress stopped at that point. Talleyrand had by this time

[1] To Liverpool, Oct. 9, 1814 : *B.D.* 202. Talleyrand to Louis XVIII., Oct. 4, 9, 1814 ; Pallain, *Correspondance inédite*, 10, 25. From Talleyrand, Oct. 1, 5, 1814 : *Projet de Declaration*, Oct. 2, 1814 : *B.F.S.P.* ii. 559, 560, 561.

come to see that it was the dissensions of the Four rather than the rights of the smaller Powers which would give France the place which he desired, and his protests subsided into silence. As will be seen, it required a diplomatic explosion to place him by the side of the Four and constitute the Committee of Five Great Powers which carried through the reconstruction of Europe.

The formal organisation of the Congress therefore continued to be the Committee of Eight, which discussed mainly the terms of the incorporation of Genoa in Piedmont, a transfer already decided at Paris, the German Committee until the middle of November, and a Committee on Swiss affairs. The territorial settlement was discussed informally without any record of proceedings. The Ministers of the Four generally met in the morning and the sovereigns in the afternoon, until relations became too strained for them to bear one another's presence so often. Castlereagh had a situation, therefore, in which his particular genius had full scope. The rôle of mediator which he had assumed made him the centre of the discussions, and his days were spent in an unending series of private interviews, in a vain endeavour to produce agreement. His patience and imperturbability were equal to all demands, and though no one spoke more vigorously to the Tsar, he never failed to secure from him a courtesy sometimes denied to Metternich and Talleyrand. He had to suffer a severe defeat which might have shaken a less courageous man or one less convinced of the necessity of his own conduct. As it was, he was able to retrieve a position which at one time seemed hopeless, by action as audacious as it was successful, and secure a great deal, if not all, of the objects which he had pursued so long with such tenacity.

2. CASTLEREAGH AS MEDIATOR

MERE questions of procedure rarely delay diplomatic discussion if the parties really desire it. Throughout all the controversy as to the rights of the Congress, as Talleyrand had to confess, the Four continued with undiminished zeal to discuss the great problems that had divided them so long. Could they come to agreement now, there was no fear but that the rest of Europe would have to accept their conclusions. But agreement was still far off. The Tsar had not yielded in the slightest degree on his Polish plans, which to Castlereagh were still the greatest menace to the new Europe. Only a union of the other three Powers, which it might be hoped the rest of Europe, including France, would join, could provide sufficient force to beat down his steadfast and prolonged resistance. For the Tsar hastened to make his intentions quite clear. He expressed them to Castlereagh in an interview which he commanded the day after his arrival. He had decided to retain the whole of the duchy of Warsaw for his new constitutional kingdom of Poland, except a small portion allotted to Prussia. Castlereagh offered the most determined opposition to this plan. An independent Poland, he said, would be welcomed by Britain, adding with some boldness that Austria and Prussia would agree. But this view was, of course, only put forward because he knew that the Tsar must refuse, as he immediately did. To a Russian kingdom of Poland, Castlereagh then proceeded to assert, the whole of Europe was opposed, including the King of Prussia, even if he appeared to the Tsar to acquiesce.

Next day Nesselrode came to weigh the effect of the Tsar's words, and perhaps offer, as Castlereagh thought, to abandon the constitutional side of the Russian proposals, if the

342

territorial were approved. Castlereagh refused this bargain in the strongest possible terms. The new Russian frontier, he said, would degrade the monarchs of Prussia and Austria in the eyes of their subjects and, whatever compensations they received elsewhere, leave them at the mercy of Russian military power. Russia, he even hinted, would have an influence over Europe to be compared with that of Napoleon. Nesselrode made no reply to this vigorous attack, which, as Castlereagh claimed, must have given him food for thought. But it was obvious that Russia would not give way unless she were compelled.[1]

To Castlereagh, therefore, the problem was how to combine Austria and Prussia together against the Tsar. Metternich's promise of Saxony had prepared the way, but at Paris the combination had broken down over the possession of Mainz, which Austria, supported by Bavaria, positively refused to allow to pass into Prussian control. To meet this situation, Hardenberg produced at the outset another of his inevitable memoranda, which transferred Prussian territory more to the lower Rhine, Mainz becoming an Imperial fortress in Prussian occupation. This scheme necessarily disappointed the expectations of Holland for a large increase of territory in Germany. Nevertheless, Castlereagh was inclined to regard it favourably, at any rate as a beginning of Austro-Prussian agreement, when he sent it to Wellington for a strategic opinion. He was always anxious to get Prussia to the Rhine to defend Germany against France, though he did not fail to recognise that she might one day become a menace to the Netherlands. This was, however, a remote danger as compared with the more immediate threat of France against Belgium and the left bank of the Rhine.[2]

The great point was, in any case, to bring Austria and Prussia together. Castlereagh had no confidence in the former's firmness, in spite of warlike words. She was far too jealous of Prussia's views on Saxony and French designs on Italy to combine easily with them. Prussia, on the other hand, had as yet no written guarantee of Saxony from Austria.

[1] To Liverpool, Oct. 2, 1814 (Nos. 3 and 4) : *B.D.* 197, 199.
[2] To Wellington, Oct. 2, 1814, with extracts from Hardenberg's Memorandum : *W.S.D.* ix. 301. To Liverpool, Oct. 9, 1814 : *B.D.* 201.

They had indeed drifted further apart than at Paris or London, and Metternich in despair was already talking of compromise. It was only Castlereagh's insistence with the King of Prussia, Hardenberg, and Metternich in repeated interviews that eventually brought them together. Whether Metternich, as has been suggested, never intended to sacrifice all Saxony to Prussia and merely yielded now to Castlereagh's insistence because he knew that Prussia would fail to carry out her promise to oppose the Tsar, it is impossible to say; but the mood in which the plan was accepted did not, Castlereagh confessed, increase his confidence in the result.

Hardenberg at any rate shewed zeal, if only to obtain Austria's formal consent to the incorporation of Saxony as well as its immediate occupation by Prussian troops. The notes which he sent both to Castlereagh and Metternich with these demands offered to make Mainz a fortress of the Federation. Castlereagh at once gave assent, stipulating, however, that Prussia must not receive Saxony as an indemnity for her Polish possessions. He also agreed to the provisional occupation. A *note verbale* accompanied the answer, which strongly supported the justice of depriving the King of Saxony of all his territory if it was necessary for the reconstruction of Europe.

This *note verbale*, drawn up by Cooke, seems to have been intended mainly for Austrian consumption. It was handed over to Gentz to translate, a task which he only undertook with the greatest repugnance. "I have translated this note with a feeling of shame," he wrote to his chief. "It is difficult to believe that men with reputations to lose could put their names to such paltry reasoning" (*Armseligkeiten*). His criticisms represented nearly all Austrian official opinion, which regarded the absorption of Saxony by Prussia as even more dangerous than the loss of Galicia to Russia. It was not easy therefore to bring Metternich to the point, and ten days elapsed before Castlereagh could even report that verbal assent had been given concerning Saxony.

In the interval there was great suspicion that Metternich was not playing the game. The Tsar increased this by telling Lord Stewart, after asserting his determination to keep the wholė of Poland, that Metternich had made no objections to it in a long conversation a day or two before. "I am afraid," reported Stewart to his brother, "that Prince Metternich is not acting with that straightforward policy which becomes him at so critical a juncture. . . . He paralyses the decided part he might take, for it is vain to expect bold language from Prince Hardenberg until Prince Metternich declares himself unreservedly. I lament that the same line of politics which I thought I observed during the whole of the last campaign still regulates this Minister, and he is rather forced into any decision by circumstances and events or by the continued goading of those whom he fears and respects, than disposed to take such manly measures as are becoming the first Minister of a great state." Cooke's account shewed even greater distrust of Metternich, who, he told Liverpool, "will never play a great, straightforward game but by mere necessity, and when he finds that all little and side games fail. . . . I have tried to force Metternich to act by goading his employés, who all profess to be of our sentiments and eager to forward them; but they do not speak with confidence of their principal. . . . In this state, you may naturally believe that Lord Castlereagh is rather fidgety." Castlereagh himself betrayed his impatience. "The whole arrangement stands still on the point of Poland," he informed the Prince Regent, "and as yet the Emperor has evinced no disposition to accommodate. We are also impeded by the succession of *fêtes* and private balls; they waste a great deal of valuable time, and prevent P. Metternich from giving his mind to the subjects that ought to engross him." "I am a little out of patience," he confessed to Liverpool, "at this waste of time. While we were actually at war, events hurried even the most temporising to a decision; at present the irresolute and speculating have full scope to indulge their favourite game." [1]

[1] From Hardenberg to Metternich, Oct. 9, 1814; to Hardenberg, Oct. 11, 1814; *Note Verbale* on Saxony : D'Angeberg, *Congrès de Vienne*, 1934, 274, 276. Gentz to Metternich, Oct. 13, 1814: Wittichen, *Briefe von und ab Friedrich Gentz*, iii. 303. To Liverpool, Oct. 14, 20, 1814: *B.D.* 206, 211 ; Oct. 20, 1814 : *W.S.D.* ix. 363. From Stewart, Oct. 15, 1814: *F.O. Austria*, 117. Cooke to Liverpool, Oct. 20, 1814 : *W.S.D.* ix. 373 (where wrongly dated). To the Prince Regent, Oct. 20, 1815 : *Windsor Arch.* This letter, which was written to enclose a " Memorandum received from Cardinal Consalvi relative to some objects

The situation was rendered all the more dangerous because, while Austria and Prussia manœuvred, the Tsar was daily committing himself in conversation to the extreme Polish view. It was to prevent this that Castlereagh solicited another interview, in which he pressed very hard the treaty rights of Austria and Prussia. When, in order to escape this attack, the Tsar took shelter under "his moral duty," stating "that if it was merely a question of territory he would yield it without a struggle, but that it involved the happiness of the Poles, and the people would never forgive his ceding them," Castlereagh asked him " how he distinguished between his duty to the Poles on one side of his [Russian] line and on the other," and added that, as the principle of moral duty was not to be followed to the extent of making Poland really free, he could not expect other states to accept it as a valid argument.

To this assault Alexander could only answer that he was in possession and meant to remain so. But Castlereagh refused to be daunted, and while disclaiming any idea of using force, pointed out that conquest in itself was no secure title if Europe refused to sanction it. In order that these arguments might be placed on record he sent to the Tsar a memorandum containing their substance, which Cooke had drawn up for Austria and Prussia in the first instance, dealing with the legal points, accompanying it with a letter of his own composition which went to the extreme limit of boldness. It recounted all that Britain had done to assist Russia in the last war by which she had already obtained Finland, Bessarabia, and a large share of Poland. Against "the fourth instance of Russian aggrandisement," which the Tsar now proposed, public duty, he said, compelled him to protest. The whole future of Europe was at the hazard. "I do not hesitate to declare, Sire, my solemn conviction," he admonished him, "that it depends exclusively upon the temper in which your Imperial Majesty shall meet the questions which more immediately concern your own empire, whether the present Congress shall prove a blessing to mankind or only

bequeathed to your Royal Highness by the late Cardinal of York," is the only one of these months not previously published which I have been able to find in the Windsor Archives.

exhibit a scene of discordant intrigue and a lawless scramble for power." [1]

Could Castlereagh have relied on similar language from Prussia and Austria he might have gained his point. But, as has been seen, the union between them was an uneasy one and they had but little trust in one another. At last, however, he was able to announce real progress. After Hardenberg had dispatched another note, Metternich sent an answer which gave a grudging assent on the Saxon point, on the explicit understanding that Poland was saved and Mainz was kept out of Prussian influence. Hardenberg was "extremely warm" on the last point, but was persuaded to meet Metternich at Castlereagh's house. There the question of Mainz was reserved; harmony produced, and the two Ministers asked Castlereagh to draw up a plan of campaign against the Tsar. He accordingly drew up a paper which based the claim of Prussia and Austria on the partition promised by the Treaty of Reichenbach, but offered an independent Poland, if the Tsar would agree. If not, they claimed the Vistula as the boundary, though Warsaw might go to Russia. If the Tsar rejected the overture, appeal was to be made to all Europe against him, the Congress being summoned together on November 1 as had been agreed with Talleyrand. Then "the several Powers of Europe should be invited to support the said overture and to declare to the Emperor of Russia to what extent and upon what conditions Europe in Congress can or cannot admit His Imperial Majesty's pretensions to an aggrandizement in Poland." And in order to make the appeal more alarming, he was to be told "that it would rest with the Powers in Congress assembled to decide upon the measures which should be called for by so alarming an infraction of treaties and by an encroachment upon the military security of independent and neighbouring allied states in contravention of the express stipulations of subsisting engagements." [2]

This bold appeal to Europe in Congress was, however,

[1] To Liverpool, Oct. 14, 1814 : B.D. 206. To the Emperor of Russia, Oct. 12, 1814, with First memorandum on the Polish Question : W.S.D. ix. 329.
[2] Metternich to Hardenberg, Oct. 22, 1814 : D'Angeberg, Congrès de Vienne, 316. To Liverpool, Oct. 24, 1814 : B.D. 212, with memorandum on the best method of handling the Polish question.

never made. Humboldt and Stein were loud in protest against it from the first, and, as has been seen, the technical difficulties of summoning Congress were never overcome. The situation was further complicated by a visit of the three sovereigns to Buda, during which the Tsar spared no pains to increase his hold on the infirm will of Frederick William. Metternich could still rely on the support of his master, but he shrank from pressing on the plan. The Congress was therefore postponed once more, never to be summoned. The Tsar meanwhile sent a vigorous and unexpected rejoinder to Castlereagh's letter and memorandum. He appreciated Castlereagh's frankness, he told Cathcart, and he claimed the same liberty for himself. He refused even to give way on Thorn or Cracow. This note at any rate exposed his position, for it was the first time he had condescended to discuss his claims in writing, and the Austrian Cabinet at a special conference decided that Castlereagh should continue the negotiation in his capacity as mediator in the name of the three Powers. This needed, however, Prussia's consent, which Metternich proceeded to demand in a note which stated the case along the lines of Castlereagh's memorandum, suggesting also that each of the three monarchs might take a Polish title in addition to his own.[1]

Since no answer came from Hardenberg, Castlereagh continued his personal attack. On November 4 a reply was dispatched to the Tsar, Lord Stewart acting as "the most respectful and least formal channel of conveyance." It was less bellicose in tone than his first one, but reasserted his arguments. The intention was to keep the negotiations alive until Austria and Prussia could agree on the terms of the mediation. He admitted that he was doing their work, but he told Liverpool: "When I saw the service suffering from

---

[1] To Liverpool, Oct. 24, 1814 : *B.D.* 212. Cooke to Liverpool, Oct. 25, 1814 : " He [the Tsar] abused Metternich yesterday and was very violent. . . . He has abused Nesselrode. The King of Prussia has promised to do nothing in the journey which can derange the plans adopted." *W.S.D.* ix. 375. From Alexander, Oct. 30, 1814, with memorandum : *W.S.D.* ix. 386. Metternich to Hardenberg, Nov. 2, 1814 : D'Angeberg, *Congrès*, 379. Gebhardt, *Wilhelm von Humboldt*, ii. 102. Humboldt's incisive criticisms of Castlereagh's plan were, as usual, put into the shape of a memorandum (Gebhardt, *Wilhelm von Humboldt's Politische Denkschriften*, ii. 179).

inaction, I found it difficult to be passive, and your Lordship
may be assured that England is the only Power that either
can, or dares, raise her voice against the powerful and the
oppressor."

Stewart found it difficult to obtain access to the Tsar, for
the height of the crisis had been reached. When at last he
secured an audience, Alexander adopted a very high tone.
He had learnt that the letter was to be sent, and began to
protest even before it was placed in his hands. Eulogies of
his own conduct in saving Europe were followed by reproaches
that Britain had become his principal enemy. He accused
Castlereagh of deliberately avoiding him at the last two balls
in spite of Stewart's protests. The possibility of war was
openly expressed on both sides.

The Tsar's frankness was doubtless due to the fact that he
knew that he was already triumphant. His manœuvres with
Frederick William attained full success on November 5, when
Hardenberg was summoned into the presence of the two
sovereigns and forbidden to act further with Austria and
Britain in the determined manner which had been agreed.
Hardenberg was astounded at this command, and even Humboldt was shocked. Prussia's good faith was lost, and with
it her claim to Austria's consent to Saxony. But there was
no appeal. The King of Prussia was, indeed, himself convinced
that he ought not to yield on Poland, and Knesebeck, his
closest confidant, tried to strengthen his resolution with a
memoir which strongly supported Castlereagh's arguments.
But he could not resist the Tsar's appeal to his feelings, and
his Ministers had no option but to let the fact be known.
When Metternich heard of it he at once wrote in furious
protest, denying also, as the Tsar had insinuated, that he
had ever offered to bargain with him Poland against Saxony.
It was clear that the Austro-Prussian agreement could no
longer be maintained, and the diplomatic edifice, so laboriously
built up, came tumbling to the ground.[1]

[1] To Liverpool, Nov. 5, 11, 1814 : *B.D.* 222, 229. To Alexander,
Nov. 4, 1814, with memorandum : *W.S.D.* ix. 410. Gebhardt, *Wilhelm
von Humboldt*, ii. 102–103. From Stewart, Nov. 6, 1814 : *F.O. Austria*,
117. Lord Stewart's memorandum of his Conversation with the Emperor
of Russia, Nov. 6, 1814 : *F.O.* (95) *Miscellaneous*, 8. Delbrück, *Historische Zeitschrift*, lxiii. 259.

Castlereagh was bitterly disappointed. He had received a humiliating check which, moreover, threw the whole situation into confusion. For if the two German Powers were not united in common opposition on the Polish point, he knew that their rivalry over Saxony and Mainz would break out with renewed force. Failure, in fact, meant the triumph of Russian influence over all Europe.

His official letter betrayed his embarrassment and chagrin. In a long explanation he tried to shew the Cabinet the motives which had led him to take so prominent a part in the negotiations: "I deemed it of great importance to contribute, as far as depended upon me, to this concert, considering the establishment of Russia in the heart of Germany, not only as constituting a great danger in itself, but as calculated to establish a most pernicious influence both in the Austrian and Prussian Cabinets; and I also foresaw, that if these two Powers, from distrust of each other, gave up the Polish point as desperate, the contest in negotiation would then turn upon Saxony, Mainz, and other German points, and through the contentions of Austria and Prussia, the supremacy of Russia would be established in all directions, and upon every question; whereas an understanding previously established on German affairs gave some chance of ameliorating the Polish arrangement, and, in case of its failure, afforded the best, if not the only means of counteracting the Russian influence in the other European arrangements."

On this settlement the future of the Netherlands depended, and Castlereagh thus claimed that he had been forced into an active policy. War, he declared, had never been in his thoughts or he would have shewn more reserve, but he had hoped to combine all Europe against Russia. He concluded with a plea for support and a statement of the principles on which his attempt to found the reconstruction had been founded: "Since I have been on the Continent, in my intercourse with the several Cabinets, I have conceived it my duty to keep in view the following principles, considering them as those on which it was the intention of His Royal Highness's Government that I should act. In the first place, so to conduct the arrangements to be framed for Congress, as to make the establishment of a just equilibrium in Europe the first object of my attention, and to consider the assertion of minor points of interest as subordinate to this great end. Secondly, to use my best endeavour to support the Powers, who had contributed to save Europe by their exertions, in their just pretensions to be liberally re-established upon the scale to which their treaties entitled them to lay claim, and not to be deterred from doing so by the necessity of adopting, for this end, measures which, although not unjust, are nevertheless painful and unpopular in themselves. And, thirdly, to endeavour to combine this latter duty to our friends and Allies, with as much mildness and indulgence even to the offending states, as circumstances would permit." [1]

This dispatch was, of course, meant for publication if necessary. His private letters took into account the personal feelings of the Cabinet and were written to overcome the reluctance which they were already displaying at his masterful policy. For some time Liverpool had been trying to put on the brake. "I am inclined to think that the less we have to do with it, except as far as regards giving our opinion, the better," he wrote as soon as the first news came of the Tsar's attitude, and the memorandum which he sent for Castlereagh's consideration stressed the fact that a united Poland under Russia would probably be preferred by public opinion in England to a new partition. At any rate, some record must be obtained of British preference for a free and united Poland in the discussions at Vienna, a point which, as has been seen, Castlereagh always kept in mind. "We must take care so to manage this question as not to get the discredit of resisting the Emperor of Russia's proposition upon a principle of partition," Liverpool wrote a week later. When the news came of Castlereagh's hot attack on the Tsar, several members of the Cabinet took alarm, which was voiced in a memorandum by Vansittart which flatly disagreed with Castlereagh's reasoning. Austria and Prussia were not to be trusted, and Britain ran the risk of producing a combination between Russia and France which might even raise the long-buried question of maritime rights. Vansittart was even disposed to

[1] To Liverpool, Nov. 11, 1814 : *B.D.* 229.

agree with the Tsar when he claimed that Russia would gain more power "by acquiring half the duchy as a province than the whole as a kingdom," and concluded, "that we ought to avoid irritating Russia by a pertinacious opposition which is so unlikely to be successful."

These warnings must have added to Castlereagh's bitterness when he saw them apparently justified by the King of Prussia, but he did not admit that he had been wrong. The Tsar must be resisted not humoured, he told Liverpool: "You must make up your mind to watch him and to resist him if necessary as another Bonaparte. You may rely upon it, my friend *Van's* philosophy is untrue as applied to him; acquiescence will not keep him back, nor will opposition accelerate his march. His Imperial Majesty is never more condescending than to those who speak plainly but respectfully to him; and if I were to speculate upon the course most likely to save your money, and to give you the longest interval of peace with such a character, I should say that it would lie in never suffering him for a moment to doubt your readiness to support the continental Powers against his ambitious encroachments." To Vansittart he wrote a cool and reasoned reply, but he warned him that the Dutch loan would have to be shouldered if the Tsar proved reasonable, while, if he did not, no one could say what the consequences would be. His last sentence alone betrayed his bitterness: "I had rather give the Prince of Orange something more to defend and fortify the Low Countries than assist the credit of a Calmuck prince to overturn Europe." [1]

If the Cabinet were little support at this anxious moment, Talleyrand's conduct was now beginning to shew some improvement. At the outset he had been of but little use. His stubbornness over the question of summoning the Congress, as well as his open advocacy of the rights of the King of Saxony, forced Castlereagh to remonstrate with him warmly at an early stage, insisting that "it was not for the Bourbons, who had been restored by the Allies, to assume the tone of

---

[1] From Liverpool, Oct. 14, 1814 (with memorandum), Oct. 21, 27, 1814 (with Vansittart's memorandum) : *W.S.D.* ix. 342, 367, 382. To Liverpool, Nov. 11, 1814 : Yonge, *Liverpool*, ii. 53. To Vansittart, Nov. 11, 1814 : *C.C.* x. 200.

reprobating or throwing odium upon the arrangements which
had kept the confederacy together." Moreover, by raising the
questions of Saxony and Naples, instead of concentrating on
Poland, "he had sacrificed all useful influence and united all
against himself." Talleyrand received these stern remonstrances with perfect good humour and promised amendment,
but they may explain the rancour with which he wrote of
Castlereagh to his King shortly afterwards, attributing to him
the isolation of France and inveighing against his policy.
Castlereagh was aware of Louis's views on the Saxon question,
but he appealed, through Wellington, to Blacas, in order to
modify the French position, and when there appeared to be
some risk of a bargain between Czartoryski and Talleyrand,
ordered the Duke to insinuate that, as such a combination
would lead to immediate hostilities, England would at once
sign a peace with Murat in order to make Austria feel secure.
He hinted, moreover, as he had continually done to Talleyrand, that if the Polish point were settled something could
probably be done for the King of Saxony.[1]

Meanwhile Talleyrand shewed some disposition to assist
matters by delaying, at Castlereagh's urgent request, the
publication of a memoir which he had written on the Saxon
question. He was naturally ready to assist in summoning
the Congress, if it was necessary, but when the situation did
not allow of it, he did not, as has been seen, offer any very
great objection. Shortly afterwards he received fresh instructions from Blacas, which, while they maintained the
French position on Saxony, urged closer co-operation with
Castlereagh. This was a result of Wellington's efforts, but it
was perhaps more Talleyrand's own conviction that induced
him to change his tactics. A complete breach in the Alliance
was now possible; indeed La Besnardière had sent home word
that war was inevitable. Talleyrand tried to draw closer to
Castlereagh and Metternich. His approaches were received with
encouragement, if not with great warmth, and he was at once

---

[1] To Liverpool, Oct. 9, 1814 : *W.S.D.* ix. 323 ; Oct. 24, 25, 1814 : *B.D.*
213, 217. From Wellington, Oct. 9, 1814 : *C.C.* x. 161. To Wellington,
Oct. 25, 1814 : *W.S.D.* ix. 372. Talleyrand to Louis XVIII., Oct. 19,
1814 : Pallain, *Correspondance inédite*, 63. Cooke to Liverpool, Oct. 25,
1814 : *W.S.D.* xi. 375.

rewarded by obtaining a French delegate on the Swiss Commission, which had hitherto been confined to the four Powers.[1]

Meanwhile Castlereagh's mediation was over. When Hardenberg, in order to make some shew of carrying out his promises, proposed that the negotiation with the Tsar should go forward, he pressed that only the most peaceful language should be used. Castlereagh's memoranda, he said, had at least caused the Tsar to consider rectifying the frontier. Perhaps Austria and Prussia ought not to expect much more. He painted the exhausted condition of Europe and suggested that in a few years they would be in a better position to resist Russia, which by that time would be realising what a Polish kingdom really meant. Though he declared Prussia was ready to go on in this very mild way, it was clear that he refused such a negotiation as had been planned. Metternich's reply maintained his position as to the frontiers, asserted that the original plan would have been successful, and insinuated that Prussia had not kept faith. In such a situation there was no possibility of Castlereagh transmitting, as he had intended, the united opinion of the three Powers to the Tsar. He withdrew, therefore, from the negotiation, explaining that if the Powers most affected would not resist then Britain could do no more. The situation was made worse by Prince Repnin issuing a public declaration that he was about to hand over Saxony to Prussia, with the consent of Britain and Austria. This move was undoubtedly planned by the Tsar to break up the opposition against him, and it produced the sensation at Vienna which he had expected. But Hardenberg's explanations were satisfactory when Castlereagh challenged him, and he immediately gave the required assent to a note which stated that Castlereagh had agreed to provisional occupation only, and that the main issue had still to be settled.[2]

---

[1] Talleyrand to Louis XVIII., Oct. 25, Nov. 6, 1814. Blacas to Talleyrand, Nov. 9, 1814 : Pallain, *Correspondance inédite*, 80, 101, 105. From Wellington, Oct. 25, Oct. 27, 1814 : *W.S.D.* ix. 371, 380.

[2] To Liverpool, Nov. 21, 1814 : *B.D.* 238. *Mémoire Confidentielle* of Hardenberg, Nov. 7, 1814 ; Metternich to Hardenberg, Nov. 12, 1814 : *F.O. Continent*, 8 (Extracts in D'Angeberg, *Congrès*, 406, 418). To Liverpool, Nov. 21 (No. 22), 1814 ; to Hardenberg, Nov. 17, 1814 ; from Hardenberg, Nov. 19, 1814 : *F.O. Continent*, 8.

All that could now be hoped, therefore, was that the Tsar would give way somewhat to Hardenberg's mild remonstrances and that Prussia would in her turn yield on Saxony. For Metternich had immediately warned Hardenberg that Austria could not give way on both frontiers, and that, as Prussia had not carried out her bargain, he considered himself released from his promise. Hardenberg had appeared to accept this point of view, and, though much still depended on whether the Tsar would now yield some portion of the duchy to satisfy Prussia, Castlereagh had some hopes that a compromise would be effected between the three Powers. While lamenting the failure of the imposing combination which he had planned, he claimed at least the credit that he had brought the Tsar down from his dictatorial position to a species of negotiation. He had tried to do so, he said, in a review of his conduct, ever since he had joined headquarters, but the Tsar had uniformly rejected formal discussion. He had always till now claimed the rights of conquest. The duchy was his, he reiterated, and he meant to keep it. Castlereagh's pertinacity had at any rate forced an opportunity for Prussia and Austria to state their case. The Tsar might perhaps shrink from estranging them both. "Although from my experience of His Imperial Majesty's character," his bitter letter went on, "I expect nothing from his friendship to his Allies, and as little from his generosity or his sense of justice, yet I still hope for something from his fears." Perhaps the erysipelas on one of the Tsar's legs, which laid him up for a week, helped to make him more yielding. At any rate he shewed, according to Hardenberg's report, signs of conciliatory behaviour now that his political plans were conceded, and Castlereagh's official dispatch of November 25 was almost hopeful as to the result of the negotiation in which he now took no personal part.[1]

[1] To Liverpool, Nov. 21, 25, 1814: *W.S.D.* ix. 447, 451; Nov. 25, 1814: " I understand from Prince Metternich that the Emperor was very conciliatory in his language, expressed his wish to come to an understanding, etc. The conversation was general, His Highness declining to enter into the discussion of the points at issue, having placed the negotiation in Prince Hardenberg's hands. The Russian Minister [Czartoryski] had a long conference with Prince Hardenberg. . . . For the reasons already stated to your Lordship it has been my wish to interfere as little as possible in the conduct of this negotiation. I have therefore avoided calling myself

These hopes were not, however, shared by many others. Talleyrand had already reported that Schwarzenberg was talking of war. He had rejected the Tsar's attempts to bring him over to the Russian side by the offer of action against Naples, but he was still critical of Castlereagh in spite of Blacas' admonitions. Castlereagh was sensible, however, of a change in the French attitude, and sent his warm thanks to Wellington, to whom he attributed it. His explanation of his method of treating Talleyrand sufficiently accounts for the latter's acid comments on British policy: "I have not deemed it prudent to disclose to him my operations in detail, finding that he was not always discreet, and that I should lose useful influence in other quarters if I was understood to be in too close confidence with the French Minister." Nevertheless, their relations had become more cordial, as Talleyrand saw the dissolution of the Alliance proceeding rapidly.[1]

Indeed the situation grew steadily worse. The whole of the smaller German Courts were up in arms about Saxony, and the Austrians felt that they would have them nearly all on their side in the event of war, which now began to be canvassed on all sides. The long and pessimistic review of the situation, which Münster, at last restored to convalescence, sent to the Prince Regent on November 27, spoke freely of the possibility of war, for which he said both the Emperor of Austria and the King of Bavaria were ready. In an even more secret dispatch three days later he recommended that in such a case Britain's best course was to win over France, who otherwise would probably join Russia, by concessions on the left bank of the Rhine, the expulsion of Murat, and even the removal of Napoleon from Elba. Next day Castlereagh sent for the boastful Wrede and tried to get him to accept a Prussian Saxony, if compensation was given to the King, but the Marshal not only professed that morality would be shocked by such a step, but insisted, with a full display of maps, that strategical necessities prevented Bavaria

on the Chancellor, but His Highness desired Count Münster to inform me ' qu'il a été très content d'un entretien qu'il a eu hier au soir avec l'Emperor de Russie. . . .' " *F.O. Continent*, 8.

[1] Talleyrand to Louis XVIII., Nov. 17, 1814 : Pallain, *Corres. inédite*, 118–34. To Wellington, Nov. 21 1814 : *W.S.D.* ix. 446.

and Austria from giving way—an aspect of the matter on which he was a better authority. Wrede and Hardenberg also had a stormy interview in which war was threatened by the latter. Even more ominous was it that Hudelist, by far the most influential of the Austrian Foreign Office officials, spoke of war as certain, and described the preparations for it already made by his Government.

It was clear that a deadlock had arisen. The Tsar's answer to Hardenberg refused to do more than make Thorn and Cracow free towns. Austria's Polish frontier was thus made no better, and no increase of territory was given to Prussia. Metternich at once declared therefore that he could not give way on Saxony, but Hardenberg, contrary to expectation, denied that he had promised concession on that point, if the Polish negotiation failed, and claimed the whole of Saxony, which the Tsar had again offered to Prussia. The situation which Castlereagh so long feared had arisen. Prussia was now considered as the hireling of the Tsar, and the bitterness of the Austrians was such that Metternich, even if he had wished, could not give way on Saxony. Moreover, the absorption of so much of Poland had increased the compensation due to Prussia, and it was difficult to find territory in Germany to restore her to a position equivalent to 1805 unless she obtained the whole of Saxony.

Castlereagh himself was now so impressed with the dangers that he wrote to the Cabinet to consider seriously the question of war. A prolonged deadlock might result, he said, but unless affairs mended, war was more likely. Such a war, he thought, was bound to become general, and Britain would inevitably be drawn in sooner or later. Should she go in at once, or attempt some species of armed mediation to try and stop it at the outset? And in the latter case, should she try to carry France with her? It was this latter expedient that most appealed to Castlereagh, though he was far from accepting the panic-stricken ideas which Münster had put forward. "I have suggested the idea of armed mediation," he wrote, "as an expedient short of actual war, because I think there may be an interval after hostilities had commenced during which Great Britain and France might assume this character, to give weight to which the army of the Low Countries and Hanover might be united under the Duke of Wellington on the Lower Rhine, while the French army was concentrated at Strasburg." But, he added, this was merely a suggestion on which he wished the Cabinet to deliberate.[1]

They were in a very different mood from Castlereagh. Far removed from, and only half understanding the intricate manœuvres at Vienna, Liverpool's constant preoccupation had been to deprecate anything that could lead to war. He had, indeed, not had much time for Vienna. The American negotiations and ominous reports from Paris of threats to the Royal Family and, what was even more important, to the Duke, had occupied his attention. He wanted to place Wellington in safety, either in command in America or as Castlereagh's substitute at Vienna. Meanwhile Parliament had assembled for a short session and the Opposition were in a fighting mood. Some of them displayed, moreover, a very inconvenient curiosity as to what was happening at Vienna. The question of Murat was raised with documents supplied by his representatives. Rumours of Saxony's impending fate had also begun to reach London. Though the systematic attempt to work on the London Press had hardly started, on November 21 and 28 there were stormy debates on Saxony in the House of Commons. No one really knew the facts, and the Government spokesmen refused all information. It was clear, however, that Castlereagh's policy would be difficult to defend, and Liverpool, as early as November 18, warned Castlereagh that Saxony's total annihilation as an independent Power would be very unpopular, however just and necessary it was. Wilson supplied Grey, who refused to leave Howick, with gleeful reports of the unpopularity of the Ministry, a rupture between Liverpool and the Prince Regent, and the loss of prestige which Castlereagh had experienced at Vienna and which would inevitably have its effect at home. Wilson's news from Vienna came mainly from Czartoryski, and his imagination was as vivid as usual. Nevertheless, he

---

[1] Münster to the Prince Regent, Nov. 27, 28, 1814 : *Hanover St. A., Appendix*, pp. 551–57 ; Nov. 30, 1814 : *Windsor Arch., Appendix*, p. 557. To Liverpool, Dec. 5, 1814 : *B.D.* 248 ; Dec. 5, 1814 : *W.S.D.* ix. 462. Wrede to Montgelas, Dec. 4, 1814 : *Munich St. A.*

was able to quote Hamilton as believing war likely, because Belgium would become involved. It was clear, at any rate, that the Government, deprived of its most important member, was daily losing ground in the House and in public estimation.[1]

The great thing, therefore, in Liverpool's mind was to impress Castlereagh that a new war in the present temper of the country, and while the American negotiation was still so doubtful, was a thing to be avoided at almost any cost. "It may be quite true," the Prime Minister wrote, "that if the Emperor of Russia does not relax his present demands, the peace of Europe may not be of long continuance; but for however short a time that peace may last, I should consider it of great advantage. . . . But if war should be renewed at present I fear that we should lose all that we have gained, that the revolutionary spirit would break forth again in full force, and that the Continent would be plunged in all the evils under which it has groaned for twenty years. A war now, therefore, may be a revolutionary war. A war some time hence, though an evil, need not be different in its character and its effects from any of those wars which occurred in the seventeenth and eighteenth centuries before the commencement of the French Revolution. In short, this appears to me to be the precise period in which the sentiment of Cicero, so often quoted by Mr. Fox, is really in point: *Iniquissimam pacem justissimo bello antefero.*"

That the Cabinet thoroughly agreed with this point of view is shewn by the transmission, two days later, of the only important official instruction which Castlereagh was to receive while he was at Vienna. "His Royal Highness," he was told, "cannot contemplate the present state of Europe, and more especially the internal state of France, Italy, and the Low Countries, without entertaining the most serious apprehensions of the consequences which would result from the renewal of war on the Continent under present circumstances. His Royal Highness has no doubt, therefore, that you will use

---

[1] Horner wrote hopefully to Mackintosh of the protests in the House " against the monstrous proceedings of the robbers at Vienna," and elicited an opinion from the historian that they were " more important and I hope more beneficial on the Continent than at any former period of our parliamentary history." Horner, *Corres.*, ii. 213, 218.

your best endeavours to prevent, by all means in your power, so great an evil. It is unnecessary for me to point out to you the impossibility of His Royal Highness consenting to involve this country in hostilities for any of the objects which have hitherto been under discussion at Vienna." [1]

How little influence this dispatch was to have on Castlereagh's conduct will be seen. But when it reached him he was still contemplating the ruins of his imposing negotiation, and watching the gradually growing hostility of Prussia and Austria. He formally withdrew his original offer of consent to the incorporation of all Saxony in Prussia, quoting Liverpool's letter of November 18 to prove that his Cabinet supported him in so doing. But Hardenberg continued to urge Metternich, in prose and even in verse, to give way, and since Castlereagh knew that Austria could not do so and was daily more anxious of the consequences, he made yet another effort to convince Hardenberg of the necessities of the situation. When the Prussian Minister, imitating the Tsar's tactics, talked of war, Castlereagh intimated that a mere refusal by other states to recognise his position could never be made a sufficient cause, and that he would do far better to secure the reconstruction of Prussia with the consent of Europe than to take the whole of Saxony in opposition to her wishes. Hardenberg promised to consider these arguments, and Castlereagh then tried to persuade Metternich to make offers of compensation elsewhere in Germany, such as would satisfy Prussia. Metternich professed his readiness to do so and was again sanguine of success.

But Castlereagh had by now grown suspicious of Metternich's hopes and Hardenberg's promises. Cooke's long letters to Liverpool at this time shew the atmosphere of intrigue and suspicion which these controversies had produced. Humboldt, he said, was intriguing against Hardenberg; the Tsar was supposed to have bribed Metternich with money and a lady; Talleyrand was improving, "but a man who has been so bribed has not much weight." The marked atten-

[1] From Liverpool, Nov. 2, 18, 25, 1814: *W.S.D.* ix. 401, 438, 285 (where wrongly dated). From Bathurst, Nov. 27, 1814: *B.D.* 247. Wilson to Grey, Oct. 31, Nov. 5, 22, 26, 1814: *Wilson MSS.* 30120, ff. 77, 81, 98, 101.

tions of the Tsar to the English at Lord Stewart's ball, where
"The Emperor danced polonaises with Lady Castlereagh,
country dances with Lady Matilda, and the Archduchess
(Catharine) polonaised with Planta," seemed only part of his
plot to obtain control over Europe. Castlereagh could hardly
view such a situation with much hope. He had given up his
rôle of mediator, but when left to themselves the continental
Powers shewed no signs of compromise. "I witness every day
the astonishing tenacity with which all the Powers cling to
the smallest point of separate interest," he wrote to Liverpool
as he surveyed the scene. It seemed possible that the whole
of his endeavours to create a peaceful Europe would be swept
away in a new cataclysm.[1]

It was, indeed, the blackest moment of all his diplomatic
career. His plans had gone astray and his judgment had
been completely at fault. The Cabinet had estimated more
correctly than he the weaknesses of the continental Powers,
though they had relied on their instinct rather than on a full
knowledge of the facts which Castlereagh believed himself
to possess. They obviously disliked his policy of giving
Saxony to Prussia, which he had himself been compelled to
abandon by the force of circumstances. War was threatening, in which he knew Britain must be involved. It was his
darkest hour. But he faced it with superb courage and
patience. He was already forming new plans to meet the
emergency, and he was soon to go into the thick of the fray
again and establish with more success his position as the
mediator of Europe.

[1] To Liverpool, Dec. 7 (No. 27) : *B.D.* 255–57. Cooke to Liverpool,
Dec. [7], 10 : *W.S.D.* ix. 473, 476. Hardenberg to Metternich, Dec. 3,
1814 : *F.O. Continent*, 8.

3. THE SECRET TREATY

THE tension between Austria and Prussia soon ended in a diplomatic explosion. Metternich's reply to Hardenberg of December 10 was a definite refusal to allow Saxony to pass into Prussian hands. It made, in accordance with Metternich's promise to Castlereagh, other suggestions for the reconstruction of Prussia, but on the main point it was peremptory. To Hardenberg, so he noted in his diary, this final refusal was as unexpected as it was unpleasant. At any rate, in his rage against Metternich he threw himself into the Tsar's hands and, moreover, communicated to him all the recent letters which Metternich had written as to their joint action against Russia. Castlereagh and Münster believed that Humboldt had pushed him into this outrageous conduct in order to overthrow him and get his place, but, however inspired, it produced, naturally, grave consequences. The Tsar immediately demanded an explanation from the Emperor of Austria, who referred him to Metternich. The latter must have been sorely tempted to produce Hardenberg's letters, which contained much more serious reflections on the Tsar, and, as has been seen, even suggested that action should only be deferred to a more convenient time. But Castlereagh pleaded urgently that this should not be done, and the Emperor of Austria and Metternich consented. Though the interview between the Tsar and Metternich was very stormy it was ended by the Tsar saying : *"C'est bon : n'en parlons plus."* As Castlereagh put it, "the climate of Russia is often the more serene after a good squall," and the meeting between the two Emperors which followed produced something like a reconciliation. Francis had always been more anxious about Saxony than Poland, and he now told the Tsar that he would abandon opposition to his Polish plans, while Alexander magnanimously offered to restore Austria the district of Tarnopol, taken by the Peace of Vienna in 1809, not a large concession but still an earnest of goodwill. Castlereagh was, indeed, inclined to think that the incident had done some good by allowing Alexander to get an impression, for the first time, of the real views of Metternich and Hardenberg on the Polish question. "Had these Ministers spoken as bold truths to His Imperial Majesty in their interviews as they did to each other in their letters," he commented, "and had they supported *me* in the clear and decisive tone which their official correspondence entitled me to expect, my persuasion is that the Emperor of Russia would have come to a suitable arrangement with respect to the point of Poland, notwithstanding the embarrassment he had previously created for himself by hopes given to the Poles. In this correspondence the Emperor clearly perceived that I had not been mistaken in representing to him the real feelings of his Allies; and I have no doubt that they made their impression even after the concert had failed." [1]

However that might be, Poland was clearly lost and Castlereagh's prestige much diminished. His new attitude towards Saxony was attributed by many to a change of instructions from London rather than to his own wishes, though, as has been seen, this was quite untrue. The reports of the Saxon debate in the House produced considerable effect. His position was held to be shaken both at Vienna and in the confidence of his own Government. Gentz, who had always hated the sacrifice of Saxony to Prussia, attributed the lack of success at Vienna entirely to Castlereagh's conduct, and Talleyrand wrote to his Court that he was like a man "who had lost his way" and would probably soon go home. Wrede reported, as an accepted fact, that Castlereagh and Münster had received final instructions from London to take up the Saxon cause on the evening of December 7. There can be

---

[1] To Liverpool, Dec. 17, 1814 : *W.S.D.* ix. 483 ; Dec. 18, 1814 : *F.O. Continent*, 9. To Wellington, Dec. 17, 1814 : *C.C.* x. 219. Münster to the Prince Regent, Dec. 17, 1814 : *Münster*, 196–207. Metternich to Count Charles Zichy [Dec. 18], 1814 : communicated by Professor Marczali. Wrede to Montgelas, Dec. 15, 1814 : *Munich St. A.*

no doubt but that this idea, which was due to a report of Merveldt's, was generally believed at Vienna. The Russians were so alarmed that Lieven was instructed to find out how far the Cabinet still supported their colleague, to press the Russian point of view on them both as to Poland and Saxony. If he failed with the Cabinet, he was then to stir up the Opposition. His instruction, doubtless written by Czartoryski, was full of bitter criticism of Castlereagh, who, it suggested, wished to preserve Britain's influence in Europe by fomenting rather than allaying the differences between the Powers. Lieven had, of course, no chance of influencing the Cabinet, and the appeal to the Opposition could have no effect till Parliament met again, but it shews how matters stood at Vienna, and how bitterly Castlereagh's conduct had been resented by the Russians.[1]

The Cabinet was, however, much harassed by Castlereagh's proposals for an alliance with France with a view to armed mediation, which, as has been seen, he had made after his first failure. The only member of it who was warmly inclined to such a project was Bathurst, whose memorandum on the state of negotiations at Vienna anticipated Castlereagh's proposal. Liverpool was so far impressed by Bathurst's views that he actually desired the Cabinet not to leave London until Castlereagh's next dispatches arrived. These included the proposal of armed mediation, and it seems to have been more seriously considered than any other which he sent home. The reply which Liverpool sent on December 23 was, however, in no sense an instruction. The Cabinet were unanimous that any settlement, provided, of course, that France's frontiers remained unchanged, was preferable to war. It would be, indeed, impossible to get the country to go to war "except upon a clear point of honour, or for some distinct British interest of sufficient magnitude to reconcile

---

[1] Wrede to Montgelas, Dec. 12, 1814 : *Munich St. A.* Talleyrand to Louis XVIII., Dec. 20, 1814 : Pallain, *Corres. inédite,* 191 ; Gentz, *Dépêches inédites,* i. 127. Nesselrode to Lieven, Dec. 15, 1814, Instructions on Poland and Saxony : *Pet. Arch.* It was on Dec. 17 that Castlereagh first definitely asked Wellington to replace him : " I consider the Polish question as settled, Prussia never contended it in earnest and Austria consequently has yielded. The Saxon question is now the only one that is of much difficulty. The point of Naples being one of principle and not of detail cannot lead to delay " : *C.C.* x. 219.

the country to it," and the defence of the Low Countries seemed to the Cabinet the only point which would be so regarded. While, therefore, the Cabinet did not reject the proposals of armed mediation with France, they refused to sanction it, and the tone of Liverpool's letter was such as to deprecate action, since Britain had no interest of her own to establish but only to consolidate peace by some kind of amicable arrangement.

The letter gave, therefore, no guidance and but little encouragement to Castlereagh in his difficulties. Other letters which accompanied it were all of a negative character. There must be no question of taking any part of the Russian debt to Holland. It was desirable to get rid of Murat, but it was far better to leave him where he was than risk a war. No countenance must be given to Münster's attempts to increase Hanover, which Liverpool thought was much safer if left as it was, since public opinion would not support any action to defend an enlarged Hanover—perhaps not to defend the old one.

Other letters that followed in the course of the year were of the same tone. Meanwhile, the essential point was to get Castlereagh home again to make the Government safe in the House of Commons. If Wilson's reports to Grey could be believed, it was almost in dissolution, and Grey might expect to be summoned to replace Castlereagh at Vienna. But, at any rate, Castlereagh was badly needed at home, and not even the American peace, which the Opposition in a special meeting decided was no great credit to the country, brought much relief to the situation. Wellington's agreement to replace Castlereagh, which Liverpool received at the end of the month, gave the Prime Minister great satisfaction. He set off, at the beginning of the New Year, to Bath, most of his colleagues were already in the country, and the devoted Bathurst alone remained in town to receive the fateful dispatches in which Castlereagh described the issue of peace or war at Vienna.[1]

[1] From Liverpool, Dec. 22, 23, 1814 (4 letters) : *W.S.D.* ix. 493, 495–97. Wellington to Liverpool, Dec. 25, 1814 : *W.S.D.* ix. 503. Liverpool to Wellington, Dec. 31, 1814 : *W.S.D.* ix. 518. Liverpool to Bathurst, Dec. 31, 1814 : *W.S.D.* ix. 519. Wilson to Grey, Dec. 8, 12, 21, 28, 1814 :

But Castlereagh had still a great rôle to play at Vienna, and there is no sign that he was moved by the jealousy around him. Doubtless but little of it was shewn in his presence. He was, moreover, still indispensable. Tne relations between Prussia and Austria had naturally been made much worse by the recent explosion. Yet if the peace of Europe was to be preserved, they had to be brought together again. The Tsar, pledged to Prussia over Saxony and convicted of underhand conduct towards Metternich, could hardly play this part. Both Hardenberg and Metternich turned once more to Castle-reagh, therefore, and asked him to mediate on the Saxon point, though the former admitted that Prussia's recent conduct might well make him reluctant to consent. Castle-reagh was, however, the last man to put his personal feelings before an obvious duty, and while he confessed that he had no desire to be mixed up in the Saxon question, consented to act, provided that Prussia would admit as a basis of discussion that the King of Saxony should keep part of his kingdom.

When Münster was sent by Castlereagh to sound Harden-berg on this last point he found a new proposal in the field. The Prussian statesmen could not yet bring themselves to renounce Saxony, which they had counted on for so long to consolidate their position in Germany. The new lands on the Rhine meant little to them in comparison, for they still thought of Prussia mainly as an eastern German state, with little affinity to the softer and Catholic Germans of the Rhineland. It was, perhaps, natural therefore that they should think of offering these lands to the King of Saxony as compensation for the loss of his kingdom, a step which was decided in a conference of December 13, at which Knesebeck, Stein, and Czartoryski took part with Humboldt and Hardenberg. This proposal was embodied in a letter of December 16, sent to the Tsar and Castlereagh. When the plan was put before Castlereagh, therefore, it had ostensibly Russian as well as Prussian support, and Stein and Czar-toryski assisted Hardenberg in a discussion which lasted nearly

---

Wilson MSS., 30120, ff. 110, 112, 114, 124, 130. It is difficult to believe Wilson that Yarmouth said to Perry, " These men cannot remain. There must be a change. . . . The Prince is of the same opinion." But in Castlereagh's absence Yarmouth had certainly quarrelled with the Cabinet.

two hours, during which time, Castlereagh reported, " I had
to sustain the united efforts of those present to convert me,
and to impeach the conduct which Austria had pursued."
No impression, however, was produced on Castlereagh, who
replied that the scheme was impossible, since the King of
Saxony would certainly not consent, and neither France nor
Austria would urge him to agree to the transfer. Prussia,
he still insisted, must find satisfaction elsewhere than in
Saxony; she had much better swim with the stream than
against it. If his arguments did not convince the Prussians,
they still wished him to continue his work of mediation,
which he now began to prosecute with great energy.[1]

It was time; for the crisis had grown daily more menacing.
Castlereagh had alluded in the last interview to the assent
of France—and with reason, since Talleyrand had begun to
have a position of great importance. Metternich was now
completely under the influence of the extreme party and
was looking for allies against Prussia. He proposed to Wrede
a treaty of alliance between Austria, Bavaria, and Hanover,
which the General in high glee recommended to his Court in
terms hardly less insulting to Metternich than to Prussia.
It was Metternich, and not Castlereagh, who still hoped to
avoid so obvious a challenge, who approached Talleyrand,
sending him his last note to Hardenberg on Saxony. There
could be no doubt of the reception which Talleyrand would give
to this confidence. He sent in reply to Metternich the note
which Castlereagh had got him to keep back, without making
any conditions, stating that France was perfectly content with
her position as laid down at Paris. He took, however, a very
lofty view of the King of Saxony's rights. It was not for
Prussia to say how much she would take, but for the King of
Saxony to say how much he would yield. In this way the
principle of legitimacy was safeguarded, while some concession
was made to Prussia's needs. Cooke was contemptuous of
Talleyrand's "tirade about the rights of Kings." "The

[1] To Liverpool, Dec. 18, 24, 1814 : *B.D.* 260, 267. Gebhardt, *Wilhelm
von Humboldt*, ii. 110. Münster to the Prince Regent, Dec. 24, 1814 :
Münster, 214–15. Note of Prince Hardenberg, Dec. 16, 1814 : D'Angeberg,
Congrès, 531. Wrede to Montgelas, Dec. 21, 1814 : *Munich St. A.* Max
Lehmann, " Tagebuch des Freiherrn von Stein während des Wiener
Kongresses, 1814," *Historische Zeitschrift*, lx. 415–16.

doctrine," he wrote to Liverpool, "is not very suitable to our meridian." He thought that Talleyrand was still open to a bargain with Prussia, and that Metternich was foolish not to abandon Murat in order to get his full support.[1]

It was this side of Talleyrand's policy which was occupying Castlereagh's attention. He was less forward in demanding his support than Metternich, but he wished to prepare the ground for it if it was necessary. While, therefore, avoiding definite commitments on the main question, he had begun some little time before conversations with Talleyrand on Naples, and had elicited from him his plans on that subject, and consulted the Home Government about them. Castlereagh's own proposals went even further than Talleyrand's, but he was as yet only preparing the way on this question, and still held Talleyrand aloof. When, therefore, on December 23 Talleyrand proposed to him that an alliance should be formed between Austria, France, and England, Castlereagh still held back and answered that the time had not yet come, and that to form an alliance prematurely "might augment the chances of war rather than of an amicable settlement, which I trusted we all had in view."

This offer of Talleyrand's was concerned with an important proposal as to the conduct of the negotiations which Castlereagh now made. The controversy as to the reconstruction of Prussia had been rendered much more difficult because neither side would accept the figures of the other of the populations to be transferred. Their arguments were thus led from the main point into side issues concerning statistics. Castlereagh now proposed to set up a Statistical Commission, which should devote itself to this question and furnish agreed figures to the plenipotentiaries.

This offer was accepted. Castlereagh had promised to include a French representative, but the Prussians violently objected. Since Castlereagh still had some hopes of settling the affair without France, he sent Lord Stewart to Talleyrand to ask him to withdraw his claim. Stewart was, perhaps, not a very tactful envoy, even if Talleyrand's account is, as usual,

---

[1] Talleyrand to Metternich, Dec. 19, 1814: D'Angeberg, *Congrès*, 540. Cooke to Liverpool, Dec. 24, 1814: *W.S.D.* ix. 502. Wrede to Montgelas, Dec. 24, 1814: *Munich St. A.*

highly coloured. At any rate, Talleyrand took a strong attitude and threatened to order his horses, as Cooke put it, unless France was admitted. Castlereagh thereupon gave way and with much difficulty persuaded Prussia to agree.

The Commission was then constituted, the best workers of the Congress were placed on it—Clancarty, d'Alberg, Wessenberg, and Münster—together with two zealous and erudite Prussian officials. It set to work immediately, and despite some controversies as to the exact method of evaluating the "souls" to be transferred, it was soon able to make much easier the task of compromise in which Castlereagh was now to be engaged.[1]

For the crisis was now at hand. The combination against Prussia was growing. Metternich had begun to organise a German League to her exclusion, a step which caused Münster considerable alarm. Nevertheless, public opinion in Germany was obviously on Austria's side. The correspondence between Metternich and Talleyrand had, in Castlereagh's opinion, now made France a principal in the question. Russia had to give her official support to Prussia, however reluctant the Emperor now was to run the risk of war over Saxony. But she was known to wish a compromise if it could be arranged. It was this last circumstance that made Castlereagh sanguine as to the result of his efforts. But it was obvious that the position was very dangerous, and that much would depend upon his conduct when the clash between the two sides arrived.

This was now precipitated by a demand from the Tsar that the questions should be officially discussed. His main object was to obtain formal ratification of the Polish settlement, but the question of Saxony had obviously to be included, since the concessions to Austria depended on it. The position of France had therefore now to be defined. With Metternich, Talleyrand had already made his terms, but it was not until December 27 that Castlereagh sent him a letter welcoming his support, so that "such an arrangement may be ultimately effected, both with respect to Saxony and Naples, as may tend to

---

[1] To Liverpool, Dec. 24, 25, 1814 : *B.D.* 268, 271 ; Dec. 25 : *W.S.D.* ix. 511. Talleyrand to Louis XVIII., Dec. 22, 1814 : Pallain, *Corres. inédite*, 198.

establish a just equilibrium among the Powers of Europe
and procure a general and solid peace." This vague statement was written with a view to being laid before Parliament
if necessary, but doubtless in conversation Castlereagh was
more definite as to the expulsion of Murat. At any rate,
Castlereagh and Metternich, at the first meeting held on
December 31, insisted that Talleyrand should be admitted to
the formal negotiations on Saxony. Prussia and Russia
opposed, the former with great vehemence. They still
claimed the total incorporation of Saxony, and Hardenberg, in
his desperation, used language of a most threatening character,
intimating that Prussia could not continue her provisional
occupation indefinitely, and that a refusal to recognise her
claims would be regarded by her as tantamount to a declaration
of war. This open threat produced an immediate effect on
Castlereagh's mind. He protested against it as "a most alarming and unheard-of menace." "Such an insinuation," he said,
"might operate on a Power trembling for its existence, but
must have the contrary effect upon all that were alive to their
own dignity," and, he added, "that if such a temper really
prevailed, we were not deliberating in a state of independence,
and it were better to break off the Congress." Others hastily
intervened to explain away the unfortunate remark, and it
was not entered on the Protocol. But the effect remained,
and its impression was confirmed by the tone of intimidation
which the Prussian soldiers were adopting in public on every
possible occasion.

Castlereagh, therefore, at once proposed to Metternich a
treaty of defensive alliance between Austria, France, and
Britain. Metternich immediately agreed, and Talleyrand was,
of course, eager to sign. It was Castlereagh who drew up the
draft, which was accepted without any substantial alterations
by both Metternich and Talleyrand. The latter stated that
he was only too glad to subscribe to the articles, which specifically described the maintenance of the Treaty of Paris as one
of the objects of the new treaty. He was perhaps wisely
content that the coalition was dissolved—"dissolved for
ever," as he falsely prophesied to his King. He has been
much criticised for not making a bargain at this critical

moment, but his previous conduct had made it impossible
unless he was to lose all the confidence of Metternich and
Castlereagh. Since Hanover was treated as if it were a British
possession—and if it were attacked the other two Powers
were bound to come to its aid—and Holland was also to be
invited to accede to the treaty, Castlereagh had thus included
all the special British interests in it.

Nevertheless it was a bold step to take, and in a sense
was in direct defiance of the last official instruction of his
Cabinet. It is true that letters were on their way agreeing,
if necessary, to some action in conjunction with France, but
these had not arrived when the treaty was signed. Castlereagh seems, however, to have been quite certain that there
would be no hesitation at home in accepting it. He was confident, he said in his official dispatch, that his conduct was
justified by the exigency of the occasion. His private letter
to Liverpool dwelt on the immense advantages obtained in
return for what was really no more than a promise of subsidies.
If war broke out "for the disgrace of the times," Britain
would be bound to be involved in any case, and with the treaty
she had her special interests in the Netherlands protected, and
France bound to respect the new frontiers. "It may save
Austria, and consequently the Continent," he concluded.
Cooke's recommendation was contained in a single phrase,
"I trust you highly approve Lord Castlereagh's great and
necessary measure." The news of the peace with the United
States came opportunely enough on the morning of January 1,
and this doubtless helped Castlereagh to make up his mind.
"We have become more European," he told Van Spaen,
"and by the Spring we can have a very nice army on the
Continent." But it was in no sense the determining factor
in the decision. Castlereagh made the treaty because the
attitude of Prussia threatened war and in the hope that the
strength which it would give to Austria would prevent war
from breaking out. Without it there might be doubts in the
minds of both Austria and France, not only as to Britain's
attitude, but even more probably as to the steadfastness of
each other. He had delayed such an irrevocable step to the
last possible moment in the hope that his mediation would

prevail on Prussia to give way—so long, indeed, that there was criticism of his backwardness in his own delegation, who feared that it might "give Talleyrand the lead." When Hardenberg's language shewed how tenacious and truculent her attitude still was, the treaty appeared to be the only way to ensure peace. It may be that all the Powers would have shrunk at the last moment from the extremity of war even if the treaty had not been made. But certainly both the Prussian and Austrian soldiers were preparing for it, and had weakness in the opposition been suspected the former would have pressed their demands so far that it might have been impossible to draw back.

, Fortunately the crisis did not last long. The news of the American peace, which had not been expected, created a great sensation at Vienna, and Castlereagh passed the evening of the day in which he drafted his treaty in receiving at a Court Ball the congratulations of the sovereigns and statesmen. To the Tsar's good wishes Castlereagh replied, "*Il commence l'âge d'or*," a phrase which Cooke thought might have been taken to mean that new subsidies were under consideration. But Castlereagh had never descended to insinuation at Vienna, and he pursued now his usual simple and direct methods. He saw Humboldt privately, and warned him that such menaces as those of the day before "Great Britain would resist with her whole power and resources, and that every man in Parliament, of whatever party, would support the Government in doing so." Such resolute language produced a due effect, and as early as January 5 Castlereagh was able to report "the alarm of war is over," and that Prussia had determined to yield. Hardenberg's only stipulation was that the negotiation was to be settled by the Powers without the King of Saxony's consent being considered necessary until they were in agreement, a condition which Castlereagh readily accepted and induced Talleyrand to accept also.[1]

---

[1] To Talleyrand, Dec. 27, 1814: *F.O. Cont. Arch.* 15. To Liverpool, Jan. 1 (Nos. 43, 44, 45): *B.D.* 276, 277, 279; Jan. 2: *W.S.D.* ix. 523; Jan. 3, 5: *B.D.* 280; *W.S.D.* ix. 527. Talleyrand to Louis XVIII., Jan. 4, 1815: Pallain, *Corres. inédite*, 209. Wrede to Montgelas, Jan. 3, 1815. Wrede appeared to think that it was Metternich who proposed the treaty

Indeed Talleyrand's conduct was now very satisfactory; for when a last effort was made to revive the idea of bringing the King of Saxony to the Rhine he strongly supported Castlereagh in his opposition. "He said for purposes of ambition and conquest," Castlereagh reported, "he must favour the plan; but as his sincere desire and that of his Court was to put a restraint upon any extension of the existing boundaries of France he was against the project." This example of wise statesmanship, rare in history, though of course Talleyrand was bound by the wishes of his King to a large extent, won Castlereagh's warm appreciation. He hastened to secure the position by a special interview with the Emperor of Russia, in which he claimed that the Treaty of Chaumont had given Britain a veto on the disposition of the Rhine territories. This and the obvious arguments against the creation of a feeble and discontented state on the Rhine produced a visible effect on the Tsar, who with his usual frankness adverted to the reports circulating of a secret treaty between Austria, France, Bavaria, and Great Britain. Castlereagh did not deny them, and the interview ended with the Tsar declaring he was satisfied with Castlereagh's plans for the reconstruction of Germany. Nor, though he shewed embarrassment, did he absolutely refuse, when Castlereagh suggested that Russia might contribute something to the common stock by concessions on the Prussian frontier.[1]

These interviews had prepared the way for the resumption of the official meetings. Talleyrand was now included, and the "Committee of Five" thus constituted, Humboldt with truth named "the real Congress of Vienna." It was in this Committee that in the next five weeks the reconstruction of

to Castlereagh: *Munich St. A.* Metternich to Merveldt, Jan. 13, 1815: *Vienna St. A.* Cooke to Liverpool, Jan. 2, 1815: *W.S.D.* ix. 521. Van Spaen to Van Nagell, Jan. 2, 1815: Colenbrander, *Gedenkstukken*, vii. 719. Apsley to Bathurst, Jan. 2, 1815: *Bathurst*, 319. The English draft of the treaty (*F.O. Continent*, 10) has only slight variations from the French text signed on Jan. 3.

[1] To Liverpool, Jan. 5, 8, 1815: *B.D.* 282, 283. Münster to the Prince Regent, Jan. 22, 1815: *Hanover St. A.* Apparently Castlereagh sometime later believed that the Emperor was unaware of the secret treaty. Van Spaen to Van Nagell, Feb. 3, 1815: "The English ministers seem to believe that the treaty is still quite unknown to the Russians and Prussians; I doubt it." Colenbrander, *Gedenkstukken*, vii. 728. Clancarty to the Prince of Orange, Jan. 6, 1815: Colenbrander, *Gedenkstukken*, vii. 721.

Europe was carried out, Castlereagh playing a dominant rôle in all the decisions, and by his energy, common sense, and fertility of suggestion gradually solving the complicated problems that arose.

In such a situation it was only natural that he should refuse to return to Britain, whatever the embarrassments of the Government, until his task was complete. He wrote at once to Wellington to delay his departure. Yet during the whole of these all-important transactions he was constantly under pressure from Liverpool to return home at the earliest possible moment. There was no suggestion that his conduct was not approved. On the contrary, the ratification of the secret treaty was decided by Liverpool and Bathurst as soon as they received it. Nothing could better illustrate the casual method in which foreign affairs were transacted by the British Cabinet than in the manner which this important step was taken. Liverpool was still at Bath and most of his colleagues were in the country. But he had no intention of interrupting his cure or summoning a Cabinet. He assumed that Bathurst, who as usual was at his post, would agree, and that the Cabinet would acquiesce. The matter was indeed decided and Castlereagh informed before the Cabinet was shewn the treaty. Bathurst sent off a handsome letter of approval, which warmly commended Castlereagh's conduct in resisting the Prussian menaces. Most of the Cabinet agreed easily enough to this summary procedure, but Harrowby refused to give an opinion until he had seen the treaty, and Westmorland seems to have definitely opposed it. When Liverpool was informed of these protests he instructed Bathurst that agreement could best be obtained by ignoring them. His approval of the treaty was not so emphatic as Bathurst's: "It will secure the Low Countries and give more *éclat* to Castlereagh's presence at Vienna, which was certainly wanting," was his first verdict, shewing how much Castlereagh's first failure had lowered his prestige. "I am not sure that in Castlereagh's place I should have proposed it," he wrote three days later; "but if it had been proposed by Austria and France I would not have refused to be a party to it, and I am sure it gives us the only chance of coming out of the Congress with credit, which we shall do, if it becomes the means of saving Saxony."

His chief preoccupation was, however, the Parliamentary situation, which indeed was serious enough. He was urgent, therefore, that Castlereagh must come home to take charge of the business as soon as it met. This was, he said, the unanimous decision of the Cabinet, though he relied even more on the opinion of the junior members of the Ministry as to the weakness of the leaders in the Commons during the autumn session. Hardly anyone in England cared much about what was going on at Vienna, he said; what they were interested in was reduction of expenditure. Castlereagh, therefore, must come home, whatever the state of the business at Vienna, and leave Wellington to finish. He could not understand, he told Bathurst, why Castlereagh should object: it was Wellington who had reason to complain—an opinion which illustrates Liverpool's inability to understand the ordeal through which Castlereagh had passed and the importance of his position at Vienna. Bathurst's sympathetic letter took a larger view, but even he had to confess that without Castlereagh's help the Government stood in great danger.[1]

Fortunately ere these letters reached him, Castlereagh had won his battle. The success of his last stand had placed him in a commanding position at Vienna, and he was able at last to play the part he had always imagined to be his, of acting as a real mediator between the continental Powers, and thus creating a new Europe in which Britain could become the defender of the peace. The urgent entreaties, and at last peremptory orders, of the Cabinet to leave this task in order to come to their help merely stimulated his energy and resolution, and were perhaps one of the main reasons why the reconstruction of all central Europe to the Alps was carried out in the short space of five weeks.

[1] From Bathurst, Jan. 18, 1815: *B.D.* 291. From Liverpool, Jan. 15, 16, 1815: *W.S.D.* ix. 536, 537, 538. Liverpool to Bathurst, Jan. 16, 18, 21, 1815: *Bathurst*, 324–26; Jan. 17, 1815: *W.S.D.* ix. 541. Harrowby to Bathurst, Jan. 17, 1815: *Bathurst*, 325. From Bathurst, Jan. 18, 1815: *Lond. MSS.* Wilson to Grey, Jan. 13, 17, 1815: *Wilson MSS.*, 30120, ff. 132, 137. Wilson confirmed, rather ruefully, Liverpool's opinion as to the interest of the public which " seem too much engaged with the Property Tax and the Legion of Honour for attention to foreign news."

CHAPTER VII

THE CONGRESS OF VIENNA II : RECONSTRUC-
TION COMPLETED, JANUARY-JUNE 1815

1. THE RECONSTRUCTION OF CENTRAL EUROPE.

2. THE SETTLEMENT OF ITALY.

3. THE ABOLITION OF THE SLAVE TRADE. GENERAL QUESTIONS.

4. THE GUARANTEE OF THE NEW EUROPE.

" Le repos sans l'équilibre est une chimère."—METTERNICH.

CHAPTER VII

1. THE RECONSTRUCTION OF CENTRAL EUROPE

THOUGH the main crisis was over by the end of the first week
of January there was still much to be done at Vienna. The
Prussians fought their position step by step, while the Austrians elated by their victory wished to press it home and drive
them back as far as possible. War was again threatened, or
at least mentioned, on more than one occasion. It is difficult
to see how, without Castlereagh's assistance, the rivals could
have come to an agreement, so deeply had passions now been
stirred and so difficult seemed the problems to be solved.
Castlereagh's position was now higher than it had ever been
before. All turned to him for advice or help, and he became
the centre of every diplomatic exchange. Though the
"Council of Five" was the official organ by which the decisions
were made, before they were recorded on its protocols much
private discussion had to take place, and each time a note had
to pass or a project to be considered it was Castlereagh who
saw both sides and endeavoured to find the compromise on
which agreement could be based. Though Talleyrand was
full of rancour at Castlereagh's determination to make a strong
Prussia, and indulged in many scornful criticisms of his
ignorance and weakness, yet he had to admit that it was
Castlereagh who made the final decisions on the Saxon
question. Gentz, who also had been a severe critic, bore
witness in his review of the Congress to his immense energy
and endurance. "He worked day and night," he wrote,
"sometimes with the King of Prussia and the Emperor of
Russia, sometimes with Prince Metternich and Prince Hardenberg." It was as a result of these amazing powers of work

that the territorial arrangements north of the Alps were complete, except for certain details, before Castlereagh left Vienna.

The key to the solution lay in the Saxon question. Castlereagh had secured the entry of France to the Committee, and, at Prussia's request, the formal agreement of Talleyrand that the settlement was not to depend upon the King of Saxony's consent. But Prussia had not yet abandoned her claim to the whole of Saxony. She kept it as a means of bargaining, and it was still included in the plan with which Hardenberg opened the game at the first meeting of the Five on January 12. That this also demanded Bayreuth and 660,000 more "souls" than Prussia possessed in 1805 shewed that she intended to push her claims hard.

Austria had to reply to this formal statement, and the spirit in which she began to consider it caused Castlereagh the greatest anxiety. The Austrian soldiers were putting pressure on Metternich in the same manner as the Prussians on Hardenberg. Schwarzenberg presented the Emperor with a memoir which on strategic grounds would have deprived Prussia of Torgau and Erfurth, the key fortresses of the Upper Elbe. He had much support in Austrian political circles, including that of Stadion. Metternich himself was eager to push Prussia back as far as possible, for he was as much alarmed at the radical spirit of the Prussian war party as at the extravagant claims which they put forward. Castlereagh at once opposed this scheme in the strongest language. In a general war Austria must rely on the support of Britain and France, he said, and not on a fortress more or less, while as regards Prussia and Austria alone he considered strategy gave Prussia the better claim. Austria had no right to dominate Saxony, which belonged to north Germany rather than south. In short, he told Metternich that while he had been ready to defend Austria against hostile invasion, he would not run the risk of war upon "a mere question of details." [1]

Metternich was himself ready to yield to Castlereagh on these points, but, as his master was not, he shrank from facing

[1] To Liverpool, Jan. 11, 22, 1815 : *B.D.* 285, 292. From Talleyrand, Jan. 8, 1815 : *F.O. Continent*, 10. Metternich to Merveldt, Jan. 13, 1815 : *Vienna St. A.* Metternich, *Memoirs*, ii. 494.

the hostile combination against him. It was left to Castlereagh, therefore, and Münster, who was a gallant second at this period, to bear down the opposition. Münster tackled both Stadion and Schwarzenberg, and secured the former's admission that war could not be risked on such a point. Castlereagh, by informing Metternich that he would withdraw all support if the demand was pressed, secured an interview with Francis, who he found in a very warlike mood, more so, indeed, than on any previous occasion. The Emperor urged the necessity of keeping Torgau and Erfurth out of Prussia's hands, and even offered to give back to Russia territory in Galicia so that Russia could indemnify Prussia on her Polish frontier. Castlereagh refused absolutely to agree to this offer, which did not, of course, meet the strategic question at issue, and on the following day met Metternich and Talleyrand to consider the Austrian answer, which he found most unsatisfactory. It had been concerted between them and Schwarzenberg, and still denied Torgau to Prussia, and also much reduced her total. Castlereagh refused to support it in spite of their determined efforts to convince him. "You can have no idea," reported Wrede in great anger, "of the number of military and political arguments used against Castlereagh. It has all been in vain." It was, Castlereagh said, a little hard that the odium of urging severe measures towards Saxony should be thrown upon him, but that he would not "sacrifice the peace of Europe to preserve to them two or three hundred thousand subjects more or less."

This firmness at last induced the Emperor to give way, and Castlereagh agreed with Talleyrand and Metternich on a plan which he could support as a fair one, though he insisted it must be open to discussion and not offered as an ultimatum. Metternich excused himself to Schwarzenberg by throwing all the blame on Castlereagh, whose support was necessary to oppose Prussia. Similarly, Talleyrand, whose conduct had been most satisfactory, took care in his letters to the King to throw all the responsibility for the reduction of the King of Saxony's dominions on to Castlereagh, whom he accused of gross ignorance—a charge which Treitschke from the opposite point of view has repeated. The truth was that Castlereagh had the whole of the negotiation at his finger-ends, and was able to state the case for either party with equal skill, and find the compromise which both could force their extremists to accept.

He had now to turn his attention to the Prussian side, and put on them the same pressure from the opposite point of view. They wanted not only Torgau and Erfurth but Leipzig as well. To Münster Hardenberg's language was as truculent as at the end of December; "he would insist," he said, "on giving his ultimatum, that if it was not accepted, Prussia, supported by Russia, would make war with 300,000 men —that in this case she would spare nothing, and she would regard as enemies all who would not join her. He particularly mentioned Hanover and England, knowing well himself that we would not take part with Prussia in such a cause."

Münster wisely refused to comment on such remarks and left Hardenberg to Castlereagh, who came with the Austrian plan. Though the Prussian Minister made no such threats to Castlereagh, his opposition to giving up Leipzig was just as strong. He could not return to Berlin, he said, without it as a trophy. In reply Castlereagh pointed out that sound policy would avoid separating Dresden and Leipzig, that the opinion of Berlin was not so important as that of Great Britain, Austria, France, and Germany, which was all on the other side. "If the British Government had listened to popular sentiment," he said, "we still should have been at war with America in pursuit of an object not essential to our honour, and too dearly purchased, even if accomplished, by a protracted war." But it was in vain. Hardenberg refused to agree, and when the Austrian projet was submitted to the Committee of Five reserved his reply. Castlereagh had, however, in a special interview already got the Tsar to view the Austrian plan favourably, and to admit that the King of Saxony should be restored.[1]

[1] To Liverpool, Jan. 29, 1815: *B.D.* 294. Münster to the Prince Regent, Jan. 21, 1815: *Münster*, 220–24; Jan. 22, 1815: *Hanover St. A.* Talleyrand to Louis XVIII., Feb. 1, 1815: Pallain, *Corres. inédite*, 252. Metternich to Schwarzenberg, Jan. 27, 1815: Klinkowström, *Oesterreichs Theilnahme*, 823. Wrede to Montgelas, Jan. 26, 1815: *Munich St. A.*

It was at this point that Castlereagh received the letter from Liverpool, positively commanding his presence in London to defend the Government's Budget, on which the Opposition promised a warm attack, especially on the unpopular income tax. Wellington had in vain urged that it was only natural that Castlereagh should want to finish his great work. He had delayed his departure for a few days, but now orders came for him to set out and relieve Castlereagh as soon as possible. Castlereagh had therefore to get ready to go, though he had no intention of leaving until he had settled the main problem. "I shall leave Vienna on my return home," he curtly informed Liverpool, "whenever I have fully communicated with the Duke of Wellington—and when I am of opinion I can do so without prejudice to the publick service in the existing critical state of our negotiations." To the considerate Bathurst he was more expansive, even jocular, but just as resolute: "You may rely on my joining you as soon as I can without essentially endangering the point immediately at issue; but you might as well expect me to have run away from Leipzig (if I had been there) last year to fight Creevey and Whitbread, as to withdraw from hence till the existing contest is brought to a point." His staff, who were not informed of this resolution, were surprised at his quietness. Young Lord Apsley expressed their feelings when he told his father: "It is a bad example to shew an opposition that they can so bully you as to force home the man whom they allowed to be the fittest negotiator." [1]

Fortunately Castlereagh was able to overcome the resistance of Prussia shortly after he received this instruction. Having failed with Hardenberg, he made an attempt on the King of Prussia himself, in an interview which he described as "the most painful in all respects that it has been my fate to undergo since I have been upon the Continent." In view of the experiences in the last twelve months these are strong words, but the King seems to have vented on Castlereagh all his spleen and disappointment at the loss of Saxony, which

[1] Liverpool to Wellington, Jan. 15, 1815 ; *W.S.D.* ix. 536. Wellington to Liverpool, Jan. 10, 13, 1815 : *Gurwood*, xii. 241, 245. To Liverpool, Jan. 30, 1815 : *Lond. MSS.* To Bathurst, Jan. 30, 1815 : *W.S.D.* ix. 551. Apsley to Bathurst, Jan. 30, 1815 : *Bathurst*, 336.

was as much due to his own weak conduct as to any other cause. But Castlereagh was by now used to the reproaches of sovereigns, and he spoke just as frankly in reply. "My duty was to discourage the King from any false move, which might compromise us all," he explained, "and as I wished to execute this without reserve, my audience terminated as unpleasantly as it had begun."

In this extremity he turned to the Tsar, by whom it will be remembered he had suggested some sacrifice should be made, and obtained the offer of Thorn and a slice of territory to Prussia. With this concession, a considerable one from a strategic point of view, as history was to shew, for Thorn commands the middle Vistula, Prussian consent was at last obtained to leave Leipzig in Saxon hands. Even now, however, Prussia's other demands for Saxon territory were such that Castlereagh had no hope that Austria or France or the King of Saxony would agree to them. The only thing to do was to find compensation for Prussia in some other part of Germany. In these circumstances Castlereagh got Münster to give up 50,000 of the new "souls" which Hanover was to obtain, and reduced on his own responsibility Holland's increase by another 50,000. Hardenberg made a last struggle for Leipzig, for which the Prussian soldiers and Stein's friends were still fighting tooth and nail, and trying to make a question of national prestige. But Castlereagh's new offers, which shewed the genuineness of his efforts, at last overcame Hardenberg's resistance and he accepted the new scheme. Metternich agreed at once; Talleyrand, whose sovereign had wished Saxony to be a second-class not a third-class Power, with some hesitation at first, but without reservation, and the long struggle was over on February 6.[1]

The Saxon question had involved concessions on so many other frontiers that with it most of Europe north of the Alps was settled. Castlereagh's share in the reconstruction had been a large one, and the final result, though he had suffered defeat on what he regarded as the most vital frontier, was not altogether incommensurate with his plans for the "just equilibrium" which he had had in his mind.

[1] To Liverpool, Feb. 6, 1815 : *B.D.* 299.

As regards Poland, the new map of Europe was very different from that which he had tried to create. Instead of being pushed back beyond the Vistula, Russia was in occupation of a country which reached within striking distance of Berlin and came close to the Carpathians. Cracow was a free town and Prussia had obtained Thorn, but this made but little impression on the Tsar's gains. In his duel with Castlereagh he had come off with flying colours.

Moreover, he had easily been able to maintain his plans of creating a Kingdom of Poland which he was to endow with a constitution, though Castlereagh was right when he insinuated that the Russians would prevent their monarch from adding any territory on the Russian frontier of the duchy of Warsaw. Castlereagh had faithfully followed Liverpool's instructions in placing on public record Britain's desire that Poland should be erected as an independent state, which he had used so much in the course of the controversy. As has been seen, he had never contemplated such a solution seriously, and it was obviously impossible under the conditions of the time. None of the three Powers concerned would have consented. He appealed, however, in his note to each of the three monarchs to treat their Polish dominions as separate parts of their realms. The Tsar had, of course, already promised to do so. It must be confessed that this appeal was partly made to satisfy Parliamentary criticism, though the wise words which it contained as to giving the Poles national institutions represented considerable feeling on Castlereagh's part. They represented, moreover, the feelings of a large part of his countrymen, and Castlereagh laid great emphasis on this point in his first speech in the House of Commons, while they served in the nineteenth century as a basis for the protests of Britain and France, when Alexander's successors destroyed the institutions with which he had endowed his new kingdom. Both Austria and Prussia were ready to agree, indeed Metternich took advantage so eagerly of the opportunity, "to prove the anxiety of the House of Austria at all times to uphold the independence of the national government of Poland," that the Tsar was alarmed, and Wellington's intervention was necessary to modify the language. The Tsar, of course, made also an affirmative reply, and he could do so with some consistency. Czartoryski was much dissatisfied with all three answers, and urged Wellington to propose that the Tsar should immediately assume the title of King of Poland, and that the declarations of the three Powers should be made more explicit. Talleyrand could also genuinely support the protection of Polish nationality in any form, however lukewarm his actions had been during the earlier crisis in Vienna, and he sent a reply approving "without reserve" Castlereagh's sentiments.[1]

The great barrier to Russia as to France was in Castlereagh's mind to be found in central Europe, and the most pernicious effect of Russia's Polish claims was the breach which they made between Prussia and Austria. His endeavour to unite them on the basis of the sacrifice of all Saxony to Prussia had failed, but he could still claim that it was his efforts that had brought them together again. The compromise which he had achieved almost single-handed was a reasonable one, and the settlement of German territory lasted till the age of Bismarck. Its essence was a strong if widely extended Prussia, which was always Castlereagh's aim as it had been Pitt's. It was his support that secured her so much in the end, though, of course, if his Polish plans had succeeded she would have had much less territory in the west. Yet Castlereagh had welcomed her presence as the guardian of the Rhine, and done his best to increase her territory there into a compact and solid mass, such as her soldiers said was necessary in so advanced a position. He would have been ready at this time to add Luxemburg, but they positively refused to accept it. This transfer of Prussian power from east to west was, in a sense, the most important decision of the Congress, and there is irony in the thought that it was Britain, with the assistance of Talleyrand, which brought it about rather than any great inclination on the part of Prussia

---

[1] To Liverpool, Jan. 11, 1815 : *B.D.* 287. Circular note, Jan. 12, 1815: *B.F.S.P.* ii. 642. The Russian, Prussian, and Austrian replies follow. From Talleyrand, Jan. 13, 1815 : *F.O. Continent*, 10. From Wellington, Feb. 15, 1815 : *W.S.D.* ix. 579. Castlereagh's defence in the House is given in *B.D.* 402.

herself. Castlereagh deliberately made the plan of bringing Prussia to the support of his new kingdom of the Netherlands, and once the opportunity was given, to make her interests there as strong as possible. As has been noted, he was not unaware that Prussia might one day become herself a danger, and her conduct at Vienna did not diminish these fears; but the history of the next fifty years shewed that he was right in considering the threat from France as the more immediate, and therefore the only one which could be taken into consideration at that time.

It may be noted also that Prussia was in support rather than in direct contact with France. The Prussian territory marched with the Netherlands during the greater part of its frontier. Talleyrand was at this time, indeed, able to claim credit for the fact that the Prussian and French frontiers nowhere touched—an object which he had laid down for himself in his instructions.[1]

In the north, the Netherlands kingdom was, of course, the special creation of Britain, and in particular of Castlereagh. It was his insistence alone that had deprived France of Belgium, as Napoleon often confessed. Though history was to shew the impossibility of fusing these Catholic provinces with Protestant Holland, yet it is difficult to see what else could have been done with them at that time, if Austria refused to resume her ancient possessions. Even Mackintosh, who loudly condemned the union of Genoa and Piedmont, had nothing to say against the incorporation of Belgium with Holland. It was Castlereagh who managed their affairs at the Congress, and decided with the other Great Powers their final shape. As has been seen, his views on this question had to change a good deal in the course of the negotiations. The early plans of 1814, which would have given the Netherlands much more of the left bank of the Rhine down to the Moselle,

---

[1] Talleyrand to Louis XVIII., Feb. 15, June [25], 1815: Pallain, *Corres. inédite*, 271, 454. Castlereagh also seems to have regarded this point as important. It was the exchanges made during the second peace of Paris that made the two Powers neighbours. To Clancarty, Sept. 20, 1815 : " The object, secured as I thought at Vienna, of interposing a third Power between France and Prussia has, I find, been defeated by the assignment to Prussia of a population of 69,000 souls in the unsettled territories on the left bank of the Rhine, for which she is to account with some minor Princes elsewhere." Colenbrander, *Gedenkstukken*, vii. 276.

were defeated by Prussia's necessities.   But Castlereagh seems
to have early had a growing conviction that the strength of
the Netherlands would not increase with such accessions of
territory, and that if he secured the line of the Meuse the new
kingdom would then be in the best position to maintain
the barrier against France.   He doubted also "the policy
of building our system of defence exclusively upon the Prince
of Orange's power, enfeebled as it must be by great military
exertions, by the genius of his people, and by the principles
of his government."   Münster's jealousy of the new state,
more than once stated in the course of the year, may have
contributed somewhat to his decision, but it was approved
also by Wellington on strategical grounds, provided only that
the Liège Bishopric, which was for some time in doubt, was
given to the Netherlands as well as both banks of the Meuse.

It was also Prussia's insistence that caused the Prince of
Orange to exchange his hereditary possessions of Nassau
for the duchy of Luxemburg, which was kept separate from
his kingdom and made him a member of the German Confederation.   Castlereagh had tried to avoid this connection,
and the Prince much resented his position in it, largely on
grounds of dignity, which was only partly assuaged by his
receiving the title of Grand Duke.   He attempted in vain to
refuse the Prussian garrison of the fortress.   He accepted,
however, the other territorial arrangements without much
demur, though his representatives, recently reinforced by
Capellen, were hardly as satisfied with the whole as Castlereagh described them in his official report.   They testified,
however, warmly to Clancarty's affection for the new state,
which had only been overcome by the necessities of politics
and Castlereagh's commands.   It is significant perhaps that
the King was in dread of Prussian neighbours almost as much
as of the French, but this was largely due to the overbearing
character of their troops of occupation, and the return of
Napoleon soon brought a change of mind.

Castlereagh's plans for the marriage had been by this time
completely defeated, and preparations were on foot to replace
them with an alliance with Russia, the one which he most
disliked for the House of Orange.   But it was hardly likely

that the connection would have obtained the importance in the future of the Netherlands which Lord Salisbury assumed in 1862. Princess Charlotte, if she had lived, would hardly have been able to have much influence on her Dutch husband, whose conduct was to cause both his father and British Ministers much anxiety in the immediately succeeding years.[1]

The eternal question of the Russian-Dutch loan had also to be tackled by Castlereagh before he left Vienna. In spite of the opposition of the home Government, which Cooke had so strongly supported, Castlereagh felt that it was necessary to pay this money, partly as a matter of good faith, since Russia had earned it in the closing stages of the negotiations, but also in the interests of the Netherlands. It was doubtful, he said, whether he could secure the signature of Russia to the frontiers of the new kingdom without it, and the authority of the Prince of Orange might thus be severely shaken. He considered that the cession of Demerara, Essequibo, and Berbice had made Britain morally responsible for some monetary compensation. In such circumstances it was only sound policy to use the money to promote the general harmony.

"If, then," he wrote, "a charge must be incurred, there seems no adequate motive, but the reverse, at the close of a Congress, which is likely to end in good humour, to disturb a temper that may improve, at least, the prospects of peace." He therefore persuaded Russia to accept one-half instead of two-thirds of the debt, as had been originally arranged, a saving of a million and a half to Britain, and agreed to pay the rest, leaving, however, the final arrangement in the Duke's hands "as a security for the due execution of what remains to be done." Perhaps even then he would have failed to obtain the consent of the Cabinet had not the return of Napoleon made Russia's recognition of the new state specially

[1] To Liverpool, Feb. 13, 1815 : *B.D.* 303. To Wellington, Oct. 2, 1814, with explanatory documents. From Wellington, Oct. 17, 27, 1814 : *W.S.D.* ix. 301, 346, 381. Van Spaen to Van Nagell, Feb. 12, 1815 ; Van Nagell to Capellen, Feb. 13, 1815 ; Clancarty to the Prince of Orange, Feb. 14, 1815. From Stuart, Feb. 14, 24, 1815 : Colenbrander, *Gedenkstukken*, vii. 733, 734, 736, 220, 223.

desirable. The problem was finally settled so far as Castlereagh was concerned by a treaty drawn up in London between
Castlereagh, Lieven, and Fagel on May 19, 1815, which was
carefully drafted to make the discharge of the debt depend
upon the maintenance of the sovereignty of the King of
Holland over Belgium—a fact which reopened the whole
question in 1831.

The whole transaction is a good illustration of Castlereagh's
use of financial assistance as a means of helping forward the
general peace of Europe. Though Liverpool and Vansittart
might protest and groan at such large-mindedness, in the long
run the money was probably well spent in relieving Britain
from any charge of meanness so likely to be brought against
the wealthiest country in the world by poorer allies who had
joined with her in a common cause. Meanwhile the new
kingdom had been formally proclaimed, for as soon as the
news of the return of Napoleon reached him, the Prince of
Orange assumed the title of the King of the Netherlands, and,
thanks to Castlereagh's efforts, all the Great Powers were
ready to acknowledge the new sovereign immediately.[1]

After the Netherlands, Hanover was the greatest charge on
Castlereagh's care. Here again extravagant schemes had been
abandoned, and the final result was one that could be defended
on every ground. Münster had shewn himself at Vienna
very moderate in his demands, and, as has been seen, allowed
his territory to be cut down at the last minute to satisfy
Prussia's claims. The new Hanover was, at any rate, more
compact and had the command of the mouth of the Ems, a
point which Castlereagh mentioned with satisfaction and
Talleyrand with some jealousy. The fact that almost the
whole of its eastern frontier was in direct contact with
Holland was also satisfactory to Britain, whose two clients
were thus placed in a position to be jointly defended, while
Münster rejoiced that he had at least one frontier out of
contact with Prussia, whose power he had learnt to dread.
The Prince Regent was much distressed at the sacrifice of

---

[1] To Liverpool, Feb. 13, 1815; F.O. Continent, 12; and the dispatch
of Clancarty in the preceding note. To Wellington, March 12, 1815;
from Wellington, March 25, 1814: W.S.D. ix. 590, 615. F. Martens,
Recueil des Traités, xi. 218–22. B.F.S.P. ii. 378.

Lauenberg for East Frisia, which he surrendered to Prussia, who used it to barter from Denmark Pomerania and the Isle of Rügen, which Sweden had ceded in return for Norway. Sentiment forbade him, he urged, from alienating the territory of his father while the old King was still alive. Münster could only "deplore a necessity which has placed me in the position of a sufferer who has sacrificed one of his limbs to save the rest of his body." The Regent's conscience caused an attempt to be made in August to buy it back from Denmark, but the King regarded the suggestion as 'most odious,' and though the British Minister strongly supported the Hanoverian envoy nothing could be accomplished. This territory would, however, have added but little strength to the new kingdom, whose title was now recognised by almost all the Powers. At any rate, there could be no substance in the charge, to which all British Governments were still liable, that they had placed Hanoverian interests before those of their own country.[1]

That these exchanges were not completed until nearly the end of the Congress was due to the conduct of Bernadotte, who, in spite of the satisfactory settlement of the Norwegian question, refused to hold Denmark guiltless, and would not, therefore, carry out the terms of the Treaty of Kiel. The question was really largely a financial one, Bernadotte hoping to evade certain payments due under the treaty by the pretext of making Denmark compensate him for the expense of reducing Norway. It was British insistence on justice being done to Denmark that finally produced a settlement. Wellington wrote one of his admirable minutes, and, when Prussia and Russia refused support, Clancarty, who saw in their conduct an intrigue of the Tsar with Bernadotte, took vigorous action. It was only, however, the fortunate fact that Britain had money to pay to Sweden for Guadeloupe that enabled her eventually to force the reluctant Bernadotte to submit, so that the exchanges between Prussia, Sweden, and Denmark could be arranged. The King of Denmark and his Ministers were full of gratitude for this timely help, though,

[1] To Liverpool, Feb. 13, 1815 : *B.D.* 303. Münster to the Prince Regent, Jan. 21, March 5, 1815 : *Hanover St. A.*; March 11, 1815 : *Münster*, 225. From Foster, Aug. 15, 29, Nov. 4, 14, 1815 : *F.O. Denmark*, 71.

of course, they thought that more money could have been obtained from Sweden.[1]

Sweden had thus given up the last of her possessions on the mainland, a step of far greater wisdom than the acquisition of Norway. This withdrawal was altogether in accordance with Castlereagh's ideas, not only because it strengthened Prussia, but because it made Sweden more insular.

This completed the arrangements in the north, but in the south of Germany matters were less settled. Castlereagh had, of course, less direct interests to defend, but, as has been seen, he had ever since the peace of Paris vainly endeavoured to get Bavaria to give back to Austria Salzburg and the Tyrol, without obtaining Mainz, which he preferred to have in stronger hands. But Bavaria had been obdurate, even truculent, playing on the necessities of Austria during the critical period. The final settlement of the Saxon question left her therefore somewhat dismayed, but it was still impossible to make her accept the situation. Castlereagh used all his influence when passing through Munich on his way home to induce her to accept the Palatinate as compensation; and Rose, at Castlereagh's instructions, continued this pressure after he had left. It would bring Bavaria, he said, into contact with Holland and Hanover, and thus with Britain herself.

Montgelas, however, was still fearful of taking responsibility on the other side of the Rhine. He would have preferred to round off his state by large contributions from his immediate neighbours. But Bavaria had overreached itself. The compensations left in Germany after Prussia had been satisfied were unequal to all the new demands. Eventually, though Bavaria secured some additions, it had to accept the Palatinate as Castlereagh had advised, while Mainz not only

---

[1] To Liverpool, Jan. 25, 1815 : *F.O. Continent*, 11. From Wellington, Feb. 18, March 4, 1815 : *W.S.D.* ix. 571, 587. From Clancarty, April 1 (" The Russian Emperor is playing us a game of delay in favour of his minion Charles Jean "), April 21, 1815 : *F.O. Continent*, 17 ; April 28, 1815 : *Lond. MSS*. Wellington's incisive note to Razumovsky is printed in the Appendix of Johan Feuk's *Sverige På Kongressen i Wien* (Lund, 1915), which also gives a detailed analysis of the negotiations. From Foster, June 3, 17, 1815 : *F.O. Denmark*, 71. Bernadotte still managed to evade some of the obligations of the Treaty of Kiel, and Castlereagh had to bring it up again at the Conference of Aix-la-Chapelle.

became a fortress of the Federation but was put under Hesse's sovereignty. The tortuous diplomacy by which Austria and the south German Courts settled these final problems gave Clancarty much trouble and extended far beyond the Congress, but Britain's rôle was merely that of a disinterested spectator who endeavoured, though generally in vain, to find some compromise acceptable to all.[1]

On the whole, Castlereagh could view the new central Europe with some satisfaction. "A better defence has been provided for Germany than has existed at any period of our history" was his final word before he left Vienna. This was true at any rate as regards France, out of whose encroachments the long war had arisen. As for the failure on the eastern frontier, its dangers would be minimised if Austria and Prussia were reconciled and set themselves to the task of organising Germany as a unit. The negotiations for the German constitution, which had been abandoned in November, could now be renewed with some hope of success. So far as Castlereagh had influence it was employed to unite Germany into as strong a state as the conditions of the time allowed, both now and in the remaining years of his tenure of office. But he kept British policy outside this complicated question, though Münster continued to be an important factor in the discussions.

In Swiss questions, both internal and external, however, Britain became gradually more and more involved, and it is hardly true that Stratford Canning's instructions, while the Cantons were engaged in drawing up their new constitution, were, as his biographer has stated, "one long panegyric on non-intervention." The Great Powers had assumed the responsibility of guaranteeing the independence and integrity of Switzerland, and therefore "felt themselves called upon to endeavour to guard against the evil of internal commotion." Stratford was ordered to co-operate in the work, though he was enjoined to make any difference with his colleagues "as little a matter of public observation as possible." Stratford's energy soon brought him into the thick of these

---

[1] From Rose, Feb. 20, 1815 : *F.O. Bavaria*, 42. Clancarty's continual disappointments in this question were reported from time to time.

problems, especially as Capo d'Istria under La Harpe's influence was violently supporting the rights of the "new" Cantons against Berne's desire to resume her old supremacy. Stratford tended to support Berne, but he sought to effect compromises as he had been ordered, and on the whole was conciliatory to Capo d'Istria, even when he opposed him.[1]

Their co-operation extended to Vienna, whither Stratford was summoned in October to advise the British delegation on Swiss affairs. He got on well with Lord Stewart, who was in charge of the British case, and with Castlereagh, who gave him such attention as he could spare and much hospitality and kindness. Stratford was given the task of secretary to the Swiss Committee, when he challenged Capo d'Istria's drafting, and British influence was used wisely in composing the differences between the "old" and "new" Cantons, without in any way attempting to alter the essentials of the constitution, to which they had agreed after much difficulty, though it was far from satisfying their wishes for a strong Switzerland.

In the small but difficult questions of the Swiss frontier Britain took a surprisingly sustained and lively interest, especially in those connected with Geneva's incorporation in the Confederation. The visit to London of Sir François d'Ivernois, whom the Genevese wisely associated with Pictet de Richemont to represent them, had caused Castlereagh to repent a little of the rather harsh attitude he had taken up at Paris. Stratford was told therefore of the anxiety "to keep up the ancient and intimate relations between this country and Geneva," and the desire to maintain "the independence and strength of that Republic and of affecting its incorporation with the Swiss Union as the most effectual barrier of Switzerland, and therefore as essential to the repose of Europe."[2]

This promise, officially transmitted to Geneva on August 4, was kept, as d'Ivernois readily admitted, and even Pictet,

---

[1] To Stratford Canning, June 16, July 25, 1814 : *F.O. Switzerland*, 40. From Stratford Canning, July 25. Aug. 6, 7, Sept. 16, 26, 1814 : *F.O. Switzerland*, 41. Lane-Poole : *Stratford Canning*, i. 226.

[2] Lane-Poole : *Stratford Canning*, i. 243. To Stratford Canning, July 25, 1814 : *F.O. Switzerland*, 40.

though he always bore a grudge against Castlereagh for his conduct at Paris, sometimes allowed. Britain certainly supported every attempt to strengthen the Swiss frontiers on the south, and it was impossible for her, as Pictet desired, to refuse Genoa to Piedmont unless the latter agreed to the Swiss claims, though she succeeded by using the 'imperial fiefs' in obtaining a slight increase of frontier. It was not her fault that Austria got the Valtelline. The greatest disappointment was, however, over the Pays de Gex, which it was hoped that France would cede against another piece of frontier. Stewart had worked hard for this, and he was greatly disappointed at the result. Castlereagh gave him no more than his due in praising him in an official dispatch for his efforts, though he refused to put pressure on France to give way. He commended, however, Swiss interests to his successors, and both Wellington and Clancarty supported Stewart in all that he did.

At the second Peace of Paris, Castlereagh was able to do a little more for Geneva, whose deputies now represented the whole Federation. A slip of territory (Versoix) was given them joining Geneva to the Canton of Vaud, and the customs frontier of a large portion of the Pays de Gex was pushed back so as to give Geneva a larger economic area, while the fortress of Huninguen which threatened Bâle was razed.[1]

In the guarantee of neutrality, by far the most important step which was taken by the Powers for Switzerland, Castlereagh does not, however, seem to have taken any lead, though he professed great interest. The neutralisation of Switzerland under the guarantee of the Great Powers, first made by declaration at Vienna, came from the initiative of the Swiss

---

[1] To Liverpool, Dec. 18, 1814, Jan. 22, 1815 : *F.O. Continent*, 9, 11. From Stewart, Dec. 6, 1814 : *F.O. Austria*, 117. From Wellington, March 25, 1815 : *W.S.D.* ix. 615. See also O. Karmin, *Sir François d'Ivernois* (1920), 562–65 ; Pictet, *Biographic de C. Pictet de Richemont* (1892) ; and L. Cramer, *Corres. Diplomatique de Pictet de Richemont et François d'Ivernois* (2 vols., 1914). The latter's eulogy of British zeal is given in ii. 744. Much of the story is shewn in the Protocols and Memoirs printed in d'Angeberg, *Congrès de Vienne*, but an important one in which Stewart's advocacy at Vienna is further emphasised is omitted. Stratford Canning warmly recommended the increase of territory in August 1815, on the ground that Geneva was too much exposed to resist France. This weakness explained its " very equivocal line of conduct " in the late war. (From Stratford Canning, Aug. 15, 1815: *F.O. Switzerland*, 42.)

themselves, and none of the Powers seem to have realised its full significance. Castlereagh expressed his great pleasure at its renewal at Paris, in the more solemn form of a treaty, which, he told Pictet, promised well for the future security of the Confederation. So great, however, was his objection to the idea of guarantee at this time that for a moment he wished to substitute a mere declaration, until it was pointed out that a 'guarantee' had already been solemnly pronounced at Vienna. Then he cheerfully acquiesced and took a great interest in the drafting of the clauses in which it was incorporated in the treaty.[1]

Though the reconstruction of Italy still remained to be decided, plans of Castlereagh and Metternich gave promise that solutions would also be found for its problems, including the removal of Murat by negotiation or otherwise. The new Europe was therefore almost in being. Castlereagh could thus leave, for the task of pacifying or mastering the House of Commons, with a consciousness of having performed nearly all that he had intended. On February 14 he set out for home *via* Munich and Paris, where he had important action to take on the way, after distributing to the principal plenipotentiaries, whom he left still labouring at Vienna, a print of himself, which Talleyrand said was "very like the donor and would always give him agreeable memories."[2]

[1] L. Cramer, *Corres. Diplomatique de Pictet de Richemont*, ii. 203. P. Schweizer, *Geschichte der Schweizerischen Neutralitat*, ii. 584–85.
[2] From Talleyrand, Feb. 3, 1815 : *Lond. MSS.*

2. THE SETTLEMENT OF ITALY

THROUGHOUT the great duel over Poland and Saxony the question of Italy, and especially of Naples, had exercised an important if subterranean influence. Talleyrand's adhesion to the Austrian side had been obtained, partly at least, because he had received assurances, even if only of a vague character, that Murat would be removed from Naples. But Metternich, with great skill and tenacity, had succeeded in postponing any attempt to deal with Italian problems until the Saxon crisis was over. In the final stages of a negotiation that reached past Talleyrand to Paris, Castlereagh had a considerable share.[1]

As has been seen, Castlereagh went to Vienna with no commitments to Murat except the armistice and in no very friendly mood towards him. His overthrow had already been considered. Castlereagh must have discussed the matter with Wellington on his way through Paris, for the latter sent to him, as early as September 12, a scheme for carrying out 'our plans' without Austrian help, by the use of the forces of the Bourbon Powers. At Vienna Castlereagh found an impression on all sides that Murat must be got rid of. The death of Marie Caroline, on September 7, had removed one obstacle to the restoration of Ferdinand, and Münster reported that Metternich was prepared to yield to the unanimous voice of Europe. Castlereagh was not so definite, though he doubtless knew more, but the instructions to A'Court from Vienna contemplated the restoration of the Sicilian Bourbons.[2]

[1] An entirely new light on these transactions was thrown by Commandant M. H. Weil in his *Joachim Murat*, 5 vols. (1909), as a result of researches in the Austrian archives. The volumes also contain a large number of documents from Italian, British, and French archives.

[2] From Wellington, Sept. 12, 1814: *C.C.* x. 114; *Münster*, 186. Münster, who had discussed the question in Paris (see his letter to the

Murat's energetic and able representatives, the Duke of
Campo Chiaro and Prince Cariati, were well aware of this
attitude and from the first made every attempt to counteract
it. Except the treaty with Austria, Murat had, as yet, no
recognition of his position. France, Spain, and, of course,
Sicily were hostile to him, the Papacy was demanding back
the Marches and the Principalities of Beneventum and Pont
Corvo before it would discuss that 'neutrality' which was all
that Murat dared to ask, while the attitude of the Tsar and
the King of Prussia was doubtful. British support might well
be all important. One of the first acts at the Congress of
Murat's representatives was, therefore, to give to Castlereagh
a *Mémoire Historique* justifying all their master's actions since
he had changed sides, an official step which was undoubtedly
meant, like their later notes, to influence public opinion as
much as the Government; for Campo Chiaro was in correspondence with Wilson, who had now become a good Muratist,
and the Opposition, which on the whole took the same side,
were informed of these documents so that they could challenge
the Government in Parliament. Indeed, throughout all these
months Naples was full of English visitors, whom Murat
entertained in royal fashion and whose flattery was perhaps
one of the causes of his final actions. Lord Oxford's papers,
seized in Paris, contained many letters of encouragement from
both French and English, though nothing that really justified
the action, which, however, pleased Castlereagh. The debate
in the House in November shewed that Naples would be used,
if possible, as much as Saxony to discredit the Government.

The *Mémoire* had but little effect on Castlereagh and he
reserved its refutation to a more suitable moment. Murat's
representatives were denied all official recognition by the
Congress, though of course they received it at the Austrian
Court. Metternich, however, remained studiously enigmatic
to the world at large. There were other Italian questions
besides that of Murat, including the Duchies of Parma, to
which, in spite of the Treaty of Fontainebleau, Talleyrand
desired the Spanish Bourbons to return, and the Legations,

Prince Regent of Sept. 2, 1814 : Dupuis, *Ministère de Talleyrand*, ii. 286), was
perhaps too vehement an opponent of Murat to give an impartial report.

including the important town of Ferrara, which Austria held, and which were sought as compensation for many parties. All these questions he wished to reserve until the struggle over central Europe was ended.

Yet undoubtedly Castlereagh and Metternich were discussing the Italian problems during this period and gradually arriving at some agreement. Metternich for a time seemed ready to agree that Marie Louise should give up the Duchies and receive compensation in the Legations. At any rate, Castlereagh believed that he was so minded, and Metternich himself, in a long intimate interview with Consalvi, in which he foretold the fall of Murat, confessed: "There are only two persons to whom I can speak as I have just done, you and Lord Castlereagh. You two alone can understand me." Naturally Castlereagh kept these confidences to himself.[1]

By December, however, the need for Talleyrand's support had made further action concerning Naples indispensable, and Castlereagh began to make preparations for the accomplishment of this most delicate task. He sent the *Mémoire Historique* to Bentinck, who had returned to Italy as Commander-in Chief, so that he, like Nugent, could traduce its statements and give evidence of Murat's treasonable intercourse with the enemy during the critical period of 1814. He invited Talleyrand's views as to how the question should be settled, and elicited from him a letter urging a declaration of the Powers recognising Ferdinand's rights to Naples. Castlereagh himself was not, however, convinced that this would be sufficient to ensure Murat's fall. He wished more direct methods—an offer to Murat of money, with the threat of force if he refused. Murat's conduct in 1814, the just claims of Ferdinand, and the wishes of all Europe would, he thought, justify such a step in the eyes of Parliament.

Such a policy, of course, implied the co-operation of Austria, and Castlereagh must have felt assured of it before he made such a proposition to his Government. Metternich had so far, it is true, refused all Talleyrand's suggestions, so that Münster could complain to the Prince Regent: "The cardinal

---

[1] To Liverpool, Nov. 21, 1814: *W.S.D.* ix. 448. "Project of arrangements for Italy," dated "Minoriten Platz, Nov. 5, 1814": *F.O. Cont. Arch.* 21 ; P. I. Rinieri, *Consalvi e Pacca*, 134.

error, for which nothing in my opinion can excuse Metternich, is the support which he gives to Murat, who quietly occupies the frontier, and who has recently bought 25,000 muskets in Austria!" But Metternich was now drawing Talleyrand closely to him concerning Saxony, on which point, as has been seen, he went in advance of Castlereagh, and it is impossible not to believe that he gave some general assurances about Naples. The time and method of the transaction, however, he left quite vague.

The only Italian question, therefore, which was dealt with officially during these months was the incorporation of Genoa in Piedmont, which had already been settled in principle at Paris. The protests of the Genoese were, however, not without result. The commercial and political interests of the town received the guarantee of the Great Powers, and it may be that Dalrymple was not far wrong when he declared that the agitation against annexation came mainly from the aristocrats and the priests, who saw their ancient domination undermined. Nevertheless, the abolition of the ancient republic became a great theme of the Opposition, who described it as a violation of 'national' rights.[1]

If Genoa could rouse so much feeling, it is not surprising that Liverpool began to be very nervous about the question of Murat. On December 7 he told Cooke that the time for frightening him out of Naples had gone by, and that he did not desire action which might lead to a general European war. When Castlereagh began to press for it and sent home Nugent's answer to the *Mémoire*, Liverpool was still doubtful of the proofs of his treachery, and still deprecated a war against him. It could only be justified, he said, if it prevented an even more dangerous war in the West. To this point of view he adhered, when Castlereagh's correspondence with Talleyrand reached him, always insisting that in any case Britain's efforts must be confined to a blockade.

At Paris, on the other hand, the desire for Murat's removal

---

[1] To Bentinck, Dec. 10, 1814: *W.S.D.* ix. 489. From Talleyrand, Dec. 13, 1814: Weil, *Murat,* ii. 172. To Liverpool, Dec. 17, 1814: *W.S.D.* ix. 485. Münster to the Prince Regent, Dec. 17, 1814: *Münster,* 206. For British policy as to Genoa, see *B.F.S.P.* ii. 316–41 ; for the Neapolitan correspondence as laid before Parliament, *B.F.S.P.* ii. 245–305.

only increased as time went on.   Blacas seems early to have
seen in the problem an opportunity for asserting himself
against Talleyrand, and he resumed a secret correspondence
with Metternich on the question, urging that, if only Austria
would promise a benevolent neutrality, France could manage
the rest.   Wellington was altogether on his side and sent home
the details of the expedition which he had already suggested
could defeat Murat.[1]

These discussions could not take place without increasing
the uneasiness of Murat's envoys.   On December 29 Campo
Chiaro sent another note to Castlereagh, insisting on Murat's
good faith and emphasising the assurances which Castlereagh
had given on April 3, 1814, in his letter to Bentinck urging
co-operation in Italy.   This was meant for the Opposition,
and indeed an extract from Castlereagh's letter had already
been published in England.   Meanwhile, the number of
Murat's British visitors continued to increase, and the King
was undoubtedly influenced by the fact that so many of good
position readily accepted his hospitality and advocated his
cause, not allowing sufficiently for party spirit and the desire
to meddle in public affairs and enjoy the winter climate of
Naples.   He made also an especial blunder in loading honours
upon the Princess of Wales, whose reported passion for him
was soon a theme for diplomats.   Throughout all Italy the
discontented intellectuals were on Murat's side, while the
restored rulers were anxious for the removal of one whom
they could not help but consider dangerous to themselves.
Burghersh reported the alarm of Tuscany's ruler and his
readiness to join in the attack.   Bentinck, on the other hand,
while ready to blacken the case against Murat to the utmost of
his power, gloomily foretold that even Austria now would find
it difficult to crush his old enemy, who would rally the whole
of Italy to his side under that standard of Italian independence which Bentinck had once hoped to unfurl himself.[2]

[1] Liverpool to Cooke, Dec. 7, 1814.   From Liverpool, Dec. 23, 1814 ;
Liverpool to Wellington, Dec. 31, 1814 ; Liverpool to Bathurst, Dec. 31,
1814 : *W.S.D.* ix. 468, 496, 517, 519.   Bombelles to Metternich, Dec. 23,
1814 : Weil, *Murat*, ii. 251.   Wellington to Liverpool, Dec. 25, 1814 :
W.S.D. ix. 503.
[2] From Campo Chiaro, Dec. 29, 1814 : *B.F.S.P.* ii. 268.   From
Burghersh, Dec. 1, 1814 : Rachel Weigall, *Corres. of Lord Burghersh*, 63.

Castlereagh no doubt did not attach undue importance to Bentinck's judgments, which were no more accurate in 1815 than they had been in 1814, but the effect of Murat upon the rest of Italy must have stimulated Metternich's desire to get rid of him. At any rate, after the crisis of the Saxon-Polish question had been surmounted, he began to take definite steps to concert action. He preferred that the matter should be arranged with the King and Blacas in Paris rather than with Talleyrand, and he intended to obtain his own way regarding the rest of Italy as a reward for his support against Murat. He asked that Talleyrand should receive orders not to protest at Metternich's insistence that the question of Murat was outside the scope of the Congress, but merely state that the Bourbon Powers maintained their claims. The matter would then be settled by Metternich in accordance with Louis' desires.

This overture was made in the greatest secrecy, but Castlereagh was fully informed and copies of the most secret letters were sent to Liverpool on January 25. It was received with some suspicion by the French Court, and at first the King refused the suggestion that Congress should dissolve without dealing with the question of Murat. But when Bombelles shewed a firm front, the King gave way, and Blacas agreed to the course proposed, on condition that Austria signed a secret treaty recognising Ferdinand's claims to Naples. The King was perhaps helped to the decision by Wellington, who informed him, in accordance with Liverpool's repeated instructions, that no British troops would take part in the expedition against Murat.[1]

Meanwhile at Vienna Talleyrand was pressing for the return of the Duchies to the Queen of Etruria as well as the Legations to the Pope, thus leaving Marie Louise without a crown. "But Italian affairs," as the French plenipotentiaries reported, "were held up in the bureaux of M. de Metternich." For

From Bentinck, Jan. 7, 1814: *F.O. Continent*, 11. Ferdinand protested against the presence of the Princess of Wales, while the Comte de Mier later reported that her conduct at Naples almost justified the Prince Regent. Weil, *Murat*, ii. 202 ; iii. 6, 65.

[1] Metternich to Bombelles, Jan. 13, 1814 (ostensible et confidentielle) : Weil, *Murat*, ii. 327, 330, and *F.O. Continent*, 11. Wellington to Liverpool, Jan. 23, 1814 : *W.S.D.* ix. 543.

Metternich, while seeming to view these propositions not un-favourably, was simply playing for time until the decision had been reached at Paris. Talleyrand also redoubled his efforts with Castlereagh on the subject of Murat and found him sympathetic but indefinite. Although he was supplied with evidence against Murat furnished by La Besnardière, he would announce his decision, he said, after he reached home. Talleyrand's letter to the King with delightful irony mocked at Castlereagh's desire not to compromise his character. British practice in India, he added, prevented them from having exact ideas on the subject of legitimacy. He little knew that the recipient of his letter was settling the business with Metternich and Castlereagh behind his back.

Louis' consent to the new plan appears to have reached Vienna just in time for Metternich and Castlereagh to consider it before the latter left for home. Metternich entrusted to Castle-reagh the negotiation at Paris, not only of the project concern-ing Murat but of the whole Italian problem, which Metternich insisted must be settled at the same time. Castlereagh saw the King on February 27 and succeeded in obtaining his con-sent to practically all Metternich's conditions. As Metternich had given way about Murat, he said, France must give way as regards the north of Italy, and eventually the King agreed that Marie Louise should keep the Duchies for life, the Spanish claimant succeeding her to the exclusion of her son. There was some discussion as to the exact method, and Castlereagh yielded on one or two points, but substantially Metternich obtained all that he desired.

The Austrian Chancellor was now confident of his posi-tion, and adopted a new and more intimidating attitude towards the Neapolitans who had just sent a third note to Castlereagh. Even before Castlereagh reached Paris, Wellington, who was no doubt fully in the secret, was able to report confidently of the measures which Schwarzenberg was taking in secret to assemble a large Austrian force in Italy. "So that I consider Murat's affair as settled," he wrote. "His recent conduct is rather fortunate." [1]

[1] Bombelles to Metternich, Feb. 4, 1815; Metternich to Bombelles, Feb. 13, 1815 (not 18 as in Weil): Weil, *Murat*, ii. 397, 453. Talleyrand to Louis, Feb. 15, 1815; Louis to Talleyrand, March 3, 1815: Pallain,

Murat was, indeed, in a state of nervous tension, and in his anxiety was taking steps of doubtful wisdom in Italy. But his fall had been determined before Napoleon's return. Unless he was prepared to acquiesce tamely in the fate which Castlereagh and Metternich had prepared for him, there was no recourse but to adopt the programme which Bentinck had foreseen and appeal to all Italy to fight on his side. Nevertheless, Murat's threatening attitude, of which Bentinck, Burghersh, and Wellington made the most, had some weight with the British Cabinet, which Castlereagh found very reluctant to adopt his plan upon his return. Their scruples were overcome by a number of documents furnished from the French archives, which, Castlereagh claimed, proved his treachery, though Wellington had already assured Blacas that they were insufficient. Castlereagh was, however, anxious to conceal as far as possible his own prominent part in the negotiations. "As there will be some nicety," he wrote to Wellington on March 12, "in giving to our line on this question the form most likely to prove satisfactory to Parliament, it might be desirable we should accede, according to our own form, to the treaty previously agreed to by Austria and France in the negotiation of which you will assist with a view of rendering the details as little objectionable as possible." [1]

By now the news had come of Napoleon's landing in France, and the shock was more than Murat's nerves could stand. Though his representatives at Vienna offered to sign the declaration against Napoleon, Murat himself felt, perhaps rightly, that his only chance lay in taking advantage of the confusion to overcome his enemies. His troops began to

---

Corres. inédite, 270, 305. From Talleyrand, Feb. 9, 1815 ; La Besnardière to Talleyrand, Feb. 9, 1815 : *F.O. Continent*, 12. To Wellington, Feb. 28, 1815 : *W.S.D.* ix. 583. From Wellington, Feb. 25, 1815 : *Gurwood*, xii. 263.

[1] From Burghersh, Jan. 31, 1815 : Weigall, *Corres. of Lord Burghersh*, 94. From Bentinck, Jan. 15, 1815 : Weil, *Murat*, ii. 288. To Wellington, March 12, 1815 : *W.S.D.* ix. 592; with Contre Projet on Naples: *F.O. Cont. Arch.* 8. The letter of Wellington to Blacas was published by Napoleon, and Wellington then alleged that the memoirs of Nugent and Bentinck made the proofs sufficient. (To Wellington, May 19, 1815 : *W.S.D.* x. 323. From Wellington, May 23, 1815 : *Gurwood*, xii. 418.) Most of the French evidence is given in *B.F.S.P.* ii. 300–305. Cooke said there was plenty of proof in the Austrian archives if only they would reveal it ! (From Cooke, April 13, 1815 : *C.C.* x. 313.)

move north to defeat the Austrian armies before they could concentrate. There was, however, a period of uncertainty, and Castlereagh, on receipt of an offer from Chevalier Toco, Murat's unofficial representative at London, to join the Allies, actually authorised Wellington to accept it, if it was considered at Vienna the best means of furthering the general cause. But before Wellington had left Vienna he had settled the Neapolitan question with Metternich and Talleyrand in accordance with Castlereagh's instructions of March 12. They were to make a treaty agreeing to the restoration of Ferdinand, to which Britain was to adhere in her own form of words. Wellington therefore, who only received the later instruction after he had set out for Brussels, advised Clancarty not to act on it. By that time the Austrians were ready to march, and Clancarty had no hesitation in declaring to Metternich that he considered the instruction as invalid. Burghersh had, indeed, anticipated events and denounced the armistice on April 3, though Austria only declared war on April 12, while Bentinck was so anxious for the complete destruction of Murat that he indulged in the most acid criticism of the Austrians, with the result that they demanded his recall. A'Court, in spite of pressure, failed to organise any assistance from Sicily. The British share in the final overthrow of Murat was therefore confined to a naval demonstration by Lord Exmouth in the Bay of Naples, after Murat had been easily defeated on land. For in spite of Bentinck's prophecies the Italians shewed no signs of rallying to Murat's banner, his own Neapolitan troops fought half-heartedly, and by May 2 the Austrians were in Naples, Murat had fled to France, and Prince Leopold of Sicily had been received with the "universal applause of the people." [1]

Castlereagh, of course, delighted in this result, though as late as April 3 he had been prepared for some sort of arrangement with Murat. He was stirred to fury by the outcry of the

[1] To Wellington, March 24, 1815 (enclosing Chevalier Toco to Castlereagh, March 24, 1815) ; from Wellington, March 25, 1815 : *W.S.D.* ix. 609, 612. From Clancarty, March 29, April 8, 1815 : *B.D.* 318, 321. From Burghersh, March 18, 24, April 3 : *F.O. Tuscany*, 22 ; May 21, 23, 1815 : Weigall, *Corres. of Lord Burghersh*, 167-70. Bentinck to Stewart, April 22, 1815 : *F.O. Austria*, 117. From Clancarty, April 22, 1815 : *Lond. MSS.*

Opposition on his conduct. "We shall have Naples on Tues-day," he informed Clancarty on April 29, "and I hope to make our shameless opponents smart for their calumnies on that subject. I am glad you felt strong enough to refuse Murat's overture. My only object was to listen to it, if the union cause upon calculation required his help, of which those on the spot could alone be competent judges." He warmly approved the energetic conduct of Burghersh, and urged A'Court to join in the attack. The discomfiture of the Opposition, and especially Sir Robert Wilson, who to the last refused to believe that Murat could be beaten, must have increased his pleasure in the good news. Metternich's request for the recall of Bentinck could now be safely granted.[1]

Moreover, according to A'Court the Sicilian problem had been solved while the fight with Naples had been in progress. The reform of the constitution for which A'Court was working had languished during April, but in May both Houses were induced to ask the King to appoint a commission for that purpose and then dissolved. A'Court's congratulations were as warm as Bentinck's had been a year before. "The credit of having emancipated the Sicilians from despotism remains to us," he assured Castlereagh, "but all our responsibility is removed. . . . Hitherto the King has been the enemy of a constitution, which he considered as having been forced upon him by a foreign Power. He must now of necessity become the supporter of his own work." How illusory this judgment was the next few years were to shew, and A'Court himself was pained to find on his arrival at Naples that Ferdinand had promised Austria, in a secret treaty of April 30, twenty-five millions of francs for the restoration of his kingdom. This sum it was quite impossible for him to pay without ruining his subjects, and in view of the fact that both Austria and Ferdinand were in receipt of special subsidies from Britain for the same purpose, the discovery came as a great shock. Nevertheless, A'Court was pleased that no bloodshed had this time accompanied the restoration, and he was as ready as

---

[1] To Clancarty, April 3, 1815 : *F.O. Continent*, 16 ; April 29, 1815 : *Lond. MSS.* To Burghersh, May 9, 1815 : *F.O. Tuscany*, 23. To A'Court, May 9, 1815 : *Lond. MSS.* Metternich to Merveldt, May 17, 1815 : *Vienna St. A.*

Castlereagh to welcome Austrian control over Naples.   When in July, by another secret treaty, Ferdinand promised not to introduce a constitution into Naples without Austria's consent he gave it warm approval.   So closed for a time Britain's attempt to introduce constitutional principles to the people of Italy.

A'Court was, however, not without influence in the last act of the tragedy of Murat.   The exiled King had fled from France to Corsica after Napoleon's defeat, and, refusing the offer of residence in Austria, he made on October 8 a mad and desperate attempt on the coast of Calabria.   He was at once arrested and in a few days shot.   "As an act of justice and policy," wrote A'Court, "it is in my mind equally to be justified, and I am not afraid to own that I gave this opinion very plainly and unequivocally to the Neapolitan Government the moment I heard of the landing.   My opinion, I have reason to believe, had some weight in the business."   Few other Englishmen, it is to be hoped, would have cared to claim credit for such an action, however imperative the duty which dictated it.[1]

Meanwhile, the settlement of the rest of Italy had been proceeding along the lines Metternich had laid down.   Talley-rand was powerless, now that his master was an exile, and it was reserved for Clancarty to play the most obstinate rôle in the only part of the settlement which gave much trouble— the fate of the young Napoleon.   As has been seen, Louis and Metternich had agreed that he should not succeed to his mother's kingdom, and though Castlereagh after his return was doubtful if the Treaty of Fontainebleau did not forbid such an arrangement, the action of Napoleon was considered to have made that treaty no longer binding as regards his son.   Accord-ingly, by the time Wellington left Vienna everything seemed settled in that sense, and Clancarty was able to report "the whole affairs of Italy may be considered as finally arranged," the only opponent being the Spanish plenipotentiary, who continued to insist on the immediate return of the Duchies to the Queen of Etruria.   This prevented signature of the articles,

[1] From A'Court, April 2, 4, 17, May 14, 31, 1815: *F.O. Sicily*, 65. From A'Court, July 18, 1815: *F.O. Sicily*, 70.   A'Court to Burghersh, Oct. 23, 1815: Weigall, *Corres. of Burghersh*, 198.

and then Metternich pleaded Murat's advance as another excuse for delay. Whether he was still anxious to keep a Bourbon out of Italy or simply waiting on events in France is not known, but the difficult legal situation enabled him to prolong the discussions into May.[1]

It was, however, the Tsar who suddenly upset the whole scheme by refusing to agree to the exclusion of the young Napoleon. Metternich asserted that he disapproved of this plan, but he gave but little support to Clancarty's obstinate and furious opposition which alone prevented it from being adopted. Clancarty's long letters to Castlereagh on the subject shew how deeply he resented the Tsar's desire to place "Buonaparte's bastard," as he called him, on a throne. It is probable that the Tsar was merely moved by a sense of chivalry, but it was not difficult to impute other motives to him, especially in view of his unconcealed dislike of the Bourbons. Clancarty, therefore, held his ground and refused to sign any part of the treaty unless he got his way. "The Emperor of Russia's tenacity to the Archduchess," he wrote in a long private letter of May 26, "is not relaxed. It seems to me to be bottomed not less in the desire to range her in his interests in the event, which he will certainly endeavour to bring about, of her becoming Regent in France, but also in the plan of availing himself of an opportunity of doing what he supposes ungrateful to us, cloaking himself at the same time with the excuse of his gallantry and chivalry in espousing her part. . . . Metternich, whatever he professes, has acted but a shabby part in all this business." It seemed, indeed, that the struggle would prevent the signature of the treaty altogether; for when the Emperor of Russia left Vienna the issue was still in doubt. Castlereagh would scarcely have approved of carrying British opposition so far, since he informed Clancarty on May 30 that Britain had not a primary interest, but simply desired "to acquiesce in whatever might best serve to conciliate the pretensions of other Powers." However, a compromise was at last found, and the Duchies were given to the Archduchess for life, while the succession was to be decided

---

[1] To Clancarty, April 12, 1815: *B.D.* 323. From Clancarty, April 1, 8, 1815: *F.O. Continent*, 17; April 28, May 1, 1815: *Lond. MSS.*

by the five Powers at a later date. This did not, however,
satisfy Labrador, who refused to sign the treaty mainly
because of this clause, while Austria and Russia actually
made a secret convention that the young Napoleon was to
succeed, which was only discovered in 1817. However, for
the moment the principal Powers were agreed and so the great
treaty could be signed.[1]

In the other Italian questions British views had not much
influence. They reluctantly acquiesced in Austria taking the
Valtelline instead of Switzerland, and, of course, approved of
her retaining the papal territory on the left bank of the Po
and the right of garrison in Ferrara. Though Consalvi had
obtained nine-tenths of his territorial demands he still thought
it right to issue a papal protest in thunderous Latin, to which,
however, nobody paid any attention. Nor had the relations
of the Papacy with Britain improved. The disposition of the
Pope to grant the power of veto remained firm for some time,
in spite of the loud clamour of the Irish, whose representatives
at Rome were received with cold comfort. But only a united
Government could have handled such a delicate question
successfully, and the British Government was split into two
irreconcilable parties. Thus, though Castlereagh discussed
the question with Consalvi at Vienna, and Cooke had hopes
of settling it during his residence at Rome, no official negotiation could take place and the opportunity was lost. Only
the British Catholics themselves, by their pressure on the
Papacy to grant the veto, could in Castlereagh's opinion make
the passage of the Emancipation Bill possible. But, as Consalvi had pointed out, it was too much to expect the Pope to
grant on his own initiative what he had only hitherto given
perforce to the demands of established Governments.

This decision carried with it a negative on the proposed
diplomatic recognition of the Pope by Britain. Cooke had

---

[1] From Clancarty, May 13, 1815 : *B.D.* 332 ; May 26, 1815 : *Lond.
MSS.* ; June 2, 1815 : *F.O. Continent*, 19. *Münster*, 263. To Clancarty,
May 16, 30, 1815 : *F.O. Continent*, 16. In a letter of May 6 Clancarty
narrates the embarrassment of the plenipotentiaries as to how to deal with
Napoleon's request to receive back his wife and child, the answer to which
Metternich said the Emperor of Austria must reserve for his own decision.
Lond. MSS. For the later history of the Duchies, see my *Foreign Policy
of Castlereagh 1815–1822*, 114–16.

discussed it with Cardinal Pacca at Rome, and suggested that
the accredited agents might be secret or public. The Cardinal
had assured him that the Pope would be strongly in favour of
some regular system. But Castlereagh on his return to England found that opinion had moved against such a course and
refused to follow up the proposition, which was not renewed
for many years. Though the Cardinal was thought by some
of the British Delegation to be too sly a bargainer for comfort,
his personal relations with Castlereagh continued to be excellent and were strengthened by British help to the Pope
at the second Peace of Paris.[1]

Once the Duchies were settled no trouble was caused by
the restoration of Tuscany and Modena to their Austrian
Grand Dukes. The only territorial point left was the fate
of the Ionian Islands. As has been seen, these were at one
time intended as compensation for Ferdinand, but, as soon as
his restoration was contemplated, Castlereagh agreed that
Austria "would object, and justly, to both shores of the entrance
to the Adriatic being in the hands of the same Power." So
long as neither France nor Russia obtained influence there,
Britain was content, and all kinds of schemes were suggested
at one time or another, including the restoration of the
Republic and the institution of a new Knights of Malta.
Castlereagh purposely delayed the settlement until the end,
and undoubtedly expected the islands finally to go to Austria,
who had claimed full sovereignty over them if Ferdinand was
restored. But Capo d'Istria was a native of Corfu, and
Alexander rewarded his services at the Congress by allowing
him full powers in this question. He objected strenuously
to Austria and far preferred Britain, who could give the
Ionians better government and better protection on the seas.
The matter was, therefore, left open until the meeting at
Paris, when Capo d'Istria insisted that Britain should have
merely a protectorate and not full sovereignty. By this time
the Cabinet had become more eager for control of the islands,

---

[1] P. I. Rinieri, *Il Congresso di Vienna e la Santa Sede*, 615–20; *Consalvi e Pacca*, 413, 416, 594. From Cooke, March 18, 1815: *F.O. Italian
States*, 8; April 13, 1815: from Consalvi, May 13, 1815; to Cooke, June 4,
1815: *C.C.* x. 309, 351, 375. *Bathurst*, 305. Bernard Ward, *Eve of
Catholic Emancipation*, ii. 132–34.

to which Bathurst had always attached importance, but Castlereagh succeeded in winning their assent since he claimed the substance of power remained. It is interesting to note that one means of pressure brought to bear on the Islanders was to delay the expedition to Algiers in order that they might the more desire the protection of the British flag.[1]

No Power was so disappointed at Vienna as Spain, which refused to sign the treaty. Labrador had been hampered by contradictory instructions from Cevallos, who succeeded San Carlos as Foreign Minister in November, but his own conduct had been foolish and inept. Spain had wasted her energies on projects which it was impossible to attain. Labrador had proved a stalking horse for Talleyrand, only to be deserted by him when his usefulness was over. A vain attempt was made to secure Louisiana during the early months through British arms, yet Labrador had shewn no confidence in Castlereagh, and Spain had been the least accommodating Power on the question of the Slave Trade. British Ministers had therefore little sympathy with her complaints.

Portugal had been more pliable, and Palmella had done as much as he possibly could to meet British views. Castlereagh had thus been able to arrange the tedious dispute with France over the Guiana frontier. He had hoped also to win back Olivenza from Spain. But Wellington reported that France would not insist upon the cession, which Spain would certainly refuse. Accordingly all that could be inserted in the treaty was a clause ensuring the good offices of the Powers on Portugal's behalf, and this question was to cause trouble for a long period. Portugal refused altogether to supply troops for the allied armies after Napoleon's return, and Castlereagh was indignant with both the Peninsular Powers at the close of these transactions. "It is somewhat singular in itself," he

---

[1] To Liverpool, Nov. 21, Dec. 24, 1814 ; from Liverpool, Jan. 6, 1815 ; Bathurst to Wellington, Jan. 13, 1815 : *W.S.D.* ix. 448, 501, 530, 535. From Clancarty, April 1, 1815 : *F.O. Continent,* 17 ; June 2, 1815 : *Lond. MSS.* ; June 10, 1815 : *F.O. Continent,* 19. To Bathurst, July 31, Aug. 17, 1815 ; from Bathurst, Aug. 25, 1815 : *C.C.* x. 449, 483, 499. To Bathurst, Sept. 24, 1815 ; from Bathurst, Oct. 3, 1815 : *F.O. Continent,* 28, 20. To Bathurst, Oct. 19, 1815 : *Bathurst,* 389. General Campbell's too vigorous rule may have influenced Capo d'Istria, but he was undoubtedly thinking also of Greece—how rightly was shewn in 1863, when the islanders were united to their compatriots.

wrote to Canning from Paris, "that the only two Courts
with which we find it difficult to do business are those of the
Peninsula. There is a temper in both which makes it more
arduous to settle a trifling matter with them than to arrange
a great measure of European policy with other Powers. It
seems as if the recollection of our services made it impossible
for them to do anything without endeavouring most unnecessarily and ungratefully to display their own independence." [1]

[1] See the Marqués de Villa-Urrutia's criticism of Spanish policy in his
España en el Congreso de Viena, 188–90. From Wellington, April 5,
1815 ; from Clancarty, June 2, 1815 : *Lond. MSS.* To Canning, Aug. 12,
1815 : *F.O. Cont. Arch.* 36.

3. THE ABOLITION OF THE SLAVE TRADE. GENERAL QUESTIONS

NOT least of all the anxieties of Castlereagh and his Government during the months in which the fate of Europe hung in the balance was the necessity of continuing unceasingly their efforts to secure the universal Abolition of the Slave Trade. The treaty with France had incurred the severest censure from the "Saints" in this respect. No sooner had Castlereagh laid it on the table of the House of Commons amid the applause of the whole House than Wilberforce rose and said, "I cannot but conceive I behold in his hand the death-warrant of a multitude of innocent victims, men, women, and children, whom I had fondly indulged the hope of having myself rescued from destruction." In this spirit the campaign for universal Abolition was renewed all over the country and met with an immediate and overwhelming response. Petitions from almost every town and village in Britain poured into the House of Commons. Addresses were carried unanimously in both Houses of Parliament. Wellington, on his short visit to receive at last the honours he had accumulated in four years of successful warfare, yet found time, amidst the enthusiasm with which he was received, to tell his brother of an indescribable "degree of frenzy existing here about the Slave Trade. People in general appear to think it would suit the policy of the nation to go to war to put an end to that *abominable* traffic, and many wish we should take the field on this new crusade."

The Government had necessarily, therefore, to make every effort to remove the blot on their record. The Opposition, as Wilberforce noted, were only too eager to make the cause a party question, and Liverpool confessed that, even if he had not desired to do so, he would have been forced to take action.

The difficulty was how to enforce Abolition on other Slave Trading Powers, whose inhabitants were completely untouched by the emotions moving the British people. Of the colonial Powers, Holland, Denmark, and Sweden had now all agreed to Abolition, and it was only the three Latin and Catholic countries which stood in the way—France, Spain, and Portugal. They had against them the whole of Europe, since the three continental allies of Britain had no colonial interests to defend and were anxious to win British favour by supporting her actions on this point. Indeed, the Tsar shewed himself almost too fervid to please the Tory Government. Wilberforce, who before his arrival had written to him after much prayer and heart-searching, had several interviews with him during his visit to London. The Tsar was ready to promise all his support. "We must keep them to it," he said of the French, and, true to his rôle at the time, was ready to score a point against Castlereagh. "What could be done," he insinuated, "when your own Ambassador gave way?" For the Catholic Powers the support of the Papal See was even more important, however the Protestant Wilberforce might distrust such an ally, and Consalvi assured Castlereagh officially that "the Pope will not lose a moment after his re-establishment at Rome in exerting the influence he may possess among the Catholic nations of the Continent, to awaken them to a due sense of the enormity of continuing to carry on a trade in their fellow-creatures, and if possible to bring about its early and complete abolition." [1]

Thus the vast majority of civilised states were now on the side of Abolition, and obviously the approaching Congress would afford an opportunity to obtain an international condemnation of the Slave Trade which would be of great value. But would this force the three Powers who still allowed their subjects to take part in the Slave Trade to abandon their legal rights? And would this abandonment be effective unless some international machinery was set up to enforce it? To these questions the practical mind of Castlereagh immediately addressed itself. Means must be found to put

[1] *Life of Wilberforce*, iv. 187–91, 209, 211.   Wellington to Wellesley, July 20, 1814 : *Gurwood*, xii. 77.   To Wellesley, July 15, 1814 : *F.O. Spain*, 158 ; F. G. Klingberg, *The Anti-Slavery Movement in England* (1926), 146.

pressure on states who obviously would not yield to an appeal to their feelings, and a system of international control established to secure what had been gained. He would endeavour therefore in the interval to induce by concession or threats the French and Spanish Governments to come further along the road to Abolition—to reduce the period of legal traffic and, above all, to grant immediate Abolition north of the Equator, where the British navy had effectively stamped out Slavery. Money might induce Spain to do something, since she was nearly bankrupt and yet eager to re-establish her power overseas. France might desire British co-operation in the reconstruction of Europe, and thus bid for the support of British public opinion by further measures against the Trade. The Portuguese Government was too far off for immediate action, but Britain had more means of control over her than over the other two states. As a last resort a new idea of a world economic boycott of the Slave Trading states, the exact origin of which is uncertain, but which doubtless arose as a consequence of the blockades and restrictions which had been employed during the world war, might be used to overcome a too stubborn resistance. As for enforcement, that could only be done by the British fleet, and this meant that some "right of visit and search" in African waters should be conceded to it by other Powers—a delicate question to raise immediately after the great war and while one was still being fought with the United States over the exercise of the right as a belligerent.

It was hoped that the Pope's spiritual influence would exercise some effect on Spain, where Ferdinand was engaged in restoring Catholicism in all its mediaeval forms, but the necessity of other means of pressure was soon realised. Henry Wellesley had been trying, though without much hope, to insert a clause on the subject in the projected treaty of alliance. But San Carlos explained that the Spanish colonies, unlike the British, were not well stocked with slaves. Only with great difficulty could Wellesley obtain, in return for a promise that Britain would prevent her subjects from supplying the revolted colonies with munitions, an article which was no more than a recognition that the traffic was inhuman, and that its abolition would be taken into consideration by the King, "with the deliberation which the state of his possessions in America demands," and a promise that Spanish ships should only supply Spanish colonies.

Castlereagh agreed to this proposal, but urged that further steps should immediately be taken, and offered considerable material inducements. If Spain would follow France's example and agree to Abolition in five years and at the same time abolish immediately all Slave Trading to the north of the Equator, the subsidies would be continued for the whole of the year 1814, a payment equal to £800,000, and the Government would not object to Spain raising a loan in Britain, though it was not likely to be a commercial proposition at present. These terms were, however, not high enough to overcome Spanish objections. San Carlos insisted on retaining the area of the Guinea Coast to 10° north of the Line, which was exactly the area which Britain was anxious to protect, nor would he promise to abolish in less than ten years. Though the negotiations continued until October no further advance could be made. Bathurst suggested that the threat of a world economic boycott of Spanish colonial products should be employed, "which might operate more prejudicially to the colonial and commercial interests of Spain than the Abolition of the Slave Trade." But this was a remote threat, and the opposing interests were close at hand. "The Abolition is vehemently opposed," reported Wellesley on August 31, "by all those who have any connection with S. America or with the Spanish West Indies; and the Government is apprehensive of the effect which it would produce in the Colonies, particularly at Havanna, where public opinion is in a very unsettled state." These motives prevailed even though the Spanish Government was almost bankrupt and was urgently in need of the money which Britain offered, indeed so urgently that Wellesley was afraid lest they would turn to other Powers, and advised that financial assistance should be granted for this reason alone, in spite of the refusal of Abolition.[1]

[1] To Wellesley, July 15, 30, 1814; Bathurst to Wellesley, Sept. 9, 1814: *F.O. Spain*, 158. From Wellesley, July 6, Aug. 26, 31, Sept. 20,

By this time, however, Castlereagh had himself taken up the question at Vienna both with Spain and Portugal, whose Court was too far away for anything to be done in this interval. France had, however, not been neglected during the months of July and August. Abolition had been made the principal point of Wellington's instructions. Castlereagh himself prepared the way with an urgent personal appeal to Talleyrand, while the Prince Regent sent an eloquent and moving epistle to his erstwhile guest. Wellington was then instructed to sound Talleyrand on the idea of the economic boycott and to endeavour to obtain immediate Abolition north of the Line. Haste was necessary, since news had already been received of slaving expeditions fitting out in French ports, some of them assisted by British capital, and it was expected that an effort would be made to recapture St. Domingo and thus create a new market for slaves. Wellington dealt with the affair with his usual energy and directness. He asked for Abolition to the north of the Line, the right of visit in African waters, and the restriction of slaves by licensing only the number absolutely necessary to the restored colonies. The King and Talleyrand were sympathetic, but they urged that public opinion in France was almost entirely against them. That this was so was admitted even by Wilberforce. He had spent July in preparing an open letter to Talleyrand, recapitulating all the arguments so powerful in Britain and which he thought must move Frenchmen also. But his correspondence with Madame de Staël, Sismondi, Chateaubriand, and others, and the visits of Stephen, Clarkson, and General Macaulay to Paris gradually shewed him the truth. Only the Jacobins supported the King, amongst them Grégoire, 'the regicide,' and this drove all good royalists on to the side of the commercial classes.[1]

Nevertheless, Wellington persisted and Castlereagh supported him in the interviews which he had with the King and Talleyrand on his way to Vienna. Wellington had secured from Talleyrand a confirmation of the King's verbal promise

Oct. 11, 1814 : *F.O. Spain*, 160, 161. Extracts from some of the dispatches are given in *B.F.S.P.* iii. 920–33.

[1] To Talleyrand, July 16, 1814 : *W.S.D.* ix. 163. Correspondence in *B.F.S.P.* iii. 900–905. *Life of Wilberforce*, iv. 212–13.

2D

that the Trade to the north of the Line should be stopped, when the negotiation was complicated by a chance remark of Talleyrand to Clarkson, who was engaged in propaganda in Paris, that some concession either of money or the return of a colony would enable the French Government to agree to total Abolition.   This was immediately urged on the British Government by Wilberforce, and Liverpool, though with no good grace or confidence in the success of the overture, was compelled to instruct Wellington to offer the return of Trinidad or a large sum of money as the price for complete Abolition.   Wellington shared Liverpool's opinion of the unwisdom of this offer, but it was nevertheless made.   By this time, however, Talleyrand had left for Vienna and the responsibility was handed over to Castlereagh.   Wellington persisted, however, in his efforts at Paris for the more limited objectives. The right of visit proved so obnoxious that he found it better to withdraw the demand altogether, but fortunately the French at last realised that St. Domingo was not worth the effort necessary for its conquest.   Affairs at Vienna were leading the Government to seek even closer co-operation with Britain, and before the end of the year Wellington was able to announce to Wilberforce that orders had been issued prohibiting French subjects from trading north of the Line. "You have inspired your hero Wellington with as much ardour to do good as to win victories," wrote Madame de Staël, "and his influence with the Royal Family has come to the aid of your poor blacks."   This was, perhaps, hardly doing justice to Wellington, but the zeal of the Abolitionists had obviously been one of the main factors in keeping the Government and the Ambassador to their work, even if it had sometimes made that work more difficult.[1]

Meanwhile, Castlereagh had found conditions at Vienna hardly propitious to international co-operation.   He immediately made the offer of a colony to Talleyrand, but obtained no reply for over a month.   When it came it was a refusal, as had been anticipated.   Still the news about St. Domingo,

---

[1] *B.F.S.P.* iii. 900–909.   Wellington to Liverpool, Sept. 2, 13, 1814; to Wilberforce, Sept. 15, 1814 : *Gurwood*, xii. 94, 113, 114.   Liverpool to Wellington, Sept. 7, 23, 1814: Yonge, *Liverpool*, ii. 119, 123.   *Life of Wilberforce*, iv. 216, 223.

on the necessities of which island Talleyrand had based his main resistance to British proposals at Paris, made Castlereagh hope that French objections could be overcome, "as the supply required for the other French colonies in the next five years must be very inconsiderable; so trifling, indeed, that the French nation might well make this sacrifice to humanity without looking either for a pecuniary or colonial compensation."

Castlereagh obviously was angry at having been forced to make this abortive offer. Indeed, the whole agitation in Britain was, in his opinion, doing more harm than good to the cause abroad. "It is impossible to persuade foreign nations that this sentiment is unmixed with the views of colonial policy," he wrote in October, "and their Cabinets, who can better estimate the real and virtuous motives which guide us on this question, see in the very impatience of the nation a powerful instrument through which they expect to force, at a convenient moment, the British Government upon some favourite object of policy." He wished, on the contrary, to prepare the way slowly for action at the appropriate moment. He circulated to the plenipotentiaries the evidence on the subject prepared for the House of Commons, taking care to emphasise the material side of the arguments, points which Clarkson's pamphlet had tended to omit. He also tried to prepare their minds for the economic boycott against refractory Powers.

Meanwhile, he had entered into private negotiations with the Spanish and Portuguese representatives, Labrador and Palmella. The former still insisted on eight years' Trade, and immediate abolition only south of the Equator; the Portuguese were more conciliatory, though their powers were limited. Both required to be bought by money and concessions in other matters, and Castlereagh asked for authority to name them.[1]

All this was, of course, preparatory to bringing the matter officially before Congress when the right moment arrived. Castlereagh had worked out a comprehensive plan. Pressure

[1] To Liverpool, Oct. 9, 1814 : *W.S.D.* ix. 323 ; Oct. 25, 1814 : *B.D.* 215; Nov. 11, 1814 : *F.O. Continent,* 8.

was to be brought to bear on the three Latin Powers to adopt, if France would go so far, three years or, if not, five as the extreme duration of their Trade. In the event of failure, he was seriously considering the proposal of economic boycott against the colonial produce of the Slave Trading Powers by the rest of the world. Above all, his mind was engaged with plans for making the Abolition effective, and for this purpose he wished to create centres of information and action at London and Paris, in Ambassadorial Conferences, which should have a permanent existence and continually review the state of the whole question. To this proposal he attached the greatest importance: "I particularly recommend," he said in his covering dispatch, "to your consideration the advantage of having a sort of permanent European Congress in existence as therein proposed upon this particular subject. I am of opinion that this may be made in itself a most powerful instrument to enforce with good faith the engagements of the several Powers." As Castlereagh confessed, this proposal was made partly with a view to conciliating public opinion at home, by shewing that the cause was still being prosecuted, even if a final victory had not been won at Vienna; but it also shews that he had already perceived what the Abolitionists at home had hardly begun to realise, that the enforcement of international Abolition would be as difficult as obtaining the legal decrees from the various countries involved. Liverpool agreed heartily to these suggestions. He was especially anxious that record should be made of all the British efforts, including the offer of an island to France, in order to satisfy Parliament.[1]

The question was at last brought before the Committee of Eight on December 14, Talleyrand proposing that a Commission of the Eight Powers should be appointed to consider the subject. To this Spain and Portugal immediately objected, on the plea that only colonial Powers were concerned. Castlereagh insisted, on the contrary, that the Slave Trade was a matter of general interest, and gave a hint of his

---

[1] To Liverpool, Nov. 21, 1814; Memorandum as to the mode of conducting the negotiations in Congress for the final Abolition of the Slave Trade : B.D. 233–35. From Liverpool, Dec. 9, 1814 : W.S.D. ix. 470.

boycott proposal by suggesting that the non-colonial Powers could refuse to buy colonial produce from Slaving states. But it was clear that the Portuguese were awaiting Castlereagh's replies to their proposals before they would consent to any joint action, and he thought it better to suspend the sitting. He had little hope, he confessed, of obtaining from the Congress "any vigorous measures at present to enforce immediate Abolition." Some interval, whether eight or five years, must be allowed. Meanwhile, neither Portugal nor Spain would do anything without compensation. "You may rely upon it," he concluded, "that nothing effectual will be done which Great Britain does not pay for, so strongly is this expectation of turning it to profit with us gone about."

In spite of the absence of authority from home, therefore, he continued to negotiate with Palmella. He could not get him to go further than his original proposal, but this was, after all, a distinct advance. Eventually Portugal agreed to abolish all Slaving north of the Line. In return Britain paid her £300,000 in satisfaction of some doubtful claims, let her off the repayment of a loan, and gave up part of the irksome treaty of Alliance of 1810, against which Portugal had never ceased to protest. This was a rather heavy price, but Castlereagh tried to shew that it was not as heavy as it looked. It was unlikely that any part of the loan would be recovered, and the treaty of Alliance he had always regarded as of doubtful value. There was, he said, in some of the articles, "some prospect of naval advantage, but in as far as they seem to give us a command of the Portuguese ports, not usual between friendly and independent states, and which, as I believe, we never have used and there is little probability of our now turning to account, I am satisfied as a record of dependence they powerfully operate to disgust and alienate." The article which prevented the return of the Inquisition he insisted on retaining, but in a secret clause "as an interference in the internal affairs of a foreign state is always odious." The whole transaction, carried on as it was amidst the immense labours of the final settlement, is yet a good example of Castlereagh's diplomacy. He gave up rights which he regarded as unwise to keep in any event, and secured something of value with the goodwill thus secured. But, of course, without the lubrication of the £300,000 the concession could not have been secured. To the Spaniard he could only send an emphatic protest against Slaving north of the Line, being unable to get anything out of him.[1]

Time was drawing short if he was to conclude his negotiations at Vienna, and it was at the very crisis of the Saxon question that he demanded audiences of the three sovereigns to urge their acceptance of the general principles which he had laid down in his memorandum. All promised him support, the Tsar being especially cordial. Though the *Conférences particulières* which followed led to some warm exchanges of opinion between Castlereagh, supported by the non-colonial Powers, and Spain and Portugal, the debates were to a certain extent staged, since it was now known exactly how far each Power would go. Nevertheless, great care was exercised in taking these public attitudes, since the Protocols of the proceedings were to be published. Castlereagh's original plan was followed. France was first entreated to substitute five years for three. When she had refused, all the Powers turned on Spain and Portugal and urged them to substitute five for eight. When these had refused to commit themselves, Castlereagh turned to the general measures. Only the three eastern Powers wholly supported him in the idea of colonial boycott, which naturally produced emphatic protests from the two threatened Powers. Palmella said it would be an unwarrantable interference with the internal affairs of an independent state. Labrador threatened reprisals if it occurred. But Castlereagh, supported by Metternich, answered that though a Power had undoubtedly the legal right "to continue in its own dominions a system which was generally held to be immoral and pernicious," other Powers had an equal right to refuse it all direct or indirect support. The proposal was, however, only a threat for the future, and

---

[1] To Liverpool, Dec. 18, 1814, Jan. 11, 22, 1815: *F.O. Continent*, 9, 10. Convention and Treaty of Jan. 21, 22, 1815, are in *B.F.S.P.* ii. 345, 348. The transaction was also used to adjust a difference between France and Portugal on the retrocession to the former of Cayenne, which had been causing embarrassment to both Castlereagh and Talleyrand.

Castlereagh relied more on temptation than threat to accomplish his purpose as succeeding years were to shew.

The proposal to set up a permanent Committee was accepted more easily, only Spain protesting against its implication of interference in internal affairs, though the three Latin Powers and Sweden could only refer it to their Governments. As for the right of visit, Castlereagh had to admit that this could only be obtained by special treaties between the Powers concerned. He was especially anxious to establish a real control over the African coast north of the Line, where immediate Abolition had now been promised by all the Powers except Spain, whose refusal was condemned by Castlereagh in the Conference in the strongest terms. But both France and Portugal refused all idea of a "wartime police," and it was obvious that this all-important suggestion must wait for a time.[1]

Finally, when the positions of the Powers had been thus defined, a general declaration was agreed to which condemned the African Slave Trade as a traffic repugnant to the principles of humanity and universal morals, and which the Powers "in accordance with the spirit of the age" were determined should be abolished. The declaration is an ironic commentary on the discussions which had preceded it. Yet Castlereagh was right in regarding it of great importance. It was the universal recognition of a principle by all civilised states, and though much had yet to be done before the principle could be enforced in anything like an adequate manner, an all-important step in the progress of human society had been made and an unshakable foundation for future action laid down.

Though these efforts met with some criticism in the House, since they disappointed the expectations of the fervent Abolitionists, even Wilberforce, after an interview with Castle-

---

[1] To Liverpool, Dec. 18, 1814 : *F.O. Continent*, 9 ; Jan. 1, 1815 : *B.D.* 274. The Protocols of these Conferences, which are exceptionally detailed, are all given in *B.F.S.P.* iii. 946–70. They were laid before Parliament on Castlereagh's return. It may be noted that in August Metternich had warmly approved a suggestion of Hudelist that Britain should only be given support on the Slave Trade on condition that she secured immunity for all states from the attacks of the Barbary pirates (B. Gebhardt, *W. von Humboldt's Politische Denkschriften*, ii. 157). But this point does not seem to have been brought up at this time, though it was to be pressed later at Aix-la-Chapelle in 1818.

reagh, was convinced that no more could have been obtained. "I believe all done that could be done," he noted in his diary.

This was true at the moment. The effect of the discussions had to be allowed to sink in before further action could be taken. As Castlereagh wrote in his final report: "Any further attempts to accelerate the epoch of Abolition will be made with a better chance of success after the discussions in Congress are promulgated, for which endeavour the proposed Commissions in London and Paris will afford the necessary facilities." How much effect the discussions had already produced is seen by the fact that Talleyrand was already seriously considering total Abolition for France in order to obtain British support against Murat. And when Napoleon returned, one of his first steps was to decree immediate Abolition in order to win over public opinion in Britain. This step, though it failed in its purpose, made it inevitable that Louis should do the same on his return, and one of Castlereagh's first actions at Paris in July was to send Wilberforce the glad news. He had full right to the claim which he then made that it was a proof of "the undeviating and earnest exertions of the Prince Regent's ministers to effectuate this great object which had been so impressively given them in charge." [1]

In the other general questions, the Emancipation of the Jews, the Navigation of International Rivers, and the Regulation of Diplomatic Rank, raised at Vienna, British influence was but little exerted, and hardly any references were made to them in the public and private correspondence of the period. The question of the Jews was dealt with by the German Committee, and the influence of the Rothschilds on Prussian and Austrian finances, apart from the *douceurs* that Gentz received, ensured that their claim to the rights of citizenship should be recognised though they did not secure

---

[1] To Bathurst, Feb. 13, 1815: *B.F.S.P.* iii. 949. Talleyrand to Louis XVIII. Feb. 15, 1815: Pallain, *Corres. inédite*, 289. *Life of Wilberforce*, iv. 224. Clancarty at Castlereagh's request made some effort, while drafting the treaty, to sharpen the declaration and insert special clauses drawn up by Gentz, but failed owing to the opposition of Spain. To Clancarty, May 16, 1815: *F.O. Continent*, 16. From Clancarty, May 1, 1815: *Lond. MSS.*; April 1, May 13, 19, 1815: *F.O. Continent*, 17, 18. Talleyrand to Jaucourt, May 16, 1815: *Corres. de Jaucourt avec Talleyrand*, 348.

all that was wanted. It is a significant fact that Liverpool wrote to Castlereagh to support these claims at the instance of the British Rothschild. No doubt Castlereagh was not unwilling, for his subsequent policy shews that he was always ready to support the principle of toleration and equality in this matter. But he had no sphere of action, and there is no record that he did anything at this time. Münster, on the other hand, who had great influence on the German Committee, shewed distinct Anti-Semite prejudices.[1]

Clancarty was the British representative on the Navigation of Rivers Committee, but neither he nor his chief seem to have taken any interest in the important international work which it achieved, while Münster was positively indignant at the idea of being "called on to make sacrifice gratuitously, at your Royal Highness's expense, to favour some vague ideas on the liberty of commerce !" Clancarty was concerned almost entirely with the question of reducing Antwerp from a fortified to an open town as prescribed in the Treaty of Paris. The British Government, in their dread of the fortified base which Napoleon had erected against them, had at first determined that this clause should be interpreted to include not only the destruction of its inner basin but also of all its land fortifications. Wellington, however, declared against this wholesale destruction as unnecessary, and even harmful to British interests. When the question came up at Vienna it was found that there would be little support for the destruction even of the basins. Clancarty, who sympathised with the desire to preserve its shipping facilities, therefore got the Committee to agree that Britain and the Netherlands should settle the matter between themselves.[2]

If Castlereagh was lukewarm towards this important proposal, he was positively hostile to the consideration of the vexed question of the Regulation of Diplomatic Rank, which, he

[1] From Liverpool, Dec. 12, 1814 : *Lond. MSS., Appendix*, p. 543; and see Max. J. Kohler, *Jewish Rights at the Congresses of Vienna and Aix-la-Chapelle*, 18. This book has greatly illuminated this subject, as also Baron, *Die Jüdenfrage auf dem Wiener Kongress*. For later action of Castlereagh, see my *Castlereagh 1815–1822*, 169.

[2] *Münster*, 233. Wellington to Bathurst, Sept. 22, 1814; from Wellington, March 3, 1815 : *Gurwood*, xii. 123, 264; March 24, 1815 : *F.O. Continent*, 14. From Clancarty, March 11, 1815 : *C.C.* x. 266; April 15, 1815 : *F.O. Continent*, 17. D'Angeberg, *Congrès de Vienne*, 949.

said, when the Committee was appointed, was likely to raise as many problems as it solved. In this he was quite mistaken, for the Committee drew up a set of rules which destroyed much unwholesome lumber regarding "precedence," which had been a frequent cause of disputes in the past and had even on occasion led to war. Perhaps he was influenced by the fact that the salutes which Britain claimed as a recognition of her supremacy on the narrow seas might be endangered. At any rate, when this question was brought before the Committee, the British Admiralty, when consulted, would not budge. "England has always claimed the sovereign dominion of the British seas," affirmed My Lords; and in deference to their view the Congress took no further action.[1]

[1] D'Angeberg, *Congrès de Vienne*, 735. From Castlereagh, Jan. 12, 1815 : *F.O. Continent*, 11. Lords of the Admiralty to Bathurst, Feb. 7, 1815 : *F.O. Great Britain*, 26. From Wellington, March 25, 1815 : " In consequence of our refusing to agree to any arrangement regarding naval salutes and explaining that our practice was by no means objectionable, all mention of that point is omitted." *W.S.D.* ix. 616. The claim was, however, abandoned in 1818.

4. THE GUARANTEE OF THE NEW EUROPE

THE reconstruction of Europe in Castlereagh's mind had always been associated with the idea of some special guarantee of the new order. This idea he had, like so many others, inherited from Pitt. The vague suggestions advanced by Russia in 1804 had been crystallised by Pitt in a paragraph which emphasised the necessity of "giving solidity and permanence" to the new system, by "a treaty to which all the principal Powers of Europe should be parties, by which their respective rights and possessions, as they then have been established, shall be fixed and recognised; and they should all bind themselves mutually to protect and support each other against any attempt to infringe them."

The idea of 'guarantee' when new territorial arrangements were made was, of course, an old one. One Power had often guaranteed the possession of a particular piece of territory to another. It was a promise constantly demanded, often conceded, and, it must be added, often broken. The originality of the proposal lay in the guarantee by all the Powers of Europe of the whole of the European settlement, which was to be comprised in one comprehensive treaty. Though it was intended, of course, mainly as a safeguard against Napoleonic France, whose power then dominated all Europe, its universality brought a new conception into European politics.[1]

Castlereagh had now carried out nearly the whole of the

---

[1] Official communication to the Russian Ambassador, Jan. 19, 1805 : B.D. 393–94. On the history and theory of the idea of guarantee, see Sir E. Satow, "Pacta sunt servanda," and Sir James Headlam-Morley, " Treaties of Guarantee," in the *Cambridge Historical Journal*, vol. i. No. 3, and vol. ii. No. 2, the latter reprinted in his *Studies in Diplomatic History*.

reconstruction foreshadowed in the dispatch, and if we remember that ten years had passed, it is a testimony both to Pitt's foresight as well as his own statesmanship that the new map of Europe should bear so close a resemblance to that which Pitt had designed before he rolled it up after the catastrophe of Austerlitz. It was the moment, therefore, for Castlereagh to complete the scheme of his master by some special guarantee, such as that which Pitt had proposed. The idea was convenient to him also, because the Tsar, doubtless as a result of what he had learnt of the secret treaty, was anxious to renew the Treaty of Chaumont, while Metternich and Talleyrand would have liked, before being left to face Russia and Prussia with the question of Murat still on their hands, to transform the treaty of January 3 into a more permanent alliance. Both these suggestions implied a division of Europe into opposing camps, which was the last thing Castlereagh desired. He proposed, therefore, to the Tsar "that the best alliance that could be formed in the present state of Europe was that the Powers who had made the peace should by a public declaration at the close of the Congress announce to Europe whatever difference of opinion may have existed in details, their determination to uphold and support the arrangement agreed upon; and, further, their determination to unite their influence, and, if necessary, their arms, against the Power that should attempt to disturb it." The idea of guarantee was thus used by him not only as a weapon against the aggressor but also as a means to unite Europe, and to prevent it from breaking up into separate groups.

The facile pen of Gentz was used to draw up the proposed declaration. It was hardly one of his best papers, but Castlereagh was able to report that the draft was accepted by the Tsar and the Ministers of the other Powers. Castlereagh considered the question, therefore, as practically decided, and indeed announced in a circular dispatch that "there is every prospect of the Congress terminating with *a general accord and guarantee* between the Great Powers of Europe, with a determination to support the arrangement agreed upon, and to turn the general influence, and, if necessary, the general arms, against the Power that shall first attempt to disturb the continental peace." [1]

The guarantee was, it should be noticed, confined to the continent of Europe. It did not extend to the British Empire. But there was one portion of Europe which was outside the Vienna Treaties, but which was now considered by both Britain and Austria as especially needing protection. This was the Ottoman Empire, whose representative at Vienna had been constantly asking for support against Russia, whilst similar demands were being made to the Austrian and British Ambassadors at Constantinople. The Porte knew that the hastily signed treaty of Bucharest was irksome to Russia, who had never given back the cessions in Asia promised in that instrument and was pressing her right of entry into the Black Sea, while the Porte was also afraid of Russian interference in the military action then being prosecuted against her rebellious subjects in Serbia.

It is doubtful whether it was to Metternich or to Castlereagh that the idea first occurred of bringing the Ottoman dominions within the general guarantee, which would then embrace all Europe, but at any rate it was Castlereagh who made the proposal to the Tsar. It may be doubted if this practical application of the general principles to which Alexander had so warmly subscribed was very welcome, but he made no objection. He made, however, the stipulation that all outstanding difficulties between Turkey and Russia should be first reviewed—an indispensable measure, indeed, if a frontier was to be guaranteed. For this purpose he was ready to accept the mediation of Austria, France, and Britain at Constantinople. Instructions were therefore sent to the Austrian and British representatives at Constantinople to urge the Sultan to take advantage of the opportunity and settle his disputes with the Tsar. Castlereagh's sense of the

---

[1] To Liverpool, Feb. 13, 1815 ; Circular Letter, Feb. 13, 1815 : *B.D.* 305, 307. Stewart to Burghersh, Feb. 17, 1815 : " Castlereagh got a guarantee from the Emperor as to Turkey previous to his departure ; this is a great point. . . . I send you the project of the Declaration at the close of Congress. It is an outline ; how far it will be ultimately *fiated* I know not. . . . It is vain for Europe to hope for a long peace while Russia is on the Oder," Rachel Weigall, *Correspondence of Lord Burghersh*, 99–100. Gentz declared that the Tsar was moved to tears when Castlereagh read the draft to him (F. von Gentz, *Tagebücher*, i. 443).

importance of the proposal is shewn by the fact that only
one hour before he left Vienna he saw Mavrojeni, the Porte's
representative there, and tried to impress upon him the
necessity for action, though he was aware that such a settlement would probably require more time than would elapse
before the Vienna Treaty was signed.   Nesselrode had, moreover, already prepared for his master a long memorandum,
which demanded the intervention of the Powers to put a stop
to the atrocities the Turks were inflicting on the Serbs, and
which incidentally approved Russian rights to interfere in
the Balkans in the name of humanity on the same footing as
Britain's championship of the cause of the Negro.   Wellington's attention was drawn to this subject at the very moment
of Castlereagh's departure, but he asked that it be deferred
"till the period at which the Powers should guarantee the
dominions of the Porte." [1]

Both Liston and the representatives of Austria and France
pressed the Sultan to accept the Tsar's offer—but in vain.
The British Ambassador alone had any influence with the
Sultan's Cabinet; but though he did his best with repeated
messages, he admitted that the Russian territorial claims
were no mere frontier rectifications, but a consolidation
of her power between the Caspian and the Black Sea, which
the Porte might well regard as a serious advance.   The
bargain would none the less, of course, have been well
worth the sacrifice, and some of the Sultan's Ministers were
anxious to accept it, but the Sultan himself refused to submit
to arbitration, even of friendly Powers, his sovereignty over
Turkish territory, and the chance was lost.   The Grand
Vizir and the Mufti, who had pressed for acceptance, were
dismissed, and the Reis Effendi was able to inform Liston,
to whom alone an answer was sent, that the Sultan's Cabinet
were unanimous in rejection.   All this occurred before the

[1] From Liston, Jan. 10, 1815: *F.O.* (95) *Misc.* 23.   Gentz, *Dépêches inédites*,
121, 142 : " Reports of an eventual attack by the Allies upon the Ottoman
Empire continue to be transmitted to this capital by the Prince of Walla-
chia" and others, says Liston.   To Liston, Feb. 14, 1815: *B.D.* 305.
Report of Mavrojeni, Feb. 15, 1815 : Fournier, *Die Geheimpolizei*, 411.
From Wellington, Feb. 25, 1815 : *W.S.D.* ix. 580.   A précis of Nesselrode's
memorandum is given in F. Marten's *Recueil des Traités conclus par la
Russie*, iii. 177–80, but Stern (*Geschichte Europas*, i. 273) is right in suspecting
that it was never communicated formally to the other Powers.

news of Bonaparte's return reached Constantinople. After that there was no possibility of renewing the negotiation, for the Turks obviously rejoiced in his threat to Europe, and hoped to enhance their own position in the conflict that would ensue.

Napoleon's return had obviously also an effect on the main proposition, the final fate of which still lies in some obscurity. Probably when he got back to London Castlereagh found his Cabinet not very anxious to accept the responsibility of guaranteeing the frontiers of all Europe. At any rate, when Gentz's declaration was reproduced in the Press—not, Gentz claimed, by his own fault—and Castlereagh was questioned in the House about it, he refused to admit that it was an official document.[1]

In the discussions at Vienna only two states had obtained a guarantee—Switzerland and Prussia, for her new Saxon possessions, the former because of her neutralisation, the latter apparently as a strategic makeweight to obtain her consent to the partition of Saxony. To the demand of Bavaria, however, for a special guarantee of her territory by the Great Powers, as the price of her acceptance of the treaty of March 25, Clancarty refused to agree, though some of his colleagues viewed it favourably, because he considered "that a guarantee on our part is looked upon by us in a light very different from that in which a guarantee is regarded by most other Powers," and the obligation therefore too onerous to undertake. When Pfeffel, at the orders of his Court, pressed the same request on Castlereagh, it was refused on more general grounds as likely to impair rather than confirm the general system of Europe. He could not even venture to propose to Parliament, Castlereagh asserted, such a guarantee for Hanover.[2]

Nevertheless the idea of a general guarantee of the treaty persisted. On May 25 a Russian circular to all the missions, drawn up on the Emperor's departure to headquarters,

---

[1] From Liston, March 10, 25, April 10, 1815; Liston to Wellington, March 25, April 4, 1815: *F.O.* (95) *Misc.* 23; Klinkowström, *Oesterreichs Theilnahme*, 530.

[2] From Clancarty, April 3, 1815: *F.O. Continent*, 17. Pfeffel to the King of Bavaria, May 26–27, 1815: *Munich St. A.*

announced "that the Cabinets intend to establish the inviolability of the acts of the Congress by reciprocal guarantees" on the initiative of Britain. Though it was admitted that the issue must be considered doubtful, yet the principle behind it was inherent in those which inspired the reconstruction of Europe.

But such an announcement implied at least that the new settlement should be contained in one comprehensive document affecting all the states of Europe. Yet just at this moment the Russians were urging that no general instrument need be drawn up at Vienna. After Napoleon's return the arrangements as regards Poland, Saxony, etc., had been put into separate treaties and signed by the Powers concerned. If they were not united in a single instrument, each Power would only be responsible for the territories with which it was specially concerned, and have no responsibility for the frontiers of Europe as a whole. Doubtless the desire to have done with negotiation and join in the military measures now proceeding apace influenced the Russians, who were the foremost advocates of dispensing with one general treaty; but Clancarty suspected, and perhaps with good reason, that they wished also to avoid putting their signature to various long controverted decisions, especially some of those concerning Italy. At any rate, it was Clancarty who, warmly supported by the Prussians, insisted on drawing up a great treaty to include the whole settlement, and it was he and Humboldt, with the indispensable assistance of Gentz, who carried out the laborious work of drafting it. By this means every Power which signed the treaty became associated with the whole of it, and, though this did not mean a guarantee, it was at any rate a recognition of the fact that all were interested in the whole of Europe, and prevented anyone from weakening any particular part of the work by refusing its consent —unless, indeed, like Spain it refused to sign at all. The point was only won by the assiduity of Clancarty. Until the last moment he was in doubt whether the signature of the Tsar's Ministers could be obtained, for they professed themselves unable to affix it without the express consent of their master. Eventually his taunts and expostulations induced them to send a courier post-haste to the Tsar, and their signature was affixed eight days after the others.[1]

In these last days the question of the general guarantee also came up once more; for amongst the documents which Castlereagh laid before Parliament to justify his proceedings at Vienna was Pitt's famous paper with such omissions as the changes made in the map of Europe dictated. This attracted apparently but little attention in Britain, where all interest was now concentrated on the approaching struggle with Napoleon. But the paper included the suggestion as to guarantee, and Clancarty, who noted that the rest of the document had been fulfilled in the treaty which he had just drawn up, sounded the Russians as to whether provisions for the questions of general guarantee, the re-establishment of public law, and the securities of general tranquillity should not be included in it. Apparently he was quite unaware of the original idea of guarantee by declaration. At any rate he makes no reference to it in the private account which he sent to Castlereagh. Though he had little hope of success, since the Russian Ministers were not likely to act without the consent of the Tsar, which could hardly be obtained in time, he thought the opportunity favourable to obtain information "as to what might be their Emperor's feelings upon propositions of this nature." The result was what he expected. Nesselrode said that he viewed the matter favourably, but time was too short to dispose of it.

This account, the authenticity of which cannot be disputed since it was written in a private letter to his chief by the most loyal of subordinates, makes it all the more difficult to understand why a few days later Nesselrode, at the orders of the Tsar in a dispatch to Lieven, inspired like all those he wrote from Vienna with the profoundest distrust of British policy, should throw on Clancarty the responsibility of abandoning the idea of a guarantee which had been originally proposed by Castlereagh. He suspected, he said, that in conjunction with Austria and France, Britain was returning to the ideas of the "old diplomacy" and special and secret

---

[1] Projet d'instruction generale pour les missions de S.M.I., May 28, 1815: Shilder, *Life of Alexander I.*, iii. 540–48. From Clancarty, May 26, June 10, 1815: *Lond. MSS.*; June 10, 19, 23, 27, 1815: *F.O. Continent*, 19.

alliances on the model of that of January 3. Clancarty's
proposals appeared to the Emperor therefore as deliberately
intended to emasculate the idea of a general guarantee of the
settlement such as Russia had desired, and to be attributed
to the personal policy of dislike to Russia now being pursued
at London, an idea which was developed in another dispatch
of the same date. This dispatch, written on June 17, shews
what jealousies existed, to be brought to the surface had
Napoleon won at Waterloo. That the same idea was given
to others is shewn by Gentz's account to the Hospodar that
both Russia and Britain opposed the guarantee at this time,
insinuating, with his usual skill, that the Russians were inspired
by the fear that the Ottoman dominions might ultimately be
included in the benefits of the treaty.[1]

Thus the project failed completely, and we may suppose,
though direct evidence is lacking, that Castlereagh by now
did not regret the fact. At any rate, at some date after his
return he completely changed his mind on this subject. He
refused to insert a similar clause in the Treaty of Alliance
which closed the second Paris Conference. By this time it
was once more France against whom the defence of Europe
had to be concentrated, and the Treaty of Alliance of March 25,
though only a partial renewal of the Treaty of Chaumont,
seemed to point the way. As will be seen, it was along the direction of conference rather than of guarantee that Castlereagh's
idea of maintaining world peace were henceforth to move.

Nevertheless, the proposal here put forward was to have its
effects in the future and in a manner often disconcerting to
Castlereagh himself. It put into the Tsar's mind the idea
of the Holy Alliance. It inspired also ideas of territorial
guarantee which Castlereagh found most embarrassing at the
Conference of Aix-la-Chapelle. The project was, moreover,
never completely lost in the spasmodic discussions of the organisation of peace, which persisted throughout the nineteenth
century, and it has survived in full force into our own time.

---

[1] The parts of the dispatch laid before Parliament is shewn in *B.D.* From
Clancarty, June 10, 1815: *Lond. MSS.* Nesselrode to Lieven, June 17, 1815:
Pet. Arch.; Gentz, *Dépêches inédites*, 165–66, 198–99. Talleyrand claims some
credit for defeating the idea of inserting the guarantee at this time, since,
though good in itself, it would have delayed the signing of the treaty, a step
indispensable to Louis XVIII.'s interests. Pallain, *Corres. inédite*, 457–59.

CHAPTER VIII

THE SECOND PEACE OF PARIS: RECONSTRUCTION RECONSIDERED, MARCH–NOVEMBER 1815

1. THE SECOND RESTORATION.

2. THE PUNISHMENT OF FRANCE.

3. FROM GUARANTEE TO CONFERENCE.

4. CASTLEREAGH AND RECONSTRUCTION.

" Victories are never so complete that the victor can disregard all considerations whatsoever, more especially considerations of justice."— MACHIAVELLI.

CHAPTER VIII

1. THE SECOND RESTORATION

CASTLEREAGH had scarcely reached London when news came of the landing of Bonaparte upon the coast of France, which resulted in the triumphal march on Paris and the ignominious flight of the Royal Family. This amazing overthrow simplified some of his problems. It prevented the Opposition from devoting all their energies to the criticism of the decisions made at Vienna, so that some of the most important of them were never debated seriously in Parliament. It helped to solve the delicate question of Murat, and it threw a merciful cloud over such quixotic transactions as that concerning the Russian-Dutch loan, which Castlereagh was hard put to defend before his own countrymen.

But it brought with it problems of the greatest complexity, which could only be solved by an extraordinary display of patience, energy, and foresight. Rarely does Castlereagh shew to better advantage as a statesman than during the Hundred Days and the peace which followed it—that is, if once his fundamental principles of the necessity of the overthrow of Napoleon, the restoration of the Bourbons, and the prevention of a revengeful peace be accepted. In only the first of these was he supported by his countrymen, and even then there was a considerable minority on the other side; on the second they were apathetic; while on the third he had to overcome the determined resistance of the Cabinet, which was supported by nearly the whole of public opinion in Britain.

The British Government were less responsible than any other of the Allies for the Treaty of Fontainebleau, which made Napoleon an independent sovereign in the island of

Elba, with the title of Emperor, a pension from France, and even a small army of 1200 men. But since they guarded the seas, they were held both by Napoleon himself and by the rest of the world as specially responsible for his safety. In fact, neither they nor anyone else had any legal right of surveillance over Elba, and Sir Neil Campbell, who remained at Napoleon's request when the other allied officers returned to their homes, was no more than a guest while he was there. Nevertheless, he was as an observer in a situation the responsibility of which he hardly seems to have realised. Certainly he never penetrated the scheme which Napoleon must have had in his mind almost as soon as he set foot on the island. He discussed with him the reports of dissensions at Vienna and discontent in France as if these events could have no influence on the Emperor's future. He praised his extraordinary cheerfulness even amidst the financial worries which the refusal of the Bourbons to pay the pension inflicted on Napoleon and his Court. Gradually his absences grew longer. He disliked his anomalous situation and thought that he could perform his duty better by occasional visits to Elba, an opinion in which he persisted in spite of the protests of Lord Burghersh and Edward Cooke.[1]

Meanwhile the Bourbons at Paris and many statesmen at Vienna were in dread of Napoleon, and unofficial proposals of many kinds were made that he should be removed to a safer place. Talleyrand of course desired it. The Prussians put it in their programme for the Congress. Münster was always a warm advocate of the idea. But it was never officially discussed, and it is quite certain that the Tsar would never have allowed his treaty to be broken, while there is not the slightest evidence that either Castlereagh or Metternich would have taken a different view. All that could be

---

[1] From Campbell, Dec. 25, 28, 1814: *F.O. Tuscany*, 22. From Burghersh, March 3, 1815 (strongly condemning Campbell's conduct): R. Weigall, *Corres. of Lord Burghersh*, 108. Campbell himself in his diary says that Cooke pooh-poohed the idea of danger and told him to inform Bonaparte, " *Nobody thinks of him at all. He is quite forgotten— as much as if he had never existed.*" Neil Campbell, *Napoleon at Fontainebleau and Elba*, 362–63. Castlereagh entirely exonerated Campbell both publicly in the House and in a letter recommending him for employment to the Duke. But he was always the last to condemn a subordinate for faults in which the Government shared. He never sought a scapegoat.

done by Napoleon's enemies was to organise a system of espionage which seems to have been more than usually inept. Italy was regarded as the natural place for him to appeal to, and his relations with Murat were especially watched. Napoleon was naturally cognisant both of the espionage and of the rumours of his removal from Elba, which were freely canvassed in the Press, and he told Campbell that he would resist any such attempt by force.

He had at any rate, as Castlereagh was acutely aware, a legitimate grievance in the fact that no money was paid to him by France. When Talleyrand took no notice of his protests at Vienna, Castlereagh pressed the matter strongly at Paris on his way home. "I cannot leave Paris," he wrote to Blacas, "without once more urging the importance of taking some immediate measure towards fulfilling the engagements made to Napoleon in April last, under such temporary modifications as the nature of his own conduct and the unsettled state of Italy may for the present suggest and justify upon principles of precaution, but which I am confident you would wish to combine with a liberal attention to Napoleon's personal comforts and ease in the retirement assigned to him." [1]

But while this letter was being written Napoleon was nearing the coast of France. His final resolution seems to have been determined on February 13 by the news of Jacobin plots against the Bourbons which might anticipate his own plans. He had already lost the golden opportunity to take advantage of the dissensions of the Allies, but so far as France was concerned the time was fully ripe. On March 1 he landed near Cannes, and in nineteen days Louis, deserted by almost the whole of the army and with no support from the people,

---

[1] To Blacas, Feb. 28, 1814 : *F.O. Continent*, 12. *Cf.* Pallain, *Corres. inédite*, 307. For Talleyrand's actions at Vienna see Pallain, *Corres. inédite*, 72, 171, 288. No weight can be attached to his statement that Castlereagh agreed to the removal of Napoleon, which is without any confirmation from other sources, though Houssaye (*1815*, 169) and others have accepted it. They have found it difficult to reconcile this view with Castlereagh's action on the money question, which resulted in Blacas dispatching a confidential envoy to Napoleon to settle the question of funds (to Sir Neil Campbell, Feb. 28, 1815 : *F.O. Continent*, 12), a fact which appears to have escaped the notice of historians. Blacas had always pressed for Napoleon's removal. (From Stuart, July 11, 1814 : *F.O. France*, 98.) See also *Münster*, 186.

fled with his Court and one or two faithful generals to Lille and then to Belgium.

The overthrow was too sudden and complete for any aid to be sent to the King. Blacas did, indeed, ask Fitzroy Somerset to send for the British troops in Belgium, but the British *chargé d'affaires* evaded a proposal which he thought would do the Bourbons more harm than good. Even the rumour of it produced bad effects. Castlereagh approved this action and urged Louis to defend himself. He hoped that the report was true that the King would retire to Bordeaux rather than to Belgium, if Paris was menaced. "Make His Majesty feel," he wrote on the 16th, "that the possibility of any movement in his favour must depend on the degree of support his own army and people give him. The Powers of Europe can assist the French nation and its lawful sovereign to restore peace, order, and obedience, but they cannot invade France to restore him if he is betrayed or abandoned by his own troops and subjects. Which God forbid!" As he explained to Wellington, for the information of the sovereigns at Vienna, while it was essential to assemble powerful forces on the Rhine to intimidate France, it was necessary to act with great caution as regards any declaration of the end for which the Allies were to fight; "although interference on the part of the Great Powers of Europe would, in the judgment of His Majesty's Government, be both wise and necessary at the instance of the King and his Government, if sustained by an adequate national support, yet, consistent with the principles on which the Allies have hitherto acted, it would be a very different question to march into France for the purpose of restoring a sovereign who had been betrayed and abandoned by his own troops and subjects." [1]

The betrayal and abandonment were, however, soon complete, and Britain and Europe were faced once more by a Napoleon on the throne of France. At Vienna the Powers instinctively drew together at the first news of the escape,

[1] From Fitzroy Somerset, March 9, 14, 16, 17, 20, 1815; to Fitzroy Somerset, March 16, 1815: *F.O. France*, 113. To Wellington, March 16, 1815: *W.S.D.* ix. 598. He used similar words to Lieven (Lieven to Nesselrode, March 18, 1815: *Pet. Arch.*).

and, though there were some sharp words exchanged as to
the responsibility for it, there was never a shadow of doubt as
to the attitude to be taken towards Napoleon himself. His
destination was unknown (Talleyrand was certain it was to
Italy), but as soon as it was revealed, a declaration was issued
by the Eight Powers which signed the Treaty of Paris deliver-
ing Napoleon to the "public vengeance." Preparations were
immediately made to assemble armies for the invasion of
France, if Napoleon succeeded; and Alexander, on whom the
main responsibility for Elba lay, offered to appoint himself
Generalissimo of the whole. Fortunately the Duke was able
to stop this design before it caused much alarm, and the old
device of a Supreme War Council was re-established. When
Napoleon sent to the Tsar the secret treaty of January 3,
which had been left in the Archives, it had no effect on his
conduct, though he affected great indignation and intimated
his displeasure to Wellington through Pozzo di Borgo.

Wellington was pressed on all hands for new subsidies, and
when it was found he had no authority to grant them urgent
demands were sent to London, each Power having cogent
reasons why it should be preferred above the others. Wellington had some trouble, therefore, in concluding a treaty on
the model of that of Chaumont, since the Allies appeared to
consider one without a subsidy hardly worth while. Moreover,
there was great rivalry for the control of the contingents of
the smaller Powers, the Prussians demanding a free hand in
north Germany outside of Hanover. However, the treaty
which bound each of the Four Powers to supply 150,000 men
against Napoleon was signed on March 25. Unlike that of
Chaumont, it applied to the present war only, its object being
to defend the new frontiers from Napoleon's attack, while it
was open to all the small Powers to join it, and all did so,
even if their zeal was not great, since it gave them some claim
to a subsidy, when such was forthcoming. Both the declaration and the treaty were signed before it was known that
Louis had fled from France. There could not have been,
therefore, in any case reference to an intention to replace
him on the throne, though he was invited by the treaty to
co-operate with the Allies against Napoleon. But after his

flight both Clancarty and Münster, fanatically desirous of
supporting Louis, were much concerned at this omission,
which it was soon seen was very significant.[1]

For although all negotiation with Napoleon was refused, it
was apparent that the Tsar at any rate had no great desire
to see the Bourbons return. Moreover, Talleyrand himself
was lukewarm, and after Montrond, an emissary of Fouché's,
had been received by Metternich, it was suggested that a new
declaration should be drawn up expressly affirming that there
was no intention of imposing a particular dynasty on France.
This was to be done with the object of conciliating the Jacobins
and undermining Napoleon's power, and the proposal was
warmly supported by the Tsar. Clancarty was eager in
defence of the legitimate interests of Louis XVIII., on behalf
of which he moved an amendment. He defended his action
in an interview with Alexander, who shewed himself favourable to the Duke of Orleans or even to a republic, though he
took care this time to exclude any idea of substitution of
another marshal in Napoleon's place. Clancarty had strangely
enough been left in ignorance by Wellington of Castlereagh's
opinion, expressed in the early stages of the struggle, that the
Bourbons could not be openly supported. Many of the
smaller sovereigns accepted Clancarty's view, and Münster
was vehement in favour of the Bourbons and described
Alexander to the Prince Regent as a greater danger than
Napoleon himself. The Tsar had declared, he said, that he
would remember the treaty of January 3, and who knew what
the future would bring forth. Stewart was equally emphatic
on the subject of the 'intrigue' and 'devilment' at Vienna.
"The Emperor of Russia hates all the Bourbons," he wrote to
Burghersh, "and is convinced they cannot reign in France."
The whole matter was held up, and news now reached Clancarty which shewed him how little he had understood the
position of his country, while Münster was reduced to an

---

[1] From Wellington, March 12, 1815: *B.D.* 312; March 12, 25, 1815:
Gurwood, xii. 266, 278. Münster to the Prince Regent, March 11, 1815:
Hanover St. A.; March 18, 25, 1815: *Münster*, 226, 232. Bavaria
demanded to sign the treaty as a principal and not an acceding party in
order to obtain an equal right with the Great Powers to subsidies. From
Clancarty, April 3, 1815: *F.O. Continent*, 17. Spain took a similar
attitude: D'Angeberg, *Congrès de Vienne*, 1457.

almost tearful resignation at the attitude which circumstances had forced his royal master to adopt.[1]

For the position of the British Government had been made exceptionally difficult when it was realised that the King had fled. No more than in 1814 could they announce that they would fight to restore Louis XVIII. Indeed, though the Government from the first had no hesitation about the necessity of overthrowing Napoleon, they had to move with the greatest circumspection in order to make the war a popular one, and enable them to put forward their whole strength. It was true that the Opposition was divided; for, though Grey and Whitbread were for peace, the Grenvilles and Grattan parted company with them. Wellesley, however, to general surprise, was on the pacific side, and a false step might have led public opinion to recoil before the expenditure of blood and treasure which a new struggle with France must involve. It was, above all, necessary to make the war one against Napoleon, and to imply that the French people were betrayed by their army and wanted to be rid of him. Thus no notice was taken of Napoleon's overtures and letters, which were sent unopened to Vienna. But war was not declared against France. Indeed, Eldon confessed when the struggle was over that he still did not know against whom Britain had been fighting.

This led to some strange consequences. The militia, for example, could not be called out, since peace was not yet broken, and there were other difficulties as to French commerce and French possessions overseas. But it made one thing absolutely certain. Britain could not declare for Louis XVIII. Indeed, the mild words of the treaty of March 25 were too strong for the Government, and they only ratified

[1] From Clancarty, April 8, 1815: *Lond. MSS.*; April 15, 1815 (3 dispatches): *B.D.* 324, 325; *F.O. Continent*, 17. Münster to the Prince Regent, April 12, 1815: *Münster*, 243; April [25], 1815: *Hanover St. A.* Stewart to Burghersh, April 15, 1815: R. Weigall, *Corres. of Lord Burghersh*, 175. While the Tsar seemed to Clancarty very hostile to a Regency, Metternich was assuring Merveldt for Castlereagh's information that Alexander preferred a Regency to Orleans (Metternich to Merveldt, April 21, 1815: *F.O. Austria*, 123); but there can be no doubt that Russian hostility to the Bourbons was as great as in 1814. Clancarty (May 8, 1815: *Lond. MSS.*) explains that the Duke took away with him several of Castlereagh's dispatches, including the vital one of March 16 on avoiding open support of the Bourbons.

it with a reservation that it was not to be understood "as binding His Britannic Majesty to prosecute the war with a view to imposing on France any particular Government." Even then the treaty was kept secret, but rumours began to leak out. In Parliament, Whitbread and his colleagues naturally tried to make the most of the anomaly and to force the Government to expose their hand. But Castlereagh evaded his dilemmas with considerable skill. The task of Britain and Europe was to overthrow Napoleon, he reiterated, knowing that the hatred and fear of him was the only cause which would secure the unity of the country, and he left the responsibility for the declaration of war on the Allies, whom Britain would support but not drive into hostilities.[1]

But there was no doubt in the minds of the Government as to their actions. Preparations were made for war on the widest scale. "If we are to undertake the job," wrote Castlereagh to Wellington, when news of the King's flight came, "we must leave nothing to chance. It must be done on the largest scale . . . you must inundate France with force in all directions." Five million pounds were promised to the three Great Powers, to be paid monthly so long as the war lasted. The British army was harder to recreate. Unfortunately many of Wellington's veterans were still in America, and it was with the greatest difficulty and at the risk of denuding Ireland that the British troops in the Netherlands could be raised to 40,000 men. But the military provisions of the treaty of March 25 were instantly accepted, and two million pounds were assigned to raise 100,000 men from the smaller Powers to bring up the British contingent to the stipulated number. This task was entrusted to Wellington as well as the command of the army in the Netherlands, a double burden which he

---

[1] To Wellington, March 26, 1815 : *C.C.* x. 285. See Eldon's analysis in *Bathurst*, 378. Hansard, *Commons*, April 7, 1815 : of which Hardy has given a brilliant and faithful summary in *The Dynasts*, Part III. Act V. Scene 5. Wellington's opinion, given in reply to one of the queries of the Cabinet, was : " I should say that the Allies are in an intermediate state between war and peace " (Duke of Wellington's reply to the Queries, *F.O. Cont. Arch.* 7). Lieven to Nesselrode, April 12, 1815 : *Pet. Arch.* Horner, who agreed with Grey on all points, admitted that the " question was a very difficult one, and upon which different views may be taken, even by those who are most agreed upon political principles and objects " (Horner, *Corres.*, ii. 249). The British reservation is given in *B.F.S.P.* ii. 450.

cheerfully assumed and executed with much diplomatic, if little financial, skill. The Cabinet sent Wellesley Pole and Harrowby to consult with him as soon as he arrived in Brussels, with a list of eighteen queries, covering the whole diplomatic and strategic situation. Wellington's answers, models as usual of concise and illuminating information, did much to clear the mind of the Cabinet. But the Duke had first to create his army. It was not easy to find recruiting grounds, for the two German Powers were his competitors for command of the German contingents; but Hanover and the Netherlands supplied the nucleus, and the Duke, at first, even hoped to bring troops from Portugal, though not too many lest Spain should succumb to temptation if her neighbour and rival was made too weak.[1]

These measures needed, of course, the assent of Parliament, and provided the Opposition with further opportunities of challenging the Government's policy. But though they could make an excellent logical case against the Government's contention that they were fighting Napoleon and not France, they were reduced to a pitiful minority. Only the *Morning Chronicle* supported Napoleon, who in gratitude supplied it with documents on the activities of Castlereagh at the Congress, drawn from the French archives. But these tactics produced but little effect. The Property Tax was reinstituted, and the huge credits necessary for the coming campaign, in which the whole of Europe was to be once more in British pay, were voted by overwhelming majorities.

All this had to be done gradually as an assistance to a Europe already determined to make war on Napoleon. Caution was necessary, as Castlereagh explained to the exiled King, who was impatient at the delay. " It is essential to the interests of Europe," he told Sir Charles Stuart, "that the

---

[1] Wellington to Beresford, March 24, 1815 : *C.C.* x. 323. The Portuguese Regency, however, declined to act, and thus no Portuguese troops shared the honours of Waterloo. To Clancarty, April 12, 1815 : *C.C.* x. 305. To Wellington, April 13, 1815 : *W.S.D.* x. 70. The queries are given in *W.S.D.* x. 36, followed by Harrowby's account of the answers, which differs considerably from Wellington's written replies in *F.O. Continent*, 14. Pfeffel (April 14, 1815) suggested that the dispatch of the two Ministers was due to a desire to counter Wellesley's criticisms of the Ministry, designed to make mischief between them and the Duke (*Munich St. A.*).

public opinion of Great Britain should be kept together. Without a conviction of the necessity of the war in the sober judgment of the Continent we should soon have a Peace Party here, as we had in the early years of the war before last, which would soon disqualify us, augmented as the public burthens are, from giving our Allies an effectual support." The treaty, with its ratification, had now to be published, for copies had appeared on the Continent, though the wording was softened somewhat in Louis' interest. "I am, upon the whole, glad we have been driven to this disclosure," it was explained to the Duke, " although somewhat irregular, as we wanted some incident to bring up the tone of Parliament to the true point. . . . Now Whitbread must either acquiesce in our line or be obliged to attack us, by moving, under circumstances of disadvantage, a peace Address." This policy had considerable effect. The Opposition had to transfer their attack to the methods rather than the objects of the Ministers, and Grey, who had opposed the war in the conviction that it would result in bankruptcy for Britain, confessed to the Bavarian Minister that he had been too ardent in the cause of peace. Castlereagh was well pleased with the result after the debate on April 28. "I never saw a more satisfactory tone," he told Clancarty, "than last night in the House of Commons. We managed well by giving Whitbread his document, to throw upon him the onus of advising against war. His interference is an admirable ally. Rely upon it, nothing but the temperans of our line would have given us the support we received last night. For the Continent and *with* the Continent the nation will fight, but the abstract question of war would have split us in fragments." [1]

In theory, therefore, the British Government was merely engaged in a crusade against Napoleon as part of a united Europe, and in no sense pledged to support the King. In fact no other Government desired so much the return of

[1] To Wellington, April 24, 1815 ; from Wellington, April 21, 1815 : *W.S.D.* x. 147, 124. To Stuart, April 19, 1815 : *Lond. MSS., Appendix,* p. 544. To Clancarty, April 29, 1815 : *Lond. MSS.* Pfeffel to the King of Bavaria, April 14 ; to Montgelas, April 21, 1815 : *Munich St. A.* Grey's second peace speech was never delivered. See G. M. Trevelyan, *Lord Grey of the Reform Bill,* 175.

Louis XVIII. or did so much to ensure it. From the first
Castlereagh made it clear to the Foreign Ambassadors that
his speeches in Parliament did not mean that the Government
had deserted Louis. On the contrary, he continued to urge
the Bourbon claims upon them from the moment he learnt
that Napoleon had reached Paris, reiterating his opinion that
Louis' restoration was essential to the safety of Europe. One
of his first actions was to recommend that a sharp watch be
kept on the young Napoleon, and that all suspected persons
be removed from his entourage. The Prince Regent was even
more emphatic on the side of his protégés, and told Merveldt
that he could not admit the possibility of making a peace
without restoring Louis to the throne of his ancestors.

The Prince Regent, however, as Merveldt pointed out, had
no more influence now than in 1814. It was Castlereagh who
was the real protagonist of the restoration. It was suspected
by some of the foreign representatives that he had not the
entire support of the Cabinet, and was only sustained by the
influence of the Prince Regent. This explained, it was said,
the contradiction between the public and private policy of the
Foreign Minister. But there is no real evidence for this view.
Castlereagh, from the first, and all his colleagues appear to
have been united on the question of opposing Bonaparte and
restoring the Bourbons if it were possible. But it was
Castlereagh who pursued the latter object by every possible
means. If the restoration of 1814 was shared with Talleyrand,
that of 1815 was brought about almost entirely by the action
of Castlereagh himself, who from the first took the exiled King
under his secret protection and advice, and, aided by Wellington, placed him in a position to take advantage of the unexpected and unexampled triumph at Waterloo.[1]

Though the restoration of Louis appeared indispensable to
the cause of European peace, there were no illusions as to the
incapacity of the King and his advisers to play the rôle which
the British Government wished to assign to him. The Duke
and Duchess of Angoulême did indeed make an attempt to

[1] Merveldt to Metternich, March 23, 26, 1815 ; April 18, 24, 1815 ;
May 8, 1815 : *Vienna St. A.* Pozzo di Borgo to Nesselrode, March 18,
1815 : *Pet. Arch.* Pfeffel to the King of Bavaria, March 24, 31, April 7,
1815 : *Munich St. A.*

raise the south, which met with some response. But Louis
himself was suspected of wishing to flee to England *via* Ostend.
He settled down at Ghent, accompanied by his favourite
Blacas and one or two Ministers, and set up the pathetic
apparatus of an exiled Court with his usual dignity and
patience. Castlereagh from the first took Louis under his
protection. Money was supplied to the King, and arms and
equipment promised for any force that he raised from French
émigrés or deserters. When this attempt proved a failure,
funds were provided to recruit the Swiss Guards, who succeeded
in getting away from France. Louis was assured of the good
intentions of the British Government, and that their public
declarations were only to make the task of restoration easier.
Sir Charles Stuart, now Ambassador to the Netherlands, was
appointed British representative at the King's Court also,
this being a method least open to criticism.

Through Sir Charles Stuart, Castlereagh sent a never-
ceasing stream of advice. He wished Louis to get rid of the
emigrant courtiers—especially his favourite Blacas, who had
done him so much harm during the first restoration—and learn
the business of a constitutional king. He warned Stuart of
the obstacles in the way of the restoration and the necessity
of Louis altering his attitude towards France. Though
Pozzo di Borgo, who represented the Tsar, professed, and
sincerely, devotion to the Bourbon cause, reports from Vienna
shewed that his master was really far from being their friend.
Louis must, therefore, build up support in France itself, and
this could only be done by getting rid of his venal and incapable courtiers and substituting men who were really responsible Ministers. This became all the more necessary when
news arrived of the Jacobin approaches to Vienna and the
manner in which Talleyrand, and even Metternich, had seemed
to receive them. The choice, he admitted, was a painful one,
but it was better to rely on competent men of depraved
character like Talleyrand and Fouché than on corrupt fools
like the returned *émigrés*: "I agree with you and Charles," he
told Clancarty in a very intimate letter, "that Talleyrand
cannot be relied on, and yet I know not on whom H.M. can
better depend. He has not a chance in the hands of those

now around him. The fact is, France is a den of thieves and brigands, and they can only be governed by criminals like themselves. The King is too pure and honest to keep them in order, and yet if he was not crippled by his emigrant followers my conviction is that he commands more of the national confidence than either of his competitors for power." With this letter he sent a report of Wellington's which took the gloomiest view of Louis' chances of restoration, though Wellington was, like Castlereagh, fully convinced of its necessity.[1]

Louis agreed that some change was advisable, and he allowed Blacas to draw up a tentative Ministry as a preliminary to his own retirement. But he refused for some time even to consider the possibility of admitting Fouché to his favour, and still regarded his Ministers as his servants. There is something almost comic in the manner in which Castlereagh tries to teach Louis the duties of a constitutional king. The only chance of winning and maintaining the throne, he urged, was for Louis to accept any man as his Minister who commanded the confidence of the nation. He admitted the pain Louis must feel in accepting a regicide like Fouché, but after all he had appealed to him in the last desperate hours before the flight from Paris, and he could not be more averse to him "than our King was to receive Mr. Fox." The only way to control bad and ambitious men was to employ them to neutralise one another. Wellington was urged to assist Stuart in these lectures on political science. "The only chance Louis XVIII. has," Castlereagh told the Duke, "is to declare against any exclusion except that of Bonaparte, to employ the strongest man he can find for his Minister, and let him, at his own peril, compose his administration as best he can."

It was impossible, however, for Louis to alter his habits or his courtiers to overcome their vices. Special care had to be taken that the money sent for the arming of such troops as deserted to Louis should not stick in their fingers. Victor and Marmont left Ghent in disgust. The Comte d'Artois prepared to place himself at the head of the Royalist forces

---

[1] To Stuart, April 19, 24, 1815: *Lond. MSS., Appendix*, pp. 544–45. To Clancarty, April 29, 1815: *Lond. MSS.* From Wellington, April 24, 1815: *W.S.D.* x. 146; *Corres. du Comte de Jaucourt avec Talleyrand*, 307, 318.

and asked for assistance from Wellington. The latter, who was engaged in bitter disputes with the King of the Netherlands and full of pessimism at the delay in furnishing a reasonable army in the Netherlands, even accusing the British Government of apathy and lack of energy, yet treated these demands with great patience and courtesy, paying several visits to Ghent, while Castlereagh could only reiterate his previous warnings and urge the importance of getting Talleyrand from Vienna as soon as possible.[1]

Talleyrand shewed, however, no signs of appearing, and reports from Vienna continued to be unsatisfactory. The line of the Allies in public had indeed followed, as Castlereagh had expressly desired, the British reservation to the Treaty of March 25. They made counter-declarations of a similar nature, and at the same time they refused to have any dealings with Napoleon, imprisoned some of the envoys which he sent to them, and practically established a blockade of the land frontier of France. Clancarty was thus able to send to Castlereagh a dispatch specially composed for the edification of Parliament, which justified the line which he had taken in the earlier debates.

But the cause of the Bourbons was not supported in the private councils of the Allies. Talleyrand, though he asserted his faithfulness, expressed the greatest contempt for Louis' advisers, and said that he could not carry on a struggle against them at Ghent for the King's favour. He had already been reduced to beg money off Wellington, and it was doubtless with the motive of removing one cause of suspicion that Castlereagh authorised his brother to pay him two sums of £5000 out of the Secret Service funds. Though Cathcart as

[1] From Stuart, April 27, May 6, 1815 : La Malet, *Louis XVIII. et les Cent Jours à Gand*, ii. 73, 90. To Stuart, May 8, 1815 : (2 dispatches) *Lond. MSS., Appendix*, pp. 545-48. To Wellington, May 9, 1815 : *W.S.D.* x. 267. Wellington to Stewart, May 8, 1815 : *Gurwood*, xii. 358. *Corrés. de Jaucourt avec Talleyrand*, 332. Castlereagh told Fagel that Wellington had greater difficulties than he had had with the Spaniards " ce qui était tout dire " (Colenbrander, *Gedenkstukken*, vii. 772). Wellington was, however, made Commander-in-Chief of the Netherlands forces, and this relieved the situation somewhat while Herries was sent out to help with the subsidy treaties which " the Chancellor of the Exchequer on the Continent," as Gentz called Wellington, was negotiating on the old model, neglecting all the experience of previous years (E. Herries, *Memoir of J. C. Herries*, i. 96, 102).

usual gave a very favourable view of Alexander, the conviction of Clancarty and Münster only increased as time went on that he was in favour of a bargain with the Jacobins by the substitution of the Duke of Orleans.

Castlereagh had approved Clancarty's opposition to the proposed new declaration, which he considered unnecessary and even dangerous, since it might reveal a lack of unity in the Allied aims. He hoped the Allies would regulate their language by the British reservation. The decisive majority in the Commons should be sufficient to convince them, he wrote, "that whilst the British Government and nation are cautious in committing their Allies in a contest with France they will never shrink from the assertion of their interests or abandon the cause of the Continent." [1]

The plan of a new declaration, however, was not allowed to drop, since it was evident the original declaration hardly applied to present circumstances now that Napoleon was on the throne of France supported by the army and at least tacitly accepted by the people. The subject was hotly discussed at intervals, but no satisfactory form could be found until it was decided merely to publish a *Procès Verbal* of the Conference of the Eight, which argued in rather verbose language that no new declaration was necessary since Napoleon's success had in no way altered the intentions of the Allies towards him or towards France. Clancarty was able to secure that this document, if it did not help Louis very much, at least did him no harm, and in the end he professed himself satisfied, while Münster and other representatives of the smaller Courts also signed it.

Still the whole situation was unsatisfactory as far as the Bourbon cause was concerned. No improvement was to be observed in the attitude of the Tsar or of Talleyrand, while Metternich's conduct in at last yielding to La Besnardière's piteous entreaties to be allowed to return to France was viewed with the greatest suspicion. Clancarty confessed that

[1] To Clancarty, April 29, 1815 : *F.O. Continent*, 16. From Clancarty, May 6, 1815 : *B.F.S.P.* ii. 1031 ; May 6, 1815 : *Lond. MSS.* ; May 13, 1815 : *C.C.* x. 354. From Cathcart, May 13, 1815 : *C.C.* x. 350. As to Talleyrand's money : from Wellington, March 28, 1815 : *Gurwood*, xii. 286 ; to Stewart, April 20, 1815 : *F.O. Austria*, 116.

he shared all Castlereagh's fears for their future. "The only chance," he wrote in his last letter on the subject, "altho' I fear a very feeble one, of amalgamating Talleyrand's cause with that of the King—certainly a very desirable object—is that of bringing him to Ghent . . . but I doubt very much whether he will be induced to stay there. His King's interests appear to me to occupy a very secondary place in his mind— and I am much deceived if he is not much more inclined to further the views of the Emperor of Russia, which I cannot but believe to be unfriendly to the restoration, than those of his own lawful sovereign. The only mode by which it seems to me practicable to obtain Talleyrand's hearty co-operation in the cause of the King is by holding out to him prospects of power, and gain of probable and early realisation—he certainly founds his present hopes of these on the Jacobin party, who, he conceives and naturally, are more likely to dispose of the future destinies of France than that of the Royal Family." Münster, on the other hand, was more suspicious of Alexander than of Talleyrand, though he deplored the latter's intrigues with the Jacobins, and advised that no Swedish troops be brought into the campaign lest Bernadotte might be again supported by the Tsar as a candidate for the French throne.[1]

Meanwhile, Castlereagh had been occupied with the education both of his countrymen and the King of France. With the first he was now quite satisfied, and on May 26 was at last able to carry an address committing the country to the war, which had already been two months preparing. It was with some relief that he got safely past this dangerous corner. "I hope you will be satisfied with our proceedings in Parliament," he told Nesselrode. "It required some management to embark the country heartily in a new war under all the embarrassments of a Congress and an escape from Elba. You may rely upon it that it has been well done and that we shall not be wanting to our Allies and to the good cause."

[1] From Clancarty, May 19, 1815: *F.O. Continent*, 18; May 26, 1815: *Lond. MSS.* D'Angeberg, *Congrès de Vienne*, 1181. Münster to the Prince Regent, May 15, 1815: *Münster*, 263; June 3, 1815: *Windsor Arch., Appendix*, p. 561. Metternich's views will always be a riddle. Probably he was merely waiting on events, but Schwarzenberg was violent against the Bourbons and eager for Orleans or a Regency (Klinkowström, *Oesterreichs Theilnahme*, 825).

The royal education in constitutionalism did not, however, lead to such good results. Castlereagh had continued to press Louis to send for Talleyrand, make him a real first Minister, allow him to make terms with Fouché on behalf of the King, and thus secure the support of the French people in order to undermine Napoleon and prepare his own way to the throne when victory was won. He had even suggested to Wellington that the King should "invite his two Houses of Parliament to assemble in the rear of armies" when once the invasion of France began. Wellington was perhaps not too anxious for such a rearguard, but he responded loyally to Castlereagh's wishes and found time amidst his military and financial duties to give Pozzo di Borgo, who had his own ideas as to how Louis should become a real constitutional king, a lesson on the restoration of Charles the Second and the part Parliament played in it. He also wrote to Metternich urging the absolute necessity of the restoration of the Bourbons, and his letter to the suspect Duke of Orleans, who was constantly urging Louis to come to England, was a model of courteous reproof and must have given that subtle but timid Prince some serious thought for reflection.

The great thing, however, was to bring about the accession of Talleyrand to power and the bargain with Fouché, and unfortunately the King shewed but little sign of yielding to Castlereagh's advice. Though Talleyrand was daily expected at Ghent, his proper reception by the King was by no means assured. The last letter that Castlereagh wrote, therefore, was an urgent appeal to the King to make Talleyrand his Minister and give him a free hand.[1]

One other service Castlereagh and Wellington had tried to render Louis, France, and their own cause during these days of preparation and anxious waiting. In the last campaign

[1] To Nesselrode, May 28, 1815 : *C.C.* x. 365. To Wellington, May 16, 1815 : *W.S.D.* x. 306. Pozzo di Borgo to Nesselrode, May 23, 1815 : *Trans. Imp. Russian Hist. Soc.* cxii. 239–41. Wellington to Metternich, May 20, 1815 ; to the Duke of Orleans, June 6, 1815 : *Gurwood*, xii. 410, 447. From Stuart, June 16, 1815 : A. Malet, *Louis XVIII. et les Cent-Jours*, ii. 176. To Stuart, June 7, 16, 1815 : *Lond. MSS., Appendix*, p. 550. Castlereagh left London on June 30, after the news of Waterloo but before that of the capitulation of Paris, with the plan of summoning the two Chambers to Lyons. Merveldt to Metternich, July 3, 1815 : *Vienna St. A.*

the British army was the only one which had paid its way and treated the inhabitants with friendliness. The Duke had even sent back the Spanish troops partly because he could not trust them in this respect. The allied armies had roused the fury of the French, and almost caused a general rising by their brutal severity and their insistence in living on the country without payment. At an early stage both Castlereagh and the Duke, no less than Louis himself, began to consider how to prevent such conduct in the ensuing campaign. How necessary it was to take some action was already seen by the complaints arising in the Netherlands and Hanover of the action of the Prussians in commandeering supplies. Louis thought that the simplest solution was that Britain should pay for everything. This, as Castlereagh had to point out, could hardly be expected. France must contribute towards the cost of her deliverance, but at least the burden might be made tolerable by regulation. It was suggested, therefore, that royal commissaries should be attached to each army, who should have the duty of seeing that the inhabitants received receipts for the food which they supplied, so that they could be compensated by the restored French Government.

But the plan met with strong opposition from the other Powers, especially the Prussian. Stein had, indeed, drawn up a plan on the model of 1813, by which various territories should be allotted to each army as supply areas, with no regard to the interests of the inhabitants. Wellington's letters shew his indignation at the rapacity of his Allies. It was not until June that he and Stuart at last got the allied representatives at Ghent to agree to a convention with Louis on the subject, and send it to their respective Courts. But it was too late to establish the organisation, and, when Waterloo had left France open to invasion, he was powerless to protect it from the actions of all the armies except his own.[1]

[1] There was a great deal of correspondence on this most thorny and controversial subject. See specially Malet, *Louis XVIII. et les Cent-Jours*, ii. 141, 147, 158, 175; *Trans. Imp. Russian Hist. Soc.* cxii. 256, 258, and Wellington's letters in *Gurwood*, xii. 383, 387, 467, 493; that to Stuart of May 14 on Stein's paper and to Metternich of June 14 on the general question are models of his concise epistolary style. I have relied also on a letter from Stuart to Clancarty of June 4 (*Lond. MSS.*) detailing the final arrangements.

Indeed, all the Powers seemed to expect that the war should bring them no financial burdens, and all were constantly applying for larger subsidies than the funds allocated by the Government allowed. When the Duke proved adamant they turned to Castlereagh and plied him with complaints, the Bavarians being especially insistent, while the Queen of Wurtemberg tried to use her family influence to secure special treatment, more, it may be imagined, at the orders of her husband than at her own desire.

These minor claimants could be ignored, but the Tsar made the same demands, and Castlereagh was specially anxious to conciliate him, both because of the revelation of the secret treaty and to obtain his support of the Bourbon cause. He sounded Wellington, therefore, as to whether a million might not be well spent to this end, the King of France being made the channel of payment so as not to offend the other Allies. In return, Russian troops were to be put under Wellington's command. The Duke, however, though he approved the objects of the plan, refused soldiers obtained in such a way, and the discussion was not completed before Waterloo made such a course unnecessary.[1]

It came not a moment too soon for the Bourbon cause. Had the Russian and Austrian armies shared in the victory and pursuit, the fate of Louis might have been doubtful. As it was, he was able to enter France in the rear of the British armies, and Wellington was his advance agent to the throne. Blacas was at last dismissed with a huge *douceur*, and Talleyrand, though coldly received, arrived at Mons in time to be made the King's Minister. When Fouché saw Napoleon's game was up he played the part that Talleyrand himself had played in 1814, and Wellington was, of course, only too ready to assist him. The Duke was in communication with him through General Nonnelin as early as June 28, and promised to see him as soon as he wished. It was Wellington also who conducted the negotiations with the French emissaries after

[1] Pfeffel's letters on the subject form a large part of his correspondence in the Munich archives. They are revealing as to the attitude of continental Powers towards the British, but are too tedious to be quoted. The Queen of Wurtemberg's letters are in the Windsor Archives. At Paris, Russia received an extra £416,000 for this offer: see *W.S.D.* x. 274, 323; *Trans. Imp. Russian Hist. Soc.* cxii. 261. Convention of Oct. 4, 1815: D'Angeberg, *Congrès de Vienne*, 1553.

Napoleon's flight from the capital, and he took care to keep
the King's cause uppermost and to refuse all suggestions of a
Regency, though he claimed no authority which he did not
possess. It was with Fouché, however, behind the backs of
the irresolute envoys that the real negotiation took place,
Wellington practically making a bargain with him on behalf
of the King in the manner which Castlereagh had so long
advocated, and which he judged, when he heard of it on his
arrival at Paris, "to have been essential to his Majesty's
restoration." The bargain with the arch-traitor was, of
course, much criticised in England, but the Duke was not
disturbed. "If I had not settled with Fouché when I did," he
told Sir John Malcolm, "the Duke of Orleans would have been
proclaimed next day, and that would have been a new trouble."
As it was, the Bourbons were restored to the throne not as "legitimate" monarchs, but by an exercise of the will of the representatives of the people—or so it could be described if necessary.[1]

The result was a Convention which opened the gates of
Paris to the King long before the Tsar or Metternich appeared
on the scene. Blücher, the only other person in a position
to influence events, was too concerned in wreaking his vengeance on France to interest himself in politics, which he did
not understand. Castlereagh's plans were, therefore, brought
to fruition with an ease that he had never anticipated. There
was no need to summon the Chambers behind the Allied lines
when Paris itself and soon all France had capitulated to the
King. Meanwhile, Castlereagh and Wellington now stood
between France and the fury of central Europe, which poured
its armies over her borders as soon as she had been rendered
helpless. Castlereagh and Wellington had saved the dynasty.
Now they had the more difficult task of saving France.

[1] J. W. Kaye, *Life of Sir John Malcolm*, ii. 108. Castlereagh to Liverpool, July 7, 1815 : Yonge, *Life of Liverpool*, ii. 187. The transactions
are well known and have been fully described by Wellington himself in
dispatches to Bathurst of July 2, 8 (*Gurwood*, xii. 532, 549). What
historians have not appreciated is that Wellington was only carrying out
plans long matured by Castlereagh. The names left blank in the dispatch
to Sir Charles Stuart (*Gurwood*, xii. 516) which described Fouché's first
overture are fairly obvious, but are supplied by a copy in the Londonderry
archives. See also Gentz's furious comments on British recognition of
the right of self-determination. (To Metternich, July 14, 1815 : Wittichen,
Briefe von und ab F. Gentz, iii. 311.)

2. THE PUNISHMENT OF FRANCE

THE conference which resulted in the second Peace of Paris
and a new treaty of Alliance between the Four Powers lasted
nearly five months, while the first conference of Paris took
less than two.   The discrepancy is partly to be explained by
the inflammatory condition of France, but still more by the
differences amongst the Allies themselves on the nature of
the peace to be made.   July was spent in regulating the
position of the allied armies on the soil of France and settling
the fate of Napoleon.   In August took place the contest
amongst the Four Powers on the terms of the treaty, which
lasted till the middle of September.   An attempt to force
Talleyrand's Government to accept these terms in the second
half of that month failed, and meanwhile he and Fouché
succumbed to the attacks of their enemies.   In October
the terms of the treaty were worked out with the new
Ministry of Richelieu, and even then three more weeks were
necessary to settle various outstanding questions amongst
the Allied Powers.   Thus Castlereagh, who arrived in Paris
on the evening of July 6, did not leave it until November 23.

Though in history his part in these transactions has been
overshadowed by the Duke of Wellington, who naturally, as
the victor of Waterloo, impressed his personality on all
observers, it was Castlereagh who took the main responsibility
and contributed more than anyone else to the final settlement.
Fortunately there was never the slightest difference of opinion
between him and Wellington, who was always ready to support
Castlereagh's plans by his prestige and authority, and indeed
incurred some odium for that reason.   It was the Cabinet
which suggested that the Duke should be a plenipotentiary,
but Castlereagh, while cordially accepting the proposal,

pointed out that the Duke must be largely occupied in military affairs at first, as indeed he was, and throughout the initiative in political matters came from Castlereagh himself.

He lived on the first floor of the new Embassy, where the most important conferences of the allied Ministers were to be held.   Besides Wellington he had a number of other helpers. Stewart and Cathcart, of course, attended their Emperors, and the former, who hired a magnificent hotel, was to play an important part at the most critical moment of the negotiations. Clancarty visited Paris on his way from Vienna, and was used to persuade the King of the Netherlands to accept British views.   Sir Charles Stuart continued to represent Britain at the King's Court, and therefore also lived in the Borghese Palace.   Lady Castlereagh would not allow him to give balls. Since Cooke was too ill to pay more than a flying visit, Hamilton arrived in August, as the principal representative of the Foreign Office staff, but he was only a technical assistant. Lord Clanwilliam, Lord Clive, and Morier were also present, while Planta was, as usual, indefatigable as principal private secretary.   Münster appeared during the earlier part of the negotiations, but he found himself in little sympathy with the British Ministers, and after protest left his subordinate, Count Hardenberg, to yield to their wishes.

Paris was again filled with the rank and fashion of London, so that Castlereagh had an almost embarrassing number of visitors, amongst them Croker and Lord Granville.   The Speaker himself came to watch with amused contempt the efforts of the newly elected Chamber to imitate British procedure.   Charles Arbuthnot was there that his wife might attend the Duke, a labour that she shared with Lady Shelley and many other ladies.   These did not, however, keep their hero from sterner duties, and he played also a magnificent rôle in the great reviews of the Allied armies, most of whom had never fought, now encamped between Paris and the frontier, with which the monarchs paid compliments to one another and to him.   Castlereagh was thus able to give more time to real business than in 1814, but he gave many great dinners, while his wife went each night to one of the four theatres, where she had a box, and as usual instituted her "evenings," which her niece describes as "far more brilliant, both as to number and rank," than in 1814. The Duke preferred less conventional society when he could manage it, and this trait gave a handle to his enemies. It was some handicap that he lived on the ground floor of Ouvrard's Hotel.[1]

The sovereigns arrived at Paris soon after Castlereagh and remained until the end of September, when the crisis was past. The Tsar was perhaps dissatisfied with his position in contrast to the victorious entry he had made in 1814, but he served both France and Russia better at this time and would have won his place in history even without the amazing proposal which he was to lay before his brother sovereigns. A great change in his psychology had been completed during the Hundred Days, and the Lothario of Vienna had already become a religious zealot of the most extravagant kind. Capo d'Istria and Pozzo di Borgo overshadowed Nesselrode, who was now nominal Secretary for Foreign Affairs. The Emperor of Austria was as null as usual, and the King of Prussia was much harried by the generals of his victorious armies, who thought that the moment of a real Prussian peace had at last arrived. Hardenberg and Humboldt only partially shared their views, but they were often unable to make head against them in the Prussian councils. Stein's appearance at a late stage was due to the militarists who wanted his support. Metternich, with whom was Wessenberg, had a difficult part, which he carried through with much address. It necessitated keeping in the background. Gentz played his usual rôles, including that of unofficial assistant to Castlereagh, who rewarded him handsomely for his services.

The smaller Powers, whose subsidised armies were the worst oppressors of the French people, were nearly all represented by their chief Ministers, and were eager for territory or money. Wrede was no less loud and bombastic than at Vienna and won even less as a result. Gagern tried to play

[1] For Wellington's position, see *W.S.D.* xi. 28–29. Good descriptions of the scene from an English point of view, of which there are many, are in the *Croker Papers*, i. 61–71 ; *Letters of Harriet, Countess Granville*, i. 59–74 ; R. Edgcumb, *Diary of Frances, Lady Shelley, 1787–1817*, 88–159 ; J. W. Kaye, *Life of Sir John Malcolm*, ii. 97–136 ; and for Castlereagh's private life, Countess Brownlow, *Slight Reminiscences*, 124–39. Castlereagh's private expenditure cost the state £9487 (*F.O. Great Britain*, 10).

a lone hand for the King of the Netherlands but was easily
checkmated by Castlereagh. The smaller Powers, in spite of
some protests, were kept as rigidly outside the negotiations as
at the first Peace of Paris, and knew little of what was going
on until the main points of the peace were settled. Prussia,
when she felt herself isolated, made some attempt to play the
part Talleyrand had initiated at Vienna and bring them into
the discussions, but she was too clumsy and arrogant to make
a success of such a manœuvre. The final result was to
establish the hegemony of the Great Powers as the creators
and guardians of the new Europe.

The problem of the dynasty had been settled by Wellington.
The restored King, it was hoped, would be more constitutional
than in 1814, and elections were to be held to give Talleyrand
and Fouché the necessary authority to represent France.
This was altogether in accordance with Castlereagh's plans,
but unfortunately the result did not correspond to his expectations. The intrigues of the Comte d'Artois and his
friends overthrew Talleyrand and Fouché at the critical
moment and the elections were overwhelmingly ultra-Royalist.
A white terror began in the south-west, while the north-east
had still to endure the brutality of the Allies. However, a
Government was secured which could sign on behalf of France,
who had the luck to obtain in Richelieu the best Prime Minister
she ever possessed.

It was some time, however, before peace discussions could
begin. Napoleon himself had in the first place to be disposed
of. When Castlereagh left Britain he had already thought
of confining him in Scotland, but Liverpool had all along
wished him to be tried by the French Government—and hung
or shot by their orders. Blücher intended to save them the
trouble, if he caught him, at least unless he paid attention to
the Duke's indignant and dignified protest at such a suggestion. Castlereagh early reported that such a course was
impossible, and that Britain must guard him if she took him.
Napoleon's sentimental appeal to the British King and people
when he surrendered seemed ludicrous to those to whom it
was addressed and to the rest of Europe, though all Frenchmen, even the Royalists, were touched by it. He gave the

British Government a thorny legal and political problem to solve, and the solution of it has been a theme of historians and others ever since. Castlereagh still thought of Scotland rather than St. Helena and the other Powers agreed, but the difficulties experienced during Napoleon's short stay at Plymouth harbour shewed that course to be impossible. It was essential for Britain to be his gaoler, since no other Power could, in Castlereagh's opinion, be trusted not to use the prisoner as a threat. Both Castlereagh and his Government wished to make Napoleon the common prisoner of the Allies, and this was accomplished by a Convention drawn up in July. It was Castlereagh's rather hasty proposal which established allied commissioners to reside on the island, a step which Liverpool deprecated, since he rightly foresaw they would intrigue and quarrel. Still, it was important that there should be foreign witnesses of the manner in which the British Government carried out its task. Liverpool wished the Allies also to share the expense, which was no light charge, but they shewed no signs of agreeing to do so, and Castlereagh, with his usual generosity in financial matters, does not seem to have pressed them. The result was to throw on Britain the odium of taking practically the whole responsibility of guarding her greatest and most dangerous enemy in a situation of which his wonderful genius took full advantage. But though a legend was created which obscured for long the history of the Napoleonic period, it is difficult to see what else, except in details, the British Government could have done in the embarrassing circumstances of the times.[1]

[1] To Liverpool, July 12, 17, 17, 24, 29, Aug. 24, 1815: *B.D.* 341, 347, 350; *C.C.* x. 435; *W.S.D.* xi. 80; *B.D.* 370. From Liverpool, July 15, 20, Aug. 18, 1815: *C.C.* x. 430; Yonge, *Liverpool*, ii. 199; *C.C.* x. 493. Merveldt to Metternich, July 3, 1815: *Vienna St. A.* Wellington to Stuart, June 28, 1815: *Gurwood*, xii. 516. In a dispatch of July 29, Castlereagh defended the appointment of allied commissioners: " I believe that without some precaution of this nature the British Government would be exposed unnecessarily to much vulgar suspicion. In proportion as the public temper dies away, which it will do when the individual ceases to occupy, as at present, the attention of Europe, the Powers will of their own accord discontinue an arrangement which in that event will become a useless charge upon themselves. In the meantime the Prince Regent's Ministers are at liberty to conduct the whole arrangement as seems to them best, and the commissioners will have no more power to interfere than the officers nominated by the British Government have when residing at the headquarters of the respective continental armies." *F.O. Continent*, 22.

Whatever may be thought of Bonaparte's punishment, there can be no question as to the treatment meted out to France by the allied armies. The plan of control by commissaries completely failed at first except as regards Wellington's own army. The Prussians, intoxicated by their success, wished to inflict every possible burden and humiliation on the conquered. It was only Wellington's influence that obtained for Paris a capitulation instead of an unnecessary attack by the Prussian army. He got small thanks for this, since Fouché tried to twist the words of the agreement into a protection of the existing authorities. It also appeared, though unwarrantably, to give a guarantee of the lives of all Frenchmen against their own King as well as the Allies. The peaceful occupation of Paris and the return of Louis was, however, secured, and Wellington and Castlereagh managed to restrain Blücher's excesses in the city itself until the sovereigns arrived. They refused to allow him to levy a contribution of a hundred million francs, and Wellington personally intervened to save the Pont d'Jéna from destruction by the Prussians.[1] No wonder that the King was grateful, and appeared at the open window of the Tuileries with Wellington and Castlereagh at his side to receive the acclamations of his subjects, though this act was perhaps hardly politic.

Outside Paris, however, the excesses of the troops, especially those of the Bavarians and other smaller German Powers, continued for a considerable time. Wellington's protests at the arbitrary character of the generals' demands were strongly supported by Castlereagh in the councils of the sovereigns, who arrived on the 10th. Fortunately the Tsar, to whom Castlereagh had sent Pozzo di Borgo to prepare him to accept the *fait accompli* at Paris, was as eager as the British to protect France. The Russian army accepted Wellington's plan of systematic assessments instead of indiscriminate pillage, and some restraint was eventually established over the German armies.

---

[1] The famous preservation of the Pont d'Jéna from destruction by the Prussians is often attributed by French historians to the influence of Louis, but there can be no doubt that it was Wellington's action which stopped Blücher until his King arrived with the Tsar. *Cf.* Houssaye, 1815, *La Seconde Abdication*, 339–41.

The dangers thus partially avoided were, in the opinion of both Castlereagh and the Duke, extreme. Nothing less than a national uprising could be expected if the Prussians and Bavarians were allowed to have their way. "If discipline and order are not upheld," wrote Castlereagh in a memorandum whose argument he claimed was accepted by the other Ministers, "King, Army, and People will forget their differences in one common feeling of resentment against the foreign troops. The regeneration of France will be disappointed and the allied armies will be involved in a protracted war, and possibly compelled to retire from France without having effectuated their purpose of restoring it to peaceful habits." Gradually these councils prevailed, and a regulated system of assessments through French officers was established, though much local tyranny remained. Time was thus given for the demobilisation of Bonaparte's troops, and the situation of the Allies was made secure.[1]

All this took time, though the allied Ministers met every day at eleven o'clock and conferred with the French in the afternoon, and produced great exasperation amongst the Prussian soldiers. Blücher had to receive a positive order from his King to stop his operations, and threatened to resign. Colonel Hardinge, who was attached to his army, reported that the King would find it hard to check "the very unusual spirit of political interference existing in this army and its reported intimate connection with popular feeling in Prussia." Wellington's disgust with the Prussians was such that at one time he proposed to confine to British, Austrian, and Russian troops the army of occupation, which it was soon decided was to be left in France under his orders. This controversy had, however, the advantage of bringing the Tsar and Castlereagh

[1] To Liverpool, July 8, 8, 12, 14, 1815 : *C.C.* x. 418, 419 ; *B.D.* 341, 342. From Wellington, July 14, 1815 : *Gurwood*, xii. 558. To Liverpool, July 16, 1815; with confidential memorandum, July 15, 1815 : *F.O. Continent*, 20. Treitschke (*History of Germany*, ii. 208) has obscured the sense of this memorandum, which applied to the temporary, not the permanent, treatment of France. Roger André (*L'occupation de la France par les Alliés en 1815* (1924)) does more justice to British action than any other French writer, though he has neglected much printed evidence of it. He calculates the total number of Allied troops in France as over 1,200,000 and the cost to France at about 700,000,000 francs, which seems a small estimate. For the Russian attitude, see F. Martens, *Recueil des Traités*, iii. 189–91.

close together, and of paving the way for their joint action on the more important question of the permanent treaty with France. Castlereagh did everything in his power to win Alexander's goodwill, and finding that the quarrel with the Prince Regent was now much regretted, got Liverpool to persuade His Royal Highness to write to the Tsar a letter of friendship. There was even a question of another visit of the Tsar to England, but fortunately the monarchs were spared this strain on their courtesy.[1]

In these measures Castlereagh had the support of his Government, but they were far from accepting the end which Castlereagh had in view—a moderate and humane treaty with France. In the memorandum which Castlereagh took with him as his general instructions it was, indeed, laid down that in the event of Louis' restoration and the death or capture of Bonaparte the "integrity" of France, as promised in the declarations of the Allies, should be respected. But public opinion in Britain rose to a high fever during July, especially after it was known that Fouché was in the new Government, and the Cabinet were much influenced by it. "The prevailing idea in this country is," wrote Liverpool, "that we are fairly entitled to avail ourselves of the present moment to take back from France the principal conquests of Louis XIV.," and Castlereagh was requested to sound the Allies on such a proposition. The Prince Regent was as usual extreme, and told the sensible Neumann that he would support the Emperor if he revived his ancient rights on Alsace and Lorraine.[2]

Fortunately the indignation of the Cabinet was largely concentrated at this time on forcing the King to punish those "traitors" whom they considered responsible for the war.

---

[1] Colonel Hardinge to Stewart, July 26, 1815 : *Lond. MSS.* Note of Pozzo di Borgo, Aug. 2, 1815 : *Trans. Imp. Russian Hist. Soc.* cxii. 297. From Liverpool, July 28, 1815 : *C.C.* x. 440. To Liverpool, Aug. 10, 1815 : *F.O. Continent,* 23. According to a witness who had access to the best information at this time, the Tsar now attributed his behaviour in London to his sister's bad advice on points of etiquette. "He seems to have regarded the Regent as a sort of first magistrate without any of the attributes of a king." R. Edgcumbe, *Diary of Frances, Lady Shelley,* 158.

[2] Memorandum of June 30, 1815 ; from Liverpool, July 15, 1815 : *W.S.D.* x. 630 ; *C.C.* x. 431. Neumann to Metternich, July 13, 26, 28, 1815 : *Vienna St. A.* Neumann pointed out that the English King had once been a Duke of Normandy and a Count of Aquitaine, but George took the sarcasm quite seriously and said he wanted nothing for himself.

This object had been specially insisted upon in Castlereagh's original instructions as "necessary with a view to the continuance of the power of the House of Bourbon, but likewise for the security of the object for which the Allies have been contending, a safe and lasting peace." It may be doubted if Castlereagh, who had forced Fouché on the King, agreed with this view; but he was urged by Liverpool to uphold it, and it must be admitted that he was responsible for bringing the matter before the allied Ministers. It was agreed that the King must act, and Pozzo di Borgo was deputed to advise him to do so, while Castlereagh put pressure upon Talleyrand. Fortunately Fouché was Minister of Police, and took care to give notice to all concerned—a step which Castlereagh obviously viewed with equanimity though he carried out his instructions to the letter. Liverpool, on the other hand, regretted the leniency, and told Canning that he could never "feel that the King is secure upon his throne till he has dared to spill traitors' blood." No wonder that Ney, who alone of the prominent men refused to escape, found no mercy in Liverpool when his friends implored British influence to prevent his execution.[1]

But if Castlereagh faithfully followed the severe instructions of his Government in respect to the traitors, he took a very different line on the much more important question of the treatment of France herself. Had he advocated the views which the Cabinet were anxious to support and which the nation would have delighted to see prevail, he could have rallied all but the Tsar to his side. But he and Wellington went in an entirely opposite direction. Castlereagh had always opposed the dismemberment of France, and he refused to yield his opinion now that the unexpected completeness of the victory seemed to make any peace possible to the victorious Allies. Opposing both the cry for revenge in Britain and the loud and greedy clamour of the Germans, he joined with the

---

[1] To Liverpool, July 14, 17, 1815 : *B.D.* 344, 347 ; Aug. 3, 1815 : *C.C.* x. 451. Liverpool to Canning, Aug. 4, 1815 ; *W.S.D.* xi. 95. Wellington, so far as I can ascertain, took no part in the episode. The attempt to involve him by quoting the Convention which he had made with the Paris Provisional Government obviously fails. Nor could he be expected later to intervene to save the life of a soldier who had committed what was in his opinion the greatest of crimes.

Tsar in an effort to obtain security and reparation without outraging French national sentiment too far.

Alexander, indeed, would have been content to impose a moderate indemnity on France and eschew all other penalties. But such a course was impossible. It might be argued—as Wellington did argue—that France had not supported Napoleon in 1815 as in 1814. But she had offered practically no opposition until the collapse came, and something must be done to compensate Europe for the effort which they had been forced to make to overthrow Napoleon. Moreover, how could Europe feel secure if after this experience France was left in exactly the same position as in 1814? Would not the absence of all penalty merely encourage her to renew the attempt at the earliest possible moment? The Prussians, at any rate, had no doubt as to the answer to these questions. Their soldiers and statesmen were already elaborating plans in a series of memoranda which recommended sweeping territorial cessions from France for the benefit of Bavaria and the Netherlands, which Prussia would utilise to add Luxemburg and Mainz to her own territory, and an indemnity which must be at least twelve hundred million francs—far less, they claimed with elaborate details of figures, than France had taken from Prussia alone in the course of the last six years. The south German states were asking for even more, while Austria was inevitably drawn in to the scramble for territory and money.

Castlereagh had hoped to meet these views by a temporary occupation of France by an allied army, by the dismantling of those fortresses which specially threatened Belgium and Switzerland, and, above all, by a renewal of the treaty of Alliance. He accordingly approached the Tsar and urged him to accept these terms, though they went somewhat beyond the imperial opinion, and to propose them to the other Allies as his own, thus committing him to enforce them on France and giving him that lead in the discussions which he always relished. The Tsar agreed, and the Russian Ministers drew up a memorandum on these lines, which Castlereagh and Wellington were allowed to see and alter before it was officially presented. Castlereagh sent this home immediately, together with a paper of his own advocating temporary occupation to his Cabinet, who thus had the arguments for moderation brought to their notice long before they saw the counter-arguments which the Austrians and Prussians hastened to present. The former's demands were fairly reasonable, amounting to little more than the detachment of a strip along the Belgian frontier and Landau from France. But the Prussian generals still had sweeping plans which they hardly dared disclose officially, involving large cessions by France to Belgium and the consequent cession of Luxemburg to Prussia, though Hardenberg, in private conversation with Castlereagh, admitted that he did not support them. When at last Knese-beck's detailed scheme was disclosed, it made such large demands that it would have severed from France every first-class fortress which she possessed.[1]

The Cabinet received Castlereagh's first proposals with coolness. They were not prepared to cancel his instructions, but they indicated their preference for stronger measures than Russia would support. A special Cabinet was summoned, and Bathurst wrote a hasty note to Castlereagh, bidding him pause before he committed himself too far. The Cabinet were afraid to give Castlereagh new instructions of a more severe kind, but their inclinations were obviously in that direction, and when they at last received the Austrian and Prussian projets they shewed a decided disposition to accept the former as the basis of the treaty.

It was becoming clear, therefore, that some permanent cessions would have to be made by France. In order to make these as small as possible and to establish them on some principle, Castlereagh now brought forward a plan of giving to France the frontier of 1790 instead of 1792. This would deprive her of some insignificant territory on the Belgian frontier and that part of Savoy which Louis had been so

---

[1] *Précis des Contributions*, June 30, 1815: *C.C.* x. 393. To Liverpool, July 17, 24, 29, Aug. 12, 1815: *B.D.* 349, 350; *W.S.D.* xi. 122–23, 125. Memorandum of Capo d'Istria, July 28, 1815; Memorandum of Harden-berg, Aug. 4, 1815; Memorandum of Metternich, Aug. 2, 1815: D'Ange-berg, *Congrès de Vienne*, 1470, 1479, 1482. Knesebeck's Memoir, Aug. 13, 1815: *W.S.D.* xi. 117. For the German memoranda and schemes, see Treitschke, *History of Germany* (Eng. ed.), ii. 207–15; Gebhardt, *Wilhelm von Humboldt*, ii. 177 ff.; Gagern, *Mein Antheil an der Politik*, Appendices IV., VI., VII.

reluctant to accept in 1814. This plan he gradually got the Tsar to accept so that the two Powers could shew a united front, and meanwhile Wellington's powerful authority was used to convince the Cabinet and the other Allies that temporary occupation was the best way to bring back peace and security to Europe. The Duke championed Castlereagh's ideas *con amore*, and the disgust which he felt at the inordinate demands of the Prussians, which he had constantly to expose in the military committee, added fire to the usual excellence of his style.[1]

Still the Cabinet were not completely convinced and refused to give Castlereagh a free hand. Moreover, the Prince Regent was fortified in his ideas by letters from Münster which attacked with much skill the arguments of Castlereagh and Wellington. Münster, like the Ministers of the other small Powers, felt acutely the impotence to which the Four had reduced the rest of Europe, and this feeling of inferiority added venom to his criticisms. Even an interview with Louis, who sent a pathetic message to the Prince Regent, did not diminish his desire to see Germany made secure by taking large slices of territory from France, as the Prussians and the smaller German Princes desired. But Münster obviously could not face the embarrassing situation in which his opposition to Castlereagh placed him. He retired from the scene after professing a conversion to the British view, which he perhaps hardly felt, leaving Count Hardenberg to receive the final orders of his master, which he knew must be determined by the British Cabinet.

Nevertheless, Münster's influence on the Prince Regent and the Duke of York, and through them on the Cabinet, whose inclinations were in the same direction, was considerable. As a consequence the Cabinet tried to insist on various points, such as the destruction of the fortifications of Lille, which Castlereagh was most anxious to waive. They were urged on by the frantic clamour of the British Press, which had now

---

[1] From Liverpool, June 28, 1815 : *C.C.* x. 441. From Bathurst, Aug. 1, 1815 : *Lond. MSS.* From Liverpool, Aug. 3, 1815 (with memorandum on the Russian memorandum) : *C.C.* x. 454 ; Aug. 11, 18, 1815 : *W.S.D.* xi. 126, 130. Lieven to Nesselrode, Aug. 22, 1815 : *Pet. Arch.* To Liverpool, Aug. 17, 1815 : *C.C.* x. 485. From Wellington, Aug. 11, 1815 : *Gurwood*, xii. 596.

become, as even Gentz, its great admirer, confessed, a "public nuisance," and which, by language as extreme as that used by the Germans, was encouraging all the opponents of Castlereagh at Paris. The Tsar was visibly affected, and through Pozzo warned Wellington that, if Britain yielded and the Prussian demands were accepted, he would march his army home and refuse all responsibility for the settlement. The Duke confessed that he and Castlereagh had been hampered by instructions which prevented them from acting as vigorously as they wished. If the Russians went home, he added, the only other army capable of fighting was his own, and the other Allies would soon find out their mistake.[1]

In these circumstances Castlereagh felt that his authority was challenged, and that he must obtain from the Cabinet a definite promise of support in his efforts to obtain a moderate peace. He had not yet ventured to send home his own opinion, recorded in the official memorandum, though this had been shewn to the Russians and other interested parties. Lord Stewart was therefore hastily dispatched to London to lay the views of the British delegation before the Cabinet and the Prince Regent. The letter which he carried with him was one of the most incisive which Castlereagh ever sent to his Government. He pointed out that the Prussian Councils were so much dominated by their soldiers that Hardenberg had confessed to Clancarty "that he felt himself in the midst of Prætorian bands." Their demands threatened Hanover and the Netherlands as much as France herself. He was sure they would give way, if faced with sufficiently strong opposition, but he could not bring that to bear unless the Cabinet maintained his instructions and gave him a free hand. With the letter were sent memoranda which gave a comprehensive view of the whole negotiation, stressing the Alliance, rather than the spoliation of France, as the great protection of Europe.

We may be sure that Lord Stewart was not behindhand in

---

[1] Münster to the Prince Regent, Aug. 17, 18, 18, 1815: *Windsor Arch., Appendix*, pp. 562–72. Nesselrode to Lieven, Aug. 22, 24 (with Rapport à l'Empereur de Pozzo di Borgo), 1815 : *Pet. Arch.* Gentz called the British Press a " public nuisance " on Aug. 31 (*Briefe an Pilat*, i. 174), and on Sept. 5 he wrote to the Hospodar : " The mass of the English nation is as embittered against the French, as puffed up by victory and as extreme in their demands, as the majority of the German peoples ": Klinkowström, *Oesterreichs Theilnahme*, 715.

vigorous language in defence of his brother, but it was hardly necessary.   For the Cabinet had already recoiled from limiting Castlereagh's power, and a letter had been sent off which grudgingly accepted his policy.   Still, Stewart's long interview with the Cabinet in which he pressed home Castlereagh's points with much address and obtained a further instruction, which gave him everything that was asked and assured him of the cordial and zealous support of his colleagues, whatever the criticism of public opinion in Britain, was a good piece of work.   Stewart had a harder task with the Prince Regent, who had been much influenced by the letters from Münster, who, he said, was the ablest man of them all.   Stewart was able to reply, however, that even Münster was now convinced of the wisdom of Castlereagh's course, and the Prince reluctantly gave his assent.[1]

Castlereagh could now tackle his opponents at Paris with confidence.   His own memorandum, which he now made official, and a magnificent paper by Wellington, justifying the scheme of temporary occupation, were the prelude to a struggle which lasted till the middle of September.   Clancarty was sent post-haste to Brussels to warn the King of the Netherlands against the intrigue in which Gagern was engaged with the Prussians of exchanging Luxemburg for extensive additions on the Belgian frontier.   This was easily defeated, for William was now too attached to his Grand Duchy to part with it lightly, though Gagern followed Clancarty home in an effort to carry his point.   Neither Castlereagh nor the Duke spared his feelings on his return, the former treating him with cutting sarcasm for his outrageous attempt to despoil France in opposition to the Power that had brought the Netherlands into existence.   " I asked Baron Gagern," reported Castlereagh, "how the King would relish having these fortresses without the guarantee of England. . . . This view of the question appeared altogether to damp his Excellency's appetite for such acquisitions."

[1] To Liverpool, Aug. 24, 1815 : *F.O. Continent*, 24.   Inadequate précis in *W.S.D.* xi. 137 ; which also gives the enclosures (138–42).   Memorandum of Lord Stewart's Conversations with the Cabinet, Lord Liverpool, and the Prince Regent : *Lond. MSS.*   From Liverpool, Aug. 28, 1815 : *C.C.* x. 506.   Lieven to Nesselrode, Aug. 29, 1815 : *Pet. Arch.*   Pellew, *Life of Sidmouth*, iii. 133.

All the other small Powers which bordered or even approached France were making demands not less absurd for cessions of territory which they expected Britain to guarantee. Castlereagh's indignation was unbounded. He had too much respect for the fighting qualities of Frenchmen to expect them to acquiesce in such humiliation. Gagern was astounded at his praise of France, but it represented the experience of twenty years of warfare. "The more I reflect upon it," he told his Cabinet, "the more I deprecate this system of scratching such a Power. We may hold her down and pare her nails so that many years shall pass away before they can wound us. I hope we may do this effectually and subject to no other hazards of failure than must, more or less, attend all political or military arrangements; but this system of being pledged to a continental war for objects that France may any day reclaim from the particular states that hold them, without pushing her demands beyond what she would contend was due to her own honour, is, I am sure, a bad British policy." [1]

The demands of the jackal German Powers, most of whom had been aggrandised by Napoleon himself, could be easily refused. It was different with Prussia, who had now brought 280,000 soldiers into France. The only thing was to isolate her. Castlereagh had the bad luck to have a serious accident at this critical moment, which kept him in bed several days. But the conferences were held in his bedroom as he refused to allow the business to be suspended. Austria was fairly easily won over, and the Tsar soon consented to accept the British propositions, *i.e.* the frontier of 1790 and an indemnity of six hundred million francs. The Prussians still stood out for the Saar Valley, cessions to Belgium equivalent to Luxemburg, and twelve hundred million. This last demand was considered outrageous and impossible, and Prussia made to abandon it. For form's sake, however, all her territorial demands had to be submitted to France in the first instance, though as Castlereagh had already assured the rejection of

[1] Memorandum of Castlereagh, Aug. 31, 1815 : *W.S.D.* xi. 147. Memorandum of Wellington, Aug. 31, 1815 : *Gurwood*, xii. 622. To Liverpool, Sept. 4, 1815 : *B.D.* 375. From Clancarty, Aug. 30, 1815 ; to Clancarty, Sept. 4, 1815 ; Gagern to Van Nagell, Sept. 4, 7, 1815 ; King of the Netherlands to Fagell, Sept. 5, 1815 ; Clancarty to the King, Sept. 5, 1815 ; Colenbrander, *Gedenkstukken*, vii. 267, 270, 802, 803, 804, 811.

the Luxemburg plan there could be no result on that point. Saarlouis was in a different character as a fortress of great strategic value in a small territory. Prussia was using every expedient to gain her ends, and now even tried to introduce the smaller German Powers into the sacred circle of the Four. This manœuvre failed, and the three Powers refused to do more than make the full demand, and Castlereagh was confident it would be rejected by France. It was imperative, however, to come to some decision in order to open the negotiation with the French Government before the newly elected Chambers met in Paris. Moreover, the Tsar was determined to leave Paris by the end of the month and the other sovereigns were also urgently required at their capitals.[1]

In the midst of this excitement there also came to a head another negotiation in which the British delegates, and especially Wellington, incurred much undeserved odium. In 1814 the French had been allowed to retain the art treasures which their armies had collected by force from every capital of central Europe. It was a generous gesture, but the Parisians had regarded it merely as a tribute to their importance. It could hardly be expected that similar generosity would now be shewn. Liverpool had, at an early stage, suggested that the art treasures should be returned to their owners, and, though both Castlereagh and Wellington had hoped to spare the King this humiliation, they were forced to take another view. The Tsar, who had none to recover, was the only opponent of the measure amongst the Allies, and the Prussians eventually began to remove their own art treasures from the gallery of the Louvre and elsewhere, under armed guard, without waiting for protocol or treaty. The King of the Netherlands pressed that the Belgian and Dutch pictures should be restored also, the Florentines naturally wanted to get back the Venus Di Medici, while the Pope sent Canova to obtain the many treasures that had been taken from Rome.

---

[1] To Liverpool, Sept. 14, 21, 21, 25 : *F.O. Continent*, 27 ; *W.S.D.* xi. 165, 167 ; *C.C.* xi. 31. Castlereagh was kicked by a horse. His house continued to be the diplomatic centre of the Conference, and after Sept. 18 all the meetings of the principal Powers were held there, as Gentz's diary reveals.

Thus Castlereagh, while he would have nothing to do with a proposal of the Prince Regent that some should be bought for his galleries, agreed that a general restoration should be made, and brought it formally before the allied Council, which ratified the demand.

Talleyrand shewed little surprise, but he insisted that the King must be made to yield to force, so as to avoid the odium of signing away the treasures to which the Parisians attached so much importance. His official reply, however, to Castlereagh's note was couched in the most insulting terms, a shabby trick, which the recipient said might be expected from a man of his character. The Netherlands pictures were, nevertheless, taken away under the protection of British soldiers, and Wellington wrote Castlereagh a letter which replied with interest to Talleyrand's insinuations. Subsequently the delighted Canova, who was given British funds to cover the expenses he had otherwise no means of meeting, was allowed to remove the Papal treasures, while other Italian states also got back some of these ill-gotten gains, the Parisians being especially furious at the removal of the Venetian horses from the Carrousel. Castlereagh's insistence on regularising the procedure and Wellington's action with regard to the Netherlands pictures, together with Talleyrand's cowardly attack, had made them the centre of the abuse which the infuriated Parisians had to hurl at somebody. The Duke was hissed publicly in Catalani's performance, at the beginning of October, when, it is true, he rather tactlessly tried to use the royal box, and after the fall of Talleyrand a number of libels were circulated about his private life. The Duke bore this abuse, in which the Pope and Canova were his only rivals, as easily as he had accepted the unprecedented honours which had fallen to his lot. There is a delightful irony that the two men who were doing most to save France from dismemberment and ruin should be made the central targets of Parisian hatred at the crisis of her fate.[1]

---

[1] From Liverpool, July 15, Aug. 3, Sept. 19, 29 : Yonge, *Liverpool*, ii. 193; *C.C.* x. 453; xi. 27, 37. To Liverpool, July 24, Aug. 17, Sept. 11, 11, 25, Oct. 1 : *C.C.* x. 435, 491; xi. 12; *F.O. Continent*, 26; *C.C.* xi. 32, 39. Hamilton to Bathurst, Aug. 24, Sept. 6, 1815 : *Bathurst*, 375, 385. Note to the Plenipotentiaries, Sept. 11, 1815; from Talleyrand, Sept. 19, 1815:

Meanwhile, the more important negotiation with France as to territory and indemnity was met by Talleyrand with a blank refusal. He gave short shrift to the allied note, which he describes in his memoirs as "insolent," and refused any cessions whatever in a reply which claimed that royalist France had never been the enemy of the Allies, and that they had no rights of conquest over her. As 900,000 men were now encamped in France this was hardly a strong argument, but the reply was in any case Talleyrand's last official action. Fouché had been subjected for long to the unceasing attacks of the ultra-Royalists, headed by the Duc d'Angoulême, who was intoxicated with delight at their success, and his overthrow, which they now obtained, brought Talleyrand's along with it. Indeed, that astute Minister had been aware of his impending fall when he penned his defiant note, and was thus able to retire to the office of Grand Chamberlain with all the honours of a patriot.

It was the poor King himself, left without a Minister, whom Castlereagh had to inform that some cession of territory was indispensable and that the dogma of the "sacred soil" of France, which had never respected the integrity of other countries, must be abandoned. Fortunately in Richelieu the King found a Minister strong enough to face the inevitable, and in a few days the basis of the treaty had been laid. The last discussions were conducted on behalf of the Allies by the Duke of Wellington, and his authority made it easier both for Richelieu and the Prussians to yield.[1]

The final result was a peace which, if it lacked the generosity of that of 1814, was yet tolerable to France. Her territorial losses were small—a few rectifications of the Belgian frontier, Saarlouis, Landau, and Savoy, which was to be neutralised.

D'Angeberg, *Congrès de Vienne*, 1510, 1521. From Wellington, Sept. 23, 1815 : *Gurwood*, xii. 641. Baron d'Uchtritz to Einsiedel, Sept. 26, 28, Oct. 1, 4, 1815 : *Dresden St. A. ; Trans. Imp. Russian Hist. Soc.*, cxii. 318, 320. Talleyrand, *Memoirs*, iii. 265, 273. Mendelssohn-Bartholdy, *Briefe von Gentz an Pilat*, i. 198, 200, 203. The British Government expended 202,180 francs in sending home the Pope's possessions : E. Herries, *Memoir of J. C. Herries*, i. 104–105. Arneth (*Life of Wessenberg*, ii. 21), who claims credit for Austria in getting back the Venetian treasures, gives an eyewitness's account of how the British tourists chipped the ornaments off the famous horses as souvenirs.

[1] To Liverpool, Sept. 25, Oct. 1, 2, 1815 : *B.D.* 374; *C.C.* xi. 38, 40. Wellington to Richelieu, Oct. 1, 1815 : *Gurwood*, xii. 652.

Of these, the Saar Valley was perhaps the most substantial loss, but its economic as distinct from its strategic importance was not known at the time. There were also rectifications of the Swiss frontier, which gave Geneva a little more breathing space. The suzerainty of Monaco was transferred to Piedmont. The indemnity was reduced to seven hundred million francs, a sum which, as was to be seen, France could quite easily pay in spite of the losses inflicted on her by the Allied occupation. She also undertook once more to satisfy the private claims which she had promised to settle in the Treaty of 1814, but had entirely neglected so far.[1]

Of her own fortifications she was to destroy only Huninguen, which was considered a serious threat to Switzerland. Meanwhile, though the Allies resisted it and wished to place the whole charge on Britain and the Netherlands, the barrier fortresses in Belgium were to be built out of part of the indemnities as well as new fortifications at Luxemburg and Mainz.

Lastly, the army of occupation of 150,000 men under the Duke of Wellington was to be stationed for five years (or perhaps three if France fulfilled her obligations) in the north of France, every care being taken by special regulations, which shew the mark of Wellington's mastery of detail, that the charge should prove as little onerous as possible. The Tsar had wished to limit the numbers to 100,000 men, but gave way on condition that the total might be reduced if necessary. Liverpool was more concerned to link up the occupation with the payment of the indemnity, but though he constantly recurred to this point, it was not inserted in the treaty, and Wellington always declared that his army was stationed in France to obtain security and not to enforce payment.[2]

Richelieu lamented that he should have had to sign so

---

[1] For details of these, see my *Foreign Policy of Castlereagh, 1815–1822*, 82. Castlereagh asked Richelieu to fix a lump sum to satisfy the British claimants under the fourth article of the Treaty of 1814, who were pressing hard for payment and even threatened to retain Martinique and Guadeloupe, which had been reoccupied during the Hundred Days, if nothing was done, but he failed to get it. To Richelieu (undated) : *Lond. MSS.*

[2] Count Hardenberg to the Prince Regent, Oct. 16, 1815 : *Hanover St. A.* From Liverpool, Sept. 29, Oct. 2, 31, 1815 : *C.C.* xi. 35, 41, 59. To Liverpool, Oct. 24, 1815 : *F.O. Continent*, 29. For the Army of Occupation, see my *Foreign Policy of Castlereagh, 1815–1822*, 78.

humiliating a treaty, but if all the circumstances be considered, France, which had inflicted so much wanton humiliation and loss on every country of Europe, had reason to congratulate herself on her escape.　The Prussians and the German Powers were naturally loud in their complaints, but Harden-berg was really well content with everything but the financial settlement.　The King of the Netherlands professed himself grateful to Castlereagh for saving Luxemburg from the Prussians, and its inhabitants were greatly relieved.[1] Metternich, who had played a useful but secondary rôle in the great discussions, was also well satisfied.　The Tsar, who left Paris on September 28, was too much occupied with the scheme of the Holy Alliance to lament much at these more mundane matters, while his Ministers were glad to have been able to pose as the best friends of France and hoped for favours in return some day.

Nor were Castlereagh and Wellington dissatisfied with the final result, however much they regretted some of the harsher details.　Their device of temporary occupation had been accepted by their Allies as a solution of the immediate problem of security and had undoubtedly saved the infliction of such permanent wounds on France as would have made a long peace impossible.　Though the financial questions were only settled after long and tedious negotiations in which Britain as usual sacrificed much to the general cause, yet the total burden on France was reasonable, and a sufficient sum had been set apart for the fortifications which the Duke thought indispensable to make the Belgian barrier a real one. Though there were still some questions outstanding between the German Powers, their unity, however inconvenient during the negotiations, was greater than ever before.　The Tsar also had behaved well and merited the constant praise which Castlereagh sent home in an effort to remove the deep-rooted hostility of the Cabinet and the Prince Regent.

The Cabinet were also in the end content.　Officially they sent warm approval when the outline of the treaty was known,

---

[1] From Clancarty, Nov. 12, 1815: *Lond. MSS.* He had to give the Prussians the right to govern the town of Luxemburg, but was glad to escape at such a cost.

in accordance with their promise to Stewart. "Your Lordship is fully aware that under your instructions," Bathurst said, "you would have been authorised to consent to terms short of those which you have obtained. It will be highly satisfactory to His Royal Highness if the concessions which have been made to the representations of the Duc de Richelieu shall have the effect of giving strength to H.C. Majesty's present administration."

Liverpool's opinion was shewn by the fact that he did not think it worth while to summon a Cabinet to ratify the final terms. "I am quite satisfied," he told Bathurst, "from all I hear that the treaty will satisfy the public in general, and that you will find it to be the opinion of most persons that the terms are as *severe upon France* as would in any way be consistent with maintaining Louis XVIII. upon the throne. With respect to those who think we ought not to have troubled ourselves about the internal situation of France, but have applied our exertions exclusively to the reduction of her power and the dismemberment of her territory, I have only to say that the policy of such a course of proceeding would have been at least doubtful, even if it had been open to us, but it would have been totally inconsistent with all the treaties, declarations, and manifestos which were formulated at the commencement of the contest, and which, in fact, have received the sanction of Parliament." The remnant of the Cabinet who were in town—Bathurst, Sidmouth, Vansittart, and Pole—agreed, though their approval was couched in distinctly a low key, since the financial settlement would probably add to, rather than reduce, the burden on the country.[1]

Thus by the first week of October the main lines of the treaty had been settled; but the negotiations lasted six weeks longer, and the French were subjected to the humiliation of witnessing the Battle of Leipzig celebrated at Paris. There was still much wearisome work to be done on the Conventions, especially that settling the reparation claims, of which Gentz made half a dozen drafts. Whereas in 1814 only

[1] From Bathurst, Oct. 4, 1815: *F.O. Continent*, 20. Liverpool to Bathurst, Oct. 12, 1815; Bathurst to Liverpool, Oct. 19, 1815: *Bathurst*, 388, 390.

private interests had been considered, the principle of compensation was now extended to certain Government claims. The smaller Powers also needed time. By the magnanimous decision of the Four all were given some share of the indemnity—even the Portuguese, to Liverpool's great indignation. There were also numerous details concerning the army of occupation to be arranged. Moreover, the Allies had still some German questions to settle, which had finally to be referred to a Commission at Frankfort. The question of Swiss neutrality had also to be settled, as well as the fate of the Ionian Isles, as has already been narrated.[1]

The treaty with France was thus not signed until November 20, 1815. On the same day the Four signed another treaty which Castlereagh regarded as of even greater importance—a renewal in a new form of the treaty of Alliance, whose significance is discussed in the following section.

[1] For the financial settlement, see A. Nicolle's *Comment la France a payé après Waterloo* (1929), and my *Castlereagh, 1815–1822*, 82.

3. FROM GUARANTEE TO CONFERENCE

THROUGHOUT all the discussions as to the best means to secure the peace of Europe Castlereagh had kept steadily in view a project which to him was of more importance than all the other expedients which had been so hotly debated by his Cabinet and his Allies. Territorial cessions he had regarded as likely to do more good than harm, and the device of temporary occupation was only for the immediate future. What was needed was a permanent Alliance of the Great Powers against any renewal of the danger which a Bonaparte on the throne of France inevitably brought upon Europe. From an early date, therefore, he had contemplated a renewal of the Treaty of Chaumont in a more extended form than had been given to it by the Treaty of March 25, 1815, which was only to meet the particular emergency of the moment. "If we make an European invasion," he wrote before the news of Bonaparte's surrender reached him, "the inevitable and immediate consequence of Bonaparte's succession, or that of any of his race, to power in France, I am confident, after the experience they have had of his impotence against such a confederacy and their own sufferings, that there is not a class in France, not excepting even the army, that will venture to adhere to him at the hazard of being again overrun by the armies of Europe, with the certainty of being dismembered and loaded with contributions." [1]

When Bonaparte was in St. Helena danger from him might seem at an end, yet his example and family, and, above all, the military class which he had created, still remained. It was problematical whether Louis could succeed better a second time in leading France back to peaceful habits. The army,

[1] To Liverpool, July 17, 1815. B.D. 349.

which had welcomed Napoleon and driven out Louis, might assert itself once more and win the acquiescence, if not the active support, of the nation. In his final propositions to his Cabinet, therefore, sent by Stewart, he had placed in the fore-front of the principles on which he based the future security of Europe, as the most important of all, the renewal of the Alliance : " In deciding upon any arrangement, the first object to attend to is that it shall preserve unimpaired the Alliance to which Europe already owes its deliverance, and on the permanence of which union it ought in wisdom to rely above every other measure of security for its future peace and preservation." [1]

For the moment this idea was confined to the immediate danger threatening from France, and used to combat the proposals of spoliation and penalty which were being advo-cated at the time; but there was also another thought in Castlereagh's mind, imperfectly understood and never ex-plicitly avowed at this time. It was born out of the experience of the last three years when he had seen Europe develop a unity and persistence of purpose, such as it had never before possessed. It is true that the return of Napoleon had made danger from France supersede for the moment those other dangers which he had felt so strongly at Vienna. But the need for the union of the Great Powers was necessary, not only to guard against that danger, but also for the general interests of Europe. Castlereagh had seen the idea of diplomacy by conference, which he took with him in his first journey to the Continent, justified again and again in the course of the last two years. The treaty of Alliance, therefore, might be the means of making permanent a system which had been tested by experience, and thus securing peace by discussion and agreement rather than by the threat of armed force. This device had now become in his mind a far better instrument than Pitt's idea of guarantee, which he had advocated at Vienna.

Some such scheme must have been running in his head throughout the Paris Conference, though we have no record

[1] " Principles upon which the proposed negotiations with France ought to be considered " : W.S.D. xi. 139.

of his thoughts until the moment for action came. Only
one other at Paris was also thinking of a system of universal
peace during these crowded days, and that in a very different
manner, though the germ of the idea had come indirectly
from Castlereagh himself. The Tsar was now in the high tide
of his mysticism. He had been in constant communication
with pietist devotees of an exalted and at the same time
essentially practical Christianity, since they believed that
it should influence all actions and not be kept separate
from mundane affairs. The origins of his new faith go back
to 1812 or beyond, and the Quakers of England had certainly
helped to confirm it. It was only since he had left Vienna,
however, that it had overcome completely his passionate and
essentially human disposition. Mme. de Krudener, probably
one of the least sincere of the votaries, had at last gained
access to him, and for a short period had great influence on
his mind. The origin of the Holy Alliance, however, so the
Tsar said, was to be found in the scheme of guarantee which
Castlereagh had proposed at Vienna, and which, it will be
remembered, had deeply moved him.[1] But translated into
the terms of the sect, it had assumed a shape as different from
Castlereagh's conceptions as it is possible to imagine. Peace
was to be found in a society on which all sovereigns and their
peoples were to act as true Christians. The mere enunciation
of so sublime a truth was sufficient in the Tsar's opinion to
secure its enforcement. The sovereigns themselves, divinely
appointed to lead their subjects to the true faith, must
solemnly declare their acceptance in the name of all, and all
would then be bound by an unbreakable bond.

The Emperor of Austria did not dare refuse the Tsar when
offered so sacred a treaty by a man whom he thought mad, but
better occupied with schemes of peace and goodwill than with
more dangerous things. He accordingly signed, after altering
only a few phrases in the document which seemed especially
ridiculous or blasphemous, and the King of Prussia, whose
simple nature was more easily satisfied, of course immediately
followed suit. Meanwhile the Tsar had himself approached
Castlereagh, who was therefore prepared when Metternich

---

[1] See above, Chapter VII, Section 4, p. 429.

in great secrecy asked his advice. In the highly irreverent account which Castlereagh forwarded home he related how the two examined unsuccessfully every expedient to stop "this piece of sublime mysticism and nonsense." For Britain the situation was especially awkward, since the British sovereign had no power to sign an international act; but Castlereagh had preferred that the project should assume the character of a personal one between sovereigns, foreseeing the reception it would be likely to receive from his Cabinet, "since Wilberforce is not yet in possession of the Great Seal." It was, as he confessed, "a scrape"; yet he hoped the Tsar might be humoured since his mind was not "completely sound," and that the Prince Regent might be allowed to accede in a personal way.

Since the Tsar had expressed his delight that his treaty had been drawn up in the most *irreligious* capital of Europe, there can be no doubt that he was anxious for the Prince Regent's signature to this affirmation of Christian doctrine. But Liverpool received the news in a most petulant manner, hinting that the Tsar ought to have been prevented from indulging himself so far. The forms of the British Constitution made it quite impossible for the monarch to sign a treaty even of this benevolent character, and all that the Prince Regent was allowed to do was to send a personal letter expressing his entire agreement with the sentiments of the treaty—and fortunately the Tsar found this support as good as an actual accession to the treaty itself.[1]

All this must have been very disconcerting to Castlereagh, for at the very moment he was engaged in debating with the

[1] To Liverpool, Sept. 28, 1815 ; from Liverpool, Oct. 3, 1815 : *W.S.D.* xi. 175, 183.   To A'Court, March 26, 1816: *F.O. Sicily*, 74. Uchtritz to Einsiedel, Oct. 1, 3, 1815 : *Dresden St. A*.

In the Londonderry Papers is a draft of the treaty, apparently the first draft shewn Castlereagh by Metternich, which contains one or two striking phrases subsequently deleted presumably by Austrian influence. Thus it would have definitely associated *les sujets* of the contracting parties as well as the sovereigns in the promise to regard one another as brothers united in an indissoluble fraternity ; and at the end of the clause added : " Il en sera de même des armées respectives qui ne s'envisageront pareillement que comme faisant parties de la même armée, appelée à protéger la paix et la justice."   These are, no doubt, the alterations which Metternich claimed that he forced the Tsar to accept (Metternich, *Mémoires*, i. 211).

Other details of drafting are given by Werner Näf, *Zur Geschichte der Heiligen Allianz* (1928), but he has not read the documents in *W.S.D.*

Tsar the form of the more practical treaty of Alliance which he had himself suggested. The Tsar was not, however, so engrossed in the spiritual as to neglect the temporal Alliance. He had been impressed with the project suggested in Castlereagh's memorandum, and it was he who in this matter also first put forward a draft shortly before he left Paris. As might be expected, Castlereagh hardly found that the Tsar's project satisfied his own ideas on the subject. It was too vague as to method and action, and too explicit in its references to keeping Louis and the *Charte* alive to suit a British Minister.

He accordingly submitted a draft of his own, and this, with a few verbal alterations, became the treaty subsequently signed. It was perhaps natural that he should say nothing to the Cabinet about it until time had been given for the effects of the Tsar's Alliance to disappear. At any rate, they accepted it with only one criticism. Liverpool, since by now most of his colleagues had departed to their usual autumn visits, did not even summon a Cabinet. He sent it from Walmer Castle to Bathurst, who, with Pole, Sidmouth, and Vansittart, examined and approved it, with the exception of a reference to the "legitimate sovereign." They couched their approval in a low key, however, and hardly appeared to regard it as Castlereagh did as of more importance in restraining France than the treaty she herself was to sign. "It is the fear of our union that will keep France down," he told them, "and the knowledge that the Duke of Wellington commands only the advance guard of the force against which they will have to contend, if they again involve themselves in war." [1]

The first five articles of the treaty are almost exclusively concerned with this idea. The Four Powers bound themselves to act against France, if necessary with the whole of their forces in case she attacked the new frontiers or allowed Napoleon or any of his family to return to the throne. If a

---

[1] To Liverpool, Oct. 15, 1815 : *B.D.* 386. From Liverpool, Oct. 20, 1815. Sidmouth to Bathurst, Oct. 18, 1815 : *W.S.D.* xi. 203, 204. Bathurst to Liverpool, Oct. 19, 1815 : *Bathurst*, 390. Liverpool : "In substance meets all our ideas"; Sidmouth : "Upon the whole, satisfactory"; Bathurst, after meeting Sidmouth, Vansittart, and Pole : " You are at liberty to give [our] approbation."

revolution occurred in France, the Four Powers were to decide in conjunction with the King what action was to be taken.[1]

It was on the sixth article that Castlereagh introduced the idea of recurring conferences of the Great Powers on all matters of European concern. It is significant that he does not draw any attention to this device in the long dispatch which he sent to Liverpool, nor is there any comment by the Cabinet upon it. Yet it cannot be doubted that Castlereagh was fully alive to the importance of his suggestion, for there was a deliberate alteration of the Tsar's words. It was, however, hardly a suitable time to descant on anything else but what was after all the main object of the treaty—the Alliance against France. For the moment this was the bond that united the Powers and won the support of the British Cabinet to so close an association with Europe. Castlereagh had secured all that he wanted in this respect. The future would shew whether he could transform it into a permanent machine for ensuring European peace. He was content, therefore, to establish the idea of recurring conferences amongst the Four Powers, and he refused to complicate matters by accepting the proposal of the Tsar that the King of France should be a party to the treaty meant mainly to safeguard Europe against the country over which he ruled.

At the same time he refused to recur to the proposal of a general guarantee of all the frontiers of Europe, such as he had himself advocated at Vienna. The new boundaries were protected against French attack by the four Great Powers. That must suffice for the moment. Peace was more likely to be obtained by the new system of diplomacy to which, as was to be shewn in succeeding years, Castlereagh attached the highest possible importance.[2]

---

[1] For an extended analysis and commentary on the treaty, see my *Foreign Policy of Castlereagh, 1815-1822*, 54-55.

[2] Count Hardenberg stated that the Russian plenipotentiary proposed that the King of France should be a party to the treaty (to the Prince Regent, Nov. 8, 1815: *Hanover St. A.*) and Gentz (*Dépêches inédites*, 198-99) that Castlereagh refused to insert the general guarantee in the treaty.

4. CASTLEREAGH AND RECONSTRUCTION

Castlereagh's work during the period of reconstruction has always been better appreciated than that of the period of the Alliance. It was better known, and foreign historians like Capefigue and Thiers ascertained some part of the truth. Castlereagh shared, of course, in the general reproach which was directed against the men who made the Treaty of Vienna, when the national movements of the second half of the nineteenth century overthrew their work. But the strength of his personality and the success of his policy were to some extent recognised. Only in Britain did the malicious criticisms of the Whigs and Canningites refuse him even a moderate amount of diplomatic skill and control over the great decisions of the time.

Recent researches have reversed this judgment in Britain, and still more effect has been produced by the Great War and the peace which followed it. There is now a standard of comparison, and the work of the autocrats and aristocrats in 1814–15 can be placed alongside that of the leaders of the democracies in 1919. It is probable that the facile criticisms of the reconstruction of 1814–15 will altogether disappear from the text-books and be replaced by others which take into more account the circumstances of the period and the occasion.

At any rate, the old assumption that Castlereagh was an irresolute and mediocre man, who allowed himself to be manœuvred by the subtler Talleyrand and Metternich, must disappear for ever in the light of recent research. The legend, which was never believed in France, was almost entirely due to the attacks of the Whigs and Canningites, who never attempted to ascertain the truth. For nothing could be plainer than that, throughout the period of reconstruction,

Castlereagh had not only a mind but a plan of his own, and if anything, criticism is needed because he too often took a lead and was too anxious to carry through his own schemes. From the moment of his entry into office he had before him the new Europe which Pitt had planned, and every step that he took was directed towards bringing it into existence. Much of his success was due, of course, to forces over which he had no control. But often he skilfully directed affairs into channels which led to the results so long desired. Many parts of the European reconstruction were more his work than that of any other statesman of the time.

It was the resources of his country, so freely expended at the critical moment, which gave him the opportunity to carry out his programme. But money alone would not have achieved so much had it not been controlled by a man who knew what he wanted. He had more sustained energy than any other of those who directed the affairs of a Great Power during the period. The Tsar's activity was liable to interruption by impulse, Metternich's by pleasure seeking, Hardenberg's by infirm health. Castlereagh's exertions never relaxed. Ceaseless vigilance, unremitting hard work, unfailing patience, undaunted courage, gave him the position to which he attained in 1814.

Such qualities often defeat their own ends in diplomacy, as well-worn aphorisms attest. Perhaps it is true of Castlereagh that, during the early part of the Congress of Vienna, he shewed too much zeal for a cause which was not really his. But generally he had the gift of getting others to adopt his point of view without intimidating or wearying them. Though no foreigner felt that he had penetrated his reserve, yet the mask was never regarded as assumed to conceal his intentions, but only his emotions. He was nearly always singularly frank with those with whom he had to do business. The prescription which he took with him to the Continent of open and formal discussion of the most delicate problems he was ready to apply on almost every occasion. The secret treaty was an exception produced by an unforeseen emergency. Castlereagh was always at his best when he placed all his cards on the table before his colleagues as a body. By the end of the period it was recognised that he was the natural leader of the European council, as the negotiations at Paris in the autumn of 1815 clearly shewed. He had reached this position because the other Ministers had learnt to trust him and rely on his word in a manner which they could not apply to one another. When it is remembered that he was almost without experience of European society, never spoke French with perfect ease or with a good accent, and had a wife whose too obvious desire to help him repelled where it was meant to attract, the triumph of his personality was a remarkable one.

His was essentially a victory for character. In imagination Alexander and Metternich, in subtlety Talleyrand, in experience Hardenberg, excelled him. Their minds certainly moved as fast, perhaps faster, than his. He won his position by the patient consideration and goodwill which he always shewed even when he differed from them. They could not help but be impressed also by the courage and firmness with which he took the responsibility for great decisions, never hedging when the crisis came or riding off on the necessity of awaiting instructions. He was fortunate, of course, in the loyalty of his colleagues at home. How important it was, and how soon such prestige could be undermined, was seen during the crisis at Vienna by the effect of even a few whispers that he had lost their confidence.

Above all, Castlereagh had the great gift of obtaining what he wanted in such a manner that others came to want it also. He had exactly the same ideal which Lady Gwendolen Cecil attributes to her father: "His own conception of a perfect diplomacy was always one whose victories come without observation." [1] At any rate, Castlereagh was very successful at persuading others that his plans were the same as theirs, or at the worst that they had gained the major part in the compromises which he was so expert in framing. It is true that he had been able to assume the position of the mediator of Europe, and that in the great controversies which arose he

[1] *Life of Robert, Marquis of Salisbury*, ii. 232. Since Lord Salisbury was the first British critic to appreciate Castlereagh's qualities at anything like their proper value, it may not be fanciful to suppose that there was some conscious imitation.

was not apparently fighting for exclusively British interests. But even in matters where those interests were paramount he succeeded in getting nearly all that he desired without incurring the resentment of others.

His success in this respect was largely due to his moderation and sense of proportion. He was always ready to give way on unessentials. Once the major point had been attained, he was very adept at making such concessions as completely satisfied his opponents. His perfect manners and handsome presence helped him to attain to this indispensable quality of the first-rate diplomatist.

He preferred to work in private, and avoided as far as possible appeals to Parliament and public opinion. In the forum a foreign Minister must always exaggerate his success and appear to have done better than his rivals. It is one of the terrible weaknesses of democratic control of foreign policy, and one of the main reasons why many of the best and most peace-loving Ministers have preferred to work in secret. Castlereagh obviously hated the kind of speech which it was necessary to make to win the approval of his countrymen. When he appealed to their patriotism, it was on duty and sacrifice that he dwelt rather than on pride or glory. He could defend a course of action by solid argument, but was quite incapable of appealing to the imagination or emotions of his audience. Indeed, he was inhibited by his character from such appeals, which undoubtedly seemed to him unworthy of the race. His Irish qualities he reserved for the family circle. In public affairs he disdained every-thing but matters of fact. Above all, he refused to flatter the national esteem. What speeches Canning would have made had he been in Castlereagh's place in 1814 and 1815! How he would have made his countrymen glow with enthusiasm at his unexampled position in the affairs of Europe! But Castlereagh probably thought that the British were suffi-ciently pleased with their importance, and he must have known how easily the place which he held in the councils of Europe could be made an object of jealousy and suspicion and lose half its value for the sake of a few moments of personal triumph.

He was not the man, therefore, to associate his countrymen with his policy, and he never tried to do so. He did not treat them with the same frankness that he treated foreign statesmen. Even his Cabinet accepted large portions of his policy rather because they trusted him than because they believed in it. Everything that he could conceal from Parliament he kept secret. His belief in himself and his distrust of his compatriots extended also to his own subordinates. Even Cooke, Clancarty, and his brother, who had more of his confidence than the others, were often left outside the inner processes of his mind. He preferred to do as much himself as one man possibly could. At Paris and Vienna he kept the threads of all the important negotiations in his own hands. His energy and mastery of detail never failed him under the inevitable mass of work, and he was doubtless right in thinking that he could do it much better than anyone else. But one result was that even those closest to him imperfectly appreciated the objects at which he was aiming, and were thus incapable of carrying them out when left to themselves. This great defect was one of the main reasons why his most important and most original plans were completely lost after his death. Unlike his master Pitt, he could leave behind him neither legacy nor disciples.

This secretiveness on one or two occasions became something which deserves a harsher word. Castlereagh deliberately misled Parliament as to the part which he had played in the Saxon and Neapolitan questions. The papers laid before the House were meant to deceive them as to the processes by which the final result had been achieved. Similarly, his public policy towards the second restoration of the Bourbons was assumed in order to make his real policy possible. The excuse that these problems were terribly difficult ones, depending on a number of factors which it was impossible to gauge accurately, hardly applies to explanations after the event. The concealment, which was known to the other leaders of the Alliance, must have led them to believe that Castlereagh was prepared to deceive his own countrymen deliberately when he could not win support for his policy in any other way. He would have been on far firmer ground had he revealed the motives which actuated him, which were quite defensible, and relied on the success of his plans to defeat the criticisms of the Opposition. No wonder that the British people never understood the principles on which the reconstruction was based! He never fully took them into his confidence. Those who admire his honesty of purpose and diplomatic skill must regret this blot on his character which no casuistry can palliate.

But within the limits of the Council Chamber he was a great diplomatist, and the objects which he sought were so original and so completely founded on a broad conception of policy, that he is fully entitled to the much abused name of statesman. He held to his course with a rare tenacity, and though often compelled to twist and turn by the startling changes in fortune which he witnessed, he always returned to the same broad principles which he had inherited from Pitt. The final result was due to his faithfulness as well as to Pitt's foresight, though of course much of it was in the nature of things and beyond their control. That they aimed at what was possible was characteristic of both.

Castlereagh's greatest period was perhaps in the early months of 1814. He obviously lacked experience, and he failed in his plan to settle the reconstruction of Europe, while Napoleon was still on the throne of France. But it is hardly too much to say that without his energy, courage, and wisdom the coalition could never have entered Paris in triumph. At the same time he laid the foundations of the Alliance and made secure the most important of all British interests—Belgium. These great achievements were carried out at the headquarters of an army in which there were no British troops and in conjunction with sovereigns and statesmen who, when Castlereagh joined them, were almost as hostile to one another as to the enemy. The restoration of the Bourbons was also very much in the interests of Britain —and perhaps of France as well, if all the circumstances be taken into account. The skill and coolness with which Castlereagh handled these difficult problems has won the admiration of all who have studied them closely, whatever judgment they may have had of the policies themselves.

Napoleon himself, though imperfectly informed, recognised that it was Castlereagh who put the final touches to his downfall—one reason no doubt why he singled him out for special condemnation and abuse in the legends which he gave to the world at St. Helena.

Both Pitt and Castlereagh were more interested in constructing the new Europe than in completing the ascendancy of the British Empire in the rest of the world. Their instinct told them that a monopoly of colonial power was unwise. Thus in 1805 Pitt had been prepared to give back all the colonial conquests. Castlereagh had no need to go so far, nor would he have been allowed to do so. The strategic supremacy of Britain in every sea was carefully guarded. But other colonial territories were nearly all surrendered. British Guiana and Tobago were the only exceptions, for at the time the Cape was not appreciated at its proper value and only retained for strategic reasons. The surrender of the Dutch possessions in the East, and the rest of the West Indian Islands to Holland and France, was deliberately adopted not only to obtain the right kind of Europe, but also to avoid the reproach of aiming at colonial monopoly. It would have been easy to take the opposite line, but who can doubt that Castlereagh did the wise as well as the right thing in refusing so obvious a temptation?

The maritime rights of Britain he refused to compromise. British arrogance was there at its highest, for in declining even to discuss them, she claimed the right to dictate sea law to the rest of the world. Castlereagh, like all his countrymen, was quite unconscious of the assumptions underlying this attitude, and could never understand the feelings which it naturally provoked in other peoples. Fortunately for Britain it was a claim which was soon forgotten once peace had come, a weapon so powerful that it could only be used with effect in a world-wide war. Since by 1812 neutrality was an impossible position for any European Power, only the Ottoman Empire endeavouring to maintain it, all attempts to raise the question were purely academic and easily put on one side. The struggle that was going on with the young Republic on the other side of the Atlantic seemed so remote to Europe immersed in its own crisis, that there was never any danger that they would seriously press for influence on it. The Tsar's suggestions were also here easily refused. Sea power and the American struggle were domestic questions in which Europe had no concern.

In financial matters Castlereagh shewed himself a true aristocrat. He never, in fact, understood them, although he had to devote much of his time in the House of Commons to endeavouring to explain them. In his diplomacy he always subordinated British financial interests to political advantage. He was dealing with countries so much poorer than his own that he was always ready to make sacrifices for them. Undoubtedly, he could have saved some money had he adopted a harsher view. But he acquired for his country influence and prestige, and perhaps even rarer advantages, worth far more than what he lost in hard cash. He extended the same generosity to the enemy as well as to the Allies, and the moderation with which France was treated made it possible for her to pay her just debts with remarkable ease. Britain was so much more advanced in industrial wealth that these sacrifices were in the end borne easily enough. But at the time her national debt was a source of much anxiety, and the financing of the Continent was only accomplished with great difficulty. Many, including Napoleon, thought that in 1814 she had reached the limit of her resources. When this is remembered, the breadth of view which Castlereagh first, but also the Cabinet and the whole nation, shewed at this time is a remarkable one. It obtained little gratitude from those it most benefited, but it prevented the creation of other feelings, which might have been dangerous to Britain in later days. In avoiding the rôle of the creditor of the new Europe and in taking the financial burden of the Alliance almost entirely on herself, Britain was probably acting by instinct more wisely than she realised.

In commercial, as distinct from financial matters, Castlereagh shewed himself well in advance of his contemporaries. He was, in fact, already aware that the mercantile age was over, and that for his own country at any rate the freer that trade was made the better. He was against the monopoly of the East India Company, and he seems even so early to have been ready to allow free trade with the British Empire. His dispatches on the colonial monopoly of Spain shew that he had gone further in this matter than most of his country-men.[1] Yet he was reluctant to bring too much pressure to bear on continental Allies to admit British goods. He saw, for example, that the Treaty of 1810, imposed on Portugal at the moment of her extreme weakness, could not be enforced in its entirety when the danger had passed. Though during the war he pressed his Allies to open their ports freely to British trade, so that the exchanges could be maintained, he made no attempt to impose commercial restrictions upon them at the peace. Nor was the territorial settlement in any way distorted so as to give free entry to British goods, a course which Napoleon thought Britain was foolish not to have adopted. This moderation the creator of the Continental System thought as curious as the refusal to keep the French and Dutch colonies. But Castlereagh realised, as Napoleon never did, that the best commercial asset was goodwill, and while he was never apparently very much interested in this aspect of British policy, so far as he did take it into account his attitude was entirely sound.

Castlereagh's main interest, like that of his master, was in the reconstruction of Europe in such a manner as to preserve the peace of the world. For that purpose he relied on the balance of power. The principle has been attached to the work of the Congress of Vienna ever since, but it was Castle-reagh more than any other statesman who consciously applied it. The others had necessarily to subordinate it to their own special claims in Europe. Each sought the hegemony of a special area—the Tsar in Poland, Hardenberg in north-east Germany, Metternich in southern Germany and Italy. Only Castlereagh could take a general view of the whole. For him the balance of power meant the reconstruction of Central Europe, which had all but disappeared under French pressure and again seemed threatened by the Russian advance. The reconstruction of Prussia and Austria as Great Powers was but a part of the whole scheme. They were to be brought

[1] See above, p. 70.

close together so as to present a united front to east and west. So long as this was done, Castlereagh cared little for the methods by which it was brought about. The sacrifice of Saxony seemed the obvious way, and he therefore warmly advocated it. But it was the creation of a strong centre at which he was aiming, and he was obviously disappointed that the two German Powers failed to make a more united Germany, with federal institutions and a federal army. It was not, however, any recognition of the principle of nationality which led him to this view, but rather the necessity of separating France and Russia by as strong and compact a mass of power as possible.

The same motive dictated his attitude towards Italy—that part of his policy which lends itself most easily to criticism. Had the Whigs concentrated on the essential points in it, instead of wasting their time in foolish championship of the rights of outworn and tyrannous republican oligarchies like Genoa and Venice, they might perhaps have done some good. In handing over Italy to Austrian influence Castlereagh had two motives: he wished to draw her attention to a sphere where she would not be in rivalry with Prussia, and he wished to protect Italy from French aggression. That these were solid reasons cannot be disputed. Nor was it possible at that date for the Italian states to protect themselves or create a united Italy strong enough to resist pressure from outside. Only Piedmont shewed promise of being able to stand by itself, and it owed its increase of territory, which eventually enabled it to become the rival of Austria in Italy, to Castlereagh more than to any other man. Had Murat shewn more sincerity and skill he might perhaps have won a similar position in the south. But circumstances were against such a solution, and however Castlereagh's methods may be condemned, the final result was almost inevitable. Austria had therefore to be the guardian of the Mediterranean against France, and to support her there remained a part of British policy until Italy could take over the task herself.

The other buttresses which Castlereagh tried to erect in Europe were well devised. The union of the Netherlands was indeed short-lived, but it kept Antwerp and Belgium out of French hands, and paved the way for the treaty which kept it safe till 1914. As Napoleon often insisted, it was only Britain's persistence which forced Europe to fight until the task was accomplished. But for Castlereagh France would undoubtedly have been given her 'natural frontiers.' The advance of Prussia to the Rhine was essential to the creation of a strong and united Germany such as Castlereagh always desired, and became the keystone of European security. It had in it dangers of its own, but it was impossible to guard against these in 1814–15. That the line established from the Scheldt to the Alps was the same, with a few insignificant exceptions as that which has now been recognised on both sides of the frontier as a just one and specially guaranteed by Britain, is a testimony to the judgment of the man who did more than any other to place it on the map. The fortresses which guarded it were not only designed by Britain, but in a sense placed under the special protection of Europe, and served their purpose until out of date. The union of Norway and Sweden Castlereagh had only accepted perforce, but he justified it on sound principles, and the separation of Scandinavia from Germany, which he always advocated, was essential for the former's happiness and prosperity.

The eastern frontier of Germany was made against Castlereagh's wishes. He undoubtedly exaggerated the menace of Russia, whose rapid advance had disturbed him more than most of his contemporaries. In refusing to recognise the possibility of recreating an independent Poland, he was only acquiescing in a fact, however lamentable, which he had no power to change. Once that is admitted, he was justified in thinking that the Poles would be as well off under Prussia and Austria as under their most bitter enemies, the Russians. His suspicions that Alexander's policy of preserving their kingdom would not last was proved true by Alexander's successors, in spite of the attempts made at Vienna to guarantee the future. The problem of Poland was beyond the power of any British statesman to solve, and the criticisms which have been levelled at Castlereagh on this head are without foundation.

In general, the Europe which Castlereagh helped to create was one in which he might have confidence so far as frontiers were concerned. The balance of power had clearly been reconstituted. The Four Great Powers were none of them a menace to the others. The smaller Powers had been made for the most part into units which would gravitate round a centre and give cohesion to the whole. For refusing to recreate the mass of tiny states, however venerable, for which Mackintosh pleaded, the statesmen of Vienna deserved praise. It was also impossible for them to recognise national forces which, except in Poland, were unconscious of their existence. No other policy but that of the balance of power was possible, and in working it out under such difficult circumstances with such success Castlereagh made the best of the opportunity that presented itself. He would have been the first to admit that it was often distorted by claims and privileges, which could not be ignored. But in the main he had accomplished all that he had set out to do.

Less satisfactory was his attitude towards the internal problems of the newly constituted states. He had no belief in the capacity of most Europeans to govern themselves, and on most occasions he was on the side of the autocrats rather than of their subjects. There were, however, exceptions. Both in 1814 and 1815 he perceived that France must have some kind of constitution under her restored king, and his advice to Louis in 1815 was a model of constitutional principle. The same conception was applied to the new kingdom of the Netherlands and to Switzerland. In all these cases Castlereagh saw that the way to avoid the extreme of democracy was by setting up moderate institutions which associated some portion of the citizens with the responsibility for rule. There are some signs that he would have been ready to support similar institutions in the south of Europe, if they could have been established there. But when he had to choose between undiluted autocracy or such monstrosities as the Spanish constitution, he took the side of the dynasts without hesitation. It may be true that it was the only safe alternative, but if Castlereagh had endeavoured to create suitable constitutions in Spain, Naples, and Piedmont, as he did in France, the whole history of Democracy in the Mediterranean regions might have been different.

Castlereagh was, however, always ready to institute new devices to protect subjects of different nationality from their rulers.   He saw from the first that some such measures were necessary to conciliate the Belgians, and he was the foremost advocate of their application to the Poles.   In the same way he warmly welcomed the concessions which Bernadotte made to his Norwegian subjects.   The Genoese also had their privileges safeguarded.   These measures were in part due to the pressure of British public opinion, but such a policy was in harmony with Castlereagh's ideas of a balanced constitution, and he advocated them from conviction as well as from necessity.   That he could not devise machinery to make such concessions a reality was inevitable, since it took a hundred years to bring it into existence.   But in accepting such restraints by treaty for themselves and not merely imposing them on some of the new states which they created, the autocrats went further than any statesman of a Great Power has since had the courage to go.

All these matters were obviously in Castlereagh's mind associated with the greater problem of ensuring the peace of Europe.   There he made his greatest and most original contribution to international politics.   The idea of a general guarantee of the new European frontiers came from Russia originally, and Castlereagh was obviously never quite happy about it.   His repeated assertions that since Britain took guarantees seriously she could not give them except where she had special interests, shew that the device was not one that he would have invented himself.   Nevertheless, he advocated it at Vienna, partly to prevent other combinations, partly for the sake of the safety of the Ottoman dominions. But once that elaborate plan had failed, Castlereagh ceased to rely upon the idea of guarantee for the maintenance of the peace of Europe.   He substituted his own specific of conference amongst the statesmen of the Great Powers.   That he more clearly than any other man of his age saw the value of this new device there is abundant evidence.   He had learnt the lesson of the closing years of the war as no other had done.   No one else had come to a similar conclusion until Castlereagh advocated the idea at the second peace of Paris, and even then he failed to make it properly intelligible either to the other statesmen or to his own Cabinet.   It was meant for a Europe in which he himself should take the lead, and he spent much of the rest of his life in a vain endeavour to make it work.

He thought, of course, only of a static Europe.   Though the world had changed so much during his lifetime, he, like nearly all his contemporaries, was preoccupied with preserving the new order as fixed and irrevocable.   Castlereagh did not, indeed, like Liverpool, wish to go back to the eighteenth century.   Legitimacy as a principle made no appeal to him; it was merely an expedient.   He recognised fully that the post-war world was different to that in which he had grown up.   But there he stopped—or nearly so.   For the device of diplomacy by conference is in some sort a recognition that change must come.   At any rate, machinery was provided by which difficulties could be met.   But Castlereagh was a true Conservative in making the preservation of the existing order the main object of his policy.

Such an outlook was a natural one after twenty years of warfare.   It was no wonder that men in Castlereagh's position dreaded fresh upheavals after the convulsions of the last few years.   Their hopes of lasting peace were not, however, high. During the Congress of Vienna Liverpool consoled himself with the thought that future wars would at least be on the eighteenth-century model and free from the passions of the Revolution.[1]   Castlereagh wrote from Paris in 1815:   "I should wish to fix the attention of the Cabinet upon the system which they may consider the best calculated to preserve the peace of Europe and to put down the revolutionary spirit during the next seven years.   I have always been taught to believe that an interval of this nature was not only essential to our finances, but that with the aid of such a breathing time there is hardly any effort to which we should not be competent."[2]   Perhaps it was because he had such modest expectations that the peace which he organised lasted for so long.

[1] See above, p. 359.   [2] To Liverpool, Aug. 24, 1815: *F.O. Continent*, 24.

That it did so is the greatest testimony to the wisdom of the settlement of 1814–15. Judged in the light of the time and the circumstance, it was a great piece of constructive statesmanship. To the overthrow of Britain's deadliest foe, and the making of the new Europe in such a manner that Britain obtained the longest interval of peace she had ever enjoyed, Castlereagh contributed more than any other statesman of his time. Such achievements should be sufficient to place him for ever amongst the greatest foreign Ministers of his country.

APPENDICES

A. LETTERS FROM CASTLEREAGH TO HIS WIFE, 1814.

B. LETTERS FROM LORD LIVERPOOL TO CASTLEREAGH, 1814.

C. LETTERS FROM CASTLEREAGH TO SIR CHARLES STUART, 1815.

D. REPORTS FROM COUNT MÜNSTER TO THE PRINCE REGENT, 1814–15.

APPENDIX A

LETTERS FROM CASTLEREAGH TO HIS WIFE, 1814[1]

(i)

Münster, *Tuesday*, 5 *p.m.* [*Jan.* 1814].

MY DEAREST EM,

We arrived here this morning at 8 o'clock having travel'd without a halt since we parted. The roads for the last 40 miles have been dreadfully bad—worse than a plough'd field frozen. The servants' coach broke down, which has given us some hours in bed whilst they were coming up in a country waggon. The last 20 English miles took us $10\frac{1}{2}$ hours and I only marvel how our English carriages could bear it. We walked a great part of the road to save the tolls. The weather is cold but wholesome and we have no right to complain.

We are just setting off by Paderborn and Cassel to Frankfort : we were strongly advised against the road by Düsseldorf.

I hope to hear from you whenever the messenger comes. God bless you dearest love.

Ever your affecte.
C.

(ii)

Frankfort, *Jan.* 15, 1814.

MY DEAREST EMILY,

I send a few lines by R. Gordon to say we are so far quite well, our bones a little sore; it is lucky I did not bring the coach, it never could have borne the frozen masses over which we bump'd. German dirt is beyond the worst parts of Scotland, and nothing after you leave Holland to amuse in the costume of the people. I hope to be more pleased on the borders of Switzerland—I set out to-morrow for Basle—I shall then know better what our plans are likely to be but I see no probability, after all the time lost at sea and on land, of our Sejour being such anywhere as could reconcile me to your undertaking such a journey

[1] From a typescript of the originals in possession of Lord Londonderry.

(600 miles) on such roads and at such a season. Robinson and I have hardly ever seen any other object than the 4 glasses of the carriage cover'd with frost which no sun could dissolve, so that we were in fact imprisoned in an Ice House for days and nights, from which we were occasionally remov'd into a dirty room with a black stove smelling of tobacco smoke or something worse.

God preserve you Dearest Em.,
Yours ever in haste,
C.

(iii)

Durlach, Monday morning, 2 a.m.

My dearest Em,

I have stopp'd at two in the morning to read some dispatches on their way home and send you a line to say I am well about 70 miles in advance of Frankfurt on Monday morning. I hope to reach Basle, 260 miles, in the night, between Tuesday and Wednesday. We have a thaw and it is pleasanter travelling. I bought you some Frankfurt finery, which you will receive in a few days. Hope I shall not be like Blackwood and my lace prove English. Thank Emma for her kind recollection.

Ever yours,
C.

(iv)

Basle, Jan. 22, 1914, 9 p.m.

My dearest Em,

I am just getting into my carriage to go to Head Quarters at Langres which Clancarty will show you on the map. Everything goes on well and I hope we shall prosper in the end. I wish I could bring you to us, but you must feel it is quite impossible when our movements are so uncertain. The Emperor of Russia went to the army the day before I came. The King of Prussia and the Emperor of Austria both gone and I am carrying out the rear. In order to move with more freedom where we may find no post horses I have bought 10 here for £25 each : we can then move at our pleasure.

I send by the messenger a little box with some of the products of this town. The lady is very pretty and a little like your Ladyship, therefore you will keep this for me. The two gentlemen I send to comfort you, which is being more generous than you were to me in giving me your last instructions. If you are satisfied with one beau, keep the handsomest, and give Emma the old fellow with beard with my love to hang about her beautiful neck.

God bless you in haste,
C.

(v)

Langres, *Jan.* 30, 1814.

MY DEAREST EMILY,

I suppose after Charles's long and humbugging epistle I shall be in your black books ; but I am the honest man and he is the gay deceiver. You are now 3 weeks journey at least from this place. The ground is covered with snow, and I ought to be in England by the time you could get here. We begin our negociation on the 3rd at Châtillon, where Caulaincourt has been waiting for some days. I have appointed the 3 ministers here negociators and shall go myself to superintend their progress, so you see I am not so great a hero as you suppose. I have now made acquaintance with all the great wigs here. The Emperor Alexander would be your favourite. He has 30,000 Guards here that are the finest soldiers I ever beheld. When I can calculate at all movements or events, you shall have my plans. Till then don't stir, lest I should give you the slip and return by Paris.

I am quite well. Work is hard—and I never see a single princess.

So God preserve you,
C.

(vi)

Langres, *Feb.* 1st, 1814.

MY DEAREST EMILY,

We move the day after to-morrow for Châtillon to pay Caulaincourt a visit who has sent me over some English newspapers. We are covered with snow—I see in Dublin they are buried in it. Charles went over yesterday to old Blücher to pay him a visit after his battle. He says the old boy invited them all to dine with him at the Palais Royal on the 20th of February with all the *Mamselles*. The army is in motion and a general action was yesterday calculated upon for to-day, but Charles thinks the French are drawing off and retiring towards Troyes. A Prussian officer said to a French vidette, yesterday, " Le Roi de Naples a déclaré pour les Alliés, et le Danemark est à nous." " Ce n'est pas vrai." " Vous combattez pour un tyran qui fait le malheur de l'univers." " Cela *est* vrai—nous le scavons."

I long for a messenger from the Hague.

God bless you,
C.

I am quite well.

(vii)

Châtillon, *February* 6.

MY DEAREST EM,

I take chance of a messenger going direct by Calais to London to send you a line to say I am quite well. This little village is quiet and clean compared with Head Quarters. There is no other society than the Diplomatic Corps. Yesterday we all dined with Caulaincourt. He is a well bred man of about 40, something like the Duke of Richmond, but better looking. I am lodged here in the house of an old lady, Madme de Marmont, mother of the Marshal: they are very civil and kind and my room is very clean. Bye the bye ought you not to send Alick back to his Porter. When I invited you to meet me at Paris, it was by the direct route, not the detour which is endless. I can find nothing pretty for you in this country, and I only touched Switzerland at Basle. If we meet at Paris, we may make amends.

God bless you, dearest friend,
Yours ever,
C.

(viii)

Langres, Feb. 8, 1814.

MY DEAREST EM,

The messenger carries the news of another victory: 60 pieces of cannon, and Blücher in march to the *Mamselles*. As I am a bad boy, I do not consider myself entitled, under your secret dispensation to Charles, to assist; so I shall go to the gentlemen at Châtillon, and leave both love and war to those to whom such pursuits appertain. Recollect that I have saved you from a 3 weeks journey in snow, and really a confusion here which you ought not to encounter. If the sky clears up I shall be too happy to embrace you in the capital of La belle France: you will prefer it to Blüchers' *best*, and we may go home by Dover—Clancarty can always judge how far this project can be safely executed. *Quite, quite well.*

God ever bless you,
C.

(ix)

Chaumont, February 28.

MY DEAREST EM,

You see we do not make much progress towards Paris, and as the negociation is also at a stand still, I have moved to Head Quarters, where I find ample employment. We have been retreating for some days which is flat work, especially in cold weather; but to-day we put the horses heads the other way, and I have just heard that Schwarzenberg has given Marshal Victor a good drubbing at Bar sur Aube, about 30 miles from hence. The negociators at Châtillon are spitting over the bridge, which Charles says is very bad fun. The French have, I believe, advanced upon Châtillon and driven the Austrians away—the last accounts left the Ministers with citizen soldiers as Guards of *Honor* at their gates—Burghersh is afraid they may carry off his wife as she is not *accredited*. Bradford I hear has been there, but I have not seen him—I have not heard from you for an age. God bless you dearest dr. Em. I am quite, quite well but hard worked.   C.

(x)

Chaumont, *March* 4.

MY DEAREST DR. EM,

I see I am in disgrace, but I do not deserve it. Whatever nonsense you may get travellers to talk to you about following the army, believe me it is not what you ought to encounter, even when everything is going smooth : but when the troops are in retreat it is still less fit for a woman. I can assure Lady B's undertaking is so commented upon, and I can promise you she is herself heartily sick of it. When Robinson left us for England, the sort of hearty wish with which she said, " how much I would give to be of your party," proved that following an army is not quite so joyous a life as you suppose it.

We are again moving the army forward—they have retaken Troyes, which puts people in spirits. The troops have fought well and taken about 2,000 prisoners.

I cannot yet fix any precise time for my return. Liverpool says I am not *absolutely* wanted till after Easter that is the 20th of April, and lays all their commands upon me not to stir till I have brought matters to some point.

Robinson just come back.

God bless you dearest friend.
Your ever affect.
C.

(xi)

Chaumont, *March* 12.

MY DEAREST EM,

I am still in this dirty and dull town, which has nothing to reconcile one to it, but a sense of public duty. I have only one small room, in which I sleep and work and the whole Chancellerie dines, when we can get anything to eat—Charles who is always full of resource sent young Wood with his caravan and so to Dijon from Châtillon. He returned in triumph with 3 dozen fowls and 6 dozen of wine—the army have eat up everything and the dogs alone live well, having plenty of dead horses at convenient distances on all the roads to feed on.

I am impatiently watching the moment when I can say something to you about our future movements, and I hope by the next messenger to throw some light upon this. I see your letters with delight : so pray don't be so stingy with them.

The Arch-Duchess Catherine is, I believe, by this time at the Hague on her way to England. She is, I understand, a very charming personage. The Emperor desires you will be very kind to her, and give her all sort of information and advice about England. Let her know that *I* particularly desire you to offer H.R.H. all possible assistance.

God bless you, dearest friend. I am call'd away. C.

(xii)

Chaumont, *March* 15.

MY DEAREST EM,

I am just setting off for Bar sur Aube, where we hardly hope to find a place to put our heads. It was very bad when I was last there, and as it has been twice since taken by assault, I fancy neither the *houses* nor their *inhabitants* are much the better of it.

Bradford is here, talking incessantly, but highly delighted with the lions. We were at the Emperor's Mass when the news of Marmont's defeat and the capture of Rheims arrived. H.I.M. order'd a *Te Deum* on the spot which was very well sung, and it was amusing enough to observe the French part of the audience kneeling down and returning thanks for their *drubbing*.

I wish you would go to Amsterdam, see the Inauguration and write me a long account of it. Tell Clancarty to find out what their new constitution is and to send me an account of it.

Love to Emma, dearest friend. God bless you. We shall *soon* meet, by hook or by crook.

Yours ever,
C.

(xiii)

Dijon, *March* 30.

MY DEAREST EM,

When I am tried for leaving my wife behind me I shall call Lady Burghersh as my first witness, who was obliged to fly from Chaumont and live in a bivouac with all the heavy baggage of the army, without the possibility of changing her chemise unperceived, except the ceremony was performed in the dark of the night. Another proof how pleasant the travelling is : Wessenberg was laid hold by the armed peasantry, plunder'd of everything, and produced for Bounaparte's inspection, I believe, without a fig leaf, there being none to be found. W. left [Napoleon] yesterday morning, at Doulevent on the Aube, in no very pleasant temper, having two days before lost 100 pieces of cannon, 8

Generals and 6000 prisoners. The Allies were near Paris, where perhaps we may yet meet on our way home.

This is a delightful town. It is the only one I have seen where the people looked clean and good humour'd. It was formerly fashionable. The Emperor of Austria and Austrian and Prussian Ministers return'd here from Bar sur Aube to avoid the enemy, we could not get to the Head Quarters—the French enter'd Bar, the enemy are left it.

I send you a washing gown made here which I hope you will like, also a cupid in the room of Tommy Tyrwhitt, who is now, I conclude, on his route to Switzerland.

Wellington has again made a great impression. Everything looks and I hope will end well.

God bless you dearest friend.
C.

Charles is with the Army.

(xiv)

Dijon, April 4.

My dearest Em,

The victories of the Allies—the occupation of Paris and the prospect of the nation adopting the white cockade, all lead me to hope that we may meet without further delay at Paris. If when you receive this Clancarty sees no objection, you have my full consent to proceed to Brussels, where you must advise with the learned as to your further movements in advance. I will meet you there with letters and take care that the Governor of the Pays Bas, General Vincent, shall be instructed to take you under his protection and forward you by the safest route to Paris. I will also send a messenger or two to assist your journey, with such instructions which I think may be of use. I flatter myself that the Declaration of Paris will tranquillize the peasants and make the roads safe, and I hope also to send you to Brussels either Bourbon passports or Talleyrand passports, in short some species of passports, which all good Frenchmen should respect in your Ladyship's fair hand.

I have laid in a stock of silks and old Sevres china for you here, but you must come for it, or else I will give it *en depit* to some belle at Paris.

God bless you dearest friend, I am a bad boy but you will forgive me when we meet which I trust will be in the fewest days possible.

Ever yours,
C.

I since thought it best to send Browne, the messenger, to be at your disposal and to arrange your journey for you to Brussels, etc.

APPENDIX B

LETTERS FROM LORD LIVERPOOL TO CASTLEREAGH, 1814[1]

(i)

Fife House, *December 29, 1813.*

. . . Bathurst will send you the copy of a private letter of Wellington's,[2] which is in all respects most important, and which will deserve your serious attention, before you arrive at your destination. I saw Monsieur yesterday. He was very full of the information they had received from different parts of France, and stated it as the opinion of all their correspondents, that if a French Prince arrived, there would be a general rising throughout the country. The point he particularly pressed was *one* of *them* being allowed under present circumstances to go to Wellington's Army, with the avowed permission of the General that they should not be molested or impeded in going to one of the ports of France occupied by the British Troops and that they would take their own measures, and at their own risk, for ascertaining the sentiments of the country. I stated the objections to both these propositions. The fact is that they might go to Germany without any manifest assistance on our part; this is scarcely possible with respect to France; otherwise, if they could reach St. Jean de Luz by stealth and without any apparent connivance on our part, the experiment might be worth trying, and I should think Wellington, from the letter to which I have alluded, would have no objection (to say the least) to their coming. I am to see Monsieur again on Thursday the 6th. of January, and I should be glad to know what you feel on this subject.

Bathurst thinks that some advantage might arise from Monsieur having some authority to communicate to his friends that, if the Bourbons were proclaimed, an immediate armistice by sea and land might be agreed to. I gave Pichegru such an authority in

---

[1] From the Londonderry Manuscripts.
[2] Wellington to Bathurst, Dec. 22, 1813 : *Gurwood*, xi. 390.

1803, and I can conceive circumstances in which much might depend upon such a declaration, but I doubt whether we could say anything positive on their head now, without the previous authority and consent of our Allies. . . .

I fear the fog still detains you at Harwich. I shall be most happy to find it clears away to-morrow, and that you will be able to sail. . . .

(ii)

Fife House, *December* 30, 1813.

I sent you the enclosed papers which Bathurst secured from the Comte de Grammont [1] (who is as you know a Captain in the 10th Lt. Dragoons) this morning. It evidently appears by them, that although Wellington does not *recommend* that a French Prince should be *sent* to this Army he clearly *wishes* one of them to come; the papers themselves are sufficient to establish this fact, but even if this were doubtful upon the face of those secured this morning, there can be no doubt of it, when connected with the letter, of which a copy was transmitted to you yesterday. Grammont is gone down to Hartwell. I have seen Monsieur, and am to see him again next Tuesday. I explained to them as distinctly as I was able, that, connected as we were by ties of alliance and concord with the allied Powers, it would not be possible for us to countenance *their* going unless upon communication with our Allies, or such a general rising in France as would justify us (in consequence of the known opinion of our Allies) in taking the step upon our own responsibility. The matter however will not rest here, he will make two propositions:

First we should send him a frigate to St. Jean de Luz with money arms etc. etc. in order that he might confer with Lord Wellington as to the measures to be adopted. If this cannot be agreed to, secondly that we would not prevent his going in a packet boat at his own risk, and only allow a frigate to convey him to his destination, or till he is safe from all chance of capture. The first must be refused, but can we in fairness refuse the second, after such a communication? At the same time I am aware of all the embarrassment in acceding to it and that his voyage will be represented as being made in concert with the Government, though not publicly acknowledged by them. I shall summon a Cabinet on Monday to talk this point over, and I intend in the mean time to see Count Lieven to show him the papers in confidence, and to endeavour to find out what he thinks it would be best to do under all the circumstances. I may likewise have an opportunity of knowing your opinion, before I see Monsieur on Tuesday. . . .

---

[1] Wellington to the Comte de Grammont, Dec. 20, 1813: *Gurwood*, xi. 381.

(iii)

Fife House, *January* 6, 1814.

I send you a copy of the papers which contain the whole of the correspondence between Monsieur and myself on the subject of the Comte de Grammont's Memorandum.[1] You will see by them, that your opinion has been adopted. I am however still of opinion that they will make an attempt to get to France before any answer can be received from the Head Quarters of the Allies. If they are determined to effect this at all risks, they will probably succeed. We should not be justified in imposing *Personal* Restraint upon them; some of them may apply for a common passport to go to Holland, I do not see how it could be refused, and they might then embark in a Dutch ship for St. Jean de Luz, which is a seaport; some may smuggle themselves out from this country under fictitious names. In short if they are determined to go, many means may be devised by which the end may be attained. All we can do is to refuse permission, to give no facilities, and to say that they cannot be received at Lord Wellington's Head Quarters, if they arrive there without our authority; our Declaration on this subject is now on record; the rest must be left to chance; we are not responsible for it.

I think it very desirable, however, that you should take an early opportunity of having a full communication with our Allies on this subject; there is certainly a growing opinion in France, in favour of the Bourbons. By the last account from Gen. Don, who (you know) is not a bright man, but on the other hand is safe and may be depended upon, it appears that he thinks for the *first time* that our opinion is gaining ground in Normandy and Britanny in favour of the ancient dynasty. Count Lieven has seen a person very lately arrived from France who relates a number of facts, which can hardly be invented and which confirm this opinion. I am persuaded Wellington does not overstate his own impressions and yet on the 22nd of November he says that if the French Princes were to come forward, and were supported by Great Britain, he is satisfied they would succeed.[2] I think more favourably of the state of opinion in the part of France occupied by our Army, than you appear to do. I have heard from experienced officers that there was one infallible criterion of the disposition of a country occupied, not the people being peaceable nor their bringing supplies as both may be occasioned by fear or money, but their giving you intelligence of the movements and proceedings of the enemy; this is an advantage which always belongs to the army which is favoured by the country.

---

[1] *W.S.D.* viii. 485–90.
[2] Wellington to Bathurst, Nov. 22, 1813: *Gurwood*, xi. 306.

It is what no money can adequately obtain, and in the American War the disposition of the different States was very justly estimated by our officers by the intelligence they secured from the people there. Now I believe it to be certain that Lord Wellington has been as well supplied with intelligence in France as he ever was in any part in Spain.

I have not entered so much into this subject for the purpose of intimating my opinion that we ought not to make peace with Bonaparte, if we can make it upon our own terms; I am satisfied we must adhere to the policy we have already adopted upon this point, but I do not think we should disqualify ourselves from playing another game, if we can not obtain peace on our own terms, by suffering the negociation to be indefinitely protracted.

It is very satisfactory to learn that the Allies have entered Switzerland and France. This will probably bring the contest to a short issue. They have no fortresses in their line of march to besiege. If they can not be successfully resisted in the field nothing can prevent their arriving in a short time in the interior of France, and even at Paris; this operation, if successful, must shortly end either in the destruction of Bonaparte's Govt. or in his accepting peace on the terms of the Allies. If on the other hand the Allies should be obliged to retreat they would probably prefer peace upon the frontier, and, though the terms would be far less favourable, yet peace must be so necessary to Bonaparte in his present situation, that it would not be possible for him to throw any very serious obstacles in the way of it. It is impossible under these circumstances not to feel the utmost anxiety that the contest in Holland and the Low Countries (particularly as far as respects Antwerp) should be brought to a successful issue, before any crisis of this nature arrives, that the question as far as respects these objects should have been decided by the war and not be left to be decided by the peace. This is at present our weakest point, but we rely with the fullest confidence on your successful exertions to bring about a large force in this direction as soon as possible. In the mean time every exertion shall be made here to enable Wellington to advance and to occupy as large a part of the south of France as he may find practicable. I send this letter by Jackson who will I hope overtake you before you get to the Head Quarters of the Emperor of Russia, which will probably be in some town in France by the time you are able to meet them.

P.S.—I forgot to state that Lieven was for allowing Monsieur to go to France.

(iv)

Fife House, *January* 12, 1814.

The Count Löwenheilm arrived here last week and I saw him on Friday. I found the principal object of his mission was to represent to the Prince Regent and to His Government the difficulties under which the Prince Royal of Sweden had been placed and the circumstances which had induced him to undertake the operations in Holstein instead of moving directly towards Holland. I did not fail to represent to him the bad effects which this determination had produced in this country—that these effects were rendered still more unfavourable from our having been led to suppose that General Winzingerode had received orders to march with a part of his army upon Holland, which orders had been subsequently countermanded. To this he replied (as we had heard from other quarters) that General Winzingerode was in possession of these orders, and that they were only altered upon his own representation that Davoust with his Corps would be able to escape to France if he had obeyed them. I stated to him that we had very different accounts of General Winzingerode's feeling on this subject, and that by the measures which had been adopted an opportunity had been lost of recovering easily what was most important to the policy and most interesting to the feelings of this country, and which would now require, I feared, a considerable sacrifice both of blood and treasure to obtain.

The only other point upon which he touched was the supposed intention of excluding Sweden from any discussions relating to peace, which might take place amongst the Great Powers previous to a Congress. I declined entering on this subject, and informed him that, as the object of sending you to the Continent was to give unity to our negociations, all discussions upon subjects of this nature must take place there, and that you were fully instructed with the sentiments of the Prince Regent's government upon them. To this he appeared entirely to assent.

The Prince Regent comes to Town to-night and will probably see him in the course of two days. I shall not fail to intimate to His Royal Highness the sort of language which it would be desirable that he should hold to him.

I received today your letter from the Hague of the 8th. and I trust you will now have a prosperous journey.

[News] . . . The disposition in this country for *any* peace with Bounaparte becomes more unfavourable every day. I hear it from all quarters and from all classes of people. I well know, however, how fleeting these sentiments are, and that we can only act right by acting steadily upon our own system.

The invasion of France will put to the test the moral disposition of the French people towards their present Government. If they are desirous of resisting it, they would hardly lose the opportunity. If on the other hand they submit to it, and support it, it will be a proof that from some cause or other they are determined to adhere to it, and in that case all foreign interference to overthrow it must in such a country be vain.

I think, however, that the feelings of the public here on the subject of the peace with Bounaparte and the circumstances of a negociation taking place whilst the Allied armies are on the French territory ought materially to influence the conditions of peace. Can it be too much to expect that under such circumstances France should be confined to her ancient limits? But, if the Allies should be so embarrassed by their Declaration as to render an arrangement on this principle impracticable, I trust that they will at least feel the importance of insisting upon the independence of the whole of the Netherlands including the fortress of Luxembourg.

Colonel Bunbury will go to Lord Wellington's Head Quarters to-morrow with full explanations on all points as to reinforcements and supplies. We are making an arrangement respecting specie, which will I trust be effected and enable Lord Wellington to put in motion the Spanish armies.

We are all here strongly impressed with the opinion that the fate of the war must be determined in the course of the next three or four months, and that every effort should therefore be made to bring it to a prosperous issue during that time.

(v)

Fife House, *January* 20, 1814.

I send you the despatch which was received last night from Sir Henry Wellesley containing the extraordinary intelligence of the signature of a treaty at Valençay between Buonaparte and Ferdinand 7th. The Spanish Government appear to have acted very properly on this occasion and I have not the least doubt that the Cortes will refuse to ratify the treaty.

This transaction is however an additional proof, if any were wanting of the baseness of Buonaparte ; especially when all the circumstances are considered under which it has taken place. Wellington justly observes in a private letter to Bathurst [1] that Buonaparte is so false and fraudulent that he even outwits himself. For what would he have lost by escorting Ferdinand to the frontier of Spain, and negociating with him there. In which case there probably would have been a large party in Spain in favour of the peace.

[1] Wellington to Bathurst, Jan. 10, 1814 : *Gurwood*, xi, 433.

I think this communication, when you have made it to the Allies, will strike them as a virtual breach of faith as to what was passing at the same time through St. Aignan and Caulaincourt, and that they will see how impossible it is to trust Buonaparte even for a day. I have the less difficulty in giving a strong opinion on this subject because I am perfectly prepared to advise peace in conjunction with the Allies, if they are of opinion that under all the present circumstances peace is desirable, and if they can make it upon the conditions to which you are authorised to assent. Our policy should be to keep the Alliance together and not to separate ourselves from it either in peace or war. But we ought at the same time not to conceal from ourselves or our Allies that any peace with Buonaparte will be only a state of preparation for renewed hostilities.

(vi)

Fife House, *January* 20, 1814.

I think it right to inform you that since I wrote to you last Monsieur desired to see me and told me that it was his intention to go to Switzerland under a *nom de voyage* and that he should apply therefore for a passport to sail from this country for Holland. I, of course, said that this would not be refused him, but that I recommended him not to go to the Head Quarters of the Allies without having first obtained their permission. I found afterwards that he had spoken on the subject both to Count Lieven and Fagel, and that they were not desirous, even if it had been practicable, to throw any obstacle in the way of his journey.

I have since learnt from a private source of information that the Duc d'Angoulême is going under feigned name to Passage. Monsieur abstained from saying anything to me on this point— and he goes of course at his own risk.

The Government did not feel that they would be justified in taking any strong measures for preventing the French Princes at such a crisis, from playing their own game. We have warned them of their danger, and refused them all facilities by which we ourselves could be committed. But we cannot conceal from ourselves that if we were in their situation we should act as they are acting—particularly after the representations, which, whether true or false, they are receiving from so many quarters, of the disposition of the people of France to rise in their favour, provided a French Prince made his personal appearance among them.

Before Monsieur reaches Switzerland the contest will probably be brought to some issue. If Buonaparte does not gain any considerable advantage over the allied armies, he will probably be compelled to sign the terms which are proposed to him. It remains only to be seen whether the advance of the Allies into the interior of France will of itself lead to the overthrow of his power, or to such a public manifestation of opinion in favour of the Bourbons as to induce the Allies to pause before they become parties to an act, which would not only re-establish but consolidate the authority of Buonaparte.

(vii)

Fife House, *January* 20, 1814.

Since you left this country I have received representations from persons interested, in almost all the foreign colonies against the restitution of them to the enemy in case of a general peace.

You are so fully aware of my sentiments upon the whole of this subject that I think it unnecessary to trouble you upon any of them except upon the memorial of the planters and merchants in Tobago, as the case of this colony does not appear to me to have been sufficiently considered before you left England. The island of Tobago is exclusively possessed by British proprietors. This is nearly the case with Demerara, Essequibo, etc. but there is a striking difference in the justice of the claims of the respective inhabitants of these colonies. A considerable part of the property vested in Demerara was vested there while they were Dutch colonies—the remainder whilst they were in the situation of conquered colonies and had no right to suppose that they might not be restored at a peace. The inhabitants of Demerara, etc. have no claim therefore on the justice of the country, whatever they may have on its policy—but the property of Tobago was vested in that island at the time it was a British colony. You are aware that it became so at the Peace of 1763—and remained in that condition till it was captured by France together with Dominica, St. Vincents and Grenada in the American War. There was certainly not an idea that it would have been left in the possession of France at the peace negociated by Lord Lansdowne, but the French made a great point in the negociation of keeping Dominique as possessing the only good harbour in the islands which they had conquered. And Lord Lansdowne at the close of the negociation for the purpose of recovering Dominica on account of its harbour agreed to cede Tobago. He had however this excuse that the island had been conquered and was actually in the possession of the French. We had no such good excuse at Amiens, and should be equally without it now, if we consented to restore the island to France.

In addition to all these considerations it is material that you should be informed of what I was not aware of till my attention was directed to it, that it appears by the Printed Papers before Parliament that during Lord Lauderdale's negociation in 1806 the French offered to restore Tobago to this country.

I have thought it right to trouble you with this detail in order that you may be fully apprized of the circumstances of this case which differ very materially from those of every other colony which can become the subject of negociation—and I have no doubt you will give them all the weight to which you may consider them as entitled.

(viii)

Fife House, *January* 21, 1814.

. . . I ought likewise to mention to you that in the last conversation I had with Monsieur he informed me that when he arrived in Switzerland he should endeavour if possible to put himself in communication with the allied sovereigns; and that he was authorized by the King of France to declare to them that in the event of his re-establishment he would be contented with ancient France and should not seek to retain anything beyond the frontier as it existed in 1789. I think it material to mention this circumstance as it differs very much from the language held by the emigrants some years ago.

(ix)

Fife House, *January* 26, 1814.

I wish you joy of the peace. with Denmark. It has taken at this moment a great weight from off our shoulders, as it sets free a large army and relieves us and our Allies from all the embarrassment of having to discuss the question respecting Norway in any negociation with France.

The ten thousand Danes for which stipulation is made in the 6th. Article, are certainly not worth the £400,000 which we are to pay for them. This calculation has been made I suppose upon the ground of the Swedish treaty, without adverting to the different circumstances of the two cases—however, as an option is left to us to retain the troops or not, there is no mischief in the stipulation. Our disposition is certainly to dispense with their services, but until we know more from you of our actual situation, it has been thought better not to come to any final determination on this head. It is conceived that no further inconvenience can arise from the delay than perhaps the necessity of paying them for a month more than would have been otherwise expected.

. . . If you cannot bring all matters to the point in which you would wish to leave them by such time as would enable you to return before the 1st of March, do not let this embarrass you. We can adjourn Parliament by authority for a fortnight, if it should be necessary, or we might go on with common business with understanding that no motion of political importance should be made till after your return. I do not believe there would be any difficulty in such an understanding for a reasonable time.

(x)

Fife House, *February* 4, 1814.

You will receive by this Messenger the answer of the American Government to our overture of the 4th of November, which they have published in all their papers. We must of course be prepared with a negociation to meet theirs at Gottenburgh. Upon talking it over with some of our colleagues, we are of opinion that a lawyer and especially a civilian, if a good one could be found, would be more proper for this business than a diplomat.

I have desired Sir William Scott would turn this in his mind, and suggest any name that may occur to him for consideration.

I think it possible you may have an application from Thornton to be engaged in this business, but I am sure it would never do. What is wanted is a man of legal mind and of a very accurate understanding. If Bragge Bathurst was not a Cabinet Minister he would be exactly the man for such a business—but there is some objection to employing a Cabinet Minister in such a negociation.

We return the Danish treaty today ratified with the exception of the 4th. Article. Thornton has committed a great mistake in adopting the conditions and principle of restitution in the convention of 1801. We were not then at war with Denmark. The colonies and prizes were taken only as hostages. Nothing was condemned, and the treaty for restitution took place three or four months after hostilities had commenced. We have now been in possession of the colonies five years. We have considered them and treated them as conquered colonies—and it could never reasonably be expected that we should make compensation for the revenues which we had enjoyed during the whole of that period.

The merchants interested in St. Croix are besides particularly clamorous on the point. In lieu of the 4th. article we have proposed the insertion of the Articles for restoring the French, Spanish and Dutch colonies in the Treaty of Amiens, which are conformable to antecedent treaties, appear perfectly equitable in themselves, and can give rise to no litigation.

We do not wish to restore the Danish colonies on less favourable conditions than other colonies have been restored, but we do not think that they are entitled in this respect to better terms.

Mr. Addington who carries over the ratification thinks the Danish Government will make no serious difficulty in acceding to this alteration.

(xi)

Fife House, *February* 8, 1814.

We have received your dispatches and the private and confidential letters which accompanied them of the 22nd January from Basle.

We are very well satisfied upon the whole with what passed at your first interview, and have little doubt you will be able to surmount the only serious difficulty that presented itself at that time.

We shall expect to hear by the next messenger of the result of your first interview with the Emperor of Russia, and I conclude, when this has taken place, you will be enabled to settle with the different ministers your plan of operation—God grant that another battle of Leipsic may occur at Châlons—this would strike at the root of the evil, and render all prospective arrangements comparatively easy. The military reports of your brother and Lord Burghersh are very encouraging. I own I wish, however, that the line of operations of the Allies was not so extended.

I am happy to find by your confidential letter that your ideas respecting the basis of a negociation, if we are to negociate in our present situation, so very much correspond with what I stated for your consideration in my letter of the 12th of last month. And if preliminaries are to be concluded with France upon this basis, I hope at least that the only condition of an armistice will be either that the Allies shall remain in possession of the provinces of France which they occupy, or if they agree to evacuate those provinces, that the fortresses out of the old limits of France, viz : Luxembourgh, Mayence, Wesel, and Huningen; and Turin, Mantua, Tortosa, Alexandria in Italy shall be put in the possession of the Allies.

You will recollect that a similar arrangement was insisted by Bonaparte in the armistice which took place in 1800 after the battle of Marengo.

I have desired Hamilton to send you copies of the dispatches from Sir Henry Wellesley, which are very satisfactory, as to the steadiness and good disposition of the Spanish Government. It is too ridiculous, however, their attempting to revive under present circumstances the question of Louisiana, and, as I understand from Fernan Nuñez, that of the former Spanish part of St. Domingo.

I trust the expedition with which you made your journey will have done no injury to your health and that you will find the means of returning home, when all your business is concluded, by a shorter and easier route.

(xii)

Fife House, *February* 12, 1814.

I received last night your despatch and letters of the 6th of February by Sylvester, through France—and this morning I have received your dispatches and letters by the messenger Williams.

The dispatches through Holland throw an entire light upon

those which came to us through France, and enable us to form a good judgement upon the present state of affairs.

The proceeding you have adopted, as to the course and form of the negociation is most highly approved.   So is the new basis which you suggested according to your dispatch No 4, and which has been so satisfactorily adopted by the Allies.[1]

I do not augur much from the first conference of the negociators on the 5th instant.   If Buonaparte feels his situation to be such as to render him sincerely anxious for peace, it is not his business to make little difficulties.

The maritime question was originally introduced as a *pomme de discorde* between us and our Allies.   As soon as he saw that we were agreed on that point, it was not to be expected that he would make any serious difficulty upon it, especially as we do not call upon him to make the sacrifice of any principle which he has advanced, but only to agree that the whole subject shall be *écarté* from the negociation.

The report of the next conference will probably throw material light on our situation—Caulaincourt will then be apprized of our basis, and of the nature of our propositions for peace, and we shall be able to judge how far they are likely to be entertained.

You can scarcely have an idea how *insane* people in this country are on the subject of any peace with Buonaparte, and I should really not be surprised at any public manifestation of indignation upon the first intelligence of a peace with him being received.

This ought not to make any substantial difference in the course of our policy—but it renders it necessary that we should not *lower* our terms.   Every Article in the peace you may be assured will be criticised with great severity ; and arrangements, which under other circumstances might even escape observation, will be looked to at the present moment with the greatest jealousy and apprehension.   Indeed I should not doubt that, if the Opposition could take up the Bourbon cause against Buonaparte, they would, upon a peace with the latter, overturn the Government.   This is however impossible—not from their forbearance—but from the impossibility of avowing that they would act upon such a principle, if they came into office.

In the midst of all these difficulties our course is clear.   Let us adhere in principle to the policy which was adopted before you left this country, but let us, at the same time, be impressed with the conviction that the events and successes which have since occurred, and the public feeling which those events and successes have excited, render it necessary to improve the arrangement, even upon the principle on which it was formed ; and particularly with the view of its becoming acceptable to the country, which can alone insure its continuance.

[1] See above, pp. 206–208.

I have thought it most prudent by this conveyance, not to enter into further particulars. I shall be obliged to you if you will acknowledge the receipt of my letters with their dates, as it enables me to know whether they have come to hand. I hope you received the one relative to the colony of Tobago. This object is of much importance to us, and can be none to France. The proprietors are all British. It is no point of strength, and it is just one of those objects which could not be conceded without strong marks of dissatisfaction in the present state of the public mind in this country.

With respect to the military movements of the Allies, God grant that they may continue to succeed, and that even if they should receive any check, they may not be discouraged from a perseverance in the contest. That such a check might materially affect the terms of peace I admit, but with perseverance and good countenance on their part, I am persuaded the enemy cannot ultimately foil them.

P.S.—I am afraid the Spaniards will be offended at not being included amongst the Great Powers in the first negociation. You know how proud they are. I have been endeavouring to manage Fernan Nuñez, and I think with some success. I recommend you strongly not to neglect Pizarro.

2nd *P.S.*—The only material point on which we differ with you is as to the *overthrowing* Buonaparte. We incline to the opinion that this event is desirable whatever might be the *immediate result* of it. No individual in France is capable of succeeding him, and if the ancient dynasty was not restored in the first instance, it would be the ultimate consequence.

No Government, be it what it may, could be so bad for Europe as Buonaparte; the very hatred which is borne to him by the people of other countries, and which he knows to exist, is for the same reason an obstacle to the continuance of peace, which would not be applicable to any other Government, however implacable in other respects. I admit, however, that if France continues to support Buonaparte, we must make peace with him, and that we ought not to look to his destruction by any means which, in progress, will tend to separate the Allies.

(xiii)

February 17, 1814.

We are anxious to hear what has been the result of the conferences which the Emperor of Russia was desirous should be renewed at Châtillon.

If a cause of delay was wanted which might not break in upon the principle of negociation, we are rather surprised that the treaty with Ferdinand the Seventh has not been made use of; requiring a preliminary explanation on that point would be fully justifiable in the eyes of all the world—and we might have a fair right particularly after the event of such a treaty to insist upon the liberation of Ferdinand as a preliminary of treating.

I state this as a good ground of delay, if delay is desirable on account of the progress of military operations. Upon this point those on the spot can be the only competent judges. Peace is as unpopular as ever.

It was reported and believed yesterday that there were divisions in the Cabinet and that I had resigned. There was as little foundation for the first of these reports as for the last. Be assured everyone is disposed to support you in what you do.

Pray secure Tobago if you can. The restitution of it would make a great clamour here, and cannot be pressed ultimately by France.

Discountenance likewise all idea of any compensation being made to France out of the colonies of Spain or Holland for the cessions she makes to us. This is a point which never should be conceded. Recollect that the Spanish part of St. Domingo is in possession of Spain. They will object to restore it and should be supported in this if possible.

(xiv)

Fife House, *February 27*, 1814.

I have received with the greatest grief and concern your private letter on the subject of the communication made by Count Lieven to the Emperor of Russia.

The nature of our constitution so entirely precludes the possibility of any communication on the part of our Government with foreign Powers, except through the accustomed official channels, that I should have trusted no misconception could have happened on such a matter. But it is most extraordinary that it should have occurred in your particular case, being entrusted as you were with this most important mission in consequence of your being Secretary of State for Foreign Affairs, a member of the Prince Regent's Government, and invested consequently with a discretion on all subjects on which you might have occasion to negotiate, which it is wholly unused to entrust to any Ambassador or ordinary Minister.

From all I have seen of Count Lieven, I am bound to do the fullest justice to the correctness and propriety of his conduct, and I am persuaded therefore that it never was his intention to represent the personal sentiments of the Prince Regent, communicated in conversation as those of an individual in favor of the Bourbon family, for whom His Royal Highness has always professed the strongest interest, as the sentiments which were to influence the Prince Regent's accredited Minister in the conduct of a negociation in which he was to act in conformity to instructions given him under the Sign Manual of His Royal Highness.

I can assure you that your conduct in every part of this business has met with the unqualified approbation of the Prince Regent and of his confidential servants; and that we sincerely regret that anything should have occurred to have given you so much uneasiness.

With respect to the sentiments stated to have been delivered by me, I have never concealed my opinion from Count Lieven, or from any other person with whom it has been proper for me to converse on such subjects :—that it would be a great blessing that we should have to conclude peace with any other person at the head of the French Government other than Buonaparte, and that I entertained hopes (though never confident ones) that the advance of the allied armies into the interior of France might make such an impression on the sentiments of the French nation as to lead to the destruction of his power : but I never intimated an opinion that these considerations ought to have any effect upon the course and policy adopted for negociating with Buonaparte. The negociation, once begun, it must proceed in the accustomed way ; and if any causes should arise for delaying it, the sovereigns or their Ministers on the spot, would be alone competent judges of them, and in such a consultation you only could speak the sentiments of the British Government.

Had any circumstance arisen which rendered it necessary to furnish you with instructions from the Prince Regent different from those which were agreed upon previous to your departure from England, such instructions would certainly have been transmitted to you through the usual channel, and in the regular official way, and not through the mediun of any Foreign Minister.

(xv)

Fife House, *March* 11, 1814.

I send you a very curious correspondence in consequence of a letter from Comte François D'Escars· on the subject of the reception of Monsieur in France.

The whole statement I have no doubt is greatly exaggerated and there are some facts in it (such as the offer of the towns to capitulate to Louis, etc.) which must be false. It will shew you, however, the temper of mind both of the emigrants and their friends in this country. Our master has got tolerably quiet and reasonable on this subject, but no effort has been spared to influence him upon it.

We have no letters from the south of France since the 22nd. Wellington had then begun his movements and I should hope the next account would inform us of his advance into the heart of the country.   It is provoking that contrary winds should have prevented our receiving any intelligence from him for 17 days at a time when we know he was beginning to move, and when the usual passage from the port of departure is not more than six or seven days.   As soon as we hear anything important from that quarter I will send a messenger to you through France.

[News] . . . Buonaparte appears to be playing again the same game as at Dresden, and God grant it may be with the same result. We shall begin to be anxious to receive some account of what passed on the 10th.   If the military events now in progress shall induce him to agree to the projet in all its substantial points, I shall feel satisfied.   It may not be considered as the best possible issue of the struggle in which we have been so long engaged ; but I am persuaded that by a continuance of it we are more likely to fare worse than better.   The great object to have in view in this case will be to prevent all disputes amongst the Allies respecting their separate interests after the great work of peace has been achieved.   I should be sorry if you were obliged to leave Head Quarters without at least bringing them to an understanding upon the general allotment of the countries out of which compensations are to be made to the respective Powers.

We shall probably hear by your next dispatches the result of the deputation from the people of the Low Countries to the allied Powers.   All our information represents them as unfavourable to a connexion with Holland.   If this should prove to be the case, might it not be arranged, after giving such a district to Holland as might be necessary for its own security, that the remainder of the Low Countries together with the electorates of Trêves and of Mayence should be placed under an Archduke of the House of Austria.   These countries combined might in time constitute a formidable state.   The people of them agree in religion, and do not materially differ in character and habits, and there is reason to believe that they would prefer Austrian connexion to any other which could be proposed for them.

P.S.—Since closing the above we have received your despatches of the 4th and 5th and your private letter of the 5th.   I am very much gratified by finding that my private letter by Robinson was so satisfactory to you.   I trust it will have removed any difficulties which may have existed.

The success of Prince Schwarzenburg on the 3rd has given us great joy, as well as the general aspect of the military movements. I now hope the Allies will really have profited by their former errors, that they will recover the confidence in themselves which they appear for a short time to have lost, and that they will, at the same time, have learnt not to despise the enemy against whom they are contending.

(xvi)

Fife House, *March* 11, 1814.

I send you a most extraordinary communication from the Prince Castelcicala on the subject of a proceeding of Lord William Bentinck of which the Foreign Office has never received any information.[1]

Although it appears by the papers inclosed that Prince Castelcicala had no orders from his Government to demand the recall of Lord William Bentinck, and that the communication in question was considered rather as a private letter than as a public despatch, yet it is most unaccountable that Lord William should have taken such a step without any authority from his Government, more particularly as the proposition, if known, would make a most unfavourable impression against us both with our Allies and with Europe.

I have thought it right to lose no time in transmitting to you these papers in order that you may explain the matter to the allied Courts, if it should be necessary—and likewise that you may take such steps as you may judge most proper for obtaining an explanation from Lord William Bentinck of his conduct on this occasion.

I believe the fact to be that he finds his *new constitution* and the *Sicilian Court* are never likely to work together, and that therefore he has no way out of the difficulties in which he has involved us but by a transfer of the island of Sicily to Great Britain. If there were no other objections to such a transaction, I believe it would be very difficult for us to manage the island through such an instrument as the new constitution, but you well know that the continental states are more jealous of our obtaining power in the Mediterranean than in any other quarter. Circumstances have induced them to make no difficulty about our retaining Malta, but the idea of our possessing Sicily by an act, which in its most favourable light must be considered as a *douce violence*, could not fail greatly to revolt them. It is to be observed likewise that this transaction is considered as depending upon the recovery of the kingdom of Naples for King Ferdinand, an event which after what has passed with Murat *can hardly* be considered as within our power.

I do not intend to return any answer to Prince Castelcicala's note respecting Lord Wm. Bentinck's recall, but if the demand should be repeated, I shall then inform him that the correspondence has been transmitted to you and I beg in the mean time to ask him whether he has received any orders from his Court to make such a demand. To this question we know he can not give a satisfactory answer.

[1] See above, pp. 255–56.

(xvii)

Fife House, *March* 17, 1814.

You will receive by Mr. A'Court the continuance of our correspondence with Prince Castelcicala, and I trust you will approve of our having refused to allow him to withdraw his notes. The truth is, he has acted not only with intemperance but with great cunning in the whole of this business. His first note in which he asks us whether we ever gave any authority to such a transaction was most insidious; and, when it was answered with a frankness which one always wishes to manifest in British correspondence, his violence and insinuation, when he found he could not carry his point, were unpardonable. He never cried mercy till he found we had got him into a difficulty by the questions we had put to him, and that out of that difficulty he could not extricate himself. Indeed his last note is not a fair interpretation of what we know to be the Prince of Sicily's letter. For that letter did not only not authorize him to demand the recall of Lord William Bentinck, but is not even written in a tone by which he could be justified in inferring that it was the wish of his Government that such a demand should be made.

The proceeding of Lord William Bentinck was certainly very objectionable and it may be very awkward for him to remain in Sicily for any length of time after such an event. It did not, however, profess to be official or anything but the private sentiments of the individual; and however it might have awakened suspicions in the minds of the King and Prince of Sicily as to the views and intentions of Lord William Bentinck, it was not a proceeding upon which an official demand of recall could be borne out.

I feel this transaction much more deeply as it regards the future situation of Sicily. I am persuaded Lord William Bentinck feels that his constitution will not work in Sicilian hands, though he does not own it, and that his suggestion to the Prince of Sicily was a device for getting out of the difficulties in which his Whig principles had involved both himself and us. I only hope it may be in our power to bring matters there to a settled state before a French Minister Resident at Palermo can commence his intrigues.

(xviii)

Fife House, *March* 19, 1814.

Whilst we have been most highly gratified by the Treaty of Alliance which you have brought with so much ability to a satisfactory conclusion, we have been a good deal annoyed at the progress of the conferences at Châtillon. We were in hopes that within a day or two after the 10th, the question of war or peace would have been decided, but we received serious mortification from finding that this was not only not the case, but that the negociations had made a retrograde movement. By a private letter of your brother to Cooke he appears to have taken a very just view of the matter.[1] I should hope therefore that the errors of the last proceeding will have been corrected, and that the Ministers of the Allies, and their plenipotentiaries, will be convinced that if their object is, as it must be, *old France*, they will never obtain it, unless they are peremptory on the subject.

As long as Caulaincourt thinks he has the least hopes of obtaining better terms for his master, he will never yield. And he will justly consider his hopes in this respect as not desperate as long as the allied plenipotentiaries appear to hesitate. He has besides every advantage from delay. He never will believe that under any success of the Allies he may not obtain peace on those terms, and if the Allies should meet with any misfortune, he can always avail himself of it to improve the conditions on the part of France. He knows moreover that, whilst the negotiation is going on, we cannot play the Bourbon game, and, whatever may be the ultimate result of an attempt of this nature, it could not fail to be very embarrassing to Buonaparte. In Brittany, in Poitou and in the south, the disposition to the old dynasty appears to be much more favourable than in the provinces through which you have passed. The advance of Wellington's army will likewise produce a considerable effect. He is personally popular in the country, and his army does not live by requisition, as the other allied armies do, but pay for whatever they receive. The result is that the French people within the British lines are better off than any other people in Europe—for they pay no taxes to their own Government, and they are not subject to military requisition. It is provoking that we should have heard nothing from him since the 23rd of February. Report says he is at Bordeaux, and I confess I incline to give credit to it. We know he has succeeded in throwing 15,000 men across the Adour below Bayonne on the 24th or 25th and an account from Morlain says he was at Roquefort, which is considerably nearer Bordeaux than Bayonne.

Blücher's success has been most glorious, and in all respects most important, but the inactivity of Schwarzenberg during these operations has produced here a very unfavourable impression against the Austrians. Count Merveldt's[2] tone is peculiarly flat. He seems to have no anxiety but about peace—though he admitted to me the other day that, if the Allies could maintain their ground

---

[1] Stewart to Cooke, Feb. 28, 1814 : *C.C.* ix. 553. See above, p. 219.
[2] The Austrian Ambassador at London.

till Lord Wellington arrived between the Loire and the Seine, the fate of Buonaparte was decided.

Pray let us know what is the full extent of the truth of the reports circulated by the emigrants respecting the reception of Monsieur in France. It is of the utmost importance that we should be able to contradict them, if they are not true.

Believe me it requires every effort of which I am possessed to keep anything like steadiness in our councils. It is not only the public mind that is inflamed, but persons of weight, character, sense and respectability partake of the popular feeling against peace, and it is difficult even to make them hear reason. If we can stand however to our question of *ancient limits* I do not despair. Independent of the advantages of a peace on such terms, it is carrying a *principle*, which will be intelligible to all the world, and for which they will give us credit as soon as the popular frenzy has subsided. It is only by dinning this *principle* in their ear that I can keep certain persons right even now. Let us therefore be steady to this point and I trust all will do well.

(xix)

Fife House, *March* 21, 1814.

We may be much embarrassed by the measure which the Prince Royal of Sweden has adopted of sending a plenipotentiary to Châtillon, as Spain will justly consider herself as having more right to participate in these negociations than Sweden. I do not like to advise Fernan Nuñez to set out, and indeed, if I did, he would probably arrive too late—but I hope you will be able to contrive, in case preliminaries shall be agreed upon, either that the Swedish minister shall not sign, or that Pizarro [1] shall somehow or other, be brought into the business. We must not forget that Spain was our first friend, and that pride is the chief characteristic of the nation. Besides, Spain has always been considered as a power *du premier ordre*, where this has not been the case with Sweden for more than a century.

(xx)

Fife House, *March* 22, 1814.

Do not be alarmed at our despatch of this day.[2] Would to God the event at Bordeaux had happened six weeks ago! But after considering the matter in every possible light, I am satisfied it was not in our power to have done otherwise than we have done.

---

[1] Spanish representative.
[2] *B.D.* 171.

The same disposition which has broken out at Bordeaux has been manifested likewise at Pau, and the letters, as you will see, of Lord Wellington speak of it as general throughout the whole of that part of the country. We understand from General Don that in Brittany and La Vendée the sentiments are not less favourable to the ancient dynasty. I should have paid little attention to all this if the explosion had not at last taken place, if it had not occurred in one of the first cities in France, and if the rising had not been sanctioned by the civil authorities and upper orders of the people as well as the lower.

[Cypher deciphered.]

We never should be forgiven if we made peace with Buonaparte under these circumstances, unless forced to it by the Allies. Our object must be now, as Caulaincourt's has been for some time past, to gain time. We must use our utmost endeavours to persuade the Allies to make common cause with us. If they do, I feel confident that the flame will spread to other parts of France, and that the fate of Buonaparte will not long be doubtful. If the Allies are however determined, under all the circumstances, to conclude the peace, we shall give due attention to all their representations, and they cannot avoid seeing that the case is one in which we are justified in demurring until we know their opinion. Every day will bring fresh information which will assist us and them in a final judgement. With respect to the avowed cause for breaking off the negociation, that must depend upon the state of it. If Caulaincourt is still equivocating upon points of importance, there can be no difficulty, if there is will to put an end to it. If on the other hand, all material points are settled and you are on the eve of signing, your reservation of the 29th January, or the principles of it, must be made use of. The event which has arisen, tho' not probable was always foreseen as possible, and was one of those which you had provided for from the beginning. The only doubt which can arise, therefore, upon our own principles, is as to the quality and magnitude of the explosion, but all proceedings of this nature must begin, and a more promising one in the first instance could hardly have been expected. At all events I think you will see that it is sufficient, if not for a final and irrevocable determination, at least for a temporary suspension of our present proceedings.

(xxi)

Fife House, *April* 9, 1814.

I trust this letter will find you at Paris. I congratulate you most cordially and sincerely on all the happy and extraordinary events which have passed since I last wrote to you. The tremendous contest in which the greater part of Europe has been engaged for the last twenty years, is, I trust, now brought (as far as essentials are concerned) to as satisfactory a termination as any person could desire. It remains only to finish the work by a solid and equitable peace.

My principle object in writing to you to-night is to entreat you not to think it necessary to return to England by the 18th, if in your judgement your continuance at Paris will be likely to be productive of general advantage to the public cause. I own I am inclined strongly to the opinion, even from circumstances which have attended the late glorious events, that much benefit may result from your remaining with the Allies for a short time—perhaps till the new Government are actually in possession, and the preliminaries of peace have been finally settled.

With respect to the preliminaries of peace I know of no better text than the projet of the 17th of February.[1]

I know not what the Emperor of Russia means by *doing more for France than respecting the integrity of the ancient territory*, and one cannot help looking at such an expression with some jealousy. I am satisfied Monsieur did not expect to obtain anything out of the limits of *ancient* France when he left this country. And I should hope that the principle to which I have referred, would (as you have most properly stated on a former occasion) be substantially, if not literally, maintained. There are certainly some points in the projet of the 17th of February which may be properly omitted in any treaty now to be signed—such as the retention or occupation, even for a time, of any of the fortresses within old France. It may likewise be advisable to bring forth the king of Sardinia and some of our other ancient Allies more prominently than was judged expedient at Châtillon. But as to all the main questions I think the nearer you can adhere to your former projet the better.[2]

I trust there will be no difficulty on the part of the new French Government, after all the exertions and sacrifices this country has made, in our keeping the islands of Mauritius and Bourbon. They may perhaps be in some measure reconciled to this by a remission on our part of any claim to the money due to us from France, for the maintenance of the French prisoners of war and for the other pecuniary charges, which might not be unfairly brought against that government. Money is that of which they will be most in want for some time, and if we deal generously by them in this respect, they ought not to grudge us a fair compensation.

Tobago will, I am convinced, make no difficulty whatever, as it

[1] See above, pp. 214–15.
[2] A translation of a few sentences of the dispatch are given by M. Charles Dupuis in his *Ministère du Talleyrand*, i. 335, from a source not stated.

stands upon ground so peculiar in itself, and can never be a question of pride with the new Government.

It is very unlucky that the Emperor Alexander should have fixed on Elba for Buonaparte's retreat—not only from the value of that island in itself, it being considered by many persons as the best naval station in the Mediterranean, but likewise from the influence which it necessarily will give the person who holds it over the adjoining parts of Italy.   I see by Cathcart's letter that he is fully aware of the objections which existed to this arrangement, and he thinks that as the other allied Powers were no direct parties to it, some less objectionable station may be substituted for it.   At all events I wish you would turn your thoughts seriously to this point.

If you determine not to come over for the meeting of Parliament, could you not spare Robinson?   It would certainly be desirable to have some person in the House of Commons who had been following the course of our foreign policy in detail, and who could assist Vansittart and Bathurst, if any discussion should arise unexpectedly respecting it.

(xxii)

Fife House, *April* 14, 1814.

I have considered with Vansittart as well as I could your private letter together with its inclosures on the subject of the Emperor of Russia's loan in Holland.   We neither of us see how it could be practicable for the Government of this country to guarantee for the first time the debt of a foreign Power contracted many years past, and not in any war in which that Power was co-operating with Great Britain.   Nay a part of it probably contracted on account of operations in which Russia was hostile to Great Britain.

Any project of guarantee of a foreign loan has since the experience of the Austrian loan always been the most unpopular finance measure that could be proposed—and I think on just ground.   It is unnecessary to add that the circumstances to which I have referred would materially aggravate all the objections which exist to such a measure abstractedly considered.

In addition to these considerations it is to be observed that both the Austrian and Prussian Governments have likewise very considerable debts in Holland, which as far as I can learn amount to (Prussia 30,000,000 Guilders and Austria 110,000,000) 140,000,000 Guilders, and it does not appear to us upon what principle this relief would be afforded to Russia and afterwards refused altogether to Austria and Prussia.

The resources of Prussia are small indeed compared to those of Russia, and the exertions she has made for the common cause in proportion to her means may justly be considered as more considerable than those of either of the other Powers.   On the other hand Austria might rest her claim as far as Holland is concerned on her ancient rights in the Low Countries, and on the equitable pretensions she may have, on surrendering those rights, to some equivalent from the Dutch Government.

In what way then can any relief be afforded by Great Britain to the finances of Russia on grounds distinct from those which may be equally stated by the other Allies ?

The only way which has occurred to us is by a continuance of the subsidy for a certain time after the return of the Russian armies to their own country—for instance by allowing twelve months instead of six after a definitive treaty for their return.   Such an arrangement might not be objectionable in principle, as the Emperor of Russia has been induced for the general benefit of Europe to carry on the war at a far greater distance from his own dominions than any other Power, and as he, of course, had a less direct and immediate interest in the operations which have been carrying on since the French armies were obliged to retire beyond the Elbe.   It is well known that the continuance of these operations, to the extent at least to which they have been carried, have been contrary to the opinion of many persons of great weight both military and civil in the Russian councils, and it appears therefore not unreasonable that some compensation should be made to the Emperor of Russia for the sacrifices which he has incurred for the common cause.

The proposition thus submitted for consideration would rest upon its own special grounds, would keep us clear of all the unpopular arguments arising out of the other idea, and would furnish no precedent of which we should have any reason to be very apprehensive in future.

You will judge of the propriety of entering upon this communication with the Emperor of Russia immediately, or of postponing it for a short time, till a favourable opportunity shall arise for bringing it forward.

(xxiii)

Fife House, *April* 14, 1814.

I enclose a letter which I have received from Wilberforce on the subject of the Slave Trade.[1]   The article in our projet of the 17th of February would I conceive, perfectly satisfy him and his friends, and I should hope the new French Government would have no difficulty in adopting it.   We have a very fair right to stipulate such a condition under present circumstances ; as our restitution

---

[1] Wilberforce to Liverpool, April 12, 1814, stating that to return the colonies except on condition that the Slave Trade be abolished would be " *absolutely irreligious and immoral.*"   *Lond. MSS.*

of the French colonies is now gratuitous, and as we do not intend to impose any obligations upon them to which we shall not be reciprocally bound ourselves.

(xxiv)

Fife House, *April* 14, 1814.

As there must unavoidably exist great awkwardness in the relations between this country and France, under present circumstances, it is very desirable that no unnecessary delay should occur in the signature of preliminaries of peace. You can, of course, have no difficulty in ascertaining whether in any or in what points the views of the Allies have altered since the rupture of the negociation at Châtillon, and when this has been ascertained, you will be able easily to learn whether the Comte d'Artois, Talleyrand and those they may be disposed to consult, are ready to agree to the peace upon the terms acceptable to us.

If every material difficulty should be removed under both these heads, it will then be of importance that matters of etiquette should stand as little in the way as possible of restoring the accustomed relations of peace between the two countries.

I do not know whether the Comte d'Artois's powers of Lieutenant General of the Kingdom would enable him to conclude peace in the name of the King as soon as the King had accepted the constitution and been proclaimed. But if there is any doubt on this head, might not the King give him a special authority for the purpose. In short, if the peace is substantially agreed upon, I should hope that it would not be difficult to devise means by which all ambiguity in our respective situations might be removed.

(xxv)

Fife House, *April* 14, 1814.

You will receive by the messenger who carries these letters a note from Prince Castelcicala on the subject of his master's rights to the kingdom of Naples, and it is certainly very desirable to prevent Murat retaining that kingdom if possible. Fernan Nuñez told me sometime ago that the Spanish Government had declared they would never be a party to the arrangement for Murat. Independent of the rights of their own connexion, they say justly, that the case is very different from that of Bernadotte—that the period at which the latter came forward in favour of the Allies gave him the strongest claim to consideration, whereas Murat held a most important command in the French Army, as late as the battle of Leipsic—that in addition to this consideration, Bernadotte had uniformly conducted himself well in all the countries in which he had been employed as a French general, whereas Murat was the instrument, if not the author, of the massacre at Madrid.

It is fortunate that we are under no positive engagements to Murat, except to give a certain notice before the armistice is denounced, and there can be no doubt that Russia and Prussia, who are likewise unshackled upon the subject, and more than all the King of France will be most anxious for the restoration of the legitimate sovereign.   I am aware, however, that Austria must be managed but I should hope with temper and judgment that this might be accomplished.

It would appear by Sir Robert Wilson's last letters that Murat has not been cordially co-operating in the common cause.   If his statement of what has passed between Murat and Lord William Bentinck is correct, Murat has given us perfectly good ground for quarrelling with him.

I wish I could suggest a good substitute for the island of Elba, but there is none to which great objections do not occur, and the whole idea of territorial possession and sovereignty for Buonaparte was unlucky, and as I cannot help believing, unnecessary.   Our friend Pozzo di Borgo would not like his having Corsica.   I should otherwise have thought that the least objectionable arrangement of the sort that could have been made for Buonaparte.   I hope his pension, whatever it may be, will be so settled that he will only receive it *quam diu se bene gesserit.*

(xxvi)

Fife House, *April* 18, 1814.

You will receive by this communication the draft of the Act of Accession, which has been prepared to the treaty signed at Paris in favor of Napoleon and his family.   There are some things in that treaty difficult to swallow—especially the recognition of his title of Emperor.   You have kept us as clear as you could, and I hope no practical mischief will result from it.   The great object will, however, be to make Napoleon's pension, and, as far as practicable, those of his family, dependent upon their good behaviour, and reliable to be stopt if they conduct themselves improperly.

It is considered by the Prince Regent's Government of great importance that the Act of Accession to this treaty should not be given without some explanation in writing of the views of the British Government with respect to the future destination of the island of Elba.   You know many persons in this country attach more importance to it than to any naval station in the Mediterranean, and as it is now French, it might revert to France after the death of Napoleon if some stipulation is not made to the contrary.   We have no desire to have it ourselves, but we wish that you would deliver a note in writing, stating that upon the death of the person to whom it is now granted it shall revert as part of those sovereignties to which it belonged antecedent to the year 1792—that is to Naples and Tuscany. This proposal cannot be objected to by the Allies, as it is wholly disinterested on our part, and is conformable to the principle on which we have been acting viz. to bring things back to their former state before the French Revolution, as far as circumstances will permit of it.

(xxvii)

Fife House, April 26, 1814.

I have received your letters of the 19th and 20th [1] by Jackson, and immediately upon my return to Town from Dover I communicated them to my colleagues.

The subject of the fleet at Antwerp is one of great delicacy—not so much with regard to the value of the fleet itself, under present circumstances (though its value is greater than you have supposed) but with reference to the impression with which its being withdrawn by the French Government may make in this country.

We cannot agree to the correctness of the principle upon which Talleyrand has advanced the claim. If a squadron from Brest or Rochfort had sought refuge in the Scheldt, or had come there for the purpose of operations, we admit that the case would be nearly parallel to that of the evacuation of the fortresses by the garrisons, but the fleet at Antwerp is a creation of that port—naturally connected with it—and has never in point of fact been out of the Scheldt. The principle, therefore, in our projet of the 17th of February, that it should follow the fate of the place, appears to be perfectly reasonable and correct.

The amount of the fleet actually in Antwerp is 21 sail of the Line complete and 11 building.

You will see that this is not a contemptible force, and many of these ships were in fact built at the expense of Holland or from articles belonging to countries which it is admitted now are not to remain a part of France.

To give, however, a proof of our liberality upon the present occasion we are ready to agree to the following arrangement. 1st. That all ships in the port of Antwerp building or not complete at the time of the signature of the suspension of hostilities shall follow the fate of the place. 2ndly. That of the ships which were then complete in the port of Antwerp the French Government shall be at liberty to withdraw two-thirds of them, the remaining

[1] C.C. ix. 472, 482.

third to belong to the Dutch, in consideration of the share which they have had in the building and equipment of the whole. I am satisfied that we are thus proposing to give as much as the French Government can expect to receive, and I am sure you will see the importance of making the most of the liberality of this concession in the settlement of other points.

You will understand that this principle must not be applied to the ships at the Helder or at Flushing—nor do I think it ought to be extended to those which are at Venice.

With regard to the Saintes, we entertain a different opinion from that stated in your letter. It is of the utmost importance for us to retain them, and they are of no value whatever to France. We have no harbour in that part of the West Indies. The French have two excellent ones at Martinique and St. Lucie. The Saintes are of no value whatever except for their harbour, and are the least invidious possession we could propose to retain. If, however, the French Government set a great value upon their restoration as an appendage to Guadaloupe, let them in that case consent to our retaining St. Lucie in the place of them. All we ask is a harbour in that part of the West Indies, where they have several, and to that we think we are fairly entitled.

I certainly admit that it is desirable to make our separate conditions of peace somewhat more favourable with the Bourbons, than those we would have made with Buonaparte. The condition respecting the fleet is already a great concession to the new Government. We should have no objection to add to this the island of Bourbon, if the French set much value upon its restoration, but we think the Mauritius, Tobago, and the Saintes or St. Lucie ought to be *sine qua non* conditions of peace, and after the six or seven hundred millions we have spent in the course of a war which has led to the restoration of the Bourbon family, the demand can scarcely be considered as unreasonable.

(xxviii)

Fife House, *April* 26, 1814.

The Prince Regent wrote from Dover to the Emperor of Austria and King of Prussia in the manner you proposed—I saw the letters and they were very proper.

I met at Dover, Pozzo di Borgo who thought it best to return to France with the King. I trust he will succeed in the object of his mission, but there are many prejudices to overcome, not so much in the King as in those who surround him. I gave Pozzo no encouragement of so favourable an arrangement respecting the fleet as is now proposed, and I must do him the justice to say I found him very reasonable upon the subject.

I hope you will be able to let us have the preliminaries soon. The point of the greatest difficulty—the arrangement respecting Naples—need not be settled till we come to the definitive treaty, but I am satisfied neither France nor Spain ever will or indeed can in honor consent under present circumstances to Murat remaining there. We must, however, manage Austria upon this question. The French are well disposed to do this, for strange as it may appear, they are in better humour with the Austrian Government, and more inclined to confide in them, than in any of the Allies, except ourselves.

The King of France, the Duchess d'Angoulême and those who attended them, left this country most fully gratified with the state of the public feeling respecting them. Indeed I never saw so much enthusiasm in my life on any occasion as was manifested from the period of their quitting Hartwell to that of their embarking at Dover.

(xxix)

Fife House, *April* 28, 1814.

We are entirely satisfied with your convention for the suspension of hostilities which is highly creditable to yourself and to all the sovereigns and ministers who have been parties to it.

I am very glad, likewise, to find that you intend at once to negociate and sign a definitive treaty of peace with France. The convention of the 23rd. inst. is, in fact, a preliminary treaty, and the course of proceeding which you have now determined to adopt will relieve us from many difficulties and give more weight to our opinions and interference in those continental points, which must be afterwards arranged and in which our own interests are less immediately concerned. I should hope now that the definitive treaty might be concluded in nearly as short a time as a preliminary treaty. You will by this time have ascertained the disposition of the French Government to the colonial points. I ought to have mentioned to you in my last letter, that I know from sources of information on which reliance can be placed, that Monsieur, when at Nancy, did not expect the restoration of Guadaloupe. This concession, therefore, may have a favourable effect in inducing him and those with whom he is connected, to give way on other points.

It will be proper, I conceive, in the definitive treaty to renew all the former treaties of peace between Great Britain and France antecedent to the Treaty of Amiens. To this the existing French Government can have no objection. It would be desirable, I am convinced, for the interests of both countries, to renew the commercial treaty of 1787, but it would require more time to look into this question than can well be spared under present circumstances, and I believe likewise, there exists a prejudice against that treaty in some parts of France, which might be an obstacle to its renewal at this time, and may render it expedient to defer any definitive stipulations on the subject of the commercial intercourse between the two countries, though some provisional arrangement in this respect will be necessary.

With regard to the Articles relative to sequestration—the period of restoration, etc.—it is always most safe to copy the Articles from former treaties.

The debt on account of French prisoners to this country is very considerable. I do not think it would be expedient, in the present state of the French finances, to press for the liquidation of it, but I think you should make the most of it as an article in your account, and endeavour to obtain some concession in return for the relinquishment of it.

We have not yet laid the subsidiary treaties and are desirous, if possible, to avoid laying anything before the House respecting our foreign relations, till we can form some judgement of the period of your return. You will perhaps be able to give me some intimation on this head, in the course of the ensuing week. You will understand that I do not wish you to return before the conclusion of the definitive treaty, if you think there is any prospect of concluding it within a reasonable time.

(xxx)

Fife House, *April* 29, 1814.

We begin to feel it of the utmost importance in the event of your absence being further prolonged (as will probably be the case for a fortnight longer) that you should send Robinson back to us. You will see by the public papers that the Opposition in the House of Commons are putting questions daily on the subject of our foreign relations, and particularly regarding the question of Norway, which is the most delicate point of all those likely to become the subject of discussion.

Neither Vansittart nor Bragge Bathurst have been in the habit of answering to questions of this nature, and neither of the Under Secretaries of State of the Foreign Office are in the House of Commons, nor any other person *au fait* of the correspondence of that department and qualified therefore to give explanation upon facts which are misstated. If you could let us have Robinson, I should feel perfectly at ease, and I should be under no apprehension of his presence provoking discussions, which are much more likely to take place when they think that they can embarrass Government by bringing them forward.

I conclude you will have sufficiently advanced in your business to be able to spare Robinson without any material inconvenience, and if any difficulty should arise, which I hope is not likely, there might be some advantage in a personal communication with him upon it.

(xxxi)

Fife House, *April* 29, 1814.

It has occurred to Vansittart and myself that in the extreme penury of the French Government at the present moment with respect to its finances, some pecuniary assistance might be of essential importance to the Government.

You have probably been informed that a hundred thousand pounds was given to the king of France just before he left this country, partly for the payment of the debts which he had contracted here, and partly for the expenses of his journey. I have now only to add that if you should find that the advance of a further sum of one hundred thousand pounds would be of any use to His Majesty under present circumstances, you are at full liberty to authorize Herries who will be at Paris to make such advance. Perhaps even the offer of it in a delicate manner may be productive of some advantage, as it may keep alive the feeling with which the Royal Family of France quitted this country, which I am satisfied it is our interest to cultivate for the welfare of both countries as well as for that of Europe in general.

(xxxii)

Fife House, *May* 3, 1814.

I have reason to believe from good authority that the Dutch Government will have no objection to our keeping the settlements of Demerara, Essequibo and Berbice, if we allow them a free trade. Indeed, I am informed, that they would, in such case, rather that they were in our hands than in their own—for they are settlements that they could not hope to defend in time of war, and they would prefer therefore that the expense of maintaining them in time of peace should rest with Great Britain.

If this arrangement should be adopted, I entirely admit that we ought to take the compensation to Sweden for Guadaloupe to ourselves, and Trinidad would be a very fair object for this purpose. I do not see why the other continental Powers should be jealous of us on this account, for of all the conquests we are desirous of retaining, these, in fact, are alone of any value—Malta and the Mauritius, though important military positions, never can be expected to pay for their own defence—the same I believe to be the case with the Cape, and the Saintes are nothing but rocks. If, however, you continue to think that we ought not to propose to keep Demerara, Essequibo and Berbice, but only one of them, (Demerara and Essequibo being now considered as one) I wish you would let me consult some persons conversant with the internal state of these settlements before our option is made. I conclude this point need not be settled in our definitive treaty with France. If anything is said upon the subject in this treaty, it may be enough to stipulate that a compensation shall be made to Sweden for the restoration of Guadaloupe to France by Holland, or in consequence of arrangements between Great Britain and Holland.

(xxxiii)

[*April* 30, 1814.]

There have arisen most unpleasant difficulties respecting the marriage of Princess Charlotte with the Prince of Orange. I have no doubt they have originated in a political intrigue, and they have been so far attended with success, that she has been induced to insist upon conditions being inserted in the contract of marriage of which she never thought until recently, and which (to the extent to which she is desirous of pushing them) can not be admitted. We have the strongest reason to believe that the Tatischeffs are engaged in this intrigue, and the object is to break off the marriage with the Prince of Orange and to form a connection between the Princess and one of the Grand Dukes of Russia.

Independant of the disgrace which will attend the rupture of this marriage there would be considerable objections to the other connection, but, at all events, it is of the utmost importance to prevent the Grand Dukes, who are now at Paris, coming over to England under the present circumstances. The Prince Regent is very desirous that you should take the most effectual measures in your power, without giving offence, for preventing this visit at this time. I should think you might be able to manage this through Nesselrode but I am aware it may be a matter of considerable difficulty.

The Prince of Orange arrived here yesterday and his communication with the Princess will probably bring the questions between them shortly to a point. I am not sanguine about the result.

(xxxiv)

Fife House, *May* 3, 1814.

You will see that we are to have, in both Houses, early in next week, a discussion upon the subject of Norway. The question is an awkward one. The Norwegian resistance is popular here, but this I should not think of much importance, as matters stand, if we had not the civilians against us upon the general principle, though I trust not so upon the particular case attended by all its present circumstances.

I was certainly not aware, that it had been laid down in the books that, though a country had a right to cede a part of its dominions for the preservation of the remainder and that after such a cession, all its rights over the ceded territory for ever ceased, yet the ceded province, or island, had a right to refuse to receive the new master. You will find this doctrine in Vattel—Book 1st. Chap. 21, Sec: 263 and 264.

The same opinion is given by Grotius, and though the general practice of Europe has been to consider cessions as binding on all the parties, yet it would be very difficult to contend against the principle laid down by such high authority, and the precedents to the contrary, it will be said, are derived from cases where no resistance was ever attempted.

We shall be obliged therefore to defend our proceedings upon the special circumstances of the case, and there can be no doubt that Prince Christian's conduct furnishes us with ample ground for saying, that the Norwegian resistance has been instigated by a Danish Prince, or Danish rebel, that it is supported by Danish officers, and that until they are withdrawn or expelled from the country and the Allies and Sweden have had a fair opportunity of communicating with the inhabitants, no one has any right to say that the opinion of the country can be fairly taken—till then it is a Danish, and not a Norwegian resistance.

I have no doubt that this view of the question will satisfy the public for the present, but we cannot conceal from ourselves, that the question may henceforth assume a shape which may make it very embarrassing and renders it highly important that every measure should be taken to conciliate the Norwegians to a connection with Sweden, and in the event of failure, I see no alternative, but Sweden being compensated by other sacrifices on the part of Denmark, which, upon the principle of the Treaty of Kiel, Denmark cannot in such case justly resist.

Augustus Foster is gone to Paris, and you had better despatch him from thence direct to Copenhagen. His credentials shall be forwarded to him there, and Thornton and young Addington, together with him, should be directed to concert their proceedings, so far as to effect the purpose of the union of Norway to Sweden upon the most liberal terms, and, if possible, without bloodshed.

In the meantime, if I can find a good man to send from hence on a temporary mission to Norway, I should be disposed to do it. Some parts of the country, and particularly Drontheim, are, I understand, favourable to the connection with Sweden. The dread of our blockade will I trust bring others to reason—I say

reason, because the Prince Royal of Sweden offers them a free
Government in the place of the arbitrary one to which they have
been subjected for nearly two centuries.

(xxxv)

Fife House, *May* 16, 1814.

We have heard nothing from you since the 5th. but I conclude
you are too hard at work to have much time to write.   As your
treaty is to be definitive, there would be some advantage if it were
possible that we could see it (to guard against *minor errors*) before
it was actually agreed.   My present anxiety is that there should
be in it no recogrition of Murat as King of Naples.   He has done
nothing to deserve a kingdom, is one of the very worst of all
Bonaparte's Generals and actually did what Caulaincourt has
been supposed to do with regard to the Duke d'Enghien.   No
arrangement in his favour such as King will ever be allowed to
stand and therefore should better not be made.   If this point can
not be satisfactorily settled I hope at least that there will be
nothing in the treaty respecting it and that it will be left over
for future adjustment.   We shall hope to see you here very soon.

(xxxvi)

Fife House, *Deecmber* 12, 1814.

Mr. Rothschild has put into my hands the enclosed letter[1]
respecting the state of the Jews in Germany and has earnestly
desired me to recommend their care to your particular attention.
  P.S.—Mr. Rothschild has been a very useful friend.   I do not
know what we should have done without him last year.

[1] Missing.

APPENDIX C

LETTERS FROM CASTLEREAGH TO SIR CHARLES STUART, 1815 [1]

(i)

April 19, 1815.

I am afraid the councils of Louis the 18th are becoming more and more emigrant, which will not diminish their difficulties.

How can M. de Blacas suppose the *Allies* can adopt measures of personal vigour, even in menace, when the King in no instance maintained his just authority by making a single example? If the principles of those about the King were less strained, and their conduct more decisive, they would maintain His Majesty's cause better.

They betray an equal ignorance of this nation when they seem to regret that we do not hurry them into the war, before the Powers of the Continent can be considered by Great Britain as having taken their decision, upon the *real* case, on which they are to act. Such precipitation is no proof either of energy or true courage.

It is essential to the interests of Europe that the public opinion of Gt. Britain should be kept together. Without a conviction of the necessity of the war in the sober judgment of the Continent, we should soon have a Peace Party here, as we had in the early years of the war before the last, which would soon disqualify us, augmented as the publick burthens are, from giving our Allies an effectual support.

The King and his friends ought to know our wishes—*we* shall not be the first to fail them, but to render them service, we must keep ourselves on the strong and tenable ground with our own parliament, and ye people. We shall be capable of rendering service in proportion as we keep down disunion, and avoid extravagant and disputable pledges, which always weaken the hands of a government in a system constituted like ours.

[1] From the Londonderry Manuscripts.

I hope you will be able to make M. de Blacas and those about the king understand, that John Bull fights best, when *he is not tied*, and that, altho' as a line of policy we can with good management connect the support of the Bourbons with the avowed object of the war, we never could sustain as a principle, that we were committed irrevocably to His Majesty to make this a *sine qua non* under every possible circumstance. Such an engagement would defeat its own purpose by rendering that questionable, which if done voluntarily, would command a general concurrence.

I suspect Pozzo di Borgo has stated rather his own principles, than his master's to the French Court. I have no doubt of H.R.H.'s decision in the war, so far as it is waged against Buonaparte, but I doubt his maintaining the Family against a national sentiment for any length of time.

P.S.—The steadiness of this country in the war will depend upon our making it clear that the Continent has *voluntarily* decided to seek its safety in arming.

I do not think in the present state of things that the Jacobins will venture to let Vitrolles be put to death. I feel the greatest personal interest in his fate. He is a most excellent man.

(ii)

April 24, 1815.

. . . I think it right confidentially to mention to you the reports that circulate here of Blacas' venality at Paris, selling officers honors, etc. I know how much favourites are traduced, and am not myself disposed to credit anything to the prejudice of his honor, but it is right that you should know that such an impression very generally prevails, which, added to his known hatred of every thing connected with the Revolution, is calculated essentially at this moment to prejudice the King's cause. I have no hope of His Majesty making any impression unless he can present himself to the nation under other advisers, and in this point of view I should hear with great satisfaction that the King had given his confidence to some individual whom he might on entering France publicly present to his subjects as his avowed Minister, with full authority to submit to His Majesty an arrangement for an effective and responsible Ministry, as early as circumstances might afford proper materials for filling up the situations. Upon the whole I know no person more competent than Talleyrand. It never could do to go on as they have done.

(iii)

May 8, 1815.

I am glad to find that the sentiments which prevail both in Vienna and in London on the necessity of a change in H.M.C. Majesty's councils are likely to be listened to.

I have given the subject every consideration in my power, and am irresistibly led to the conclusion, that in the present state of parties, or rather factions, civil and military, in France, there are only two practicable modes of Government, either to subdue or restrain all by the power of a military despotism, or to make the parties govern each other, and so contend for authority as not to implicate the Crown in the overthrow of their opponents—any middle course of forming a government, of which the *personal* influence of the King is to be a support, cannot last, and the fall of the administration will always involve necessarily the existence of the royal authority.

If I am right in this, it is in vain for the King to suppose he can maintain himself on his throne, unless he will submit himself to the necessities of his situation. He cannot establish a military despotism. He has no army to support him in the attempt, and if he had, his character and principles do not qualify him for such a task—he has no other resource then than to abstract himself as much as possible from all personal or party preferences, to give up every principle of individual exclusion and to declare his fixed determination to govern by responsible advisers. On his restoration last year, His Majesty perhaps was bound in character to exclude the regicides. He was supposed to have the means of exercising a personal authority; now he owes it to France, and to his own family to make every sacrifice of personal feeling to preserve the dynasty of which he is the head.

I am aware how painful this view of the subject must at first be to His Majesty. His virtues will lead him to repugn the idea, but reflection will reconcile him to it. When a sovereign condescends to exclude certain persons from his councils, he confers upon them at once an infinitely augmented capacity of doing mischief. They become immediately objects of unlimited confidence to all wicked and discontented men, and if they have no ostensible sphere of exertion, they become conspirators, instead of oppositionists.

Louis the 18th cannot be more averse to seeing Fouché in his councils, than our King was to receive Mr. Fox. When we retired in 1806, I then concurred in giving His Majesty the same advice I now should give to the King of France, viz., not to suffer a personal question to expose the public safety to hazard. It is not necessary that His Majesty should entrust his *immediate* confidence to any individual, who may be personally obnoxious to him, but if the Minister, who conducts the affairs of France should state to the King that the assistance of a certain individual or individuals is essential to enable him to conduct the public business, then my opinion is, as sovereign, the King ought not to oppose to that recommendation a principle of exclusion.

Fouché and men of his stamp are nowhere so little to be dreaded as in office, mixed up with other materials. Tyrants may poison or murder an obnoxious character, but the surest and only means a *constitutional* sovereign has to restrain such a character is to *employ him*. Office soon strips him of his most dangerous adherents —he becomes unpopular, can be laid aside at pleasure, and sinks to his true lead. So far from making himself visibly responsible for everything, the King ought to throw upon his Ministers the odium and risk of conducting his service. His Majesty ought to turn the political control towards the Minister for the time being and not entertain it himself beyond affording him the due support which his services may deserve. This is the true strength of a constitutional king. All paper constitutions are of comparatively small importance ; the essence of a free state is so to manage the party warfare, as to reconcile it with the safety of the sovereign— to do this, the King must give the contending parties facilities against each other, and not embark himself too deeply with any.

I had a very sensible letter from Pozzo a few days since, in which however he bears, or rather relies, too much on the *principle of exclusion*. He talks of getting rid of perhaps 50 of the worst characters, as a means of regeneration. If they were to cease to exist, they could well be spared, but that the King could put them to death with character is very improbable. Should they remain and stay in France, or retire to Switzerland or some other neighbouring state, as a species of banishment, their means of conspiring and their power of mischief will be unempaird.

From the above reasoning you will see, that I do not think Blacas's suggestions satisfactory—they do not go to the root of the evil. His own effectual retirement, I am confident, is an indispensable preliminary, but beyond that, the King must suffer the person whom he employs, to *lay before him for his approbation* a plan of arrangement and not thus previously create, limit and proscribe. If he does, the system will not work by its own strength, and the political contest will be again against the Crown, and not against the administration.

The surest way effectually to control a party is to employ them. Our King has often sustained his own authority by this expedient. The King of France may do the same, and if he wishes to serve the emigrants, his best means of doing so, is not to assemble them around the throne, as a feeble, odious and exclusive party, but to leave them through the parties of the country to struggle for and partake of their share of power.

The subject will present itself in many other points of view to your own observation, accustomed as you are to remark what constitutes the real power of the Crown in this country. You will be enabled to convince H.M. that, as he cannot rely upon the idle clamour of *Vive le Roi* nor upon the army. He must maintain his authority by useing the active political characters that have sprung up during the Revolution. It appears to me that theoretical principles form no longer the point at issue between the contending factions. It is a struggle for power, and, if the King will make himself the umpire and exclude no man for past conduct, who can be made useful, H.M. may preserve his crown and bring the system gradually to its true bearings, but to do so, he must cover himself with the protection of a responsible Minister and retire in appearance himself from the conflict. Such is my deliberate opinion and I give it from a sincere wish to contribute to his restoration.

P.S.—I hope you will be enabled to convince the King that councils held in the presence of the sovereign, except for the mere purpose of formally carrying into effect matters previously decided on, are wholly inconsistent with the march of a free Govt. Ministers will never speak their mind freely in presence of their monarch and the Princes of the blood. The secrecy and separation of the Cabinet is of the essence of our constitution. All the sovereign can, or for his own interest ought to desire is, that his pleasure should be taken by the Ministers of the respective departments before the decisions of Cabinet are carried into actual execution.

(iv)

May 8, 1815.

Since I closed my private letter of this day's date, yours of the 5th from Ghent has been received. I am not convinced of the policy of the King's imposing any restrictions in the formation of his Government upon the person he entrusts with his confidence. As far as the exigencies of the public service will admit of it, the Minister of the Crown can have no motive for bringing unacceptable individuals in contact with his sovereign, but the principle of exclusion is full of danger and weakness, and the King can have the less hesitation in proclaiming a political amnesty at such a crisis, after proposing to Fouché before he left Paris to become his Minister of Police. Much of his success and future stability may depend not only upon separating the Jacobin party from Buonaparte, but upon dividing them amongst themselves by a moderate admixture of some of their body into his Government. I do not believe that the leaders will now quarrel about principles, if they are suffered to take their share in the administration of public affairs.

(v)

May 20, 1815.

I transmit to you a letter from the Prince of Castelcicala to M. de Blacas. The object of this letter is to call upon him to make such a report, in refutation of *The Moniteur*, relative to the Murat papers transmitted by him officially to me, as may be laid by me in his justification, before Parliament. I beg you will urge H.Exc. that this may be done with the least practicable delay, and as circumstantially as he can.

I send you also a confidential paper received from *one* of the French Mission at Vienna, by my brother. You will see the sentiments that are entertained there, and that reach them from Ghent. I can also venture to inform you that Monsieur's views are anything but consonant to the notion of the King's adopting a system of governing by responsible Ministers.

Is it true that the Marshals Victor and Marmont have retired in disgust from Ghent to Aix-la-Chapelle?

The British Government have sufficiently evinced their disposition to assist the King with the means of aiding the first efforts of those troops or subjects who choose to fight under his banners, but how can they countenance an effort which is to be led by Monsieur, who may be a high bred Prince, but is no soldier. The King of France ought to perceive that the Princes of the blood are not at the head of the other armies of Europe. War is now too serious a question for etiquette, and altho' it is very fit his family should expose *themselves*, it is not right they should expose his armies, when he has any, or the cause for which they contend, by taking upon themselves a charge for which they are wholly incompetent.

I am anxious to hear what may be the result of the invitation to Talleyrand; until there is a better system at Ghent, it is in vain to suppose that the Duke of O[rleans] or any of those who have remonstrated against what is going on, will embark with the King.

I differ with the Duke of O[rleans] in his opinion that the King ought to be inactive, till the Allies have got to Paris, and have prepared his throne for him, but unless His Majesty embarks with an ostensible and acceptable system to the nation, he had better do nothing, and altho' the Duke of Wellington can only decide what military aid can be afforded, yet I must see a great deal more than I yet do before I can politically recommend any concert in such a plan as you have transmitted for consideration.

Until P. Talleyrand's arrival, perhaps it might be premature to continue your representations officially with the Ministers of the other Powers, but under the uncertainty and intrigue which appears to prevail at Ghent, we must all know without delay on what we have to depend.

(vi)

May 20, 1815.

Your private letter of the 16th arrived after I had closed the letter to you which accompanies this. Altho' the King seems prepared to go considerable lengths, yet I must still fear, giving him credit for the best intentions, that there is an indecision, if not an insincerity, in the course he is to pursue, which is calculated to expose all his prospects. Did you represent to him his own proposition to Fouché thro' Monsr. d'Embray to have him Minister of Police before he left Paris ? After this how can H.M. put a false point of honour in contrast with public expediency. Whether Fouché can really render service, I know not, but, if he can, to discourage him by silence, which means exclusion, appears to me wholly unwarranted, when the extent of interests at issue are considered.

The King having made up his mind to suffer his Cabinet to deliberate as ours does, not in the presence of the sovereign, there is no difficulty in rendering, at least at the outset, the personal intercourse merely formal ; but why should the Govt. of Bonaparte be consolidated by these new scruples ?

I beg you will consider these letters altho' conveying the sentiments of the Govt. as in their form merely for your own eye. The freedom with which they are written will apprize you that they are not intended for communication. The sentiments they contain I have no desire to conceal, but I beg you will not allow them to be copied or place them amongst the official correspondence. I observe an emissary of the name of Chaptre is to be sent to Sweden, I think you cannot be too attentive to arrest any person sent by the existing French Government to the Prince Regent, and especially from the Jacobin part of it.

I must again repeat that except thro' the medium of the Conventionalists, I think the King can do nothing, and that even with their aid, he will find it necessary to break in upon the Jacobin strength by conciliating some of their leaders.

(vii)

June 16, 1815.

I beg you will understand that when I have argued the point of Fouché, it has not been as to the *period* of his being admitted to office ; this is altogether a question of expediency. What I have deprecated is such a reception of his advances (or of those of other leading persons) as precluded him from saving France without sacrificing himself. I wish only to have the principle of exclusion generally got rid of, in *feeling*, as well as in *name* : that this un-matured marriage between Bonaparte and the Jacobins may not be indissolubly cemented against the Bourbons, because whatever may be the success of our arms, with a view to the future, I do not see how the emigrants, and the constitutionalists are ever to secure the King against the Jacobins and the army. . . . [The rest of the letter is printed in Mrs. Edward Stuart Wortley's *Highcliffe and the Stuarts*, 229.]

APPENDIX D

REPORTS FROM COUNT MÜNSTER TO THE PRINCE REGENT [1]

(i)

Vienna, *November 27*, 1814.

Le simple récit de la marche des négociations, contenu dans ma dépêche [2] d'aujourd'hui doit faire naître la crainte que le congrès de Vienne pouvait bien se dissoudre sans avoir consolidé le repos de l'Europe. Les principaux cabinets sont encore tellement éloignés d'un accord sur les principales questions qui les agitent, qu'il paraît même douteux s'ils se sépareront par une rupture ouverte, ou bien, si en refusant de sanctionner les usurpations que médite la Russie, (et dont ceux qui ne croyent pouvoir consentir a l'anéantissement de la Saxe Royale accuseront de même la Prusse), ils laisseront subsister, pour le moment, le status-quo, comme un état simplement de fait, et non de droit?

La situation de l'Europe qui serait la suite de cette dernière attitude ne manquerait pas de rallumer la guerre ou bout d'un interval plus ou moins considérable. Mais il me semble que l'alternative, bien que déjà fort déplorable en elle-même (celle, si nous retomberons sans délai dans une nouvelle lutte, ou si on nous laissera au moins le temps de respirer et une chance quelconque d'une perspective moins funeste), me parait être d'un intérêt si immense, à l'égard des mesures à prendre, que je ne voudrais pas négliger d'informer Votre Altesse Royale sur les données que j'ai recueillies a cet égard.

J'ai eu depuis quelque tems des notions positives que le Cabinet Autrichien réuni est beaucoup moins coulant sur l'affaire de la Pologne et de la Saxe que, n'a du moins paru l'être, le Prince Metternich. Dans une séance qui a eu lieu il y a trois semaines, les personnes qui passent ordinairement pour les plus pacifiques des alentours de l'Empereur François, entre autres le Général

[1] The first report is from the Staats Archiv at Hanover, the rest from the Windsor Archives.

[2] *Münster*, 187.

Ducas, et le Comte de Zichy, ont opiné pour la guerre dans le cas que la Russie et la Prusse inisteraient sur la possession des points que les militaires Autrichiens regardent comme menaçants pour eux.

L'Empereur d'Autriche, à ce qu'on m'assure, doit être d'opinion que si la guerre deviendrait probable, qu'il vaudrait mieux la faire sans délai. Le Roi de Bavière ne parle que dans le même sens et je n'ai pas de doute qu'il ne soit d'accord avec l'Autriche sur la co-opération. Un mémoire que Mr. de Gentz a composé, il y a quelque tems, pour prouver la necessité d'une alliance entre l'Autriche, la France et la Bavière, la manière dont ce savant, qui jouit d'une certaine influence sur le prince Metternich, est fêté par Talleyrand, rendent la supposition probable que la France vise à ce but. La mission de Louis XVIII. au Congrès croit peut-être que les dangers qu'une guerre pourrait avoir pour la Famille Royale seraient plus que contrebalancés par le moyen qu'elle lui fournirait de contenter et d'employer beaucoup de militaires mécontents et peut-être même de satisfaire la nation, qui difficulement se consolera sur la perte de la rive gauche du Rhin. Or les complications du moment présent offriront la chance de reconquérir ce territoire *comme une Province Prussienne*. Le moment actuel serait à plus propice à pareille entreprise, puisque plus tard la rive gauche du Rhin se trouverait sous la protection de la Ligue Germanique, qui aujourd'hui n'est pas conclue encore ! Ce sont là, indépendamment de l'intêret réel et raisonnable que la France doit naturellement prendre à la conservation de l'équilibre politique de l'Europe et surtout de l'Allemagne, quelques raisons accessoires qui font probablement désirer la guerre à la France. Sa haine contre la Prusse, la crainte de l'avoir pour voisine contribue au même but. Il faut avouer que les négociateurs Prussiens n'ont pas mis assez de prudence à éviter ce qui pourrait blesser l'amour-propre des Français. Ce sont eux qui ont souvent tenté d'écarter la mission du Roi de France de la participation aux affaires du congrès qu'aucune Puissance du premier ordre ne saurait se laisser ravir. Le ton taquin de Mr. de Humboldt a surtout paru mettre de l'aigreur dans ces sortes de discussions.

Je viens d'avoir avant hier un entretien confidentiel avec une personne, qui se trouve à la tête d'un des départements de la Chancellerie d'État d'Autriche,[1] qui m'a fait craindre, plus que toute autre chose, que nous en viendrons à une rupture ouverte. M'étant trouvé en rapport intime avec cette personne, pendant ma mission en Russie, elle me parla à cœur ouvert. Elle blâma hautement la conduite de sa Cour de ce qu'elle ne déclarait pas de suite la guerre à la Russie et me témoigna même ses regrets de ce que probablement les mesures énergiques que l'Autriche pouvait prendre,

---

[1] Hudelist, the most important of Metternich's permanent officials.

amèneraient probablement, plus que toutes les négociations, un accommodement avec cette Puissance. Elle ajouta que tout accommodement, tel qu'on pourrait le faire aujourd'hui, serait plus défavorable à l'Autriche que ne saurait l'être la guerre, vu que l'Autriche resterait, tout comme pour le présent, dans la nécessité de tenir son armée sur le pied de guerre, chose que ses finances ne pouvaient supporter. Elle m'assura qu'on n'avait encore risqué de vendre aucum cheval du train de l'armée et qu'on payait dans ce moment cinq cent mille soldats. Indépendamment du danger auquel la monarchie resterait exposée par le mauvais état de ses frontières, en les traçant même d'après les lignes sur lesquelles on insistait encore, la même personne m'assura que les vexations du gouvernement Russe étaient telles que l'Autriche ne pouvait plus les tolérer et qu'elle avait en vain épuisé les moyens de conciliation. Elle me cita comme exemple ce qui est arrivé en Moldavie. Les habitants de la Transylvanie vivent principalement de leurs troupeaux et, leurs montagnes ne leur fournissant pas de pâturage durant l'hiver, les conventions existantes avec la Porte Ottomane permettaient aux Transylvains de conduire leurs troupeaux durant l'hiver dans les vastes plaines de la Moldavie, contre une petite redevance. Depuis que les Russes ont conquis cette province, loin de confirmer ce privilège ils en ont non seulement interdit la jouissance mais ont même retenu quelques centaines de millier de chevaux, de bêtes à cornes et de brebis, avec les hommes qui en avaient eu la garde. Un second fait qui fut cité c'est qu'au lieu d'admettre d'après les traités les sujets mixtes en Pologne, ceux du territoire autrichien ont été arrêtés aux frontières par les Russes et l'entrée ne leur a été accordée qu'en signant l'engagement de rester pour toujours en Russie. Je tâchai de convaincre Mr. de H[udelist] que la guerre dans le moment présent serait le plus grand des malheurs, qu'il fallait surtout songer aux flammes révolutionnaires qui encore couvent sous les cendres. Je lui représentai l'état de l'Italie tant par rapport au sentiment général de ce pays, qui désire l'indépendance et qui est contraire à la domination Autrichienne, que surtout par rapport à Murat et des relations qu'il conserve probablement (malgré l'apparence du contraire affectée par Napoléon), avec le ci-devant Empereur des Français. J'ajoutai que les habitants de la rive gauche du Rhin et ceux même du sud de l'Allemagne étaient prêts a la révolte parce qu'au lieu d'avoir recueilli le fruit de la victoire et de la paix ils étaient ou plus opprimés que par le passé, au point que plusieurs des provinces provisoirement occupées par les différentes trouppes se plaignaient d'avoir quatre fois payé durant l'année les taxes énormes imposées auparavant par les Français ! Je suis fermement convaincu, d'un côté que l'Europe ne saurait rester en paix si l'Empereur de Russie veut, l'épée à la main, décider de ses intérêts

sans écouter les autres Puissances qui lui opposent la sainteté des
traités. Cet état de choses deviendrait encore plus intolérable
encore, si la Prusse, soit par le penchant personnel de son Roi,
soit parce que la Russie favorise ses vues, que toutes les autres
Cours désapprouvent, devenait un instrument dont cette dernière
Puissance pourrait se servir à volonté. Mais lors même qu'on
regarderait la guerre comme inévitable, je suis convaincu qu'il
serait d'un intérêt immense d'en différer l'explosion. Je dirai
plus : lors même que nous dussions nous considérer dès ce moment
même comme en état de guerre, je suis convaincu que la manière
la plus avantageuse de la faire, ce sera de gagner du tems et d'en-
dormir la Russie. Dans le moment présent elle est préparée à la
faire. Ses troupes sont rassemblées et ses chefs ont appris à faire
la guerre sans argent. Il faut surtout songer que si la guerre
éclate sous les circonstances présentes, que les Polonais se battront
pour la liberté, les Russes pour la conquête, tous deux des objets
faits pour les enflammer. Plus tard la haine la plus mortelle
divisera ces deux nations, et l'Empereur de Russie en réunissant
ses anciennes provinces Polonaises au duché de Varsovie, coupera à
son Empire, tôt ou tard, une partie vitale qui a fait de la Russie
un pays Européen, et il s'attirera en Russie même des embarras
qui le paralyseront pour longtems ; les Russes eux-mêmes ne feront
plus les sacrifices pour une cause qu'ils désapprouvent tous, qu'ils
ont portée pour le salut de leur patrie. Ajoutons que les Prussiens
se battront mieux aujourd'hui, si leur gouvernement leur fera
croire, ce qui n'est pas le cas, qu'on veut leur ravir leur juste part
aux fruits de la victoire, que lorsqu'ils verront qu'on ne refuse
nullement à leur valeur ce qui a été stipule par les traités, mais
qu'il s'agit de ne pas empiéter sur les droits d'autrui, ou de voir la
Prusse s'abaisser à devenir une province Russe. Les dangers dont
nous menace l'état de la France et Napoléon devraient surtout
donner du poids aux arguments de ceux qui voudraient conserver
la paix, du moins pour quelque tems. — Mr. de H[udelist] ne parut
guère convaincu par ces arguments et m'assura que ce n'était que
la poltronnerie de Mr. de Metternich qui différait la guerre ; que
l'Empereur aimerait mieux la faire aujourd'hui qu'au bout de six
mois ; que la plupart des Ministres pensaient de même ; et que
l'armée brulait du désir de punir l'arrogance des Russes. Quant
à l'Italie, ce croit que l'Autriche n'aurait à craindre en y laissant
80 mille hommes des cent trente mille qu'elle y avait aujourd'hui.

Le tableau des forces, que le Prince Metternich s'est fait présenter
porte l'armée Autrichienne avec les Bavarois à 630,000. Il se
pourrait bien que l'Autriche se trompa elle-même sur l'état de
ses armements, comme elle l'a si souvent fait, et qu'elle ne songea
pas à l'immense différence qu'on trouvera toujours entre les
nombres de ses soldats sur ses listes et de ceux qu'elle peut conduire

devant l'ennemi. — L'Autriche doit avoir $\frac{75}{m}$ hommes en Galicie.

Les Bavarois avaient offert de marcher deux divisions vers Bayreuth. On dit que les Russes ont de beaucoup diminué leurs troupes en Pologne.

Je n'ai encore pu approfondir quelle est la reponse que la Russie a donné au Prince de Hardenberg sur la Pologne. J'ai, je crois, réussi de convaincre Czartorysky de la nécessité de négocier sur les questions qui se lient à celle de la Pologne conjoinctement, et que sans un arrangement relativement à la Saxe rien ne serait terminé au Congrès. Je tâcherai de tirer la chose au clair, mais si je n'y réussis pas, je croirai ne pas oser retenir le courrier que Lord Castlereagh a mis a ma disposition pour avertir le Gouvernement Hannoverien sur l'état des affaires.

November 28, 1814.

Je viens de voir le Prince Czartorysky et Stein. La réponse de l'Empereur de Russie est telle que je l'avais prévue d'après mon entretien avec le premier de ces ministres : l'Empereur veut faire de Thorn et de Cracovie des points neutres, des villes libres en leur donnant un Rayon et en cédant une ligne du côté de la Silésie. Je sais d'avance que l'Autriche n'acceptera pas cette condition. Metternich est dans ce moment avec le Chancelier de Prusse. J'ai dit à Stein et à Czartorysky que j'étais loin de discuter avec eux sur la justice de la question, que je n'étais en tout cela qu'un particulier assez heureux de posséder la confiance des gouvernements intéressés et pénétré des malheurs que la guerre amènerait sur l'Europe. Ils parurent l'un et l'autre surpris de la probabilité de la guerre et Czartorysky insistait surtout à dire que la Grande-Bretagne pourrait l'empêcher, en déclarant à l'Autriche qu'elle ne l'assisterait d'aucune façon. Je lui dis simplement qu'il serait difficile de se déclarer contre une puissance qui paraissait avoir les traités en sa faveur et qui, de l'opinion des autorités militaires, n'osait pas céder au-delà de ce qu'elle avait fait. Tous les deux se récrièrent sur la folie de l'Autriche qui perdrait la Galicie au premier coup de canon. J'ai simplement observé que la Saxe et la rive gauche du Rhin se perdraient de l'autre côté et que le sort de toute l'Europe serait en danger.

Les choses en sont venues à une crise assez omineuse pour que l'on songe sérieusement au parti qu'il faudra prendre si la guerre éclate. Pour juger de cette question il faut tâcher de prévoir jusqu'à où le feu de la guerre pourrait s'étendre ?

L'Autriche et la Grande-Bretagne ont offert à la Prusse de lui assurer toute la Saxe au cas qu'elle voudrait se ranger de notre côté dans la question Polonaise. Malgré cette offre, malgré que

l'intérêt le plus clair devrait lui dicter cette ligne pour sa conduite,
je n'ai aucune raison de croire que la Prusse le suivra.   Si la guerre
aura lieu entre l'Autriche et la Russie, le Roi de Prusse ne se
déclarera certainement pas contre l'Empereur Alexandre.   Pourra-
t-il rester neutre ?   J'en doute, puisque la question de la Saxe est
trop intimement liée avec celle de la Pologne et parce que la Prusse
occupe la totalité de ce pays, que ni l'Autriche, ni la France, ni
la Bavière ne veulent lui laisser.   De l'autre côté, si la guerre
éclate, ne nous trompous pas au point de croire que le Roi de
France, même s'il le voulait, pourrait éviter d'y prendre part.   Il
devra occuper la rive gauche du Rhin en autant que les Prussiens
l'occupent.   De là naîtra un danger trop grand pour les Pays-Bas
et pour la Hollande, pour que l'Angleterre puisse rester neutre.
Se ranger du côté de la Russie dans cette cause serait impossible :
il faudrait donc qu'elle se mette sans délai bien avec ia France,
c'est-à-dire sur un pied assez intime à pouvoir s'entendre cordiale-
ment avec elle sur la limite des Pays-Bas et de la Belgique.   Cette
intimité ne sera jamais bien établie tant que Murat reste sur le
trône de Naples.   Les Bourbons doivent l'y regarder comme un
épouvantail qu'on conserve pour garde afin de se ménager une
ressource contre eux.   Le Prince Metternich a trop souvent
defendu l'existence politique de Napoléon par l'argument qu'il
était nécessaire contre la Russie.   Il l'a laissé tomber à regret
l'année passée et aujourd'hui encore il redoute moins Murat à
Naples et Napoléon à l'Ile d'Elbe que de voir les Bourbons en
Italie !

Il me semble absolument essentiel d'en venir avec l'Autriche et
la France à un accommodement sur ce point ; ce n'est qu'après
cette mesure qu'on pourra convenir de bonne foi sur un arrangement
relativement à la Belgique et la rive gauche du Rhin.

J'en viens à la question : ce que nous aurons à faire relativement
à l'Hannovre.   Je n'ai pas pu tirer au clair si l'armée de Bennigsen
a commencé sa marche vers la Russie.   Le 18 Novembre elle en
avait l'ordre, mais l'execution en fut différée jusqu'au retour d'un
courrier expédié en Suède.   A Hannovre on sera à. même d'en
avoir davantage.

Ce serait ce corps de troupples Russes qui nous menacerait, surtout
si la Russie et la Prusse nous regardaient comme ennemis.   J'ignore
si l'Angleterre et la Holiande pourront garder une attitude de
neutralité ; je le désirerais, mais quel que soit le parti que la Grande
Bretagne adoptera, nous devrons pour l'Hannovre rester étroite-
ment liés avec elle et la Hollande.   Il sera important de ne pas
trahir de l'inquiétude ou d'en répandre.   Mais il est également
important d'empêcher que les trouppes qui se trouvent dans le
Hannovre ne soyent coupées de celles qui sont dans la Belgique.
Nous ne pouvons pas défendre notre pays seul ; l'armée Anglo-

Hannoverienne sous le Prince d'Orange le pourra, et c'est à elle que nous devons réunir ce qui nous reste de trouppes en cas de danger. J'ose espérer que la Grande-Bretagne nous mettra au moins en continuant les subsides, de faire continuer nos trouppes qui se trouvent avec l'armée Anglaise dans leur position actuelle.

Après avoir conféré avec Lord Castlereagh, j'ai jugé néc ćssaire de mettre S. A. Royale Monseigneur le Duc de Cambridge et notre Cabinet au fait, en leur communiquant, sous le sceau du secret, copie de cette depêche. Le Duc fera prendre les mesures nécéssaires, dont je ne saurais juger puisque j'ignore la position des Russes et celle des Prussiens à Minden et en Ost-Frise. La perte de la Saxe et du Rhin ferait bien vite revenir la Prusse sur les cessions qu'elle nous a fâites et auxquelles nous avions droit de nous attendre.

Je finis cette dépêche par le désir ardent que la paix puisse être conservée. Votre Altesse Royale daignera donner les ordres nécessaires à son Gouvernement. Hannoverien. Il nous importe surtout que nous ne donnions pas l'alarme, pour qu'on ne tombe pas sur nous plus tôt qu'il sera absolument nécessaire de renoncer à une attitude pacifique.

J'ose encore ajouter deux données sur les souverains Jacobins qui nous restent en Europe. On m'assure ici que Charles-Jean a offert aux Turcs il y a six mois de faire cause commune avec eux en cas qu'ils auraient la guerre contre la Russie. On pourrait donc le voir en Finlande. Murat de son côté a offert ses services au Roi de France ; Talleyrand a communiqué sa lettre au Prince Metternich.

(ii)

Vienna, *November* 30, 1814.

Lord Castlereagh ayant eu la complaisance de me céder un de ses couriers pour le faire retourner à Londres par Hannovre, je l'ai expédié avant-hier afin de mettre notre gouvernement sur ses gardes pour le cas que la guerre eût lieu entre l'Autriche et la Russie. Ces dépêches ne pouvant manquer d'arriver à Londres peu de jours après Mr. Canning, qui doit se mettre aujourd'hui en route par Bruxelles, je me borne à mettre sous les yeux de Votre Altesse royale un extrait d'une lettre confidentielle que je lui ai adressé. Il m'est impossible de tracer la marche que je crois devoir Lui recommander pour l'Hannovre sans discuter la question : quels sont dans la crise actuelle les vrais rapports de la Grande Bretagne, vis-à-vis des autres Puissances continentales—et quelle devrait être sa marche politique ? Si j'ai énoncé mon opinion que la Grande Bretagne ne pourait pas rester spectatrice tranquille de la lutte qui va s'engager—cette opinion était fondée sur la

circonstance qu'il est *plus* que probable que la Prusse se verra
entraînée dans la guerre tant par l'occupation de la totalité de
la Saxe Royale, dont elle ne veut pas démordre, que par le désir
qu'elle a de se défaire de ses possessions Polonaises afin d'en obtenir
une compensation dans des provinces moins exposées et plus
à son gré. Ce désir seul met la Prusse en opposition avec les
principes que toutes les Puissances Européennes devraient soutenir
contre la Russie. Il ne faut pas se dissimuler que la disposition
personelle du Roi de Prusse l'assujettit à la dictée d'Alexandre.
J'ai dû considérer comme une suite naturelle de ces données que
la Prusse se rangerait du côté de la Russie. La France dans sa
situation présente ne peut rester neutre dèsque deux ou trois des
grandes Puissances se trouveront en guerre. Le cri de la nation
est trop prononcé pour que Louis 18 puisse se dispenser de le
calmer en revendiquant une partie du territoire sur la rive gauche
du Rhin. C'est ici que je dois développer d'avantage mes idées
sur la maînère dont un pareil plan pourait s'exécuter. L'une et
la plus naturelle serait de se rendre mâitresse du territoire occupé
par la Prusse entre Meuse et Rhin.

Mais il ne faut pas se dissimuler qu'il y aurait une autre voye
pour la France de parvenir à son but. Ce serait par une alliance
avec la Russie laquelle dans le cas supposé, on transigerait sur la
Belgique—ou même sur le territoire destiné à la Prusse en pro-
mettant à celle-ci des compensations plus commodes—par exemple
le Hannovre. Il ne faut pas se dissimuler que l'alliance Russe
serait beaucoup plus populaire en France qu'une union avec la
Cour d'Autriche, qui est aujourd'hui un objet de haine à Paris,
tandis que les générosités d'Aléxandre, bien que prodiguées au
dépens d'autres, lui ont fait des partisans.

J'ai assés d'indices pour être persuadé que le Russie brigue
l'alliance de la France. Un pareil malheur serait trop énorme
pour ne pas justifier des précautions même un peu prématurées.
J'ai parlé dans mon très humble rapport de la nécessité de s'entendre
avec la France sur le sort de Naples et sur celui de Napoléon. Je
dois ajouter à ce que j'ai dit une notion que j'ai recueillie, et qui
prouve le mauvais usage que les ennemis de l'Angleterre font de la
condéscendence qu'elle a eu pour les appréhensions de l'Autriche,
en ne pas brusquant Murat au point de rallumer la guerre en Italie.
Voici comment on l'explique—on dit que l'Angleterre vise, comme
l'Autriche, à conserver un moyen de troubler de nouveau le repos
de la France et surtout qu'elle tâche se prévaloir de l'existence
politique de Murat pour avoir la suprématie de la Méditerranée,
la Sicile devant rester à son pouvoir tant que Naples se trouvera
entre les mains des Jacobins couronnés. Je le répète, il est de la
dernière nécessité de s'entendre avec la France, sans quoi elle
s'alliera avec la Russie. Cette alliance lui assurerait deux grands

intérèts, celui d'écarter l'Autriche de l'Italie en disposant de ce pays à son gré et de rendre à la France la Belgique et la rive gauche du Rhin. Ces deux objets seraient tellement populaires en France que le Roi Louis 18 assure-t-il son règne à toujours. Que fait-on de l'autre côté pour ménager ce Prince? On traite sa mission avec le même soupçon comme si Napoléon se trouvait à sa tête et souvent, on lui dispute même la concurrence que nulle Puissance, du premier ordre, ne peut abandonner lorsqu'il est question de l'équilibre politique de l'Europe.

J'ai eu hier des entretiens avec le Comte Stadion et le Prince Metternich. J'ai été bien aise de les trouver tous les deux de mon opinion sur le point qu'il faudrait éviter pour le moment l'éclat de la guerre, même dans le cas que l'on devrait se regarder en effet comme sur un pied hostile vis-à-vis la Russie. Stadion partageait de même en tout mon opinion sur Naples. Le Prince Metternich veut au contraire que le Congrès en se séparant ne se prononce pas sur ce point et que les Puissances qui ont reconnu Murat y persévèrent de même que celles qui sont dans le cas contraire. Je ne déciderai pas si les ennemis de Metternich ne lui font pas tord en attribuant sa conduitte à sa partialité pour M. Murat. Le Ministre d'Autriche à Naples c'est le Comte de Mier—confident de cette aventure ! Mais je n'ai aucun doute que la déchéance de Murat devrait être clairement prononcée au Congrès. Quant à Bonaparte, un article de la Gazette de Vienne de la date d'hier, est assés remarcable en ce qu'il prouve que Napoléon a ravi injustement cette possession au Prince Ludovisi. Je crois qu'on ne se fâcherait pas ici si la France ou l'Angleterre faisaient enlever Napoléon.

Quant aux affaires de l'Allemagne le Prince Metternich se déclare hautement contre ces cercles, puisqu'il ni voit qu'un moyen d'étendre l'influence de la Prusse dans le nord. Si telle devait être la suite d'une pareille mesure je me rangerai se son côté—surtout sous les circonstances présentes.

(iii)

Vienna, *December* 7, 1814.

J'apprends ce moment, que Lord Castlereagh va expédier un courier qui est sur le point de partir. J'ai peu de chose à ajouter à mes très humbles raports de 29 Novembre et 1 Décembre. La réponse du Prince Hardenberg à Metternich sur la médiation,[1] dont il s'était chargé auprès de l'Empereur de Russie, porte que Sa Majesté Impériale en consentant à se désister de Thorn et Cracovie,

---

[1] *Note verbale* of Hardenberg to Metternich, Dec. 2, 1814 : d'Angeberg, *Congrès de Vienne*, 1941.

en les érigeant en villes indépendantes et neutres, insiste que les questions sur Mayence et sur la Saxe soyent décidé avec celle sur la Pologne, et que Mayence soit destiné à devenir une forteresse de la Ligue Germanique en général et que la totalité de la Saxe Royale reste à la Prusse.　Il n'est pas question dans cette réponse ni de Zamose ni de la frontière en Pologne.　Elle a été communiquée au Prince Metternich Vendredi passé, mais aujourd'hui sa réponse n'etait pas rédigée encore.　Je sais qu'elle sera négative, surtout sur le point de la Saxe.　Malgré cette divergence dans les opinions des principaux cabinets plusieurs de leurs Ministres croyent remarquer des dispositions pacifiques.　On assure même que l'Empereur Alexandre serait bien aise si le Roi de Prusse voulait le dégager de Sa promesse relativement à la Saxe.

J'ai vu ce matin sous le sceau du secret ches Metternich le plan du Chancelier de Prusse sur le partage de l'Allemagne et le contre-projèt de l'Autriche.　Dans le premier la Prusse se donne toute la Saxe, et la majeure partie de Hesse-Darmstadt.　Celle-ci, elle compte la dédomager sur la rive gauche du Rhin en l'étendant jusqu'à Luxembourg et évitant par là la contiguité de la Prusse avec le territoire Français.　L'Autriche prouve dans son contre-projet que la Prusse, même en ne comptant pas la lisière en Pologne, qui est encore en discussion, et en ne lui donnant du royaume de Saxe que les Lusaces, et quelques autres parcelles (renfermant une population de 432,000 âmes) aurait non seulement la population de près de 10 million, à quoi, d'après ses propres calculs, se montait l'état de sa Monarchie en 1805 — mais qu'il lui reviendrait encore un accroisement de plus de 400,000 âmes.　D'après ce calcul il serait clair que la Prusse ne saurait alléguer pour elle la *nécessité* de détruire la Saxe afin d'obtenir ce que les traités *lui* ont assuré.　L'Autriche a d'autres objections très solides contre ce plan. 1me Elle ne resterait en contact avec l'Allemagne que par la Bavière et la Prusse ; et cette dernière, (par le plan qu'elle médite relativement à la division de l'Allemagne en cercles) étendrait son influence sur toute lá Hesse, sur les maisons ducales de Saxe et enfin sur tout le nord de l'Allemagne, à l'exception du cercle qui tomberait sous l'influence de l'Hannovre.　Cette perspective serait trop menaçante pour tout le nord de l'Allemagne et surtout pour les intérèts de Votre Altesse Royale pour ne pas me décider à accéder à l'opinion de Metternich, qui tâche de parer le coup en revenant-entièrement sur les cercles et en ne voulant plus que des divisions militaires.

N'ayant vu le plan qu'un moment je ne puis en parler en détail. Le partage qui nous concerne ne parait point changé.　On nous assigne encore l'Ostfrise en se reservant une lisière pour réunir le Ecchsfeld aux autres possessions prussiennes. . . . [Princess of Wales has taken a house at Naples for 6 months.]

(iv)

Vienna, *June* 3, 1815.

... J'ai peu de choses à dire sur la politique en général. La terminaison glorieuse de la campagne d'Italie est une chose de la dernière importance pour le bien être général de l'Europe. Elle ne laissera pas d'allumer la jalousie des Puissances qui envient à l'Autriche la suprématie en Italie. Mais le poids que l'extinction de ce foyer d'intrigues lui ajoute, ne saurait qu'être salutaire. Je me flatte que !e système de la France, lors même que le Roi remonterait sur le trône, ne changera pas essentiellement par cette jalousie, car ce que l'Autriche gagne d'un côté en Italie la maison de Bourbon le gagne de l'autre, en voyant rendre le trône de Naples à l'une de ses branches.

Je fais mention de cette circonstance puisque je connais les données sur lesquelles plusieurs personnes ont basé, depuis quelque tems, le soupçon que le Prince Talleyrand avait été gagné par l'Empereur de Russie.

J'ai tâché de m'éclairer sur ce fait qui est d'autant plus important que ce Ministre jouit d'une grande influance sur les affaires de France et qu'on n'ose douter de l'autre que l'Empereur Alexandre tient de nouveau à toutes ses idées de Régence sous Marie Louise et peut-être même d'un protectorat sous Bernadotte !

Je crois que l'idée de donner la couronne au duc d'Orléans n'est que subordonnée au premier plan et pour le cas que celui-ci ne pût s'exécuter. De la manière dont j'ai ammené cette matière dans ma conversation avec le Prince Talleyrand et de la façon dont il l'a traitée, je ne crois pas qu'il ait caché sa véritable façon de penser. J'ai trouvé qu'il défend toujours sa thèse qu'il faudrait tâcher de transiger avec les Jacobins — hérésie que j'ai combattue derechef par les argumens exposés dans le mémoire que j'ai eu l'honneur d'envoyer le 23 avril à Votre Altesse Royale. Mais cette thèse, il la soutient toujours comme le moyen de faire remonter le Roi sur le trône. Dans cette discussion il traitait les projets de l'Empereur Alexandre avec peu de ménagement et ne leur attribuait d'autre motif que celui de vouloir s'arroger de plus en plus la direction des affaires de l'Europe qui ne sauraient sortir d'un état d'agitation sous une régence. Quant au Duc d'Orléans Talleyrand lui est décidément contraire, et il prétend même que son parti est peu important en France. Il se servit même de l'expression que l'échaffaud, si bien mérité par son père, ne devait jamais servir de marche au fils pour monter sur le trône.

Une seconde conversation que j'ai eue au sujet de l'article inséré par le Ministre de Suède dans la Gazette de Hambourg du 28 May (article qui est directement contraire aux Bourbons) m'a confirmée dans l'opinion que Talleyrand ne favorisera point les projets de la Russie. Il me répéta à cette occasion que l'Empereur

Alexandre ne favorisait Bernadotte qu'afin d'entretenir en France un état d'agitation qui servirait toujours de motif à ce souverain, pour s'emmiscer dans les affaires de l'Europe et pour différer le retour de l'ordre qui ne convient plus à ses nouvelles habitudes.

Votre Altesse Royale saura sans doute de quelle maniere Bernadotte s'agite pour prendre part aux affaires de France. On dit qu'il désapprouve beaucoup que le Ministre de Suède ait signé la nouvelle déclaration du Congrès. Je conjure Votre Altesse Royale de ne pas accorder à la Suède les moyens pour envoyer de nouveau des trouppes sur le continent — au lieu d'être utiles elles ne serviraient qu'à épuiser nos resources et à fomenter des troubles.

(v)

Mémoire confidentielle sur les affaires de France par rapport à la conduite politique que devraient tenir les Cours Alliées.

Paris, *August* 17, 1815.

Votre Altesse Royale m'a ordonné de Lui communiquer mon opinion, sur les rapports actuellement existans, entre les Puissances Alliées et la France, ainsi que sur les conditions, qui devroient servir de base, à la paix future.

J'ai différé cette tâche jusqu'à la fin de mon sejour à Paris, tant pour être à même de recueillir les notions nécessaires que pour m'instruire, sur les vues des différentes Cours.

L'union parfaite des Cabinets sur les moyens propres à detruire le pouvoir révolutionnaire, qui venoit de s'emparer de nouveau du trône de France, et l'énergie déployée dans l'application des moyens, ont ammené des succès très glorieux. Maîtres de la Capitale et des plus belles provinces de France, avec huit cent mille hommes dans ce pays, dont l'armée est ou détruite ou licentiée, les Alliés seroient sans doute à même, d'y établir tel ordre de choses qu'ils jugeront le plus propre, pour assurer, sur des bases solides, le repos futur de l'Europe.

Mais l'union, qui a ammené le succès de la campagne, a cessé de guider les conseils des Cabinets alliés. On n'est pas d'accord sur la question, si le but de la guerre est obtenue ou non ; beaucoup moins encore, sur les moyens qu'il faudroit choisir, pour assurer la durée des avantages remportées.

Je bornerai l'analise des diverses opinions, manifestées sur ces questions, aux mémoires donnés par les Ministres et généraux des quatre *grandes Puissances* alliées. C'est une appellation, qui a commencé à s'introduire dans la diplomatie, depuis la paix de Paris ; epoque à laquelle, on professoit, vouloir rendre hommage, aux droits des plus foibles et de faire cesser l'ascendant destructeur de la simple prépondérance.

L'origine, ou du moins l'une des causes de la différence des opinions, qui se manifeste aujourd'hui, doit se rechercher, dans la divergence des principes qui s'est trahie, dès le moment, que le trône de Louis XVIII. fut de nouveau ébranlé. Le principal danger de l'usurpation de Bonaparte, se trouvait dans l'atteinte qu'il portoit à la légitimité, et dans le retour des principes destructeurs des Jacobins. Mais il a paru à plusieurs Cours, qu'on ne devoit pas faire la guerre à la France, pour l'obliger à reconnoître Louis XVIII. L'Angleterre même a cru devoir en cette occasion, faire hommage au prétendu principe ; qu'un peuple a toujours le droit de changer la forme de son gouvernement. De là la tentative de Napoléon après sa défaite, de céder la couronne à son fils, ainsi que les diverses propositions des députés françois, au quartier général des Alliés.

Les doutes qui existoient sur les projets, qu'on pourroit nourrir à l'égard du pouvoir suprême en France, ont fait accélérer le retour du Roi à Paris.

Les Alliés avoient déclaré la guerre à Napoléon et à *ses adhérens*. La France presqu'entière, s'étoit identifiée avec ce parti, en lui prêtant contre nous, des secours volontaires ou peut-être forcés, mais toujours généraux. Les Royalistes même étoient coupables par leur submission passive.

Le mémoire du Duc de Wellington dit : que le parti du Roi avoit beaucoup contribué au prompt succès de la campagne, il ajoute même : qu'il seroit ridicule de supposer, que les Alliés eussent pu avancer, en si peu de jours, qu'ils l'ont fait, sur Paris, si le peuple n'avoit pas été pour le Roi. C'est sans doute un témoignage auquel on ne sauroit refuser une foi plénière. Mais on osera répliquer, que la soumission passive des François bien disposés, a du moins autant accéléré les succès de Bonaparte, que les nôtres. Si le peuple avoit fait son devoir, auroit-il pu marcher, en vingt jours, de Cannes à Paris ? lui n'avoit d'abord que quelques milliers d'hommes ; notre armée victorieuse en comptoit 150,000.

La France n'étoit guère subjugée à l'entrée du Roi à Paris, et les Alliés se trouvoient dans la situation bizarre, d'être en paix, ou même en alliance, avec Lui, et en guerre avec son peuple.

De là les discussions sur l'administration des provinces, sur le droit de faire des réquisitions.

Dans cet état choses, comment les mêmes Cours, qui avoient déclaré, ne pas vouloir faire la guerre uniquement pour soutenir les droits de Louis XVIII., croyent-elles aujourd'hui ne pas être autorisés par des considérations purement personelles au Roi, à demander à la France, les conditions que la sûreté de l'Europe paroit exiger ? On prétend : que le but de la guerre est atteint par la chute du pouvoir de Bonaparte, et que les déclarations des Cours alliées, et leur traité du 25 Mars, les obligent à se borner

aux stipulations du traité de Paris, telles qu'elles ont été complet-
tées, par le recès de Vienne. J'examinerai cette question, d'abord
sous le point de vue du droit, et ensuite sous celui de la politique.

Quant au droit, je ne saurai que souscrire au raisonnement
logique, contenu dans le mémoire du Baron de Humboldt. La
déclaration du 13 Mars, fut dirigée contre Napoléon, lorsqu'il ne
se trouvoit à la tête que de quelques milliers de complices ; de
là au traité d'Alliance, les Puissances n'ont fait que publier le
rapport d'une Commission nommée pour examiner la question,
s'il faudroit donner une déclaration ultérieure, par rapport aux
événemens qui avoient replacé Napoléon sur le trône ? La réponse
a été négative.

Le traité du 25 Mars, a admis Louis XVIII. au nombre des
Alliés. Mais il s'est trouvé, qu'il n'avoit nul secours à Ses ordres,
Ses proclamations disent même, qu'il a défendu aux Princes de Sa
maison, de combattre contre la France ; la Grande Bretagne la
première, a limité les droits que l'Article 8me du traité donnoit au
Roi de France, et toutes les autres Cours y ont accedé. Le fait
est : que toute la discussion devient oiseuse. Soyons de bonne foi.
Il semble que toutes les Cours concourent à montrer au Roi de
France les égards que les circonstances permettent: mais qu'aucune
d'elles ne Le traite vraiment en souverain allié. Sa Capitale
même, est sous le gouvernement militaire des étrangers, et on
continue à assiéger les forteresses, malgré que le pavillon blanc soit
déployé de leurs tours, tant qu'elles ne se rendront pas aux conditions, prescrittes par les Alliés, et sans le concours du Roi de
France.

Cette anomalie provient, comme je l'ai dit, de ce que nous sommes
en paix avec le Roi seul, mais non avec la France. Personne n'a
plus que moi désiré, à l'époque du 25 Mars, de voir le principe
clairement établi, qu'on feroit la guerre aux François rebelles,
pour soutenir les droits sacrés de la légitimité.

On a craint d'offenser par là le grand parti, affecté de la manie du
siècle, celle de faire de nouvelles constitutions. Toujours la guerre
a été déclarée, à Napoléon et à *ses adhérens*. En effet, quel avantage aurions-nous remporté, en n'abattant Napoléon, que pour
mettre le Jacobinisme victorieux à sa place ? Le seul mérite que
Bonaparte ait eu, ce fut d'avoir délivré le monde de Jacobins.
Qu'est-il arrivé ? Simultanément avec le rassemblement des
armées, le Prince de Talleyrand a commencé à travailler sur un
plan, qui avoit pour but de transiger avec les Jacobins. Il ne
s'en est pas caché. Il a hautement déclaré qu'il falloit s'allier à
un parti actif, et qu'il n'y avoit dans le parti du Roi que des gens
ou incapables ou pacifiques. Ce parti actif, a-t-il donc facilité la
conquête ? Certainement non ; à moins qu'on donne du prix aux
sourdes menées d'un Fouché. Son parti a continué à exercer des

actes de trahison, lors même que Paris avoit été livré aux Alliés.
Il doit constamment tenir la Cour dans l'allarme, afin de se rendre
toujours nécessaire. Il n'y a pas huit jours, que le Journal, l'Indé-
pendant, auquel Fouché avoit part, a osé dire, que Labédoyère
n'avoit fait que choisir entre un souverain de 15 ans, et un souverain
de 11 mois !

Plût au ciel que les Alliés se fussent strictement tenus à leur
déclaration de vouloir faire la guerre à Napoléon et à *ses adhérens*.
Mais ils n'ont abattu que lui, et quelque peu de traîtres. Le parti
révolutionnaire est resté, dans le Gouvernement même. Maîtres
de 800,000 hommes, en France, nous aurions dû détruire le Jacobinisme et les Jacobins jusque dans leurs dernières ramifications; ils
s'étoient tous fait connoître. Le mal d'exiler, ou même de détruire
quelques milliers de gens criminels, ou dangereux, est-il comparable
à la destruction, causée par une bataille de Waterloo ?

C'est ici que gît le fonds véritable de notre désunion. Le plus
ou le moins de confiance, qu'on croit pouvoir accorder à la durée
de l'ordre présent des choses, porte les uns à exiger plus, les autres
à vouloir moins de gages de sûreté. Si on avoit terminé la révolution de la manière indiquée, L'Europe auroit pu se promettre la
paix, et on auroit pu se passer de discuter, s'il falloit pour sa
sûreté, arracher des provinces ou démolir des forteresses Françoises ?

Depuis qu'on a permis au Roi de transiger avec les Jacobins,
que la France se trouve sous un nouveau Major Domo, dans la
personne de l'hideu Fouché, qu'on a donné, (pour plaire aux faiseurs
de constitutions) plus d'extension à l'acte constitutionel dans des circonstances, qui auroient engagé tout gouvernement sage, à suspendre
les formes constitutionelles, toute la question change de face.

Qu'on ne dise pas qu'on a été forcé à cette mesure ; qu'il n'y
a pas en France assez de gens intègres et actifs, pour conduire
les affaires de l'état. Cette assertion ne peut être vraie, lorsqu'on
parle d'un peuple éclairé, et qui n'est pas sans exemple de vertu
publique, qui en a un modèle sur le trône même. Pour ajouter
foi à une telle assertion, il faut en croire les factieux, qui repré-
sentent tous les amis du Roi, sous l'appellation burlesque " de
voltigeurs de Louis XV.," comme des imbéciles décrépités. Mais
il n'est pas étonnant que des gens intègres, ne voudront pas
s'associer à des régicides et à des gens déshonorés.[1]

[1] *Note by Münster :* Pour donner une preuve, qu'il est impossible de
s'attendre à un changement sincère dans la disposition des révolutionnaires
et combien il est par conséquent imprudent de composer avec eux, on n'a
qu'à jetter un regard sur les acquéreurs des biens nationaux. Le Roi,
pour les contenter, a donné les assurances les plus solemnelles, il a été
jusqu'à mécontenter les victimes de leur loyauté, qui avoient sacrifiés
leurs biens dans Sa cause. Cela a-t-il tranquillisé les acquéreurs ? bien
loin de là ; — ce sont eux qui intriguent contre le Roi, pour ammener un
changement. Ne voudroit-il pas mieux frapper le coup, et les priver
de leurs biens mal acquis ?

On n'ose plus se flatter aujourd'hui, qu'après six semaines de séjour à Paris les Alliés voudront revenir sur leurs pas, et terminer la Révolution Française, en détruisant le Jacobinisme? Il faudra donc considérer l'état de la France vis-à-vis de nous, tel qu'il est.

Peu de personnes en France, croyent à la stabilité de l'ordre actuel des choses. Ces gens à talent, dont on a cru devoir se servir pour rétablir l'ordre, soutiendront mal le trône des Bourbons. Mais lors même qu'ils le feroient, de pareils soutiens offriroient un foible gage pour la tranquillité future de l'Europe. Ecoutons l'auteur de l'Histoire de la Révolution du 20 Mars 1815. Il dit page 4me : " L'idée d'une Puissance légitime, n'est plus comprise en France, que dans le sens nouveau d'une puissance, voulue par le peuple, établie par le peuple etc. Le souverain légitime, est celui qui se trouve à la tête de ce contrat, bon ou mauvais, bien ou mal exécuté, et vouloir disputer sur ce subjet avec la jeunesse actuelle, autant voudroit-il faire reculer les Alpes."

Les quatre partis en France, dont parle cet auteur, les Jacobins, les Constitutionels, le pouvoir militaire, et les Royalistes, se disputeront de nouveau le pouvoir suprême, et ces derniers, auront à combattre de plus l'accusation, que le Roi a été imposé par les Puissances alliées à la France, et que c'est pour atteindre ce but, qu'elle souffre sous une invasion ennemie.

Les Alliés ont traité la France, comme le Général des Samnites traita l'armée romaine réduite en son pouvoir. Il demanda conseil à son père. " Tués les tous," fut sa réponse. Cela lui parut trop cruel. " Mettés les donc tous en liberté " reprit le père. Cet extrême lui parut trop modéré. Il se décida à insulter l'armée romaine, en la faisant passer sous le joug. Les suites sont connues. Nous avons agi de même. Le séjour de nos armées en France irrite au dernier degré un peuple naturellement vain et orgueilleux d'une longue suite de victoires. Nous devons prévoir avec certitude une nouvelle attaque, ne fût-ce que pour venger l'affront; avec cette conviction, nous sommes trop délicats, sur les mesures de précaution, qui deviennent nécessaires. Le mémoire du Duc de Wellington admet que la France est trop puissante pour la sûreté de ses voisins, mais il déconseille de l'affoiblir par des cessions territoriales, en alléguant, que la séparation de la Belgique et de la rive gauche du Rhin et le peu de disposition montrée par le Roi pour les reconquérir, avoit été l'une des principales causes du succès de l'entreprise de Bonaparte. Ce motif ne continue-t-il pas d'exister, et n'ammènera-t-il pas de nouvelles guerres? Tout le monde convient, qu'il n'y a pas un François, de quel parti qu'il soit, qui ne songe à reconquérir ces provinces. Ne pouvant raisonnablement les rendre à la France, et voyant par l'expérience, que la foi des traités ne suffit pas pour les assurer, il devient indispensable de songer à de nouvelles garanties. Le mémoire du

Prince de Metternich a rappellé avec raison, que la France monarchique a été conquérante, tout comme la France révolutionnaire. Toutes les Cours conviennent de la nécessité de se procurer des garanties. La plus part des opinions sont contraires à un démembrement, tellement considérable, qu'il pourroit changer l'état de possession établi par le Congrès de Vienne. Je suis du même avis, persuadé que l'union des Cabinets finiroit au renouvellement des discussions sur un nouveau partage de provinces. Mais un pareil revirement ne seroit nullement la suite nécessaire d'un nouvel arrangement de frontières, qui n'auroit pas pour objet l'agrandissement de tel ou tel état mais la sûreté de tous. C'est sur cette question surtout que se manifeste une suite fâcheuse, de ce que les grandes Puissances ne consultent pas avec leurs Alliés, sur une question qui *les* intéresse principalement. C'est l'Allemagne qui a été constamment la victime de l'esprit de conquête de la France. L'Allemagne comme telle, ne peut devenir dangereuse à la France, tandis que celle-ci appuye des dispositions hostiles par des positions militaires, des forteresses qui la mettent en état de porter à volonté le théâtre de la guerre sur la rive droite du Rhin. Des quatre grandes Cours, il n'y a que la Prusse qui soit limitrophe de la France.[1] Ses demandes pour cette raison, peuvent être moins modérées que celles de l'Autriche. Celle-ci se rappelle cependant, que la position de Strasbourg, conduit les armées Françoises sur le Danube, sans que rien ne les arrête, la Forêt Noire étant facile à tourner par le Nord et par le Sud. L'Autriche insiste donc sur la démolition de Strasbourg. La Russie, qui ne risque rien elle-même, est la plus généreuse. L'Angleterre, s'intéresse surtout pour les Pays-Bas. Le Duc de Wellington propose l'occupation de 17 forteresses[2] (ou du moins de 13[3] de ce nombre) pour un tems limité, mais il n'en demande *aucune*, depuis *Landau* jusqu'a *Huninguen*, espace sur la quelle, l'Allemagne n'a que Mayence pour défense. Le mémoire de Lord Castlereagh finit par dire : que les Alliés, s'ils se verroient de nouveau provoqués, par l'ambition de la France, pourroient se réunir de nouveau, sous l'avantage des positions qu'ils occuperoient, et forts par cette puissance morale, qui seule peut réunir une pareille Alliance et assurer son succès. Mais osera-t-on jamais se promettre un concert aussi général, que celui qui a produit les heureux résultats de l'an 1814 et 1815. Que seroit-il devenu de l'Europe, si le Congrès de Vienne avoit terminé par une querelle, ou même si sa durée, et l'incertitude

[1] *Note by Münster :* Et celle ci même ne l'est pas strictement parlé.
[2] *Note by Münster :* Lille, Condé, Valenciennes, Le Quénoi, Maubeuge, Philippeville, Givêt, Mezières, Sedan, Montmedi, Longoy, Thionville, Sarrelouis, Sarguemines, Bitche, Landau, Huninguen.
[3] *Note by Münster :* Condé, Valenciennes, Bouchain, Maubeuge, Landreci, Le Quénoi, Avesnes, Rocroi, Philippeville, Givêt, Bitche, Landau, Huninguen.

de son résultat, n'avoit engagé toutes les Puissances, à complletter leurs armées et à les mettre sur le meilleur pied possible ?   Mais supposant même, que tous les moyens dont nous nous sommes servi, se trouvassent de nouveau à notre disposition, que de souffrance et de pertes de tout genre, sont inséparables du passage d'armées nombreuses par un pays !   Veut-on de nouveau y assujettir l'Allemagne, après que l'expérience en modération de l'année passée a si mal réussie.   On ose hardiment supposer, que si les Cours d'Autriche, de Russie et d'Angleterre pouvoient se trouver dans le cas d'avoir à discuter la question, dont il s'agit, comme ayant à redemander à la France des provinces limitrophes, qui leur auroient été arrachées, qu'elles ne balanceroient pas à les réclamer.   Pourquoi l'Allemagne, considérée comme un corps politique, ne les revindiqueroit elle pas ?   Les Pyrennées, les Alpes et la mer, préscrivent des bornes à l'ambition de la France ; pourquoi le Jura, les Vosges et les Ardennes ne rendroient-elles pas à l'Allemagne, les garanties dont jouissent sur un autre point l'Espagne et l'Italie ?   On a donné la Belgique à la maison d'Orange, sans que cette cession ait causé des discussions sur l'état des possessions des grandes Puissances.   Qu'on dispose de la même manière des provinces, qu'on ne sauroit laisser avec sûreté à la France.

Mais si les grandes Puissances se refusent à rendre à l'Allemagne, ce qu'elle pouvoit réclamer avec justice et ce qui ne feroit nullement descendre la France du rang d'une des Puissances du premier ordre, qu'on lui ôte du moins les agrandissemens ajoutés à la paix de Paris à ses limites de 1792.   L'expérience a prouvé, combien ces cessions ont été nuisibles à l'Allemagne, aux Pays Bas et à la Savoye.   Dans les Pays Bas, les premières familles ont maintenant des possessions en France et s'attachent par là à son système.   En Savoye, les habitans des montagnes, dépendent de ceux des plaines, cédées à la France.

D'après ce que j'ai dit, j'ai suffisament indiqué, que je ne suis pas d'avis, qu'on osera se borner à laisser seulement une armée d'observation alliée en France, et de n'occuper, que pour un tems limité, les places fortes indiquées.   L'armée d'observation me paroîtroit nécessaire, ainsi que la cession permanente des points d'attaque.

Quoiqu'on fasse, je suis moralement persuadé qu'on ne portera pas le Roi de France, à consentir de bon gré, aux propositions les plus modérées, indiquées dans les différens mémoires.   Celui de Lord Castlereagh observe même avec raison, qu'il faudroit imposer à Sa Majesté, les arrangemens dont on conviendroit, comme des conditions inévitables.   Je ne répondrai pas, que ces conditions, bien que trop modérées, celon mon humble avis, n'ammèneront les suites, qu'on paroit craindre, en voulant demander des cessions permanentes.

Le Roi connoit le danger des concessions qu'il faudra nécessaire-
ment Lui demander. Il sait, que Sa résistance réuniroit tous les
partis et Sa lettre au Prince Talleyrand contient même la menace,
que, lorsqu'Il ne pouvoit rien faire pour Son peuple, Il Se retireroit
en Espagne, espérant que les François sauroient organiser une
guerre, semblable à celle, qui avoit soutenue l'indépendance de la
Péninsule.

J'ai passé sous silence, les garanties morales dont parle le
mémoire de Monsieur le Comte de Capo d'Istria, mais j'ai suffisament montré, que le ne saurai y attacher du prix dans les circonstances présentes. Elles ne me paroissent plus ou moins que cette
garantie, vantée dans la lettre du Duc de Vicence à plusieurs
Cabinets, lorsqu'il vouloit les rassurer sur le repos de l'Europe,
par ce que Napoléon avoit imaginé, " de placer la paix sous le
sauve garde de l'honneur François."

Le résumé de l'opinion énoncée dans ce mémoire est : que les
Alliés ont le pouvoir d'établir, relativement à la France, l'ordre
des choses qu'ils jugeront nécessaire pour le repos de l'Europe.

Qu'ils ont, outre le pouvoir, le droit de le faire et que les traités
existans, ne les en empêchent pas.

Qu'on n'ose se fier aux garanties morales, qui doivent assurer
le repos de la France.

Qu'une guerre prochaine, paroit inévitable, à moins qu'on la
prévienne, par des moyens plus efficaces, que ceux proposés par
plusieurs Cours.

Que l'armée d'observation et la possession temporaire de
certaines forteresses, ne suffiroient pas pour atteindre le but.
Qu'il faudoit rendre à l'Allemagne ses limites naturelles, ou du
moins, se défaire des points militaires d'agression, comme Strasbourg. Qu'en tout cas, il faudroit réduire la frontière de la
France, à ce qu'elle étoit en 1792.

(vi)

Paris, *August* 18, 1815.

J'ai l'honneur de Vous présenter ci-joint[1] le resultat de mes
réflexions sur les affaires de France. Votre Altesse Royale trouvera
que j'ai le malheur de différer de l'opinion de Ses Ministres pour la
Grande Bretagne. Il me parait évident que les 4 Cours qui ont
discuté entre elles la grande question l'ont chacune jugée d'après
leur intérêt particulier mais que celui de l'Allemagne proprement
dite a été négligé parce qu'elle n'a pas eu voix en chapitre. Plusieurs
Ministres m'ont fait observation que les Pays Bas et le Hannovre
n'étaient relativement à la Grande Alliance qu'une partie de
l'Angleterre — et que l'opinion de ces deux Cours serait perdue pour

[1] Number (v) above.

le bien de l'Allemagne. Votre Altesse Royal daignera juger d'après tout quelles instructions Elle jugera convenable de donner au Comte de Hardenberg qui devra voter pour le Royaume de Hanovre après que j'aurai quitté Paris. Il serait imprudent de nous attirer la haine de la France sans pouvoir parvenir à convaincre les premières Puissances qu'elles agissent sur un principe erroné.

J'ai la conviction morale que la grande modération de la Russie tient 1er : à la situation de ses provinces qui n'auront rien à craindre de la France 2d : à la vanité de l'Empereur qui veut être proné comme libérateur de la France, 3.mement à Son désir de se rapprocher d'elle. Loin d'avoir ressenti l'Alliance du 3 Janvier, 15, Le Roi de France ne reçoit aujourd'hui de l'Empereur Alexandre que des marques d'amitié et d'intérêt.

Personne qui réfléchit sur l'état de l'Europe n'oubliera que la France doit rester forte pour pouvoir résister à la prépondérance de la Russie. Mais que serait ce si ces deux Puissances s'unissaient? J'observe ici que les cessions considérées nécessaires dans mon mémoire seraient loin d'affaiblir la France. Il faut en général abandonner l'idée qu'on pourait réduire la nation Française à un état absolu de faiblesse. Elle ne se laissera pas partager, et son sol reproduit toutes les années tous et plus qu'il ne lui faut pour être puissante. Les provinces coupées par la ligne de ses frontières vraiment naturelles sont resté allemandes malgré la longue durée de leur séparation. Leur mauvaise conduitte dans la guerre actuelle tient à des causes connues.

J'ai eu des entretiens confidentiels avec Mr. de Gagern et le Général Fagel. Le Roi des Pays Bas envisage la situation des affaires à peu près comme moi. Mais Il croit ne pas oser manifester publiquement Ses voeux [de] crainte d'être accusé de vouloir aggrandir Son territoire après avoir été doté avec une libéralité sans exemple.

Il me reste encore à rendre compte à Votre Altesse Royale de l'entretien particulier avec le Roi de France auquel j'ai été invité par le Prince de Talleyrand. La situation de ce Souverain est vraiment des plus affligeantes. Il daigna m'en tracer le tableau de la manière la plus touchante, puis après avoir montré l'importance du repos de la France, sous le règne de la maison de Bourbon, pour le reste de l'Europe, Sa Majesté parla des obligations personelles qu'Elle Vous devait, Mon Seigneur, et m'engagea à Vous représenter que toutes les cessions qu'on demandrait à la France, meme que ce ne serait que pour un tems limité, rendraient sa position plus difficile ; que la nation lui imputerait chaque concession comme une perte encourrue à cause de Son retour au trône. J'aurai cru manquer au devoir d'un honet homme, honoré de la confiance d'un Roi, si je n'avais répondu avec franchise à ce discour—j'aurai même placé Votre Altesse Royale, qui Se trouve obligée par Ses devoirs à tenir une conduite à l'égard de la France différente de celle que le Roi Lui demande, dans une situation pénible vis-à-vis de ce souverain qui réclame Son amitié personelle, si je n'avais indiqué les difficultés qui se présentent.   J'ai donc observé au Roi que l'opinion publique et la voix de la Presse en Angleterre, si puissantes dans ce pays, demandaient hautement des garanties qu'on ne croyait pas trouver dans le choix de quelques personnes en place.   Le Roi me reprit : " Vous voulés dire que mon ministère, surtout que Fouché n'inspire pas de confiance ? "   " Oui Sire, lui dis-je cela ne saurait être — mais je sais ce qui a engagé Votre Majesté à ce choix."   Le Roi se plaignit alors que les journaux Anglais après l'avoir autrefois bien servi, le traitaient aujourd'hui avec dureté — que Fouché lui avait été utile, mais qu'Il le faisait observer de près et qu'Il l'avait sous Son pouvoir — qu'Il avait besoin de rassembler les Chambres avant que de pouvoir agir librement et qu'Il se flattait d'obtenir de bonnes élections.   Après avoir promis de faire un rapport fidèle mais secret à Votre Altesse Royale sur cette conversation, le Roi me congédia avec bonté mais non sans un peu d'émotion.

P.S.—Je ne suis pas plus avancé que je ne l'étais il y a huit jours pour notre traité des subsides.   Le Duc de Wellington parait indisposé à ce projet.   Après tout ce que j'ai vu ici je ne pourai plus proposer à l'avenir à Votre Altesse Royale de consentir que Ses trouppes Allemandes soyent confondues dans l'armée Anglaise. On les traite, quand même plusieurs généraux leur rendraient justice, comme des êtres inférieurs — d'ailleurs la différence de la solde n'admet pas la même discipline.   Je ne crois pas que le Duc de Wellington ait jamais vu un seul de nos officiers excepté aux revues et sur le champ de bataille.   Hier après un grand dîner à l'honneur des nouveaux Chevaliers de l'ordre militaire du Bain le Duc a donné un grand bal auquel la ville et les fauxbourgs ont été invité.   Je doute qu'il s'y soit trouvé un seul hanovérien — ni Hardenberg ni Grote ni moi n'avons été invités — ce sont là des bagatelles — mais elles irritent l'esprit des trouppes — et les suittes ne sont plus des bagatelles.

Jérôme Bonaparte se trouve ici ches le Ministre de Wurtemberg. Son Beau-père le réclame pour le garder.

Post Scriptum.

August 18, 1815.

Le Général Blomfield ayant différé son depart à demain matin j'ajouterai quelques lignes à ma très humble dépêche.   J'ai eu un long entretien avec le Ministre de Russie, Pozzo di Borgo, et avec le Baron Stein, qui a été appellé ici par le Prince Hardenberg pour servir de renfort à ce qu'on appelle la question allemande (c'est à dire les sûretés demandées pour la garantie des frontières de ce

pays). Le Br. de Stein est venu me lire son mémoire qui est en
partie tracé sur le mien, dont il m'avait demandé la lecture. En
général il est modéré et pour ne pas demander ce que les Cours
ne se réuniront pas d'exiger — il se borne à représenter comme
indispensable la cession *permanente* des places fortes représentées
comme formant une base d'opérations agressives contre les
voisins de la France.

Le Général Pozzo impute la nomination des Ministres Jacobins,
qu'il blâme hautement, à l'Angleterre, mais il persiste à soutenir
l'opinion que le Roi parviendra, à l'aide des deux chambres, qui
d'après le succès des élections promettent beaucoup en sa faveur,
à établir solidement Son pouvoir. Sur cette supposition il base
l'espoir du retour de l'ordre en France. Insister sur les conditions
proposées par la Prusse, ce serait celon lui, degrader le Roi et
boulverser la France.

Le Prince Metternich tient toujours à son opinion — mais il
ajoute qu'il serait très dangereux de laisser à la Russie le mérite
d'avoir seule réussi à sauver la France des conditions dures que
les autres Cours auraient proposées de lui imposer. Il tient
d'ailleurs, avec raison à l'union parfaitte des grandes Cours, et à
ce que finalement les termes de la paix paraissent être fixées d'un
accord commun et entier. Il est à prévoir de là que l'Autriche
cédera. La Russie se rangera du côté de l'opinion de la Grande
Bretagne. J'ai voulu lire mon mémoire à Lord Castlereagh mais
comme la conférence est fixée pour demain matin entre les Ministres
des 4 Cours principales, mes observations pouraient bien être tar-
dives. Le Chancelier Prince Hardenberg m'a cependant dit qu'il
était résolu de résister et de demander que les principales Cours
d'Allemagne soyent écoutées avant qu'on décide la question.

Cette situation des affaires exige que Votre Altesse Royale munisse
le Comte Hardenberg de Ses ordres pour le Hannovre. Je conviens
de-la grande difficulté de la question. Elle jugera des argumens
pour ou contre.

P.S.—On m'a encore renvoyé à demain pour l'expédition de
nos affaires territoriales avec la Prusse. Le Chancelier n'a pas
trouvé le Roi.

Je dois me corriger sur le bal du Duc de Wellington. On me
dit qu'il y a eu quelques officiers hanovériens.

INDEX